FREEDOM AND TERROR IN THE DONBAS

A Ukrainian-Russian Borderland, 1870s–1990s

This book discusses both the freedom of the Ukrainian-Russian borderland of the Donbas and the terror it has suffered because of that freedom. In a detailed panorama the book presents the tumultuous history of the steppe frontier land from its foundation as a modern coal and steel industrial center to the post-Soviet present. Wild and unmanageable, this haven for fugitives posed a constant political challenge to Moscow and Kiev.

In light of new information gained from years of work in previously closed Soviet archives (including the former KGB archives in the Donbas), the book presents, from a regional perspective, new interpretations of critical events in modern Ukrainian and Russian history: the Russian Revolution, the famine of 1932–33, the Great Terror, World War II, collaboration, the Holocaust, and de-Stalinization.

Born in Japan in 1953, Hiroaki Kuromiya was educated at Tokyo University and Princeton University. He is also the author of *Stalin's Industrial Revolution: Politics and Workers, 1928–1932*. Formerly a Mellon postdoctoral fellow at Harvard University's Russian Research Center and a Research Fellow at King's College, Cambridge, Kuromiya now teaches history at Indiana University, Bloomington.

FREEDOM AND TERROR IN THE DONBAS

Cambridge Russian, Soviet and Post-Soviet Studies: 104

Editorial Board

Stephen White (*General Editor*)
Roy Allison Mary Buckley Julian Cooper Paul Dukes
Saul Estrin Catherine Merridale Hilary Pilkington

Cambridge Russian, Soviet and Post-Soviet Studies, under the auspices of Cambridge University Press and the British Association for Slavonic and East European Studies (BASEES), promotes the publication of works presenting substantial and original research on the economics, politics, sociology and modern history of Russia, the Soviet Union and Eastern Europe.

Books in the Series

Series list continues after index

FREEDOM AND TERROR IN THE DONBAS

A Ukrainian-Russian Borderland,
1870s–1990s

Hiroaki Kuromiya

CAMBRIDGE
UNIVERSITY PRESS

PUBLISHED BY THE PRESS SYNDICATE OF THE UNIVERSITY OF CAMBRIDGE
The Pitt Building, Trumpington Street, Cambridge, United Kingdom

CAMBRIDGE UNIVERSITY PRESS
The Edinburgh Building, Cambridge CB2 2RU, UK
40 West 20th Street, New York NY 10011–4211, USA
477 Williamstown Road, Port Melbourne, VIC 3207, Australia
Ruiz de Alarcón 13, 28014 Madrid, Spain
Dock House, The Waterfront, Cape Town 8001, South Africa

http://www.cambridge.org

First published 1998
First paperback edition 2002

Typeface Times Roman 10/12 pt, in LATEX 2_ε.

A catalogue record for this book is available from the British Library

Library of Congress Cataloguing in Publication data
Kuromiya, Hiroaki.
Freedom and terror in the Donbas: a Ukrainian-Russian borderland,
1870s–1990s / Hiroaki Kuromiya.
        p.   cm. – (Cambridge Russian, Soviet and post-Soviet studies: 104)
Includes bibliographical references and index.
ISBN 0 521 62238 7
1. Donets Basin (Ukraine and Russia) – History – 19th century.   2. Donets Basin
(Ukraine and Russia) – History – 20th century.   3. Political persecution – Donets Basin
(Ukraine and Russia).   I. Title.   II. Series.
DK511.D7K87   1998
947.7′4–dc21   98-15789   CIP

ISBN 0 521 62238 7 hardback
ISBN 0 521 52608 6 paperback

Contents

Maps and Figures

Maps

Figures

Notes on Names

Names in a linguistically mixed area are a familiar problem to historians. Fortunately, the case of the Donbas is not as complex as the infamous case of L'viv (Lemberg, L'vov, Lwów, Leopolis). There is no satisfactory solution for everyone, however. For example, Nikita S. Khrushchev (an ethnic Russian), Nikolai, and Aleksandr are respectively M. (Mykyta) S. Khrushchov, Mykola, and Oleksandr in Ukrainian. The Russian name for Lugansk is Luhans'k (or Luhans'ke) in Ukrainian, but most locals call their city Luhansk in Russian under the influence of the Ukrainian language. John Hughes's town was Iuzovka for most of its residents, but Iuzivka for the local Ukrainians. In the case of Ukrainian names, the matter is compounded by several changes in orthography, the most infamous being the 1933 abolition by the Soviet government of the special Ukrainian letter Ґ. In both Russian and Ukrainian cases, the problem is further complicated by frequent changes in the official names of places.

In this book, for the sake of consistency, I have generally followed Ukrainian geographical names for the present-day Ukrainian Donbas and Russian names for the Russian Donbas. The personal names are harder to deal with, but I have generally used Russian names for Russians and Ukrainian names for Ukrainians. In all cases, I have followed the Library of Congress transliteration rules. Hence Luhans'k (rather than Lugansk or Luhans'ke), Donets'k (rather than Donetsk or Donets'ke), Kharkiv (rather than Khar'kov), Taganrog (rather than Tahanrih), M. S. Hrushevs'kyi (rather than M. S. Grushevskii or M. S. Hruševs'kyj), M. O. Skrypnyk (rather than N. A. Skrypnik). I have also employed established English usages for well-known names such as Moscow (instead of Moskva), St. Petersburg (not Sankt-Peterburg), Kiev (rather than Kyiv or Kyyv), and Chernobyl' (not Chornobyl').

However, it is impossible to be entirely consistent, because, for example, there were many Ukrainians who primarily wrote in the Russian language. In confusing cases, I have listed both Ukrainian and Russian names.

The following is a partial list of important changes in geographical names:

Artemivs'k: Bakhmut (to 1924).

Donets'k: Iuzivka (to 1924 and during the German occupation of 1941–43), Stalino (1924–61).

Kadiivka: Stakhanov (1978–91).

Krasnoarmiis'k: Hryshyne (to 1934), Postysheve (1934–38), Krasnoarmiis'ke (1938–64).

Krasnodon: Sorokyne (to 1938).

Luhans'k: Voroshylovhrad (1935–58, 1970–90).

Mariupol': Zhdanov (1948–90).

Shakhty: Aleksandrovsk-Grushevskii (to 1920).

Donets'k *huberniia* formed in 1919. After a series of complex administrative changes (including a 1924 territorial concession of the easternmost part to Russia's northern Caucasus *krai* [see Map 1.2]), Donets'k *oblast'* was established in 1932. In 1938 it broke into Stalino and Voroshylovhrad *oblast'*s, subsequently Donets'k and Luhans'k *oblats'*s respectively.

Acknowledgments

For the nearly nine years I have worked on this book, I have received generous help from numerous institutions and individuals. Many archives, particularly those in Moscow, Kiev, Donets'k, and Luhans'k, have helped my research. When I began to work on this book in 1988, I could not imagine that I would ever be able to access some of these archives. I appreciate the generosity of the archivists of some twenty institutions (listed in the Sources) in which I have worked for this book. I also would like to express my gratitude to the libraries where I have read much of the published material used in this book: the former Lenin Library in Moscow, the Vernads'kyi Library in Kiev, the public libraries in Donets'k and Luhans'k, the British Library, the Cambridge University Library, the Alexander Baykov Library at the University of Birmingham, the New York Public Library, the Indiana University Library, and Harvard University's various libraries.

This work was begun while I was at King's College, Cambridge. Its generous fellowship, as well as the British Council's scholarships, helped me to work in the former Soviet Union for extended periods. Since I moved to the United States in 1990, many institutions have allowed me to make numerous research trips to Ukraine and Russia: at Indiana University, the Department of History, the Russian and East European Institute, Research and the University Graduate School, and the President's Council on International Programs; the Midwest Universities Consortium for International Activities; the National Endowment for the Humanities; the International Research and Exchange Board; and particularly the National Council for Soviet and East European Research whose 1994–95 grant allowed me to work full time on this book and complete a first draft. Many institutions have aided me in research: the former Moscow Historical Archival Institute, Moscow State University, the Ukrainian National Academy of Sciences, Donets'k State University, Luhans'k Pedagogical Institute, King's College, the University of Cambridge, the Center for Russian and East European Studies at the University of Birmingham, Indiana University, and Harvard University's Davis Center (formerly Russian Research Center) and Ukrainian Research Institute. I would like to express my gratitude here to all these institutions.

Discussion with many fellow scholars has been indispensable. Gábor T. Rittersporn, whom I have known since our Tokyo years in the 1970s, inspired some of the ideas discussed in this book. For intellectual discussion over the years, my special thanks go to John Barber, Yitzhak Brudny, Jeffrey Burds, Bill Chase, R. W. Davies, Sarah Davies, Orlando Figes, Sheila Fitzpatrick, Greg Freeze, the late Ernest Gellner, Arch Getty, Jonathan Haslam, Jochen Hellbeck, Manfred Hildermeier, Peter Holquist, Aileen Kelly, Oleg Khlevniuk, George Liber, Lars Lih, Roberta Manning, Terry Martin, Norman Naimark, Lewis Siegelbaum, Robert Thurston, Takeshi Tomita, and Amir Weiner. My Russian and Ukrainian colleagues have helped me out on many occasions: Oleg Khlevniuk, Sergei Karpenko, V. S. Lel'chuk, and the late V. Z. Drobizhev in Moscow, Iu. I. Shapoval and S. V. Kul'chyts'kyi in Kiev, Hryhorii Nemyria and Volodymir Nikol'skyi in Donets'k, and Volodya Semystiaha in Luhans'k.

I have benefited enormously from the valuable comments and penetrating criticisms by people who have read part or all of the manuscript at its various stages: John Barber, Orlando Figes, Peter Holquist, Jochen Hellbeck, Lars Lih, Roberta T. Manning, Norman Naimark, Roman Szporluk, William Taubman, Amir Weiner, and two anonymous referees of Cambridge University Press. Carolyn Morley's relentless critique of my ideas and their exposition forced me to revise the manuscript further when I thought it was all right. Without these comrades, this book would not have been what it is. My sincere thanks go to all of them.

My students at Indiana University as well as many people who commented on talks I have given in various parts of the world have also helped me to formulate and clarify many of the ideas in this book.

Frank Smith and Michael Holdsworth, my editors at Cambridge University Press, have rendered me indispensable encouragement and support. Brian R. MacDonald of the Press has carefully copyedited my book manuscript.

An earlier and much shorter version of Chapter 3 appeared as "Donbas Coalminers in War, Revolution, and Civil War," in *Making Workers Soviet: Power, Class, and Identity*, edited by Lewis Siegelbaum and Ronald Grigor Suny (1994), pp. 138–58, and used here by permission of the publisher, Cornell University Press. Maps in this book were prepared by John Hollingsworth. The University of Toronto Press and Columbia University Press have granted me permission to publish Map 1.2 and Map 1.3 respectively in an adapted form. Illustrations are published by the kind permission of Ukrainian and Russian archives and museums.

Last but not least, this book grew with my family. They lived with it. Without their support, tolerance, and good spirit I would not have been able to complete it. So I dedicate this book to Carol, Jun, and Naomi.

Introduction

RUSSIA IS A BIG COUNTRY. So is Ukraine, at least by European standards. This book is about the Donbas, or Donets Basin, a relatively small area (somewhat smaller than the state of Indiana but much larger than Massachusetts) that straddles Ukraine and Russia. Small though it may be, the Donbas, located far from the political metropolis of Moscow or Kiev, has always remained a political problem for the power center. When I was writing a book on Stalin's industrial revolution in the mid-1980s, I came to recognize the importance of this coal mining and metallurgical center, Russia's (and Ukraine's) Ruhr and the problem child of Moscow and Kiev. In 1988, after the book was published,[1] I decided to write a monograph on the tumultuous history of the Donbas.

In the meantime, several books dealing with the Donbas (up to 1924) were published in English.[2] I have benefited from these publications, particularly that of Charters Wynn. I challenge some of their conclusions and assumptions, but my primary concern in this book is with political terror in the period not covered by my predecessors, namely, the Stalin era. I place my discussion within a much larger chronological context, from the Cossack era to the 1990s, in order to emphasize the central theme of this book: throughout its history the Donbas has embodied freedom and it was this freedom that defined the extraordinarily brutal and violent political history of the Donbas.

Speaking of freedom in the autocratic Russian Empire or Stalin's Soviet Union may seem to be a contradiction in terms. In fact, this book shows that

---

[1] Hiroaki Kuromiya, *Stalin's Industrial Revolution: Politics and Workers, 1928–1932* (Cambridge University Press, 1988).

[2] Theodore H. Friedgut, *Iuzovka and Revolution*, vol. 1, *Life and Work in Russia's Donbass, 1869–1924*, and vol. 2, *Politics and Revolution in Russia's Donbass, 1869–1924* (Princeton University Press, 1989–94); Charters Wynn, *Workers, Strikes, and Pogroms: The Donbas-Dnepr Bend in Late Imperial Russia, 1870–1905* (Princeton University Press, 1992); and Susan P. McCaffray, *The Politics of Industrialization in Tsarist Russia: The Association of Southern Coal and Steel Producers, 1874–1914* (Northern Illinois University Press, 1996). Also note a book on the contemporary Donbas: Lewis H. Siegelbaum and Daniel J. Walkowitz, *Workers of the Donbas Speak: Survival and Identity in the New Ukraine, 1989–1992* (State University of New York Press, 1995).

I

while political violence was part and parcel of the history of the Donbas, paradoxically, the Donbas, the steppe land once controlled by Cossacks, symbolized freedom both in the popular imagination and in the perception of Moscow (or Kiev). I use the term freedom in its "negative" sense, namely, "freedom from" and not "freedom to."[3] With its highly developed underground (both literal and symbolic), the Donbas collieries served as a refuge for freedom seekers. This does not mean that no economic exploitation or ethnic conflict existed in the Donbas. On the contrary, attracted by the freedom and opportunities this frontier region provided, all sorts of people came to settle there from all parts of the country and beyond, and harsh economic exploitation and brutal ethnic conflict were part of the everyday life of the Donbas. In this sense, the Donbas may be somewhat analogous to Siberia, the American West, or even medieval European cities.

What is remarkable about the Donbas is that even at the height of Stalinism it continued to maintain some elements of the free steppe,[4] providing refuge to the disenfranchised, to outcasts, fugitives, criminals, and others. So important were some of these people to the operation of Donbas industry that when the politically suspect were being expelled from the cities and towns of the Donbas and the rest of the country, they were allowed to continue to work in the Donbas mines. When war and other cataclysmic events produced a large number of helpless people, they were either wooed to the Donbas by Moscow or dumped there as undesirable and dangerous elements. Consequently, the Donbas was politically suspect from the point of view of Moscow. When Stalin decided to eradicate his political enemies (real and potential), the Donbas inevitably became a target for extensive terror. Indeed, there is some evidence that the Donbas was among the areas in the country hardest hit by Stalin's Great Terror.

It is not that the Donbas was wholly unique in maintaining a degree of freedom and therefore in being terrorized by the state. The present book is a

---

[3] For the positive and negative concepts of freedom and their political implications, see Isaiah Berlin, *Four Essays on Liberty* (Oxford University Press, 1969). As Berlin explains, while negative freedom (or liberty) was and can be used to legitimate the status quo of, say, despotism and poverty, it was the positive conception of freedom that, historically speaking, tended to be "inflated into some super-personal entity – a state, a class, a nation, or the march of history itself" (p. 134). As the present book demonstrates, the Donbas indeed rejected "class," "nation," and "the march of history" for much of its history, and that was why it remained Moscow's or Kiev's problem child.

[4] The steppe and freedom were inexorably associated in the minds of Ukrainians, Russians, and other residents of the empire. Note, for example, N. Gogol's description of the "limitless, free [vol'naia], beautiful steppe." N. V. Gogol', *Polnoe sobranie sochinenii*, vol. 2 (Moscow, 1937), p. 60. I owe this citation to Judith Deutsch Kornblatt, *The Cossack Hero in Russian Literature: A Study in Cultural Mythology* (University of Wisconsin Press, 1992), p. 54. Note also Mykola Cherniavs'kyi's "free sons of the steppe" [Vil'nykh stepu syniv] and Khrystia Alchevs'ka's "embraces of the free steppe" [V obiimakh voli steppovoi], in Vadym Olifirenko, *Duma i pisnia. Dzherela literaturnoho kraieznavstva* (Donets'k, 1993), pp. 125 and 177. The Donbas folklore abounded with the same kinds of notions. See Vira Bilets'ka, "Shakhtarski pisni," *Etnohrafichnyi visnyk*, no. 5 (1927).

case study, and it will require many more detailed case studies of cities and various regions of the Russian Empire or Soviet Union to place the Donbas in proper comparative perspective. The cities, particularly Moscow, St. Petersburg (Leningrad), Kiev, and Kharkiv, also provided a degree of anonymity to their residents, but residency in the capitals and other major cities was tightly controlled by the police during the Soviet period. So, as a rule, it was far more difficult and hence much less attractive for people who wanted anonymity to live in these cities than in the Donbas. Siberia, which also symbolized freedom, may have been as attractive as the Donbas in this respect, but Siberia embodied hell as much as heaven.[5] Even though Siberia had attracted many settlers (including Ukrainians) before the revolution, after the revolution it became more a symbol of exile, convict labor, and death, particularly for Ukrainians who preferred to try their luck in the more proximate Donbas.[6]

Nor was political terror the monopoly of the Donbas. Violence was no stranger in Russian or Ukrainian history. It is evident that the whole nation, all cities and all villages, suffered from terror under Stalin. It would be inappropriate to overemphasize terror in the Donbas. The fact that the Donbas coal-mining industry and quite a few of its workers were critically important to the country's economy (and hence to its military) mitigated Stalin's terror in all likelihood. Nevertheless, the terror of the 1930s in the Donbas was extraordinary, and violence was an integral part of political life in the Donbas both theretofore and thereafter. In other words, the present monograph maintains that the Donbas was an extreme example of the contention between freedom and terror and that an extreme case can be extremely revealing.

Throughout its history, the Donbas has been politically unmanageable. Forces from the political metropolises have tried to capture the hearts and minds of the Donbas only to get burned. This has been most clearly demonstrated at times of crisis such as the revolution and civil war period, the World War II years, and at the collapse of the Soviet Union. For example, unlike the neighboring Don, which articulated political ideas in 1917 (such as "Cossack republicanism" and "Soviet republicanism"),[7] the Donbas rejected all political groups. The political atmosphere of the Donbas appeared noxious and dangerous to all parties concerned. It was Leon Trotsky, Stalin's archenemy,

---

[5]Galya Diment and Yuri Slezkine, eds., *Between Heaven and Hell: The Myth of Siberia in Russian Culture* (New York, 1993).

[6]Stephen Kotkin, *Magnetic Mountain: Stalinism as a Civilization* (University of California Press, 1995), presents a more heavenly picture of the Russian East (despite a hellish climate and all the horrors of everyday life), but for Ukrainians, particularly the dekulakized, the Donbas was a temporary refuge from which one day they hoped to return to their native villages, whereas Siberia was too distant and too horrible for them to entertain hopes of one day reclaiming their homelands.

[7]Peter I. Holquist, "A Russian Vendee: The Practice of Revolutionary Politics in the Don Countryside, 1917–1921" (Ph.D. diss., Columbia University, 1995).

who best described the political history of the Donbas: "One can't go to the Donbas without a [political] gas mask."[8]

This book belongs to the genre of *kraieznavstvo* (*kraevedenie*), or regional studies. In focusing my study on one region in Ukraine and Russia, I have benefited particularly from the concept of "exit" (as opposed to "loyalty" and "voice") in Albert O. Hirschman's work.[9] It is my contention that the Donbas has always functioned as an "exit," or refuge, an alternative to political conformity or protest. Various analyses of frontiers and borders[10] and historical geography[11] have also been very useful in constructing my own ideas, even if many of the works are concerned with national identities whereas the Donbas case shows how little they mattered.

In both a geographical and symbolic sense, the Donbas constitutes a particular community, just as a nation, city, or village does. It is a space, a frontier land, where inner yearnings for freedom, wild exploitation, and everyday violence have competed for dominance. Like other communities, the steppe, with all its freedom and terror, was an imagined community.[12] Like others, this imagined community enjoyed myths. The peculiarity of the Donbas was that however differently it may have been imagined by various groups of people, the Donbas lived up to its reputation of freedom and terror.

At one point in the course of working on this book, I wanted to write a microhistory,[13] something that would explore Soviet politics from a microscopic

---

[8] Quoted in *XI z'izd Komunistychnoi partii (bil'shovykiv) Ukrainy, 5–15 chervnia 1930 r. Sten. zvit* (Kharkiv, 1930), p. 373.

[9] Albert O. Hirschman, *Exit, Voice, and Loyalty: Responses to Decline in Firms, Organizations, and States* (Harvard University Press, 1970).

[10] Peter Sahlins, *Boundaries: The Making of France and Spain in the Pyrenees* (University of California Press, 1989); William Cronin, George Miles, and Jay Gitlin, eds., *Under an Open Sky: Rethinking America's Western Past* (New York, 1992); Catherine Wendy Bracewell, *The Uskoks of Senj: Piracy, Banditry, and Holy War in the Sixteenth-Century Adriatic* (Cornell University Press, 1992); and Linda Colley, *The Significance of the Frontier in British History* (Austin, Texas, 1995). See also *Russian History / Histoire Russe*, 19:1–4 (1992), devoted to the frontiers in Russian history.

[11] Of particular interest are Mark Bassin, "Inventing Siberia: Visions of the Russian East in the Early Nineteenth Century," *American Historical Review*, 96:3 (June 1991), pp. 763–94, and "Turner, Solov'ev, and the 'Frontier Hypothesis': The Nationalist Significance of Open Spaces," *Journal of Modern History*, 65 (September 1993), pp. 413–511; and David Hooson, ed., *Geography and National Identity* (Oxford, 1994). Note also Patricia Yaeger, eds., *The Geography of Identity* (University of Michigan Press, 1996), particularly Pieter M. Judson, "Frontiers, Islands, Forests, Stones: Mapping the Geography of a German Identity in the Habsburg Monarchy, 1848–1900," pp. 382–406

[12] For an analysis of how a particular place, in this case, the Don (part of which belonged to the Donbas) in southern Russia was imagined, see Holquist, "A Russian Vendee."

[13] The most interesting recent work of this type on the Stalin era is Jochen Hellbeck, ed., *Tagebuch aus Moskau 1931–1939* (Munich, 1996). Note also Orlando Figes, *A People's Tragedy: A History of the Russian Revolution* (London, 1996), which combines both macro- and microperspectives.

point of view à la, for example, Robert Darnton, Natalie Zemon Davis, and Carlo Ginzburg. Such a history may become my next work, and the challenge of the so-called subjectivist school will have to be taken up,[14] but the sources I unearthed in Ukrainian and Russian archives pushed me instead toward an abstraction of the notion of "space," the "free steppe" in the case of the Donbas, almost a macrohistory as opposed to my earlier intent. The late Ernest Gellner's influence as well helped me to analyze the Donbas in macrohistorical terms, for example, in terms of nations and nationalism (or, to be more precise, nonnations and nonnationalism in this case).[15] Nevertheless, this book is still about the "ordinary," nameless "common" people in the Donbas (although I have tried to identify them wherever possible), and how their lives were affected by state terror.

Through abundant cases of individual lives, I demonstrate the complexity of the place and the period for the masses of the people involved. Because the main concern of the book is with the Donbas as a region, I can provide only snippets of individual lives. Nevertheless, the number of cases is overwhelming. As well as interviewing people in Ukraine and Russia, I have been able to unearth numerous stories in various libraries and newly opened archives in Donets'k, Luhans'k, Kiev, and Moscow. I have collected them ad nauseam. Tragedies, crushed lives, incidents of state as well as popular terror, heroism, villainy, cowardice, and gallantry are discussed here in great detail.

Of all the sources I have consulted, the formerly closed archives have been the most useful. Notably, "criminal" files of repressed individuals in the former security police archives in Donets'k and Luhans'k, Ukraine, are the source of many hitherto unknown stories on those repressed during the 1930s (Chapter 6) and in the war and postwar years, as well as on the Holocaust and war criminals in the Donbas (Chapter 7). I have been less successful in accessing archival sources on the more recent years, in part because of the official secrecy laws in Ukraine and Russia. Nevertheless, I have found considerable new information on the tumultuous lives of people in the Donbas (Chapter 8). All in all, these three chapters, along with Chapters 3 and 5 (on war, revolution, and civil war, and the 1932–33 famine, respectively) compose the core of this book.

To write about how "ordinary people" experienced terror is a formidable challenge. What terror meant to the people and how they felt, thought, and acted can not be answered without examining their world views. Yet one knows well, empirically, that belief and ideology determine action as much as they do not. To examine an era of rapid change and transformation, both

---

[14]Manfred Hildermeier organized a conference on this challenge in Munich in June 1996, "Stalinismus vor dem zweiten Weltkrieg."

[15]Ernest Gellner, *Nations and Nationalism* (Cornell University Press, 1983), and *Encounters with Nationalism* (Oxford, 1994).

synchronic and diachronic analysis is needed. While historical sources, even hitherto secret archival documents, cannot tell the "truth" in and of themselves, historical documents and events cannot be treated merely as texts or semiotic fields.[16] Historical events took place under real material and human constraints. Such universal constraints as power, greed, fear, hope, and hunger have to be entered into the equation. Only then do the questions of how people lived in a historically specific context and how their perceptions changed become comprehensible.[17] I have tried to do this in the present book through the use both of detailed statistics when available and personal case histories.

In writing on terror in the Soviet Union, one must state categorically that political terror on a mass scale in the modern era is not unique to the Soviet Union. Adolf Hitler, Mao Tse-tung, Idi Amin, Pol Pot, to name just a few, perpetrated mass terror. This fact does not mitigate the monstrosity of the terror in the Soviet Union. However, its enormity has sometimes been downplayed for other reasons, for example, in recognition of Stalin's victory over Nazi Germany. A similar phenomenon might have occurred with regard to Germany had Hitler won the war, as Saul Friedlander posits in his criticism of Hayden White for the implications of White's epistemological relativism:

> For instance, what would have happened if the Nazis had won the war? No doubt there would have been a plethora of pastoral emplotments of life in the Third Reich and of comic emplotments of the disappearance of its victims, mainly the Jews. How, in this case, would White (who clearly rejects any revisionist version of the Holocaust) define an epistemological criterion for refuting a comic interpretation of these events, without using any reference to "political effectiveness"?[18]

This hypothetical case was a reality for the Soviet Union. Consequently the Soviet case is significantly more complex than it might otherwise have been. Stalin's terror was monstrous. Its operations were complex and extensive, writing about it is extremely painful, and its analysis is daunting for historians, but

---

[16]There is a vast literature on the subject. Note, however, Gabrielle M. Spiegel, "History, Historicism, and the Social Logic of the Text in the Middle Ages," *Speculum*, 65 (1995), pp. 59–86; a discussion ("History and Post-Modernism") in *Past and Present*, nos. 131 (May 1991), 133 (November 1991), and 135 (May 1992); and Ernest Gellner, *Postmodernism, Reason and Religion* (London, 1992).

[17]For an interesting discussion of these issues of belief and action, see Marshall Sahlins, *Islands of History* (University of Chicago Press, 1985), and *How "Natives" Think: About Captain Cook, for Example* (University of Chicago Press, 1995); and Gananath Obeyesekere, *The Apotheosis of Captain Cook: European Mythmaking in the Pacific* (Princeton University Press, 1992).

[18]Saul Friedlander, "Introduction," in Friedlander, ed., *Probing the Limits of Representation: Nazism and the "Final Solution"* (Harvard University Press, 1992), p. 10. For White, see his *The Content of the Form: Narrative Discourse and Historical Representation* (Johns Hopkins University Press, 1987), p. 75, where he contends: "[W]hen it comes to apprehending the historical record, there are no grounds to be found in the historical record itself for preferring one way of constructing its meaning over another."

this book suggests that there is no denying Stalin's direct role in it.[19]

I am less interested in examining Stalin's culpability, however, than in analyzing the political mechanism of his terror.

The fundamental issue here is the construction of "enemy." The Donbas, in Moscow's imagination, was fraught with "enemies." Moscow's perception may well have been accurate, as the present book suggests. Yet political authorities lacked effective means by which to gauge the political mood of the population, notwithstanding the seemingly almighty secret police with its extensive surveillance network. This was because virtually all critical political thought was driven underground. From the 1932–33 famine crisis onward, in its efforts to eradicate the invisible, imagined "enemies," Moscow constructed a new image of enemy, the class-neutral "enemy of the people," instead of the "class enemy," which was constrained by Marxist ideology.

This new image was not simply imposed from above upon a politically passive population. The Donbas case demonstrates that people created their own images of enemies, using the official political discourse to suit their purposes.[20] People who had suffered oppression for generations seized on the concept of "enemy" as a focus for their frustration and anger. Traditional prejudices surfaced and received popular affirmation under a new label, the "enemy." Anti-Semitism is one disturbing example. Before World War II, the Soviet authorities had discouraged this prejudice of long standing, but it died hard in society. Such was the case, at least in the Donbas, where few Jews were among the mining population.

The problem was that the "enemy of the people" was so inclusive that it embraced the "people" themselves. The otherwise safest political option of passivity was not safe in the case of Stalin's Soviet Union, because the enemy hunt concerned precisely those hidden, invisible enemies who, in Stalin's imagination, feigned passivity. Thus, as if caught in a maelstrom, virtually everyone got involved in the terror in some capacity or another at some stage or another. The Donbas case demonstrates how blurred and confusing the concept of the "enemy of the people" became. Even though Moscow tightly controlled its terror against the "enemies of the people," the operations became so extensive as to be self-defeating.

There is no need to assume the impossibility (or difficulty) of "subjectivity," or the "private sphere," in Stalinist society, as some historians contend.[21]

---

[19]Note the uncritical and unsubstantiated contention by Robert W. Thurston, *Life and Terror in Stalin's Russia, 1934–1941* (Yale University Press, 1996), p. 227: "Stalin was not guilty of mass first-degree murder from 1934 to 1941."

[20]One form of this practice is denunciation. For a perceptive analysis of this in a European context, see Sheila Fitzpatrick and Robert Gellately, eds., *Accusatory Practices: Denunciation in Modern European History, 1789–1989* (University of Chicago Press, 1997).

[21]See, for example, Hellbeck, *Tagebuch*. Note also Kotkin, *Magnetic Mountain*, and Igal Halfin and Jochen Hellbeck, "Rethinking the Stalinist Subject: Stephen Kotkin's 'Magnetic Mountain'

For one, as Manfred Hildermeier has argued, just as the "objective" world is not the whole world, so "the 'inner world' and 'self-consciousness' do not compose the whole world."[22] Indeed, one can safely assume that in a country like Stalin's Soviet Union, a complete break between an individual's thought and action was possible. This break explains why Stalin needed his own version of trials of conscience.[23] For another, much of the argument of the "subjectivist" school seems to assume implicitly or explicitly the immutability of the regime in discussing an individual's action (or practice). The regime was not at all immutable in parts of the Soviet Union: the war with Germany did away with Stalin's power in occupied territory. (This is a fact very often missed by studies focused on Moscow or St. Petersburg – hence the importance of regional studies.) The German occupation brought entirely new factors into politics. Even at the height of the Great Terror, individuals no doubt imagined political alternatives. It was patently clear both to the ruler and the ruled that war brings such alternatives. This indeed became the case for large areas of the Soviet Union, including the Donbas.

An apparent contradiction has always been inherent in both traditional and new approaches to the subject of Stalin's terror. In condemnation of Stalinist terror, historians implicitly assume that there was no serious political resistance to Stalin. At the same time, in support of Stalin's political foes, historians also assume that there actually was considerable resistance.[24] While the subjectivist interpretation allows for little or no room for dissent, historians who focus on dissent, resistance, and subversion tend to take too uncritically official archival documents full of fabricated information.[25] I contend that it would be more fruitful to conceptualize the "frontiers," for example, the free steppe and the

---

and the State of Soviet Historical Studies," *Jahrbücher für Geschichte Osteuropas*, 44:3 (1996), pp. 456–63.

[22] Manfred Hildermeier, "The Circular Flow of Theory: Some Interpretive Problems of Prewar Stalinism in the 1990s" (paper presented at the "Stalinismus vor dem zweiten Weltkrieg" conference, June 1996).

[23] For the best analysis of the similarity between the Inquisition and the Great Terror, see Kotkin, *Magnetic Mountain*, pp. 336–38. However, Kotkin tends to minimize Stalin's terror by treating it as intraparty business.

[24] Note Conquest, *The Great Terror*, and Stephen F. Cohen, *Bukharin and the Bolshevik Revolution: A Political Biography, 1888–1938* (New York, 1973).

[25] This tendency is blatant in many works by historians of the former Soviet Union. For more careful approaches, see Jeffrey J. Rossman, "The Teikovo Cotton Workers' Strike of April 1932: Class, Gender and Identity Politics in Stalin's Russia," *Russian Review*, 56 (January 1997); Sarah Davies, *Popular Opinion in Stalin's Russia: Terror, Propaganda and Dissent, 1934–1941* (Cambridge University Press, 1997); and Leslie A. Rimmel, "Another Kind of Fear: The Kirov Murder and the End of Bread Rationing in Leningrad," *Slavic Review*, 56:3 (Fall 1997). I have explored this problem in more detail in "How Do We Know What the People Thought under Stalin?" (paper prepared for the conference "The Stalin Period: New Ideas, New Conversations," University of California, Riverside, 12–15 March 1998).

minds of the people, which the powers that be could not fully control.[26] This case study suggests a new way of studying Stalin's terror.

[26]Note J. Arch Getty's important concept on center-local relations in his *Origins of the Great Purges: The Soviet Communist Party Reconsidered, 1933–1938* (Cambridge University Press, 1985).

I   Life on the Wild Field

A VISITOR TO THE DONBAS, even today's industrialized Donbas, will marvel at the vast, open steppe land that surrounds it. The Donbas is part of the area which used to be called the "wild steppe" (*dyke pole, dikoe pole*). In an analogy with the American expression "wild west,"[1] one might call the area the "wild south." In any case, it was so called because it was historically a theater of continuous military operations. Its geographic peculiarities made the steppe a wild, dangerous area: it "stretches from Mongolia westward to the Carpathians and has an extension into the middle Danubian area. In old times it offered an excellent road for the Mongolian nomads, with no natural obstacles to bar their way until the Carpathian Mountains." Therefore, according to George Vernadsky,

> In a sense, the steppe may be likened to the sea. With sufficient forces it could be blockaded but it was impossible for either the Russians or the Cumans [i.e., Polovtsians, or Kipchaks] to control or guard every section of it. The Cuman horde made yearly rounds of the steppe, men following their grazing horses and cattle; the section in the vicinity of the nomad tents could not be entered by any outsider but the rest of the steppe was practically no man's land, at least periodically.[2]

It was here where Slavs, numerous nomadic peoples such as Pechenegs and Polovtsians (Kipchaks), and later Tartars staged long and bloody battles for many centuries. In the psyche of Russians (and Ukrainians), again according to Vernadsky, the steppe had special meaning:

> This was the *pole* ("prairie") of the old Russian epic poems, the sense of the heroic deeds of Ilia Muromets and other Russian legendary *bogatyri*

---

[1] William Cronin, George Miles, and Jay Gitlin, eds., *Under an Open Sky: Rethinking America's Western Past* (New York, 1992), is an inspiring work.

[2] George Vernadsky, *Kievan Russia* (Yale University Press, 1948), pp. 13 and 157. For the meaning of the steppe in Kievan Rus', see also Charles J. Halperin, *Russia and the Golden Horde* (Indiana University Press, 1985), ch. 2. Even now a newspaper called *Dikoe pole* is published in Alchevs'k, near Luhans'k.

("valiant knights"); also that of actual battles – of the exploits of thousands of real Russian warriors, whether victorious, like Vladimir Monomakh, or vanquished like Igor of Novgorod-Seversk. Covered with *kovyl* (a special kind of grass peculiar to south Russia) and abundant in animal life, but also in Cuman archers, the steppe held out a strong attraction to the adventurous, while repelling the weak. It is poetically, if tersely, described in the *Lay of Igor's Campaign* of the late twelfth century and hardly less poetically but with much more elaborate verbosity in Nikolai Gogol's *Taras Bulba* seven centuries later.

Vernadsky goes on to add:

> In the course of the fifteenth and sixteenth centuries this no man's land be-came the abode of the Ukrainian and Russian Cossacks, who eventually or-ganized themselves in strong military communes ("hosts"), of which the Za-porozhie – beyond the Dnieper cataracts – and Don hosts – the latter in the lower Don region – were the most important two.[3]

The wild field of the Donbas is situated between these two historically Cossack areas.[4] It was not fully incorporated into the Russian Empire until the era of Catherine in the late eighteenth century.

Today the Donbas straddles Ukraine and Russia, but its history, up to the present time, embodies the characteristics of the wild field – freedom, mili-tancy, violence, terror, independence – that transcend the borders of Russian and Ukraine. The political history of the Donbas has been defined by these characteristics even after "modernity" came to the wild field. If anything, "modernity" seems to have recreated these very characteristics of the steppe frontiers in the Donbas (see Chapter 2).

Part of what came to be called New Russia,[5] the Donbas lies in south-eastern Ukraine (present-day Donets'k and Luhans'k *oblast'*s) and extends to southwestern Russia (part of Rostov *oblast'*), the area surrounded roughly by

[3] Vernadsky, *Kievan Russia*, pp. 157–58. For a critical review of Vernadsky's view of the steppe, see Charles J. Halperin, "Russia and the Steppe: George Vernadsky and Eurasianism," *Forschungen zur osteuropäischen Geschichte* (Berlin), 36 (1983), ch. 4.

[4] For the Donbas and the wild steppe, see Petro Lavriv, "Dyke pole: pravda i mify. Populiarnyi narys pro nashe minule," *Donbas*, 1992, nos. 9–10, and "Dyke pole: pravda i mify. Litopys zemli Donets'koi," *Donbas*, 1992, nos. 11–12. For the interaction of the two Cossack groups in the Donbas, see V. A. Pirko, "Kozatstvo na Donechchyni," in *Ridnyi krai. Istoryko-kraieznavchyi al'manakh*, vol. 1 (Donets'k, 1995), and "O vzaimootnosheniiakh zaporozhskikh i donskikh kazakov v XVI–XVII vv.," in *Donbass i Priazov'e: problemy sotsial'nogo, natsional'nogo i dukhovnogo razvitiia* (Mariupol', 1993). For the contemporary politicization of the Donbas's pre-carious position between Ukraine and Russia, see Andrew Wilson's excellent article, "The Donbas between Ukraine and Russia: The Use of History in Political Disputes," *Journal of Contemporary History*, 30 (1995).

[5] For a very good description of New Russia at the beginning of the twentieth century, see V. P. Semenov-Tian-Shanskii, ed., *Rossiia. Polnoe geograficheskoe opisanie nashego otechestva. Natsiol'naia i dorozhnaia kniga. Tom 14. Novorossiia i Krym* (St. Petersburg, 1910).

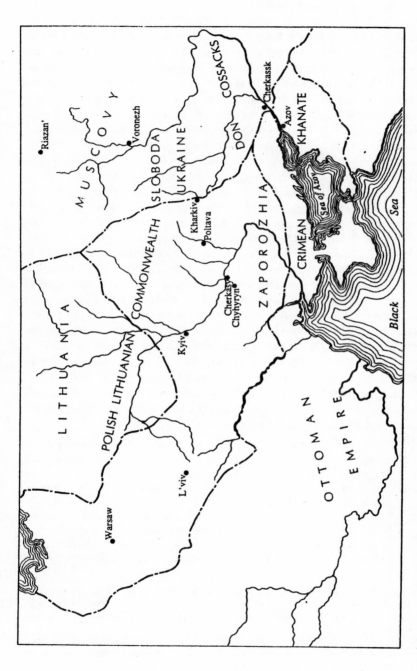

Map 1.1. Ukraine in the sixteenth and seventeenth centuries. Adapted from M. M. Arkas, *Istoriia Ukrainy-Rusi z 210 maliunkamy i portretamy ta 9 kartamy* (St. Petersburg, 1908).

the middle and lower Donets River (a tributary of the Don River) and the Sea of Azov. In a more limited sense, the Donbas refers to the coal-steel industrial region that has developed in this area and is as large as the state of Vermont in the United States. It was Russia's (and Ukraine's) Ruhr.[6] On the eve of 1917, the year of revolutions, the heartland of the Donbas, which included major cities or settlements such as Bakhmut, Iuzivka, Luhans'k, and Mariupol', belonged to Katerynoslav (Ekaterinoslav) province (*huberniia, guberniia*), and its eastern part, with major cities or settlements such as Makiivka, Taganrog, and Aleksandrovsk-Grushevskii, to the Don Cossack Host (*Voisko*) province.

The Donbas has never been a single administrative unit, making statistical compilations difficult for historians. However, its population grew very rapidly through intense migrations, once it was fully integrated into the empire,[7] and it developed into an ethnically diverse border area united by economic factors. After the Bolshevik Revolution the coal-mining industry in the Shakhty area in North Caucasus *krai* of the Russian Republic was subordinated administratively to the management in the Ukrainian Donbas. When, in 1928, it was announced that "economic counterrevolution" had been uncovered in the Shakhty coal mines, the Soviet government contended that such incidents were common in the whole of the Donbas, that is, on both sides of the border.

The climate of the Donbas is temperate-continental. Still its physical environment is harsh. The Soviet dissident Petro Grigorenko, whose son died of dysentery in August 1934 in Stalino (Iuzivka until 1924), called its climate "murderous."[8] Any visitor to Stalino will confirm Grigorenko's observation.

The harsh climate was made worse by a dull social environment. A Russian engineer who in the early 1890s landed a position in Rutchenkove, just outside Iuzivka, left the following impression of the Donbas:

> The boredom, the monotony, of this exceptionally dull life were truly debilitating. All around was the steppe, flat as a board, lacking even so much as a gulch, in the winter blindingly white, in the spring all black except for patches of snow. It was fair only in early summer when the wild peonies tinted the steppe red, and the song of hundreds of larks rang almost like chimes. But even this beauty was marred by the deliberately prosaic setting of the mine, which seemed incompatible with spring – especially the great mounds of grey-white rock, reeking of sulphur, where, through pale smoke, one watched the jerking outlines of the workman's figure, endlessly emptying

---

[6] In 1917, the year of revolutions, the Donbas produced 87% of the country's coal output, 70% of pig iron, 57% of steel, more than 90% of coke, and more than 60% of soda and mercury. Iu. V. Afonin, "Monopolistychna burzhuaziia Donbasu v 1917 r.," *Ukrains'kyi istorychnyi zhurnal*, 1990, no. 9, p. 45.

[7] In 1897 the population of the (present-day Ukrainian) Donbas was less than 700,000, but it grew to more than two million by 1920 and to nearly seven million by 1959. Petro Lavriv, *Istoriia pidvenno-skhidnoi Ukrainy* (Kiev, 1996), pp. 175–74.

[8] Petro G. Grigorenko, *Memoirs*, tr. Thomas P. Whitney (New York, 1982), p. 61.

wagonloads of rocks. I recall the strange sense of bondage that often seized me in my first years at the mine, most acutely in spring. I felt a strong urge to run away, and I was weary to tears.[9]

Makiivka on the western edge of Don Cossack Host province is an important site of colliery and metallurgy. It was here that in 1895 the Makeevka (Makiivka) Coal Company was founded by the Länderbank of Austria with the Société Générale of France.[10] A French Catholic visitor to Makiivka noted in July 1908 that "the climate is trying. . . . At present, I think it is hotter than Palestine and I am told that, in winter, it is colder than St. Petersburg." He continued to write of his impression of the Donbas and Makiivka:

> It is a strange country. The soil is as black as the coal they take from it. There are no trees and no grass and it seems even more of a desert than those I saw beyond the Jordan. The only vegetation is an unusual kind of plant with twisted leaves which are greyish-green in color. The sweeping undulations of the terrain are pitted, here and there, by deep gullies torn out by the rains which rush along the rich soil and disappear leaving scarcely any moisture. The air is hot and dry, and the driving wind that comes off the steppe must make this a terrible place in winter.[11]

Come spring, the streets of Makiivka "were running with water": "If only there had been a few gondolas in sight," one could "easily have imagined himself in Venice." After the floods, mud was everywhere – "the mud of Makeyevka [Makiivka] could never be imagined by one who has not seen it with his own eyes."[12]

Just thirteen kilometers to the west, in Iuzivka in Katerynoslav province, the Menshevik George Denike had a similar impression when he went there after the 1905 revolution:

> There were nice houses and apartments for workers, but the strongest impression that remained with me from Iuzovka was that I got stuck in the mud in the street and barely managed to get out. It was an unpaved street, and there was such an unbelievable amount of mud that I got stuck. I floundered

[9] Aleksandr I. Fenin, *Coal and Politics in Late Imperial Russia: Memoirs of a Russian Mining Engineer*, tr. Alexandre Fediaevsky and ed. Susan P. McCaffray (Northern Illinois University, 1990), p. 43.

[10] John McKay, *Pioneers for Profit: Foreign Entrepreneurship and Russian Industrialization, 1885–1913* (University of Chicago Press, 1970), pp. 392 and 395. For more of Makiivka history, see *Makeevka: spravochnik* (Donets'k, 1981).

[11] Patrick A. Croghan, *The Peasant of Makeyevka: Biography of Bishop Pius Neveu, A.A.* (Worcester, Mass., 1982), pp. 14 and 15.

[12] Ibid., pp. 31 and 121. To serve the Catholic community, mainly of French and Belgian nationals, the Catholic Church maintained parishes in various places in the Donbas. (See Cl. de Boisanger, *Vivre en Russie an temps de la N.E.P.* [Paris, 1961], p. 54.) In Ienakiieve, for example, in 1915 there were "about 3,000 Catholics, most of whom were employed in the huge Russo-Belgian metallurgical works." (Croghan, *The Peasant of Makeyevka*, p. 32.)

around for a long time, and finally had to use my arms to help myself crawl out.[13]

It was such that in spring and autumn Iuzivka was unreachable for two to three weeks.[14] Even in 1923, of 334 settlements in Donets'k province, only 11 had paved streets, 212 had unpaved streets, and 111 had no streets at all. Workers had to wade in mud to go to work.[15] Mud would soon be replaced by frequent duststorms. Despite the inhospitable climate, the foreign visitor to Makiivka was optimistic about its future:

> In this comparative desert, one senses an intense life. The steppe is criss-crossed with telephone wires and with cables which distribute light and power. Not many large cities have such facilities. Makeyevka, of course, is officially only a village, but it is a village with a future. They tell me that ten years ago you would scarcely see a dog here. Now there are almost 25,000 people and more dogs – all of them black – than I have seen anywhere except perhaps in Constantinople. I am sure that in thirty years, Makeyevka will have a population of over 200,000 people.[16]

Twenty-nine years later, in 1937, Makiivka had a population somewhat short of his prediction, 160,239,[17] but, according to the 1939 census (which is widely believed to be exaggerated), Makiivka exceeded the Frenchman's prediction: 241,897.[18]

The "nice houses and flats for workers" Denike observed in Iuzivka may have actually been the "little red-brick houses" for technicians and administrators that the Welshman John Hughes (who had founded Iuzivka and after whom the city was named) built, "just like the ones I [Khrushchev] saw on my trip to England [in 1956]."[19] Certainly, in some areas nice houses were built for workers,[20] and, as Theodore H. Friedgut has shown in his detailed study of life in Iuzivka, by the time of World War I, "the civilizing influences" of education and, more generally, of "a modern culture" came to be felt in the

[13]Leopold H. Haimson in collaboration with Ziva Galili y Garcia and Richard Wortman, *The Making of Three Russian Revolutionaries: Voices from the Menshevik Past* (Cambridge University Press, 1987), p. 356.

[14]P. Surozhskii, "Krai uglia i zheleza. Ocherk," *Sovremennik*, 1913, no. 4, p. 301.

[15]*Itogi sploshnoi podvornoi perepisi Donetskoi gubernii (ianvar'–fevral' 1923 g.)*, vol. 1 (Kharkiv, 1923), p. XXI.

[16]Croghan, *The Peasant of Makeyevka*, p. 15.

[17]RGAE, f. 1562, op. 329, d. 151, l. 167, and d. 141, ll. 22–23 (for the full name of archives cited here and hereafter, see Sources). See also *Vsesoiuznaia perepis' naseleniia 1937 g. Kratkie itogi* (Moscow, 1991), p. 66.

[18]*Itogi vsesouznoi perepisi naseleniia 1959 goda. SSSR (Svodnyi tom)* (Moscow, 1962), p. 30. *Materialy k serii 'Narody Sovetskogo Soiuza'. Ch. 5. Perepis' 1939 goda* (Moscow, 1990), pp. 913–14, gives a slightly lower figure: 240,145.

[19]*Khrushchev Remembers*, tr. and ed. Strobe Talbott, introduction, commentary, and notes by Edward Crankshaw (Boston, 1970), p. 403.

[20]See, for example, Fenin, *Coal and Politics*, pp. 79–80.

Donbas. This may have been true for some factory workers who enjoyed much better housing, education, and medical care than did the colliers.[21] Denike, no doubt working mainly with factory and railway workers, even went so far as to note that "I didn't feel that there was the kind of poverty in Lugansk which I sensed in other places."[22]

Yet other accounts are not so favorable. The "civilizing influences" of modernity were hardly to be seen; on the contrary, modern industrial development came to recreate the wildness of the steppe engraved in the Russian and Ukrainian imagination. A mining engineer observed on life in the 1890s: "The uncleanliness and filth in the barracks was so awful that, when I decided to inspect them in my first days as manager, the above-ground senior miner [*poverkhnostnyi*] warned me threateningly: fleas. In fact, after visiting three or four such barracks, I had suffered innumerable bites and noticed with horror that the tops of my high boots were alive, so to speak." With much condescension, he went on to say that the peasant worker in the Donbas "was capable of turning a decent lodging into a virtual cesspool, as was the fate of the model barracks built at the Verovka mine."[23] Another, sympathetic observer noted in 1913 that Iuzivka was "awfully filthy and sickly," while Horlivka, another settlement to the north of Iuzivka, was "quite a cesspool": "I have never seen such a dark and hopeless life as in Horlivka."[24] According to the writer Konstantin Paustovsky who lived in Iuzivka during World War I, it was "a disorderly, dirty settlement, surrounded by hovels and mud huts. Different neighborhoods were called by words like 'dog' and 'filthy,' and the gloomy humor of the names was the best proof of how wretched and miserable they were."[25]

The artist N. A. Kasatkin, who lived in Aleksandrovsk-Grushevskii in 1894, noted his impression of the city: "The city is dirty . . . and dusty. Hither and thither squalid men, women, and children roam between a sooty city and black coal mines."[26] The image was black all over. A similar impression was received by a visitor to the city from nearby Kamensk in 1917:

---

[21] Theodore H. Friedgut, *Iuzovka and Revolution*, vol. 1, *Life and Work in Russia's Donbas, 1869–1924* (Princeton University Press, 1989) (quotations from pp. 330 and 334).

[22] Haimson, *The Making of Three Russian Revolutionaries*, p. 356.

[23] Fenin, *Coal and Politics*, pp. 51 and 53.

[24] Surozhskii, "Krai uglia i zheleza," pp. 300, 304, and 315. For extremely poor living conditions in Horlivka and in the Donbas in the early twentieth century, see also Loren R. Graham, *The Ghost of the Executed Engineer: Technology and the Fall of the Soviet Union* (Harvard University Press, 1993), pp. 8–10 (P. I. Pal'chinskii, who was to be executed in 1929 by the Soviet government, investigated the living conditions in the Donbas and reported to his superior on his findings, whereupon he was dismissed).

[25] Konstantin Paustovsky, *The Story of a Life*, tr. Joseph Barnes (New York, 1964), p. 429. See also Charters Wynn, *Workers, Strikes, and Pogroms: The Donbass-Dnepr Bend in Late Imperial Russia, 1870–1905* (Princeton University Press, 1992), p. 30.

[26] *Shakhty. Istoriko-kraevedcheskii ocherk o gorode* (Rostov on the Don, 1974), p. 23.

Figure 1.1. Miners' settlement in Horlivka, at the end of the nineteenth century. From *Ocherki istorii Donetskoi oblastnoi Komsomol'skoi organizatsii* (Kiev and Donets'k, 1987), insert.

> The miners in the surrounding district lived very wretchedly. . . . Everything was black in this mining settlement, even in summer. The mud in the streets was black like liquid soot after a downpour of rain, and so deep and sticky that not only passers-by, but even horses, could hardly pull their feet out of it. The faces of the people and their children were also black because there was no soap. They lived in small and primitive huts infested with vermin.[27]

The conditions barely changed even after the October Revolution. Victor Kravchenko, who in 1922 went to the Donbas to become a miner, noted: "A walk through the miners' settlement scarcely raised our spirits. It was a long, dingy lane flanked by time-worn shacks and raw-new barracks. A pall of coal dust enveloped everything. The romance of 'building socialism' with our own hands ebbed rapidly, and it took many weeks to restore some of the zest with which we had started."[28] Khrushchev tells us the following horror story: "At the [Rutchenkove] mine where I worked after the Civil War, there was a latrine, but the miners misused it so badly that you had to enter the latrine on stilts if you didn't want to track filth home to your own apartment at the end of the workday. I remember I was once sent somewhere to install some mining

---

[27] N. M. Borodin, *One Man in His Time* (London, 1955), pp. 15–16. The Donbas settlements were "buried in black coal dust mixed with sticky dirt," so much so that alongside the barracks "not one blade of grass grew." See Mikhai l Baitalsky, *Notebooks for the Grandchildren: Recollections of a Trotskyist Who Survived the Stalin Terror*, tr. Marilyn Vogt-Downey (Atlantic Highlands, N.J., 1995), p. 106.

[28] Victor Kravchenko, *I Chose Freedom: The Personal and Political Life of a Soviet Official* (New York, 1946), pp. 34–35.

Figure 1.2. A colliers' settlement, Red October Mine, Ienakiieve, 1924, with the vast steppe land in the background. From TsDKFFA, od. zb. 0-181508.

equipment and found the miners living in a barracks with double-deck bunks. It wasn't unusual for the men in the upper bunks simply to urinate over the side."[29]

In any case, on the eve of World War I, according to one survey, 40.4 percent of Donbas colliers lived in "dugouts" (*zemliankas*), half buried in the earth, most of which had no floor or windows and were said to be unfit even for livestock; 2.5 percent in barns and summer kitchen houses; 22.3 percent in stone or brick houses; and 25.8 percent in peasants' huts. The average living space was small: 64.8 percent of them had less than 4 square meters a person. Of the 9,658 workers surveyed, only 3,253 had sleeping places with only 21 mattresses and 54 pillows for every 100 workers. According to another survey,

---

[29] *Khrushchev Remembers: The Last Testament*, tr. and ed. Strobe Talbott, foreword by Edward Crankshaw and introduction by Jerrold L. Schecter (Boston, 1974), p. 88. No doubt, housing conditions were spartan, to put it mildly. According to the 1923 Donbas city census, of 159,007 families surveyed, only 1,695, or 1.1% had a toilet in their flats. In Starobil's'k, Lysychans'k, Shakhty, and Iuzivka, no family lived in a flat with a lavatory. (*Itogi sploshnoi podvornoi perepisi Donetskoi gubernii*, p. xxiii.) Yet, as an official from the miners' union put it in 1933, attitudinal problems, perpetuated by misery and despair, may have been partly responsible: embarrassed by foreign workers' questions about why the toilets and the dining rooms were so dirty, he had no answer. (TsDAVO, f. 2605, op. 3, spr. 1129, ark. 55.)

Figure 1.3. Miners' dugouts, Shevchenko Coalfield, Hryshyne, 1927. From TsDKFFA, od. zb. 0-35409.

there were only 6,793 sleeping places for 18,624.[30]

The October Revolution hardly changed this difficult situation. No systematic data are available, but according to the miners' union in 1924 per capita living space in the Donbas was 5.3 square meters and in 1926–27 it was 5.8.[31] The 1926 census, however, shows that in the city of Stalino, per capita living space was 4.4 square meters for those living in houses and flats and 3.6 for those living in dormitories.[32] (Some miners could not find any place to live but on the boilers, perhaps a substitute for the fireplaces in peasants' huts.)[33] According to another report, in 1928 there were 3.8 square meters per mine worker, but in 1932 only 3.5.[34] Yet another survey shows that in 1929 40 percent of Donbas workers (not just colliers) occupied less than 2 square meters

[30]P. A. Pokrovskii, "Kak zhivet donetskii shakhter," *Russkoe bogatstvo*, 1913, no. 12, pp. 243–47. For discussion of earlier periods, see M. I. Masterova, "Materialy fonda Iugo-vostochnogo gornogo upravleniia o polozhenii gornorabochikh na Iuge Rossii (1900–1917 gg.)," *Istoricheskii arkhiv*, 1957, no. 2, p. 600.

[31]TsDAVO, f. 2602, op. 1, spr. 2320, ark. 21.

[32]*Statisticheskii spravochnik Stalinskogo okruga* (Stalino, 1928), p. 35.

[33]*Deviatyi s"ezd Kommunisticheskoi partii bol'shevikov Ukrainy. Stenograficheskii otchet, 6–12 dekabria 1925 g.* (Kharkiv, 1926), p. 108.

[34]*Industrializatsiia SSSR, 1929–1932 gg. Dokumenty i materialy* (Moscow, 1970), p. 183. This seems to refer to the miners in the country as a whole.

Figure 1.4. People living in a dugout in 1934 in Hryshyne. From TsDKFFA, od. zb. 3-1105.

of living space a head and 11.7 percent less than 3 square meters.[35] Archival data reveal that in 1931 only 2.8 square meters of living space was available per capita as opposed to 7 square meters, the norm prescribed by the People's Commissariat of Labor.[36] By 1936, however, the per capita living space of workers was said to have increased to 4.9 square meters.[37] These figures do not adequately represent the problem. Huge housing facilities may have been built, but because of poor planning, they often had no electricity, running water, or sewage; in the surrounding areas there were no paved roads or even roads of any kind.[38]

The wages of the Donbas workers were relatively high by national comparison, in part because the Donbas was a center of heavy industry which generally paid higher wages than did light industry. (At the turn of the century, "Donbas coal miners were averaging 266 rubles per year and factory workers

[35]A. Abramov, *Zhilishchno-bytovoe stroitel'stvo Donbassa* (Moscow and Leningrad, 1930), p. 12.

[36]GARF, f. 7416, op. 1, d. 2, l. 117.

[37]*Donbass v tsifrakh. Statisticheskii spravochnik* (Stalino, 1936), p. 110, which refers to "the socialized housing fund." See also Z. G. Likholobova, *Rabochie Donbassa v gody pervykh pi-atiletok (1928–1937 gg.)* (Donets'k, 1973), p. 132.

[38]*Udarnik uglia*, 1933, nos. 10–11, p. 26.

323 roubles per year, compared with a national average of 203 rubles annually.")[39] However, this did not deter high labor turnover. This was particularly the case with the colliers. The persistent seasonality of labor was one reason for high turnover, and the poor housing situation in the Donbas was another. Data are scant, but before World War I labor turnover in terms of the annual rate of discharge to the average number of employed records over 100 percent among Donbas colliers; the turnover of factory workers was smaller, ranging from two-thirds to three-quarters.[40] This trend continued well into the 1920s and 1930s, or if anything, intensified even more.

Among the colliers of the nation, turnover in 1930 was an astonishing 295.2 percent (which meant that, on average, each collier changed jobs three times a year); the rate of turnover then dropped to 95.4 percent in 1934 as a result of harsh administrative pressure to contain it, but soon rose to 112.7 percent in 1936 and 114 percent in 1937. In other industries, including metallurgy, the rates were usually dozens of points lower.[41] In the years immediately before World War II, turnover seemed to have risen further. In 1939, for example, the average work force of coal miners was 373,700 and the discharges 487,300, for a turnover rate of 130.4 percent.[42] The overall high turnover rate led to the binding of labor to the workplace on the eve of World War II. Ironically, in the coal-mining industry the most important category of colliers, hewers, were the most unstable with the highest labor turnover. Much of the industry's seasonality was due to these colliers.[43]

Many other factors made life in the Donbas difficult and promoted the instability of the labor force. Then as now air pollution was so strong as to make people ill. The sky glowed in various colors at night from the constant smoke emitted from the factory chimneys.[44]

[39]Susan P. McCaffray, "Origins of Labor Policy in the Russian Coal and Steel Industry, 1874–1900," *Journal of Economic History*, 47:4 (December 1987), p. 957.

[40]See Friedgut, *Iuzovka and Revolution*, pp. 225–27. Note also S. I. Potolov, *Rabochie Donbassa v XIX veka* (Moscow and Leningrad, 1963), pp. 144–45. This was much higher than that of coal miners in other countries that suffered from the same problem. The turnover of Ruhr colliers in Germany, for example, fluctuated between 37% and 69%, with the exception of 1914, which recorded 102%, an impact of war. See Gerhard Adelmann, ed., *Quellensammulung zur Geschichte der sozialen Betriebsverfassung Ruhrindustrie unter besonderer Berücksichtung des Industrie- und Handelskammerbezirks*, vol. 1 (Bonn, 1960), pp. 145–46. See also Elaine Glovka Spencer, *Management and Labor in Imperial Germany: Ruhr Industrialists as Employers, 1896–1914* (Rutgers University Press, 1984), pp. 46–47.

[41]*Trud v SSSR. Statisticheskii spravochnik* (Moscow, 1936), pp. 95 and 109; Ia. Kats, "Tekuchest' rabochei sily v krupnoi promyshlennosti," *Plan*, 1937, no. 9, pp. 21–22, and Likholobova, *Rabochie Donbassa*, p. 116.

[42]GARF, f. 8225, op. 1, d.700, l. 15.

[43]*Sezonnost' i sezonnye kolebaniia v promyshlennosti i narodnom khoziaistve. Sbornik statei* (Moscow, 1930), pp. 387–88.

[44]See an interesting description in Surozhskii, "Krai uglia i zheleza," pp. 292 and 304.

As serious as air pollution was the chronic water shortage that plagued the Donbas both before and after the October Revolution. On the eve of World War I, workers, who received much less water than white-collar employees, were able to use only one-ninth of what was considered the minimum daily allotment of four *vedros* (1 vedro = 12.30 liters). Water was often not available for days (even today a visitor to the Donbas may have to endure the same problem). Human waste would seep into mine water deposits, which, for want of clean water, were consumed by Donbas residents. Hence the chronic outbursts of cholera and other epidemics in the Donbas. Once cholera broke out, it spread quickly to central Russia and Ukraine through residents who fled by way of the Donbas's well-developed railway network. Thus, the Donbas was said to be a nest and distributor of all kinds of epidemics. Other, nonepidemic diseases assaulted the Donbas workers with equal ferocity. Even now typhoid fever, for example, is not rare in the Donbas. A 1908 comparison of sickness rates between peasants and colliers in Katerynoslav province shows that the latter suffered two to three times more than the former who, as was well known, the author contends, by no means enjoyed a good life.[45] Venereal disease was said to be particularly widespread among the Donbas work force.[46] Life in the Donbas was such that a "man at the age of thirty-five looked fifty or fifty-five."[47]

One area where a noticeable improvement was made in the late imperial period and in the Soviet period in particular was literacy. According to the 1897 census 38 percent of the Donbas population was literate. In general, workers were more literate than peasants, who constituted the majority of the population: 60.2 percent of metalworkers, 46.4 percent of chemical workers, but only 31 percent of colliers were literate.[48] It was another peculiarity of the coal-mining industry that the most important category of colliers, the hewers, had the lowest literacy rate among the colliers as a whole.[49] By 1926, 56.6 percent of the Donbas population was literate, among industrial workers 85 percent. According to the 1929 trade-union census, the illiterate accounted for only 15.2 percent and 9.5 percent among the Donbas colliers and metallurgical

[45]See Pokrovskii, "Kak zhivet," pp. 250–55 and 260–61. For a case of cholera outbreak in the Donbas, see Theodore H. Friedgut, "Labor Violence and Regime Brutality in Tsarist Russia: The Iuzovka Cholera Riots of 1892," *Slavic Review*, 46:2.

[46]GARF, f. 5459, op. 4, d. 80, l. 198 (referring to 1923). See also *Gornorabochie*, 1923, no. 9, p. 34.

[47]Jacques Sandulescu, *Donbas* (New York, [1968]), p. 125.

[48]Potolov, *Rabochie Donbassa*, p. 133. In this census and the 1926 census, "literacy" meant the ability to read only: it was sufficient to be able to read printed words if only by syllables.

[49]In 1923–24, 70% of Donbas colliers were literate, but the literacy rate of hewers was 60.2%. 27.1% of the former were "totally illiterate," and 36.2% of the latter could not read or write at all. *Khoziaistvo Donbassa*, 1924, nos. 7–8, p. 95.

workers respectively.[50] By 1935 only 2.9 percent of the Donbas workers were said to be illiterate.[51] In 1937, however, of those employed in the Donbas coal-mining industry 3.4 percent were illiterate and 7 percent were half illiterate (*malogramotnye*).[52] How much literate culture was created is another matter. In 1922, for example, more than two-thirds of miners were reported never to have read a newspaper or a book.[53]

Working conditions were as difficult as living conditions in the Donbas. Coal mining in general was one of the most strenuous industrial trades. A Russian engineer who visited an anthracite mine in the Donbas before the revolution noted:

> To study the actual operation of modern equipment I went down to the 3,000-foot level in the mines and saw the difficulties confronting the miners in their work. As the thickness of the anthracite layer did not exceed three feet, the miners had to crawl into the narrow gangways and then out again with their coal loaded on sleds drawn by ropes tied to their waists. Special training was needed for this work and few could stand the strain. I was told by an engineer who accompanied me that a healthy young student who wanted some practical experience would last only three days at the job.[54]

Fatigue and inertia were such that material incentive often did not work in motivating colliers to harder labor. At the turn of the century, managers observed with despair that "with very rare exceptions," higher wages did not lead to higher productivity. The higher the wages of colliers, the fewer days they worked and the less strenuous their work became. Consequently, their earnings remained more or less constant, usually at subsistent levels, independent of the rates.[55]

The following commentary on the British coal-mining industry is equally true of Ukraine and Russia: "The most painful feature of the coalmining industry is the heavy toll it takes on human life by accidents causing death or injury; this statement . . . merely echoed similar remarks made by generations of observers, within and outside the industry."[56] By most accounts, data on industrial accidents were far from complete. According to available data, in

[50]Likholobova, *Rabochie Donbassa*, p. 41, and A. G. Rashin, *Sostav fabrichno-zavodskogo proletariata v SSSR. Predvaritel'nye itogi perepisi metallistov, gornorabochikh i tekstil'shchikov v 1929 g.* (Moscow, 1930), p. 97.

[51]Likholobova, *Rabochie Donbassa*, p. 122.

[52]*Istoriia rabochikh Donbassa*, vol. 1 (Moscow and Leningrad, 1963), p. 263.

[53]Kir'ianov, *Rabochie Iuga Rossii, 1914–fevral' 1917 g.* (Moscow, 1971), p. 105.

[54]*The Life of a Chemist: Memoirs of Vladimir N. Ipatieff* (Stanford University Press, 1946), p. 160.

[55]E. Taskin, *K voprosu o privlechenii i uderzhanii rabochikh na kamennougol'nykh kopiakh Donetskago basseina* (Kharkiv, [1899]), p. 15.

[56]Roy Church, with the assistance of Alan Hall and John Kanefsky, *The History of the British Coal Industry*, vol. 3, *1830–1913: Victorian Pre-eminence* (Oxford, 1986), p. 582.

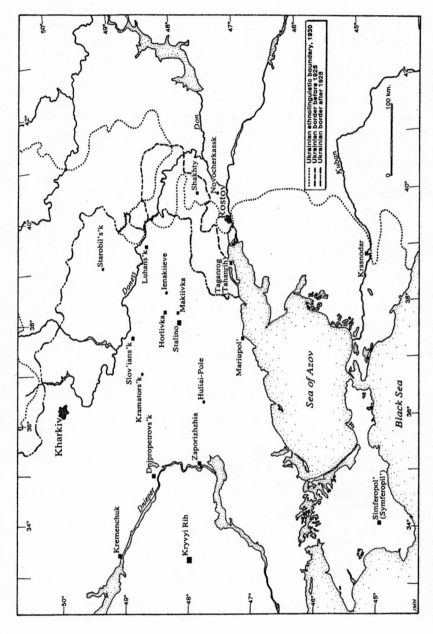

Map 1.2. The Donbas in the 1920s and 1930s. Adapted from *Nash krai* (Rostov, 1963), insert, and Paul Robert Magocsi, *Ukraine: A Historical Atlas* (University of Toronto Press, 1985), p. 22.

1906–10, of every 1,000 Donbas colliers 329 were maimed at work, whereas of every 1,000 factory workers only 33 were injured.[57] According to another report, in 1906, of the 100,000 Donbas miners, 40,000 were injured. These figures appeared, according to a contemporary observer, as if they had come straight from the "battlefields."[58] Industrial fatalities among miners were also high. In 1904–13, 2.6 deaths for every 1,000 colliers were recorded in the Donbas. This compared with 3.7 casualties in the United States, 2.9 in Japan, and 2.1 in Germany for the period 1901–10.[59] Yet for deaths per 1 million poods of coal production, the Donbas (0.306) stood much higher than Germany (0.186) or the United States (0.082).[60]

From 1893 to 1915–16 the total death toll in the Donbas collieries was 5,152.[61] The following *chastushka* of the miners sadly reflects reality:

> Sirens blare alarmingly,
> People flock to the drift,
> And they carry out a young horsehand
> With a smashed-in head.[62]

The Donbas metallurgy industry was an equally dangerous workplace. Its fatalities (1.2 and 1.5 per 1,000 in 1913 and 1914 respectively) were fewer than in coal mining, but accident rates (450 and 435 per one 1,000 in the same periods) were higher.[63]

After the October Revolution, the accident rates remained high: there was little improvement from the prerevolutionary years. In 1924–25 the fatality

---

[57] Lev Liberman, *Trud i byt gorniakov Donbassa, prezhde i teper'* (Moscow, 1929), pp. 20–22. Liberman was an expert of industrial hygiene and mining safety who widely published both before and after the revolution.

[58] Quoted in V. N. Rubin, "Rabochii vopros na S"ezdakh gornopromyshlennikov Iuga Rossii," *Uchenye zapiski* (Moskovskii gosudarstvennyi pedagogicheskii institut im. V. I. Lenina, Trudy kafedry istorii SSSR), no. 249 (1966), p. 30.

[59] *Voprosy tekhniki bezopasnosti i travmatizma v gornoi promyshlennosti SSSR. Doklady gornoi sektsii II Vsesoiuznogo s"ezda po profgigiene i tekhnike bezopasnosti* (Moscow, 1928), p. 36, and Liberman, *Trud i byt*, p. 22. In Britain between 1906 and 1913, 1.4 deaths were recorded for every 1,000 miners. Church, *History*, p. 586. For similar comparisons, see *Statistika neschastnykh sluchaev s rabochimi gornoi i gornozavodskoi promyshlennosti iuzhnoi Rossii za 1908–1904* [sic] *gg.* (Kharkiv, 1910), pp. 92–93, which quotes 3.19 deaths per 1,000 for 1893–1903 in the United States. According to Albert H. Fay, comp., *Coal-Mine Fatalities in the United States 1870–1914 with Statistics of Coal Production, Labor, and Mining Methods, by States and Calendar Years*, Department of the Interior, Bureau of Mines, Bulletin 115 (Washington, D.C., 1916), pp. 10–11 and 21, 3.32 deaths occurred per 1,000 miners between 1870 and 1913.

[60] D. M. Kirzhner, *Gornaia promyshlennost' v tsifrakh. Kratkii spravochnik* (Moscow, 1926), p. 36.

[61] *Voprosy tekhniki bezopasnosti i travmatizma v gornoi promyshlennosti SSSR*, pp. 36–37, and *Statistika neschastnykh sluchaev s rabochimi gornoi i gornozavodskoi promyshlennosti iuzhnoi Rossii*, p. 90.

[62] *Shakhty*, p. 4.

[63] Kir'ianov, *Rabochie Iuga Rossii*, p. 79. See also Friedgut, *Iuzovka and Revolution*, pp. 280–81.

rate was 1.36 per 1,000 miners. It rose to 2.9 in 1929,[64] remaining almost constant at 2.84 in 1934, 2.84 in 1935, and 2.45 in the first months of 1936.[65] This may not have been unique, because in the British coal-mining industry, too, in approximately the same periods, deaths and accidents failed to decline.[66] Theodore H. Friedgut may be right in saying that in the prerevolutionary years both managers and workers shared "the passive fatalism of traditional society in regarding work accidents as phenomena of nature about which little or nothing could be done."[67] The same thought was expressed in a *chastushka* recorded in Stalino in the 1920s:

> A collier goes down the pit,
> Farewell to the bright world,
> There he walks with a candle,
> Carrying death on his shoulder.[68]

Mining was such a dangerous job that fatalism was not merely resignation, but one way of contending with fear, a counsel of despair. Recklessness was part of the miners' manly culture, and some, for example, dared light their cigarettes in gaseous pits or near dynamite warehouses.[69]

Mining was dreaded as the most dangerous and least attractive employment. When Victor Kravchenko declared to his parents that he would go to work in the Donbas, "father looked sad. Mother wept softly and reminded me that I was only a boy and that I would have plenty of time to work later."[70] Unlike sons and daughters of factory and railway workers, who often went into the profession of their parents and thus formed a "workers' dynasty," children of miners generally avoided following in their parents' footsteps. Those who entered mining work did so for economic reasons and not from interest in the job.[71] A contemporary *chastushka* conveys the popular image of a miner's life:

> Mummy, I'm done for –
> I've fallen for a collier:

---

[64]GARF, f. 5459, op. 10, d. 11, l. 110 (the figures in this document are 13.6 and 29, obvious errors). Published figures are much lower: 0.84 in 1923–24, 0.93 in 1924–25, and 1.45 in 1927–28. See *10 let soiuza gornorabochikh SSSR* (Moscow, 1930), p. 75. *Voprosy tekhniki bezopasnosti i travmatizma v gornoi promyshlennosti SSSR*, p. 37, lists 1.15 for 1923–24; 1.10 for 1924–25; and 1.31 for 1925–26.

[65]RGAE, F. 7566, op. 1, d. 2522, l. 4. The figures for the Donbas per se were 2.71, 2.68, and 2.48 in the respective periods.

[66]Barry Supple, *The History of the British Coal Industry*, vol. 4, *1913–1946: The Political Economy of Decline* (Oxford, 1987), p. 427.

[67]Friedgut, *Iuzovka and Revolution*, p. 288. See also p. 276.

[68]Vira Bilets'ka, "Shakhtarski pisni," *Etnohrafichnyi visnyk*, no. 5 (1927), p. 59.

[69]See, for example, GARF, f. 5459, op. 10, d. 11, ll. 63 and 137 on the 1920s.

[70]Kravchenko, *I Chose Freedom*, p. 34.

[71]I. I. Moshkovskii and R. L. Natanzon, "Nekotorye dannye o professional'noi ustoichivosti shakhterov na osnovanii professional'nogo anamneza," *Vrachebnoe delo*, 1934, no. 1, p. 58.

A collier is sooty, he is dirty,
Always drunk, and disgraceful.[72]

For many people mining labor was something to be avoided.

Drinking was a favorite escape for miners. As the just quoted *chastushka* suggests, heavy drinking was an integral part of collier life. To many pre-revolutionary observers, colliers lived only by work and drink.[73] Often the miners would insensibly drink away their wages. As one engineer noted of the Donbas miners in the 1890s, "The plague of the miner's life was heavy drinking after the monthly paydays; sometimes work stopped for two or three days."[74] Conveniently, there were numerous taverns to serve miners.[75] In 1892 in Katerynoslav province there was one Orthodox church for every 3,094 inhabitants, one school for every 2,040, and one public house (*piteinoe zavedenie*) for every 570![76]

Even under the Soviet regime with all its "enlightenment" programs, miners were said to justify drinking with misguided notions of the effects of alcohol: they would drink to ease fatigue and stimulate the body for work and, in cold weather, to feel warmer. Consumption under such circumstances only helped to ruin their health. Managers, when hard pressed for cash, gave workers alcohol in lieu of wages, premiums, and overtime.[77] Thus, more than half of their wages were spent on vodka, the trade of which, unlike that of food and other goods, was well organized in the Donbas.[78]

Drinking led to absenteeism, which increased on Saturdays and Mondays and declined in the midweek. Miners' absenteeism was in fact by far the highest of all industrial workers in the 1920s and 1930s. In 1930, for example, the average number of days absent without permission was 13.78 among the colliers and 4.4 days in industry as a whole.[79]

---

[72]Mikh. Donbasskii, "Pesni shakhterov Donbassa," *Revoliutsiia i kul'tura*, 1928, nos. 23–24, p. 112.

[73]See, for example, see A. Shestakov, "Na zare rabochego dvizheniia v Donbasse. Vospominaniia," *Proletarskaia revoliutsiia*, 1921, no. 1, p. 160.

[74]Fenin, *Coal and Politics*, p. 49. For the same picture after the October Revolution, see the 1925 report from Shakhty in Nichoas Werth and Gaël Moullec, eds., *Rapports secrets soviétiques. La société russe dans les documents confidentiels 1921–1991* (Paris, 1994), p. 195.

[75]See, for example, the map of Iuzivka in the 1890s in Friedgut, *Iuzovka and Revolution*, pp. 74–75 and 201, on tavern keepers.

[76]*Robitnychyi rukh na Ukraini (1885–1894 rr.) Zbirnyk dokumentiv i materialiv* (Kiev, 1990), p. 284.

[77]I. Kuznetsov, "Rabochii klass i alkogol'naia problema," *Gornorabochii*, 1922, nos. 7–8, pp. 43–44.

[78]*Desiatyi Vserossiiskii S"ezd Sovetov rabochikh, krest'ianskikh, krasnoarmeiskikh i kazach'ikh deputatov (23–27 dekabria 1922 goda). Sten. otchet s prilozheniiami* (Moscow and Leningrad, 1923), p. 46.

[79]*Trud v SSSR* (1936), pp. 96 and 110. Note also *Trud v SSSR. Spravochnik, 1926–1930 gg.* (Moscow, 1930), pp. 18–19.

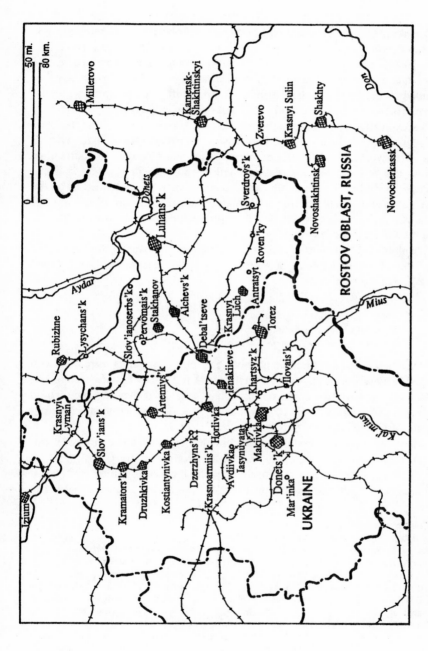

Map 1.3. The Donbas, circa 1950. Adapted from Theodore Shabad, *Geography of the USSR: A Regional Study* (Columbia University Press, 1951), p. 451.

Drinking was an important part of the miners' observance of religious holidays and saints' days.[80] This was particularly the case before the revolution when priests rang the church bells even on holidays not sanctioned by the mines and factories: "The miners, with a never-come-Monday alacrity, responded to the call, and, having missed their shift anyway, went on to the tavern. The result . . . was a work-month of only twenty days."[81]

Yet even after the revolution their work-month hardly changed: in the Donbas coal-mining industry in 1924–25 it was 20.7 days and in 1926–27 21.4 days. The work-month for the most important, but also the most strenuous of jobs, that of the hewers, was even smaller: 18.6 days in 1926–27.[82] Thus, unlike other industries where the key categories of workers tended to be the most stable and reliable, in the coal-mining industry the core of the miners, the hewers, whose labor decided much of production, were the least stable, the least reliable, and the least literate.[83]

Drinking led to everyday violence. Wife abuse appears to have been common even after the October Revolution, as is shown in a *chastushka* recorded in Stalino in the 1920s:

> He rakes up money from the earth,
> On Sunday he drinks vodka,
> He drinks vodka on Sunday,
> On Monday he beats his wife.[84]

In Makiivka, in the last three months of 1928, 600 complaints were filed with the police by wives beaten by their husbands.[85] In Luhans'k, wife beating was widespread, but women could not complain because if they did they would be beaten even harder.[86] In 1937 a man in Makiivka was sentenced to four months of forced labor for wife beating.[87]

Many observers testified that men's brutality was matched by that of women. A mining engineer recalls his life in the Donbas in the 1890s: "My social circle consisted of poorly educated people, the junior mining staff. Their manners were such that once two of the 'ladies' started a quarrel that led to

[80]Taskin, *K voprosu*, p. 9.

[81]Friedgut, *Iuzovka and Revolution*, pp. 322–23.

[82]A. D. Ratner and V. P. Renke, *Kamennougol'naia i antratsitovaia promyshlennost' Donetskogo basseina. Obzor sovremennogo sostoianiia* (Kharkiv, 1928), pp. 21 and XLV.

[83]*Sezonnost' i sezonnye kolebaniia v promyshlennosti i narodnom khoziaistve*, p. 388.

[84]Bilets'ka, "Shakhtarski pisni," p. 55 ("V zemli hroshi ohribaiet, / U nidiliu vodku piot, / On v nidiliu vodku p'ie, / V ponedilok zhinku b'ie"). Bilets'ka notes that this song refers to miners' negligent attitude toward work in the field. Incidentally, this verse is not grammatically correct. As is often the case in the Donbas, Russian and Ukrainian are mixed here.

[85]*Protiv "Rozhdestva." Materialy antirozhdestvenskoi kampanii 1928–1929 g.g.* (Kharkiv, 1928), pp. 6–7. See also *Deviatyi s"ezd Kommunisticheskoi partii bol'shevikov Ukrainy*, p. 187.

[86]TsDAVO, f. 2605, op. 2, spr. 602, ark. 58.

[87]*Makeevskii rabochii*, 4 October 1937.

blows."[88] The writer Konstantin Paustovsky also observed the following scene in Iuzivka during World War I:

> The women also had a vulgarity of speech attainable only by Philistines in the south of Russia, an evil gossip compounded of impudence, dirt, and hatred. Each of these women was, of course, "the main one in her own yard." In spite of the slander and the chewing of sunflower seeds, they still had time to fight. As soon as two women had grabbed each other's hair with animal shrieks, a crowd would form around them and the fight would be turned into a gambling game: bets of two kopecks were placed on which one would win. Old drunkards of the neighborhood were always the bankers. They would hold the money in a torn cap.
>
> The women were deliberately provoked to this fighting. Sometimes a fight would spread to include a whole street. Shirt-sleeved men would join in, using brass knuckles and lead-tipped whips, and cartilages would crack and blood would flow. Then a patrol of Cossacks would ride up at a trot from Novi Svit, where the administration of the mines and factories lived, and disperse the crowd with knouts.[89]

Even today a visitor to Iuzivka, now Donets'k, or Luhans'k may encounter a similar scene.[90]

What outside observers considered violence was part of the Donbas workers' everyday life. Fistfighting, for example, which Daniel R. Brower has described as nineteenth-century entertainment among workers,[91] was still frequently observed in the late 1920s among Donbas colliers: barracks fought against barracks, Riazaners against Orelians. Deaths were not infrequent on these occasions.[92] Children would imitate adult entertainment and beat each other half to death.[93] In fact, fighting was a form of pastime brought from the countryside. (In the Donbas countryside today similar fighting can be observed.)[94] Even so, the violence in the Donbas was said to be extraordinary. In

---

[88] Fenin, *Coal and Politics*, p. 43.

[89] Paustovsky, *The Story of a Life*, p. 430. See also Wynn, *Workers, Strikes, and Pogroms*, p. 88.

[90] On 23 June 1992 on Donets'k's main street one observed two women, a seller and a buyer, in a fight, grabbing each other's face. For beatings in the marketplace, see, for example, *Luganskaia pravda*, 2 July 1994.

[91] Daniel R. Brower, "Labor Violence in Russia in the Late Nineteenth Century," *Slavic Review*, 41:3 (Fall 1982).

[92] See, for example, GARF, f. 5459, op. 10, d. 9, ll. 114–15 and *Rabochaia gazeta*, 2 March 1929, p. 2. For more detailed discussion, see Wynn, *Workers, Strikes, and Pogroms*, pp. 89–94.

[93] The future Ukrainian dissident, Mykola Rudenko, born in 1920 in Iur'ivka near Luhans'k into a collier family, was almost beaten to death with stones in such a fight among children and went blind in one eye. See Mykola Rudenko, *Ekonomichni monolohy. Narysy katastrofichnoi pomylky* (Munich, 1978), p. 46.

[94] See B. V. Gorbunov, "Narodnye vidy sportivnoi bor'by kak element traditsionnoi kul'tury russkikh (XIX–nachalo XX v.)," *Sovetskaia etnografiia*, 1989, no. 4, p. 93. For this pastime in the countryside in the 1920s, see Helmut Altrichter, *Die Bauern von Tver. Vom Leben auf dem russischen Dorfe zwischen Revolution und Kollektivierung* (Munich, 1984), pp. 105 and 107.

Luhans'k, for example, one prerevolutionary observer noted that people would beat even the fallen fighters, whereas in Russia proper it was a rule not to do so. This inevitably took a heavy toll. The observer had to wonder whence such bellicosity came.[95]

To some extent, high absenteeism and violent entertainment were due to the nature of mining labor itself. It was "a cripplingly fatiguing task," and there was "in any case an extremely powerful social inertia surrounding traditional rest days." Recreation was therefore "of enormous importance to mining communities."[96] However, contemporary – that is, both pre- and postrevolutionary – discussion almost invariably attributes violence to the lack of "virtue," "culture," and "respectability" among the Donbas workers.

Then, as now, crime in the Donbas was high in comparison with other industrial areas.[97] Then, as now, there was a widespread belief that the Donbas attracted numerous criminals. In the prerevolutionary years criminal gangs operated widely in the Donbas: the largest in Iuzivka, for example, being the Malakhovs and the Sibiriakovs, who fought constantly with each other.[98] People romanticized the life of criminals. In the 1920s, for example, "hooligan songs" with much of the jargon of thieves were popular among young Donbas workers.[99]

Yet crime was different from violence. However prevalent violence may have been in everyday life in the Donbas, crime was limited largely to professional criminals, who were legion. For all its violence, the Donbas lived its own moral life. As one prerevolutionary resident of an eastern Donbas town noted, "Their [Donbas people's] code of ethics was high, there were almost no thefts, either in the town [Kamensk] or in the surrounding miners' settlements, and yet there were always a lot of newcomers to the mines."[100]

Many observers, both pre- and postrevolutionary, failed to see the social underpinnings of violence, however.[101] Much like Paustovsky, who seems to

[95]I. Nikolaenko, *Revoliutsionnoe dvizhenie v Luganske* (Kharkiv, 1926), pp. 6–7.

[96]Supple, *History*, pp. 58–59.

[97]See Wynn, *Workers, Strikes, and Pogroms*, p. 89.

[98]See, for example, F. Zaitsev, "Bol'sheviki Iuzovki do 1918 goda," *Literaturnyi Donbass*, 1933, nos. 10–12, p. 156, and "Nravy Donetskogo basseina," *Donetskii kriazh* (Donets'k), no. 119 (26 May–1 June 1995), p. 3.

[99]Donbasskii, "Pesni shakhterov Donbassa," p. 112.

[100]Borodin, *One Man in His Time*, p. 6.

[101]The values of a society do inform violence, as some historians of the United States assert (see, for example, Richard M. Brown, *No Duty to Retreat: Violence and Values in American History and Society* [Oxford University Press, 1991]), but there are also social underpinnings not specific to a particular culture or nation. An overwhelmingly male (and young, to boot) environment is one. According to David T. Courtwright, *Violent Land: Single Men and Social Disorder from the Frontier to the Inner City* (Harvard University Press, 1996), p. 79, "Put formally, the assortment of traits found in frontier mining regions – violence, cruelty, recklessness, irreligion, dissipation, neglect of hygiene, bad cooking, and widespread bachelorhood on the one hand; friendliness,

have seen only "Philistines" amid the Donbas inhabitants, a Russian engineer saw only a crowd in a crowd. He noted of the Donbas miners:

> It seemed as if these people lacked something essential, strong, and basic: perhaps the *muzhik* [peasant] way of life had never given them any kind of economic "upbringing," which was the root of the peasant psychology. They were incredibly ignorant; it seemed that neither religion nor tradition had left any trace on their souls. They were somber, and if not empty, at least they were not touched by anything, living more by instinct than by reason.[102]

This view of workers and peasants as animal-like creatures was indicative of the social cleavage that plagued the old regime.

Such a view is more than a mere reflection of the cleavage. The "wildness" of the southern steppe land in general and the Donbas in particular, in its modern incarnation, was a creation of the imagination of contemporaries. What is more, in many respects the modern political history of the Donbas did indeed embody this imagined wildness, as the following chapters demonstrate.

---

camaraderie, sharing, and democratic decision-making on the other – was a biologically, culturally, and socially determined byproduct of an economically driven migratory process that initially screened out the very young, the very old, and women."

[102] Fenin, *Coal and Politics*, pp. 48 and 50.

2   Political Development to 1914

Politics and Geography

The political development of the Donbas was affected by its geographic location in the "wild field," at least in terms of Moscow's perception of it. In three respects, the impact was perceptible. First, the militant traditions of the Cossacks continued. Second, the Donbas (and the steppe in general) served as a haven for many fugitives from political and economic oppression. Third, ethnic tensions were inevitable in the multiethnic steppe.

The Cossacks (*kozaki*, *kazaki*, horsemen or brigands in Turkic) formed martial communities in the wild field, composed of those who fled the oppression of Polish-Lithuania and Muscovy, dreaming of a free, independent, and better life in the new land. In the free steppe, life forced them to live as "free warriors," fighting both against their enemies in the north and against the Tartars and Turks in the steppe. Being free warriors often meant in practice fighting as mercenaries, allying with this or that camp depending on political, military, economic, and other exigencies. Apart from fighting, the Cossacks made their living by a combination of fishing, hunting, commerce, agriculture, and plunder. Life itself was at once brutal, savage, ruthless, and heroic. Whatever the mythology of the Cossacks,[1] they came to be integrated into the Russian Empire in the course of the seventeenth, eighteenth, and nineteenth centuries, as Moscow expanded its control over the steppe.[2] This long and complex process involved give and take, both material and symbolic. In the

---

[1] For a judicious discussion of Cossack mythologies, see, for example, Linda Gordon, *Cossack Rebellions: Social Turmoil in the Sixteenth-Century Ukraine* (State University of New York Press, 1983), and Serhii M. Plokhy, "Cossack Mythology in the Russian-Ukrainian Border Dispute," in S. Frederick Starr, ed., *The Legacy of History in Russia and the New States of Eurasia* (Armonk, N.Y., 1994).

[2] For a similar process of the Hetmanate (Little Russia, referring to the Kiev-Poltava-Chernihiv area, as opposed to New Russia), see Zenon E. Kohut, *Russian Centralism and Ukrainian Autonomy: Imperial Absorption of the Hetmanate 1760s–1830s* (Harvard Ukrainian Research Institute, 1988).

case of the Zaporozhian Cossacks, in 1775 their host was altogether abolished by Catherine the Great. (Some fled to the south, to the Ottoman Empire, but many of the Zaporozhian Cossacks were "transplanted to become the Chernomorskoe [Black Sea] voisko [host]" in the Kuban region in the northern Caucasus.)[3] By the nineteenth century, the Don Cossacks, the largest host in the Russian Empire, like other Cossack groups, came firmly under tsarist control.[4] In exchange for loyalty and military service, they were granted a degree of self-government under the jurisdiction of the War Ministry; even after civil self-government (*zemstvo*) was introduced in most localities of European Russia following the 1861 Emancipation, the Don Cossack Host was exempted from this invasion of civil authority right up until 1917 (with the brief existence of a temporary *zemstvo* in the 1870s). Cossack leaders were co-opted into nobility and officialdom. Cossackdom in general was given a special legal status (*soslovie*, or estate), and most importantly the Cossacks were never obliged to pay poll (soul) tax (before it was abolished in 1887) or labor or money dues. In short, the Cossacks became an important military power of the empire. Ironically, the Cossacks were thus viewed by revolutionaries as the embodiment of counterrevolution, the oppressor of revolutionary movements.[5]

Nevertheless, Moscow feared the Cossacks' passionate aspiration for independence. The Zaporozhian Cossacks' participation in the 1768 peasant (*haidamak*) rebellion on Right-Bank Ukraine (*Koliivshchyna*) served as the immediate reason for their disbandment. The Don Cossacks produced many leaders of large-scale peasant uprisings: Stenka Razin (1672), Kondratii Bulavin (1707–9), and Emel'ian Pugachev (1792–94). The relationship between tsars and Cossacks was so important that "When Nicholas I appointed the first most august ataman [chieftain] he journeyed with his son to Novocherkassk, the Don Cossack capital, for the presentation. . . . Each successive tsar from Nicholas I managed to make at least one ceremonial visit to the Don, the largest and senior surviving Cossack community."[6] In the imagination of the common people, too, the Cossacks "personified the yearning for a better world and a kind of anarchistic freedom."[7]

[3] Robert H. McNeal, *Tsar and Cossack, 1855–1914* (Houndmill and London, 1987), p. 15.

[4] For an excellent account of this process, see Bruce W. Menning, "The Emergence of a Military-Administrative Elite in the Don Cossack Land, 1708–1836," in Walter McKenzie Pintner and Donald Karl Rowney, ed., *Russian Officialdom: The Bureaucratization of Russian Society from the Seventeenth to the Twentieth Century* (University of North Carolina Press, 1980), pp. 130–61.

[5] For an excellent study of how each political actor imagined the Don and the Don Cossacks in their multiplicity of roles, see Peter I. Holquist, "A Russian Vendee: The Practice of Revolutionary Politics in the Don Countryside, 1917–1921" (Ph.D. diss., Columbia University, 1995).

[6] McNeal, *Tsar and Cossack*, p. 1.

[7] Jeffrey Brooks, *When Russia Learned to Read: Literacy and Popular Literature, 1861–1917* (Princeton University Press, 1985), p. 177.

The Cossack militant traditions were to become most evident in the civil war that followed the 1917 October Revolution. The Donbas was to become a theater of fierce battle in which, as narrated in Mikhail Sholokhov's famous stories on the Don, many Don Cossacks participated on the White side. The militant traditions of the Cossacks also helped the Reds, as Sholokhov's stories show or as seen in Isaak Babel's *Red Cavalry*, yet even the Red Cossacks were not easily brought under Bolshevik control. This is clear from the case of the civil war hero and Red Army Cossack officer Filip K. Mironov, whose independent mind aroused suspicion in Moscow and led to his arrest and execution.[8]

Like other frontier areas, the Russian-Ukrainian south had an antimotherland tendency. It had traditionally attracted Old Believers and sectarians who sought freedom there. The Donbas and New Russia in general were bastions of "tremendous sectarian activity."[9] According to a Kuban Cossack ataman, "the genius of the Russian people" had always been attracted by the south; therefore the reform of Peter the Great was a mistake; the Cossacks embodied for the Russians the attraction of the south. In 1919 the ataman emphasized this point to the White Army leader A. I. Denikin, who had fled to the free south from the north conquered by the Bolsheviks.[10]

The Cossack militancy or its mythological power was still feared even in the 1960s. At the first news of the famous 1962 strike uprising in Novocherkassk at the outer edge of the Donbas, a Soviet military commander of the northern Caucasus reacted by claiming "the Cossacks are in rebellion [*vzbuntovalis' kazachki*]." The people's outrage against Moscow was such that they beat a woman and tore out her hair simply because her surname was Khrushcheva,[11] a feminine form of the name Khrushchev, the Soviet leader in Moscow.

Even in the former area of the Zaporozhian Cossacks, civil war seemed to revive their militant traditions in the form of a large-scale, anarchistic peasant war (*Makhnivshchyna, Makhnovshchina*), which engulfed the Donbas. During the civil war fought from 1918 to 1920–21, the Bolsheviks condemned the Ukrainian peasants for "an extremely clearly crystallized individualistic consciousness and strong anarchistic tendencies." The Ukrainian peasants, allying neither with the Soviet power nor with the White Army, did not resemble their Russian counterparts.[12] More generally, the Cossack heritage was at the

---

[8] Sergei Starikov and Roy Medvedev, *Philip Mironov and the Russian Civil War*, tr. Guy Daniels (New York, 1978).

[9] V. P. Semenov-Tian-Shanskii, ed., *Rossiia. Polnoe geograficheskoe opisanie nashego otechestva. Nastol'naia i dorozhnaia kniga. Tom 14. Novorossiia i Krym* (St. Petersburg, 1910), p. 182.

[10] A. G. Shkuro, *Zapiski belogo partizana* (Moscow, 1991), p. 149.

[11] Ol'ga Nikitina, "Novocherkassk: khronika tragedii," *Don* (Rostov), 1990, no. 8, p. 124.

[12] *Vos'maia konferentsiia RKP(b), dekabr' 1919 g. Protokoly* (Moscow, 1961), p. 81.

core of Ukrainian national consciousness[13] and, in the eyes of Moscow, provided separatist aspirations for a free, independent Ukraine. Under Soviet rule, therefore, academic research on the Ukrainian Cossacks was greatly restricted and "at times virtually taboo." "All Ukrainian political groups, including the early Soviet Ukrainian republic, used Cossack symbols," and when recently the chance for independence has loomed and become real, the Cossack past has served as "a focus for national self-identification."[14]

As the formation of the Cossacks illustrates, the wild steppe served an important function in the history of Ukraine and Russia. Many of the Cossacks were originally fugitives, freedom seekers. The poet Tymko (Khoma) Padura (1801–70) sang:

> The Cossack never knew a master,
> for he was born on the steppes.[15]

Over the years the Cossacks were joined on the steppe by numerous peasants fleeing political and economic oppression from the north. Ivan the Terrible's famous Oprichnina, for example, caused much ruin in the country and numerous peasants found refuge on the steppe.[16] It was in part in response to the service class of landlords who demanded that Moscow stem the loss of their peasants to the free steppe in the south and elsewhere that Muscovy established serfdom in the heartland of Russia in the sixteenth and seventeenth centuries.[17] The deprivation of freedom of movement did not stop the exodus of peasants. On the contrary, it gave them all the more reason to flee. Some were caught and returned to their owners, but others gained freedom on the steppe. Their settlement was not entirely negatively perceived by Moscow, however, which deemed it helpful for the defense of the southern frontiers against the Muslim "infidels."

The steppe also attracted all kinds of criminals and the politically or religiously persecuted who sought a haven: there "they felt like fish in water."[18] Many protestants, Catholics, and Old Believers, those who adhered to the old

[13]For this as reflected in literature, see George Grabowicz, "Three Perspectives on the Cossack Past: Gogol', Ševčenko, Kuliš," *Harvard Ukrainian Studies*, 5:2 (June 1981), pp. 171–94.

[14]Frank Sysyn, "The Emergence of the Ukrainian Nation and Cossack Mythology," *Social Research*, 58:4 (Winter 1991), pp. 846, 848, and 864. See also O. W. Gerus, "Manifestations of the Cossack Idea in Modern Ukrainian History: The Cossack Legacy and Its Impact," *Ukrains'kyi istoryk* (New York), 19:2 (1982). Gerus maintains that the Central Rada of 1917–18 "in many ways saw itself as an extension of the Zaporozhian republican traditions and its social myths" (p. 33).

[15]Dmytro Čyževs'kyj, *A History of Ukrainian Literature (from the 11th to the End of the 19th Century)*, tr. Dolly Ferguson, Doreen Gorsline, and Ulana Petyk (Littleton, Colo., 1975), p. 568.

[16]See, for example, S. F. Platonov, *Ivan the Terrible*, ed. and tr. Joseph L. Wieczynski (Gulf Breeze, Fla., 1974).

[17]See Richard Hellie, *Enserfment and Military Change in Muscovy* (University of Chicago Press, 1971).

[18]P. Surozhskii, "Krai uglia i zheleza. Ocherki," *Sovremennik*, 1913, no. 4, p. 300.

rituals after the church schism in the seventeenth century, for example, came to settle on the steppe. Non-Orthodox Christians composed a considerable percentage of the local population (including the Cossacks). As the revolutionary movement gathered momentum, and political persecution intensified, revolutionaries also fled to the south as fugitives.

Economic development on the steppe, particularly in the latter half of the nineteenth century, lured many people from central Russia and Ukraine who sought there a freer and better life than they could have found back home. The presence of growing economic opportunities also attracted many Jews to the steppe, the area west of Don Cossack Host province being within the pale of settlement.[19]

Much of the imagery associated with the free steppe was mythology, however. Many people who fled oppression were again subjected to harsh exploitation by serfdom reintroduced or reinforced in the eighteenth century. After the Emancipation of 1861, gentry "latifundia" and "kulak" farming became strong. True, the peasants, the majority of whom were Ukrainians, tilled land allotments substantially larger than the Russian peasants to the north, and before 1905 arrears in redemption payments in the Donbas were much smaller than in, say, Tula. Indeed, this was why local Ukrainians as a whole were much more reluctant to go to work in mines and factories. Yet the economic differentiation of the peasantry was more intense in the Ukrainian steppe than elsewhere.[20] The popular enmity toward kulaks was therefore very strong in the steppe.[21] After the emancipation act, in both agriculture and industry, an unmistakably capitalist logic was always present in the life of the population, but there was a peculiarly southern twist to it here, as the writer Konstantin Paustovsky observed:

> It was hard to understand who had settled Yuzovka [Iuzivka]. The imperturbable hall porter in the hotel explained to me that it had been chiefly "illegals" – buyers of secondhand goods, small usurers, market traders, richer farmers, tavern keepers, all of them living off the surrounding workers' and miners' settlements.[22]

The steppe was far from "free."

Nor did the free steppe always live up to its reputation in a political sense.

[19] John D. Klier and Shlomo Lambroza, eds., *Pogroms: Anti-Jewish Violence in Modern Russian History* (Cambridge University Press, 1992), pp. 140 and 334 (Alexander Orbach and Hans Rogger).

[20] Iu. I. Kir'ianov, "Krest'ianstvo stepnoi Ukrainy v gody pervoi mirovoi voiny (1914–1916 gg.)," in *Osobennosti agrarnogo stroia Rossii v period imperializma* (Moscow, 1962), pp. 225 and 253.

[21] See, for example, the memoir of Volodymyr Sosiura, who grew up in the Donbas, "Tretia rota," *Kyiv*, 1988, no. 1, pp. 88 and 90.

[22] Konstantin Paustovsky, *The Story of a Life*, tr. Joseph Barnes (New York, 1964), p. 430. For a similar statement, see GARF, f. 5459, op. 7, d. 2, ll. 83–84.

For example, the formally democratic Don Cossack government in the form of *krug* (assembly) and ataman was largely legendary, losing what little substance it had as the Cossacks became incorporated under Moscow's rule.

The romantic image of the steppe was also absent from the Donbas. A visitor to the Donbas would be disappointed not to find there the "sweet bitterness of the wormwood," traditionally associated with the steppe. Instead the Donbas smelled of dust and smoke. Everywhere was "just the same: the steppe, factories, mines, and the steppe."[23]

Yet the "myth itself was of the greatest importance for it provided everyone with a paradigm of problem-solving," as Albert Hirschman once remarked concerning the American West.[24] Similarly, the mythology (and the image) of the free and wild steppe influenced politics.[25] Just like the Cossacks, the non-Cossack residents in the steppe appeared to Moscow as unruly fighters for freedom and independence. Indeed, their record was hardly encouraging to the center. It was here on the steppe that major peasant uprisings, usually led by Cossacks, took place in the seventeenth and eighteenth centuries. In the twentieth century, this history was to repeat itself, reinforced by new elements in the cities (the labor movement). To Moscow the image was more than just a myth.

One has to be careful in emphasizing the force of myth, culture, and tradition. Thirty years ago, Barrington Moore Jr. warned against the assumption that "cultural and social continuity do not require explanation":

> To maintain and transmit a value system, human beings are punched, bullied, sent to jail, thrown into concentration camps, cajoled, bribed, made into heroes, encouraged to read newspapers, stood up against a wall and shot, and sometimes even taught sociology.[26]

Apart from whether people were taught sociology, Moore's contention applies to the Russian-Ukrainian steppe with the roles reversed: the tsarist government

---

[23]S. Borisov, "Po Donetskomu basseinu," *Novyi mir*, 1929, no. 12, p. 124.

[24]Albert O. Hirschman, *Exit, Voice, and Loyalty: Responses to Decline in Firms, Organizations, and States* (Harvard University Press, 1970), p. 107.

[25]The myths and images of a geographical region are often politically influenced constructions. For an excellent discussion on this point regarding the Don, see Holquist, "A Russian Vendee," and for Siberia, see Mark Bassin, "In venting Siberia: Visions of the Russian East in the Early Nineteenth Century," *American Historical Review*, 96:3 (June 1991). The Donbas, sandwiched by two historically Cossack areas, also inherited some of the image of the *slobidshchyna* ("the land of free communes") created in the seventeenth century by refugees from the Polish-Cossack wars to the present Kharkiv–North Donbas region. For *slobidshchyna*, see Michael Hrushevsky, *A History of Ukraine*, ed. O. J. Frederiksen (Yale University Press, 1941), p. 274. For the importance of geography to historians, see David Hooson, ed., *Geography and National Identity* (Oxford, 1994), and Patricia Yaeger, ed., *The Geography of Identity* (University of Chicago Press, 1996).

[26]Barrington Moore Jr., *Social Origins of Dictatorship and Democracy: Lord and Peasant in the Making of the Modern World* (Boston, 1967), p. 486.

took violent measures to suppress the spirit of the free steppe while making efforts to integrate the borderland Cossack states into the empire.

Even under the Soviet regime the steppe in general and the Donbas in particular provided a refuge for those politically disenfranchised, especially the dispossessed kulaks who fled collectivization and famine, as will be discussed in later chapters. The horror and charm of the Donbas was well described by the writer Borys Antonenko-Davydovych who visited there in 1929. The wide open spaces of the Donbas steppe, punctuated by waste tips (*terakony*), were so different from the Donbas of his imagination: they aroused in him no sentiments, no "historical romanticism," so intimately associated with the wild steppe. Yet it appeared to him that there a new history, some new peculiar romanticism, was unfolding. Maybe even a new Ukraine was being born.[27] Despite all the oppressive measures of the Soviet government, the Donbas retained an aspect of freedom.

Part of the "wildness" of the steppe was ethnic tension. Because so many ethnic groups crisscrossed the steppe, it was a battleground for constant ethnic wars. Even after the Russian Empire conquered the south and colonized it mainly with Slavic populations, still the steppe (including the Donbas) retained a multiethnic character. According to the 1897 first general census of the country, the "ethnic" composition of the Donbas population (in Bakhmut, Slov'ianoserbs'k and Mariupol' *uezd*s) was (in percent) Ukrainians, 52.4; Russians, 28.7; Greeks, 6.4; Germans, 4.3; Jews, 2.9; Tartars, 2.1; Belarusian, 0.8; and Poles, 0.4.[28]

How ethnically diverse the Donbas was may be seen from the case of the Ukrainian poet Volodymyr Sosiura (1898–1965) who was born in Debal'tseve in the Donbas. He could count at least six ethnic groups in his ancestry: Serbian, Hungarian, Jewish, Ukrainian, French, and Karachai.[29] The Don Cossacks, a blend of Russians and Ukrainians, included a special rank of non-Slavs: Kalmyks.[30] Similarly, the Zaporozhian Cossacks included many non-Slavs: Jews, Tartars, Poles, Turks. Nikita Khrushchev fondly remembers Bulgarian farmers in the prerevolutionary Donbas "who ran many of the best agri-

[27]Borys Antonenko-Davydovych, *Zemleiu Ukrains'koiu* (Philadelphia, 1955), p. 141 (this is a reprint of a 1942 L'viv edition).

[28]Calculated from *Pervaia vseobshchaia perepis' naseleniia Rossiiskoi imperii, 1897 g.* (St. Petersburg, 1904–5), 13:74–75. (In the 1897 census, "nationality" [*natsional'nost'*] was defined by the "mother tongue" [*rodnoi iazyk*].) The Don province to which the eastern part of the Donbas belonged, the Russians accounted for 67.2% and the Ukrainians 28.1%. (See Semenov-Tian-Shanskii, *Rossiia*, p. 182.) The Greek population was concentrated on the shore of Azov, particularly in the Mariupol' area, as this Greek name suggests. The Jews resided mainly in the western part, since the Don as well as the Kharkiv area was outside the Jewish pale of settlement.

[29]Sosiura, "Tretia rota," p. 63. The Karachais are Muslims and mountain tribes by origin from the North Caucasus.

[30]McNeal, *Tsar and Cossack*, p. 10.

cultural enterprises. They were marvelous organizers. They literally showered the markets with high-quality, low-price produce."[31] In the Donbas there were many German farmers, descendants of those who came to colonize the steppe under Catherine the Great.

Many languages were spoken in the Donbas, but the dominant ones were Russian and Ukrainian. The Don Cossacks spoke a "Cossack language," Russian with Ukrainian and Tartar influences. The dominant language in the cities was and is Russian, as the Menshevik activist George Denike said of Luhans'k in the prerevolutionary years:

> I was really struck by the fact that I never heard a single word of Ukrainian in Lugansk itself. When I went around to where the workers were, as I did fairly often, no one ever spoke Ukrainian. But when I encountered a non-worker, peasants or petty bourgeoisie, it was sometimes difficult to make myself understood. It was a striking contrast between the town and industrial population in general, and the peasantry.[32]

Some less educated Donbas residents spoke (and to some extent still do) a language that blended Russian and Ukrainian, a "Ukraino-Russian dialect."[33] Often people in the Ukrainian-Russian borderlands identified neither with U-kraine nor with Russia, calling themselves *pereverteni* or *perevertyshi* (converts).[34]

Ethnic coexistence almost inevitably meant ethnic conflict, however. In the industrial Donbas, the Tartars, Muslims, were ready victims of violence by Slavs. Local authorities persecuted the Tartars whom they regarded, it was said, as nonhumans.[35] In 1902, in the Iakobenko coalfield, Russian colliers, incited by rumor that their low wages were due to the influx of Tartar workers, broke into their barracks and beat and stabbed them.[36]

The relations between Russians and Ukrainians were sometimes strained. In the countryside, they lived a very similar life, but villages were either Rus-

---

[31] *Khrushchev Remembers: The Last Testament*, tr. and ed. Strobe Talbott, foreword by Edward Crankshaw and introduction by Jerrold L. Schecter (Boston, 1974), p. 187. For Bulgarian farmers in the Donbas, see also GARF, f. 5459, op. 9, d. 145, l. 167.

[32] Leopold Haimson, in collaboration with Ziva Galili y Garcia and Richard Wortman, *The Making of Three Russian Revolutionaries: Voices from the Menshevik Past* (Cambridge University Press, 1987), p. 354.

[33] See Bohdan Krawchenko, *Social Change and National Consciousness in Twentieth-Century Ukraine* (New York, 1985), p. 79. For more details, see I. Nimchynov, "Do iazykovoi problemy v Donbasi," *Kul'tura i pobut*, 15 November 1925 (supplement to *Visty VUTsVK*).

[34] L. N. Chizhikova, *Russko-ukrainskoe pogranich'e. Istoriia i sud'by traditsionno-bytovoi kul'tury (XIX–XX veka)* (Moscow, 1988), p. 49.

[35] F. Zaitsev, "Bol'sheviki Iuzovki do 1918 goda," *Literaturnyi Donbass*, 1933, nos. 10–12, p. 156.

[36] *5-letnii obzor deiatel'nosti Soiuza gornorabochikh v Donetskom basseine (1920–1925 gg.) i kratkii ocherk rabochego i professional'nogo dvizheniia gorniakov Donetskogo basseina do 1920 goda* (Artemivs'k, 1925), p. 18.

sian or Ukrainian, and they hardly mixed with each other. Some ways of life, such as the Russian custom of building fences around their houses, were not liked by Ukrainians.[37] Relations seem to have been more strained in cities and workers' settlements. Russians and Ukrainians would insult each other with derogatory names (*khokholy* [the tuft of hair on a Cossack's shaven head] for Ukrainians, *katsapy* [a standard derogatory term meaning billy goat], *hrachi* [gamblers], *kuhuty* [roosters] for Russians, etc).[38] Russian miners "were constantly at odds with" local Ukrainians, mainly over women. Workers would steal things from peasants simply "to spite the hated *khokhol*."[39] In the Donbas, according to a former Bolshevik activist, their hostility "systematically took the form of the most wild forms of knife fights."[40] In prerevolutionary Luhans'k, there was constant enmity among its three districts, the city itself where Russian workers lived, the left-bank village Kamennyi Brod, and the right-bank Gusinovka populated by artisans (many of whom were Jews). Their hostility was such that it was dangerous to cross the line into another district: one would be forced to "swim in dust and dirt," subjected to all kinds of mockery, and finally beaten repeatedly. Local Ukrainians seem to have had the upper hand in many cases: four to five Ukrainians could beat up twenty-five Russians; if a Ukrainian in Luhans'k was in a good mood on a holiday, he would go to the working-class district "to knock out *katsapy*." He might break into the church during the service to fight.[41]

The most complex and serious conflict involved Jews. According to one account, "The whole policy and work of the authority was directed against the Jews. The church, the school, and the whole police apparatus were adapted to persecution and oppression."[42] In the Donbas, as in other parts of Ukraine and Poland, there were periodic pogroms. The Jews were confined to the pale of the settlement, living under a host of officially sanctioned restrictions on their material and spiritual life. Some were able to attend technical schools such as

[37] Semenov-Tian-Shanskii, *Rossiia*, p. 189. See also K. E. Voroshilov, *Rasskazy o zhizni. Vospominaniia. Kniga pervaia* (Moscow, 1968), p. 11, and Chizhikova, *Russko-ukrainskoe pogranich'e*, p. 47. For a similar, mutually suspicious attitude of Ukrainians and Russians in Poltava in the early 1930s, see Lev Kopelev, *I sotvoril sebe kumira* (Ann Arbor, Mich., 1978), pp. 135–36.

[38] Zaitsev, "Bol'sheviki Iuzovki," p. 156. Sholokhov's classic, *And Quiet Flows the Don* (1934), also includes vivid descriptions of such discord in the Don.

[39] A. A. Auerbakh, "Vospominaniia o nachale razvitiia kamennougol'noi promyshlennosti v Rossii," *Russkaia starina*, 1909, no. 12, p. 555. For the enmity between Russians and Ukrainians in the Donbas, see also *5-letnii obzor*, p. 19.

[40] T. Kharechko, "Sotsial-demokraticheskii soiuz gorno-zavodskikh rabochikh. Iz istorii revoliutsionnogo dvizheniia v Donbasse 1900–1908 g.g.," *Letopis' revoliutsii*, 1925, no. 3, p. 13. See also Aleksandr Gambarov, "Ocherki po istorii revoliutsionnogo dvizheniia v Luganske, 1901–1921 gg.," *Letopis' revoliutsii*, 1923, no. 4, p. 46.

[41] Voroshilov, *Rasskazy o zhizni*, pp. 121–22, and I. Nikolaenko, *Revoliutsionnoe dvizhenie v Luganske* (Kharkiv, 1926), pp. 7–8.

[42] Zaitsev, "Bol'sheviki Iuzovki," p. 156.

mining institutes, which provided a growing number of Jewish technicians and engineers.[43] Yet the majority of the Jews engaged in "traditional" trades such as "mercantile and artisanal occupations, dominating the provisions of services for the rapidly growing settlements of the Donbass." Here, as elsewhere within the pale of Jewish settlement, they had to compete in their trades with Russians and Ukrainians who, like themselves, had come to seek new opportunities. Few Jews engaged in physical labor in mines and factories. Thus not only their ethnicity and religion but their occupational concentration contributed to their isolation from the working population in the Donbas. Workers viewed Jewish shopkeepers and tavern keepers as outsiders who, in collusion with mine and factory managers, exploited them. Yet for the gentiles they were not merely "exploiters" but "Jewish exploiters." In the famous Iuzivka cholera riot of 1892, for example, which led to pogroms against the Jews, "the mob at first looted only the Jewish shops, and, where a merchant proved his Russian identity by displaying an icon, the rioters paid for all goods taken. Only after they were senseless with drink did the rioters burn and loot indiscriminately."[44]

In the Donbas, as elsewhere in Ukraine, anti-Jewish pogroms took place periodically, particularly in the late nineteenth and early twentieth centuries. The Donbas was largely spared the first large-scale pogroms of 1881–82,[45] but the specter of pogroms haunted the Donbas in 1892[46] and 1903. In the latter case, the pogroms that took place in Kishnev in the spring of that year led to a widely circulated rumor of imminent pogroms in the Donbas. Jews evacuated to safer places, and mine officials fled to avoid danger. The Social Democrats who had prepared for May Day demonstrations had to cancel them lest, according to their own account, the miners take part in pogroms. The timely dispatch of Cossack troops, however, prevented any pogroms from taking place in 1903.[47] A small-scale pogrom did occur in February 1905 in the Rykove coalfields (near Luhans'k): three thousand striking miners assaulted and destroyed the shop of Davydovich.[48]

Here, as elsewhere, the most destructive pogroms occurred in October 1905, during the few days immediately after Nicholas II issued the famous

---

[43]Theodore H. Friedgut, *Iuzovka and Revolution*, vol. 1, *Life and Work in Russia's Donbass, 1869–1924* (Princeton University Press, 1989), pp. 197–98.

[44]Ibid., p. 201.

[45]*Materialy dlia istorii anti-evreiskikh pogromov v Rossii*, vol. 2 (Petrograd and Moscow, 1923), p. 531, lists only two in the Mariupol' area. For the 1881 pogroms in general, see I. Michael Aronson, *Troubled Waters: The Origins of the 1881 Anti-Jewish Pogrom in Russia* (University of Pittsburgh Press, 1992). See also the articles by the same author, Moshe Mishinsky, and Erich Haberer in Klier and Lambroza, *Pogroms*.

[46]See Theodore H. Friedgut, "Labor Violence and Regime Brutality in Tsarist Russia: The Iuzovka Cholera Riots of 1892," *Slavic Review*, 46:2 (Summer 1987).

[47]*Iskra* (Geneva, Switzerland), no. 45 (1 August 1903), p. 7.

[48]V. Nevskii, "Ianvarskie dni 1905 goda v Ekaterinoslave i Donetskom basseine. Po arkhivnym dokumentam," *Proletarskaia revoliutsiia*, 1923, no. 3, pp. 55 and 60.

October Manifesto, promising political concessions, when anxiety for the future of the autocracy mobilized conservative elements.[49] In Iuzivka, where one of the biggest pogroms in the Donbas broke out, at least twelve Jews were murdered.[50] The Iuzivka pogrom started when a small group of people, said to have been made up mainly of Jews, demonstrated in order to acquaint the workers with the October Manifesto. Workers instead countered with a savage pogrom. Almost all Jewish properties were destroyed, so was the synagogue in Iuzivka. Workers, both from factories and mines, chased the fleeing Jews (among whom were women and children) to infirmaries with axes. Miners went around searching for Jews hiding in surrounding villages.[51] Some Jews were tossed alive into blast furnaces.[52] Nikita Khrushchev, an eleven-year-old boy at the time, was a witness to this pogrom:

> In my childhood in the Donbass, I once witnessed a pogrom with my own eyes. . . . It was a lovely, sunny, autumn day. . . . The mob surged to the south side of the slope, but the soldiers didn't let the workers into the city. A volley of rifle fire rang out. Someone shouted that they were shooting in the air. Someone else shouted that they were shooting with blanks and that only one or two soldiers were shooting with live bullets, just to scare the Jews a little. Everyone was inventing his own version of what was happening. The crowd dispersed late in the evening. The workers from our mine were bragging the next day about how many boots and other trophies they'd picked up during the looting. One man said he had made off with ten pairs of boots. Some of the miners were telling about how the "yids" marched around calling the Russians abusive names, carrying banners, and bearing their "yid tsar" on their shoulders. When the Russians attacked them with clubs, he hid in a leather factory. The Russians set this factory on fire, and the "yid tsar" was burned alive inside. The day after the pogrom started I ran straight from school to Yuzovka [Iuzivka] to see what was going on here. There was still a lot of looting. I saw clock repair shops which had been broken into, and feathers were flying along the streets where the looters were ripping open mattresses and shaking the feathers out the windows of Jewish homes. . . . I heard that many of the Jews who had been beaten were in the factory infirmary. I decided to go there and have a look with one of my friends, another little boy.

[49]See Shlomo Lambroza, "The Pogroms of 1903–1906," in Klier and Lambroza, *Pogroms*. For Odessa, the most pogrom-prone city, see Robert Weinberg, *The Revolution of 1905 in Odessa: Blood on the Steps* (Indiana University Press, 1993), ch. 7.

[50]A. Linden, ed., *Die Judenpogrome in Rußland* (Cologne and Leipzig, 1910), p. 217.

[51]*Voskhod* (St. Petersburg), 1905, nos. 42–43, col. 34, and nos. 47–48, cols. 18–21. See also Heinz-Dietrich Löwe, *Antisemitismus und reaktionäre Utopie. Russischer Konservatismus im Kampf gegen den Wandel von Staat und Gesellschaft* (Hamburg, 1978), pp. 240–41 (Iuzivka is misspelled Iuzokov), and S. A. Stepanov, *Chernaia sotnia v Rossii (1905–1914 gg.)* (Moscow, 1992), p. 77.

[52]L. Shklovskii (Sergei), "Vospominaniia o 1905 gode," *Proletarskaia revoliutsiia*, 1926, no. 1, p. 201, and Surozhskii, "Krai uglia i zheleza," p. 304.

We found a horrible scene. The corpses of Jews who had been beaten to death were lying in rows on the floor.[53]

No one can be certain whether all the details of this reminiscence and its explanation of the cause of the pogrom are accurate.[54] Yet Khrushchev's comments are a valuable testimony to the tension that obtained in Iuzivka.

In Luhans'k, the pogroms were more limited with only one reported death.[55] However, there was much robbery, and a woman was raped while her daughter was forced to look on with a candle in her hand. People could not get away by showing a cross on their chest: they had to show "more material evidence,"[56] most often the absence of circumcision. In Luhans'k the perpetrators of the pogrom, initially a crowd of 150, carried a portrait of the tsar and a red flag. An observer, a Social Democrat, could not understand what this apparent contradiction meant: a patriotic manifestation or a revolutionary demonstration.[57]

Ethnic and religious hatred and prejudice were no doubt responsible for the pogroms, but there were other important factors. Take the geography of pogroms, for example. As many students of pogroms have noted, both the 1881–82 and the 1903–6 pogrom waves were concentrated largely in several provinces: Kiev, Poltava, Chernihiv, Kherson, Bessarabia, Podilia, Katerynoslav, in other words, by and large the southern Ukrainian steppe. In the northwest (Lithuania and Belarus), which had an equally large Jewish population, pogroms did not take place or were limited.[58] This was often attributed by some Russians to the "Cossack traditions" of the Ukrainian people (which

---

[53] *Khrushchev Remembers*, with an introduction, commentary, and notes by Edward Crankshaw, tr. and ed. Strobe Talbott (Boston, 1970), pp. 266–67. Black Hundreds refer to organizations of the extreme right.

[54] For pogroms in Iuzivka and elsewhere, see Charters Wynn, *Workers, Strikes, and Pogroms: The Donbass-Dnepr Bend in Late Imperial Russia, 1870–1905* (Princeton University Press, 1992), ch. 7.

[55] It was, according to S. M. Ryzhkov, due to a teacher and delegate to the first Duma from Katerynoslav province: "an unarmed teacher" (Ryzhkov?) and "unarmed workers" dispersed the *pogromshchiki* (pogrom perpetrators). He emphatically declared that the Russian people had no enmity toward the Jewish people. *Gosudarstvennaia Duma. Stenograficheskii otchet. 1906 god. Sessiia pervaia. Tom II. Zasedaniia 19–38 (s 1 iiunia po 4 iiulia)* (St. Petersburg, 1906), p. 956.

[56] DALO, SIF 94f.

[57] Nikolaenko, *Revoliutsionnoe dvizhenie*, p. 28. For pogroms in other parts of the Donbas, see Linden, *Die Judenpogrome*, pp. 204–10 (Bakhmut), 227–40 (Mariupol'), 245 (Iasynuvata and other stations). See also T. Kharechko, "Oktiabr'sko-dekabr'skii pod"em 1905 g. v Donbasse," *Letopis' revoliutsii*, 1925, nos. 5–6, pp. 8–10 and 13–14. Pogroms also took place in the eastern Donbas in Don Cossack Host province, where relatively few Jews resided. See the case of Aleksandrovsk-Grushevskii in Kharechko, p. 14. In the Don anthracite mines, the victims of pogroms were said to be the " 'seditious' intelligentsia." (*Proletariat v revoliutsii 1905–1907 gg. K 25-letiiu revoliutsii 1905 g.* [Moscow and Leningrad, 1930], p. 203.) In the city of Rostov, just outside the Donbas, where of its 144,000 population 14,000 were Jews, pogroms also took place. See Linden, *Die Judenpogrome*, pp. 488–98.

[58] See the maps on Klier and Lambroza, *Pogroms*, pp. 43 and 194.

included the massacre of Jews by Cossack Hetman Bohdan Khmelnytsky in 1648 and by the peasants and Cossacks who took part in the 1768 Koliiv-shchyna).[59] Yet the later pogroms were not so much a new version of old atrocities as events caused by tensions from rapid economic development, and indeed it was in the steppe that the old social structure was under the severest strain.

As Hans Rogger has convincingly shown in his recent essay, the pogroms were "primarily and originally an urban phenomenon and a projection of the fast growing southern cities' social and ethnic tensions." The main perpetrators were members of urban lower middle classes (*meshchane*) and "migrants from the inner-Russian provinces, from which most Jews were barred." These were "railway and construction workers, the day laborers, freight handlers, and vagabonds" (one might add factory workers and colliers in the case of the Donbas) who "fled from poverty to the towns, ports, factories, and workshops of the south." Yet "in raw settlements or urban slums" they clashed with Jews (who, like themselves, came to the steppe seeking a better life), viewing "this despised and alien group as rival job seekers, as employers, as buyers or sellers of prime necessities."[60] The conservative elements, in turn, were alarmed by rapid economic developments, which assaulted the rural old regime and caused much tension in the cities. These people regarded the Jews as the embodiment of all they feared: change, modernity, and an uprooted life.[61] When these two forces merged, as was the case in 1905, the effect proved deadly.

Without popular Judeophobia, anti-Jewish pogroms could not have taken place, but it alone cannot explain their geography. Certainly, as Shlomo Lambroza maintains, the fact that in the steppe Jewish community organization was limited and the Bund (General Jewish Workers' Union in Lithuania, Poland, and Russia) "had not yet established significant self-defense units" may also account for the concentration of pogroms in the south.[62] Yet part of the reason for these weaknesses was that the Jews in the steppe were more assimilated in a more competitive economic environment than those in the northwest. Few Jewish workers spoke Yiddish, which made it difficult for the Bund to organize them.[63] As Hans Rogger has suggested, in western Europe the liberation of Jews and the competition offered by them were important causes for pogroms. "Had Jewish emancipation been a fact in Russia rather than a chimera of the

[59]John Klier, "The Pogrom Paradigm in Russian History," in Klier and Lambroza, *Pogroms*, p. 14.

[60]Hans Rogger, "Conclusion and Overview," in Klier and Lambroza, *Pogroms*, p. 336.

[61]See Löwe, *Antisemitismus und reaktionäre Utopie.*

[62]Lambroza, "The Pogroms in 1903–1906," in Klier and Lambroza, *Pogroms*, p. 230. For the Bund, see Henry J. Tobias, *The Jewish Bund in Russia: From Its Origins to 1905* (Stanford University Press, 1972).

[63]Friedgut, *Iuzovka and Revolution*, p. 204. The Bund had thus to compete with the Russian Social Democrats. See Tobias, *The Jewish Bund*, p. 117.

Right, its anti-Semitism might possibly have found a wider echo" than it actually did after 1905.[64] Rogger has also suggested that antiblack riots in the American north in the nineteenth and twentieth centuries have much in common with anti-Jewish pogroms in Russia's south. Even though these took place in radically different bodies politic, one an autocracy, the other a liberal democracy, the antagonism in both countries stemmed from "the stress of change in the urban environment."[65]

Geography is important to understanding the politics of the Donbas. The Donbas was located between two historically Cossack areas. The Cossack forces as oppressors of popular demonstrations symbolized the old Russia, the status quo, and their presence in and near the Donbas provided a powerful conservative force to Donbas politics. At the same time, however, the Cossack spirit of freedom continued to pose a threat to the central authorities, whether tsarist or Soviet. For all its economic exploitation, the Donbas was a haven for refugees from poverty and oppression. Finally, the Donbas was a place where, historically, many ethnic groups gathered. Ethnic tensions were exacerbated by rapid economic development. In the Donbas, political battles were fought against this historical and geographical background.[66]

Labor and Violence

The emergence of modern industry and its rapid expansion in the Donbas in the latter half of the nineteenth century recreated symbolic frontiers by offering tremendous opportunities and thereby attracting numerous people from various parts of the empire. The Donbas came to embody many of the characteristics of the historical wild steppe – freedom and violence – in their modern incarnations.

Industrial development created numerous workers' settlements and colonies in the Donbas. These were typical company towns, where almost everyone was connected with the company and almost everything was run by it. Iuzivka was a good example, as Theodore T. Friedgut has shown.[67] There was a peculiarly feudal atmosphere about it. According to Nikita Khrushchev, who worked for the Hughes company,

[64]Hans Rogger, *Jewish Policies and Right-Wing Politics in Imperial Russia* (University of California Press, 1986), p. 227.

[65]Rogger, "Conclusion and Overview," in Klier and Lambroza, *Pogroms*, p. 361. For a more general argument linking nationalism and industrial society, see Ernest Gellner, *Nations and Nationalism* (Cornell University Press, 1983).

[66]For an excellent discussion on the competing identities in "New Russia" in general, see Terry Martin, "The Empire's New Frontiers: New Russia's Path from Frontier to *Okraina*, 1774–1920," *Russian History/Histoire Russe*, 19:1–4 (1992).

[67]Friedgut, *Iuzovka and Revolution*.

It is interesting to note that at the mine there was no financial office, not even a single accountant or payroll clerk. The owner did it all himself. He handed out the pay, calculated production figures, and kept track of it all. He really did control the entire mine, acting as manager, bookkeeper, and cashier. He knew how much each worker should get and he paid them.[68]

Makiivka possessed similar characteristics, as a French visitor observed in 1908:

> At the same time, the Makeyevka region is one of the most important in the Donetz Basin which itself is one of the most highly industrialized in Russia. Apart from the soil which is immeasurably rich, the subsoil holds treasures which, until thirty years ago, had not been tapped or exploited. Both soil and subsoil are owned by the various industrial concerns, many of which are French; and it is they who, around the mine-shafts and the blast furnaces, build towns and villages, administer them and collect taxes from the inhabitants. We have here a real feudal system in which the tall chimney has replaced the castle.[69]

These settlements and towns differed from other industrial centers such as St. Petersburg and Moscow where industry was developed at least partially based upon existing resources. True, these cities and centers, as Daniel R. Brower has argued, lacked adequate human resources and had to rely on migrant labor (hence he has called them "migrant cities").[70] Yet the sparsely populated Donbas had to build its industry from scratch, relying almost entirely on migrant labor. Similarly, while private, state, and foreign capital financed industrialization in Moscow and St. Petersburg, in the Donbas foreign capital was the driving force behind its economic development. On the eve of World War I, twenty-six of the thirty-six joint-stock companies in the Donbas coal-mining industry had almost exclusively foreign capital. These firms yielded 95.4 percent of coal output by the joint-stock companies and more than 70 percent of all coal production in the Donbas. The boards of nineteen of the twenty-nine companies were situated in France and Belgium.[71]

Foreign and Russian managers in the Donbas lived a lavish life. Direc-

---

[68] *Khrushchev Remembers: The Glasnost Tapes*, foreword by Strobe Talbott, tr. and ed. Jerrold L. Schecter with Vyacheslav V. Luchkov (Boston, 1990), p. 7. Khrushchev referred to 1909.

[69] Patrick A. Croghan, *The Peasant from Makeyevka: Biography of Bishop Pius Neveu, A.A.* (Worcester, Mass., 1982), p. 14.

[70] Daniel R. Brower, *The Russian City between Tradition and Modernity, 1850–1900* (University of California Press, 1990).

[71] V. S. Ziv, *Inostrannye kapitaly v russkoi gornozavodskoi promyshlennosti* (Petrograd, 1917), p. 59; G. D. Bakulev, *Razvitie ugol'noi promyshlennosti Donetskogo basseina* (Moscow, 1955), pp. 150–53; and V. I. Vovykin, "Frantsuzskii kapital v aktsionernykh predpriiatiiakh v Rossii nakanune Oktiabria," *Istoriia SSSR*, 1991, no. 4, p. 180. Anthracite production, particularly in the eastern Donbas, was mainly in the hands of Russian capital financed by St. Petersburg's credit institutions, foreign firms accounting roughly for 15% to 20% of Donbas anthracite production (Ziv, *Inostrannye kapitaly*, p. 64).

tors lived in "palaces" with large yards planted with rare trees, while foremen, shop directors, and chief accountants lived in attractive flats with four to twelve rooms and with free servants.[72] Their extravagance sometimes assumed a peculiar form. The director of Makiivka Mine in the early 1890s was A. N. Glebov, a transport engineer. "Living about 25 versts [26.5 kilometers] away from the mine at Ilovaiskii's country estate, Zuevka, Glebov used to arrive at the mine in a wild troika amidst great uproar and ringing of bells, either late at night or at dawn – these unexpected visits were the way he 'controlled' the works."[73]   Another director at a mine near Iuzivka was reported in 1892 to practice the same flaunting of power and wealth.[74] Naturally they lived totally isolated from the workers. The peasants in the area, in turn, treated the managers as new noblemen: "They used to come to pay their respects very solemnly on major holidays, when it was traditional, alas, to give them some money 'for vodka' – there was no escaping it."[75]

The wild steppe was a stage for wild exploitation. In the workplace, managerial authority was often unbridled. The workday of the average collier was characterized by brutal exploitation and affront. Foreign foremen were said to be extremely arrogant and often beat Russian workers.[76] The mining engineer Aleksandr Fenin maintained that he and his fellow engineers "were able to win the strong sympathy of the workers," but a 1903 leaflet contended that Fenin treated workers worse than animals.[77]

Even *artel*'s (independent work gangs) were not free from exploitation. Workers often organized *artel*'s to cope with hard, dangerous work and to fight against exploitation. Generally speaking, *artel*'s were tightly knit organizations which ensured (or at least sought to ensure) equality, mutual assistance, and autonomy. In other words, *artel*'s were a sort of transplanted village commune (*mir*, *obshchina*), which the peasants idealized and which preserved their distinct communities. *Artel*'s could be very paternalistic, as was often the case, but its chiefs, (*artel'shchiks*), or elders (*starshinas*), were usually elected, and respected, by their members. Such communities were particularly important

[72]Zaitsev, "Bol'sheviki Iuzovki," p. 153. See also Levus, "Iz istorii revoliutsionnogo dvizheniia v Donetskom basseine," *Narodnoe delo. Sbornik*, 3 (1909), pp. 47–48. For more examples, see Wynn, *Workers, Strikes, and Pogroms*, pp. 35–36.

[73]Aleksandr I. Fenin, *Coal and Politics in Late Imperial Russia: Memoirs of a Russian Mining Engineer*, tr. Alexandre Fediaevsky and ed. Susan P. McCaffray (Northern Illinois University Press, 1990), p. 56.

[74]See V. Veresaev, "V studencheskie gody," in his *Sobranie sochinenii*, vol. 5 (Moscow, 1961), p. 333.

[75]Fenin, *Coal and Politics*, p. 93.

[76]See, for example, Voroshilov, *Rasskazy o zhizni*, pp. 57 and 63. However, Voroshilov has added that he has a fond memory of foreigners, too. See also, Wynn, *Workers, Strikes, and Pogroms*, p. 64.

[77]Fenin, *Coal and Politics*, p. 45, and "Poslednie novosti," *Letopis' revoliutsii*, 1923, no. 2, p. 242.

for dangerous underground work, and the dissolution of *artel*'s after the 1917 revolution destroyed the traditional bonds underground and resulted in danger and confusion.[78] Yet exploitation existed in *artel*'s. In Russia, unlike in Italy, according to one account, *artel*'s somehow became dependent on contractors for their labor (for whom the *artel*' elders often doubled) and were exploited by them.[79]

To regiment labor, managers imposed fines for the smallest violation of workplace rules, depriving workers of 10 to 25 percent of their wages.[80] (This offset the relatively high wages of Donbas workers.) Mining engineers were thus referred to as "mining officers."[81] Fenin suggested that historically, in Russia, the word engineer had been synonymous with "money grubber," "an almost utterly shameless plunderer."[82] In the case of the Donbas, moreover, they could even have been branded lackeys of foreign capital because many of them worked for foreign concerns. Management tended to pay wages late to retain the work force, but the wages were often merely credits or coupons for the company shop and taverns. Workers, many illiterate or barely literate, were cheated at work, in shops, and in the office.[83] Labor was not free but hard, as workers would say: "Why Siberia, we have our own Siberia."[84]

Almost all accounts of the Donbas labor movement maintain that it was difficult to organize workers, particularly colliers. The coalfields were scattered around the steppe, and there was little contact among them. Disaffected workers moved from one colliery to another; so did those persecuted by managerial personnel and fugitives without proper documents. Ethnic diversity made the task of organization all the more difficult, yet antagonism and separation remained strong even within a single ethnic group, for example, the Russians, whose loyalty often belonged to their barracks or *zemliachestvos* (groups of people from the same family, clan, village, district, or region).[85] Moreover,

---

[78]For *artels*, see my "Workers' Artels and Soviet Production Relations," in Sheila Fitzpatrick, Alexander Rabinowitch, and Richard Stites, eds., *Russia in the Era of NEP: Explorations in Soviet Society and Culture* (Indiana University Press, 1991).

[79]See B. Boronov, *Artel'nyi trud. Kak organizovat' trudovye arteli*, 2nd ed. (Moscow, 1918), p. 11.

[80]This was the case even on the eve of the 1917 revolution. See Iu. I. Kir'ianov, *Rabochie Iuga Rossii, 1914–fevral' 1917 g.* (Moscow, 1971), p. 64.

[81]Gambarov, "Ocherki," p. 49.

[82]A. I. Fenin, *Vospominaniia inzhenera. K istorii obshchestvennago i khoziaistvennago razvitiia Rossii (1883–1906 g.g.)* (Prague, 1938), p. 40. The English translation is inaccurate. (Fenin, *Coal and Politics*, p. 36.)

[83]*Proletariat v revoliutsii 1905–1907 gg.*, p. 190; *Robitnychyi rukh na Ukraini (1885–1894 rr.) Zbirnyk dokumentiv i materialiv* (Kiev, 1990), p. 321; and G. Novopolin, "Pervye 'besporiadki' gornorabochikh (1887 god)," *Proletarskaia revoliutsiia*, 1923, no. 2, p. 13.

[84]A. N. Pasiuk, "Rabochee dvizhenie na predpriiatiiakh Novorossiiskogo O-va (1872–1905 g.g.)," *Letopis' revoliutsii*, 1926, nos. 3–4, p. 205.

[85]See Voroshilov, *Rasskazy o zhizni*, p. 67, Kharechko, "Sotsial-demokraticheskii soiuz gornozavodskikh rabochikh," pp. 12–13, and Gambarov, "Ocherki," pp. 46–47.

as Theodore H. Friedgut has shown, there was a marked differentiation between factory workers ("advancing into a modern culture set in something that grew to resemble an urban settlement") and colliers ("stuck in the throes of the unsettling transition from village to industry"), "two totally different societies."[86] Add to these differences divisions by skill, earnings, religion, age, and regularity of employment, and one had very disparate groups of workers.

By contrast, the southern industrialists (of whom the Donbas entrepreneurs composed a majority) were among the most organized in the empire. As early as 1874 they formed the Association of Southern Coal and Steel Producers, which "advocated speedy economic modernization for their country." Many of the southern entrepreneurs also pressed for the formation of syndicates to promote "a centralization and control of industry well suited to absolutism." In 1902 the Prodamet (of steel producers) was sanctioned by the government, and in 1904 it was followed by the Produgol' (of coal producers).[87] The association became a large and influential interest group with many lobbyists placed in strategically important organizations.[88]

Historians concur that the Donbas industrialists were of the relatively "enlightened" sort. Alfred J. Rieber has maintained that they "displayed toward their workers a concern which was hierarchical rather than paternalistic. That is, the workers were perceived as contractual employees rather than as 'members of the family,' as they were in Moscow."[89] The need to attract and retain the work force in a labor-shortage region was said to be one reason why they concerned themselves with the welfare of workers. Indeed, without governmental legislation the southern industrialists took the initiative to create a disability fund in 1884 and expended as much as one-third of the association's budget to this end.[90] Their political orientation was nonpartisan. Even when the 1905 revolution was taking place, one prominent Donbas engineer recalled, "I am quite embarrassed at the difficulty of defining the political orientation of most of my friends or even of my own views."[91] Susan P. McCaffray has called

---

[86]Friedgut, *Iuzovka and Revolution*, p. 330.

[87]Susan McCaffray, "The Association of Southern Coal and Steel Producers and the Problems of Industrial Progress in Tsarist Russia," *Slavic Review*, 47:2 (Fall 1988), pp. 464 and 478. See also Alfred J. Rieber, *Merchants and Entrepreneurs in Imperial Russia* (University of North Carolina Press, 1982), pp. 222–43 and 333–45, V. Liashenko, "Torgovo-promyshlennaia burzhuaziia Donbassa v 1861–1917 gg.," *Gorod* (Donets'k), 24 (61) (22–28 June 1992), p. 7; and René Girault, *Emprunts russes et investissements français en Russe 1887–1914* (Paris, 1973), pp. 364–71 and 449.

[88]In 1917 it had more than 200 lobbyists. See Iu. V. Afonin, "Monopolistychna burzhuaziia Donbasu v 1917 r.," *Ukrains'kyi istorychnyi zhurnal*, 1990, no. 9, p. 49.

[89]Rieber, *Merchants and Entrepreneurs*, p. 235.

[90]Ibid.

[91]Fenin, *Coal and Politics*, p. 134. Many of them were to join the liberal party, the Kadets (the Constitutional Democratic Party). Yet Fenin still found "the demand for universal suffrage . . . absolutely unacceptable, as I knew the Russian peasantry well" (p. 156).

their position "welfare capitalism," or "welfare liberalism."[92]

Despite all this, as the report of the Katerynoslav governor on the 1892 cholera riot in Iuzivka pointed out, there was a gross imbalance of power between labor and management: the former's welfare was completely dependent on the latter's goodwill; and, in fact, the former was exploited by the latter with impunity. (Marginalia jotted down by the minister of the interior read: "Isn't this the crux of the matter?") In this sense, in the Donbas industrial towns and settlements strong paternalistic relations pertained. As elsewhere and in other countries, strong paternalism often made labor passive. Yet once conflict occurred, savage force was used; and workers were flogged as if they were children and slaves whose misbehavior ought to be corrected by paternal whipping. Everyday life in the Donbas was so brutal that the Russian press attributed savage exploitation to brutal capitalism alien to Russia, a convenient device because the Donbas was dominated by foreign capital:

> Exploitation exists everywhere, wherever there are people who work and people who utilize the labor of others. But never in Russia, not at a single factory, has it taken on such grandiose proportions of "misunderstanding." . . . Mortality among the Hughes workers significantly exceeds that among prisoners in the Siberian mines.[93]

Not surprisingly, the history of the Donbas was marked by periodic outbursts of violent protest.

One of the first conflicts in the Donbas took place in Iuzivka in 1874. Colliers demanded a wage hike; they wanted the rolling-mill operatives to join them in halting work. The Hughes administration provided the operatives (who were much better paid) with some barrels of vodka. When the colliers came unarmed, the operatives attacked them with iron bars under the command of the Hughes clan. The operatives chased the workers for a mile, but then stopped "as if they felt ashamed of their deed," but in fact they were simply drunk. Then the Hughes officials mounted on horseback, pursued the colliers, and captured them one by one, beating one of them with an iron bar. The leaders of the "rebellion" (*bunt*) were deported to their native village under police guard. In summer, to prevent the seasonal exodus of workers, Hughes did not return passports to workers who wished to leave. When they began to leave without their documents, Hughes had the railway station master deny tickets to those

---

[92] Susan P. McCaffray, *The Politics of Industrialization in Tsarist Russia: The Association of Southern Coal and Steel Producers, 1874–1914* (Northern Illinois University Press, 1996). Their outlook may be comparable with that of Baku oil industrialists. See Ronald Grigor Suny, "A Journeyman for the Revolution: Stalin and the Labour Movement in Baku, June 1907–May 1908," *Soviet Studies*, 23:3 (January 1972).

[93] Quoted in Louise McReynolds, *The News under Russia's Old Regime: The Development of a Mass-Circulation Press* (Princeton University Press, 1991), pp. 110–11.

without passports and send them back to the company.[94] In the following year, workers of the Hughes company, angry with a delay in payments, pillaged shops and taverns when their promised credit was rescinded.[95]

On 5 May 1887 colliers of Mines 11, 18, and 19 in Rutchenkove near Iuzivka struck and then robbed and ravaged shops, the reason being that the seasonal wage hike (every spring, when the supply of labor became short, the wages were raised to retain workers) was smaller than the previous year. Because there was no technician who spoke Russian in the mines, they could not convey their demands. Finally, fifteen hundred colliers gathered at the management office, and when the director Vincent refused a further wage hike, the workers verbally threatened him, and Vincent reported the occurrence to the police chief in Bakhmut. When this report became known to the miners that evening, several hundred of them raided a brewing factory, drank up the beer, and then broke into a tavern and consumed the vodka on the spot. The following morning several hundred miners congregated again at the brewery, this time breaking into the locked storage, and again drinking up all the beer. At midnight of that day about fifteen hundred colliers again gathered and proceeded with their head lamps on (according to some reports, armed with hacks) to the Hughes company, three miles away. On their way, they destroyed some houses, robbed a tavern, and drank its vodka. Armed workers gathered by the police at the Hughes factory broke up the demonstration, pursuing the demonstrators all night. Forty-seven workers (according to some reports, forty) were detained. Still for two days the Rutchenkove workers refused to work. When the vice-governor of Katerynoslav province arrived in Rutchenkove with two battalions of soldiers and the miners were ordered to resume work, the strike ended.

It was pointed out in official reports that workers' wages were reduced by heavy fines "for their insolence toward the bosses" and that the mine administration gave the colliers coupons (in lieu of wages) for purchase at the company shops at higher than market prices. According to the gendarme officer, the workers presumed that "they will be punished for the disorders but at the very least others will understand their situation and improve it, even if just a little." After the strike, Cossack regiments were stationed to guard the mines and factories.[96]

A much more destructive event, the so-called cholera riot, took place in 1892 at the Hughes company, taking a heavy toll in lives. Troops fired more than 150 live cartridges and used sabers and lances on a rioting crowd. At

---

[94]*Robitnychyi rukh na Ukraini. Stanovyshche ta borot'ba robitnychoho klasu, 1861–1884 rr. Zbirnyk dokumentiv i materialiv* (Kiev, 1986), pp. 124–25.

[95]Ibid., p. 127.

[96]*Robitnychyi rukh na Ukraini (1885–1894 rr.)*, pp. 113–31; Novopolin, "Pervye 'besporiadki,'" p. 13; and Brower, *The Russian City*, p. 216.

least 23 workers were killed (according to some reports, 50 or more) and 7 were burned to death. A total of 182 shops, 11 taverns, 7 private houses, and 1 synagogue were burned and looted. Up to 500 people were arrested. The riot soon spread to Don Cossack Host province. Colliers fled from the mines en masse to escape the epidemic and persecution, with the result that coal production declined by 60 percent. Still from the beginning of July to 6 November cholera accounted for 738 deaths in the steppe industrial belt.[97]

The immediate reason for the riot was fear of the epidemic, which had spread to the Donbas from Astrakhan on the Volga. The epidemic revealed a profound social cleavage in the mining community. Every year the number of "homeless, wandering" migrants was increasing. According to a report of the Katerynoslav province governor, people harbored resentment against those responsible for their lot and against those who took advantage of their weakness, and were ready for revenge at the earliest opportunity. When the cholera epidemic broke out, one peasant woman was ordered into isolation in the sick barracks. Workers, suspecting that doctors would finish her off, rioted. An estimated fifteen thousand to twenty thousand participated. The riot continued for more than 24 hours, and was suppressed by the Twelfth Don Cossack Regiment and the police. Hughes had complacently believed that their workers (five thousand), many of whom were already settled there, were therefore content and loyal. In fact, when the riot began, "all of the workers" abandoned the factory and joined the crowd of rebels. They did not listen to company officials' refutation of the rumor of the doctors' sinister plot. The crowd did listen to a clergyman's sermon and kissed the sacred cross as a gesture of deference, but advised the clergy to hurry home and rioted all the same. The crowd trusted and obeyed only their own leaders "from among the unknown vagrant people."[98]

The leaders of the riots were arrested and subjected to public flogging in the burned down main square of Iuzivka. Local peasants were mobilized to administer the punishment, which continued for three days. Even the strongest were unable to scream after ten strokes. A military doctor decided, judging by appearance, how many blows the workers could withstand. Appearance was deceptive, and some were carried out dead. Others were tried by a military court; eight of them were sentenced to death.[99]

Less destructive disturbances were numerous in the 1890s, a time of vast

[97]*Robitnychyi rukh na Ukraini (1885–1894 rr.)*, pp. 285, 297, and 318; V. Kolpenskii, "Kholernyi bunt v 1892 godu," *Arkhiv istorii truda v Rossii*, vol. 3 (Petrograd, 1922), p. 112; and Surozhskii, "Krai uglia i zheleza," p. 303. For a detailed work of this riot, see Friedgut, "Labor Violence and Regime Brutality in Tsarist Russia."

[98]*Robitnychyi rukh na Ukraini (1885–1894 rr.)*, pp. 280–87.

[99]Kharechko, "Sotsial-demograficheskii soiuz gornozavodskikh rabochikh," pp. 9–10; Zaitsev, "Bol'sheviki Iuzovki," p. 157; and *Staraia Iuzovka 1869–1905* (Moscow, 1937), pp. 91–92.

industrial expansion in the Russian Empire.[100] In the mid-1890s, for example, in Holubivka, three thousand colliers ravaged the administration building, dropped a mining crane down the shaft, and damaged draining machines. (The reason for this riot is not known.) The authorities armed peasants of surrounding villages and pitted them against the miners. Then two Cossack squadrons joined in. Arrested workers were birched sixty times each.[101] In 1900 strikers at the Makiivka and Prokhorivka Coalfields who demanded better working conditions were subjected to flogging.[102]

Until 1904 flogging (and corporal punishment in general) of peasants (the majority of workers belonged to the peasant estate) was legal.[103] Yet this practice (which did not stop even after 1904, as will be seen) was symbolic of the deep social divide that characterized the tsarist regime. It was far from befitting the supposedly liberal ideals of the Donbas industrialists, replicating instead the old noble-serf, master-servant relations. The old regime actually survived. Its endurance is often attributed to the lack in the Donbas of civic experience. According to this view, so-called third elements, professional groups such as doctors, teachers, agronomists, and statisticians who would have promoted such experience from their base in the *zemstvo* (local governing body), were "minimal in the Donbas."[104] It is not clear whether this was indeed the case in statistical terms as far as the western, Ukrainian part of the Donbas was concerned.[105] (The eastern Donbas in Don Cossack Host province had no *zemstvo*.) Yet the third elements with whom workers came in contact were employed largely by the Donbas companies, private employers. (However big the company towns may have been, they were not elevated to the status of municipalities.) From the workers' point of view, these professionals belonged to the administration. (Hence doctors were viewed as enemies.) Extreme though the Donbas may have been, the vast gulf between ideals and harsh reality was observed in Russian cities in general. Daniel R. Brower has called this "the confrontation between the visionaries and the business elite, on the one hand, and the migrant city, on the other."[106]

The Donbas riots were directed against those whom workers considered

[100]For a list of such events, see S. I. Potolov, *Rabochie Donbassa v* XIX *veke* (Moscow and Leningrad, 1963), the insert between pp. 248–49. See also Iurii Gessen, *Istoriia gornorabochikh SSSR. Tom vtoroi. Vtoraia polovina 19-go veka* (Moscow, 1929), pp. 141–49.

[101]Levus, "Iz istorii," pp. 53–54.

[102]Ibid., p. 57.

[103]For the history of corporal punishment in Russia, see N. Evreinov, *Istoriia telesnykh nakazanii v Rossii* (New York, 1979).

[104]This is one of the conclusions of Friedgut's study of the Donbas. See his *Iuzovka and Revolution*.

[105]Note various statistical data in B. B. Veselovkii, *Istoriia zemstva za sorok let*, 4 vols. (St. Petersburg, 1909–11).

[106]Brower, *The Russian City*, pp. 225–26.

their oppressors and their accomplices: managers, merchants, tavern keepers, physicians, and foreigners in general. It is often suggested in the Leninist framework of spontaneity versus consciousness that they did not seem to concern themselves with "fundamental social, economic, and political changes."[107] In the post-Soviet 1990s some observers would make the same argument about the Donbas colliers' lack of concern with "fundamental" issues (Chapter 8).

Yet they may have viewed fundamental issues in terms of autocracy. The tsarist myth, the benevolent tsar and evil officials, is said to have obtained widely among the Russian and Ukrainian peasantry.[108] Destructive though the riots were, they were, as the 1887 incident in Rutchenkove discussed earlier in this chapter suggests, "ritualized violence in which the workers appealed to the tsarist officials."[109] According to Aleksandr I. Fenin, the colliers, still tied to the countryside, were "inclined to feel that taking part in a strike was a kind of 'rebellion' [*bunt*], something that is punishable by the authorities [*nachal'stvo*] but that is full of rakish protest."[110] In other words, according to this view, the workers' sense of the world in which they lived, their perception of their self-identity, and their concept of the moral economy were defined and shaped by official political discourse: benevolent autocracy, loyal *narod*, and abusive elements in between. Doctors, trained in modern medical science, fit easily into this view of the world. Even flogging was consistent with the view of the *narod* as the tsar's repentant subjects.

One could argue, however, that in fact workers simply used such concepts to their own ends. Like the peasants Daniel Field has studied, workers were cunning, opportunistic, and calculating. There is evidence that the Donbas workers were shrewd operators in the market and understood its mechanism well. For instance, they often struck in the spring, as they did in 1887, for maximum effect when the labor market became a sellers' market with the seasonal exodus of the work force.[111] Clearly, the kind of market force that operated in the south was an enormous transformational force and was a threat to the traditional social and moral fabric of the autocracy, and that is why the autocracy remained ambivalent all along about rapid capitalist development.[112]

[107]See Wynn's Leninist-sounding interpretation in Wynn, *Workers, Strikes, and Pogroms*, p. 128.

[108]Daniel Field, *Rebels in the Name of the Tsar* (Boston, 1989). One of the two cases Field has analyzed comes from Ukraine (Chyhyryn, south of Kiev).

[109]Brower, *The Russian City*, p. 223. His examples include the Donbas riots of 1887 (pp. 216–17).

[110]Fenin, *Vospominaniia inzhenera*, p. 148. The English translation of this phrase, Fenin, *Coal and Politics*, p. 140, is inaccurate.

[111]For this bargaining tactic, see E. Kolodub, *Trud i zhizn' gornorabochikh na Grushevskikh antratsitnykh rudnikakh*, 2nd ed. (Moscow, 1907), p. 44.

[112]See the classic by Theodore von Laue, *Sergei Witte and the Industrialization of Russia* (Columbia University Press, 1963).

Yet the tsarist officials were convinced, despite frequent riots, that the colliers were not inclined to get organized (why should they if it was assumed that they operated in the traditional manner), and, in this sense, it appeared to officials that the colliers were politically less disloyal than the factory workers.[113] (Studies show that even though the mining industry in other countries, too, is prone to strikes and violent protests, it can also be peaceful.)[114] Until the turn of the century, to the satisfaction of the tsarist officials, revolutionaries were unable to organize Donbas miners.[115] The behavior of Donbas miners was so similar to Field's peasants that one might conclude, following Field, that "we cannot establish the balance of sincerity and dissembling within the peasants themselves."[116]

From the turn of the century onward, however, underground organizations of Social Democrats (Marxists), Populists (later Socialist Revolutionaries, SRs), and anarchists came to operate in the Donbas on a sustained basis.[117] How effective they were in organizing workers, especially colliers, is difficult to ascertain. Anarchists were not very organized by definition; the SRs were diverse groups. As for the Marxists, in the wild steppe of the Donbas the moderate Mensheviks were much stronger than the Bolsheviks. This may suggest that the organized segment of the Donbas workers, which was very small, preferred open, economic struggle for tangible gains.[118]

The 1905 revolution, which took place during a losing war against Japan, was a watershed for the Donbas as elsewhere in the empire. Both the privileged and educated and the lower classes were united in their political dissatisfaction with a regime that allowed no political input from society. The tsarist moral order failed in 1905, symbolized by Bloody Sunday, urban and rural unrest

[113]Kharechko, "Sotsial-demokraticheskii soiuz gorno-zavodskikh rabochikh," pp. 13–14.

[114]Note Gaston V. Rimlinger, "International Differences in the Strike Propensity of Coal Miners: Experience in Four Countries," *Industrial and Labor Relations Review*, 12:3 (April 1959). ("Four countries" refers to Britain, France, Germany, and the United States. The reason for miners' contradictory behavior is attributed to their social and geographic isolation and their intense solidarity.) For an interesting comparison of German colliers and iron and steel workers, see Barrington Moore Jr. *Injustice: The Social Bases of Obedience and Revolt* (London, 1978), ch. 7. For a more recent examination of miners' militancy, see Roy A. Church, Quentin Outram, and David N. Smith, "The Militancy of British Miners, 1893–1986: Interdisciplinary Problems and Perspectives," *Journal of Interdisciplinary History*, 22:1 (Summer 1991), which emphasizes three factors: structure, consciousness, and organization.

[115]Some members of the People's Will, a populist party, worked in the late 1880s, but their impact seems to have been minimal. See Levus, "Iz istorii," p. 50. For the People's Will in the South in general, see Norman M. Naimark, *Terrorists and Social Democrats: The Russian Revolutionary Movement under Alexander III* (Harvard University Press, 1983), ch. 4.

[116]Field, *Rebels*, p. 214.

[117]See Wynn, *Workers, Strikes, and Pogroms*, ch. 5.

[118]See George Denike's interesting account in Haimson, *The Making of Three Russian Revolutionaries*, pp. 355–56. Luhans'k had "all the things that in most cases distinguished the Mensheviks from the Bolsheviks," but there the Bolsheviks were predominant.

with much bloodshed, and the continuing battle in 1906–7. Charters Wynn has described this process in the Donbas.[119]

An attentive observer of the revolution in the Donbas noted that by 1905, a tangible change had occurred in the Donbas workers' political outlook. The revolutionaries' agitation was probably one factor, and, no doubt, workers had learned lessons from their struggle for the redress of what they regarded as injustice. Fenin, for instance, has noted that 1905 and the preceding few years "brought something new in the workers' mood, which became generally excited. Now and then we met downright arrogance, something inconceivable before." With "the old authority . . . strongly shaken," workers "started perceiving us as direct enemies."[120] According to another observer, owing to the "liberation movement" of that period, the old "patriarchal" relations between workers and their bosses were replaced by hostile ones. Now some workers, however small they might be in number, viewed the industrialists as exploiters, not as employers. "Having lost belief in God," they understood "freedom" simply as a personal freedom to attack the bosses with a knife or a revolver.[121] In fact, in the Donbas, political terrorism came to be practiced by worker-revolutionaries under the influence of the SRs.[122]

These individual observations should be qualified. First, in everyday life, the workers' "downright arrogance" took the form of maximum humiliation rather than terrorism. The carting off of rude bosses in a wheelbarrow was their favorite ritual. "Small villains" were simply carted out of factories and mines and dumped in the street. The bigger ones were treated with much pomp. For example, a guard of honor, workers with brooms, was set up to haul out one Zakopyrki, a foreman in Luhans'k. Managers were subjected to harsher treatment. "Tauson" (probably Tawson or Towson, an Englishman), in Luhans'k, was first put in a bag and then thrown into the mud before being dragged out.[123] Second, workers may not have discarded their "belief in God." On 14 December 1905 in Debal'tseve, for example, a large crowd went to attend the funeral of fallen comrades at a church. With no sense of contradiction, they sang a hymn and then revolutionary songs.[124]

---

[119] Wynn, *Workers, Strikes, and Pogroms.*

[120] Fenin, *Coal and Politics*, pp. 140–41.

[121] A. A. Auerbakh, "Vospominaniia o nachale razvitiia kamennougol'noi promyshlennosti v Rossii," *Russkaia starina*, 1909, no. 12, p. 560.

[122] Levus, "Iz istorii," p. 68, and Zaitsev, "Bol'sheviki Iuzovki," p. 161. No doubt, terrorism was in part a response to official terror. In February 1905, for example, miners' strikes in two Donbas coalfields led to shooting by the police, which left seven workers dead. See *Materialy po istorii Ekaterinoslavskoi sotsial-demokraticheskoi organizatsii bol'shevikov i revoliutsionnykh sobytii 1904–1905–1906. K 20-ti letnemu iubileiu revoliutsii 1905 g.* (Katerynoslav, 1924), p. 223.

[123] Gambarov, "Ocherki," pp. 73–74.

[124] Ibid.

Still, the language of politics had begun to change in the Donbas.[125] The workers in the Donbas began to speak openly against the tsar.[126] The old tsarist myth appeared no longer to be tenable (if it had been tenable at all). In 1905 Donbas workers marched singing, characteristically in Russian:

> In Piter [St. Petersburg] on the throne
> Sits a scarecrow with a crown.[127]

Another song from December 1905 went: "From Warsaw to the Altai there is no one more evil than Nicholas."[128]

Opinion among the workers was not unanimous, however. In the December 1905 armed uprising in Horlivka, the "cesspool" of the Donbas, many fighters uttered, "The tsar is a swine." Yet, as one Donbas collier later testified, he did not know whether the tsar was a swine or not, but all the same he went to help the armed comrades.[129] The uprising originated in a local labor dispute in this settlement, developing into armed conflict with the authorities in which several thousands of railwaymen, miners, factory workers, and others from all over the Donbas participated. In one of the largest and bloodiest battles in the empire in 1905, the several thousand strong workers were routed by several hundred Cossacks. The workers had 250 rifles, 500 revolvers, 400 guns of other types, and thousands of lances, as well as plenty of dynamite and other ammunition. Still they were defeated, because, apart from the lack of leadership and military training, they had hoped that the troops would retreat and that the matter would not become serious.[130] More than one thousand mutineers knelt down in defeat, asked for mercy, cried, and sang the national anthem. The military commander Ugrinovich was so shaken by their wailing, "unfeigned desperation," "miserable look, and faint-heartedness" that he did not even make a list of the arrested.

The "unfeigned desperation" and penitence of the rebels may have been a shrewd tactic to save their lives, rather than a manifestation of their belief in the tsar's benevolence. In fact, their "unfeigned desperation" did not save them from humiliating punishments. Those detained were forced to take an oath (which probably involved kneeling down before the portrait of the tsar and even kissing the imperial flag) and then to sing "God Save the Tsar." Others were whipped by Cossacks until they could not move.[131] After 1904 such

---

[125]For the link between language and "class" action, see Gareth Stedman Jones, *Language of Class: Studies in English Working Class History, 1832–1982* (Cambridge University Press, 1983).

[126]Levus, "Iz istorii," p. 66.

[127]Sosiura, "Tretia rota," p. 78.

[128]K. G. Ershov, "Dekabr'skoe vooruzhennoe vosstanie v Donbasse," *Katorga i ssylka*, 1930, nos. 8–9, p. 12.

[129]Ibid., p. 13. For an interesting account of popular attitude toward the tsar, see Wynn, *Workers, Strikes, and Pogroms*, p. 249.

[130]Ershov, "Dekabr'skoe vooruzhennoe vosstanie," pp. 56 and 61–62.

[131]Ibid., pp. 60 and 65–66. Fearful of terror, Donbas miners fled en masse with the result that

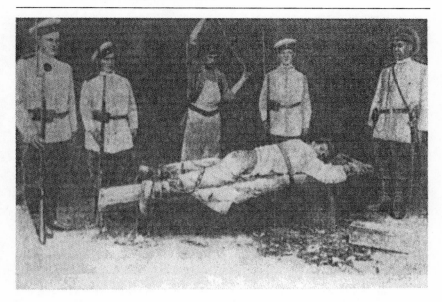

Figure 2.1. A Donbas worker being whipped for participation in the revolutionary struggle in 1905. From A. N. Shcherban' and A. A. Rutenka, *Stranitsy letopisi Donetskoi* (Kiev, 1963), p. 74.

punishment was illegal but was still widely meted out. The whip was in great demand in the Donbas "as a means of 'reproof'" for the colliers.[132] (Punishment and humiliation by whipping remained a source of bitterness for many years among the Donbas workers. When, for example, the engineer N. N. Berezovskii, who worked at the Uspenskii coalfield near Luhans'k from 1905 to 1910, was implicated in the famous Shakhty trial of 1928, sixteen former workers from the mine wrote to the public prosecutor's office, accusing him of lashing and torturing his colliers in 1906.)[133]

Eventually, dozens were tried, but the majority were acquitted on the grounds that they were "utterly dark masses" [*sovershenno temnye liudi*].[134] Whatever the tactics of the "utterly dark masses," the tsarist myth appears to have still retained some power in official discourse. As is clear from the executions in 1909, of the thirty-two rebels who were sentenced to death, the

the number of colliers almost halved after the uprising.

[132] P. Pokrovskii, "Kak zhivet donetskii shakhter," *Russkoe bogatstvo*, 1913, no. 12, p. 256.

[133] GARF, f. 9474, op. 7, d. 259, ll. 89–90.

[134] *Materialy po istorii Ekaterinoslavskoi sotsial-demokraticheskoi organizatsii bol'shevikov*, pp. 460–61.

twenty-four who repented escaped execution, while the eight who did not repent were executed in 1909.[135]

The political behavior of the Donbas workers, particularly the miners, posed some troublesome questions for the revolutionaries. For one, unlike the workers in the capitals and other industrial centers,[136] the Donbas miners showed little interest in organizing themselves. (I shall discuss this issue later in this chapter.) For another, revolution and reaction appeared to merge in the wave of anti-Jewish pogroms. As Khrushchev has discussed in his memoirs quoted earlier, ordinary Donbas workers were among the active participants. Surely, some segments of the working class, particularly colliers, were recruited into the company posses or stood on the side of counterrevolution, attacking their fellow workers with arms.[137] In 1905 and the following few years the notorious Black Hundreds, radical right-wing groups, also recruited Donbas workers, including colliers.[138] Similarly, in some coalfields the Black Hundreds succeeded in recruiting colliers into the "Union of the Russian People," often said to be a protofascist organization.[139] Yet in 1905 many workers participated in both strikes and uprisings and pogroms.[140] Indeed, an observer of the Iuzivka pogroms stated that the "dark masses" a thousand strong had surpassed the Black Hundreds in their "cruelty and inhumanity." He despaired of the "awfully difficult and awfully long" process of educating these "dark masses."[141]

The revolutionaries had difficulties in dealing with these seeming contra-

---

[135]*Donbas v revoliutsii 1905–1907 godov* (Stalino, 1955), p. 71, and Kharechko, "Oktiabr'sko-dekabr'skii pod"em v Donbasse," p. 51.

[136]Laura Engelstein, *Moscow, 1905: Working-Class Organization and Political Conflict* (Stanford University Press, 1982), and Gerald D. Surh, *1905 in St. Petersburg: Labor, Society, and Revolution* (Stanford University Press, 1989). Even the oil workers in Baku seem to have been much more eager to get organized. See Ronald Grigor Suny, *The Baku Commune, 1917–1918: Class and Nationality in the Russian Revolution* (Princeton University Press, 1972), ch. 2.

[137]See the case of Dolzhansk coalfield miners in *5-letnii obzor*, pp. 18–19.

[138]Linden, *Die Judenpogrome*, p. 211; P. A. Moiseenko, *Vospominaniia, 1873–1923* (Moscow, 1924), pp. 146–49; and T. Kharechko, "Iz istorii RSDRP v Donbasse," *Letopis' revoliutsii*, 1927, no. 2, pp. 165 and 167, and "Iz istorii RSDRP v Donbasse (1906–1909 g.g.)," *Letopis' revoliutsii*, 1927, no. 3, pp. 129–31. Generally speaking, the Black Hundreds also included "pure proletarians," skilled workers of long standing. For this point, see Stepanov, *Chernaia sotnia*, pp. 224–25.

[139]Kharechko, "Iz istorii RSDRP v Donbasse" (1927, no. 3), pp. 130–31. In 1905–7, there were 17,386 union members in Katerynoslav province, more than in Moscow (12,000) or St. Petersburg province (11,081). In the Don there were 3,059. See I. N. Kiselev, A. P. Korelin, and V. V. Shelokhaev, "Politicheskie partii v Rossii v 1905–1907 gg.: chislennost', sostav, razmeshchenie. (Kolichestvennyi analiz)," *Istoriia SSSR*, 1990, no. 4, p. 77. See also I. H. Samartsev, "Chornosotentsi na Ukraini (1905–1917 rr.)," *Ukrains'kyi istorychnyi zhurnal*, 1992, no. 1, p. 99.

[140]This is one of the major conclusions of Wynn, *Workers, Strikes, and Pogroms*. See also Löwe, *Antisemitismus und reaktionäre Utopie*, p. 90. For pogroms in miners' settlements in Slov'ianoserbs'k near Luhans'k, see Stepanov, *Chernaia sotnia*, p. 58.

[141]V. Iulii, "Chernye ili temnye? (Poezdka v Iuzovku)," *Voskhod*, 1905, nos. 47–48, p. 21.

dictions: the "Russian revolutionary parties with one or two notable exceptions rarely intervened to fight the October pogroms." Their problems had historical roots. As Jonathan Frankel has perceptively noted,

> That the revolutionaries in Russia generally welcomed the pogroms was in reality not surprising. The inherent tendency of revolutionary populism to idealize the *narod* was here reinforced in varying degrees by Bakunist *buntarstvo* (the ideology of the peasant jacquerie) and by Tkachev's or even Nechaev's Jacobinism (the justification of the means by the ends). Moreover, the struggle – literally for life or death – against the tsarist regime, the constant depletion of the ranks by arrests, and the failure of the assassination of Alexander II [in 1881] to shake the regime inevitably drove many revolutionaries to read an apocalyptic meaning into the pogroms.[142]

Some Jewish revolutionaries, too, "considered the antisemitic massacres to be a good omen."[143] Even in 1905 and beyond anti-Semitism and ethnic issues were not high on the agenda of revolutionaries. Khrushchev has maintained that "Later the workers came to their senses. . . . The workers realized that the Jews were not their enemies when they saw that many leaders of the factory strikes were Jews, and the main speakers whom the workers eagerly listened to at political meetings were Jews."[144] Yet, as he also admits, "the germs of anti-Semitism remained in our system."[145] They were to manifest themselves in various forms throughout the period under study.

The militancy of Donbas workers, as of those workers in Moscow who retained a strong nexus with their village,[146] may be understood from their life goals. Because many Donbas workers wanted to save and return to their native villages, their temporary tenure made militancy less risky. Such patterns have been observed in other countries, for example, with regard to immigrant workers in the United States. The workers did not need permanent organizations. To prove this, one would have to analyze carefully, among others, the economic fluctuations in agriculture and the pattern of industrial actions.

One can hypothesize here, however, that in their struggle the Donbas work-

[142]Jonathan Frankel, *Prophecy and Politics: Socialism, Nationalism, and the Russian Jews, 1862–1917* (Cambridge University Press, 1981), pp. 150, 101. (Bakunin, Tkachev, and Nechaev were all Russian revolutionaries.)

[143]Erich Harber, "Cosmopolitanism, Antisemitism, and Populism: A Reappraisal of the Russian and Jewish Socialist Response to the Pogroms of 1881–1882," in Klier and Lambroza, *Pogroms*, p. 111. As a sad commentary on the plight of the Iuzivka Jews, it is said that, save for a few exceptions, the majority of the "more or less well-off" Jews in Iuzivka "obstinately would not give anything to support their poor brethren." See *Otchet o deiatel'nosti pravleniia obshchestva posobiia bednym evreem v Iuzovke, Ekat. gub. za 1907 god* (Iuzivka, 1908), p. 3.

[144]*Khrushchev Remembers*, p. 267. According to Denike, the Mensheviks in the Donbas were "virtually all Jewish." In Haimson, *The Making of Three Russian Revolutionaries*, p. 345.

[145]*Khrushchev Remembers*, p. 269.

[146]See Robert Eugene Johnson, *Peasant and Proletarian: The Working Class of Moscow in the Late Nineteenth Century* (Rutgers University Press, 1979).

ers sought to defend their own space of freedom. The workers wished to protect their freedom and independence and their sense of dignity, the actual or symbolic guardian of which was their actual or imagined communities.[147] The revolutionaries failed to understand that these communities were not necessarily political parties, trade unions, or other forms of their own making. Rather, these communities could be paternalistic and fluid and could be as small and concrete as transplanted village communes (*artel*'s), barracks, *zemliachestvos*, and neighborhoods, and as large and abstract as the "free steppe," the "working class," and even "Ukraine" and "Russia." Thus one could simultaneously be a Donbas worker from Kursk, a Russian patriot and anti-Semite, a pious churchgoer and wife-beating drunkard, a fierce defender of the free steppe and a participant in the revolutionary events of 1905. People identified themselves with a multitude of actual and imagined societies and communities, which, in turn, constituted their moral universe.

The church was part of their moral universe, and the revolutionaries and the tsar were their protectors or foes depending on specific circumstances, but there were clear outsiders such as managers, engineers, educated people, Jews, and foreigners. There was little need for workers to organize if they understood that their communities were already there. People were able to choose, ideologically, existentially, and emotionally, where they belonged (a Ukrainian could become a Russian nationalist, a Russian could turn against Russia, and so on), but in real life they played particular roles according to their actual sense of belonging. When they perceived a threat to their moral communities, for example, this justified violence. At least to the extent that their belonging was moral and emotional, they used violence as much out of morality and emotion as out of calculated reasoning. This hypothesis is further supported by what was to happen in 1917 (see Chapter 3).

The Donbas workers' sense of community is similar to what Mark Steinberg has discussed concerning the printers in Moscow and St. Petersburg.[148] Yet, unlike the printers Steinberg discusses, the Donbas workers, particularly miners, laid little claim to the universality of their fight for freedom, dignity, and moral order. They made little effort to link their narrow, particularistic demands to universal liberation of the laboring population and of humankind. This was not a sign of their "backwardness." As Isaiah Berlin has shown, the claim to universal liberation was a dangerous element of "rational" reason-

[147]Here one may draw an analogy with Benedict Anderson's study of nationalism as an imagined political community. See Benedict Anderson, *Imagined Communities: Reflections on the Origins and Spread of Nationalism* (London, 1983).

[148]Mark D. Steinberg, *Moral Communities: The Culture of Class Relations in the Russian Printing Industry, 1867–1907* (University of California Press, 1992), and "Workers on the Cross: Religious Imagination in the Writings of Russian Workers, 1910–1924," *Russian Review*, 53:2 (April 1994).

ing,[149] and there was no historical necessity for the Donbas miners to acquire a class-based, Marxist world view. Steinberg maintains that the "discovery of self" was an important stage in the development of Russian printers' consciousness. Yet the Donbas colliers did not have to discover their "selves": the Cossack myth, reinforced by the open space in the steppe and the dark, yet uncontrollable underground, provided, almost by default, a community for them. They were more interested in protecting their space than in liberating it. Their struggle was more defensive than offensive. Their sense of community was akin to the peasants' view of their community, *mir*.[150] Unlike the *mir*, however, which excluded outsiders, the open steppe, like the American West and Siberia, was inclusionary: the steppe did not reject those who sought freedom there.[151]

The extent of peasant militancy in the Donbas in 1905–6 matched that of the workers: arson, destruction and plunder of noble estates, armed attack on the authorities.[152] In 1905 Fenin felt lucky to be an engineer when he heard a Ukrainian peasant woman shout to workers: "Just let me get my hands on the *pan*s [noble landowners]. I'll cut their throats."[153]

Among the Donbas peasants (the majority of whom were Ukrainian-speaking), however, national sentiments were not articulated, not only because of political repression and organizational problems, but also because of the "intellectuals' unrealistic statements, which often did not correspond to the interests of the peasants being addressed."[154] The Ukrainian peasants in the east did not necessarily need Ukrainian nationalism to articulate what they wanted. They had their own cultural and ideological heritage, the Cossack past, which helped them to formulate their dreams and demands. This tendency would manifest itself during the civil war from 1918 to 1920–21. After the 1905–6 revolution, outright violence declined in the countryside in general, but instead, throughout the European provinces of the empire, peasants came to express their "open

---

[149]Isaiah Berlin, "Two Concepts of Liberty," in his *Four Essays on Liberty* (Oxford University Press, 1969).

[150]See Ben Eklof and Stephen P. Frank, eds., *The World of the Russian Peasant: Post-Emancipation Culture and Society* (Boston, 1990).

[151]For the inclusionist hospitality of the frontiers, see Leonard Thompson and Howard Lamar, "The North American and Southern African Frontiers," in Thompson and Lamar, eds., *The Frontier in History: North America and Southern Africa Compared* (Yale University Press, 1981), p. 18.

[152]See, for example, *Nash krai. Dokumenty po istorii Donskoi oblasti* (Rostov, 1963), pp. 373–75. For geographical analysis of peasant disturbances, see S. M. Dubrovskii, *Krest'ianskoe dvizhenie v revoliutsii 1905–1907 gg.* (Moscow, 1956), pp. 61–62, which lists the steppe area of Ukraine among the most active areas.

[153]Fenin, *Vospominaniia inzhenera*, p. 169.

[154]See the discussion on 1905–7 in Rudolf A. Mark, "Social Questions and National Revolution: The Ukrainian National Republic in 1919–1920," *Harvard Ukrainian Studies*, 14:1–2 (June 1990), p. 118.

hostility to, and rejection of, authority" in the form of widespread, spontaneous "hooliganism" (which ranged from public obscenity and brawling to "assault and battery, rape, arson, and murder").[155]

Violence had long been a way of life in the steppe. After 1905, violence came to assume a more explicitly political character than before. It became common for workers to swear at managers with obscenities and threaten them. It was therefore considered dangerous (and, here and there, impossible) for the mine officials to walk around the coalfields without a revolver in the pocket and a whip in hand.[156] Political meetings sometimes ended in shootings involving the police and troops.[157] In 1907 in Luhans'k the Hartman factory police chief Grigor'ev, reputed to have been extraordinarily savage, was assassinated by three Social Democrats while he was strolling in a city park.[158] Here and there bombs were thrown, and guns fired, "against the protectors of the old regime."[159] Until the end of 1906 Mine 21 of the Voznesensk Company remained inaccessible to the police and dragoons: at every crossing they would encounter bomb throwers.[160] The Black Hundreds caused disturbances on the street and in public places. Workers were beaten and flogged, and their living quarters attacked. In return, from time to time bodies of murdered constables and Cossacks were found in various corners of the Donbas.[161] When the Social Democratic party prohibited terrorism against individuals, terrorists drifted to the SR party and anarchist groups.[162]

The steppe provided a certain freedom in the Donbas. For example, workers' political meetings often were held at night not surreptitiously but in the open steppe, because the police and Cossacks, afraid of bomb attacks from unknown quarters, would not approach them.[163] The fact that the mines, dispersed widely in the steppe, were isolated from one another also helped the working population to flee from oppression and exploitation: they moved from

---

[155]Neil B. Weissman, "Rural Crime in Tsarist Russia: The Question of Hooliganism, 1905–1914," *Slavic Review*, 37:2 (June 1978).

[156]Pokrovskii, "Kak zhivet donetskii shakhter, p. 256.

[157]See the case of Iuzivka in May 1907 in TsDIA, f. 705, op. 2, spr. 4, ark. 67.

[158]Gambarov, "Ocherki," pp. 76–77 (the three assassins escaped). See also Voroshilov, *Rasskazy o zhizni*, pp. 331–32. Levus, "Iz istorii," p. 82, claims that it was an act of the SRs. For other cases, see TsDIA, f. 705, op. 2, spr. 4, ark. 301.

[159]Levus, "Iz istorii," p. 82. For cases of murders of engineers, see TsDIA, f. 705, op. 2, spr. 4, ark. 79, and *Trudy ekstrennago s"ezda Gornopromyshlennikov iuga Rossii (15–21 maia 1907 g.). Chast' 2-ia. Stenograficheskii otchet* (Kharkiv, 1907), pp. 76–77.

[160]Kharechko, "Iz istorii RSDRP v Donbasse" (1927, no. 2), p. 168. Dynamite was easily available in mines and was frequently stolen. See TsDIA, f. 705, op. 2, spr. 4, ark. 93, 98, 101, 112, etc.

[161]T. Kharechko, "Iz istorii RSDRP v Donbasse (1906–1909 gg.)," *Letopis' revoliutsii*, 1927, no. 1, p. 195, and Voroshilov, *Rasskazy o zhizni*, pp. 363–64.

[162]Kharechko, "Iz istorii RSDRP v Donbasse" (1927, no. 1), p. 196, and (1927, no. 3), p. 129.

[163]Kharechko, "Oktiabr'sko-dekabr'skii pod"em 1905 g. v Donbasse," p. 6, and "Iz istorii RSDRP v Donbasse" (1927, no. 2), p. 156.

one mine to another and hid there. (High labor turnover was in part an expression of this geographical peculiarity.) Furthermore, the nature of mining labor itself restricted managerial control: underground work was difficult to supervise. In other words, if neither conformity, nor rebellion, nor exit was possible or preferable,[164] there was still a fourth possibility or option: everyday forms of resistance were readily available.[165]

The political violence of the Donbas lower classes was emblematic of the political and social rifts that divided Donbas society. It was in the Donbas, perhaps more than anywhere else because of its Cossack association, that the specter of a Pugachev rebellion and popular uprisings haunted "respectable society." Alexandr I. Fenin, who happened to see armed workers in Debal'tseve in December 1905, recalled "a large crowd of people armed with the most incredible weapons – home-made pikes, shotguns, even scythes, which gave the gathering the appearance of one of Pugachev's bands."[166] The colliers' militancy reminded the mayor of Luhans'k of Pugachevshchina (the Pugachev rebellion).[167] In popular perception, the Cossacks as a political force still embodied the coercive power of the state, but here as elsewhere some Cossack regiments engaged in mutiny, expressing resistance to military mobilization and dissatisfaction with the bleak status of their farms.[168] The unrest was not merely economic, but political: some Cossacks evoked "that old Cossack spirit of freedom which created the Cossacks, which lived in them and which in the course of centuries our Russian autocratic bureaucratic government destroyed in the Cossacks."[169] These mutinies foreshadowed the failure of Cossack soldiers to support the tsar in February 1917. Many impoverished Cossacks and retired soldiers had no choice but to work in collieries.[170] While their presence was feared by workers and revolutionaries, the entry of people from the military estate into industrial labor did signify that the old order was being eroded by economic development. "Respectable society" in the Donbas, as elsewhere, was horrified at the specter of Pugachevshchina. What they saw right under their noses, offense to person and property, went against their liberal beliefs.[171]

[164]Here I have in mind Hirschman, *Exit, Voice, and Loyalty.*

[165]See James C. Scott, *Weapons of the Weak: Everyday Forms of Peasant Resistance* (Yale University Press, 1985). Yet another option was famous: heavy drinking. Severe political repression paralyzed the activity of miners, some of whom sought refuge in drinking.

[166]Fenin, *Coal and Politics*, pp. 158–59.

[167]Shklovskii, "Vospominaniia," p. 207. For liberals' fear of Pugachevshchina, see also Rogger, *Jewish Policies*, p. 199.

[168]See John Bushnell, *Mutiny amid Repression: Russian Soldiers in the Revolution of 1905–1906* (Indiana University Press, 1985). For a case of support of workers' struggle by Cossacks in 1906, see *Donbass v revoliutsii 1905–1907 godov*, pp. 76–77.

[169]Quoted in McNeal, *Tsar and Cossack*, p. 133.

[170]Levus, "Iz istorii," p. 84, and Kolpenskii, "Kholernyi bunt," p. 112.

[171]The best account is Roberta Thompson Manning, *Crisis of the Old Order in Russia: Gentry*

The fate of the sick fund law of 1912 was symbolic of these fissures which entailed no political compromise. In Moscow, St. Petersburg, and elsewhere, the sick funds were accepted by both labor and management, and contributed quickly to the creation of surrogate trade unions and cultural organizations of labor.[172] Yet in the Donbas they were rejected in most cases by both parties: labor was angered by a stipulation that required workers' contribution to the funds, while the employers, disappointed as they were by the financial burden imposed upon themselves, were apprehensive that reductions from workers' wages would cause labor unrest. The industrialists' demand that the government provide national sick funds was not met. Consequently, few sick funds existed in an industrial center with notably high accident and illness rates.[173]

Workers' organizations, particularly, trade unions, were legalized after the 1905 revolution. Some formed but were soon disbanded.[174] In the Donbas only two metalworkers' unions in Luhans'k and Sulin and about ten small unions of artisans (tanners, tailors, dockers, printers) existed on the eve of World War I.[175] Revolutionaries were literally hounded by gendarmes and Okhrana (the secret police) underground or into exile, or were sent to jail. As a result, it was said that after the 1905 revolution no other industrial center was as devastated as the Donbas.[176] The social and political rifts thus created in the Donbas may correspond roughly to what Leopold H. Haimson has called a dual polarization in Russian society on the eve of World War I: a rift "between workers and educated, privileged society," and a chasm between "the vast bulk of the privileged society" and "the inept, helpless tsarist regime."[177] It was not that elements of modern civility, which might have helped to create a modern, civil society, were absent in the Donbas, but that the Donbas lower classes challenged the very notion of civility through their deep suspicion of "respectable" society. Unlike the St. Petersburg workers Haimson analyzed, the Donbas

---

and Government (Princeton University Press, 1982).

[172]For example, see the case of Moscow in Diane Koenker, *Moscow Workers and the 1917 Revolution* (Princeton University Press, 1981), pp. 73–74. For a more critical view of the sick funds in St. Petersburg, see Robert B. McKean, *St. Petersburg between the Revolutions: Workers and Revolutionaries, June 1907–February 1917* (Yale University Press, 1990), pp. xiii, 163–64, 182, and 489.

[173]Iu. I. Kir'ianov, *Rabochie Iuga Rossii. 1914–fevral' 1917 g.* (Moscow, 1971), pp. 197–203. The industrialists had also been in dispute with the zemstvo concerning their cost sharing of local administration.

[174]See *Professional'nye soiuzy rabochikh Rossii. 1905 g.–fevral' 1917 g. Perechen' organizatsii,* vol. 1 (Moscow, 1985), pp. 89, 90, 103, 104, 105, 108, and 109.

[175]Kir'ianov, *Rabochie Iuga Rossii,* p. 190.

[176]T. Kharechko, "Nakanune Fevral'skoi revoliutsii v Donbasse," *Letopis' revoliutsii,* 1927, no. 4, p. 175.

[177]Leopold H. Haimson, "The Problem of Social Stability in Urban Russia, 1905–1914," *Slavic Review,* 23:4 (December 1964), and 24:1 (March 1965).

workers were not easily susceptible to the influence of the Bolsheviks, as 1917 would witness (Chapter 3).[178]

In the meantime, as one perceptive observer noted, Donbas society was stuck in "a relationship of eternal and sharp enmity": industrial managers looked on colliers as dirty, stinking humans of inferior stock, while the latter saw in the former their most malicious enemy.[179]

---

[178]This is similar to McKean's criticism of Haimson regarding St. Petersburg: "None of the socialist groups, including the Bolsheviks, entered the new free Russia [in 1917] with solid legal or illegal structures or anything other than a minute following among a minority of skilled male workers." (McKean, *St. Petersburg*, p. 494.) A sophisticated cultural study by Joan Neuberger, *Hooliganism: Crime, Culture, and Power in St. Petersburg, 1900–1914* (University of California Press, 1993), points to the same conclusion (see pp. 24, 261–64, and 271). Another sophisticated cultural study, of *Petrushka* ("the Russian equivalent of *Punch and Judy*"), which "altered and developed . . . above all in the Ukraine and in the south," also points to the existence, in urban popular culture, of the same kind of profound distrust of any authority. See Catriona Kelly, *Petrushka: The Russian Carnival Puppet Theatre* (Cambridge University Press, 1990) (quotation from p. 78). It is not known, however, whether even this form of "popular culture" ever existed in the Donbas.

[179]Pokrovskii, "Kak zhivet donetskii shakhter," p. 256.

3   War, Revolution, and Civil War

THE SEVEN YEARS from 1914 to 1921 reveal just how distant relations were between the Donbas and the political power centers of Moscow and Kiev. Although patriotism of a kind was observed among the Donbas colliers, in the revolutionary era they demonstrated a distinct lack of awareness or concern for national politics. The interests of the people of the Donbas lay in protecting their freedom and the space that guaranteed it. Neither the "class" ideology (represented by the Bolsheviks in the Russian capitals) nor "nation" (represented by the Ukrainian nationalists based in Kiev) mattered much to them. Their apparent lack of political commitment baffled and angered both the Bolsheviks and nationalists, while their insistence on freedom brought about a siege of terror by the counterrevolutionaries.

War and Patriotism

The outbreak of war in the Balkans in 1914, soon to become World War I, was an important event for the Donbas as for the country as a whole. Few people appeared to think that another war might lead to another revolution. The initial reaction of the population to the war seems to have been positive, even enthusiastic. Many European socialists and Russian Marxists (including the father of Russian Marxism, G. V. Plekhanov) supported the war, abandoning "proletarian internationalism." In the Donbas, a future leader of the Workers' Opposition within the Communist Party noted that "a significant number of the workers" had been caught up in a wave of chauvinism.[1] Another account contends that the colliers were the most belligerent: they were "blinded by 'patriotism,'" from which they were to be freed only by military failures at

[1] A. Shliapnikov, *Nakanune 1917 goda. Vospominaniia i dokumenty o rabochem dvizhenii i revoliutsionnom podpol'e za 1914–1917* (Moscow, 1920), p. 276.

71

the front, economic collapse on the home front, and the underground antiwar propaganda by the Bolsheviks.[2]

In Iuzivka, when the war began, according to one observer, a crowd gathered in the main street, and agitators made patriotic speeches: "Death to Austria and Germany. Long live Russia. Hurrah!!!" (According to this observer, "many, many workers" believed in the war. The market was filled with portraits of "tsars, kings, presidents, and various generals" on sale. People thought it necessary to hang a portrait of the tsar not only in their homes but in the barracks as well. In this observer's barracks, too, a man named Surzhak Tishka, theretofore known as a curser of God and the tsar, hammered in a nail, strung up a portrait of Nicholas, and hung it on the wall.)[3] Another observer described the event in Iuzivka in somewhat different terms. The gathering had been organized by the leader of the Black Hundreds Zuzulia. There were only several hundred demonstrators who carried banners and sang "God Save the Tsar." Yet he conceded that "the majority of workers" were "patriotically minded."[4]

As was the case with inductions in general, however, the mobilization of the people for war was often accompanied by rioting. In July 1914, for example, twenty thousand young Donbas residents were mobilized from villages and mines and assembled in the city of Luhans'k. Many were said to be "chauvinistically minded." At their request, services were performed in churches. Then they asked for drink before departing for the front. They believed that in other places in the Donbas the mobilized were given free liquor. When their demand to open a state wine warehouse was denied their anger escalated into a full-scale riot, which ended in looting and anti-Jewish pogroms: they destroyed almost all the shops in the main street. A drunken crowd, perhaps following their fighting traditions, attacked a fallen policeman. The police and the soldiers mobilized to deal with the riot shot three men dead, according to official data.[5]

Other reports paint a very different picture of the Donbas population.[6] In Katerynoslav, just west of the Donbas, the chairman of the Union of the Russian People, Kuz'm Martynov, was beaten by reservists for his patriotic

---

[2]Iu. I. Kir'ianov, *Rabochie Iuga Rossii. 1914–fevral' 1917 g.* (Moscow, 1974), p. 221.

[3]GARF, f. 6870, op. 1, d. 150, ll. 1–2 (memoirs of V. Galuzin). Galuzin was a Menshevik, and he probably tended to describe the people as patriotic to defend his wartime position.

[4]F. Zaitsev, "Kak my tvorili Oktiabr' (1917–18 gg. v Iuzovke)," *Letopis' revoliutsii*, 1925, no. 4, p. 132.

[5]Aleksandr Gambarov, "Ocherk po istorii revoliutsionnogo dvizheniia v Luganske, 1901–1921 gg.," *Letopis' revoliutsii*, 1923, no. 4, p. 80; *Rabochee dvizhenie na Ukraine v period pervoi mirovoi imperialisticheskoi voiny, iiun' 1914 g.–fevral' 1917 g. Sbornik dokumentov i materialov* (Kiev, 1966), pp. 12–17; A. Rashkov's review in *Litopys revoliutsii*, 1929, nos. 5–6, p. 352; and Iu. I. Kir'ianov, "Krest'ianstvo stepnoi Ukrainy v gody pervoi mirovoi voiny (1914–1916 gg.)," in *Osobennosti agrarnogo stroia Rossii v period imperializma* (Moscow, 1962), p. 244.

[6]O. K. Koshyk, "Antyvoienni vystupy robitnykiv i selian Ukrainy na pochatku pershoi svitovoi imperialistychnoi viiny," *Ukrains'kyi istorychnyi zhurnal*, 1959, no. 3, p. 34.

speeches. Further attempts by him to appeal to patriotism met with the same treatment. An anonymous observer noted that he did not see any enthusiasm, or any "cheerful faces" among the mobilized: they were apathetic toward "the identity and intentions of the foreign enemy," but they had a very clear and hostile attitude toward the internal enemy, in this case the police.[7] Thus, people in the Donbas declared, "Why not mobilize the police constables for war?"[8] When colliers of the Varvaropol' coalfield were horded to a railway station, they disarmed the guards and went back home singing revolutionary songs.[9] In July 1914 in Makiivka, reservists and factory workers clashed with the police and Cossacks. One gendarme officer and a shopkeeper who helped the police by firing at the demonstrators were killed by the rioters. The rioting continued the following day. The reservists hijacked the train to be used to transport them to the front. Fifteen people, according to the police report, were shot dead, and the riot was quelled.[10] Similar riots, with shootouts with the police, Cossacks, and shopkeepers, took place in other parts of the Donbas at that time.[11]

The majority of the mobilized, however, did go to war. They did so, because, according to a Bolshevik activist in the Donbas, "others went."[12] Allan K. Wildman has noted that the typical mood of the mobilized was that "the rest of society seemed to be telling them they must go. Unable to sort out the reasons, they simply surrendered to the current and kept their thoughts to themselves."[13] It is not certain, however, whether the mobilized men were "unable to sort out the reasons."

Even in 1917, when the general mood of the country turned against the war, the Donbas workers in general would continue to express support for the

[7]*Rabochee dvizhenie na Ukraine*, pp. 16–17, Koshyk, "Antyvoienni vystupy," p. 35, and A. B. Berkevich, "Krest'ianstvo i vseobshchaia mobilizatsiia v iiule 1914 g.," *Istoricheskie zapiski*, vol. 23 (1947), pp. 23–24.

[8]A. P. Hritsenko, "Selians'kyi rukh u Donets'komu promyslovomu raioni v roky pershoi svitovoi imperialistychnoi viiny (lypen' 1914 r.–sichen' 1917 r.)," *Ukrains'kyi istorychnyi zhurnal*, 1958, no. 4, p. 79.

[9]Kir'ianov, *Rabochie Iuga Rossii*, p. 219.

[10]Koshyk, "Antyvoienni vystupy," p. 36, and Hritsenko, "Selians'kyi rukh," p. 77. ("Ulichnye besporiadki i vystupleniia rabochikh v Rossii," *Istoricheskii arkhiv*, 1995, no. 4, pp. 95–96, reports thirteen people dead.) See also Iu. I. Kir'ianov, "Byli li antivoennye stachki v Rossii v 1914 godu," *Voprosy istorii*, 1994, no. 2, p. 47.

[11]Koshyk, "Antyvoienni vystupy," p. 36, and Hritsenko, "Selians'kyi rukh," pp. 77–78 (Bakhmut, Khrustal's'k, and Iasynuvata). See also Berkevich, "Krest'ianstvo," p. 24.

[12]A. Batov, "V Donbasivs'komu pidpilli," *Litopys revoliutsii*, 1930, no. 1, p. 152. See also Kir'ianov, "Krest'ianstvo stepnoi Ukrainy," p. 243.

[13]Allan K. Wildman, *The End of the Russian Imperial Army: The Old Army and the Soldiers' Revolt (March–April 1917)* (Princeton University Press, 1980), pp. 78–79. Yet Wildman goes on to say that the induction riots suggested that many of them "regarded the war as a fruitless venture of the upper class for which they would have to pay, and they took their vengeance in various subtle and not-so-subtle ways" (ibid.).

war, baffling the antiwar Bolshevik party. Because they kept their thoughts to themselves, it is difficult to know exactly what kind of patriotism obtained among them, but popular patriotism did not necessarily spell loyalty to the tsar.[14] As would become clearer in 1917, the war assumed a moral, anti-"bourgeois" character in political discourse.

In the meantime, those who stayed in the Donbas were "militarized." By August 1914 30 percent of the Donbas miners were mobilized for the front. Their mobilization created a labor shortage, particularly of skilled workers, and the Donbas industrialists pleaded with Moscow for their return to the coalfields. Thus by September 1914 7 to 10 percent of the mobilized colliers were brought back to the mines.[15] With some exceptions such as messengers and cooks, many of those working in the mines were thereafter exempted from war mobilizations. Instead, they were obliged to work in the mines as if called up for military service. In March 1917 these *voennoobiazannye* with a deferred call-up accounted for 45 percent of the almost 290,000 workers in the Donbas collieries. (Prisoners of war constituted more than a quarter of them. The Donbas managers preferred to use the POWs because they could not strike.)[16] The *voennoobiazannye* were bound to their workplace. This created a strong dissatisfaction among them: "We are like serfs here." Some restrictions were removed later, but still they were not free to move.[17]

The militarization of mining had the additional advantage of curbing the notoriously high labor turnover. The war created coal hunger in the country, even though coal production rose almost without a break from 1913 to 1917. This was achieved exclusively by adding labor, which increased rapidly. The productivity of labor, however, declined accordingly.[18] There was all the more reason to minimize labor turnover, which adversely affected labor productivity. Summer field work under the sun in which many engaged normally was part of their work cycle: it was seen as a seasonal break from hard underground work; so the miners did not want to work underground all year round. They had to be goaded underground.[19] Despite the ban on seasonal work, up to 30 percent of

---

[14]For this point, see Hubertus F. Jahn, *Patriotic Culture in Russia during World War I* (Cornell University Press, 1995).

[15]Iu. I. Kir'ianov, "Vliianie pervoi mirovoi voiny na izmenenie chislennosti i sostava rabochikh Rossii," *Voprosy istorii*, 1960, no. 10, p. 91.

[16]Ibid., p. 94.

[17]Lev Liberman, "Shakhtovladel'tsy i shakhtery," *Russkiia zapiski*, December 1916, pp. 241–42.

[18]See the table in *Gornozavodskoe delo*, 1919, nos. 3–4, p. 16640; M. Ostrogorskii, "Rabochee dvizhenie v Gorlovsko-Shcherbinovskom raione Donbassa (v gody imperialisticheskoi voiny)," *Litopys revoliutsii*, 1928, no. 3, p. 80; and S. O. Zagorsky, *State Control of Industry during the War* (Yale University Press, 1928), appendixes XXI, XXII, and XXX.

[19]Liberman, "Shakhtovladel'tsy i shakhtery," pp. 240–41 and 244.

the miners left for the countryside, which also suffered from a severe shortage of male hands during the war.[20]

Wartime conditions made the exploitation of labor easier. By 1917 the real wages of miners and factory workers in the Donbas declined by 42.6 percent from 1913.[21] Their wages were further reduced by all kinds of fines and deductions for the church, school, and *soldatki* (wives of soldiers). Underground work was now legalized for women and minors, and for "all without any exception" the work day lasted twelve hours.[22] Consumers' cooperatives exploited workers more than helped them. Hence workers referred to them as "robbers' cooperatives."[23] Many of the new recruits were said to be sons of rich peasants who bought their way into factories and mines to evade military service. They were among "the most conservative and most cowardly" and were willing to break strikes.[24] Strike leaders and participants were arrested and dispatched to the front.

Still, strikes continued.[25] Many accounts contend that during the war the Mensheviks, with their emphasis on legal, economic struggle, gained considerable influence in the Donbas.[26] Yet, according to contemporary observers, the strikes were all spontaneous, without the leadership of political parties or even the most primitive strike committees.[27] Both metalworkers and miners struck, but the former, better paid and better provided for, often failed to support the latter's strikes morally or materially.[28]

In April–May 1916 a general strike of colliers took place in Horlivka-Shcherbynivka. It was, according to an official report, a purely economic strike demanding a 50 percent wage hike; no political party activity was observed

[20]*Gornozavodskoe delo*, 1915, no. 8, p. 10510, and 1916, no. 4, pp. 12844–45, and Kir'ianov, "Vliianie pervoi mirovoi voiny," pp. 98–99.

[21]*Bor'ba za Oktiabr' na Artemovshchine. Sbornik vospominanii i statei* (Kharkiv, 1929), p. 25. See also Kir'ianov, *Rabochie Iuga Rossii*, p. 77, which reports a 30% to 50% decline.

[22]Ostrogorskii, "Rabochee dvizhenie," p. 83.

[23]Ibid., p. 86.

[24]T. Kharechko, "Nakanune Fevral'skoi revoliutsii v Donbasse," *Letopis' revoliutsii*, 1927, no. 4, p. 166, and F. Zaitsev, "Bol'sheviki Iuzovki do 1918 goda," *Literaturnyi Donbass*, 1933, nos. 10–12, pp. 166–67. For anti-German assaults in general, see Iu. I. Kir'ianov, " 'Maiskie bespori-adki' 1915 g. v Moskve," *Voprosy istorii*, 1994, no. 12, especially p. 143.

[25]For the strikes during the war, see Iu. I. Kir'ianov, "Stachechnaia bor'ba rabochikh Eka-terinoslavskoi gubernii v gody pervoi mirovoi voiny (iiul' 1914–fevral' 1917 g.)," *Istoriia SSSR*, 1960, no. 4.

[26]Kharechko, "Nakanune," pp. 179 and 184–85; *Bor'ba za Oktiabr' na Artemovshchine*, pp. 31–32; Kir'ianov, *Rabochie Iuga Rossii*, p. 187; R. Ia. Terekhov, *Tak nachalas' bor'ba. Iz vospominanii* (Stalino, 1957), p. 52, etc.

[27]Kharechko, "Nakanune," pp. 171 and 176, and Ostrogorskii, "Rabochee dvizhenie," pp. 93–94.

[28]See, for example, Ostrogorskii, "Rabochee dvizhenie," p. 92, and *Bor'ba za Oktiabr' na Artemovshchine*, p. 31.

(such activity took place only among the factory workers).[29] Yet according to another, it was organized by a Bolshevik strike committee.[30] Whatever the case, the dayworkers, those least provided for, threatened the better-paid workers with force if they refused to join the strike. Altogether, thirty thousand (according to some accounts, forty-five thousand), including women and children, joined in the strike, but mechanics and electric station workers did not. The administration responded to the walkout by sending in soldiers. They clashed, leaving four (five, according to some data) dead. More than three hundred workers were arrested. They were whipped and beaten with sabers by the soldiers.[31] Moreover, more than a thousand colliers of draft age were arrested and sent to the front.[32] The lost workers were replaced by "yellow labor," cheap and unorganized Chinese workers. After the strike was put down, the embittered workers were described as being inclined to "break machines, flood the mines, and attack the administration."[33]

In the eyes of the workers, the mines and factories had made a considerable profit from the "coal hunger" created by the war and from the steel and coal production quotas imposed by the Association of Southern Coal and Steel Producers.[34] The German firm Hartman in Luhans'k, for example, was believed to have increased its profits by 75 percent from 1913 to 1915–16.[35] By contrast, workers had good reason to feel that they were being more harshly exploited than before the war.[36] Moreover, even in what were identified as "purely economic strikes," "political" demands that the administration treat the workers courteously were evident.[37] By the end of 1916 the specter of hunger began to

[29]"Stachka shakhterov Gorlovsko-Shcherbinovskogo raiona Donbassa (19 aprelia–11 maia 1916 g.)," *Istoriia proletariata SSSR*, 1934, no. 2, p. 131.

[30]Ostrogorskii, "Rabochee dvizhenie," p. 95. See also L. R. Nikiforova, "Gorlovskaia zabastovka 1916 g.," *Istoricheskie zapiski*, vol. 4 (1953). For this bone of contention, see Theodore H. Friedgut, "Professional Revolutionaries in the Donbass: The Characteristics and Limitations of the *Apparat*," *Canadian Slavonic Papers*, 27:3 (September 1985), p. 293.

[31]Ostrogorskii, "Rabochee dvizhenie," pp. 95–101, and "Stachka shakhterov Gorlovsko-Shcherbinovskogo raiona Donbassa," pp. 105–32.

[32]Kir'ianov, *Rabochie Iuga Rossii*, p. 252.

[33]Batov, "V Donbasivs'komu pidpilli," p. 158. See also A. Batov and M. Ostrogorskii, "Pis'mo v redaktsiiu zhurnala 'Letopis' revoliutsii,' " *Litopys revoliutsii*, 1928, no. 1, p. 340.

[34]For the quotas, see V. A. Manzhosov, "Predstavnyts'ki orhanizatsii hirnychopromyslovtsiv Pivdnia Rosii v 1917–1919 rr.," *Ukrains'kyi istorychnyi zhurnal*, 1991, no. 10, p. 78.

[35]Kharechko, "Nakanune," p. 165.

[36]Iuzivka was perhaps an exception. Here the New Russian Company created its own networks of supply of food and other consumer goods and rationed them. As a result, there was no inflation between 1914 and 1917 and there were no strikes by workers. (Zaitsev, "Bol'sheviki Iuzovka do 1918 goda," p. 168.) Elsewhere, however, Zaitsev says that even in Iuzivka a strike occurred at the end of 1916; people were searched in the street and at home ("Kak my tvorili Oktiabr'," p. 133).

[37]See, for example, the case of the 1916 Horlivka-Shcherbynivka strike in "Stachka shakhterov Gorlovksko-Shcherbinovskogo raiona Donbassa," p. 123. Kir'ianov, "Stachechnaia bor'ba rabochikh Ekaterionoslavskoi gubernii," lists twenty-seven "political strikes" with more than half a million participants.

haunt the Donbas, even though the fertile southern steppe was better supplied than the northern provinces.[38]

By 1916, according to one observer, cries of "To the devil with your war" came to be heard openly in the Donbas. By "your war" was meant "the war of the Tsar and his government who were daily becoming more and more unpopular": "The people were half openly saying that the Tsar was a drunkard, that the Tsarina was corrupt and a German spy and that the Court ministers appointed by the Tsar were selling Russia to the Germans."[39]

The Inversion of the Old Order

The food crisis prompted female workers in the capital to walk out on International Women's Day, 23 February 1917. The strike and demonstration quickly gained momentum. Within a week, on 2 March the tsarist government collapsed with the abdication of Nicholas II and the refusal of his brother Michael to succeed.

The news of revolution in the capital soon reached the Donbas by way of the grapevine. Much of the local press was censored. In Kamensk (later Kamensk-Shakhtinskii), when rumors of the revolution were confirmed, "there were endless speeches in the streets and a great number of pamphlets were distributed to the people, who were all singing the 'Marseillaise' and 'We fell as victims in the fatal struggle.' All the Tsar's pictures were burned or torn."[40]

The old order was overturned and revolutionary politics became fluid in the extreme. In the process, no political parties succeeded in capturing the hearts and minds of the Donbas workers, who followed their own notions of justice and morality in their political life.

Here as in the capital, one of the immediate effects of the revolution was a steep rise in crime.[41] Along with political prisoners, criminals were released from the tsarist prisons in the spirit of revolutionary freedom. The old police force was disbanded or disabled, and a new militia was not immediately formed. Thus, in Luhans'k, for example, criminals committed "an unbelievable number of thefts" every night. Workers' militias (*rabochie druzhiny*) were

---

[38] In the autumn of 1916 many miners who had gone to summer field work did not come back from the countryside where the food situation was better. Kir'ianov, *Rabochie Iuga Rossii*, pp. 47–48.

[39] N. M. Borodin, *One Man in His Time* (London, 1955), pp. 12–13.

[40] Ibid., p. 14.

[41] For an interesting account of crime in the capital in 1917, see Tsuyoshi Hasegawa, "Crime, Police, and Mob Justice in Petrograd during the Russian Revolution of 1917," in Charles E. Timberlake, ed., *Religion and Secular Forces in Late Tsarist Russia: Essays in Honor of Donald W. Treadgold* (University of Washington Press, 1992).

hurriedly organized, often under the leadership of the Socialist Revolutionaries (SRs). They organized raids and "punished [most likely, executed on the spot] criminals caught red-handed." Others were forced out of the city and fled to the countryside where they perpetrated more crimes. Workers' militias made expeditions to villages in lorries. Then crime declined, according to one account.[42] (In June, however, a Luhans'k newspaper still maintained that the city was in a war situation with many thieves and murderers. Clearly some criminals must have been lynched, as in the capital, because newspapers urged the residents not to resort easily to lynching.)[43] In Makiivka, soon after the February Revolution, colliers set up "workers' control" everywhere. Distrustful of specialists and intellectuals, they staffed the militia and even took up the duties of judges. All organizations were thus said to be in their hands.[44]

Some revolutionaries punished former *Okhrana* spies and police agents brutally. Here the wild steppe did not betray its reputation for violence. In Huliai-Pole at the western edge of the greater Donbas area, for example, Nestor Makhno (1889–1934), the famous anarchist leader who was released from the tsarist prison on 2 March by the Provisional Government amnesty after a nearly nine-year incarceration, returned from the capital to his native land to take immediate revenge. Back in 1905, in Huliai-Pole, whoever was caught on the streets "was brutally whipped. Those who were arrested in their homes were led through the streets and beaten with the butts of muskets to instill fear among the people." In 1908 Makhno had been arrested, tried, and sentenced to death by hanging (which was subsequently commuted); he had been betrayed by members of his anarchist-Communist group who were police informers.[45] Makhno found the names of the agents in the police archives. He dragged out Kirik Basetskii from his house and shot him on the street. He caught Sergei Martynenko at a meal and shot him dead through a window, a dumpling in his mouth. Dmitrii, a priest, was taken to a clay quarry, beheaded, and the head was dragged around town in a cart.[46]

Anti-Semitic sentiments also surfaced immediately. As in October 1905, the revolution caused anxiety over the future of the new state. Political uncertainties, food shortages, and inflation heightened social tensions. Newly freed from legal restrictions, the Jews were regarded in the country as the main ben-

[42] I. Nikolaenko, "Fevral'skaia revoliutsiia v Luganske (Iz vospominanii)," *Letopis' revoliutsii*, 1927, no. 3, pp. 38–39.

[43] *Donetskii proletarii* (Luhans'k), 21 June 1917.

[44] *Sed'maia (Aprel'skaia) Vserossiiskaia konferentsiia RSDRP (bol'shevikov). Petrogradskaia obshchegorodskaia konferentsiia RSDRP (bol'shevikov). Aprel' 1917 g. Protokoly* (Moscow, 1958), p. 160.

[45] Michael Palij, *The Anarchism of Nestor Makhno, 1918–1921: An Aspect of the Ukrainian Revolution* (University of Washington Press, 1976), p. 68.

[46] Taras Bespechnyi, "Nestor Makhno – buntar' s rozhdeniia," *Donbas*, 29 February 1992.

eficiaries of the revolution. Small-scale pogroms took place in reaction here and there in Ukraine.[47]

The collapse of the old regime was accompanied by the formation of new alternative organizations to fill the power vacuum. In the Donbas, as elsewhere, soviets of workers' and peasants' deputies were organized. In the case of the Donbas, however, industrialists initially led some of the coalfield soviets.[48] N. F. von Ditmar (fon Ditmar), the president of the Association of Southern Coal and Steel Producers, declared that "the only possible form of government in Russia is republican . . . there is a real need to abandon the fallacy of monarchism once and for all." He and other industrialists considered themselves "participants in the revolution" and in March adopted a resolution to donate money to help former political prisoners by collecting one ruble from each worker! They proposed an eight-hour workday and some wage hikes.[49] Yet the workers did not seem to accept the new political stance of their bosses. In Luhans'k, for example, it became difficult after the February Revolution to restrain workers from using force against their supervisors.[50]

In 1917 the deep sociopolitical division in the Donbas manifested itself in violent explosions of conflict between labor and management. It appeared that, unlike the more "sophisticated" workers of Moscow or Petrograd, the Donbas colliers struck back with a vengeance in the immediate aftermath of the February Revolution. They showed only mild interest in such institutions as collective agreements and conciliation boards. When unionization became possible and fashionable, they, unlike many other groups of workers and artisans, hardly bothered to unite themselves in trade unions.[51] Instead they took direct action against managers in the form of search (obysk), removal from the mines, and arrest.[52] When the autocracy fell, the Donbas colliers had little illusion about any form of politics.[53] What Leopold H. Haimson has called the "absence of a

[47]I. Cherikover, Antisemitizm i pogromy na Ukraine 1917–1918 gg. (K istorii ukrainsko-evreiskikh otnoshenii) (Berlin, 1923), pp. 29–31.

[48]See, for example, F. Zaitsev, "Oktiabr' v Iuzovke," in Oktiabr'skaia revoliutsiia. Pervoe piatiletie (Kharkiv, 1922), p. 619, and Manzhosov, "Predstavnyts'ki orhanizatsii," p. 79.

[49]Manzhosov, "Predstavnyts'ki orhanizatsii," p. 79.

[50]Nikolaenko, "Fevral'skaia revoliutsiia," p. 32. For a similar contest of new republican and new socialist visions in the Don, see Peter I. Holquist, "A Russian Vendee: The Practice of Revolutionary Politics in the Don Countryside, 1917–1921" (Ph.D. diss., Columbia University, 1995).

[51]Ziva Galili, The Menshevik Leaders in Russia's Revolution: Social Relations and Political Strategies (Princeton University Press, 1989), p. 98, speaks of "the highly organized workers of the Donbas mining regions," but it did not seem to have been the case except for a few factories. The unionization of miners proved difficult even after the February Revolution. See V. L. Meller and A. M. Pankratova, eds., Rabochee dvizhenie v 1917 godu (Moscow, 1926), p. 246.

[52]See V. Ia. Boshcherskii, "Stachechnoe rabochee dvizhenie v Donbasse v period podgotovki Oktiabria," Rabochii klass i rabochee dvizhenie v Rossii v 1917 g. (Moscow, 1964), and A. M. Lisetskii, Bol'sheviki vo glave massovykh stachek (mart–oktiabr' 1917 g.) (Kishnev, 1974), pp. 267–68.

[53]They may be compared with the Russian and Armenian workers of Baku who through 1917–

Figure 3.1. A meeting at the Gustav Mine, Lutuhyne, near Luhans'k, in the spring of 1917. Note the cross on the banner on the left-hand side with an inscription which reads: "For the eternal memory of the heroes who fell for freedom." From DALO, f. P-7118, op. 1, spr. 111.

minimal consensus – not merely about an institutional framework and a political and social order but also about a moral order"[54] – manifested itself in an extreme form in the Donbas. What happened in the Donbas in 1917 was thus characterized as "unbroken, continuous conflict."[55]

The February Revolution was followed immediately by what mine administrators termed "excesses" on the part of colliers: the introduction of a de facto eight-hour workday and willful removal of contractors, senior officials, engineers, and technicians, followed by their "forcible arrests."[56] Throughout

18 "were concerned about safeguarding the freedoms won in February and consolidating their economic position through the labor contract." See Ronald Grigor Suny, *The Baku Commune, 1917–1918: Class and Nationality in the Russian Revolution* (Princeton University Press, 1972), p. 346.

[54]Leopold H. Haimson, "The Problem of Social Identities in Early Twentieth Century Russia: Observations on the Commentaries by Alfred Rieber and William Rosenberg," *Slavic Review*, 47:2 (Fall 1988), p. 516.

[55]M. Balabanov, "Konflikty v Donbasse v 1917 godu," in *Materialy po izucheniiu istorii professional'nogo dvizheniia na Ukraine. Sb. 1. Professiona'noe dvizhenie v 1917 godu* ([Kharkiv], [1928]), pp. 65–66.

[56]See DADO, f. 306, op. 1, spr. 3, ark. 28, and the complaints of managers cited in Meller and

1917 the Donbas industrialists bombarded the Provisional Government with requests for assistance and intervention. According to one such proclamation of 27 May 1917, "the dictatorship of the working class has been established in its most primitive form. The working class, carried away by tempting perspectives depicted to it by irresponsible leaders [*vozhaki*], awaits the advent of a golden age. Terrible will be its disappointment, which it is impossible not to foresee."[57] By August 1917, it was reported that in the Donbas no state authority, inviolability of domicile, or personal safety existed at all.[58]

Between March 1917 and January 1918, 149 instances of violence occurred in the Donbas collieries, of which 127 were concentrated in the summer and autumn (from 1 July to 20 September). The main reasons for conflict were "interference with internal order" (72 cases) and wages (38 cases), followed by work hours (15 cases) and the closure of mines and firing of workers (15 cases).[59] The preponderance of "interference with internal order" meant workers' challenge to managerial authority in the workplace. In other words, these data suggest that power in the workplace was the major bone of contention and that the colliers were as concerned with settling old scores with management as with demanding sharp increases in wages and deductions in work hours.

What happened in the Chystiakove pit of the South Russian Coal Company at the end of March is typical and instructive. One day workers' delegates came to the main office of the company and demanded, among other things, the removal of a mechanic, against whom three accusations were lodged: (1) before the revolution he imposed excessive fines; (2) he did not let workers earn proper wages, by placing only two workers where three or four were needed; (3) he did not place the order for a spare gear for a steam winch, even though its cogs had long been broken and threatened to disrupt work. The mechanic responded: (1) fines were necessary because of the miners' "poor work," but they were assessed in accordance with the company rules, and after February he had not fined them; (2) he had a long experience in the mining business, and therefore he knew better how many hands were adequate and where; (3) the gear, ordered fourteen months before, had not been delivered yet. The main office found the accusations unfounded, and the mechanic went on a "holiday." When he came back, workers dumped him in a wheelbarrow and carted him around "all the mines." Simultaneously, his telephone line was cut, and his horses taken away, so as to prevent him from working. (Engineers

Pankratova, *Rabochee dvizhenie*, p. 123. See also *Gornozavodskoe delo*, 1917, nos. 13–14 (15 April), p. 15605, and *Robitnychyi kontrol' i natsionalizatsiia promyslovosti na Ukraini. Zbirnyk dokumentiv i materialiv, berezen' 1917–berezen' 1921 rr.* (Kiev, 1957), pp. 140–41.

[57]Meller and Pankratova, *Rabochee dvizhenie*, p. 126.

[58]See *Bor'ba za vlast' Sovetov na Donu, 1917–1920 gg. Sbornik dokumentov* (Rostov-on-Don, 1957), pp. 78–79.

[59]Balabanov, "Konflikty v Donbasse," pp. 52–54. These are far from complete data on "more or less big conflicts" that were eventually solved.

were usually provided with a horse to facilitate their travel and work.) The conciliatory board, recommended by the management, refused to elaborate on this affair on the grounds that the case was not one of a conflict of interests, but of a "mutual misunderstanding." The workers refused the mechanic any guarantee of safety.

Eventually the case was handed over to the "comrades' court" of miners. Held in early June, the court declared: (1) that before the revolution the mechanic dealt despotically with his subordinates; (2) that of late he still maintained the same attitude toward workers and acted disrespectfully toward their organizations; (3) that holding a responsible position, he left the mines without reporting to the miners' committee, which had to take the responsibility on itself for the order of work. The court decided to force him to quit his position. The management, however, preempted the inevitable outcome by dismissing him first, yet allowing him to live in his flat until a new mechanic took over. Thereupon, the workers forced him out of both his flat and the coalfields.[60]

Similar events were legion. Those flats taken away from engineers and white-collar employees were either occupied by workers or wrecked by them.[61] Neither the newly created workers' Soviets nor the prosecutor's office was said to have done much to calm the situation.[62] When a fire broke out at the Iakovenko Brothers Coalfield in June, for example, a crowd of agitated workers arrested the director, Engineer Kogan. Taken to the executive committee of the Soviet, he was threatened by the crowd with a *samosud* (which meant anything from a kangaroo court to lynching). Eventually Kogan was released at the request of some workers, whereupon he promptly passed out.[63] In August the director of the Russian Providence Company (Providence russe) in Mariupol', "Fer'e" (Ferié?), a French citizen, was detained by a crowd of workers and his house was searched. Workers seized his revolver and a box of wine. At the Kamyshevats'k coalfield as elsewhere the food shortage was severe. The owner of the coalfield was beaten and robbed by his workers.[64] Many other directors, engineers, and foremen were subjected to house arrest and beating, their weapons and horses confiscated.[65] Vladimir Ipatieff, a chemist who visited the Donbas in September 1917, was not beaten but met with the following reaction at a chemical (explosive) plant: "I gave a speech [no doubt a prowar speech] to the workers, which on the whole was favorably received; but as I was leaving the plant someone shouted at me, 'Sing your tune while you

[60] Ibid., pp. 60–61.

[61] DADO, f. 306, op. 1, spr. 32, ark. 2.

[62] See *Robitnychyi kontrol' i natsionalizatsiia promyslovosti na Ukraini*, pp. 135–36.

[63] *Gornozavodskoe delo*, 1917, nos. 24–25 (24 June), p. 15938. This attack may have been anti-Semitic, because Kogan was probably Jewish.

[64] GARF, f. 393, op. 3, d. 150a, ll. 1–2.

[65] See, for example, GARF, f. 1255, op. 1, d. 31, ll. 48–50 (Makiivka).

can!' " Ipatieff sensed that "another revolution was in the offing, with peace its first objective."[66]

Miners often organized a large meeting for a *samosud* of engineers and foremen, just as peasants did for criminals and violators of community rules and customs. It was intended as the ultimate humiliation. For instance, in August 1917, the foreman at the Union Coal Company, Vasilii Maikut, was condemned for having demanded order at work. (Demands like this one were regarded by workers as an encroachment on their hard won freedom.) After much altercation, Maikut was told by the crowd of workers that the only way out was for him to take off his service cap (*furazhka*, a symbol of elevated status), kowtow in all directions, and beg the workers for mercy. Maikut was fortunate to be able to steal a moment to escape, but he could no longer go to the mine.[67] *Samosud* occasionally resulted in lynching. At the Iasinivka coalfield, for example, an assistant mine director was killed by workers.[68]

Coal managers bitterly complained that such anarchy sharply decreased labor productivity. Indeed, in the course of 1917 both production and productivity declined. According to one account, in the first half of 1917 the average collier produced 521 poods of coal a month, but in the latter half of the year, 421.[69] Yet it was not clear whether this was due to the alleged lack of work discipline or the shortage of food. In any case, the industrialists, panicked, appealed to the workers to "postpone your class struggle until the end of the war." Yet they noted in alarm that by June the workers had become increasingly convinced that they could manage on their own the factories and mines in administrative, economic, and technical respects, without their owners and administrators, who therefore could be dismissed.[70] How concerned the managers were can be seen by looking at their organ *Gornozavodskoe delo*. In 1917 the journal is full of references to crowds of people, who are depicted as anarchists and terrorists.[71]

Many humiliated and threatened managers refused to return to work unless

---

[66]*The Life of a Chemist: Memoirs of Vladimir N. Ipatieff* (Stanford University Press, 1946), p. 257.

[67]*Gornozavodskoe delo*, 1917, nos. 36–37 (25 November), pp. 16342–43, and DADO, f. 306, op. 1, spr. 3, ark. 28–28zv.

[68]DADO, f. 305, op. 1, spr. 6, ark. 38. In June, when the question arose as to what to do with former policemen and gendarmes, the Donbas industrialists jumped on the suggestion that they be sent to the mines. See E. Osipov, "Gornorabochie i gornopromyshlenniki v 1917 godu," *Materialy po istorii professional'nogo dvizheniia v Rossii, Sbornik 4* (Moscow, 1925), p. 402.

[69]*Narodnoe khoziaistvo*, 1919, no. 5, p. 76.

[70]*Gornozavodskoe delo*, 1917, nos. 26–27 (12 June), pp. 16012 and 16045. Indeed, some mines were taken over and managed by workers themselves. For the case of Khanzhenkove (Khanzhonkove), near Makiivka, see A. Frolov, "Oktiabr' v Khanzhonkove," in *Proletarskaia revoliutsiia na Donu. Sbornik vtoroi* (Rostov, 1922), p. 68.

[71]See, for example, *Gornozavodskoe delo*, 1917, nos. 22–23 (12 June), p. 15861, and nos. 34–35 (15 November), p. 16309.

apologies and a guarantee of safety were offered. When such offers were not forthcoming, they did not go back to the mines.[72] To counter the workers, industrialists resorted to lockout and closure. By the beginning of September, two hundred coalfields were said to have been closed, with perhaps a hundred thousand workers thrown into the streets.[73]

If in the summer of 1917, "illegal" acts, strikes, and workers' control in the capital cities of Moscow and Petrograd were largely motivated by a desire to maintain production,[74] the concern of Donbas colliers was elsewhere. They maintained, for example, that horses taken from management were to be used to transport workers' families in case of imminent civil war.[75]

What appeared to respectable society as a general breakdown of order was symbolic of the inversion of order brought about by the February Revolution. Once the formerly underprivileged classes realized that they could attack the privileged classes with impunity, they began to do so with vengeance. Such attacks were not unique to the city and industry. Soon after the revolution, the peasantry began to mount the same kind of violent attack upon the landed gentry to take back land.[76] Soldiers and sailors, in the midst of the war, challenged their officers' authority.[77]

The inversion of the old order would not have occurred without a concomitant inversion of the concept of the "enemy." If before the revolution the enemy was the subversive, revolutionary element (or, to reverse the point of view, tsarism and its supporters), then in the postrevolutionary months the enemy became the *burzhui*. This word, a popular term referring pejoratively to "bourgeoisie,"[78] was appropriated and politically constructed in 1917 not just by the Bolsheviks but by the Mensheviks, the SRs, and even some church reformers. Even the liberals could not resist the anticapitalist, antibourgeois rhetoric of the revolution, which gained wide popularity. In the political discourse of 1917, *burzhui* came to refer to a greedy egoistic person regardless of his or her social origin. The term became such an all-inclusive dirty word that both the right and the left were able to proclaim: "Down with the provisional Government. Beat the *burzhui*s and the Yids [*zhidov*]."[79] Thus, navy officers,

[72] See, for example, DADO, f. 306, op. 1, spr. 41, ark. 4–11.

[73] Meller and Pankratova, *Rabochee dvizhenie*, p. 228. See also Manzhosov, "Predstavnyts'ki orhanizatsii," p. 82.

[74] See William G. Rosenberg and Diane P. Koenker, "The Limits of Formal Protest: Worker Activism and Social Polarization in Petrograd and Moscow, March to October, 1917," *American Historical Review*, 92:2 (April 1987), p. 319.

[75] *Robitnychyi kontrol' i natsionalizatsiia promyslovosti na Ukraini*, p. 156.

[76] See K. G. Kotel'nikov and V. L. Meller, eds., *Krest'ianskoe dvizhenie v 1917 godu* (Moscow and Leningrad, 1927), which also covers the Katerynoslav and Don provinces.

[77] See, for example, Wildman, *The End of the Russian Imperial Army*.

[78] See André Lirondelle, "Bourgeois et 'Bourjoui,' " *Le Monde Slave* (Paris), 2:8–9 (February–March 1918).

[79] For an excellent discussion of this construction of the *burzhui* in 1917, see B. I. Kolonitskii,

angry with demands of the sailors, could denounce them as *"burzhuis."* Likewise, supporters of the Provisional Government could contend that its ministers were not *burzhuis*, because they were selfless patriots. In both popular consciousness and political propaganda, economic and other difficulties obtaining in society came to be explained by "conspiracies of *burzhuis*."[80]

This construction of *burzhui* is similar to that of "speculator." As Lars T. Lih has shown, "The Bolsheviks' crusade against speculation should thus be seen less as an offshoot of socialist ideology than as a precapitalist attitude they shared with the rest of the Russian political community. Analogues to medieval English laws against 'engrossers,' 'forestallers,' and 'regrators' are still on the books in the Soviet Union."[81] The terms *burzhui* and "speculator" thus came to function politically just like the notorious term *kulak*, rich peasant or rural *burzhui*, which was similarly constructed.[82]

This political construction did not imply a complete inversion of the old order, however. It incorporated both new and old elements, as, for example, the inclusion of anti-Semitism. In Petrograd some food riots in the summer of 1917 were "accompanied by pogroms against Jewish merchants."[83] In the Donbas, anti-Semitic propaganda was widely distributed in the streets. Socialists feared that "dark forces," who they claimed "formed a bloc with the Jewish Bund," would fight against them.[84] When workers' strikes were organized, rumor circulated that the strikes were calls for pogroms.[85] In September 1917 a crowd broke into a Bakhmut liquor storage of 100,000 vedro (1 vedro = 12 liters) of vodka and 600,000 vedro of other kinds of liquor. The drunken crowd then assaulted grocers to obtain food to go with the vodka and rampaged through the city. Jews fled the city in fear of pogroms. (The crowd accused the militia of "defending *burzhuis*.")[86] Even within the Bolshevik party, in the

---

"Antiburzhuaznaia propaganda i 'anti-burzhuiskoe' soznanie," in *Anatomiia revoliutsii. 1917 god v Rossii: massy, partii, blast'* (St. Petersburg, 1994), p. 194. For the historical origin of the pejorative term *zhid* for Jew in Russian, see John D. Klier, "Zhid: Bibliography of a Russian Epithet," *Slavonic and East European Review*, 60:1 (January 1982).

[80] Kolonitskii, "Antiburzhuaznaia propaganda," p. 201. This construction of the term seems to incorporate much old usage. See Louise McReynolds, *The News under Russia's Old Regime: The Development of a Mass-Circulation Press* (Princeton University Press, 1991), pp. 110 and 270, and Lirondelle, "Bourgeois et 'Bourjoui.' "

[81] Lars T. Lih, *Bread and Authority in Russia, 1914–1921* (University of California Press, 1990), p. 242.

[82] For an excellent discussion of this, see A. N. Solopov, "Kogo schitali kulakom v 20-e gody. (K istorii predposylok peregibov v derevne)," *Voprosy istorii KPSS*, 1990, no. 10.

[83] Hasegawa, "Crime, Police, and Mob Justice," p. 260.

[84] *Donetskii proletarii* (Luhans'k), 16 (3) August 1917.

[85] A. M. Lisetskii, "Bol'sheviki vo glave stachechnoi bor'by proletariev Donbassa v period podgotovki oktiabr'skogo shturma (sentiabr'–oktiabr' 1917 g.)," *Sbornik nauchnykh rabot kafedr istorii KPSS vuzov g. Kharkova* (Kharkiv), vol. 3 (1960), p. 70.

[86] G. Kuranov, "Sovety na Artemovshchine mezhdu Fevralem i Oktiabrem 1917 goda," *Letopis' revoliutsii*, 1927, nos. 5–6, p. 187. When initially liquor was dumped into the river, Bakhmut

midst of revolutionary events in the autumn of 1917, anti-Semitism persisted, to the extent that on 18 November 1917, for example, the Iuzivka Organization of the party placed the problem of intraparty anti-Semitism as the second item on the agenda: some Bolsheviks treated "members of other nationalities" badly, heaping "all kinds of insults" on them.[87]

Many observers noted that in places like the Donbas collieries where literate culture was minimal and few elements of modern politics and civil society had ever existed, rumor and demagogy found fertile ground. Such perceptions reflected the prejudices of the observers, in this case both industrialists and Bolsheviks. To determine the extent to which press reporting in the Donbas influenced the ways in which political identification was formed would need the kind of careful analysis done by Diane P. Koenker and William G. Rosenberg, with regard, mainly, to Moscow and Petrograd.[88] Yet the press played a far more limited political role in the Donbas than in Moscow or Petrograd. By nearly all accounts, anti-Bolshevik agitation proved very effective, even though it was the Bolsheviks who supported workers' "excesses," while the SRs and particularly the Mensheviks called for moderation. In Hryshyne, for example, popular sentiment was so strongly against the Bolsheviks that they were not able to engage in open political activity until mid-July 1917. Bolsheviks, when identified, were subjected to a *samosud* even without any provocation. Such was the case in a significant part of the Donbas, as one witness has observed. Their antiwar campaign was so unpopular with miners and peasants that some Bolsheviks were lynched by the *samosud* of crowds in Iuzivka.[89]

In the Donbas, anti-Bolshevik forces branded the Bolsheviks as German spies, who worked for the defeat of Russia and the reinstatement of the tsar. They evoked Lenin's "sealed train" constantly. Such demagogy, according to observers, "confused workers, who leaned both to the right and left. In those days [March 1917] whoever told them whatever, they applauded everyone all the same."[90] Workers' meetings often were filled with a "pogromlike mood": "Beat the Bolsheviks." The arrest of Trotsky and Lunacharsky, and retreat into hiding of Lenin and Zinoviev, in the aftermath of the July events

residents flocked to the river to recover vodka floating on the surface.

[87] *Bol'shevistskie organizatsii Ukrainy: organizatsionno-partiinaia deiatel'nost' (fevral' 1917–iiul' 1918). Sbornik dokumentov i materialov* (Kiev, 1990), p. 445.

[88] Diane P. Koenker and William G. Rosenberg, *Strikes and Revolution in Russia, 1917* (Princeton University Press, 1989), ch. 7. See also Koenker and Rosenberg, "Perceptions and Reality of Labour Protest, March to October 1917," in Edith Rogovin Frankel, Jonathan Frankel, and Baruch Knei-Paz, eds., *Revolution in Russia: Reassessment of 1917* (Cambridge University Press, 1992).

[89] E. Medne, "Oktiabr'skaia revoliutsiia v Donbasse," *Letopis' revoliutsii*, 1922, no. 1, p. 49.

[90] P. Kazimirchuk, "Revoliutsionnoe dvizhenie v Gorlovo-Shcherbinovskom raione Donbassa (Vospominaniia)," *Letopis' revoliutsii*, 1923, no. 3, pp. 45 and 47. See also Kuranov, "Sovety," p. 179, and I. Nikolaenko, "Lugansk. Istoriia odnoi organizatsii kompartii," in *Oktiabr'skaia revoliutsiia*, p. 632.

(armed demonstrations in the capital and other cities), were said to have like-wise sparked hostilities against the Bolsheviks among Donbas miners: Bol-shevik agitators were beaten up and had to be rescued from the *samosud* of crowds, whose mood was "pogromlike."[91] In Iuzivka, a Menshevik center according to V. M. Molotov,[92] miners chased their Bolshevik fellow workers with picks, forcing many activists to recant.[93] Workers' prejudice was fully utilized: they were fed propaganda to the effect that Lenin, Trotsky, and others were all Jews who were guilty of the ruin of Russia.[94] Rumors about German gold, allegedly received by the Bolsheviks, were insidious in the Donbas.[95]

All this suggests that a significant segment of the Donbas workers believed in patriotism, an abstract, emotional attachment to one's country, which was, in the Bolshevik view, at odds with proletarian internationalism. Violent attacks against Bolsheviks were hardly surprising, given that in the political discourse of 1917 a lack of patriotism was considered part of the despised *burzhui* char-acteristic. Thus, the anticapitalist Bolsheviks became *burzhui*! (Indeed some regarded the Bolsheviks as the enemy of the revolution.)[96] Patriotism tran-scended ideology, as was clear from the fact that not only nonsocialists but even the majority of socialists in and outside Russia supported the war. At a miners' meeting in May 1917 in Hryshyne, most of the men supported the war, and only an insignificant number were against the war. Yet, at the same time, it turned out that there was a strong anti-Menshevik, anti-SR ferment taking place among them.[97]

In the summer of 1917, for example, at a miners' meeting in the town of Aleksandrovsk-Grushevskii, the following incident occurred. The chairman of the local revolutionary committee, who was a lawyer, spoke at the meeting. "He wore a shiny bowler hat, his plump body was clothed in a clean smart suit and his pomaded moustache was stiffened like a corkscrew." The chairman

> spoke very well and his audience listened with attention, but when he said, "Everybody must be ready for further sacrifices in the name of the immortal ideals of the Revolution and in the name of our victory in the war with Ger-

---

[91] Kazimirchuk, "Revoliutsionnoe dvizhenie," pp. 51, 53, and 55, and *Shestoi s"ezd RSDRP (bol'shevikov). Avgust 1917 goda. Protokoly* (Moscow, 1958), pp. 92 and 362. See also the protocols of the Iuzivka party meetings where these anti-Bolshevik actions were discussed in *Bol'shevistskie organizatsii Ukrainy*, pp. 175, 215, 216, and 242. For a more favorable view of Donbas miners, see I. Vishniakov, "V bor'be za diktaturu proletariata v Donbasse (1916–1918 gg.)," *Litopys revoliutsii*, 1928, no. 2, p. 225.

[92] *Sto sorok besed s Molotovym. Iz dnevnika F. Chueva* (Moscow, 1991), p. 352.

[93] See Zaitsev, "Kak my tvorili Oktiabr'," pp. 136–37, and "Oktiabr' v Iuzovke," in *Oktiabr'skaia revoliutsiia*, p. 622.

[94] Kazimirchuk, "Revoliutsionnoe dvizhenie," pp. 63–64, and *Donetskii proletarii* (Luhans'k), 16 (3) August 1917, p. 2.

[95] See, for example, *Donetskii proletarii* (Kharkiv), 9 (22) December 1917, p. 3.

[96] Kazimirchuk, "Revoliutsionnoe dvizhenie," p. 55.

[97] Medne, "Oktiabr'skaia revoliutsiia," p. 50.

many," the mood of the crowd changed. On to the speaker's platform jumped a miner, his face black with coal dust. "Smell that!" he cried, shaking his fist under the nose of the speaker. "We want none of your ideals and your war to . . . !" There followed the recommended place of destination in very strong and colourful words.

"Right! Down to hell with this fat belly!" shouted the crowd, and the meeting broke up amidst pandemonium.[98]

They had their own ideals and their own sense of war. Few revolutionaries understood exactly what they were.

In fact, no one seemed to understand the complex political development in the Donbas in 1917. The evident anti-Bolshevism was certainly nightmarish for the Bolsheviks. Yet this same development was hardly a comfort to the Mensheviks and SRs, because their counsel for moderation was not sought by the Donbas miners. Leon Trotsky, later in exile, sought to understand this seemingly contradictory process of political identification in the Donbas in the following fashion:

> An excellent example of this *quid pro quo* between the Compromisers [Mensheviks and SRs] and the masses, is to be seen in an oath taken at the beginning of July by 2,000 Donetz [Donbas] miners, kneeling with uncovered heads in the presence of a crowd of 5,000 people and with its participation. "We swear by our children, by God, by the heaven and earth, and by all things that we hold sacred in the world, that we will never relinquish the freedom bought with blood on the 28th of February, 1917; believing in the Social Revolutionaries and the Mensheviks, we swear we will never listen to the Leninists, for they, the Bolshevik-Leninists, are leading Russia to ruin with their agitation, whereas the Social Revolutionaries and Mensheviks united in a single union, say: The land to the people, land without indemnities; the capitalist structure must fall after the war and in place of capitalism there must be a socialist structure. . . . We give our oath to march forward under the lead of these parties, not stopping even at death." This oath of the miners directed against the Bolsheviks in reality led straight to the Bolshevik revolution. The February shell and the October kernel appear in this naive and fervent picture so clearly as in a way to exhaust the whole problem of the Permanent Revolution.
>
> By September the Donetz miners, without betraying either themselves or their oath, had already turned their back on the Compromisers.[99]

---

[98] Borodin, *One Man in His Time*, p. 16.

[99] Leon Trotsky, *The History of the Russian Revolution*, tr. Max Eastman (London, 1977), pp. 792–93. Appeal to patriotism by their bosses did not always work, however. In the summer of 1917 the Donets-Grushevsk coalfield director urged the colliers to work harder to help the country's war efforts ("so that they would not end up under the rule of the German Emperor"). Yet the miners responded: "Let us, all the same. You know the [German] POWs, even though they've lived under the kaiser, they aren't any more stupid than us, they're clever." DADO, f. 306, op. 1, spr. 3, 29zv.

The influence of the Mensheviks and SRs may hypothetically be explained in sociological terms. Those workers who settled in the Donbas had much to lose and were more receptive to moderation, whereas peasant workers were attracted to the SRs' agrarian platforms. Yet Trotsky's description also suggests that the Donbas miners followed the direction of no single political party: they rejected the Bolsheviks on the issues of land and peace while spurning the Mensheviks and SRs on direct action.

The scene described by Trotsky is similar to an event witnessed by another Bolshevik in the autumn of 1917 (probably shortly after the October Revolution) at the Eristovo coalfields. There about five thousand colliers worked, half of whom were Tartars. It was a revolutionary center. The director of the coalfields was a man named Konopliannikov, who was also a political leader [*vozhd'*]. Konopliannikov, like a boa, was said to "hypnotize the whole of this brave militant 5,000 strong collective." He had the power of suggesting to the colliers that "he, Konopliannikov, and only he was the embodiment of revolution, truth, and justice." He did not subordinate himself to the Provisional Government, according to one acute observer, "quite rightly calling it counterrevolutionary." Yet at the same time he inspired the miners to believe that all the parties, including the Bolsheviks, were "enemies of the people and the revolution." This Bolshevik visitor encountered the following "crazy and wild scene":

> Konopliannikov gives a speech from the balcony of a two-story house to six to seven thousand colliers.
>
> "On your knees. Kiss the earth!" orders Konopliannikov imperiously in the shrill voice of a gallant commander. The six thousand strong, like cut grass, fell to their knees. "Raise your hands and take this oath after me."
>
> "We swear!" issues forth from the six thousand miners' mouths, resounding in a booming echo in the wood. "We swear! We'll all die for Konopliannikov. For our republic-commune. We'll all die! We'll betray him to no one. We will not. We'll die [first]."
>
> I don't understand this, I who have seen the world. Is it a comedy? A melodrama?[100]

It turned out that this was a rehearsal for "genuine class war": the meeting was followed by an attack by an "armed band of the Provisional Government." The colliers faithfully defended their ataman and repelled the attack, with forty-nine deaths on the enemy side and none on the Konopliannikov side. (Yet soon thereafter the "Konopliannikov republic-commune" was destroyed by the bands of Kaledin, the Don Cossack ataman, and Konopliannikov was arrested and sent to Novocherkassk. His fate is unknown.)[101]

---

[100]Puchkov-Bezrodnyi, "Oktiabr' v Donbasse. (Iz zapisok krasnogvardeitsa)," *Katorga i ssylka*, 1932, nos. 11–12, pp. 192–93.

[101]Ibid., pp. 193–94.

The famous Makhno movement shared similar charismatic dimensions. In the course of 1917 the peasants in Huliai-Pole area simply confiscated gentry lands and divided them up among themselves. When the Provisional Government sent its representatives there they were kicked out. Some Mensheviks who were elected to the city Soviet were forced out by Makhno on threat of execution. When land was given to the peasants after the October Revolution, the peasants and workers believed that it was given not by the Soviet government but by Nestor Ivanovich Makhno.[102] These accounts imply that the free steppe had a very strong localism, with allegiance owed to its atamans. Anti-Bolshevism was part of a centrifugal force.

This implication may not be as peculiar to the steppe as first appears, and, moreover, it still explains far from everything that took place in the Donbas. Patriotism, for example, appeared to merge with localism. As Donbas political activists knew well, each mine, each coalfield, each factory operated under very different conditions, with links among them often absent. Thus, in some places in the Donbas, the Bolsheviks were extremely weak, in others they were very strong.[103]

This may support the hypothesis proposed earlier that the Donbas workers, particularly colliers, fought for ideas, values, and symbols they believed protected their communities. These communities could be as small as *artel*'s, barracks, and *zemliachestvo*s and as large as the Konopliannikov commune, the "free steppe," the "working class," and even "Ukraine" and "Russia"; they could be paternalistic; but they had to ensure freedom, welfare, and personal dignity. In real life, one could belong to a number of such groups, by being, for example, a Tambovite, a patriot, a militant revolutionary, and an anti-Semite. Allegiance to a group or a sense of belonging necessarily included an exclusionary orientation against those deemed outsiders. Hence the managers and engineers were outsiders or even enemies (because they appeared to deprive the workers of freedom and to denigrate them). So were many others, including foreigners and some ethnic and religious minorities. They were all *burzhui*s, in the parlance of the time. The church still appeared to be part of the workers' moral universe, but war and Bolshevism could be their allies or enemies, depending on specific circumstances.

For the Bolsheviks, it was a historical necessity that, with proper outside guidance, the workers would come to identify themselves with the "working class" and its self-professed vanguard, the Bolshevik party, over and above allegiance to all other groups. For workers, there was no reason to subscribe to any political party, because its politics could not encompass the whole of their lives. Yet even within the narrow confines of politics, it was not illogical

---

[102]Bespechnyi, "Nestor Makhno."
[103]*Shestoi s"ezd RSDRP (bol'shevikov)*, p. 92.

at all for them to remain patriots and denounce the Bolsheviks as German spies while actively fighting for freedom and their atamans. Such behavior appeared to the Bolsheviks to be a manifestation of petit bourgeois mentality. Even the language of class, as reflected in, for example, the use of *burzhui*, did not necessarily follow the party line.

The political identification of Donbas colliers in 1917 was thus a very complex process. The autocracy was discredited; so was liberalism, long regarded as the bosses' politics, which was, in any case, utterly incompatible with workers' action. (Among the workers the word Kadet meant "obscene.")[104] It was left to the Mensheviks, the SRs, the Bolsheviks, the Ukrainian nationalist groups, and to a lesser extent the anarchists to fight for political hegemony. (Once the tsarist regime collapsed, Ukrainian nationalism became a political force in the Donbas. Slogans such as *Het' z nashei khaty* (Get out of our home) and *Het' z Ukrainy zhydiv ta katsapiv* (Get Jews and Russians out of Ukraine) began to be heard in the Donbas.)[105]

In the Donbas, as elsewhere, Bolshevik influence did surge in the summer and autumn of 1917.[106] For example, in the August elections to the Luhans'k City Duma, the Bolsheviks gained 29 seats out of 75 (the SRs 18 seats, the houseowners' group 11, the Mensheviks 10, etc.).[107] (In Iuzivka, however, the Bolsheviks won only 6 seats out of 73, the SRs acquiring 50 seats, the Mensheviks 10, the Kadets 5, etc.).[108] In the September elections to the Luhans'k Soviet, the Bolsheviks won 82 seats out of 120.[109] In Iuzivka, the Bolsheviks gained one-third of the Soviet delegates, a sharp rise from only a handful (5–6) out of 200 in July.[110]

The political ascendancy of the Bolshevik party in the Donbas reflected the political discredit of the Mensheviks and the SRs in Ukraine and Russia.[111] When in the summer "hunger revolts" were threatening the Donbas, the

[104]Iu. V. Afonin, "Monopolistychna burzhuaziia Donbasu v 1917 r.," *Ukrains'kyi istorychnyi zhurnal*, 1990, no. 9, p. 51.

[105]See, for example, Kuranov, "Sovety," pp. 184–85, *Bol'shevistskie organizatsii Ukrainy*, p. 428; and *Gornorabochii*, 1927, no. 41, p. 35.

[106]See Alexander Rabinowitch, *The Bolsheviks Come to Power: The Revolution of 1917 in Petrograd* (New York, 1976).

[107]*Donetskii proletarii* (Luhans'k), 22 (9) August 1917. See also Iu. I. Tereshchenko, *Politychna borot'ba na vyborakh do mis'kykh dum Ukrainy v period pidhotovky Zhovtnevoi revoliutsii* (Kiev, 1974), pp. 108–9.

[108]Zaitsev, "Kak my tvorili Oktiabr'," p. 137. In Ienakiieve, the Bolsheviks won 27.2% (or 11 seats out of 42), the SRs 38.9%, the Mensheviks, the Bund, and the Ukrainian socialist bloc 19% of the votes. (Tereshchenko, *Politychna borot'ba*, p. 110.)

[109]N. Goncharenko, *Oktiabr' v Donbasse* (Luhans'k, 1961), pp. 165–66. The majority of the Bolshevik delegates were representatives of metalworkers from the Hartman factory.

[110]Zaitsev, "Kak my tvorili Oktiabr'," pp. 136–37.

[111]For the precipitous decline of the Mensheviks, see Iu. M. Hamrets'kyi, "Bil'shovyky ta ikhni politychni protyvnyky na Ukraini v 1917 r.: spivvidnoshennia syl," *Ukrains'kyi istorychnyi zhurnal*, 1987, no. 11, pp. 66–67.

Soviets failed to cope with the deepening food crisis.[112] The persecution of the Bolsheviks by the Menshevik-SR dominated militia was said to have militated against the Mensheviks and the SRs.[113]

In the November elections to the All-Russian Constituent Assembly, the Bolsheviks won a victory, albeit insignificant, being challenged by Ukrainian national groups (including the Ukrainian SRs and the Peasant Union) and the Russian SRs. Out of 577,010 votes cast in "the most important districts and cities in the Donets-Kryvyi Rih Basin," the results were as follows:

Bolsheviks	186,543	(32.3%)
Ukrainian national groups	132,604	(23.0)
Russian SRs	107,917	(18.7)
Kadets	42,606	(7.4)
Mensheviks	30,899	(5.4)
Others	76,441	(13.2)

In some cities the Bolsheviks fared far better, receiving 48 percent in Luhans'k and 47 in Iuzivka.[114] In the coal mines in particular, the Bolsheviks defeated the Mensheviks, the SRs, and the Ukrainian nationalists by a wide margin (16,775, 362, 2,043, and 889 votes respectively).[115] How complete the available data on the Donbas mines are is far from clear, however, because the total votes cast amounted to only 20,279.[116] An SR newspaper bitterly complained that Donbas miners, carried away by bootleg vodka and gambling, forgot their "civil duty – voting in elections."[117] According to another account, only 5 to 8 percent of miners participated in various organizations.[118] Historians can

---

[112]See, for example, L. S. Gaponenko, *Rabochii klass Rossii v 1917 godu* (Moscow, 1970), p. 451. For the best study of the food crisis in general, see Lih, *Bread and Authority in Russia.*

[113]Zaitsev, "Kak my tvorili Oktiabr'," p. 137. See also Kazimirchuk, "Revoliutsionnoe dvizhenie v Gorlovo-Shcherbinovskom raione Donbassa," *Letopis' revoliutsii,* 1923, no. 4, pp. 55–56.

[114]I. K. Rybalko, "Rabochii klass Ukrainy na vyborakh vo Vserossiiskoe i Vseukrainskoe uchreditel'nye sobraniia," *Istoriia SSSR,* 1965, no. 1, pp. 119–20.

[115]*Donetskii proletarii* (Kharkiv), 18 November (1 December) 1917. See also GARF, f. 7952, op. 6, d. 13, l. 3, and Steven L. Guthier, "The Popular Base of Ukrainian Nationalism in 1917," *Slavic Review,* 38:1 (1979), p. 44.

[116]There are well-preserved archival data on the election results in the Don. The Bolsheviks won large numbers of votes in the coalfields. See Iu. K. Kirienko, *Revoliutsiia i Donskoe kazachestvo (fevral'–oktiabr' 1917 g.)* (Rostov, 1988), pp. 208–18.

[117]See *Klich naroda* (Iuzivka), 5 November 1917, p. 4.

[118]*Gornozavodskoe delo,* 1917, nos. 34–35 (15 November), p. 16279. The elections for the All-Ukrainian Constituent Assembly, held in January 1918, were even less popular: the turnout was only about one-third of that of the All-Russian elections. (TsDAVO, f. 1146, op. 1, spr. 2, ark. 24 and 199, and Rybalko, "Rabochii klass Ukrainy," pp. 121–25. See also F. I. Zaitsev, *Zhovten' na Stalinshchyni* [Kharkiv, 1933], p. 42.) The result was favorable to the Bolsheviks. "In the major towns and districts of the Donets-Kryvyi Rih Basin," the Bolsheviks gained 38.5% of the votes, the Ukrainian SRs, the Peasant Union, and other Ukrainian groups 31.6%, the Russian SRs 9.9%, the Mensheviks 2.2%. (In Iuzivka the Bolsheviks won only 18.3%.) At the Mykytivka coalfield only 585 of the 3,101 electors participated. (Rybalko, "Rabochii klass Ukrainy," p. 124.) The

hardly assume that the election results reflected the political configuration of the Donbas at the time.

As it turns out, even where the Bolsheviks prevailed, the workers often did not follow the Bolsheviks. In Makiivka, for example, it was reported in October that "even the most influential party of Bolsheviks" was losing popularity with workers."[119] In the Donbas as a whole the Mensheviks and the SRs still combined to present a formidable challenge to the Bolsheviks. For example, when the unionization of the miners finally took place in October 1917, much more belatedly than for other trades, the Bolsheviks sent the largest contingent, forty-seven, to the first union conference, but they were outnumbered by the Mensheviks and the SRs combined, seventy-eight. The leadership of miners' unions remained in the latter's hands until 1919.[120] On 31 October 1917 the Iuzivka Soviet adopted a resolution proposed by the Menshevik Internationalists, which condemned the Bolshevik seizure of power in Petrograd and appealed for a "homogeneous democratic government."[121] In some other Soviets in the Donbas, the Bolsheviks gained leadership with great difficulty.[122] Because no one party could manage the Soviets in the name of the workers, recalls of delegates and reelections took place frequently.[123] When the Bolsheviks disbanded the Constituent Assembly in January 1918, "some coalfields, which have always followed us [Bolsheviks]" became troublesome. At meetings, many workers asked why the Bolsheviks dissolved the assembly: "You yourselves held the elections, didn't you? But now you've disbanded it."[124]

Soon after the Bolshevik seizure of power, the new government appeared to the Donbas miners to have deprived them of "the freedom bought with the blood of the 28th of February, 1917," which they had sworn never to relinquish "by our children, by God, by the heaven and earth, and by all things that we

general chaos and the civil war, which had already started in the Donbas, adversely affected the turnout.

[119]GARF, f. 1255, op. 1, d. 31, l. 49.

[120]Meller and Pankratova, *Rabochee dvizhenie*, p. 248, and *5-letnii obzor deiatel'nosti Soiuza gornorabochikh v Donetskom basseine (1920–1925 gg.) i kratkii ocherk rabochego i professional'nogo dvizheniia gorniakov Donetskogo basseina do 1920 goda* (Artemivs'k, 1925), p. 35.

[121]See *Donetskii proletarii* (Kharkiv), 9 (22) December 1917, and *Pobeda Velikoi Oktiabr'skoi sotsialisticheskoi revoliutsii i ustanovlenie Sovetskoi vlasti na Ukraine, okt.–dek. 1917 g.*, vol. 2 (Kiev, 1957), p. 285. In February, in the Iuzivka Soviet the Bolsheviks still accounted for only 65 seats out of 143, or 45%. See P. M. Tryhub, "Pro kil'kist', partiinyi ta sotsial'nyi sklad Rad Ukrainy v hrudni 1917–kvitni 1918 rr.," *Ukrains'kyi istorychnyi zhurnal*, 1972, no. 1, p. 113. In April it still maintained that it did not have authority or real power. See the 13 April 1918 protocol of the Bolshevik organization in Iuzivka in *Bol'shevistskie organizatsii Ukrainy*, p. 622.

[122]See N. G. Goncharenko, *V bitvakh za Oktiabr' (mart 1917–mart 1918 gg.)* (Donets'k, 1974), pp. 144–50, 155–57.

[123]Meller and Pankratova, *Rabochee dvizhenie*, pp. 242–43. The state of affairs in Iuzivka, for example, was described as "multiple power" (*mnogonachalie*). *Litopys revoliutsii*, 1928, no. 3, p. 371.

[124]Kazimirchuk, "Revoliutsionnoe dvizhenie," p. 125.

hold sacred in the world." The arrest of opposition party members on whom the new government spied prompted Donbas colliers to describe the Bolsheviks as "gendarmes of the revolution."[125] Rumors of German gold, allegedly received by the Bolsheviks, kept circulating in the Donbas.[126] From late 1917 onward, the worsening economic situation further complicated matters. New Bolshevik masters soon became as harsh as old masters and, in difficulties, threw workers out into the streets.[127] Some party members came to behave like dictators, and those who had entered the party on the spur of the moment turned against the party.[128]

Civil War

The experience of civil war and foreign intervention on the periphery of the former Russian Empire differed sharply from the experience of the heartland: it restored the old regime. As was characteristic of the civil war in the south, the Reds, Whites, Blacks (anarchists), and Greens (peasant armies) fought against each other.[129] In the Donbas, the battle was so fierce that some twenty political regimes were set up one after another.[130] Like Mikhail Bulgakov's Kiev, the Donbas repeatedly changed hands among the Reds, Whites, and the Blacks. In the particularly chaotic months of February through May 1919 Kostiantynivka in the center of the Donbas changed hands twenty-seven times.[131] In the process, the Donbas turned into a truly "wild field" of carnage and savagery. Thirty percent or more of the Donbas colliers were said to have perished.[132]

In the Donbas, unlike the capital cities, "the victory of labor over capital" was not "achieved remarkably, and perhaps deceptively, easily."[133] Many col-

---

[125]*Klich naroda*, 8 November 1917.

[126]*Donetskii proletarii* (Kharkiv), 9 (22) December 1917.

[127]See *Protokoly I-go delegatskago oblastnogo s"ezda professional'nago soiuza gornorabochikh Donetskago, Krivorozhskago i Solianogo Basseinov, 25 March–1 April 1918* (Kharkiv, 1918), p. 22.

[128]*Bor'ba za vlast' Sovetov Donbassa. Sbornik dokumentov i materialov* (Stalino, 1957), p. 313 (Gorlovka-Shcherbinovka party conference in February 1918).

[129]See Holquist, "A Russian Vendee"; and Peter Kenez, *Civil War in South Russia, 1918: The First Year of the Volunteer Army* (University of California Press, 1971), and *Civil War in South Russia, 1919–1920: The Defeat of the Whites* (University of California Press, 1977).

[130]*5-letnii obzor*, pp. 8–9.

[131]*Istoriia rabochikh Donbassa*, vol. 1 (Kiev, 1981), p. 182. For a kaleidoscopic picture of Donbas life with various armies, "fightings, funerals, shootings, retreats, offensives," see Vasil' Haidarivs'kyi, *"A svit takyi harnyi . . . "* (Buenos Aires, 1962), p. II.

[132]GARF, f. 5459, op. 1, d. 1, l. 62.

[133]Sheila Fitzpatrick, "New Perspectives on the Civil War," in Diane P. Koenker, William G. Rosenberg, and Ronald Grigor Suny, eds., *Party, State, and Society in the Russian Civil War: Explorations in Social History* (Indiana University Press, 1989), p. 15. See also Fitzpatrick, "The

liers did flee the Donbas to avoid the war, but unlike in Moscow, where "this confrontation was removed from the direct daily experience of most workers,"[134] in the Donbas, the war was the "direct daily experience" of those who chose to stay.

Labor's violent attack on management, as some workers were well aware, led inevitably to the latter's retaliation. The Donbas industrialists were embittered by the brutal assault of labor on them and their liberal beliefs. On 30 November 1917, for example, the director of the Petrovsko-Khrustal'sk Anthracite Company, S. G. Violin, was dragged from his house to the general meeting of workers and employees. They demanded a 50 percent wage hike above the previously agreed-upon level and the immediate introduction of an eight-hour workday without a paycut. He was given ten minutes to sign the "agreement" with the threat that if he refused he would not be able to leave the meeting alive. The threat was supported by the menacing cries of workers. Violin had no choice but to accept the demands.[135] In December the Donbas industrialists declared: "The inevitable has occurred. The Donbas has been destroyed, the fuel and metal supplies of the country are almost completely lost. The moment of the collapse of economic life in the Donbas is near."[136]

From August 1917 onward, in fact, the Donbas industrialists importuned the Provisional Government to dispatch Cossack regiments and declare martial law in the Donbas. The Kornilov affair delayed the implementation of this scheme. By early October Ataman General A. K. Kaledin's squadrons had occupied almost the entire region.[137] On 25 October, in connection with the loss of the telegraph connection with the capital Kaledin declared martial law in the Donbas coal-mining area. Kaledin justified this measure by citing anarchistic disorder caused by "agitators who have come in large numbers from Germany" (an allusion to the Bolsheviks).[138] Martial law was met with threats of strikes by workers.[139] As the seizure of power by the Soviets spread through the Donbas, the confrontation developed into armed fighting. Already in December, White terror was in full swing in the Donbas. In Iasynivka, for example, the Kaledin bands dissolved the workers' Soviet, tore up Red banners, broke the furniture, murdered twenty workers, and dumped their bodies into cesspools

Bolsheviks' Dilemma: Class, Culture, and Politics in the Early Soviet Years," *Slavic Review*, 47:4 (Winter 1988), p. 600.

[134]Diane P. Koenker, "Urbanization and Deurbanization in the Russian Revolution and Civil War," in Koenker, Rosenberg, and Suny, *Party, State, and Society in the Russian Civil War*, p. 99.

[135]DADO, f. 305, op. 1, spr. 6, ark. 29–29zv.

[136]*Gornozavodskoe delo*, 1917, nos. 40–42, p. 16427.

[137]Meller and Pankratova, *Rabochee dvizhenie*, pp. 229–35. See also *Bor'ba za vlast' Sovetov Donbassa*, p. 143, and P. V. Volobuev, *Proletariat i burzhuaziia Rossii v 1917 godu* (Moscow, 1964), pp. 248, 256–61.

[138]DADO, f. 305, op. 1, spr. 6, ark. 47.

[139]GARF, f. 1255, op. 1, d. 56, ll. 136–38, and RTsKhIDNI, f. 71, op. 33, d. 241, l. 5.

Figure 3.2. The bodies of 118 workers killed at Iasynivka and Makiivka by the Kaledin men on 31 December 1917. From TsDKFFA, od. zb. 2-28891.

and dung. In Makiivka, in revenge for armed resistance, the Kaledin forces plucked out the eyes of arrested workers and cut their throats. Workers who came up from the underground were chopped up and shot, while others were thrown alive down mine shafts. Altogether, 118 miners (including 44 Austrian POWs) were shot in Iasynivka and Makiivka.[140] In Ienakiieve, an anti-Soviet raid resulted in the execution of all the workers caught.[141] In January 1918, all Red Guard commanders congregating in Debal'tseve were caught and shot by the men of the Don Cossack Captain Chernetsov.[142] Elsewhere White officers showed up at mines, rounded up all the workers, and exiled them to places unknown; managers evicted the families of arrested workers from their flats.[143] In the surrounding villages, the White officers flogged peasants and raped women.[144]

Red terror was likewise brutal. Officers, cadets, and other anti-Soviet

[140]Vishniakov, "V bor'be za diktaturu," pp. 228, 230–31, and *5-letnii obzor*, pp. 38–39. See also T. Kharechko, "Bor'ba za Oktiabr' v Donbasse. Organizatsiia biuro revkomov i Tsentroshtaba v Donbasse," *Letopis' revoliutsii*, 1927, nos. 5–6, pp. 141–42.

[141]E. Kholmskaia, "Iz istorii bor'by v Donbasse v oktiabr'skie dni," *Letopis' revoliutsii*, 1922, no. 1, pp. 55–56.

[142]Gregory P. Tschebotarioff, *Russia, My Native Land* (New York, 1964), pp. 147–49.

[143]*Donetskii proletarii* (Kharkiv), 13 (26) December 1917.

[144]I. Nikolaenko, "Grazhdanskaia voina v Luganske," *Litopys' revoliutsii*, 1928, no. 1, p. 202.

forces were arrested and shot, and their bodies displayed in public.[145] Sometimes, the Reds selected "nonproletarian" people on the basis of outlook (or
on the basis of whether one's hands had calluses or not) and summarily executed them.[146] In the eastern Donbas, Red Guards arrested and brutally executed many clergymen, one of whom was found later with his sexual organ
cut off.[147] On 7 January 1918 the Red Guards arrested the director of the
Berestovo-Bogodukhovska coalfield, Engineer Porakov, and a cadet (son of
an employee) for alleged cooperation with the Whites. On the same day, the
court sentenced them to be shot and executed them.[148] Managers, engineers,
foremen, and other specialists suspected of sabotage were subjected to harsh
treatment.[149] On 7 January 1918, for example, a riot by hungry colliers in the
Nikolai coalfield resulted in the murder of a foreman, the only remaining member of the administration.[150] The Bolsheviks, according to some observers,
were given to drinking and to looting not only rich estates but peasants' huts
in their class war.[151]

To complicate matters, terror was not committed just by the Reds and
Whites. In the Donbas, as in much of Ukraine, numerous armed bands of
unknown or vague ideological persuasion were soon to take advantage of civil
war and plunder the helpless population. In Iuzivka, for example, shortly before it was occupied by the Germans and Austrians, the Bolsheviks fled, and
power moved into the hands of anarchists. They terrorized the population and
engaged in "the most extensive and unrestrained robbery."[152]

While the steppe did not provide as good a hideout as the green forests
did for the peasants in the north and in the south, it did allow the Cossacks
to retreat far across the open and inaccessible parts of the Don steppe, "as far
away from railroads as possible, where the Red Guards would have difficulty
in following us."[153]

---

[145]See P. V. Kovalev, *Sostoianie Donetskogo Basseina v oktiabre–ianvare mesiatsakh 1917/18
g.* ([Moscow?], [1918]), p. 3.

[146]VMA, box 111, folder 5 (Akt razsledovaniia po delam o zlodeiianiakh bol'shevikov . . .), and
James E. Mace and Leonid Heretz, eds., *Oral History Project of the Commission on the Ukrainian
Famine*, 3 vols. (Washington, D.C., 1990), 2:1156.

[147]VMA, box 111, folder 9 (Soobshchenie o goneniiakh bol'shevikov . . .). For more cases,
see A. A. Valentinov, comp., *Chernaia kniga* (Paris, 1925), p. 38. For Bolshevik atrocities in the
Don, see also G. Ianov, "Don pod bol'shevikami vesnoi 1918 goda i vozstanie stanits na Donu,"
Donskaia letopis' (Belgrade), 1924, no. 3, p. 17.

[148]DADO, f. 306, op. 1, spr. 32, ark. 3zv. See also Terekhov, *Tak nachalas' bor'ba*, p. 84.

[149]Kovalev, *Sostoianie Donetskogo Basseina*, p. 3, and P. Kazimirchuk, "Revoliutsionnoe
dvizhenie," 1923, no. 3, p. 65, and 1923, no. 4, p. 126.

[150]Kovalev, *Sostoianie Donetskogo Basseina*, p. 4.

[151]*Bol'shevistskie organizatsii Ukrainy*, pp. 618, 622–23, and 631, and VMA, box 111, folder 5
(Akt rassledovaniia).

[152]*Gornozavodskoe delo*, 1918, nos. 5–6, p. 16535.

[153]Tschebotarioff, *Russia*, pp. 170, 208, and 250–51. Those peasant detachments in the north
and the south were called "Greens." For the most famous Greens (the Antonov movement), see

After the October Revolution in Petrograd the Donbas fell under crossfire from Novocherkassk and Kiev. Kiev became the center of the Ukrainian independence movement, represented by the Central Rada, while Novocherkassk, the Don capital, assumed the role of the capital of counterrevolution, or Russian Vendée.[154]

The Don provided the best hope for counterrevolution, and Novocherkassk (and Ekaterinodar, the capital of the Kuban Cossacks) attracted many anti-Bolshevik forces, who sought political refuge and a new basis for political struggle, in Cossack lands. These included prominent generals such as M. V. Alekseev, A. I. Denikin, and A. S. Lukomskii, Kadet leaders such as P. N. Miliukov, V. A. Stepanov, A. I. Shingarev, and P. B. Struve, the Octoberist M. V. Rodzianko, and the former SR terrorist and Kerensky's aide B. V. Savinkov.[155] Some Donbas industrialists, including A. A. Svitsyn, the director of the New Russian Company of Iuzivka, also fled to Novocherkassk and Ekaterinodar.[156] They were often followed by intellectuals such as professors and Academicians, and specialists such as engineers and technicians who sought safety and employment in anti-Bolshevik territory.[157] It was in the Don that in December 1917 the Volunteer Army, the most powerful anti-Bolshevik armed force in the civil war, was formed.

Kiev's nationalism prompted the cession of the Donbas from Ukraine. To counter the Kiev-based Central Rada, which declared the independence of Ukraine in January 1918,[158] in February 1918 the more industrialized eastern part of Ukraine and the industrial area of the Don formed the Donets'k-Kryvyi Rih Soviet Republic, with Kharkiv as its capital.[159] How much support the

Oliver Radkey, *The Unknown Civil War in Soviet Russia: A Study of the Green Movement in the Tambov Region, 1920–1921* (Hoover Institution Press, 1976).

[154] The best work on this is Holquist, "A Russian Vendee."

[155] William G. Rosenberg, *Liberals in the Russian Revolution: The Constitutional Democratic Party, 1917–1921* (Princeton University Press, 1974), pp. 308 and 311, and Kenez, *Civil War in South Russia, 1918*, p. 74. See also Richard Pipes, *Struve: Liberal on the Right, 1905–1944* (Harvard University Press, 1980), pp. 246–67. See also Anna Prosyk, *Russian Nationalism and Ukraine: The Nationality Policy of the Volunteer Army during the Civil War* (Edmonton, Canada, 1995), p. 39.

[156] Manzhosov, "Predstavnyts'ki orhanizatsii," p. 83.

[157] See, for example, S. Timoshenko (a metal specialist who later emigrated and became a professor at Stanford University), *Vospominaniia* (Paris, 1963), pp. 170–83.

[158] For the Ukrainian revolution, see Pavlo Khrystiuk, *Zamitky i materiialy do istorii ukrains'koi revoliutsii. 1917–1920 rr.*, 4 vols. (Vienna, 1921–22); John S. Reshetar Jr., *The Ukrainian Revolution, 1917–1920: A Study in Nationalism* (Princeton University Press, 1952); Taras Hunczak, ed., *The Ukraine, 1917–1921: A Study in Revolution* (Harvard University Press, 1977); and Richard Pipes, *The Formation of the Soviet Union: Communism and Nationalism, 1917–1923* (Harvard University Press, 1954).

[159] Evgeniia Bosh, *God bor'by. Bor'ba za vlast' na Ukraine s aprelia 1917 g. do nemetskoi okkupatsii* (Moscow and Leningrad, 1925), p. 108, and "K materialam o Donetsko-Krivorozhskoi respublike," *Litopys revoliutsii*, 1928, no. 3. For the uneasy relationship between the Donbas and

new republic received from the population is difficult to tell. There were few representatives from the Donbas per se, and none from its miners (because, according to one account, "the majority of the Donbas colliers," whose "political level" was very low, simply were "not up to [even] the provincial level of work").[160] This suggests that it was a bureaucratic creation. Even V. I. Lenin opposed the formation of the republic on the grounds that it would split the Ukrainian front.[161] The republic hoped that by declaring independence from Ukraine it would be saved from occupation by the German armed forces, which, according to the Brest-Litovsk treaty concluded with Ukraine, came to occupy Ukraine. (For similar reasons a Don Soviet Republic was also formed at that time.) They hoped in vain: much of the Donbas was occupied by late April and early May 1918, and the republic evaporated.

Lenin's disapproval, however, had a long-standing impact on the territorial demarcation of Ukraine: Moscow acknowledged that much of the Donbas, including the Russophone industrial towns and settlements, belonged to Ukraine.

The Occupation

The occupation of the Donbas by German and Austrian troops and the Skoropads'kyi coup d'etat in April 1918 (which toppled the socialist-oriented Ukrainian Central Rada) helped to restore the old regime to the mines and factories. Those managers who had fled returned to recover their mines, and those who had stayed reasserted their authority. The triumphant former masters sent their regards and devotion to Pavlo Petrovych Skoropads'kyi, the hetman of Ukraine. The president of the Association of Southern Coal and Steel Producers, N. F. von Ditmar, even addressed him with the grandiose title *Iasnovel'mozhnyi Pan Hetman*, His Highness Hetman.[162] The managers soon called for a thorough review of all labor legislation enacted under the Provisional and the Soviet Governments.[163] Thus, working hours were increased, wages cut, the unions ignored or closed, and strikes virtually outlawed.[164]

Ukraine, see Mykola Skrypnyk, "Donbas i Ukraina," in *Statti i promovy z natsional'noho pytannia* (Munich, 1974), pp. 9–18.

[160]M. Ostrogorskii, "Istoriia odnoi nepravdy," *Litopys revoliutsii*, 1928, no. 2, p. 338.

[161]V. I. Lenin, *Polnoe sobranie sochinenii*, vol. 50 (Moscow, 1965), p. 50. For Trotsky's opposition to Donbas separatism, see *The Trotsky Papers, 1917–1922*, ed. and annotated by Jan M. Meijer, vol. 1 (The Hague, 1964), p. 500 (doc. 267).

[162]*Gornozavodskoe delo*, 1918, nos. 7–8 (31 June), pp. 16554–55 (18 May speech by von Ditmar).

[163]Ibid., pp. 16574–75.

[164]See B. Kolesnikov, *Professional'noe dvizhenie i kontr-revoliutsiia. Ocherki iz istorii professional'nogo dvizheniia na Ukraine* (Kharkiv, 1923), pp. 46–50. See also the case of Adam Svitsyn, director of the New Russian Company, in *Gornotrud*, 1919, no. 2, p. 9.

Figure 3.3. A group of German officers with the administration of Iuzivka's metallurgical factory, 1918. From Donets'kyi kraieznavchyi muzei.

The restoration of the old regime meant not just the denationalization of nationalized industry[165] but also terror. In Nesvetai in the Don, for example, forty-five miners were caught and executed by the Germans on the first day of the fight, 18 May 1918.[166] In Aleksandrovsk-Grushevskii, colliers were executed en masse or dropped down the mine shafts.[167] In this mining town, the site of the future Shakhty affair, as many as eight thousand to ten thousand workers were shot in the civil war.[168]

It was symbolic of the restoration that savage corporal punishment was widely reintroduced by anti-Bolshevik forces, including former factory and mine owners.[169] In Iuzivka, for example, forty politically suspect workers were subjected by Skoropads'kyi's men to twenty-five or more blows by a ram-

[165] For the nationalization of Donbas coalfields, see I. Sh. Chernomaz, *Bor'ba rabochego klassa Ukrainy za kontrol' nad proizvodstvom (mart 1917–mart 1918 gg.)* (Kharkiv, 1958), p. 159.

[166] L. V. Karasev, *Shakhterskaia letopis'. Iz istorii shakhty im. Lenina* (Rostov, 1960), p. 37.

[167] I. Borisenko, *Sovetskie respubliki na Severnom Kavkaze v 1918 godu*, vol. 1 (Rostov, 1930), p. 103.

[168] Kh. Rakovskii, *Donbas (iz materialov o Donetskom basseine i Donetskoi gub.)* (Kharkiv, 1921), pp. 12–13 and 22.

[169] Manzhosov, "Predstavnyts'ki orhanizatsii," p. 84.

Figure 3.4. Red Guards after battles near Morozovs'ka railroad station, 1918 or 1919. The left banner reads: "Proletarians of all countries, unite! Long live freedom, fraternity, equality. Long live . . . " From TsDKFFA, od. zb. 0-10951.

rod; one of them died from this punishment.[170] Striking colliers in Horlivka were declared traitors and flogged to death.[171] Women, too, were subjected to flogging.[172] Yet terror was often met with terror. Here and there, anti-Bolsheviks disappeared one by one without trace or were found murdered.[173]

The old regime was also restored in the countryside. Peasants were flogged by German troops and Skoropads'kyi's men for having taken the lands and estates of former nobles.[174] The German colonists, who had suffered much during World War I and were suffering from the new regime's policy because of their relatively large landholdings, actively collaborated with the German forces.[175] Greeks, who like Germans, tended to have larger landholdings and

[170] *5-letnii obzor*, p. 48. For the flogging practice, see Lev Liberman, *V ugol'nom tsarstve. Ocherki uslovii truda, byta i razvitiia promyshlennosti v Donetskom basseine*, 3rd ed. (Moscow, 1924), p. 153.

[171] Khrystiuk, *Zamitky i materialy*, 3:46.

[172] See, for example, Kazimirchuk, "Revoliutsionnoe dvizhenie," p. 123 (1923, no. 4).

[173] GARF, f. 6870, op. 1, d. 150, l. 13.

[174] G. A. Kolos, *Zametki o podpol'i i vooruzhennoi bor'be 1918–1919 g*. (Dnipropetrovs'k, 1927), p. 9, and Volodymyr Sosiura, "Tretia rota," *Kyiv*, 1988, no. 1, pp. 109 and 114, and no. 2, p. 76. However, the flogging was not the monopoly of the Whites. Peasant rebels against grain requisitioning were mercilessly flogged by the Bolsheviks, regardless of their sexes; for a case in Kaluga, see *The Life of a Chemist*, p. 273. Makhno often flogged his own men. See Natal'ia Sukhogorskaia, "Vospominaniia o makhnovshchine," *Kandal'nyi zvon* (Odessa), no. 6 (1927), p. 39.

[175] See, for example, *Mizhnatsional'ni vidnosyny na pivdni Ukraini*, pt. 3 (Zaporizhzhia, 1993),

to be more prosperous than Ukrainian and Russian peasants, were likewise said to be no friends of the Soviet government.[176]

The violence and brutality of the political revenge frightened even the managers who feared that the workers would flee the mines en masse.[177] Their fear was justified: numerous colliers deserted the mines to avoid the famine and fighting.[178] Donbas miners "now were enrolled in the Red Army, now left the coalfields retreating with the Soviet Government, now went to the Kuban or other grain-producing areas to escape famine, now returned to their native villages, now went back to the coalfields." The population movement was such that it was described as a "great migration of peoples."[179] According to one account, the number of Donbas miners thus declined progressively from 215,000 in March 1918 to 78,239 in October 1918, a 64 percent drop in seven months.[180] Coal production accordingly plummeted from 24,836 to 8,910 thousand tons from 1917 to 1918.[181]

The dire shortage of labor led the desperate managers to round up recalcitrant workers by force from their flats and barracks.[182] Yet they often did not pay wages. Strikes erupted everywhere. In the Sofievka coalfield, for example, on 24 September 1918 a spontaneous strike took place over payment of August wages. On that day, the trade union under Menshevik leadership managed to convince the strikers to end their action, but the following day the strike resumed. The administration promised to pay by 28 September, and the union's appeal ended the strike. The promise was not kept, however, and the colliers struck anew.[183] "All during the summer of 1918 spontaneous strikes remained a mass phenomenon."[184] To the surprise of the Bolsheviks, in spite of the strike waves and the material hardships under which the Donbas colliers lived, the restored "capitalist" regime managed to increase the productivity of labor.[185]

---

p. 176. During World War I the ethnic Germans were often physically assaulted by local (Russian and Ukrainian) peasants for being German. In 1915 the government confiscated more than three million desiatinas (1 desiatina = 2.7 acres) of land from the ethnic German citizens of the empire. See Hritsenko, "Selians'kyi rukh," pp. 81–82, and Kir'ianov, "Krest'ianstvo stepnoi Ukrainy," pp. 246 and 249.

[176] V. N. Nikol'skyi, "Natsional'nye problemy 20-kh godov i ikh reshenie," *Novye stranitsy v istorii Donbassa. Stat'i*, vol. 2 (Donets'k, 1992), p. 54.

[177] *Gornozavodskoe delo*, 1918, nos. 5–6 (15 May), p. 16524.

[178] See, for example, *Donetskii proletarii* (Kharkiv), 23 March 1918, and *Protokoly I-go delegatskago oblastnogo s"ezda*, p. 47.

[179] *5-letnii obzor*, pp. 9–10.

[180] E. M. Skliarenko, *Robitnychyi klas Ukrainy v roki hromadians'koi viiny (1918–1920 rr.). Narysy* (Kiev, 1960), p. 24.

[181] G. D. Bakulev, *Razvitie ugol'noi promyshlennosti Donetskogo basseina* (Moscow, 1955), p. 662.

[182] *5-letnii obzor*, p. 47.

[183] DADO, f. 306, op. 1, spr. 25. ark. 9.

[184] Kolesnikov, *Professional'noe dvizhenie*, pp. 103–4.

[185] See the case of Iuzivka in RTsKhIDNI, f. 71, op. 35, d. 436, l. 89, and *Narodnoe khoziaistvo*,

The remaining work force, composed largely of "old" (i.e., skilled) workers with families, exerted themselves to their limits in order to feed their families. The same pattern was repeated in 1919 under the Denikin regime.[186] The bewildered Bolsheviks almost certainly wondered where the political loyalty of these Donbas workers lay.

Civil war was complicated by the intervention of capitalist powers against the new regime. They, particularly the Entente countries, still at war with Germany, wished to push Russia back into the war by toppling the Bolshevik government. They were deeply disturbed by the emergence of an openly anti-capitalist power on the world scene. The new government nationalized foreign concerns without compensation and annulled foreign debts. France, for example, which had heavily invested in the southern industrial belt in general and in the Donbas in particular, had much reason to want to regain the area.[187]

In the Crossfire: Revenge

The surrender of Germany and the end of war in the autumn of 1918 weakened the Skoropads'kyi regime in Ukraine, which had relied on the German armed forces. From late 1918 (when Skoropads'kyi was toppled by the socialist and nationalist Directory) to mid-1919 (when almost the entire Donbas fell to A. I. Denikin and his Volunteer Army), the Donbas again became a theater of savage warfare and class revenge. In Makiivka, hostilities "had broken out again not long after the departure of the Germans," and "for four long months" people lived "with the constant sound of gunfire."[188] Workers were terrorized by the Whites simply because they were workers.[189] In December 1918 in Iuzivka, for example, according to General S. V. Denisov's order, one out of every ten arrested workers was hanged. Hundreds of corpses were kept hanging for days in major streets; all others were flogged.[190] In January 1919, in Ienakiieve, Horlivka, and Shcherbynivka, more than five hundred workers were shot; others were hanged in the city centers and left on the gallows for two or three days. This was repeated each time the Whites came.[191] In Ukraine captured

[186] *Oktiabr' i gorniaki* (Moscow, 1927), pp. 49–50.

[187] Michael Jabara Carley, *Revolution and Intervention: The French Government and the Russian Civil War, 1917–1919* (McGill-Queen's University Press, 1983), p. 133.

[188] Patrick A. Croghan, *The Peasant from Makeyevka: Biography of Bishop Pius Neveu, A.A.* (Worcester, Mass., 1982), p. 41.

[189] See *Robitnychyi kontrol' i natsionalizatsiia promyslovosti na Ukraini*, p. 495.

[190] *Pravda*, 4 December 1918, and I. Lukomskaia, "Proletariat Donbassa i realizatsiia Stalin-skogo plana razgroma Denikina," *Istorik-marksist*, 1940, I (77), p. 106. See also GARF, f. 6870, op. I, d. 150, l. 13, and Kolos, *Zametki o podpol'i*, p. 20, where the order was "to hang all arrested workers in the main streets and not to remove them for three days."

[191] *Gornotrud*, 1919, no. I (10 April), p. 20.

Reds were forced to dig their own graves before being shot. A popular song from that time runs:

> A young [White] general went up to them:
> – Now, I hope that you'll understand:
> You have asked for land, I'll give you land,
> But find freedom [*voliu*] in heaven![192]

Many workers managed to flee with the retreating Reds, fearing White terror. In April 1919, for example, forty thousand workers (obviously with their families) left Iuzivka with the Red Army soldiers.[193] Those who stayed were subjected to savage terror. They were often recruited at gunpoint for the Volunteer Army. Resistors to call-ups were flogged severely.[194] In May 1919 the divisions of the Cossack General A. G. Shkuro captured "many prisoners – Reds and Makhnovites" in Iuzivka and hanged all the arrested Communists.[195]

With Denikin, former managers returned again. This time they criticized the Ukrainian nationalists, Skoropads'kyi and Symon Petliura (the leader of the Directory), with whom they had opportunistically collaborated. Only with the Volunteer Army and its leader General Denikin did they declare, "we have that national power . . . to revive and create a Single and Great Russia."[196] In Iuzivka the former director of the New Russian Company, Adam Svitsyn, came back with the Volunteer Army and restored the pre-February regime.[197] As in 1918, public flogging was widely practiced. Often the victims were subjected to this pre-1905 form of corporal punishment in markets and town squares for everyone to see.[198] The Whites used corporal punishment because they believed that the miners were an "extremely embittered and immoral element with rude instincts and without the slightest value for their own or anyone else's life."[199] As in previous times, such savage treatment embittered workers. When Aleksandr Nekrasov, for example, was indicted at the famous Shakhty trial of 1928, a worker named V. P. Saksonov wrote to the prosecutor that in 1919 Nekrasov worked at the Paramonov mines under the Whites, beating and

---

[192]Moris Simashko, "Pisanie po Bondariu," *Literaturnaia gazeta*, 1 June 1988.

[193]V. A. Antonov-Ovseenko, *Zapiski o grazhdanskoi voine*, vol. 4 (Moscow and Leningrad, 1933), p. 63. See also Zaitsev, "Oktiabr' v Iuzovke," p. 630.

[194]A. V. Turkul, *Drozdovtsy v ogne. Zhivye razskazy i materialy obrabotal Ivan Lukash* (Belgrade, 1937), p. 71.

[195]A. G. Shkuro, *Zapiski belogo partizana* (Moscow, 1991), p. 125.

[196]*Gornozavodskoe delo*, 1919, nos. 1–2 (5 September), p. 16595 (editorial written by A. I. Fenin. The president of the Association of the Southern Coal and Steel Producers, von Ditmar, died from typhus on 5 January 1919).

[197]*Gornotrud*, 1919, no. 2, p. 9, and Kolesnikov, *Professional'noe dvizhenie*, p. 172.

[198]*Bor'ba za vlast' Sovetov na Donu*, p. 423.

[199]See the report in VMA, box 41, folder 10 ("Svodka").

insulting workers. Because of him, thirteen arrested workers were flogged to death.[200]

This time around the former factory and mineowners were said to be concerned not so much with increasing their profits as with getting revenge.[201] The workers were ruthlessly exploited, in any case, and deaths from starvation and epidemics were "not rare in Ienakiieve, Kadiivka and other districts."[202] Captured Red Army soldiers who were lucky enough not to be shot or hanged were used as slave labor. At the New Russian Company of Iuzivka, for example, where 1,406 soldiers worked in September 1919, every day ten to sixteen bodies had to be buried. By December only 458 of the 1,406 Reds remained alive.[203] In Aleksandrovsk-Grushevskii, half of the population was sick with typhus. No medical help was given, nor were patients isolated, and the epidemic spread uncontrollably. Mortality reached 20 percent, hitting hardest the thirty-five- to fifty-year age group.[204] Here and there desperate wildcat strikes occurred.[205] Yet, as in 1914–1917, strikers were threatened with, and punished by mobilization to the front with the result that the strike movement was more limited under Denikin than under Skoropads'kyi.[206] Anti-White armed insurrections, too, were organized, but they were brutally suppressed.[207]

The Whites justified their terror as revenge. Colonel Drozdovskii, who operated in the Don and Kuban area, for example declared that "we live in a terrible time, when man is becoming an animal. These unbridled hooligans understand only one law: an eye for an eye, a tooth for a tooth. But I would propose two eyes for one, and all teeth for one."[208]

Red terror was as savage as White terror. This was particularly the case in the Cossack area of the eastern Donbas. The Reds looted Cossack settlements (*stanitsy*), captured local residents, sent them to Luhans'k, and executed them. The executions involved the cutting off of ears and noses, the gouging out of

---

[200]GARF, f. 9474, op. 7, d. 259, l. 110.
[201]Kolesnikov, *Professional'noe dvizhenie*, p. 172. More generally, see M. Mal't, "Denikinshchina i rabochie," *Proletarskaia revoliutsiia*, 1924, no. 5.
[202]*Gornotrud*, 1919, no. 3 (25 September 1919), p. 7. See also TsDIA, f. 2161, op. 1, spr. 279, ark. 91.
[203]Manzhosov, "Predstavnyts'ki orhanizatsii," p. 86.
[204]A. Nebotov, *Boevye gody. Proletarskii Donbass v bor'be za Sovetskuiu vlast' (1919–1920 gg.)* (Stalino, 1959), p. 39.
[205]Note, for example, the Makiivka case in *Professional'noe dvizhenie*, no. 40 (5 December 1919), p. 3, and VMA, box 28, folder 4 (Obzor o nastroenii . . .).
[206]Kolesnikov, *Professional'noe dvizhenie*, p. 308.
[207]L. A. Pavlova, "Rabochie Donbassa v usloviiakh Denikinskogo voennoi diktatury (po materialam TsGASA)" (unpublished paper, Russian State Humanities University, 1992), pp. 75, 76, and 78.
[208]Quoted in Viktor G. Bortnevskii, "White Administration and White Terror (The Denikin Period)," *Russian Review*, 52:3 (July 1993), p. 357.

Figure 3.5. Burial of colliers in Iuzivka, killed in action by the Denikin army, 1919. From TsDKFFA, od. zb. 0-53773.

Figure 3.6. Bodies of prisoners, poisoned by the Denikin army before retreating from the city of Artemivs'k (Bakhmut), 1919; the bodies were also mutilated and their lower parts left exposed. From TsDKFFA, od. zb. 0-8596.

eyes, and dismemberment.[209] In Luhans'k, the Cheka (Soviet secret police) killed all the ex-officers found in the town.[210] The engineers and technicians were battered by the workers. When the Whites retreated, workers would attack engineers and technicians, even those sympathetic with the Soviet government, rationalizing that the time for revenge had come.[211] Many tragic deaths resulted.[212] Nor did the Soviet government trust the specialists as a whole, many of whom had cast their lot with the Whites.[213] In December 1919, half of the mining specialists fled the Donbas with the defeated Whites.[214]

In Kamensk, east of Luhans'k, "there were always a lot of corpses lying in the streets for quite a few days before they were removed." A witness recounted the following horror story:

[209]VMA, box 111, folder 8 (Akt razsledovaniia . . .).

[210]Robert Argenbright, "Red Tsaritsyn: Precursor of Stalinist Terror," *Revolutionary Russia*, 4:2 (December 1991), p. 171. Luhans'k provided some of the important Cheka members in Tsaritsyn where Stalin used them to apply extensive terror against the Whites and his own opponents.

[211]*Protokoly III-go oblastnogo delegatskogo s"ezda professional'nogo soiuza "Gornotrud" Donetskogo Basseina, Krivorozhskogo i Solianogo raionov, 26 aprelia–6 maia 1919 g.* (Kharkiv, 1919), p. 67.

[212]For concrete cases, see V. A. Manzhosov, "Oktiabr' 1917 goda i tekhnicheskaia intelligentsiia Donbassa," in *Novye stranitsy v istorii Donbassa. Stat'i*, vol. 1 (Donets'k, 1992), p. 110.

[213]*Narodnoe khoziaistvo*, 1919, no. 5, p. 29.

[214]*Ekonomicheskaia zhizn'*, 25 February 1920.

One day the rebellious Red Cossacks with the Red Guard miners pulled out the local governor – the ataman – from his house and slashed him with sabres in the street, with several captured White officers. Colonel "Bloodsucker" [who used to beat his batmen] was amongst them. The officers died hard. One of them, a handsome, tall, strong man with black hair and a haughty face, tried to cover his head with his arms, but his wrists were slashed in two. Lying with his face on the ground the officer screamed, moving his arms with the severed wrists as if he was swimming in the mixture of his blood and the road's dust. The ataman was sitting with his back supported by the leaning fence of a garden in front of his house. He pressed his large hands with outstretched thick fingers to his slashed chest as if he would prevent his soul from leaving his mutilated body. His eyes in his pale face with the thick moustache were wide open. Tears were running from them like streams, and dripping from his moustache. Colonel "Bloodsucker's" face was a mass of bloody flesh, his mouth had been slashed by a slanting stroke and it produced the impression of a horrible smile. One of the Cossacks swore, "so you are smiling, son of a bitch" and brutally struck him with the butt end of his rifle. After this blow, the colonel began to snore like a horse.

"Finish them off," cried one of the crowd.

The reply came: "Shut up, you dirty dog! Do you want to get the same punishment? They will cough until they have coughed out all the blood they drank from us. Understand?"[215]

When the Whites returned, they captured about two hundred Red Cossacks and Red Guard miners. Some died soon "because their genitals were gradually screwed with wire to compel them to give up their leaders." The Whites shot every fifth man from the captured Reds. The executions attracted a crowd:

The common grave was already dug by the condemned men themselves. It was long like a trench but not very wide or deep. After the first layer of soil there was bright yellow clay, and a heap of it rested on the other side of the grave. It was sticky and heavy after the rain, and here and there was a trickle of yellow water running down into the grave.

There was unusual silence only broken by discharges from the rifles of the firing squad. It seemed as though both the executioners and the condemned were obliged to carry out some dirty and tiresome work and hurried to finish it as soon as possible. When their turn came, each condemned man quickly undressed, as soldiers do, and having put their folded clothes aside walked in their worn-out dirty underwear to their last resting place, trying not to step into the cold rain-pools with their bare feet. At the edge of the grave some of them were whispering and nobody knew whether it was their last oath or their last prayer. Some crossed themselves with the orthodox cross, then all quickly disappeared into the grave.[216]

[215]Borodin, *One Man in His Time*, p. 19.
[216]Ibid., p. 20.

Others were flogged "with the thick metal rods which were used for cleaning rifles. After a few blows of the rods the backs of the scourged men were like chopped meat and at the end of the beating each of the punished men was carried away from the bench either unconscious or dead."[217]

Friends and Foes

The Donbas miners were no blind followers of the Reds. In May 1919 in Iuzivka, for example, before the Bolsheviks marched to the city, workers gathered and adopted a resolution that if the Bolsheviks showed disrespect for the church and clergy, they would stage an uprising. The resolution was handed to the Bolsheviks and the church and clergy were saved.[218]

The mass movements of Ukrainian nationalism seem to have largely bypassed the Donbas. It is not that the nationalist groups had little support. As the elections to the two constituent assemblies demonstrated, they had considerable popular support, especially among the peasants, and people like the poet Volodymyr Sosiura participated in the movements as recruits.[219] Yet the nationalists hardly succeeded in organizing their supporters. The peasants would stage an uprising against their enemies and go back home once the fight was over.[220] In the Donbas, according to a testimony by a Ukrainian resident, the names of the Central Rada and Skoropads'kyi were not spoken of or even mentioned.[221] Peasant aspirations for land and freedom were stronger than the appeal of Ukrainian nationalism, a creation of intellectuals. Popular aspirations were manifested largely in the form of armed movements of warlords against Reds, Whites, Germans, Skoropads'kyi, and Petliura. These movements were modern-day *haidamatstvo* (steppe fighters' rebellion), which had been glorified for centuries in Ukraine and in the steppe in particular for their resistance to "every would-be conqueror."[222] The warlords, like their predecessors, the Cossacks, acted like mercenaries, allying with this or that camp, depending on the situation, and in the process perpetrated as much terror as did the Reds and Whites.[223]

---

[217] Ibid., p. 21.

[218] Valentinov, *Chernaia kniga*, p. 42.

[219] See Sosiura, "Tretia rota."

[220] Maksimenko, "Iz istorii partizanskoi bor'by v Donbasse i Ekaterinoslavshchine v 1918–19 godu," *Letopis' revoliutsii*, 1925, no. 4, p. 163.

[221] Mace and Heretz, *Oral History Project*, 1:35.

[222] Arthur E. Adams, *Bolsheviks in the Ukraine: The Second Campaign, 1918–1919* (Yale University Press, 1963), p. 234. See also his "The Awakening of the Ukraine," in Donald W. Treadgold, ed., *The Development of the USSR: An Exchange of Views* (University of Washington Press, 1964).

[223] Adams's *Bolsheviks in the Ukraine* has much information on these various brigands. See also his "The Great Ukrainian Jacquerie," in Hunczak, *The Ukraine*.

The most notable of these was the Makhno movement. Whether or not its followers were anarchists is less important than the fact that they supported their leaders in their fight against all outsiders. Cossack traditions of independence and freedom shaped the movement.[224] The following proclamation attributed to Makhno attracted many followers:

> Down with all authority . . . so that we can have what we want. Kill the Jews who bleed us. Kill the generals who wish to establish what they call law and order. Kill the landowners who keep us from our own, and then kill all Communists who would make us share with the towns. When we've killed the lot we'll divide the land, and then we will dictate to the towns what they must give us, and we can *make promises* as to what we will give them in exchange.[225]

The Soviet grain requisition detachments became the favorite targets of terror. "Hundreds and thousands of them" were murdered by peasants and Makhnovites.[226] (So were Volunteer Army soldiers who often looted towns and villages.) Sometimes the skin was torn from the victims still alive.[227] When chased, the Makhnovites were given refuge by peasants who saw a savior in the Russophone Ukrainian Makhno.[228] Makhno had some followers among the workers as well.[229] His popularity, according to contemporary observers, was such that even some Bolshevik party organizations, in Hryshyne and Iuzivka, for example, were "contaminated with the Makhno movement."[230] For other contemporaries, it was simply unclear whom Makhno was serving.[231] Many other "bandit" groups similarly captured and killed Communists. (Therefore, Red terror against Makhnovites and their sympathizers was particularly savage.)[232] According to a Ukrainian resident in the Donbas, these warlords did not rob the people and enjoyed popular support.[233]

They did, however, perpetrate anti-Jewish pogroms. So did the Whites, the Ukrainian nationalists, and the Reds. (In the Don, Kalmyks were subjected

[224]Palij, *The Anarchism of Makhno*, pp. 57–60.

[225]Quoted in John Ernest Hodgson, *With Denikin's Armies: Being a Description of the Cossack Counter-Revolution in South Russia, 1918–1920* (London, 1932), p. 118 (emphasis in the original).

[226]Viktor Prudnikov, "Ataman iz Guliai-Polia," *Vechernii Donetsk*, 7 September 1990.

[227]*Bor'ba za Oktiabr' na Artemovshchine*, pp. 370–71.

[228]DADO, f. R-1146, op. 2, spr. 26, ark. 240, and VMA, box 49, folder 14 (Obshchestvennaia i politicheskaia zhizn' . . .).

[229]See, for example, D. Kin, *Denikinshchina* (Leningrad, 1927), p. 116.

[230]*Revoliutsionnyi front* (Kharkiv), 1920, no. 5, p. 56.

[231]Mace and Heretz, *Oral History Project*, 1:206. Some peasants confused these "bandits" with the Reds. See *Ispytanie dolgom. Vospominaniia chekistov*, 3rd ed. (Donets'k, 1989), p. 27.

[232]See V. A. Savchenko and L. I. Basanets, " 'Chervonyi teror' proty makhnovtsiv i selian pivdnia Ukrainy u 1917–1920 pp.," in *Shosta Vseukrains'ka naukova konferentsiia z istorychnoho kraieznavstva (m. Luts'k, veresen'–zhoven' 1993 p.)* (Luts'k, 1993).

[233]Mace and Heretz, *Oral History Project*, 1:37 and 57.

to similar terror.)[234] The pogroms in the south during the civil war were the bloodiest in modern history. They began in 1917, continued in 1918, and reached a peak in intensity and frequency in 1919, the climax of the civil war. The pogroms were perpetrated by all sides, including the Red Army led by the Jew Leon Trotsky[235] and the soldiers of Makhno, one of whose close comrades was V. Volin (Eikhenbaum), a Jew.[236] According to a recently declassified account by Trotsky, Trotsky had resolutely declined to become the leader of the Red Army on the grounds that he was a Jew, but eventually was persuaded to do so by Lenin. In 1923 Trotsky told the party that he should not have assumed the leadership of the Red Army because, at critical moments of the civil war, the agitation of the Whites, "At the head of the Red Army stands a Jew," undermined the Red Army.[237] In any case, slogans such as "Beat the Jews and Save Russia," "Soviets, but no Jews," "Death to the Jews and Communists," and "Jews and Russians, Get Out of Ukraine" were used according to the needs of the perpetrators.[238] The estimated number of deaths in Ukraine and Belarus from 1917 to 1921 is 180,000 to 200,000.[239]

As in the previous waves of pogroms, the pogroms in the Donbas during the civil war were fewer and more limited than in the western parts of the country where there were larger and more concentrated Jewish populations. Still at least twenty-four pogroms were recorded in Luhans'k, Iuzivka, Hryshyne, Ienakiieve, and other places in the Donbas: six by the Denikin men and eighteen by "bandits" such as Makhnovites.[240]

[234]Pavlova, "Rabochie Donbassa," p. 47.

[235]See V. L. Genis, "Pervaia Konnaia armiia: za kulisami slavy," *Voprosy istorii*, 1994, no. 12; Orlando Figes, "The Red Army and Mass Mobilization during the Russian Civil War, 1918–1920," *Past and Present*, 129 (November 1990), pp. 195–96; Iu. Delevskii, "Bol'shevizm i pogromy," *Evreiskaia tribuna* (Paris), 8 (20 February 1920); and Oleh Romanchuk, "Zirka Davyda i tryzub Volodymyra na tli Kremlia," *Dzvin* (Kiev), 1991, nos. 9 and 10. Stories on the pogroms committed by Red Army men, contained in Lenin's papers, have been withheld from publication. See *Istoricheskii arkhiv* (Moscow), no. 1 (1992), p. 217.

[236]N. Gergel, "The Pogroms in the Ukraine in 1918–1921," *YIVO Annual of Jewish Social Science*, 6 (1951), and Henry Abramson, "Jewish Representation in the Independent Ukrainian Governments of 1917–1920," *Slavic Review*, 50:3 (Fall 1991), both of which have statistical data with breakdowns of pogroms by the parties that committed them. For pogroms by Makhnovites in the Donbas, see, for example, DADO, f. R-2593, op. 1, spr. 1. One of Makhno's bodyguards was a Jew. See *Zhertvy repressii* (Kiev, 1993), pp. 255–62 (L. N. Zin'kovskii-Zadova, who returned to the Soviet Union from exile in Rumania, worked for the GPU-NKVD, and was shot in 1938 as a "spy"). See also *SB* (Moscow), 1992 (probnyi nomer), pp. 24–25.

[237]"L. D. Trotskii zashchishchaetsia," *Voprosy istorii KPSS*, 1990, no. 5, p. 36.

[238]See, for example, RGVA, f. 199, op. 3, d. 900, l. 1.

[239]*Evreiskie pogromy 1918–1921* (Moscow, 1926), p. 74. See also Peter Kenez, "Pogroms and White Ideology in the Russian Civil War," in John D. Klier and Shlomo Lambroza, eds., *Pogroms: Anti-Jewish Violence in Modern Russian History* (Cambridge University Press, 1992), p. 302.

[240]*Evreiskie pogromy 1918–1921*, p. 76, and I. B. Shekhtman, *Pogromy Dobrovol'chskoi armii na Ukraine (K istorii antisemitizma na Ukraine v 1919–1920 gg.)* (Berlin, 1932), p. 385. For cases of pogroms, see also S. Pogrebnoi, "Lugansk i ego proletariat," *Letopis' revoliutsii*, 1924,

Clearly the traditional images of enemies persisted. Peter Kenez's argument that "the Jews awaited the coming of the Volunteer Army with high hopes" is arguable (the majority of the Jews were artisans and traders who were hurt by the antitrade policies of the Bolsheviks).[241] According to Henry Abramson, Zionist parties were the most popular among the Ukrainian Jews.[242] Yet Jews were killed because many Whites believed Bolshevism was a Jewish conspiracy, because they suspected Jews of sympathy with the Bolsheviks, and because they viewed the Jews as *burzhuis*, however poor they may have been in actuality.

The Bolshevik leaders and the Soviet government, partially in a move to protect the oppressed Jews and counter anti-Semitism, sought to construct new images of enemies: counterrevolutionaries of all sorts under the general rubric of class enemies, wreckers (*vrediteli*), or saboteurs. With this went "the call (and the menace) to volunteers to engage in 'espionage' work – an order issued by Piatakov, head of the Donetz Che-Ka [*sic*], and proclaiming that 'any failure of any Communist to denounce a traitor will be regarded as an offense against the Revolution, and punished with all the vigour of the laws of the present war-revolutionary period."[243] Already in 1917, "sabotage" and "saboteur" became key words in political discourse in Petrograd.[244] By 1919, these terms supplanted anti-Semitism as a catchphrase for political scapegoat:

> Formerly, during the time of the tsarist government, it was said that "Jews are to blame," but now, when our system is bad, it is said that "Saboteurs are to blame." Of course, sabotage is a criminal act, but small defects are the result of a misguided system.[245]

This construction became even more expedient politically after the civil war, when the enemies were militarily defeated (Chapter 4).

Some workers were faithful and courageous Volunteer Army soldiers. Donbas miners recruited in Horlivka, for instance, were the best of the patriotic soldiers who fought "for the sake of Russia": they were valued by the

no. 4, pp. 63–64; DADO, f. R-1146, op. 2, spr. 26, ark. 52; RGVA, f. 198, op. 3, d. 553, l. 61; and *Grazhdanskaia voina na Ukraine*, 1 (Kiev, 1967), p. 326.

[241]Kenez, "Pogroms," p. 300. See also Kenez, *Civil War in South Russia, 1919–1920*, p. 169.

[242]His lecture at the Harvard Ukrainian Research Institute on 16 March 1995.

[243]Sergey Petrovich Melgounov, *The Red Terror in Russia* (London, 1926), p. 142, citing *Kharkovskaia zvezda*, 7 June 1919. Iu. (G.) L. Piatakov did not seem to have ever been the "head of the Donets Che-Ka," however. In 1919, he did work in the Donbas area as a member of the Revolutionary-Military Council of the Thirteenth Army at the Southern Front. See V. F. Soldatenko, "H. L. Piatakov: epizody zhittia i diial'nosti na Ukraini," *Ukrains'kyi istorychnyi zhurnal*, 1989, no. 4, p. 102.

[244]See S. A. Smith, *Red Petrograd: Revolution in the Factories, 1917–1918* (Cambridge University Press, 1983), p. 167.

[245]*Vtoroi Vserossiiskii S"ezd professional'nykh soiuzov, 16–25 inavaria 1919 goda. Stenograficheskii otchet. Chast' 1-ia (plenumy)* (Moscow, 1921), p. 180.

Whites as being "worth their weight in gold."[246] Yet by the admission of the Whites, the Donbas miners as a whole were not on their side.[247] In the Donbas, workers protested White rule by cutting out the eyes in the portraits of Shkuro, Mamontov, and other generals.[248] In fact, from the very beginning the battle for the support of the workers was a lost cause for the Whites who correctly understood this and treated the workers as enemies. This contrasts sharply with the way the Whites made every effort to woo the peasantry as political allies.[249]

Certainly, the political identification of the Donbas workers was complex and problematic. Bolshevik ideology was only partially accepted by workers and peasants, which may be seen from the following observation of the French Catholic bishop, Father Neveu, in Makiivka in 1919, as recounted by his biographer:

> Four of the five Orthodox priests in Makeyevka had fled, leaving behind only one old priest who was escorted to and from his church by a band of women who were determined to ensure that no harm would come to him. On the other hand, Fr. Neveu saw many of the Red soldiers go openly into his church to pray, and, once again, he had to confess that it was not easy to understand the soul of Holy Russia.

Father Neveu further noted, perhaps optimistically:

> This [sic] poor people has [sic] always been ill-treated, distrusted, despised and exploited by their masters. Nobody has ever tried to serve them or show them any kindness. On the day when they see nuns like our Little Sisters of the Assumption working freely among the sick poor, they will be already halfway into the Catholic Church.[250]

However hard the Bolsheviks tried to "serve them or show them any kindness," the political process of 1917 discussed earlier indicated to the Bolsheviks that they were in for trouble.

Under war conditions, some societal fissures were repaired but others widened. The coercive measures of the Soviet government and the Red Army had a strong negative political impact. Like the Whites, the Red Army engaged

---

[246]Turkul, *Drozdovtsy v ogne*, p. 75. For more famous cases of workers' anti-Bolshevik fighting, see Stephen M. Berk, "The 'Class-Tragedy' of Izhevsk: Working-Class Opposition to Bolshevism in 1918," *Russian History*, 2:2 (1975). For the attack on these workers by the Bolsheviks, see *XI s"ezd RKP (b), mart–aprel' 1922 g. Stenograficheskii otchet* (Moscow, 1961), pp. 387–88 and 455.

[247]See, for example, V. E. Pavlov, comp., *Markovtsy v boiakh i pokhodakh za Rossiiu v osvobod-itel'noi voine 1917–1920 godov. Kniga vtoraia. 1919–1920 gg.* (Paris, 1964), pp. 2 and 27–28, and M. B. Shteifon, *Krizis dobrovol'chestva* (Belgrade, 1928), p. 6. For the same view by Soviet intelligence, see RGVA, f. 198, op. 3, d. 552, l. 23.

[248]Pavlova, "Rabochie Donbassa," p. 45.

[249]Kenez, *Civil War in South Russia, 1919–1920*, p. 102.

[250]Croghan, *The Peasant from Makeyevka*, pp. 42–43.

in looting, requisitioning, and murder.[251] The Red Army also forcibly recruited civilians. In May 1919, for example, "units of the 8th and 13th Armies
in the Donbas region carried out forcible mobilization at the Bakhmut coal-
mines by occupying the pits and simply rounding up at gunpoint all the miners
under the age of forty." The complaints by concerned local Soviet authorities were not accepted by Lenin for military reasons.[252] Elsewhere the Red
Army surrounded settlements and mobilized men. Such mobilizations did not
create the desired effect: some men were able to hide and others deserted
later.[253] Tartars were described as being particularly unreliable, because they
went back and forth between Red and White.[254] In May 1919 various groups
of roaming armed deserters numbered thirty thousand to forty thousand in
the Lysychans'k-Bakhmut-Kupians'k area alone, neither moving to the Soviet
north nor wishing to be enlisted in the Volunteer Army. They were reported "to
be extremely embittered against the Commissars, Communists, and Jews."[255]

The Outcome

The Donbas population underwent terrible sacrifices during the civil war. In
December 1919 a Bolshevik described "this economic center of the Soviet
Republic" as "having become a cemetery of Donbas miners and metalworkers."[256] A journal of the miners' union congratulated their members on their
brave fight:

> Among the miners there was not such deep degradation and depravity as seen
> in the ranks of other industrial workers, not excluding even the vanguard met-
> alworkers. In the Donbas [we] didn't even know what the Kirstov movement
> was. The dark, ignorant miners have come out honorably from the ordeal of
> those gloomy days. . . . With the exception of some rare instances in which
> individual workers or groups of workers showed a friendly attitude toward
> the [White] authorities, the miners as a whole, after a brief depression, were
> opposed to the Voluntary Army.[257]

[251] See, for example, VMA, box 47, folder 20 (Svodka svedenii . . . za fevral' i mart 1919 g. . . . v
Luganske).

[252] Figes, "The Red Army and Mass Mobilization," p. 190.

[253] VMA, box 47, folder 20 (Svodka svedenii o prebyvanii bol'shevikov v Bakhmutskom raione).

[254] GARF, f. 452, op. 1, d. 42, l. 11.

[255] Ibid. See also VMA, box, 47, folder 20 (Svodka svedenii po oprosu lits pribyvshikh iz Sovde-
pii). Even many Red Cossacks under S. M. Budennyi's command maintained independence and
separatism, proclaiming such slogans as "Beat the Jews, Communists, Commissars, and Save
Russia." See Genis, "Pervaia konnaia armiia, pp. 70–77.

[256] Vos'maia konferentsiia RKP(b), p. 86 (Ia. A. Iakovlev).

[257] Gornotrud, 1920, no. 1 (22 March), p. 16. The Kirstov movement was a kind of Zuba-
tovshchina (police socialism) under the Denikin rule, strong in Kiev and Odessa. For a view more
favorable of miners than of metalworkers, see also Kolesnikov, *Professional'noe dvizhenie*, p. 113.

Surprisingly, then, once the Whites were gone and the Reds came back, some eighty thousand remaining Donbas colliers, among others, found themselves decried by the Bolshevik party:

> All the best [elements] of the [Ukrainian] proletariat have gone to Russia and to the Red Army, and few have returned. The remainder are those who have families and private property: not a few have a house by the coalfields and factories and have stayed there. They are psychologically crushed. They have no work, but engage in petty speculation. This is understandable, because they want to eat, but their proletarian consciousness, which wasn't very high to begin with, has now been completely crushed.[258]

The colliers were even told that in the Donbas the working class had disintegrated into the Makhno movement and that the proletariat did not exist.[259] Some workers did join the Makhno insurrections. Yet this disparagement by the Bolshevik party was symptomatic of the troubles lying ahead, which it attributed to the "declassed proletariat."[260] The civil war had brought the Bolsheviks and the miners closer in their fight against common enemies. With the end of the war came not a peaceful but a turbulent time. In the years of economic crisis that followed the civil war, the Donbas miners resorted repeatedly to strikes, and the "great migration of peoples" could not be halted.[261]

Implicit in the reproach by the Bolsheviks, however, seemed to be the party's suspicion of the political loyalty of those who stayed on under the Whites. (Moreover, some workers were refugees from the north under the Soviet government to the Donbas under White rule. The migration of people embittered by the Bolsheviks, according to a White newspaper, "improved the mood of workers" in the coalfields.)[262] To be sure, the suspicion was not explicitly stated, but it would have been absurd for the party to assume their loyalty without reservation. It feared that the frequent change of powers, that is, the availability of political alternatives, made the population less firm in its support of the Soviet government.[263] The restoration of the old regime during the civil war distinguished the Donbas from other industrial centers in the Russian heartland. The civil war gave the Donbas workers political choices that Moscow or Petrograd workers did not have. Even though the war united the Bolsheviks and workers against their common enemies, the former remained suspicious of the latter. Those miners who remained and worked in

---

[258] *Vos'maia konferentsiia RKP(b)*, p. 104 (V. P. Zatons'kyi). For a similar criticism of Donbas colliers, see *Gornorabochii*, 1920, no. 3, p. 44.

[259] *Vos'maia konferentsiia RKP(b)*, p. 107 (D. Z. Manuil'skii).

[260] For this problem in general, see Fitzpatrick, "The Bolsheviks' Dilemma."

[261] See Chapter 4.

[262] *Poslednie novosti* (Iuzivka), no. 1 (6 December 1919).

[263] This fear is clearly seen in *Sbornik otchetov Narodnykh komissariatov USSR, Upolnomochennykh Narodnykh komissariatov RSFSR pri Sovnarkome USSR i tsentral'nykh uchrezhdenii Ukrainy* (Kharkiv, 1921), p. 23.

the Donbas were suspected of sympathy if not collaboration with the Whites and the war lords. As a Ukrainian Bolshevik leader declared in December 1919, in Ukraine, where many powers alternated, "there is deep distrust of any power."[264] The same kind of suspicion would be exhibited by the Soviet government toward people who lived under the Germans during World War II. In any case, that many workers chose to remain, and even recorded a high productivity, under the Whites was not palatable to the Bolsheviks.

The civil war experience posed a very serious conceptual and practical challenge to the Bolsheviks. If the Bolshevik party regarded as true proletarians those Moscow or Petrograd workers who held out through the civil war years and as "semiproletarians" those who fled to the countryside, then could the same criteria be applied to the Donbas colliers? Should those workers who settled in the Donbas and stayed on under the Whites and the warlords be labeled "true proletarians"? Should those migrant peasant workers who fled from the Donbas, presumably with the retreating Bolsheviks, be viewed as "semiproletarians"?

To the specific circumstance of civil war must be added the historical heritage of the steppe. In the Donbas, political alternatives were not necessarily created by the civil war, but were readily available in the traditions and myths of the Cossacks and the free steppe. As the political developments in 1917 show, the Bolsheviks came to garner an increasingly strong support among the Donbas workers. Yet the allegiance of workers was far from limited to the Bolshevik party. They were willing to resist all outside forces and fight for whatever they believed protected their freedom and dignity. The Bolshevik suspicion of the post–civil war Donbas was thus compounded by the historical legacy of the Donbas.

From the party's point of view, this lingering suspicion was counteracted by the profound enmity of workers toward the representatives of the old regime. Those workers who had stayed on under the Whites and the warlords had worked desperately to survive. Yet their enmity hardened with their bitter civil war experiences. The civil war was not just any kind of civil war, but one in which almost all major capitalist countries, including those which had invested much capital in the Donbas, intervened in support of the Whites and Ukrainian nationalists. Therefore, the supporters of the old regime appeared in the minds of workers as representatives of foreign interests. Such a view was supported by the service rendered by the anti-Soviet forces to foreign concerns that dominated the Donbas economy. In Luhans'k, when the Bolsheviks came back, few intellectuals remained, the majority having fled with the Whites. So the Bolsheviks treated the few remaining intellectuals (who may well have been

---

[264] *Vos'maia konferentsiia RKP(b)*, p. 97 (K. G. Rakovskii).

Bolshevik sympathizers) "extremely harshly."[265] Thus, even in the peacetime that followed the civil war, "specialist baiting" (*spetseedstvo*) was kept alive among the Donbas colliers.

[265] VMA, box 47, folder 20 (Dolkad o deiatel'nosti Luganskoi Chrezvychainoi Komissii . . .).

4   The New Economic Policy

THE NEW ECONOMIC POLICY was generally successful in its immediate goal of restoring an economy ruined by war, revolution, and civil war. However, the economic benefit to the Donbas in particular was far from evident. Nor was the political goal, the restoration of civil peace in the aftermath of the class war, categorically achieved in the Donbas. Peace remained precarious, and the Donbas was difficult to manage. As before, the Donbas continued to attract numerous outlawed people. Not only did the disenfranchised find refuge and work in the Donbas collieries, but the former "capitalist" enemies (mainly technical specialists) returned to restore industry, this time as nominal subordinates of new, Communist bosses. Friends and foes of the new government had to work side by side in a new political and economic order. Few people believed that the New Economic Policy (NEP) would be the final settlement of the revolution.

Precarious Peace

> When Nikolas the fool was with us,
> Bread was five kopeika,
> But then the clever Communists came,
> And there was nothing left to eat,
> No bread at any price.[1]

The outcome of the civil war was decided by and large by the beginning of 1920. However, for many Ukrainian peasants the new regime compared poorly with the old, as the preceding folk song demonstrates. Makhno's troops and

---

[1] "Iak buv u nas Mykola-durachok, / To khlib buv piatachok, / A iak priishly rozumny kommunisty, / To nicheho stalo liudiam isty, / Khliba ni za iaki hroshi ne distanesh'," in Vladimir Korolenko, "Pis'ma k Lunacharskomu," *Novyi mir*, 1988, no. 10, p. 211, a complaint by a peasant in Poltava. This Ukrainian song contains Russianisms.

other "bandits" continued to disturb the hard-won peace for a few more years.[2] Characteristically of the "wild steppe," there were many of these "bandit" groups in the Donbas: Makhno, Sabonov, Belash-Kurilenko, Foma-Kozha, Kameniuk, Zolotoi-Zub, Pogorelov, Hromov, Miliushchenko, Shkipko, Syrovatskii, Zhugin, Donchenko, Maslakov, Sychev, Zhorzh-Babitskii, to name just a few. Even in December 1921, it was reported that there was "not even a hint of the consolidation of Soviet power" in the Donbas countryside.[3] These "bandits" were said to enjoy "the full support of the peasant population."[4] In the meantime, the Red terror continued. The Donets'k province Cheka shot thirty-one people in June 1920, fifteen in the latter half of July, thirty in the latter half of August, and twenty-two in the first half of September.[5]

Conditions in 1920 also posed a formidable industrial challenge for the Soviet government: production had to be restored. Coal production had dropped by more than 80 percent from 1,751 million poods in 1916 to 338 million poods in 1919; none of the sixty-five blast furnaces that had operated to full capacity in 1913 worked at the beginning of 1920.[6] Even at the end of 1920 pig iron production was a mere 0.5 percent of the prewar level.[7] Overall, by 1921 nearly half of all the Donbas industrial plants had been closed down.[8] There was little with which to feed and clothe the Donbas population in general. By the autumn of 1919 80 percent of the horses used in the Donbas mines had either been taken by the Whites or died from lack of fodder.[9] There was no communication, telegraphic, postal, or personal, between the Donbas and Moscow; official correspondence from Moscow took several months to reach the Donbas.[10]

To increase coal production in the Donbas, the Soviet government took many harsh measures: it introduced "political departments" to tighten discipline and political control; it used Red Army soldiers as labor; and it militarized the Donbas coal-mining industry (which involved the binding of workers

[2] See O. O. Kucher, *Rozhrom zbroinoi vnutrishn'oi kontrrevoliutsii na Ukraini u 1921–1923 rr.* (Kharkiv, 1971).

[3] TsDAVO, f. 3204, op. 1, spr. 25, ark. 44zv.

[4] *Donetskii shakhter*, 1921, no. 1, p. 23.

[5] DADO, f. R-1146, op. 2, spr. 26, ark. 44, 226zv., 242zv., and 235zv.

[6] N. P. Prokopenko, "Bor'ba za vozrozhdenie ugol'nogo Donbassa v 1920 godu," *Istoricheskie zapiski*, 25 (1948), p. 25, and E. Kurdiumova, "Bol'sheviki Donbassa v bor'be za vosstanovlenie promyshlennosti v period perekhoda partii na mirnuiu rabotu (1921–1925 gg.)," *Voprosy istorii*, 1951, no. 12, p. 4.

[7] G. D. Didenko, *Rabochii klass Ukrainy v gody vosstanovleniia narodnogo khoziaistva (1921–1925)* (Kiev, 1962), p. 17.

[8] *Itogi sploshnoi podvornoi perepisi Donetskoi gubernii (ianvar'–fevral' 1923 g.). Tom pervyi. Promyshlennost' Donbassa* (Kharkiv, 1923), p. 16.

[9] Prokopenko, "Bor'ba," p. 26.

[10] *Gornorabochii*, 1920, no. 3, p. 14.

to the mines).[11] "Many [Terek] Cossacks," who had fought against the Bolsheviks during the civil war, were sent to forced labor in the Donbas mines.[12] The trade unions of the miners were taken away from the Mensheviks in 1920, and, as M. P. Tomskii, the head of trade unions, later described, the miners' unions were recreated from above.[13] Iu. (G.). L. Piatakov, the chief manager of the Donbas coal industry in 1920–21, in whose cabinet the trade-union bureau meetings were held,[14] was so dictatorial as to be described as "a conquistador among the Papuans."[15] Under his direction the unions were merged with the political departments to tighten discipline in the mines.[16]

Emma Goldman, an American anarchist who visited Kharkiv in 1920, gives an indication of the dire conditions that prevailed. She reports that an engineer who had worked in the Donbas informed her that

> In reality, the Donetz mines were in a most deplorable state. . . . The miners were herded like cattle. They received abominable rations, were almost barefoot, and were forced to work standing in water up to their ankles. As a result of such conditions very little coal was being produced. "I was one of a committee ordered to investigate the situation and report our findings," said the engineer. "Our report is far from favourable. We know that it is dangerous to relate the facts as we found them: it may land us in the Tcheka [Cheka]. But we decided that Moscow must face the facts. The system of political Commissars, general Bolshevik inefficiency, and the paralysing effect of the State machinery have made our constructive work in the Basin almost impossible. It was a dismal failure."[17]

Other accounts give a similarly dismal picture.[18] Trotsky, a man known for his harsh and authoritarian administrative style, was sympathetic to the Don-

[11]See "Iz istorii ukrainskoi trudovoi armii (obzor dokumentov i materialov) 1920 g.," *Proletarskaia revoliutsiia*, 1940, no. 3. See also V. Bazhanov, *Kamennougol'naia promyshlennost' za 1920 g. Pervaia proizvodstvennaia programma Glavnogo ugol'nogo komiteta i ee vypolnenie* (Moscow, 1920), p. 6.

[12]N. F. Bugai, "20–40-e gody: deportatsiia naseleniia s territorii evropeiskoi Rossii," *Otechestvennaia istoriia*, 1992, no. 4, p. 38. The Terek Cossacks were based in the northern Caucasus with Vladikavkaz as its capital.

[13]RTsKhIDNI, f. 17, op. 2, d. 354, l. 55.

[14]GARF, f. 7920, op. 1, d. 1, l. 29. For Piatakov in the Donbas, see Andrea Graziosi, "At the Roots of Soviet Industrial Relations and Practices. Piatakov's Donbas in 1921," *Cahiers du Monde russe*, 36:1–2 (January–June 1995).

[15]V. F. Soldatenko, "H. L. Piatakov: epizody zhittia i diial'nosti na Ukraini," *Ukrains'kyi istorychnyi zhurnal*, 1989, no. 4, p. 104. Later Piatakov was said to have fed his pet, a bear, on white bread, while the Donbas workers had to live on oil meal (*makukha*). Once his bear fled to a market where it caused "calamities," for which Piatakov had to pay dearly. *Persha Vseukrains'ka konferentsia KP(b)U. 17–21 zhovtnia 1926 roku. Sten. zvit* (Kharkiv, 1926), p. 63.

[16]See *600,000,000. Sbornik. Stat'i i materialy, vypusk II. Posviashchaetsia Velikomu Organizatoru Kommunisticheskogo Khoziaistva – X s"ezdu RKP* (Kharkiv, 1921), pp. 52–55 and 146.

[17]Emma Goldman, *My Disillusionment in Russia* (New York, 1923), p. 181.

[18]See, for example, TsDAVO, f. 2602, op. 1, spr. 2, ark. 10–11.

bas miners after a visit there in November and December 1920. He dispatched a telegram to Lenin on 19 November: "The situation in the Donbas is extremely serious. The workers are starving; there is no clothing. In spite of the revolutionary-Soviet mood of the masses strikes are flaring up here and there. One cannot help being surprised that the workers are working at all."[19]

The transition in the Donbas from the "war communism" of the civil war to the market-oriented NEP proved a very painful process both for workers and for Moscow. As Trotsky noted, strikes demanding wages, food, and clothes engulfed the Donbas.[20] Many workers could not work simply owing to the lack of shoes or clothes, or both.[21] To weaken "counterrevolution" in the countryside and to compensate for the shortage of labor, the Cheka took kulaks as hostages and forced them to work in the mines.[22] From 1920 onward, "concentration camps" were set up in the coalfields both for violators of discipline and for criminals and political prisoners.[23] Whatever peace the end of the war brought about proved precarious. It is no surprise, then, that in the recollections of Soviet citizens who grew up in the 1920s, the era is associated more with hunger, pain, and bitterness than with pleasure.[24]

Moscow gave a great deal of material assistance to the Donbas. Yet with the country as a whole in deep economic crisis, the assistance was not sufficient to ease the Donbas's hardship. In an attempt at rationalization, the authorities heaped political denunciations upon the workers, accusing them of counterrevolutionary thought. Such was the case not only of public statements but in numerous, secret reports by the Cheka. A Donets'k province Cheka report for June 1920, for example, cited food strikes in Iuzivka and elsewhere and contended that such "selfish matters" dominated the minds of workers, which only demonstrated their lack of "consciousness and political literacy."[25] Another secret Cheka report for September 1920 maintained that workers demanded only shoes, clothes, and food and that they lacked "consciousness"

---

[19]*The Trotsky Papers, 1917–1922*, ed. and annotated by Jan M. Meijer, vol. 2 (1920–22) (The Hague and Paris, 1971), pp. 360–61, and L. Trotskii, *Sochineniia*, vol. 15 (Moscow and Leningrad, 1927), p. 32. See also Trotsky's speech in *Biulleten' V Vseukrainskoi konferentsii KP(b)U*, no. 5 (Kharkiv, 1920), p. 9.

[20]For more information on strikes, see DADO, f. R-1146, op. 2, spr. 26, ark. 94, 205, 225zv; *Gornorabochii*, 1920, nos. 2–3, p. 21; and *Diktatura uglia. Sbornik. Stat'i i materialy, vypusk III. Posviashchaetsia II-mu Donetskomu s"ezdu gornorabochikh* (Kharkiv, [1921?]), pp. 88 and 167.

[21]*Narodnoe khoziaistvo*, 1921, nos. 8–9, p. 102.

[22]DADO, f. R-1146, op. 2, spr. 26, ark. 45.

[23]*Diktatura uglia*, p. 177, and *Gornorabochii*, 1921, nos. 1–3, p. 35. Until 1924 the GPU, the successor to Cheka, operated several mines in the Donbas. See *Promyshlennost' SSSR v 1924 godu. Ezhegodnik VSNKh. Otchet III s"ezdu Sovetov SSSR* (Moscow and Leningrad, 1925), pp. 4, 15, and 17.

[24]See V. A. Bykov, " . . . prostupaiut cherty pokolenii," *EKO* (Novosibirsk), 1987, no. 10, p. 60.

[25]DADO, f. R-1146, op. 2, spr. 26, ark. 26 and 42zv.

at a time when the whole country was suffering from economic devastation. The demands were the result, according to the secret police, of "suspicious persons" with anti-Soviet views who had infiltrated the working class.[26]

On the other hand, a quite different "strictly secret" (as opposed to "secret") Cheka report for December attributed workers' strikes to the actual shortage of food, clothes, and shoes, and reported on the disturbing mood of the population in general, quoting the people as complaining that "previously we were downtrodden by the *burzhui*s, and now the Soviet government exploits us . . . but the children of the *burzhui*s and the *burzhui*s themselves have crept into [Soviet] institutions and are living in clover . . . while those who fought for freedom, our fathers and brothers, died in the battle against counterrevolution, and we are starving and freezing."[27] Such candid reporting was limited even among "top secret" documents.

In any case, the question of political motivation among workers living in such circumstances was not easily understood. Concern about "suspicious persons" stemmed in part from the recognition that the Donbas had historically provided a haven for refugees and fugitives. During the civil war, many kulaks and others who had reason to flee from Bolshevik rule in various parts of the country were suspected of escaping to the Donbas.[28] Moreover, in 1917 the Donbas was a stronghold of the Socialist Revolutionaries (SRs) and the Mensheviks, and the Cheka suspected that their influence was still strong.[29] How strong these political parties still were is difficult to determine. The secret police closely monitored these and other non-Bolshevik groups. In its July 1920 report, for example, the secret police disclosed that in Iuzivka there were thirty-five Menshevik members and listed the names of all activists. In Alchevs'k there was an organization of Borot'bisty (an offshoot of the Ukrainian SRs, many of whom joined the Bolshevik party in 1920), with thirty-one members, almost all miners. In Chystiakove there were thirty-two SRs, twelve rightists and twenty leftists.[30] Many SRs and Mensheviks, according to other reports, had crept into the Bolshevik party. The Ienakiieve committee of the Bolshevik party, for example, consisted "entirely of SRs."[31] The secret police applied various measures of repression to all non-Bolshevik parties.[32] The Menshevik

---

[26] Ibid., ark. 334.

[27] Ibid., ark. 222.

[28] See, for example, GARF, f. 3984, op. 1, d. 8, l. 7.

[29] DADO, f. R-1146, op. 2, spr. 26, ark. 240, and L. N. Maimeskulov, A. I. Rogozhin, and V. V. Stashis, *Vseukrainskaia chrezvychainaia komissiia, 1918–1922* (Kharkiv, 1971), p. 173.

[30] DADO, f. R-1146, op. 2, spr. 26, ark. 42. See also RTsKhIDNI, f. 5, op. 1, d. 2617, ll. 30b and 50b.

[31] DADO, f. R-1146, op. 2, spr. 26, ark. 48.

[32] On 26 November 1920, for example, 346 prominent anarchists were arrested in the Donbas. See *Edinozhdy priniav prisiagu . . . Rasskazy o chekistakh* (Donets'k, 1990), p. 12.

party was thus driven underground, but in the Donbas its influence was felt well into the 1920s.[33]

The challenge to Bolshevik power also came from within the party itself. The so-called Democratic Centralism faction within the Ukrainian Communist Party, critical of the lack of concern among the party leadership for democratic principles, was strong enough to outvote the supporters of Moscow and Lenin at its fourth conference in March 1920.[34] Of the twenty-four delegates from the Donbas, twenty-one voted against the principle of one-man management in industry advocated by Lenin and in favor of collective management.[35] Another faction, the Workers' Opposition, which had similar concerns with democracy and the defense of workers' interests, also retained considerable influence in the Donbas in 1920–21. In February 1921, for example, the Iuzivka party organization had forty-five supporters of Lenin, eighteen of the Workers' Opposition, and seven of Democratic Centralism. Some of the strikes were organized by these dissenters.[36]

The apparent lack of political commitment among the Donbas workers exasperated all parties. Ivan Maistrenko, who was sent to the Donbas at that time by the Ukapisty (the Communist left wing of the Ukrainian Social Democrats, which was to be absorbed by the Bolsheviks in 1925), has left this impression: the Ukapisty appeared to have more support among the Donbas workers than did the Bolsheviks. Yet those workers who supported the Ukrainian Communists had no sense of nationality issues. They just wanted to see how the Ukrainian Communists would improve their lives, their thought being "Well, if nothing comes of the All Russian party (Bolsheviks), let's try the Ukrainian one."[37]

In fact, there were many signs of trouble brewing for the ruling (all-Russian) party. In Nesvetai in the eastern Donbas, the press reported worker sentiment that the party had become a closed caste and that therefore the rank-and-file workers, miners, and "honest laborers" in general were disaffected. The

[33] See Boris Dvinov, *Ot legal'nosti k podpol'iu (1921–1922), Prilozhenie: G. Kuchin-Oranskii, Zapiski* (Stanford, Calif., 1968), pp. 49, 90, 172, and 173. The writer Vladimir Korolenko, who closely observed the civil war in Poltava, noted in 1920 that, because of the mistaken policies of the Bolshevik administration, the Mensheviks strengthened their influence among the workers. See Korolenko, "Pis'ma k Lunacharskomu," p. 211.

[34] See R. Pirog, "Chetvertaia konferentsiia KP(b)U," *Pod znamenem leninizma* (Kiev), 1990, no. 2.

[35] *Deviatyi s"ezd RKP(b). Mart–aprel' 1920 goda. Protokoly* (Moscow, 1960), p. 177.

[36] R. Terekhov, *Storinky heroichnoi borot'by. Spohady staroho bil'shovyka* (Kiev, 1963), pp. 200–1. For the Workers' Opposition in the Donbas, see also M. Zorkii, ed., *"Rabochaia Oppozitsiia." Materialy i dokumenty 1920–1926 gg.* (Moscow and Leningrad, 1926), pp. 41 and 51–53.

[37] Ivan Maistrenko, *Istoriia moho pokolinnia. Spohady uchasnyka revoliutsiinykh podii v Ukraini* (Edmonton, Canada, 1985), p. 171. Ten years later Maistrenko categorically refused to go back to the Donbas ("this culturally joyless province") to work (p. 251).

deeds of local Communists were such that the party appeared to be merely a means of achieving wealth, leading some old colliers to declare: "I'm sick of working. I'd like to join the party of the Communists."[38]

With the end of the civil war came a severe famine, brought on by economic ruin, Soviet seizure of grain, and drought. The famine hit the Volga basin hardest, but a large area of Ukraine, including the Donbas, also suffered severely. According to one observer, N. M. Borodin, a Don Cossack boy who later wrote of his experiences in the book *One Man in His Time*, in Kamensk the "people died like autumn flies." Cats and dogs "disappeared from the streets, either they had been eaten or were kept under lock and key by a few people who had enough food. . . . Even the fish disappeared from the river Donetz [Donets] and it was said that the water had been poisoned by the corpses which were thrown into the river during the Civil War. . . . There were many murders for a piece of bread."[39] Armed bands took advantage of the situation and assaulted villages, railways, mines, and factories. In October 1921 their activity had "reached an incredible scale" in some areas of the Donbas. They shot "many good colliers."[40] Trade in human meat was widely rumored. For example, in the former Aleksandrovsk-Grushevskii, renamed Shakhty in February 1920, an old woman was arrested at a market near the railway station on suspicion of selling human meat. According to N. M. Borodin (who, swollen from hunger, bought and ate cooked meat from her and witnessed the subsequent event), her house was searched, and there "were discovered two barrels containing parts of children's bodies, sorted and salted, and scalped heads." Borodin goes on to report that people said that

> these sellers of human flesh had lured homeless waifs from passing trains and enticing them to their house had killed them; and that it was not until they began boldly to steal children from the neighbourhood that they were discovered. I did not try to find out any details. I left the place as soon as I could, using the moment of confusion when the crowd began to lynch the old man [the husband of the old woman] and his wife, a business which the militia tried in vain to stop. The couple must have been beaten to death. The last I saw was the man kneeling on the snow which was red with blood.
> "Get him —!" "Kick out their — brains!" the crowd shouted, and the victims were screaming like pigs.[41]

In Kamensk, there were trials of cannibals.[42]

---

[38] *Trud*, 3 March 1921.

[39] N. M. Borodin, *One Man in His Time* (London, 1955), pp. 26–27 and 30.

[40] Kucher, *Rozhrom*, p. 11.

[41] Borodin, *One Man in His Time*, pp. 39–40. Railway stations were convenient places for mothers from famished areas to abandon their children. See *Gornorabochii*, 1922, no. 11, p. 26.

[42] Borodin, *One Man in His Time*, p. 35.

Figure 4.1. Abandoned children in the Donbas, 1921. From Donets'kyi kraieznavchyi muzei.

In Makiivka the situation was similar. Father Neveu, who stayed through the terrible period in Makiivka, wrote in February 1922:

> We are witnessing scenes reminiscent of Flavius Josephus' description of the siege of Jerusalem. Mothers kill their children and then commit suicide to put an end to their sufferings. Everywhere we see people with haggard complexions and swollen bodies, people who can hardly drag themselves around, and who are driven to eating dead cats, dogs, and horses. Small wonder that there is so much typhus, cholera, scurvy and even the glanders. . . . The famine continues. We feel almost guilty whenever we eat a piece of bread, and we have seen so many horrible things and heard of others, including cannibalism, that our sensitivities are becoming numb. There are still two long months until the harvest. . . . People are dying like flies from hunger and typhus, now the dreaded cholera has made its appearance.[43]

In Donets'k province, in the first half of April 1922 alone, 1,075 children and 1,038 adults were registered as dead from starvation.[44] In Ienakiieve, every evening a hospital horse cart went around the streets, collecting for burial dead and half-dead people whose eyelashes still moved.[45]

In enacting repressive measures, the Cheka chairman F. E. Dzerzhinskii warned that only by improving the conditions of workers would political repression work.[46] Even the Cheka operatives lived under terrible material conditions, and some of them as well as famished Red Army soldiers joined the "bandit" guerrillas.[47] As a song of that time recorded in Iuzivka goes,

> Eh, Apple,
> What a nation . . .
> All around robbery,
> Speculation.[48]

Hungry workers continued to strike. Communist managers enjoyed little authority over them as the workers suspected that their new bosses were merely pursuing their own selfish interests.[49] In July 1921 in the famine-struck Iuzivka coalfields, miners walked out, "incited by Mensheviks." At one of the meetings, "counterrevolutionary slogans" were voiced, and the party secretary and a member of the Soviet executive committee of the district were not allowed

[43]Patrick A. Croghan, *The Peasant from Makeyevka: Biography of Bishop Pius Neveu, A.A.* (Worcester, Mass., 1982), pp. 56 and 59–60.

[44]DADO, f. R-1146, op. 2, spr. 140, ark. 2zv.

[45]Ivan Il'in Uksusov, "Posle molchaniia," *Sovetskii shakhter*, 1989, no. 11, p. 9.

[46]*Iz istorii Vserossiiskoi Chrezvychainoi komissii, 1917–1922 gg. Sbornik dokumentov* (Moscow, 1958), pp. 427–28.

[47]DADO, f. R-1146, op. 2, spr. 140, ark. 3 and 3zv.

[48]A. V. Piaskovskii, *Kollektivanaia proletarskaia poeziia. Pesni Donbassa* (Moscow and Leningrad, 1927), p. 79.

[49]Note the complaints in *Biulleten' 1 Donetskoi gubernskoi konferentsii soiuza gornorabochikh*, no. 3 (Bakhmut, 1921), p. 2 (November 1921).

to speak.[50] In August, at the Auerbakh and Prokhorivka coalfields, rightist SRs appealed to workers for an armed uprising, declaring that the Communists were to blame for the food crisis. Strikes started. In view of the strikers' "counterrevolutionary mood," local authorities declared martial law in the coalfields.[51]

Food supply was the most serious political and economic problem at that time. When payment in kind was introduced in 1921 and supply was increased, the productivity of emaciated colliers jumped beyond the 1913 level. This surprised the Donbas officials. The desperate workers, in fact, sought to secure as much grain as possible by exerting themselves beyond their strength and often working two shifts.[52] When in December 1921 food supply was curtailed, the industry fell into chaos again. Twenty-five thousand workers recruited in the autumn had to be returned to their villages; many of them did not make it home, dying along the way.[53] Predictably, the following year 1922 was punctuated by numerous strikes, often described by the authorities as "anti-Soviet."[54]

The famine subsided by 1923, but its end did not significantly improve the overall political and economic situation. The hyperinflation of 1921–24, reflecting the economic breakdown in the aftermath of war, revolution, and civil war, frustrated all attempts at alleviating prevailing conditions. In June 1922, in Iuzivka, one pood of wheat flower cost 9.5 million rubles and ten eggs 1 million.[55] This hyperinflation was "one of the largest and longest in world history," and at its close 50,000 million rubles of Soviet monetary tokens were exchanged for 1 new ruble.[56]

A wave of industrial strikes swept the country in 1923, perhaps the largest in the decade or, for that matter, for most of the Soviet period, and were, for the most part, in reaction to delays in wage payment.[57] Such delays were critical for workers already living in hand-to-mouth conditions. In the Donbas, there were almost two hundred strikes with more than sixty thousand miners partic-

---

[50]Terekhov, *Storinky heroichnoi borot'by*, pp. 208–9.

[51]DADO, f. R-1146, op. 2, spr. 77, ark. 79.

[52]*Donetskii shakhter*, 1922, no. 4, p. 34, *Khoziaistvo Donbassa*, nos. 30–31 (15 June 1923), p. 7, and *Promyshlennost' i rabochii klass Ukrainskoi SSR v period vosstanovleniia narodnogo khoziaistva (1921–1925 gody)* (Kiev, 1964), pp. 37–38, 128, and 134.

[53]*Narodnoe khoziaistvo Rossii za 1921 g.* (Moscow and Berlin, 1922), p. 91.

[54]See, for example, DADO, f. R-1146, op. 2, spr. 140, ark. 4, and *Gornorabochii*, 1922, no. 20, p. 26.

[55]Vladimir Nikol'skii, "Povtorenie proidennogo. NEP vo vtorom prochtenii," *Donbas*, 1991, no. 2, p. 143.

[56]See Judith Shapiro, "The Cost of Economic Reform: Lessons of the Past for the Future?" in Catherine Merridale and Chris Ward, eds., *Perestroika in the Historical Perspective* (London, 1991), pp. 139–40.

[57]For this, see Gert Meyer, *Studien zur sozialökonomischen Entwicklung Sowjetrußlands 1921–1923. Die Beziehungen zwischen Stadt und Land zu Beginn der Neuen Ökonomischen Politik* (Cologne, 1974), pp. 393–402.

ipating in them, far more than metalworkers.[58] Loss of production owing to strikes in the first nine months of the year equaled a two-month output.[59] The strike wave peaked in the summer when timely payments were particularly important for workers to return to field work. The June wages, for example, were paid on 25 July for 39 percent, and the remainder on 3 August.[60] Often wages were paid in the form of bonds, the redemption of which was not easy and took some time. In the meantime, hyperinflation rapidly decreased the purchasing power of the wages. Thus, miners' labor appeared to inspectors from Moscow as "voluntary penal servitude."[61] The unions of colliers did virtually nothing to help the members. According to M. P. Tomskii's subsequent account, in 1923 the miners' unions, virtually created from above in 1920, still "didn't resemble trade unions."[62] Almost all strikes were reported to be "spontaneous" with the unions and the party standing by or unaware of strike initiatives.[63] Harsh reality, according to a trade-union report, had disillusioned workers about NEP.[64]

The strikes thus inevitably carried elements of political protest. This is clear from archival data as well. Secret police reports note that labor's view of Communist managers was very negative. The director of Makiivka Coal and Steel Combine, Comrade Liaksutkin, treated workers rudely. According to the report, he considered speaking to workers' meetings beneath his dignity. When workers came to him, he berated them, not letting them finish their sentences. Liaksutkin reportedly spent his free time sipping tea or drinking with specialists. He thus appeared to workers as "a lackey of specialists" who would indict ten innocent workers to spare one guilty *spetsy* (specialist).[65] In other coalfields, striking workers condemned the "extravagant way of life" of their Communist bosses, calling it "bourgeois."[66] They accused other Communist officials of using orphans (of whom there were many in the Donbas) as their servants.[67] At a June 1923 miners' strike in Krasnodon, the party cell sec-

---

[58] *Otchet Gubotdela Vserossiiskogo Soiuza Gornorabochikh za 1923* (Bakhmut, 1924), p. 183, lists 193 strikes with 61,833 participants from January to November. (GARF, f. 374sch, op. 27sch, d. 1535, l. 7, lists 91,829 person days for the first nine months alone.) In December there were two strikes. See GARF, f. 5459, op. 4, d. 80, ll. 63 and 208–9.

[59] Volodymyr Nikol's'kyi, "Same toi dokument," *Ukraina*, 1992, no. 1, p. 2.

[60] *Otchet Gubotdela Vserossiiskogo Soiuza Gornorabochikh za 1923*, p. 158.

[61] RTsKhIDNI, f. 76, op. 2, d. 133, l. 123.

[62] Ibid., f. 17, op. 2, d. 354, l. 55.

[63] GARF, f. 5459, op. 4, d. 14, l. 53, and f. 374sch, op. 27sch, d. 1535, l. 7.

[64] *Otchet Gubotdela Vserossiiskogo Soiuza Gornorabochikh za 1923 g.*, p. 5.

[65] DADO, f. 9p, op. 1, spr. 80, ark. 28.

[66] V. Nikol'skii, "Svidetel'stvuiut GPU. Iz arkhivov," *Sovetskii shakhter*, 1990, no. 12, p. 13.

[67] GARF, f. 5459, op. 4, d. 141, l. 28ob. In December 1921, there were nearly 40,000 orphans in Donets'k province. Some of them were fostered by factories, mines, and individual households. The fostering was done first voluntarily and later compulsorily. See *Vozvrashchaias' k istokam. Nauchno-populiarnye ocherki* (Donets'k, 1990), p. 56.

retary I. Revin, who doubled as secretary of the miners' union in Krasnodon, treated the striking miners just as the much detested former owners had. The workers were understood to be mindless followers of agitators, a very familiar view to students of the prerevolutionary labor movement. Revin denounced the strikers as gangs of demagogues and had the following altercation with them:

> I began to argue with them sharply, "Agitators have muddled you. You are following agitators. Such despicable scum engaged in provocation ought to be shot!" The outcry grew fiercer. I said to them, "Comrades, if it's necessary for the Soviet government to arrest an agent provocateur, and if he turns out to be Stupivtsev [a member of the strike committee], he will be shot." At this moment, several fists were raised in the crowd with the shout: "Kill him, tear him to pieces." I responded, of course, indignantly. I said that I was there and that they could go ahead and tear me to pieces and kill me. I said this moving toward the crowd. When I told them to go ahead and kill me, they became quiet.

In commenting on this incident the secret police noted that the reason for the strikes had been forgotten by both Revin and other leaders.[68]

In some areas, strikes involved violence. In Krindachevka, a strike committee was formed by the trade union headed by a Communist. It appears to have been a desperate attempt by the union to contain the demands of workers within what it considered reasonable limits. But workers beat up the Komsomol members and strikebreakers. Dynamite was thrown into the yard of the local miners' union secretary. After the strike ended, nonparty members of the strike committee were arrested.[69] In another incident in the Sovetsk coalfield, miners' had been given rotten flour and potatoes, resulting in illness, by cooperatives at higher than market prices. Other consumer items were available only to the wives and daughters of their bosses. The miners struck, but their strike ended with the appearance of the secret police (GPU) officials who discussed the international situation and accused the strikers of having counterrevolutionary intentions. In fact, the mining officials had contemplated assassinating the worker leaders Tolmachev and Savin on their way to Holrivka and then declaring that the two had deserted the mine and were subsequently shot.[70]

Perhaps the most serious disturbance occurred in Shakhty in October–November 1923, when five thousand colliers from four coalfields struck. A certain Kapustin, a former party member, was said to have agitated workers against the party. Kapustin contended that the party was living well at the ex-

---

[68]V. N. Nikol'skii and V. I. Iziumov, *NEP v Donbasse. Istoricheskoe issledovanie* (Donets'k, 1992), p. 88, and Nikol'skii, "Svidetel'stvuiut GPU," p. 12.

[69]GARF, f. 374sch, op. 27sch, d. 1535, ll. 8 and 14–15.

[70]Ibid., f. 5459, op. 4, d. 141, ll. 127–28.

pense of workers and issued the slogan: "Down with the party cell and the union committee. Long live the C[central]C[ommittee] of RKP(b) [Communist Party] and VSR [?]." Kapustin was also said to have circulated various rumors, for example, on the schisms in the party. (Later the local party was accused of not discrediting him, assigning him responsible positions in cooperatives or mine administration, and giving him other "dangerous" jobs!) On 1 November the local party organization arrested Kapustin. That evening workers gathered, demanding his release. They even demanded the release of six arrested former White officers. The workers threatened to detain the coalfield manager, the *okrug* party secretary, Ravich, who came to the meeting, and the chairman of the *okrug* Soviet executive committee, if their demands were not met. When Ravich condemned former White officers for the strike, a concerted outcry came from the crowd: "There are among us many who were White officers. The Soviet government has given us amnesty." The Communists and Komsomol members present at the meeting backed down and did not vote against the demand to free Kapustin. At the critical moment, the party cell secretary fainted and had to be carried out.

The following morning, a small group of workers (100 to 150), carrying a red trade-union banner, together with an amateur orchestra, made a procession to the prison in the city. As they progressed, the crowd expanded to 1,000, including women and children. The delegation scuffled with the police and the guard, seizing the weapons of several soldiers, and shooting a horse dead. Kapustin shouted from a prison window, demanding immediate release; otherwise, he threatened, it would be too late. When the police began to use their revolvers, Kapustin ordered the crowd to disperse. Shots were fired into the air, and water was poured onto the crowd. Only then did the crowd break up. A commission sent by the party Central Committee, while admitting the difficult living conditions, concluded that there were counterrevolutionary elements among the colliers, particularly among the former Cossacks who had been obliged to work in mines after losing their land, and among White émigrés who, given amnesty by the Soviet government, had returned to their homeland.[71]

Whether Kapustin's authority represented the kind of power held by Konopliannikov in 1917 (see Chapter 3) is not clear. Yet what is clear is that the party Central Committee commission ignored the widespread resentment of

---

[71]GARF, f. 374sch, op. 27sch, d. 1535, ll. 8–12, 19, and 22. This "Kapustin affair" was remembered in 1928 when the Shakhty affair was discussed by the party's Central Committee. According to the 1928 discussion, in 1923 L. B. Kamenev, a Politburo member, was not convinced by the conclusion of the commission: if it is right, then Soviet power is nonexistent in Shakhty. Kamenev suggested that to blame only "counterrevolutionary elements" was to misunderstand the problem. In 1928 Kamenev was accused of not having taken the presence of counterrevolutionary elements seriously in Shakhty in 1923. (RTsKhIDNI, f. 17, op. 2, d. 354, l. 70.)

Figure 4.2. "Assault on distinguished newcomers," 1923. From GARF, f. 324, op. 27, d. 64, l. 40.

workers, blaming instead so-called counterrevolutionary elements.

The Central Committee commission was, by its own admission, greeted with suspicion in the Donbas. Very few locals held out any hopes for the commission. The main reason was that the commission was just another of numerous such commissions sent by Moscow (said to be the thirty-fifth – or the forty-third, according to another account – since 1920) arriving with much pomp, occupying whole trains.[72] The pomp, pretense, and arrogance of the commission was caricatured by Donbas workers in songs and cartoons. One song opens with

> They pondered and predicted in Moscow
> At last to the Donbas they went.
> > Zh.Zh.Zh.[73]
> The thirty fifth [commission] by count
> To show, they say, they cared.
> > Zh.Zh.Zh.

[72]GARF, f. 374sch, op. 27sch, d. 1535, l. 6.

[73]It is not clear what this refrain means, but it most likely is a sound effect. It may be taken from the name of some mine boss, or from the often used refrain "Zhura, zhura, zhuravel', zhuravushka molodoi," signifying a merry mood (see, for example, Piaskovskii, *Kollektivnaia proletarskaia poeziia*, pp. 98–99). If the latter is the case, of course, the refrain is used ironically.

Come sirs no ordinary powers
Powers big!

        Zh.Zh.Zh.

Iaroslavl', Goncharov,
And Chubarov and Bubnov

        Zh.Zh.Zh.

Seniushkin, Akulov with them
And Ugariushka – hefty chaps!

        Zh.Zh.Zh.

The song goes on to ridicule the method of investigation, discussion, and reasoning, and concludes ironically with the following:

We'll wait for Moscow
So impatiently.[74]

        Zh.Zh.Zh.

There'll be credits and wages
And the collier'll have a house

        Zh.Zh.Zh.

There'll be a house, not a hen cage
He'll be more literate and cultured

        Zh.Zh.Zh.

The Donbas'll begin to live again,
To sing its merry songs.[75]

Evidently this last part referred to promises that would never be realized. Such evidence of a "counterrevolutionary" mood was collected by the commission and brought back to Moscow.

In 1924 the stabilization of the currency realized whatever merit the NEP had to offer by restoring market relations to the economy. In the Donbas, industrial production gradually revived, but the benefit of the NEP was not noticeable everywhere. The Donbas was again haunted by the specter of famine. The 1924 famine, which the party attributed to drought and bad crops, was less extensive than the 1921–22 famine, but, as reports from the Donbas noted the situation was "very, very difficult."[76] Workers began to sell whatever they possessed in order to secure as much bread as possible, and there was a run on the market.[77] The kulaks were said to have bought up whatever livestock the poorer peasants possessed, thereby widening the stratification of the countryside. Because of the pessimistic mood created by the famine, religious activity

---

[74]The original is "Budem zhdat' my iz Moskvy, / Slovno s nebushka krupy." Literally, this phrase, which evokes the Russian idiom "kak manny nebesnoi zhdat'," can be translated: "as if to wait for goats from the sky."

[75]GARF, f. 374sch, op. 27sch, d. 64, l. 5.

[76]RTsKhIDNI, f. 76, op. 3, d. 338, ll. 1–2, 28, 42, and 45.

[77]See, for example, *Kochegarka*, 3, 18, and 27 July 1924.

Figure 4.3. "Visit by Kirilkin before wage payment" and "After payment." From GARF, f. 324, op. 27, d. 64, l. 37.

"increased noticeably."[78] Closure of churches, banning of processions, and other antireligious campaigns at a time of famine, according to official reports, allowed the clergy and the kulaks to shift the blame for drought onto the Soviet government.[79]

Industrial strikes never ceased in the Donbas. Workers accused the Soviet government of being incapable of feeding the population. In August 1924 at the Rykove coalfield, for example, five hundred miners struck, demanding an immediate payment of their outstanding wages for June. During the strike one policeman, who detained a miner suspected of stealing a piece of coal, was beaten up by a crowd with cries of "Beat the foremen [*desiatniki*] and those who live in plenty." The ringleaders of the strike were interrogated by the GPU. It turned out, according to a secret GPU report, that the workers were very angry with the mine manager Tarenko, who would rudely kick them out of

---

[78]RTsKhIDNI, f. 17, op. 16, d. 1448, ll. 1 and 261, and DADO, f. R-1146, op. 2, spr. 317, ark. 120zv.

[79]DADO, f. 9p, op. 1, spr. 29, ark. 33 and 33zv.

his office.[80] Various secret reports expressed considerable concern about local Communists' life-styles. Many Communists, including some from the much praised "Lenin recruits," were alleged to appear drunk at meetings, practice polygamy, engage in moonshining, and even rape young girls.[81] Some Communists were even accused of murdering defiant but helpless Soviet citizens. A report from Iuzivka warned of a possible lynching of Communists by angry workers.[82]

Whether the remaining Mensheviks incited strikes, as was often alleged, is almost impossible to ascertain. As of October 1923, according to a "top secret" document of the party, Donets'k province had the largest number of "organized Mensheviks" (160) in Ukraine,[83] but they were closely monitored and hounded by the GPU. What is apparent is that there was a Menshevik-like mood and, perhaps, Menshevik sympathizers. For example, Donbas workers characterized the drive for cost reduction as "exploitation of labor," as the Mensheviks had.[84] Trade unions enjoyed little authority among the workers. At the Pastukhov coalfield, for example, in February 1924, two workers, angry that the mine union committee office was always closed, broke into it, smashed the windows and chairs, and turned everything upside down.[85] Another incident is also illuminating. When Lenin's death was announced in January 1924, a cleaning woman at Donbas Coal, named "Matiumi," clearly underpaid and poorly treated by her bosses, reacted in an emotional outburst: "To hell with him, he died, so what" [*Chort s nim, chto on vzdokh*].[86]

Negative sentiments toward the Soviet government were often tinged with anti-Semitism. It was particularly strong, according to a secret report, among low-paid workers engaged in heavy work.[87] Some miners asked: "Is it true that Lenin didn't die from an illness, but was poisoned by Trotsky?" Others responded openly: "Yids [*zhidy*] poisoned him and now say that he died." In Shakhty, workers reasoned that "Lenin has died, the Jew Trotsky'll be put in his place, then there'll be more tax."[88]

Even 1925, supposedly the height of the much praised economic prosperity brought about by the NEP, was not a good year in the Donbas. Again there was a relatively localized famine, caused by harvest failure. In Luhan'sk, Mariupol', and Starobil's'k *okruhs*, according to a GPU "top secret" document,

---

[80] Ibid., op. 2, spr. 317, ark. 455.

[81] RTsKhIDNI, f. 17, op. 16, d. 1448, ll. 262–63. The Lenin recruits were those new party members, mainly from the factory bench, who were recruited in connection with Lenin's death.

[82] Ibid., and DADO, f. 9p, op. 1, spr. 80, ark. 28–30.

[83] DADO, f. 9p, op. 1, spr. 29, ark. 30zv. The next largest number was Katerynoslav's 140.

[84] GARF, f. 5459, op. 5, d. 16, l. 118.

[85] *Gornorabochii*, 1924, no. 2, p. 29.

[86] DADO, f. R-1146, op. 2, spr. 322, ark. 12.

[87] RTsKhIDNI, f. 17, op. 16, d. 1448, l. 262.

[88] DADO, f. R-1146, op. 2, spr. 322, ark. 10, 13, and 14.

Figure 4.4: "Attention to the trifles! Don't walk barefoot, or catch cold. Or are you better off on your own? From the speech of a Kulturträger to dirty Donbas people," 1923; note that the Kulturträger addresses the workers with "*ty*," just as the bosses did before the revolution. From GARF, f. 374, op. 27, d. 64, l. 33.

people were swollen with hunger. As much as half of the population in Staro-bil's'k *okruh* fed on a mix of grain substitutes such as oilcakes and weeds. A number of deaths from starvation (mainly among the poor peasants) were recorded in 1925. Many hungry children roamed the countryside, begging.[89] And the Donbas saw an "enormous rise in criminal elements," committing armed robbery and murder.[90]

Often Communists and Komsomol members could not cope with the massive problems associated with the NEP. It is indicative of these difficulties that the number of suicides in the country rose sharply in the first half of the 1920s from the prewar years and that many of those were Communists and Komsomol members.[91]

Old and New "Enemies"

The end of civil war and the consolidation of the new regime did not mean that the old enemies of Bolshevism had been eliminated. However, the establishment of a new order meant that perceptions of who the "enemy" was did change. The image of the "class enemy" promoted by the Soviet authorities was not necessarily identical to the image of "enemy" as it was generated by the working population, which refused to accept the regime's civil peace with old enemies such as the specialists. Moreover, the Communists as new bosses also began to enter the popular perceptions of enemies at this time.

The most serious problem was that it became increasingly difficult to identify the "enemy" as political expression was driven underground. Macabre and ghastly the civil war may have been, but the world was relatively simple: there were enemies and allies, even though sometimes enemies became allies and vice versa. Once the war ended, however, the situation became more complex in spite of the fact that the enemies had been defeated militarily.[92]

In the 1920s there were still many supporters of the Whites, Makhno and other numerous atamans, the Mensheviks, the SRs, and the Ukrainian nationalists who had fought in armed combat against the Bolsheviks. Summary executions, which characterized the period of the civil war, gave way to more formal legal punishment. In the first half of the 1920s, particularly in 1920, 1921, and 1922, the revolutionary tribunal, which dealt with "counterrevolutionaries," remained very active. The Donets'k province revolutionary tribunal handled thousands of cases against alleged enemies of the Soviet government,

[89] Ibid., spr. 348, ark. 160, 363, 376, 650–52, and 941.
[90] Ibid., f. R-129, op. 1, spr. 6, ark. 9–10.
[91] See V. S. Tiazhel'nikova, "K analizu suitsidnosti revoliutsii," reported in *Otechestvennaia istoriia*, 1993, no. 4, pp. 214–15.
[92] Borodin, *One Man in His Time*, p. 54.

spies for foreign countries, and traitors, sentencing the defendants to death and other harsh forms of punishment. An archival fund of the tribunal for 1921–1925, which is far from complete, lists almost seventy thousand cases brought before the tribunal.[93]

Some of those who had fallen under the general rubric of "enemy" during the civil war, like the intelligentsia, were placated as a conciliatory measure, and some of those who had emigrated came to terms with the Soviet government and returned to their homelands (the so-called *smenovekhovstvo*, the Change of Landmarks movement). Of the Mensheviks and SRs who had been outlawed, some went underground and obstinately fought against the new regime. The famous SR trial in 1922 shows that they were still a force to be reckoned with.[94] Yet others, who believed in the consolidation of the NEP, did moderate their opposition and in 1923–24 made their peace with the Soviet government.[95]

Similarly, the policy of *korenizatsiia* ("indigenization," or, in the case of Ukraine, Ukrainization) placated at least some Ukrainian nationalists. It was designed to maintain civil peace among the Ukrainians, whose national ideology, according to Trotsky, was "an explosive force of immense proportions."[96] According to Frank Sysyn, after 1917, a "revolution in perception" had occurred in Ukraine, that is to say, "the acceptance of the idea of an entity with fairly well-defined borders called the 'Ukraine,' and the self-identification of the masses living in this area as 'Ukrainians.' "[97] This revolution was made possible, at least in part, by the new conciliatory policy to contain the potentially explosive nature of national ideology. Ukrainization was officially approved and promoted by Ukrainian Communists. (Hence their ideology came to be called "national Communism.")[98] Ukrainization promoted Ukrainian culture and the Ukrainian language in education, publication, and administration.[99] Even the Orthodox Church in Ukraine was now allowed to have its own head (the Autocephalous Church).[100] The symbol of the reconciliation

[93] See DADO, f. R-2740sch, op. 1sch.

[94] This is the conclusion of Marc Jansen, *A Show Trial under Lenin: The Trial of Socialist-Revolutionaries, Moscow, 1922*, tr. Jean Sanders (The Hague, 1982).

[95] For a good discussion of this phenomenon, see P. A. Podbolotov, *Krakh esero-menshevistskoi kontrrevoliutsii* (Leningrad, 1975), pp. 113–15.

[96] Quoted in Bohdan Krawchenko, *Social Change and National Consciousness in Twentieth-Century Ukraine* (New York, 1985), p. 58.

[97] Frank Sysyn, "Nestor Makhno and the Ukrainian Revolution," in Taras Hunczak, ed., *The Ukraine, 1917–1921: A Study in Revolution* (Harvard University Press, 1977), p. 277.

[98] See James E. Mace, *Communism and the Dilemmas of National Liberation: National Communism in Soviet Ukraine 1918–1923* (Harvard University Press, 1983).

[99] See, for example, George Liber, "Language, Literacy, and Book Publishing in the Ukrainian SSR, 1923–1928," *Slavic Review*, 41:4 (Winter 1982).

[100] See Bohdan R. Bociurkiw, "The Ukrainian Autocephalous Orthodox Church, 1920–1930: A Case Study in Religious Modernization," in D. Dunn, ed., *Religion and Modernization in the*

was the 1924 return to Kiev from abroad of the dean of Ukrainian studies and the former president of the Ukrainian Central Rada, M. S. Hrushevs'kyi.[101] Ukrainization helped Moscow to maintain civil peace in Ukraine. As one prominent Ukrainian put it, without Ukrainization, "we would have a civil war in Ukraine under nationalist slogans."[102]

By contrast, the NEP did little to moderate the confrontation between religious groups and the explicitly atheist Soviet government. In the Donbas, eight churches were closed in Artemivs'k (Bakhmut) and its surroundings, five in Petrovs'kyi (Horlivka), eight in Rykove (Ienakiieve) and its suburbs – altogether at least forty-two (all appeared to be Orthodox churches). In addition, six synagogues, thirty-five chapels (mainly Baptist), two Roman Catholic churches, and three monasteries were shut down.[103]

Father Neveu in Makiivka had been the subject of search twenty-two times in 1917 and 1918 and was sentenced to death, only narrowly escaping execution.[104] In 1922–23 he was again subjected to the same number of searches. In May 1922,

> All the clergy in town were summoned to the local Soviet where we were told that the Government is going to requisition all sacred vessels and precious objects from churches, temples and synagogues and intends to use them to buy wheat from abroad. Since then, I have been sent for six times. The only thing of value that I possess is a crucifix, but they rejected this because it was not in the Russian style, having only one nail in the feet of our Saviour instead of two. I must say that on each occasion I was treated with great respect.[105]

On other occasions he was not so lucky. When he was ordered to leave his house in July 1923, he asked the police officer for the document ordering the eviction and was told: "I am the document." On 14 November "the search party decided to come at 1:00 A.M. We were awakened by a thunderous hammering on the door." He "could no longer walk down the street without being insulted" and "was stoned several times by conscientious young citizens."[106]

From time to time in the 1920s, the government accused religious groups of having ties to the monarchists, the Whites, and foreign countries. Catholics were particularly suspect because of their alleged connection with Poland, the Soviet Union's hostile neighbor on the western border. In November 1923 in Makiivka and Iuzivka all Catholics, specifically those associated with Father

---

Soviet Union (Boulder, Colo., 1977).

[101] For Hrushevs'kyi, see Thomas M. Prymak, *Mykhailo Hrushevsky: The Politics of National Culture* (University of Toronto Press, 1987).

[102] Krawchenko, *Social Change and National Consciousness*, p. 111.

[103] Taras Bespechnyi, "Kak rushili tserkov' v Donbasse," *Vechernii Donetsk*, 21 September 1990, and GARF, f. 374sch, op. 27sch, d. 1535, l. 15.

[104] Croghan, *The Peasant from Makeyevka*, p. 55.

[105] Ibid., p. 60.

[106] Ibid., pp. 71 and 84.

Neveu, were arrested, and he was subjected to a search and had his few possessions (including his letters) confiscated.[107] Later he reported that "there were spies and informers everywhere."[108] Still, many religious groups remained active. The Baptists, for example, were "very organized, and even had their own religious publications."[109] A number of Communists in Stalino were ousted by the party for observing religious rites: thirty-seven members on 20 December 1924, fifty-four on the following day, and so on.[110]

Clearly the attitude of the populace toward religion was conflicted. From the point of view of the atheist regime, on the other hand, the question was rather simple: religious groups were at best political irritants, at worst outright enemies. In any case, the government did not need their service.

The question of technical and other specialists was much more complex, because the regime needed their services to restore an economy ruined by war, revolution, and civil war, and simply to run the country. In the 1920s, these *spetsy* (a frequently used pejorative word for specialists, particularly "old" or "bourgeois" specialists, i.e., those trained under the old regime) were given incentives to work for the new rulers, but they remained among the most damned enemies among the workers. How to use experts and professionals was part of the larger problem of how to deal with the political and cultural legacy of the old regime. In this sphere, as Sheila Fitzpatrick has shown, there was constant conflict between moderates and hard-liners throughout the 1920s.[111]

The government had no other choice but to use the old specialists, just as they had used former tsarist military officers to win the civil war. When the civil war came to a close in 1920, the government sent special trains to Rostov, where many Donbas experts had fled, to recruit old specialists back to work.[112] By the end of 1920 the Donbas succeeded in bringing back 65 percent of the prewar technical experts.[113] Some were sent into forced labor as punishment for retreating with the Whites.[114] Still, emotional resistance to their use remained strong, hardly surprising in light of what had happened in the Donbas mines and factories during the civil war. The families of specialists were persecuted, making it impossible for them to live in the Donbas.[115] Antispecialist

[107]Neveu Documents, 2EQ-197, p. 2.

[108]Croghan, *The Peasant from Makeyevka*, p. 120. For the infiltration of religious groups by the GPU, see V. Nikol's'kyi, "Taiemni ahenty v riasakh," *Skhidnyi chasopys* (Donets'k), March 1992, p. 6. Apart from informers, many priests, engaged in infighting, informed on each other. DALO, f. P-34, op. 1, spr. 17, ark. 9a.

[109]Croghan, *The Peasant from Makeyevka*, p. 119.

[110]Bespechnyi, "Kak rushili tserkov' v Donbasse."

[111]Sheila Fitzpatrick, "The 'Soft' Line on Culture and Its Enemies: Soviet Cultural Policy, 1922–1927," *Slavic Review*, 33:2 (June 1974).

[112]V. Drobizhev and N. Dumova, *V. Ia. Chubar'. Biograficheskii ocherk* (Moscow, 1963), p. 38.

[113]Prokopenko, "Bor'ba," p. 36.

[114]RTsKhIDNI, f. 17, op. 2, d. 354, l. 4.

[115]See, for example, *The Life of a Chemist: Memoirs of Vladimir N. Ipatieff* (Stanford University

feelings had considerable support in the party leadership. T. V. Sapronov, a prominent Left Communist who would become the leader of the Democratic Centralism faction, declared to a Soviet Congress in December 1919: "The specialist? He won't do. He'll work not for revolution but for counterrevolution."[116] At the first all-Russian congress of the miners' union in April 1920, A. I. Rykov declared that without science and technology "we will go back to the time of Ivan the Terrible." Yet he was rebuked by a delegate who declared that the fist ought to lead the brain.[117]

In industrial communities, the old *spetsy* became the symbol of the old regime with all its injustice, because the real capitalists and their associates had largely disappeared. Only a few, for example, Adam Svitsyn, the former director of the New Russian Company in Iuzivka, returned and worked in the Donbas, apparently with the reassurance of the Soviet government. (Svitsyn was to be arrested in 1928.) When the former Paramonov coalfield in Nesvetai decided to hire back the former manager P. E. Kalnin as chief engineer, the engineer I. I. Nekrasov as his assistant, and another engineer V. M. Kuvaldin as mechanic, many openly demanded that the party secretary K. M. Gorlov intercede: "Throw him [Kalnin] out on his ear, Kostia. However much you may feed a wolf, he still looks to the wood!" Kalnin appeared to the miners to be Paramonov's manager, a lord, just as before.[118] (Kalnin, Nekrasov, and Kubaldin were all indicted at the famous Shakhty trial in 1928.)[119]

The old engineers, whose return to work disturbed many, were harassed by workers and Communists in every possible way. Indeed, workers complained that the revolution brought nothing good.[120] The way of life of the specialists was said to be very lavish while workers went hungry and naked. At the Shcherbynivka coalfield, experts lived in houses of three to eight rooms, with baths, electricity, and running water, as well as a barn in which to keep livestock, and were served by a servant and a driver at the expense of the administration. Some even had a field to sow, also at the expense of the administration. Their wages were only 20 percent of what they had been before the revolution, but they had many privileges and were paid regularly.[121] None of the conveniences and privileges were enjoyed by most of the workers. Consequently, workers turned to physical and verbal assault and "emotional torture" in their

Press, 1946), p. 300.

[116]7-i Vserossiiskii s"ezd sovetov rabochikh, krest'ianskikh, krasnoarmeiskikh i kazach'ikh deputatov. Sten. otchet (Moscow, 1920), p. 201.

[117]GARF, f. 5459, op. 1, d. 1, ll. 147 and 159.

[118]L. V. Karasev, Shakhterskaia letopis'. Iz istorii shakhty im. Lenina (Rostov, 1960), pp. 47 and 49.

[119]For the Shakhty trial, see my "The Shakhty Affair," South East European Monitor, 4:2 (1997).

[120]DADO, f. R-1146, op. 2, spr. 348, ark. 932.

[121]Khoziaistvo Donbassa, no. 29 (15 May 1923), p. 18. For their salaries, see DADO, f. 1p, op. 1, spr. 1871, ark. 2–3.

negotiations with specialists.[122] Their sentiments are well expressed in the following *chastushka*, heard in Stalino in the mid-1920s:

> The collier works at night,
> He cares nothing for the rich,
> Show me a rich man
> And I'll mash his mug.[123]

The phenomenon of antispecialist attack became so common that it acquired a special term *spetseedstvo*, or specialist baiting.

Workers frequently attacked the specialists savagely,[124] outraged that the Soviet government treated the *spetsy* too humanely.[125] When a Communist tried to kill the director of the Artem Coalfield in Debal'tseve, the party organization asked for his release on the grounds that he acted according to his proletarian instincts. The secretary of the party bureau of the Ol'hoversk Coalfield shot a technician dead. In 1924, at another mine near Artemivs'k a Communist shot an engineer who made him stay at work until the end of his shift.[126] In Ukraine, Makhaevshchina, violent hostility toward the educated, was said to have worsened with the NEP: the word "intellectual" had become an abusive word, and "not belonging to the working class is becoming a crime."[127]

There were bizarre incidents as well. On 14 June 1922 in Dolzhano-Rovenets'kyi, Popov, the director of Mine 1, was killed and his wife and child injured by dynamite placed on the window sill of his flat. Popov was a former Kadet party member, and rumor had it that the party officials Buliukin, Zhikharev, Pashin, Abramov, Kovalevskii, and Kornev, as well as Boiko (who made every effort to acquire the directorship of the mine) were guilty of the murder. Two weeks earlier, a leaflet was circulated that stated, not quite grammatically, that Popov had come back to suck the workers' blood and appealed to the people to throw over Popov and all Kadets and Cossacks. Even before the murder, rumors circulated that the Communists were trying to assassinate Popov. The investigation commission concluded, however, that some political organization (an SR circle was implicated) hostile to the Communist Party had committed the murder to discredit the party's authority. The leaflet had been a

---

[122] *Otchet IV-go gubs"ezda gornorabochikh Donbassa*, pp. 9–10, and *Inzhenernyi rabotnik*, 1924, no. 5, p. 58. This was both literal and actual. For an actual case, see DADO, f. R-2607, op. 1, spr. 1326, ark. 29. Interviewee 2 used the term "moral terror." According to him, "all colliers" were hostile to the engineers.

[123] Vira Bilets'ka, "Shakhtars'ki pisni," *Etnohrafichnyi visnyk*, no. 5 (1927), p. 55.

[124] DADO, f. R-1146, op. 2, spr. 77, ark. 2 and 20, and GARF, f. 5459, op. 5, d. 223, ll. 1, 2, 190b., and 59. *Donetskii shakhter*, 1922, no. 4, pp. 26–27, and *Gornorabochii*, 1922, no. 12, p. 7.

[125] DADO, f. R-1146, op. 2, spr. 317, ark. 145.

[126] V. A. Noskov, "Rukovodstvo Kommunisticheskoi partii vosstanovleniem ugol'noi promyshlennosti Donbassa v 1921–1925 gg." (Kand. diss., Rostov State University, 1966), pp. 107–8.

[127] *Biulleten' VIII-i Vseukrainskoi konferentsii Kommunisticheskoi partii (b) Ukrainy. Stenogramma. 12–17 maia 1924 g.* (Kharkiv, 1924), pp. 41 and 64–65.

preparation for this act. The case was then handed over to the secret police.[128] One might wonder who actually committed the crime: the Communists, the SR circle, or the local GPU.

Such a state of affairs deeply concerned those who were in charge of coal mining. The noted professor L. K. Ramzin (who was to become the chief defendant at the famous Industrial Party trial in 1930) maintained that much of the problem the Donbas was experiencing in restoring its economy was the result of the engineers being terrorized and subsequently fleeing the Donbas.[129] The press attacked Ramzin for his views, but it was certainly the case that even a small accident at work could land the engineers in jail. In 1926, no less than 50 percent of the Donbas technical staff was on trial, mainly for industrial accidents.[130]

Specialist baiting also encompassed anti-Semitism. In Horlivka, for example, when Jewish university students (prospective specialists) came to the mines, angry workers protested: "Look, are there many of them among the workers? Fewer than Russians. But only Yids become the bosses."[131]

The NEP was a compromise. At all levels of the political hierarchy there was strong discontent over the civil peace with suspected political enemies. Much anxiety was expressed over Soviet policies being distorted by the specialists working for the Soviet government. The anxiety continued to torment the authorities. Consequently, the Bolshevik government's policy toward the specialists was contradictory.

In a conference in the spring of 1923, for example, I. S. Unshlikht (1879–1938) of the GPU warned against overconfidence in the *spetsy*: among them were those with aspirations for "economic counterrevolution." A certain large organization abroad, Unshlikht contended, with the aim of "economic counterrevolution," was in contact with *spetsy*. To prove this link was difficult, because it was as yet impossible to demonstrate the existence of the organization, but correspondence with the overseas leaders had been intercepted.[132]

As if to placate the workers, the government staged a number of show trials during the NEP. In the first half of the 1920s several Shakhty-style show trials of *spetsy* took place in the Donbas. (These were a part of the many show trials staged in the 1920s against the Ukrainian intelligentsia, including

---

[128]DADO, f. R-2470sch, op. 1, spr. 7, ark. 24–25.

[129]GARF, f. 5459, op. 11, d. 139, l. 6ob., and *Ekonomicheskaia zhizn'*, 27 April 1923.

[130]GARF, f. 5459, op. 7, d. 2, ll. 139 and 150.

[131]DADO, f. R-1146, op. 2, spr. 348, ark. 964. See also "Monarkhiia pogibla, a anti-Semitizm ostalsia. Dokumenty Informatsionnogo otdela OGPU 1920-kh gg.," *Neizvestnaia Rossiia*, vol. 3 (1993), pp. 331–32 and 339, and *Khoziaistvo Donbassa*, no. 29 (15 May 1923), p. 22. For strong anti-Semitism among Ukrainian workers, see also *Desiatyi z'izd Komunistychnoi partii (bil'shovykiv) Ukrainy. 20–29 lystopada 1927 r. Sten. zvit* (Kharkiv, 1928), pp. 214–15.

[132]"Soveshchanie v Sovnarkome o gosapparate [1923g.]," *Sovetskoe gosudarstvo i pravo*, 1990, no. 9, p. 116. This view was doubted by Foreign Trade Commissar L. B. Krasin (1870–1926).

groups of *zminovikhivstvo* [*smenovekhovstvo*].)[133] One of the most important trials against the technical experts was the Kadiivka trial, or the "case of economic espionage at the Kadiivka coalfields," in 1924.[134] At the end of 1923 and the beginning of 1924 a number of mining engineers in Kadiivka were arrested by the GPU.[135] Some of them were put on trial in June 1924 in Kharkiv, then the capital of Ukraine. The chief defendant was the former chief engineer Guliakov; in addition to him four more engineers, Manuk'ian, Baltaitis, Godzevich, and Ovsiannyi, and the wives of Guliakov and Manuk'ian were indicted on charges of economic espionage and counterrevolution. Guliakov was accused of providing data concerning the coalfields to the former owners residing in Poland. Guliakov admitted having had correspondence with his former bosses through "Ruzhitskii," a councillor of the Polish Embassy in Kharkiv, who before the revolution was a shareholder of the former Dnipro Company. Guliakov also confessed to having received money from his former bosses for his service, but he contended that the data he provided was not secret because he collected them from newspapers and that correspondence with them was not illegal. The money he received, Guliakov maintained, was meant to help those former employees who were living under very difficult circumstances. Guliakov and his company were also accused of willfully mismanaging the coalfields, as a result of which production lagged, machinery fell into disrepair, and labor discipline was lax.

According to the local newspaper *Kochegarka*, the alleged crimes of Guliakov and company came to light "only because" his estranged wife, the daughter of an old Donbas worker, informed the authorities, and their guilt was "proved solely by her testimony."[136] Guliakov was declared guilty and sentenced to death, which, "in view of the strength of the Soviet government," was commuted to ten years of imprisonment. Other defendants were given various lengths of prison terms ranging from two years to seven years. Guliakov's wife was reprimanded, and Manuk'ian's was sentenced to one-year incarceration, which was suspended, however. A *Kochegarka* article accompanying the report on the sentences contended that not all of the intelligentsia had "burned all their bridges behind them" and that a considerable stratum still harbored hatred toward the Soviet government, spat on its effort, and dreamed of a return of the capitalists. Hence, the Guliakov spy clique.[137]

[133]See H. V. Kas'ianenko and V. M. Danilenko, *Stalinizm i ukrains'ka intelihentsiia (20–30-i roky)* (Kiev, 1991), and Heorhii Kas'ianov, *Ukrains'ka intelihentsiia 1920-kh–1930-kh rokiv: sotsial'nyi portret ta istorychna dolia* (Kiev, 1992).

[134]The following discussion is based on *Kochegarka*, 16, 17, 18, 19, 22, and 23 July 1924, and *Pravda*, 16, 18, 19, 20, 22, and 23 July 1924. See also Kas'ianov and Danilenko, *Stalinizm*, pp. 40–41.

[135]DADO, f. R-2607, op. 1, spr. 1326, ark. 20, 24, 396, 421, and spr. 1363, ark. 8.

[136]*Kochegarka*, 22 July 1924.

[137]Ibid., 23 July 1924.

A very similar case, again involving the Pole Ruzhitskii, and staged in Katerynoslav (later Dniproptrovs'k), was discovered in April 1924, and twenty people (engineers, technicians, accountants, including some people in the Donbas) were tried in June 1925 and sentenced to various terms of imprisonment.[138]

Both the Kadiivka and the Katerynoslav cases were to be mentioned at the 1928 Shakhty trial; they implied the continuity of "economic counterrevolution."[139] Regarding the former case, E. F. Domchenko, then the director of the Snizhne coalfield, wrote to the prosecutor in 1928: when Manuk'ian was arrested, two future defendants at the Shakhty trial, N. P. Boiarshinov and L. G. Rubanovich [Rabinovich] of the Donetsk Coal to which the coalfields were subordinated, "scolded" him for "not supporting" Manuk'ian and allowing him to be arrested. Domchenko concluded from this episode that Boiarshinov and Rabinovich were associated with, or even directed, the Kadiivka group of wreckers (*vrediteli*). Soon Demchenko was fired from his post by both men.[140]

Whatever the case, after the two "espionage groups" were discovered, the Donets'k party secretary A. Krinitskii circulated a secret letter, suggesting that a series of recent fires in large factories and mines was not accidental but that there was ground to suspect the existence of "economic counterrevolution." He urged the GPU and the police to pay special attention to the observation of people of foreign origin and those on the GPU black list.[141] The hunt for enemies never abated.[142] The secret police agent, Viacheslav Galitskii, thus succeeded in unmasking "a series of underground counterrevolutionary and espionage organizations."[143]

Complicating the issue of the "enemy" was the fact that the wounds of the civil war had not healed in the people's minds. The war had been brutal and internecine, as one Kamensk schoolboy later recalled:

> The Reds shot our headmaster Bogaevsky dead, because he was White. The Whites hanged the teacher Gorobtsov because he was Red. The Reds shot my schoolmate Obukov and his six-year-old sister, because they sympathised with the Whites. The Whites shot the boy Soloviev and his old mother, because they sympathised with the Reds. Our school no longer existed. The teachers and pupils were either fighting or helping one or other of the sides,

[138]See *Pravda*, 12, 16 April 1924, and 16 May 1925. See also, Kas'ianov and Danilenko, *Stalinizm*, pp. 41–42, and D. P. Golinkov, *Krushenie antisovetskogo podpol'ia v SSSR*, vol. 2, 2nd ed. (Moscow, 1978), pp. 178–80.

[139]GARF, f. 9474, op. 7, d. 256, ll. 135–39, and d. 258, ll. 208–9.

[140]Ibid., d. 258, ll. 208–9.

[141]DADO, f. 1p, op. 1, spr. 1862, ark. 4.

[142]For the zeal to find enemies, see, for example, *Rytsari dolga. Vospominaniia chekistov* (Donets'k, 1982), p. 37.

[143]See a "top secret" GPU document in DADO, f. R-129, op. 1, spr. 6, ark. 135–135zv.

and many of them had been killed, some by stray bullets during street fighting.[144]

Another witness, a White Army officer, testified that revenge was an important part of the savagery. In 1918 he saw an "illustration of this" in Zverevo, south of Kamensk:

> A Red Guard prisoner was brought in past our train by one of our infantrymen from a forward patrol – he was a shabby-looking young fellow. Suddenly, one of our own young volunteers jumped off the car, rushed up to the prisoner and held the muzzle of a revolver close to his head, repeating, his face distorted with hatred: "See this? . . . See this?" Before anyone could intervene, he pressed the trigger and killed the prisoner by a bullet through his brain. It turned out that shortly before that he had found the mutilated body of his uncle, a stationmaster who had been killed by the Reds for having co-operated with the Whites. The nephew was thirsting for vengeance. And so it went on – one act of brutality produced another, causing what nowadays would probably be called an "escalation" of reciprocal terror.[145]

For much of the Donbas, to this Red-White scene must be added the various warlords and Ukrainian nationalists. Instead of fighting, people were now supposed to live peacefully without mutual slaughter. It would be absurd to assume, however, that the NEP successfully introduced peace among the people in places like the Donbas where internecine war had been fought. There were too many scores to settle. In Iuzivka, for example, one armed band named itself "Sons of Offended Fathers" (*Siny obizhennykh otsov*).[146] Some former Cossacks were openly hostile and regarded Ukraine as their haven:

> We are Cossack heroes
> The Communists are fools
> We'll smash the commune
> And go to Ukraine to live.[147]

The ways in which people related to one another were not just ideological but also highly emotional. The questions people had of others were not just of their social origins or party status, but also of a deeply personal nature: what had they done during the civil war?

The peculiarity of post–civil war Soviet society was that the state did not allow the war wounds to heal. The civil peace of the NEP did not preclude the final showdown with class enemies. In fact, the fight continued in various forms. Denunciations, which had begun on a mass scale during the civil war years, for example, continued.[148] As Borodin recalled, during the civil war,

[144]Borodin, *One Man in His Time*, p. 18.
[145]Gregory P. Tschebotarioff, *Russia, My Native Land* (New York, 1964), p. 163.
[146]Kurdiumova, "Bol'sheviki Donbassa," p. 9.
[147]RF IMFE, f. 1-7/866, ark. 15.
[148]The practice of denunciations, however, was not peculiar to the Soviet period. Denunciations

Denunciations became a deadly weapon and a very convenient one for people who were too fastidious to dirty their own hands with the blood of their personal enemies. Both fighting camps encouraged denunciations and eagerly shot down the "enemies" who were pointed out to them by the finger of a "loyalist."[149]

This practice remained vigorous even after the civil war ended. No doubt, all kinds of human emotions (revenge, envy, love, jealousy, greed) entered into the equation. Borodin was able to go on to university, but some of his friends were not allowed to take the entrance examinations, because they were falsely denounced as "bourgeois litter." Borodin says, "There were a great many similar denunciations and the social selection committees were kept busy reading them, and had not the time or opportunities to check up on the truth."[150]

Jews remained old enemies among some segments of the population, even though "many Jews" in the Donbas "were very, very poor."[151] This sentiment may have been a reflection of the larger representation of ethnic Jews in positions of responsibility. According to a 1923 survey, of 601 "leading figures" in the Donbas (party and Komsomol leaders, technical experts, and others) 77, or 25.8 percent, were said to be Jews.[152] Jews appeared to be designated as enemies even within the Communist Party. Borodin recounts the following conversation with a Novocherkassk Communist in 1927:

> "I'm not anti-semitic, I am a Communist and former Red Guard, but you know, all the members of the opposition are Jews. Trotsky, Zinoviev, Kamenev, Buckarin. . . . "
>
> "Buckarin is not a Jew," I contradicted.
>
> "A masked Jew," the man replied with conviction, "and if the opposition were allowed to rule, we would become a Jewish kingdom, they will put in their Jews everywhere. I was secretly told this by a reliable man who was sent from the propaganda group of the Central Committee of the Communist Party to deliver lectures in our district."[153]

Even though Borodin's memory is somewhat unreliable (Bukharin was Stalin's ally in 1927), his account is consistent with popular anti-Semitic views. One is reminded that in 1922 when Lenin suggested Trotsky assume the position of

---

of fellow villagers were widely practiced in the prerevolutionary Russian village. See Jeffrey Burds, *Peasant Dreams and Market Politics: Peasant Labor Migration. Culture and Community in Old Regime Russia, 1861–1914* (University of Pittsburgh Press, forthcoming).

[149] Borodin, *One Man in His Time*, p. 18.

[150] Ibid., pp. 52–53.

[151] Interview 2, according to whom they spoke poor Russian while the rich Jews spoke good Russian.

[152] V. M. Nikol's'kyi, "Natsional'nyi sklad kerivnykh ta vidpovidal'nykh pratsivnykiv Donbasu na pochatku 20-rokiv," *Mizhnatsional'ni vidnosyny na pivdni Ukrainy*, pt. 3 (Zaporizhzhia, 1993), pp. 222–23.

[153] Borodin, *One Man in His Time*, p. 59.

vice-chair of the cabinet (Council of People's Commissars), Trotsky declined on the grounds that by taking up the number 2 position in the Soviet government, he would only help the enemy by inciting popular anti-Semitism. A year later, Trotsky reminded his colleagues of the serious consequences of a Jew's leading the Red Army during the civil war, and asserted that Lenin, while dismissing Trotsky's reasoning as "nonsense," had implicitly accepted it.[154] In 1925, colliers at Mine 15 of the Snizhne Coalfield were reported to believe that "Trotsky wants to become a tsar": "The Jews have taken power into their hands and want to seat their own Jewish tsar."[155]

There were enemies from without as well. The nobles and landowners had been dispossessed, politically suppressed, and deported;[156] some emigrated abroad. Likewise, former capitalists were dispossessed and many of them fled and revived their organizations abroad. These people, along with many others (intellectuals, White officers, Ukrainian nationalists, local warlords such as Makhno) were constantly described by the Soviet government as "enemies from without," who, supported by capitalist countries, were still attempting to restore capitalism in the Soviet Union by armed intervention. The deeply "offended fathers" remained belligerent and dreamed of overthrowing the Soviet government.[157] These dreams were unrealistic, however, because the offended fathers lacked strong military forces. At the time, however politically dangerous it may have been, foreign correspondence was still relatively free and possible; so was border crossing.[158]

The identity of the enemy was far from clear, however. There were old enemies such as the *spetsy*, kulaks, and Jews, but the "official" and "popular" enemies were not identical, as was the case for the Jews, whom the government never officially regarded as enemies at that time.

The complicating factor and that which exacerbated the growing divide between the perceptions of the workers and those of the party was the rise of Communists to power. During the civil war the Communists had proved to be

---

[154]"L. D. Trotskii zashchishchaetsia," *Voprosy istorii KPSS*, 1990, no. 5, pp. 36–37.

[155]The GPU's "top secret" report in DADO, f. R-1146, op. 2, spr. 348, ark. 249.

[156]As of March 1928, in Stalino *okruh*, there were fifty-four former landed gentries and large landowners; of them twenty-nine had been exempted from deportation. DADO, f. R-129, op. 1, spr. 13, ark. 27–28.

[157]See, for example, B. A. Starkov, "Utverzhdenie rezhima lichnoi vlasti I. V. Stalina i soprotivlenie v partii i gosudarstve (itogi i uroki politicheskoi bor'by v 30-e gody)" (Doktorskaia diss., St. Peterburgskii politologicheskii institut, 1992), ch. 3, which uses Soviet secret police documents.

[158]See, for example, James E. Mace and Leonid Heretz, eds., *Oral History Project of the Commission on the Ukrainian Famine* (Washington, D.C., 1990), 1:284 and 287. According to this testimony, in 1928 it became impossible to cross the border, in this case, to Poland. In 1922–25, however, at five western border checkpoints alone, 11,641 persons were detained. Of these, 675 were "spies and terrorists" and 2,604 were smugglers. See *Pogranichnye voiska, 1918–1928. Sbornik dokumentov i materialov* (Moscow, 1973), p. 525.

staunch patriots, but they also proved to be no democrats. The Donbas colliers found themselves disparaged by the party once the civil war came to a close and their religious beliefs derided and attacked even after the NEP was introduced. They had reason to believe that a new autocracy had been restored in the country: the new regime had enforced a one-party dictatorship, organized a powerful secret police, the GPU, and deprived the parliament (Soviets) and the trade unions of power, turning them into largely cosmetic devices, with Lenin and then Stalin presiding as a new tsar.

Indeed, this view had been propounded since the October Revolution by influential intellectuals, many of whom were eventually forced out of the country or chose to emigrate abroad. From this perspective, the new ruler became the enemy of the oppressed. Many of the new bosses were of humble origins and had been promoted to positions of responsibility. Yet, as was discussed earlier, at least some of them soon acquired "bourgeois tastes," behaving much as the old enemies had. It was as if the enemies of enemies had become new enemies.

Nor, from the point of view of Moscow, was the image of the enemy easy to draw. Take the 1923 Kapustin affair in Shakhty. Kapustin's identity remains ambiguous; he may have been a Red Cossack ataman. Whatever the case, the workers appeared to Moscow to have been incited by former Communist and former White Cossack officers. In comparison, the civil war period was indeed much simpler.

Under one-party dictatorship, nonparty associations were politically suspect by default. One could fool the authorities and protect religious practice by displaying portraits of Lenin, Zinov'ev, and Kalinin along with those of Jesus and Virgin Mary.[159] The free steppe continued to provide a refuge for kulaks, former Whites, Makhnovites, and other fugitives who came to the Donbas, hiding or changing their identities, and working.[160] The moral strength of communities varied. The practice of denunciations undoubtedly threatened to divide them; so did the network of police informers. Suspicious of nonparty associations, the party mounted intermittent attacks on them in the 1920s.

Police agents could not easily penetrate the Donbas communities, however. The aforementioned agent Viacheslav Galitskii, for example, was almost lynched by a crowd. His secret work became known to the party secretary of the factory in which he worked, because the GPU asked the secretary not to include him among those to be made redundant. One day, the secretary, when drunk, caught Galitskii in the street and declared that the man was a

[159]DADO, f. R-1146, op. 2, spr. 348, ark. 364. Different interpretations are possible, however: they were ambivalent about their religiosity, or they created new gods out of Communist leaders.

[160]See cases of hunting of such enemies in DADO, f. R-391, op. 1, spr. 77, and f. R-129, op. 1, spr. 7. For an interesting personal account, see Vladimir A. Bohdan, *Avoiding Extinction: Children of the Kulak* (New York, 1992), pp. 15 and 18–19.

GPU agent collecting information and that people ought to be careful, otherwise they would be put in jail. Galitskii was chased by a crowd of hundreds of children and idlers, but he managed to escape.[161]

From the party's point of view, the question, "Who is the enemy?" – that is, the identification of political enemies – was supremely important, almost a life-or-death matter. It became such an obsession that the party even searched for enemies within its own ranks. The party leaders invariably explained divisions within the party in class terms, and branded defeated opponents as agents of enemies, that is, bourgeois and petit bourgeois forces.

Clearly there was a grave danger of enemies becoming all-inclusive. Willful abuses were legion, such as listing critics as counterrevolutionaries.[162] Yet there was more to this problem. Because the government had banned any method for measuring the popular mood, such as free elections and polls, information gathering became difficult. The party encouraged all institutions to collect data in order to gauge the popular mood: the party, the trade unions, the Komsomol, and the Soviets and their inspection organizations all made a considerable effort in this respect. When the people understood the new rules of the game, they found it safest to keep silent. Occasionally people spoke out and even staged collective action; yet they knew well that freedom was severely restricted, that collective action, unless sponsored by the authorities, was dangerous, and that the law provided no protection.

Many people did petition, often at great risk, to the local and central authorities and to the local and central press for assistance and intervention. Yet, apart from these actions, secret police surveillance often became virtually the only means by which to fathom the thoughts and moods that had gone underground. The surveillance reports, usually classified "top secret," detailed various cases of remarks critical of the party and the government, but almost none of these reports ever attempted to give the policy makers an accurate sense of popular political mood other than general remarks such as "Generally good, but . . . ," or "Much discontent was observed in connection with . . . " To identify who was the enemy among the silent masses was no easy matter. It was therefore as easy for the party to have an exaggerated sense of enemy strength as it was expedient to manipulate information to suit political purposes.

[161] DADO, f. R-129, op. 1, spr. 6, ark. 135–135zv.
[162] See, for example, *Stenograficheskii otchet plenuma Donetskogo gubkoma KP(b)U. 9–10 iiunia 1925 goda* (Artemivs'k, 1925), p. 45.

5 The Famine Crisis

THE GREAT ECONOMIC TRANSFORMATIONS of the late 1920s and early 1930s brought political upheaval: millions were disenfranchised. In its drive for industrialization and collectivization Moscow waged war against presumed enemies, many of whom sought refuge in the Donbas. The 1932–33 famine crisis, a result of the economic and political upheaval, brought Stalin's leadership into question. Even some of his own erstwhile supporters within the Communist Party were alienated by the severe measures taken during the crisis. Faced with this new political tension, Moscow began to paint the image of enemies in different colors; a conceptual shift was under way from "class enemy" to the class-neutral "enemy of the people." The famine crisis was critical to this shift, a shift that led to the Great Terror.

Collectivization and Industrialization

From 1927 to 1928 onward, Moscow terrorized "class enemies" and "wreckers" in an effort to overcome economic and political crises. The deeper the crises, the harsher the terror became. The famous Shakhty affair of 1928, directed against "bourgeois" specialists, became the hallmark for Moscow's war against the NEP.[1] It was no accident that the Donbas coal-mining industry, of which Shakhty was an important part, played a central role in this "revolution from above": it was there that tension had been running exceptionally high. Political terror against alleged "class enemies," symbolized by the Shakhty affair, had proved very popular.[2] The atmosphere of the time is well described by a British journalist who visited the country in 1929 and 1930: "I was not

[1] See Hiroaki Kuromiya, "The Shakhty Affair," *South East European Monitor*, 4:2 (1997), pp. 41–64.
[2] See Hiroaki Kuromiya, *Stalin's Industrial Revolution: Politics and Workers, 1928–1932* (Cambridge University Press, 1988).

Figure 5.1. Defendants listening to their sentences at the Shakhty trial, 1928. From TsDKFFA, od. zb. 2-31336.

quite certain whether I was moving in an atmosphere of revolution or of war. The atmosphere seemed to contain elements of both."[3]

The imperative of industrialization diverted resources increasingly rapidly from consumption to capital accumulation. This, in turn, destabilized the market. When the resultant grain procurement crisis broke out in late 1927, Stalin and his close associates responded with "extraordinary measures" – extralegal measures against kulaks and other wealthy residents who were suspected of hoarding grain. Stalin and L. M. Kaganovich declared the crisis to be "a grain strike," an "expression of the first serious action, under the conditions of the NEP, undertaken by the capitalist elements of the countryside against the Soviet government.[4] The crisis created a food shortage in the cities where by 1929 rationing began to be introduced widely (later Stalin called the situation *golod*, i.e., famine or hunger).[5] When the use of force overcame the immediate crisis, V. V. Kuibyshev proudly declared: "The will of the party can create

[3]*An Impression of Russia: Reprinted from the Economist, November 1st, 1930* (London, 1930), p. 10.

[4]Kuromiya, *Stalin's Industrial Revolution*, p. 6.

[5]RTsKhIDNI, f. 85, op. 28, d. 8, l. 189. Indeed in some areas in Ukraine small-scale famine did take place. See Valerii Vasiliev, "Krest'ianskie vosstaniia na Ukraine. 1929–1930 gody," *Svobodnaia mysl'*, 1992, no. 9, p. 71.

miracles . . . and is creating and will create miracles despite all these market phenomena. . . . The will of the state has crushed the market [*gosudarstvennaia volia slomila kon"iunkturu*]."[6]

The use of force split the party leadership. For N. I. Bukharin and other "rightists" it spelled the end of civil peace with the peasantry and the possible eventuality of the government's defeat in a war with the peasantry and foreign powers.[7] They proposed as a solution to the crisis, not the use of force, but an import of grain. Yet, in the view of Stalin and his supporters, such a solution was merely a palliative: if it solved the problem that year, then what was to be done the following year?[8] So the use of force did not cease. In the meantime the collectivization of agriculture (the creation of collective farms) as a permanent solution to the vexing problems of the peasantry loomed large on the political agenda for the Stalin leadership: it believed that collective farms would ease the difficulty of the procurement of grain.[9] The right never questioned the ultimate goal of collectivization, but it regarded the speed and the ways in which collectivization was being carried out as a sure way to civil war with the peasantry.

As the right feared, the 1929–30 wholesale collectivization and dekulakization ("elimination of the kulaks as a class") campaign strained the political situation. In one Artemivs'k village, the day after the 1929 October Revolution anniversary, Ia. P. Trufanov, a Ukrainian peasant who was working in the Red Army coalfield and who owned seventeen desiatinas of land with his father and therefore was regarded as a kulak, appeared before the village Soviet along with the Perepechaienko brothers, in order to lodge a protest against collectivization. Trufanov attacked the village Soviet secretary T. Tereshchenko and the worker brigade representative Vysots'kyi, yelling: "I'll hang these Communist reptiles. You rob the peasants, you take our grain and estates. I'll show you how to rob." Trufanov was arrested. The younger Perepechaienko shouted: "Why do you mock a person who speaks the truth?" The Perepechaienkos too were arrested. Trufanov was sentenced to eight years of imprisonment (which subsequently was commuted to five years), the Perepechaienkos to three years each.[10]

A large number of peasants were dispossessed and deported to various parts of the country. As people would sing in Stalino in 1929,

[6]Kuromiya, *Stalin's Industrial Revolution*, p. 8.

[7]Bukharin intimated this to Iu.(G.) L. Piatakov. See "Materialy fevral'sko-martovskogo plenuma TsK VKP(b) 1937 goda," *Voprosy istorii*, 1992, nos. 2–3, p. 19.

[8]See G. K. Ordzhonikidze's response to Bukharin in *N. I. Bukharin, Problemy teorii i praktiki sotsializma* (Moscow, 1989), p. 289.

[9]For the events leading up to the all-out collectivization campaign, see R. W. Davies, *The Socialist Offensive: The Collectivization of Agriculture, 1929–1930* (Harvard University Press, 1980).

[10]"Rozkurkulennia v USSR," *Ukrains'kyi istorychnyi zhurnal*, 1992, no. 3, pp. 77–78.

Figure 5.2. Dekulakized peasants in the village of Udachne, Hryshyne in the early 1930s. From TsDKFFA, od. zb. 3-1101.

> Oh, the apple ripens
> The kulak surrenders grain
> And bows down.[11]

The secret police (GPU) was involved directly in this dekulakization campaign, deciding the fate of each kulak and his family.[12] Among the dekulakized were many peasants with a perfect political past, former Red partisans.[13] An untold number of peasants were executed; some of those on their way to exile were beaten to death by convoys or could not survive the brutal deportation process, which took months or more.[14]

The brutality with which collectivization and dekulakization were carried out led here and there to "armed uprisings" by peasants. In 1930 in the village Ievhenivka in the Donbas, a large group of armed men (Communists, Komsomols, and policemen) arrested at night those who did not wish to join the collective farm. The following morning the peasants gathered at the village Soviet and demanded the release of those arrested. Polina, the seventeen-year-

---

[11] RF IMFE, f. 1-7/816, ark. 74.

[12] See, for example, DADO, f. R-391sch, op. 1, spr. 218, ark. 71–73.

[13] "Rozkurkulennia," pp. 81 and 83–84.

[14] For these cruelties, see, for example, N. Mikhailov and N. Teptsov, "Chrezvychaishchina," *Rodina*, 1989, no. 8.

Figure 5.3. Dekulakized peasants in the village of Udachne, Hryshyne, in the early 1930s. From TsDKFFA, od. zb. 3-1102.

old daughter of the arrested I. K. Makovets'kyi, cried and entreated, but she was shot dead on the spot. The armed men did not allow the Makovets'kyi family to take away the body of Polina and bury it. Instead, during the night her body was removed to an unknown place. The arrested were sent to the district center, so the villagers assembled there armed themselves with sticks and forks. Their protest resulted in the release of some, but the fate of others is unknown to this day.[15] Similar and more violent protests were observed all over the country.[16]

Stalin halted collectivization temporarily and sought to overcome the political crisis by creating the ghost of pervasive enemies bent on restoring the old regime to the country and sabotaging "socialist construction." Recently declassified archival data clearly show that already in 1930 Stalin had had a substantial number of "enemies" shot.[17]

[15] *Put' k kommunizmu*, 23 May 1989 (Memoir of A. S. Iablons'kyi).

[16] See, for example, peasant uprisings in Ukraine in Vasil'ev, "Krest'ianskie vosstanie," and Lynne Viola, *Peasant Rebels under Stalin: Collectivization and the Culture of Peasant Resistance* (Oxford University Press, 1996).

[17] *Vecherniaia Moskva*, for example, began publishing execution lists (*rasstrel'nye spiski*) on 6 December 1990, which include many executions in 1930. This, however, does not imply that before 1930 executions did not take place.

In the Donbas as elsewhere, after a short break, the collectivization and dekulakization campaign resumed with as much ferocity as before. In 1931 in Novopskovs'k district in the northern Donbas, a report was sent to Moscow stating that, although 85 percent of the district had been collectivized, 10 percent of the collective farmers had no bread. Those unwilling to join collective farms, whether they were poor or middle peasants, were declared kulaks, dispossessed, and confined to the ravines, where they lived in utter poverty and hunger in dugouts. The kolkhoz officials looted and drank away the estates of the dekulakized. At night shootings took place, and the police were in a combat situation.[18] The GPU reported with alarm that some kulaks sent to the north had come back.[19] In 1931 arson and armed assaults had become common in the Donbas countryside.[20]

Collectivization and dekulakization were accompanied by antireligious campaigns. Churches were closed or destroyed, and the clergy arrested or deported. Already in 1928, Bishop Neveu reported from Makiivka that "arrests among our Orthodox brethren have multiplied to an alarming extent." In 1929, "even families with whom I used to be very friendly were afraid to show their faces in church in case they should lose their daily bread." In 1930 his church was placed under seal, to be converted into a cinema. "The crosses in the cemetery had been knocked down in preparation for turning it into a public park."[21] From April 1929 to April 1930, thirty-six chapels were closed in Artemivs'k *okruh*, and a synagogue was closed in Rykove. Komsomol activists of the "Union of Militant Atheists" went through the peasant huts, seized icons, and then burned them in bonfires in the market squares.[22] In a Donbas city an American engineer saw "a clergyman, tired and overwrought, and weak from hunger, attempt to get on a street car, five young Communists spat on him, and one kicked him in the chest, and he fell off the car and swooned into the gutter."[23]

Collectivization and dekulakization were particularly devastating for certain ethnic groups. The dekulakization rates among the Bulgarian, German, and Greek farmers were much higher than the average.[24] Ten percent of the

---

[18]"Rozkurkulennia v USRR," *Ukrains'kyi istorychnyi zhurnal*, 1992, no. 6, pp. 111–13.

[19]DADO, f. R-391sch, op. 1, spr. 218, ark. 101.

[20]See, for example, GARF, f. 7416, op. 1, d. 8, l. 43.

[21]Patrick A. Croghan, *The Peasant from Makeyevka: Biography of Bishop Pius Neveu, A.A.* (Worcester, Mass., 1982), pp. 183, 201, and 206.

[22]T. Bespechnyi, "Kak rushili tserkov' v Donbasse," *Vechernii Donetsk*, 22 September 1990.

[23]William H. Grady, "Communistic Russia: The Viewpoint of an American Mining Engineer," *Mining Congress Journal*, 17 (August 1931), p. 5.

[24]*Vtoroe Vseukrainskoe soveshchanie po rabote sredi natsional'nykh men'shinstv, 27–30 noiabria 1930 goda. Sten. otchet i postanovleniia* (Moscow, Kharkiv, and Minsk, 1931), pp. 46, 54, 122, 128, and 131. See also L. P. Pol'ovyi and B. V. Chirko, "Natsional'ni menshyny ukrains'koho sela v umovakh kolektyvizatsii," *Ukrains'kyi istorychnyi zhurnal*, 1993, nos. 4–6.

Greek farmers were deported. In Hryshyne, 40 percent of the German peasants were dekulakized.[25] Old conflicts that dated from the prerevolutionary years resurfaced with collectivization and dekulakization.[26] Minorities would say, "*Katsapy* have invaded our land from Russia," or "A Ukrainian has come . . . to rule us." Thus, in Mar'iupol' Greeks and Ukrainians came to blows.[27] Many Greeks and Germans made largely futile attempts to emigrate abroad.[28] Many poor Jews, dispossessed for their trade activity, were driven into Jewish collective farms. Thirty percent of the Jews were said to have been disenfranchised at this time.[29]

One important consequence of collectivization and dekulakization was that many peasants were pushed from the countryside into industrial and construction labor. In 1928 the Donbas was still suffering from many unemployed workers who upset the towns and settlements by causing disorder and engaging in "anti-Soviet" propaganda.[30] By 1929, however, the number of unemployed dropped dramatically and by 1930 unemployment had virtually disappeared.[31]

The Donbas had always attracted labor, but the absence of unemployment and the labor shortage that resulted from rapid industrialization made the Donbas an irresistible magnet for labor. The Donbas had historically provided a haven for fugitives, and it continued to retain its reputation as the free steppe during and after collectivization: many who had reason to flee believed that they could "hide" in the Donbas.

As pressure mounted against the market in general in the late 1920s, NEP-men, artisans, priests, and kulaks (including former Cossacks) were forced out and sought employment in the Donbas.[32] At Chubar' Mine, one report noted, 28 percent of the workers were "anti-Soviet elements: former officers, gendarmes, and other scum."[33] According to Sheila Fitzpatrick's calculation, in the country as a whole, at least ten million peasants entered the wage- and

[25]TsDAVO, f. 413, op. 1, spr. 591, ark. 2.

[26]V. N. Nikol'skii, "Nemetskoe naselenie Donbassa 20-kh gg. (nekotorye problemy)," *Donbass i Priazov'e: problemy sotsial'nogo, natsional'nogo i dukhovnogo razvitiia* (Mariupol', 1993), p. 96.

[27]TsDAVO, f. 413, op. 1, spr. 561, ark. 44 and 50–51.

[28]*Vtoroe Vseukrainskoe soveshchanie po rabote sredi natsional'nykh men'shinstv*, passim, and "Raskulachivali dazhe . . . inostrantsev. Dokumenty perioda kollektivizatsii," in *Neizvestnaia Rossiia*, vol. 2 (Moscow, 1992), p. 329.

[29]*Vtoroe Vseukrainskoe soveshchanie po rabote sredi natsional'nykh men'shinstv*, pp. 30 and 55. Many Greek merchants met the same fate.

[30]DADO, f. R-1490, op. 1sch, d. 28, ll. 131–32, and RTsKhIDNI, f. 17, op. 85, d. 307, ll. 23 and 78.

[31]TsDAVO, f. 2623, op. 1, spr. 3312, ark. 8, and Z. G. Lykholobova, "Do istorii likvidatsii bezrobittia v Donbasi (1926–1930 rr.)," *Ukrains'kyi istorychnyi zhurnal*, 1971, no. 5, p. 114.

[32]See Z. G. Likholobova and Iu. N. Krasnosov, *Kolichestvennyi rost i sotsial'no-demograficheskie izmeneniia v sostave shakhterov Donbassa v 1926–1932 gg.* (Donets'k, 1986), pp. 16–17.

[33]GARF, f. 5459, op. 10, d. 10, l. 186.

salary-earning work force, and "three out of ten peasants migrating to town or entering the wage labor force in the years 1928–1932 were probably departing wholly or essentially involuntarily from the villages in connection with dekulakization." This calculation does not include those "self-dekulakized" who "left on their own initiative out of fear of being expropriated by the authorities."[34] There were many of them. In 1930 in the northern Caucasus that included part of the Donbas, for example, eleven thousand households were to be resettled as "third-category" kulaks (i.e., those who were spared imprisonment or outright deportation), but only five thousand were actually resettled, "since the rest turned out to have disappeared from the locality."[35] In October 1930 the mass employment of kulaks and other "undesirable elements" in industry prompted the government to issue a secret order to purge the enterprises of these elements.[36] Yet the real problem for the authorities was that many of these people concealed their identity and kept quiet; some of them even became exemplary workers such as shock workers and, later, Stakhanovites.

The order and campaign to remove enemy forces proved ineffective: the Donbas (or, for that matter, the country as a whole) was hungry for labor, people of whatever origin found employment easily in a sellers' labor market. No one was to be hired without proper documentation, and yet many were employed without any check; others used forged documents. While many workers lived and worked in fear of exposure, testimony after testimony suggests that it was indeed very easy to find work in the Donbas at this time.[37]

The constant threat of arrest, however, made labor transient. One witness, for example, who was dekulakized in Kirovohrad in 1929 and fled to the Donbas in 1930, has given this testimony:

> If no one who knows you notices you, then you can work [in the Donbas], only keep silent about who you are, where you are from. This was never spoken. This was all locked up in the individual. People worked in this way. As soon as someone notices, then you become frightened and wonder where to hide, because if someone notices you, then people will know that you are there. So people leave.[38]

---

[34] Sheila Fitzpatrick, "The Great Departure: Rural-Urban Migration in the Soviet Union, 1929–1933," in William G. Rosenberg and Lewis H. Siegelbaum, ed., *Social Dimensions of Soviet Industrialization* (Indiana University Press, 1993), pp. 22 and 25.

[35] Ibid., pp. 37–38, n. 53.

[36] GARF, f. 5515, op. 33, d. 11, ll. 53–54.

[37] Note many testimonies in James E. Mace and Leonid Heretz, eds., *Oral History Project of the Commission on the Ukraine Famine*, 3 vols. (Washington, D.C., 1990). See also Dmytro Solovey, *The Golgotha of Ukraine* (New York, 1953), pp. 11–15 and 17–20; Vladimir A. Bohdan, *Avoiding Extinction: Children of the Kulak* (New York, 1992), p. 78; Antonina Khelemendyk-Kokot, *Kolhospne dytynstvo i nimets'ka nevolia. Spohady* (Toronto, 1989), pp. 61 and 82; and Jochen Hellbeck, ed., *Tagebuch aus Moskau 1931–1939* (Munich, 1996), pp. 81 and 87.

[38] Mace and Heretz, *Oral History Project* 2:1136–37.

People moved from mine to mine and were able to hide. The Donbas remained the free steppe, but the fear of loss of freedom was also evident in the Donbas.

There was another kind of fear, fear of "wrecking." One of the accusations against the "bourgeois" specialists at the Shakhty trial was wrecking, which included the destruction of expensive mining equipment and the willful causing of accidents and deaths of colliers.[39] Mining was, and is, highly prone to accidents. (In the mining community of Shakhty, for example, eight out of every ten colliers had had some kind of industrial injury in 1927.)[40] So the accusations of wrecking struck a responsive chord in the workers. Yet suspicions of wrecking were cast not only upon the *spetsy* but also upon "class enemies" among the workers – kulaks, NEPmen, priests, and so forth.

There are many frightening cases. In November 1928 at a Donbas mine dynamite was found underneath the rails.[41] Here and there electric cables were severed, ventilation tubes damaged, sand thrown into roll bearings, bolts and nails into machines, motors broken, and dynamite stolen.[42] Soviet officials described these incidents not as accidents but as deliberate sabotage by class enemies. In one case, an electric cable was cut, with seven meters of it missing. (Most likely, someone stole it to use for other purposes, because it was *defitsitnyi material*, material in short supply.) In another, a Tartar, who did not know the Russian language and hence did not understand the safety instructions, if such had been given at all, hung his lamp on a naked electrical cable and was electrocuted. In yet another, a worker was crushed to death on an underground rail by a wagon without lights. All these incidents were ascribed to wrecking.[43]

Dangerous working conditions caused numerous injuries and deaths throughout the 1930s. As in the case of the Shakhty affair, whether deliberate wrecking had been committed was impossible to prove. Whatever the case, what struck American engineers who worked in the Donbas at that time was the general indifference to human life.[44] Angry workers may have believed in wrecking by "class enemies," but they were also well aware that many Communist bosses were not overly concerned with securing workers' safety, often attributing accidents to wrecking or to the carelessness of the miners themselves. At one mine, a worker refused to go to the pit face because it was

[39] See Kuromiya, "The Shakhty Affair."

[40] B. I. Bakulin and O. L. Leibovich, "Rabochie, 'spetsy,' partiitsy (o sotsial'nykh istokakh 'velikogo pereloma')," *Rabochii klass i sovremennyi mir*, 1990, no. 6, p. 104.

[41] GARF, f. 5459, op. 9, d. 136, l. 7. For another case, see ibid., op. 10, d. 33, l. 18.

[42] Ibid., op. 10, d. 33, l. 18; op. 11, d. 139, ll. 68–68ob, and d. 155, l. 26. See many cases reported in, for example, Bor. Galin, *Perekhod. Kniga ocherkov (1929–1930)* (Moscow, 1930), p. 57; V. Turov, *Na shturm uglia* (Moscow, 1931), pp. 8–10, and *Donbass udarnyi* (Moscow and Leningrad, 1930), pp. 115–16.

[43] GARF, f. 5459, op. 11, d. 139, l. 75.

[44] Note, particularly, the Clarence Starr Collection, Hoover Institution Archive, Stanford, Calif.

not properly consolidated. So the managers sent a norm-busting shock worker (*udarnik*), who was killed in a cave-in. It took four days to recover his body.[45] The workers might well have wondered whether this was also wrecking. Their distrust is clearly seen in letters written to the authorities (including the GPU) asking for intervention in order to hold managers responsible for accidents and deaths.[46]

Ethnic animosity only reinforced fear of and anger with the imagined enemy. There were cases in which people from capitalist countries (Germany and the United States) were beaten by Russian workers.[47] Jews remained popular enemies in the Donbas. In 1928 the murders of a Jew and a Chinese were reported from Luhans'k. The murderer, a blacksmith and apparently a Ukrainian, was quoted to have said that he killed Jews, and not Russians, because there were not many Jews but there were too many Russians.[48] (Nor, no doubt, were there many Chinese.) In Artemivs'k, the food shortages, which began in 1928, led immediately to a rise in anti-Semitism.[49] Many Jews, particularly young Komsomols, came to work in the Donbas mines during the period of rapid industrialization. Some came voluntarily, others through Komsomol mobilizations. There, they were spat on, beaten, and referred to contemptuously as Yids (*zhidy*). At one mine, a Jewish Komsomol worker was whipped while bathing in a bathhouse.[50] Colliers in Luhans'k refused to sit in the shaft cage with Jews and beat them in the dark underground with rocks.[51] Beatings of Jewish farmers frequently took place in the countryside as well.[52] In Stalino, a Jewish worker named Davidzan had tar smeared on his face, while "sensible schoolchildren" attacked Jewish schools with stones and beat the children bloody.[53] Official campaigns against anti-Semitism led nowhere in Ukraine, according to an official report, with the children resembling Janus: an official face at school and an anti-Semitic face outside.[54]

The secret police constantly uncovered and punished alleged political enemies and wreckers: *spetsy*, kulaks, NEPmen, priests, former Whites, Makhnovites. (Some of these came to be referred to as *byvshie liudi*, or "has-beens,"

[45]GARF, f. 5451, op. 14, d. 259, l. 27.

[46]See, for example, ibid., f. 5515, op. 33, d. 24, ll. 29–31. According to a government report, deaths by accidents in the Donbas coal-mining industry increased by 29.6% from 1929 to 1930. Ibid., d. 36, ll. 135–37 and 155–57.

[47]Ibid., f. 7416, op. 1, d. 8, l. 58ob.

[48]TsDAVO, f. 2605, op. 2, spr. 602, ark. 53. His reference to "Jews" may imply that he had murdered more than one Jew.

[49]RTsKhIDNI, f. 17, op. 85, d. 307, l. 67.

[50]GARF, f. 5459, op. 11, d. 173, l. 50b.

[51]TsDAVO, f. 2605, op. 2, spr. 602, ark. 63, and TsDAHO, f. 1, op. 20, spr. 3021, ark. 5.

[52]DADO, f. R-1202, op. 2, spr. 48, ark. 120.

[53]TsDAHO, f. 1, op. 20, spr. 3021, ark. 5 and 9.

[54]Ibid., op. 20, spr. 2894, ark. 26. See also *Ievreis'ke naselennia pivdnia Ukrainy: istoriia ta suchasnist'* (Zaporizhzhia, 1992), pp. 81–82.

implying people who ceased to exist as a social and political group.) On the popular level, however, there were the unofficial enemies such as the Jews.

The problem was that it became increasingly difficult to identify the alleged enemies: "The enemy, beaten in open battle, is seeking detours to undermine the foundations of proletarian dictatorship. The enemy has changed colors according to the latest in the technology of social mimicry."[55] This was particularly the case in the Donbas where many individuals fled and changed their identities to live a new life. Hence came the vigilance and denunciation campaign.

However popular political repression of class enemies may have been in the Donbas, the party and the government could hardly rely on the Donbas politically. The popular perception that the Communist bosses were a new kind of enemy strengthened at this time with the growing discontent among the workers. One party leader, who journeyed to the Donbas after the announcement of the Shakhty affair, was asked at a Shcherbynivka mine: "Weren't Communist Party members among the arrested traitors?"[56]

The impact of the food shortage was reflected immediately in the popular perception of the party. In February 1928 rotten meat was knowingly sold in Artemivs'k. Workers bitterly complained that the promises of a better life given by the party were just fairy tales of Communist spongers.[57] In the summer of 1928 several strikes by miners broke out, with strikers demanding higher wages, lower work quotas, and better food supply. A hewers' strike that took place on 27 June 1928 at the "Italy" mine in Makiivka was initiated by a group of seven that included two party members and one Komsomol member. The outcome of the strike is not known.[58]

The crassness of some Communist bosses surely antagonized many people. After the Shakhty affair, many party dignitaries were dispatched to the Donbas for an inspection. One of them, Molotov, along with the local bosses, visited miners' living quarters. He met a miner's wife and told her that he, secretary of the party Central Committee, wished to know how she was living. She answered that she lived so-so, but that because the floor of her living place was cement her first child had died and now her second child was ill. Molotov said that it was too bad and was about to leave when the woman yelled after him: "Comrade Molotov, we need to lay a floor." Molotov agreed that the floor needed to be laid and left. Instead of offering any practical help, however, Molotov merely scolded the local bosses, who told Molotov that such floor problems were legion and that little money was available to repair the

---

[55] *Makeevskii rabochii*, 30 December 1931.
[56] GARF, f. 374sch, op. 27sch, d. 1332, ll. 91 and 128.
[57] RTsKhIDNI, f. 17, op. 85, d. 311, l. 80.
[58] Smolensk Archive, WKP 250, pp. 47–48. See also DADO, f. R-129, op. 1, spr. 24, ark. 253.

workers' living quarters.[59] British miners who visited the Donbas in 1929 were impressed by the sharp contrast between the grandiose theaters and monuments and the humble houses of the workers. They confronted the local Soviet official:

> The local Soviet official was asked why they spent a huge sum of money in building the theatres while allowing the workers to live in overcrowded hovels, and his reply was: "If we make the workers too comfortable they will refuse to fight, or take any active part in politics."

So the British miners responded that

> the rising generation will say: "Where are the houses you promised us? Where the prosperity, wages, pleasures, comforts?" Then there will be another revolution.[60]

The disregard for workers is clear from the following anecdote in which, at a Donbas mine, a Communist manager constantly spit on the floor during his report to a meeting. One of the cleaning people brought a spitoon and put it beside him, but the manager stubbornly kept spitting on the floor, completely ignoring the spitoon. He did not understand that after the meeting people would have to clean the floor.[61]

As in the 1923 Kapustin affair (see Chapter 4), certain outspoken figures, usually non–party members, who enjoyed much authority among the Donbas miners were considered suspect. The accounting clerk at the Shchyhliivka Coalfield near Stalino, Mironenko, was such a one. In the autumn of 1928, when he heard that the chairman of the Ukrainian Council of People's Commissariats, V. Ia. Chubar', was to speak in Stalino, Mironenko took the trouble to walk eight kilometers through mud, appear before the meeting, and, along with other "anti-Soviet elements," assail the party for its "suppression of the working class and for the lack of democracy in the country." The party organizations asked the GPU to take appropriate measures. Subsequently, when on May Day of 1929 Mironenko gave an "anti-Soviet" speech to a large crowd of workers, he was arrested. He then roused the workers, calling the GPU agents gendarmes. The GPU contended that Mironenko had served in the White Army; however, the prosecutor's office thought it impossible given his age (sixteen years old in 1918). The GPU maintained that Mironenko had won many workers to his view, but the prosecutor's office disagreed. Conflict with

---

[59]TsDAVO, f. 2602, op. 1, spr. 2320, ark. 39.

[60]W. Haydon, ed., *Russia as Seen by Two Tilmanstone Miners: A Record of a Tour to the Donetz Basin in Aug.–Sept. 1929* (Dover, 1929), p. 18, and *Our Journey through Russia. A First-Hand Account by Two British Working-Men of a Journey through Russia* (London, 1929), p. 27.

[61]GARF, f. 5459, op. 9, d. 23, l. 82.

the prosecutor's office led the local GPU to complain to Kiev. What happened to Mironenko eventually is unknown.[62]

Even among party members, the GPU reported that there were enemies. One member named Stepura, a Makiivka worker, was said to have boasted to his fellow workers that he had served in the Denikin army and that he and his soldiers had slaughtered all the scum: Communists and Russians. He urged his men to wait for the return of the Whites and butcher the *katsapy* (Russians) and the Reds.[63]

Many accounts also suggest that religious opposition strengthened noticeably in the Donbas.[64] While the Orthodox church was under attack, other sects, which had always been strong in the Donbas, became larger by absorbing many of the refugees and kulaks from other parts of the country. Baptist preachers, reportedly with financial support from foreign bourgeoisie, traveled around the Donbas.[65] In 1929 in Artemivs'k *okruh*, for example, there were 175,000 members of various religious sects whereas there were only 118,000 trade-union members.[66]

Violence was used not just against the alleged class enemies. Many managers beat miners.[67] New workers, who might have been kulaks, or who might have been poor peasants full of youthful expectations for a new life in the industrial Donbas, were badly treated. Most new workers (nearly 80 percent in 1930) were peasants, and at least half were ethnic Ukrainians. At one mine, the peasants were forced to cut their characteristically long hair.[68] Moreover, they were given virtually no care or respect by anyone, so they came and went. "They did not even claim their pay."[69] In 1930 more than half of those peasants were said to have deserted the Donbas.[70] An American journalist who visited the Donbas in 1930 recounted:

> "This is the best mine we have," said the engineer. "It is the most highly mechanized. With 250 workers we produce 120,000 tons a year. They only work a six-hour shift."
>
> A younger engineer, manager of the mine, burst into the room and with a curse exclaimed: "They've skipped."

[62]DADO, f. R-391, op. 1sch, spr. 213, ark. 131–131zv.

[63]Ibid., f. R-129, op. 1, spr. 23, ark. 93 and 110.

[64]See, for example, *Kochegarka* (Artemivs'k), 15 October 1928, and DADO, f. 5459, op. 10, spr. 9, ark. 152, and spr. 11, ark. 207.

[65]*Protiv "Rozhdestva." Materialy k antirozhdestvenskoi kampanii 1928–1929 gg.* (Kharkiv, 1928), p. 27.

[66]GARF, f. 5459, op. 10, d. 9, l. 148. In 1930 37.4% of the male miners in the Donbas were not trade-union members. See ibid., op. 11, d. 172, l. 46.

[67]See, for example, ibid., f. 5517, op. 17, d. 313, l. 125.

[68]Ibid., f. 7416, op. 1, d. 50, l. 84.

[69]Grady, "Communistic Russia," p. 5.

[70]TsDAVO, f. 2623, op. 1, spr. 4638, ark. 66.

"Who've skipped?"

"Those blasted fellows from the farms. Came up last week, worked five days, and now the half of them have left."

"Why?" came in a chorus from the chief and the others in the room.

"Lily livered – still wet behind the ears," yelled the mine manager, slamming the door.[71]

In the hot summer of 1930 virtually none of the bathhouses had water.[72] Poor living conditions spread typhoid fever and dysentery. In 1930 60 percent of all the antiepidemic funds of Ukraine was used in the Donbas.[73] In some districts there were only half-a-day food reserves left. Even with the help of the GPU, the mine officials had to scramble for foodstuffs.[74]

An American mining engineer testified that in the summer of 1930 the Donbas coal-mining industry was in deep crisis, because the miners "were not being properly fed. They were not receiving even enough for them to live on." Many workers left or did not show up for work. So in the autumn, the GPU issued an edict "to the effect that every man must get back into the mines and work on this production":

> To accomplish that they discharged all the officers of Ugel Trest [Ugol', or Coal Trust, the trust that controlled the Donbas coalfields] and put in command a man by the name of Deisch [M. A. Deich]. . . . Mr. Deisch, in his capacity as a G.P.U. (Secret Police) surrounded himself with the G.P.U. agents, and from the beginning of his career as Director of the Ugel Coal Trust, there were hundreds of arrests amongst the miners, which very promptly brought the return of miners to the mine because of the threat of arrest by the G.P.U.[75]

According to another American mining engineer, in the winter of 1930–31

> it was impossible to freely obtain coal for ordinary household use and heating, at the very mouth of the mine, even though thousands of tons of coal were stored, ready for export. At one of the mines, Mine No. 5, a resolution of protest was sent to the central committee of the Communist Party at

[71]H. R. Knickerbocker, *The Soviet Five-Year Plan and Its Effect on World Trade* (London, 1931), pp. 167–68.

[72]GARF, f. 5459, op. 11, d. 155, l. 16.

[73]Ibid., f. 7416, op. 1, d. 2, l. 148.

[74]Ibid., f. 5459, op. 11, d. 102, l. 270b.

[75]Clarence Starr Collection, Hoover Institution Archive, Testimony before the Commissioner, pp. 7–8 and 10. Deich was appointed director of the Coal complex on 6 October 1930 and removed on 18 April 1931. *Sbornik postanovlenii i prikazov po promyshlennosti* (Moscow, 1930), 75:1138, and *Za industrializatsiiu*, 19 April 1931. Another American engineer also discussed Deich's GPU connections. Deich was chosen, according to this account, "because of his 'iron willed achievements.'" (See Grady, "Communistic Russia," p. 4. See also Knickerbocker, *The Soviet Five-Year Plan*, p. 174.) It cannot be confirmed whether Deich was a GPU official, but he may well have been: Deich came to the Donbas from an appointment in the garment industry, an odd transfer. He was later criticized for his lack of expertise in coal mining. See GARF, f. 7416, op. 1, d. 88, l. 67.

Moscow. Deutsch [Deich] dissolved the [workers'] committee and arrested all its members. They were charged with counter-revolutionary activities.[76]

Coercion was prevalent in the free steppe.

The high-handed manner in which the party and the government dealt with the workers reinforced their resentment. In 1930, at the funeral of a fellow collier killed in an accident, a man with the Red Banner Order gave a speech to workers from the mine Ivan near Stalino: "In the USSR as in the West people are being mutilated in the mines. Down with the USSR."[77] Many miners declared openly that unless they were fed properly they would not work, and demanded that the wages of specialists and managers be cut.[78] Like the battleship *Potemkin* sailors in 1905, Donbas workers became extremely agitated to find worms in the canteen food. The GPU reported nineteen strikes in the Donbas mines and factories in May and June 1930.[79] At the mine Mariia, Egorov, a party member, collected workers' signatures to appeal to the GPU to release a man accused of having been a White officer. At the workers' meeting, Egorov exploded: "We should shoot all these snakes for this."[80] Hungry workers even went so far as to hold Stalin responsible for their hunger: "We need to appeal to Moscow, maybe Stalin is dizzy with success."[81] In 1930, Ia. Golyshenko, a worker from the Millerovo-Shakhty area, wrote to M. I. Kalinin, the nominal head of the Soviet government, "no one believes in anything" and "The people have gotten angry. They curse Stalin."[82]

The old division into the privileged upper classes (*verkhi*) and the downtrodden masses (*nizy*) became evident, as one party member, a worker at Mine 10 in Artemivs'k, said, "The *verkhi* are sitting on the *nizy*."[83] In the Donbas this was almost literally true: workers toiled in the dark and dangerous underground and the bosses sat comfortably on the bright and safe surface.

The food situation remained acute in 1931. Meat was not sold at all, or sold infested with worms.[84] Flour was of such poor quality that workers became ill from consuming it.[85] Surprisingly, then, Stalin declared in June 1931 that in comparison with the hunger of 1928–29, the food situation had improved and that the government was now able to export grain, indeed more grain than in any year since the October Revolution.[86] In 1932 5.2 million tons of grain

[76] Grady, "Communistic Russia," p. 4.
[77] GARF, f. 5451, op. 14, d. 259, ll. 24 and 133.
[78] Ibid., f. 5459, op. 11, d. 35.
[79] TsDAHO, f. 1, op. 20, spr. 4227, ark. 2 and 4.
[80] GARF, f. 5459, op. 11, d. 35, l. 1240b.
[81] Ibid., l. 27.
[82] *Neizvestnaia Rossiia. XX vek. I* (Moscow, 1992), pp. 203–4.
[83] GARF, f. 5459, op. 11, d. 35, l. 156.
[84] Ibid., f. 7416, op. 1, d. 8, l. 41.
[85] Ibid., d. 2, l. 163.
[86] RTsKhIDNI, f. 85, op. 28, d. 8, l. 190. (This part of his speech to industrial managers was

and flour were exported in comparison with 0.3 million tons in both 1928 and 1929 and 4.8 million tons in 1930.[87] Famine ensued.

The Harvest of Sorrow

The famine of 1932–33 affected many parts of the country: Ukraine, Kazakhstan, the northern Caucasus, the lower Volga, western Siberia, and even Russia's heartland, the Central Black Earth Region. How many people died in the famine is a bone of contention, and perhaps the exact figures will never be known, but what is clear is that the number of deaths were in the millions. The areas hit by the famine were mostly grain-producing areas (save Kazakhstan, where the brutal policy of settling nomadic people was the major factor in the death toll). Various regions of the country were affected to different degrees, and the deliberate ethnic genocides, particularly of the Ukrainians, have been put forward as the politics of the famine.[88] Available data do not conclusively prove that the famine was ethnic genocide.[89] The famine was, as Robert Conquest has aptly titled his book on the famine (borrowing a phrase from the tale of Igor'), the harvest of sorrow,[90] and the Donbas was hard hit by the famine.

There seems to be little doubt that the main cause of the famine was the brutally excessive seizure of grain from the peasantry. In the same vein, there is little doubt that collective farms (along with state farms working on similar principles) as a productive system did not prove to be a viable alternative. Note the following *chastushka*, which was branded as a verse of the kulaks:

> They've signed men up for the kolkhoz
> Now they lay their plans
> Potatoes the men will eat
> Without butter, without cream.[91]

not published.) Already in October 1930, "for the most successful shipment of coal and grain for export," the Ukrainian Politburo ordered the creation of a troika on the railways to consist of a railway local director, an OGPU representative, and an official in charge of grain or coal procurements. See TsDAHO, f. 1, op. 16, spr. 7, ark. 180–83.

[87] Michael R. Dohan, "The Economic Origins of Soviet Autarchy, 1927/1928–1934," *Slavic Review*, 35:4 (December 1976), p. 616.

[88] This was thoroughly discussed in Robert Conquest, *The Harvest of Sorrow: Soviet Collectivization and the Terror-Famine* (Oxford University Press, 1986), and *Report to Congress: Commission on the Ukraine Famine* (Washington, D.C., 1988). For a more cautious view, see R. W. Davies, M. B. Tauger, and S. G. Wheatcroft, "Stalin, Grain Stocks and the Famine of 1932–1933," *Slavic Review*, 54:3 (Fall 1995).

[89] See Hiroaki Kuromiya, "Ukraine and Russia in the 1930s," forthcoming in *Harvard Ukrainian Studies*, and Terry Martin, "An Affirmative Action Empire: Ethnicity and the Soviet State, 1930–1938" (Ph.D. diss., University of Chicago, 1996).

[90] Conquest, *The Harvest of Sorrow*.

[91] Iu. M. Sokolov, *Russkii fol'klor, vyp. IV. Chastushki, meshchanskie i blatnye pesni, fabrichno-zavodskii i kolkhoznyi fol'klor* (Moscow, 1932), p. 30.

The sorry state of Soviet agriculture that ensued seems to prove the overall failure of the collectivization movement.[92]

The bumper crop of 1930 was soon followed by poor performances in 1931 and 1932, as a result of, among other things, the savagery used to collectivize agriculture, which demoralized the farmers. According to S. G. Wheatcroft, R. W. Davies, and J. M. Cooper, "the decline in grain production in 1931 and 1932, and the recovery in 1933 and 1934, were both far more substantial than indicated by other estimates, whether western or Soviet." They estimate that grain production in the country declined from 73.3 and 76 million tons in 1928 and 1930 respectively to 61.8 (error margin 9 percent) and 61.1 (error margin 10 percent) million tons in 1931 and 1932 respectively.[93]

Nevertheless the state procurements increased from 28.2 percent of grain production in 1930 to 32.8 percent in 1931, and were projected to rise to 40 to 50 percent in 1932.[94] Moscow knew that the country was in danger of famine. In the summer of 1932, Molotov reported to the Politburo after returning from Ukraine that "we are indeed faced with the specter of famine and in rich grain districts to boot."[95] The specter did not daunt Stalin. As Stalin boasted, in 1931 a record amount of grain (grains and flour) was exported (5.2 million tons), but even in the famine years of 1932 and 1933 1.8 million tons of grains and flour were sold in overseas markets. In these famine years animal products, too, were exported in considerable quantity.[96]

The Donbas may have been better protected from the famine than other parts of Ukraine and the northern Caucasus because the government gave it priority in food supply. Yet the Donbas countryside was devastated, and the impact of the famine on the Donbas as a whole is very important to understanding the political terror that was to envelope it in succeeding years. Since 1928 the food supply had never been good in the Donbas as was true elsewhere, but already in 1931 the food situation had deteriorated considerably, and in 1932–33 the Donbas population was starving. In the winter of 1931–32 poor supply led to "colossal queues" for bread in the Donbas.[97] In the Don part of the Donbas in March 1932, only 15 percent of the supply plan was fulfilled; there was no milk, no cheese – "such things have never reached us during this

---

[92] For the latest work on this, see Stephan Merl, *Bauern unter Stalin. Die Formierung des sowjetischen Kolchossystems 1930–1941* (Berlin, 1990).

[93] S. G. Wheatcroft, R. W. Davies, and J. M. Cooper, "Soviet Industrialization Reconsidered: Some Preliminary Conclusions about Economic Development between 1926 and 1941," *Economic History Review*, 2nd ser., 39:2 (May 1986), pp. 282–83.

[94] Kuromiya, *Stalin's Industrial Revolution*, p. 292.

[95] N. A. Ivnitskii, *Kollektivizatsiia i raskulachivanie (nachalo 30-kh godov)* (Moscow, 1994), p. 203.

[96] Dohan, "Economic Origins," p. 616.

[97] GARF, f. 7416, op. 1, d. 118, l. 310b.

quarter."[98] From the spring to the summer of 1932 the city of Stalino was haunted by the specter (and then the outbreak) of typhus and dysentery, which spread quickly,[99] no doubt as a consequence of the famine that killed not only humans but also horses; the meat of dead horses was then eaten by hungry people.

Widespread rumor, which was mostly true, that in the Donbas wages were not being paid and that the Donbas also was suffering from the famine,[100] did not prevent hungry people from fleeing to this industrial center from various parts of Ukraine and Russia. Yet the outflow of people in the summer of 1932 appeared to be greater than the influx. The Donbas mining industry, for example, lost 17.3 percent of its work force, declining from 407,400 in January to 337,700 in September 1920. The average daily output of coal in the Donbas fell in the same period from 199,000 tons to 154,400 tons, a 22.4 percent drop.[101] Hungry workers left en masse in search of food and work elsewhere; some, particularly those who retained ties to the Russian countryside, may have gone back, believing that the food situation would be better there. The Horlivka Coalfield needed 1,870 workers to keep up with its production plan, and sent out 25 recruiters throughout the country, but in October it found only 16 new workers to come and work in the Donbas.[102] Many of the few recruited workers soon fled in hunger.[103] Those who stayed starved and often could not come out for work.[104] In the Don part of the Donbas, in 1932 80 percent of the horses were said to have been lost owing to the lack of fodder.[105] As early as the spring of 1932 the alarmed people's commissar of heavy industry, Ordzhonikidze, came to the Donbas to inspect the situation and excoriate the Donbas managers. In response to workers' complaints about the lack of food, he indeed harshly attacked the Donbas managers, accusing them of allowing workers to go hungry. Yet Ordzhonikidze had to concede that in the following two or three months the government would not be able to improve the food situation to any significant degree.[106]

According to Olksiy Keis, who lived in the Donbas at that time,

[98] Ibid., d. 204, ll. 123 and 203.

[99] Diktatura truda, 9 May 1932, and Sotsialisticheskii Donbass, 21 August and 2 September 1932.

[100] See, for example, GARF, f. 5515, op. 17, d. 312, l. 188.

[101] Hiroaki Kuromiya, "The Commander and the Rank and File: Managing the Soviet Coal-Mining Industry, 1928–1933," in Rosenberg and Siegelbaum, Social Dimensions, p. 149.

[102] Sotsialisticheskii Donbass, 22 October 1932.

[103] See, for example, GARF, f. 5515, op. 17, d. 618, l. 9.

[104] TsDAVO, f. 806, op. 1, d. 287, l. 51.

[105] GARF, f. 7416, op. 1, d. 118, l. 105. According to published data, the number of horses in the Donbas declined by 50% from 1928 to 1933. See Donbas v tsifrakh. Statisticheskii spravochnik (Stalino, 1936), p. 50.

[106] RTsKhIDNI, f. 85, op. 29, d. 36, l. 5, and d. 44, l. 4.

The terrible famine began in the fall of 1932. My family was living in the town of Enakievo [Ienakiieve] in the Donbas area. Frequently, we witnessed how hungry people from collective farms gathered along the railroad lines Zverovo-Kiev and Zverovo-Miullerovo, thinking that travellers on the trains would throw them a piece of bread. All along the railroad you could see the corpses of people who had died begging for food, corpses that lay on the ground like sheaves.

Once he and his brother were walking along a street in Ienakiieve and

saw the corpse of a young woman propped up against a plank fence. As we approached we saw there was a child on her breast who sucked the breast without realizing there was no milk left. A sanitary truck, whose job it was to collect the dead bodies from the streets, pulled up as we watched. Two men jumped out of the truck, grabbed the body by the leg and dragged it up on top of the pile of bodies in the truck. Then they took the living child and threw it up with the dead bodies. My brother and I wept in pity for the child, but we realized that there was little that we or anyone else could do to help it, for we were all hungry.[107]

According to Keis, as in the 1921–22 famine,

There were also instances of cannibalism in Enakievo. Nobody, as a rule, bothered merchants. However, if a person was selling meat, the police would immediately seize the meat to check if it was human or dog meat. There were people who had no qualms about cutting off a piece of flesh from a dead body, which they would then sell in order to get money for bread.[108]

Archival data indeed show that the GPU closely followed the sale of meat.[109]

By 1933 the situation became catastrophic. The famine was aggravated by official silence. Indeed, it was impossible to speak of the famine without risking being branded as a right deviationist or even a counterrevolutionary. A woman named E. D. Ialynycheva, for example, who was a member of the All-Union Central Executive Committee of the Soviets, told her colleague that in the village Chabanivka in the Donbas sixteen people had died before her eyes and that the bodies were not buried for several weeks. She was expelled from the party, allegedly as a former kulak. It was reported that the village had experienced "frequent uprisings by kulaks," the last one in early 1932. If this was the case, Chabanivka was most likely targeted for merciless grain requisitioning. The party members were urged by the local party secretary to watch everyone carefully, because even some Communists were enemies engaged

---

[107] *Second Interim Report of Meetings and Hearings of and before the Commission on the Ukraine Famine Held in 1987* (Washington, D.C., 1988), pp. 20–21. For similar scenes in Maki-ivka and Kadiivka, see Mace and Heretz, *Oral History Project*, 2:875, 3:1455.

[108] *Second Interim Report*, p. 21.

[109] DADO, f. R-835, op. 1sch, spr. 79, ark. 69.

in "counterrevolutionary agitation."[110]   In the meantime famine continued to rage.

In the village Shapars'ke in Novopskov district, there were 212 kolkhoz households and 18 individual households; of them 190 households had absolutely no foodstuffs. Five hundred people were lying sick from hunger. From 1 January to 20 February 1933 seventy-four people died of hunger; most of the dead were the very young and the old. How many died after 20 February is not known.[111] In a village near Luhans'k no cats, dogs, or birds remained alive, all had been eaten. Livestock was often stolen, and even dead livestock was eaten.[112] Dead animals were also eaten by starving dogs and birds, which were then consumed, in turn, by hungry humans. Some horses were infected with glanders. All of this caused enormous health problems. Typhus, as usual, assumed epidemic proportions in the Donbas.[113] In Mariupol', the city on the Sea of Azov, many died from eating spoiled fish on the beach.[114] In Donets'k *oblast'*, four thousand deaths were registered in just five days between 27 February and 3 March 1933.[115] And the famine showed no sign of abating.

According to Vasyl Mivutenko, the Donbas was the "mecca and nadir of the starving." In February 1933 in Khartsyz'k, a major railway junction in the Donbas, the station was filled up with people fleeing to the Donbas from various parts of Ukraine such as Kiev, Vinnytsa, and Poltava:

> I walked to work past this station every day, and saw those ragged, dirty, hunger-distended people with all their worldly goods stuffed in sacks. They would come up to me and beg for bread or something to eat. The militia-men chased them away from the station time and again, but they would always return. Some of those starving people hanged themselves on the trees or in the sheds belonging to the railway workers who lived in the town.
>
> With the coming of spring the flood of the starving increased. By March these people, black as shades, roamed not only the station, but the whole of Khartsizk [Khartsyz'k] as well. The station house and platform could not accomodate [sic] them all. They filled up all the floor space and the overflow lay, slep [sic], and died on the streets beneath the hedges of the public gardens. Every morning at seven o'clock I noticed piles of untidy, quite [sic] dead bodies, while next to them members of their families already clearly exhibited complete indifference to the surrounding sights. The militia would disperse the local working people so as not to have them looking at the

---

[110]Ibid., op. 1, spr. 77, ark. 6–10.

[111]Ibid., spr. 15, ark. 124.

[112]*33-i: holod. Narodna knyha-memorial* (Kiev, 1991), p. 228.

[113]DADO, f. R-835, op. 1, spr. 83, ark. 24, and spr. 25, ark. 107–8; RGAE, f. 7566, op. 1, d. 4, l. 20, and "To buv strashnyi sud," *Ukraina*, 1989, no. 29, p. 17.

[114]Mace and Heretz, *Oral History Project* 1:201 and 202.

[115]Vladimir Zaika, "Golodomor. 1933 v Donbasse," *Pervaia liniia* (Donets'k), no. 48 (19 June 1991).

corpses or talking to any of the starving, and would gather up the cadavers and somewhere dispose of them. Each day they would also carry many people who had died of hunger out of the railway carriages.

By April the starving had overrun the entire town of Khartsizk. They lay in every street, at every intersection, their arms were outstretched and they begged for alms with remarks like, "You can see for yourself why we are begging." The famished people died right in the streets, still clutching the stray coins they had succeeded in obtaining by begging.[116]

Mivutenko has further narrated the following horror scene at the state farm Hornyak 5 outside Khartsyszk:

As I was going there one day, I happened to hear a groan coming from the shrubbery at the side of the road. I approached and saw a large, handsome grey-haired man about 65 years of age lying on the bare earth, covered with a peasant jacket, with his mouth agape and his eyes shut. His whole face was covered with flies.

I brushed away the flies, looked around to see that no one was watching, and asked, "Where are you from, grandfather?" "I'm from Vinnichchina. . . . I heard there's bread here in the Donbas. . . . I've come here to save myself from starvation. . . . Now, please, let me have a little thin soup, not bread, because I'll die if I eat bread now. . . . " whispered the old man in reply.

I then went to the Soviet state farm and recounted all this to the administration. They promised to send some soup to [the] old man, but I know that no one saw to it that it was done, because everyone was afraid to take the responsibility, since it was forbidden to help the starving in an official capacity. The next morning a militiaman from Khatsizk discovered the old man's body among the nettles.[117]

The Donbas had indeed become the mecca and nemesis for the famished.

These testimonies pale in comparison with many gruesome acts of violence committed by people. In 1933 in Mariupol', for example:

One day, as I waited in a queue in front of the store to buy bread, I saw a farm girl of about 15 years of age, in rags, and with starvation looking out of her eyes. She stretched her hand out to everyone who bought bread, asking for a few crumbs. At last she reached the storekeeper. This man must have been some newly arrived stranger who either could not, or would not speak Ukrainian. He began to berate her, said she was too lazy to work on the farm, and hit her outstretched hand with the blunt edge of a knife blade. The girl fell down and lost a crumb of bread she was holding in the other hand. Then the storekeeper stepped closer, kicked the girl and roared:

"Get up! Go home, and get to work!" The girl groaned, stretched out and died. Some in the queue began to weep. The communist storekeeper noticed

---

[116]*The Black Deeds of the Kremlin: A White Book*, vol. 2, *The Great Famine in Ukraine, 1932–1933* (Detroit, 1955), pp. 615–66.
[117]Ibid., p. 616.

it and threatened: "Some are getting too sentimental here. It is easy to spot enemies of the people!"[118]

In another part of the Donbas, a man who could not resist stealing a cucumber in the railways was shot on the spot.[119]

In the Donbas as elsewhere there were cases of cannibalism. On 19 February 1933 in a village of Novopskov district, the collective farmer Domna Khripun, together with her sixteen-year-old daughter, killed her eleven-year-old daughter for consumption.[120] In the village Bilokurakine of the same district, the peasant M. (her real name was withheld) lost her husband who she claimed had simply disappeared. In February 1933 their two children died, and M. and her twenty-year-old daughter ate their bodies. In March, they also killed and ate M's sixteen-year-old son. On six collective farms of the district, 578 people died in January-March 1933. On 28 March Luka Babenko severed the head, arms, and legs of his brother who had died of hunger, threw them into the river, and consumed the rest. Irina Khripunova strangled her nine-year-old granddaughter and prepared meals from her meat. Anton Khripunov ate his eight-year-old sister who had died of hunger.[121] In another village the Khmyza family killed their son's wife Kateryna. Her head was chopped off and given to the hungry pigs of their collective farm and her body was cooked and eaten by the Khmyzas.[122] In Stalino and other parts of the Donbas, rumor circulated that meat pies (*pyrohy*) were being sold in markets and that people had found in them human nails and fingers.[123]

Fear was widespread. Throughout the famine-stricken areas, parents were afraid of letting their children out at night lest they be abducted and killed for meat. Indeed, it appears that they had good reason to fear, and the fear was further reinforced by rumor.[124] It was said that "many fat people, and this included the wives of Party members, were afraid to go out in the dark, because they would be more ready targets for the sausage-makers than skinny people, who were just skin and bones."[125] Another testimony: "One day I [an eighteen-year-old girl] went to the center of that coal mining town, and there were people who were running after other people. Swollen, hard-looking people. I didn't know what they were doing, then. Later on I was told that if

---

[118]*The Black Deeds of the Kremlin: A White Book*, vol. 1, *Book of Testimonies* (Toronto, 1953), p. 284.

[119]Mace and Heretz, *Oral History Project*, 2:1137.

[120]DADO, f. R-835, op. 1, spr. 15, ark. 125.

[121]*Holod 1932–1933 rokiv na Ukraini: ochima istorykiv, movoiu dokumentiv* (Kiev, 1990), pp. 448 and 495.

[122]Mace and Heretz, eds., *Oral History Project*, 2:737.

[123]Ibid., 3:1438.

[124]See Iurii Chernichenko, "Dve tainy," *Literaturnaia gazeta*, 13 April 1988, p. 11; Mace and Heretz, *Oral History Project*, 2:628–29; and *Second Interim Report*, p. 54.

[125]Mace and Heretz, *Oral History Project*, 3:1237.

they caught me they would kill and eat me."[126] Hungry parents, who could not feed their children, would, out of desperation, bring their children to stations and markets and leave them. A small number of them were taken in by kind people, but others were rounded up by the police. In Luhans'k, from 30 April to 7 May 1933 alone, 1,842 homeless people were taken into police custody; of them 232 were children. Still many homeless children roamed around the Donbas, perpetrating crimes, big and small.[127]

In the famine, as in other times of crisis, women were the first to be exploited. For example, a worker and his wife at a tractor-machine station in the Donbas survived the famine by the wife's agreeing to sleep with the station's plenipotentiary at night in return for a little flour in the morning. After Stalin's death, the man recounted the story and cried in his wife's presence to the visitor who recorded it.[128] Such and more blatant practices were widespread. Hence, perhaps, came this *chastushka*:

> All the wheat goes abroad,
> The oats go to cooperation,
> The women go to meat procurement,
> The girls go to bonds.[129]

The famine often broke up families. Women, the traditional mainstay of family life, could not bear the brutality against the family. The whole of life had become insane, and under such circumstances women were driven to destroy their own families out of desperation or insanity. At least this appears to have been the assumption of society. If my impression is correct that women, rather than men, are more often described as the perpetrators of cannibalism, this was probably due to the assumption, which in turn was tinged with popular fears of witchery. There is evidence for the link made between cannibalism and witchery in an event that took place in the village Iankivka in Kiev *oblast'*. In July 1933 Nastia Mitriakova killed the children of Kiril Kusha on their way from the nursery. Her house was searched and parts of their bodies were found there. The village Soviet gathered people together, made a bonfire and burned her on the spot.[130]

The towns were no doubt better shielded from the impact of famine than the countryside. Yet, to reiterate, it was far from the case that the industrial Donbas was, as is often said, free of famine. In 1932 one Don Cossack collier

---

[126]Ibid., 2:787. See also p. 857.
[127]*First Interim Report of Meetings and Hearings of and before the Commission on the Ukraine Famine* (Washington, D.C., 1987), pp. 166–67; *Sotsialisticheskii Donbass*, 13 December 1989; and Mace and Heretz, *Oral History Project*, 2:857, 3:1455.
[128]*33-i: holod*, p. 230.
[129]Andrei Sinyavsky, *Soviet Civilization: A Cultural History*, tr. Joanne Turnbill with the assistance of Nikolai Formozov (New York, 1988), pp. 222–23.
[130]DADO, f. R-835, op. 1sch, spr. 105, ark. 17.

wrote that he sat hungry all day long. The bread given to the workers was such that even the cat refused it. He feared that he and his fellow workers would soon die, and he spent his wages on vodka lest the money be wasted. Colliers were saying: "What did we fight for?"[131] Here and there in the Donbas workers were swollen with hunger, and children became ill from malnutrition.[132] Hungry children in the Donbas demonstrated, demanding food, destroying shops, and breaking into bakeries.[133] A Donbas secret police document lists seven instances of strikes in January and early February 1933.[134]

By 1934 grain production had increased and exports declined. The famine subsided. Nevertheless, famine lingered in the Donbas. In 1934 people would wait all night in queues to buy the bread that would be delivered and sold in the morning, and still people went hungry.[135] Some collective farmers suffered so severely that they could not go out to work in the fields.[136] In 1935 the mines could not pay wages for six months.[137] Grain went to the state, and the Donbas lived in half-starvation till 1936.[138] The wounds left by the famine were felt for a long time. For example, because in 1932–33 infants died en masse and the birthrates declined sharply, in the late 1930s, when these children would have reached school age, Donbas schools had no first graders.[139]

External Threats and Internal Enemies

The famine was not merely an economic crisis. It constituted a grave political crisis as well. The economic crisis put the defense capability of the country at risk precisely at a time when foreign threats loomed large. The famine also posed a domestic challenge to Stalin and his policy. How significant the famine crisis was to the subsequent development of political terror in the country may be seen from the fact that, as Jonathan Haslam has aptly remarked, "every reference to the origins of the so-called Trotskyist terrorist conspiracy dates

[131] "Krestnaia nosha. Tragediia kazachestva," *Don* (Rostov), 1990, no. 7, p. 77.
[132] DADO, f. R-835, op. 1sch, spr. 84, ark. 18, and op. 1, spr. 51, ark. 73. See also I. Zhukov, "My shli cherez trudnosti i poiski," *Vsegda vosemnadtsat'* (Donets'k, 1968), p. 72.
[133] E. A. Osokina, *Ierarkhiia potrebleniia. O zhizni liudei v usloviiakh stalinskogo snabzheniia 1928–1935 gg.* (Moscow, 1993), p. 26.
[134] DADO, f. R-835, op. 1sch, spr. 79, ark. 18–21.
[135] F. Shamrai, "Strashnishie za smert' – holod 1932–1933 r.r. ochima svidka," *Nasha gazeta* (Luhans'k), 12 June 1993, and Mace and Heretz, *Oral History Project*, 3:1390.
[136] DADO, f. 326p, op. 1, spr. 290, ark. 19–20.
[137] Mace and Heretz, *Oral History Project*, 3:1384.
[138] *33-i: holod*, p. 230.
[139] Mace and Heretz, *Oral History Project*, 3:1436, 1437, 1455, and 1457.

back to 1932."[140] It was this grave economic and political crisis that laid the foundations for the Great Terror.

External threats were not new to the Soviet Union. This time the threat came from both the West and the Far East: Hitler's ascension to power in Germany and the setup by Japan of a puppet government in Manchuria. In due course, the threat loomed ever more real.[141]

In Ukraine, as in the Far East, people who had come into the country from across the border became suspect. The most glaring case was the fictitious Ukrainian Military Organization (UVO), the arrests of whose "members" began in 1933 and continued into 1937. (In the 1920s there was a namesake organization in Galicia, which in 1929 in Vienna formed the core of the new Organization of Ukrainian Nationalists, or OUN. Both the UVO and the OUN practiced political terrorism, including the assassination of Soviet officials in Poland and elsewhere. Clearly the GPU meant to link the old and new UVOs.) The arrested included many Communist Party members from Galicia. They were forced to admit their membership in the UVO. The Galicians came to the Soviet Ukraine, according to the indictment, to organize counterrevolutionary fascist organizations. They were accused of attempting to overthrow the Soviet government through armed uprisings in alliance with Nazi Germany, Poland, and Ukrainian émigré organizations. The attempt was to take place in the spring of 1933 at the peak of the famine. To gain the support of the population, the UVO was said to have deliberately disrupted the food supply (no doubt, a euphemism for causing famine, in this case).[142]

Ethnic Germans and Poles became politically suspect as potential fifth columns. In 1933 the Soviet secret police uncovered a German espionage organization whose cells were found in major Ukrainian cities. Many writers and artists were implicated in this affair.[143] In the same year attacks against the Poles took the form of liquidating the Polish Military Organization. "Members" of the organization were ethnic Poles in the party and prominent cultural and social leaders of the Polish community in Ukraine. The organization was alleged to be "in the service of Polish landowners and Ukrainian nationalists"

---

[140]Jonathan Haslam, "Political Opposition to Stalin and the Origins of the Terror in Russia, 1932–1936," *Historical Journal*, 29:2 (1986).

[141]See Jonathan Haslam, *The Soviet Union and the Threat from the East, 1933–1941: Moscow, Tokyo and the Prelude to the Pacific War* (University of Pittsburgh Press, 1992), and *The Soviet Union and the Struggle for Collective Security in Europe, 1933–1939* (New York, 1984).

[142]Shapoval, "Stalinizm i Ukraina," *Ukrains'kyi istorychnyi zhurnal*, 1991, no. 10, p. 42, and no. 11, pp. 20–21. See also T. Postolovskaia, "Osobennosti klassovoi bor'by na Ukraine v period mezhdu XVI i XVII parts"ezdami, razgrom kontrrevoliutsionnykh organizatsii i rol' organov iustitsii v razgrome," *Pod markso-leninskim znamenem*, 1934, no. 1, pp. 41–47.

[143]B. A. Starkov, "Utverzhdenie rezhima lichnoi vlasti I. V. Stalina i soprotivlenie v partii i gosudarstve (itogi i uroki politicheskoi bor'by v 30-e gody)" (Doktorskaia diss., Sankt-Peterburgskii politologicheskii institut, 1992), ch. 5.

scheming to invade and destroy the Soviet Union. The Polish districts, with their national self-government, began to be abolished. The Soviet government branded them as "a potential anti-Soviet base for Polish operations."[144] In 1934 the secret police uncovered "fascist cells" in many German colonies in the Donbas. They were accused of conducting "counterrevolutionary agitation to disintegrate the collective farm system and undermine the Soviet government."[145] These incidents foreshadowed more destructive attacks against them in the coming years.

The Ukrainians also became suspect because Moscow feared Ukrainian anger. Indeed, numerous testimonies suggest that Ukrainians believed that they were being punished by the Moscow-made famine, which they believed did not affect Russia proper.[146] There was a widespread belief among the Ukrainians, according to a January 1934 report by the German consulate in Kiev, that the Soviet government promoted the spread of the famine "in order to bring the Ukrainians to their knees."[147] This perception is evident in the following Ukrainian *chastivka*:

> Lenin plays the accordion,
> Stalin dances the hopak,
> While Ukraine lives on
> But one hundred grams [a day].[148]

In case of war, it appeared to Stalin that there would be no guarantee that nationally minded Ukrainian groups would support the Soviet government. Hence came political terror against not only Ukrainian nationalists but also Ukrainian "national Communists."[149]

This wave of purges against Ukraine naturally affected the Donbas as well. In 1933, "counterrevolutionary" Ukrainian nationalist groups were uncovered and destroyed by the secret police at the Luhans'k Institute of People's Enlightenment, the journal *Literaturnyi Donbass*, the collieries in Lysychans'k, some factories in Makiivka and Slov'ians'k, and elsewhere.[150] In attacking the

---

[144]Hryhory Kostiuk, *Stalinist Rule in the Ukraine: A Study of the Decade of Mass Terror (1929–39)* (New York, 1960), pp. 94–95.

[145]DADO, f. 326p, op. 1, spr. 290, ark. 21.

[146]See Mace and Heretz, *Oral History Project*, 3 vols.; *The Black Deeds of the Kremlin*, 2 vols.; and *33-i: holod*.

[147]D. Zlepko, ed., *Der ukrainische Hunger-Holocaust* (Sonnenbühl, 1988), p. 261.

[148]*Literaturna Ukraina*, 7 May 1992, p. 7. The hopak is the Ukrainian national dance.

[149]For a classic work, Kostiuk, *Stalinist Rule in the Ukraine*, and James E. Mace, *Communism and the Dilemmas of National Liberation: National Communism in the Soviet Ukraine, 1918–1933* (Harvard University Press, 1983).

[150]DADO, f. 326p, op. 1, spr. 128, ark. 47–52 and 63–66. See also Hryhorii Kostiuk, *Zustrichi i proshchannia. Spohady. Knyha persha* (Edmonton, Canada, 1987), pp. 456 and 549–51. For the closure of *Literaturnyi Donbass* and the rumor that Moscow wanted to incorporate the Donbas formally into Russia, see Vasil' Haidarivs'kyi, *A svit takyi harnyi. . . .* (Buenos Aires, 1962), pp. iv–v. Haidarivs'kyi was arrested in this affair. The GPU closed the printing house and placed

Ukrainian "enemies," P. P. Postyshev emphasized that the "enemies" might or might not have a party card in their pocket, implying that party membership was no guarantee of safety.[151] In 1932 and 1933 the party began to imply that there were many hidden enemies within its ranks.

Indeed, because of the famine, Stalin had to face challenges to his power from within the party. The most famous and serious was the so-called Riutin affair of 1932. It was this affair that the Moscow trials of 1936–38 referred to repeatedly as the beginning of the alleged conspiracies against the party and Stalin.[152]

Doubts about Stalin's leadership appeared widespread. Riutin-like groups were uncovered and eliminated by the secret police in various parts of the country.[153] The Donbas was no exception. As far as the Donbas was concerned, archival material shows that indeed this period was characterized by the uncovering of numerous "enemies with a party membership card in their pockets." Witness the Nechaev affair in the autumn of 1932. A party member since 1925, I. P. Nechaev was born in 1905 into the family of a Ukrainian collier who was killed by the Makhnovites. He was sent in 1931 to his native Donbas from a Leningrad higher school where he had been studying. He worked as the director of the department of people's enlightenment in the Svatove district near Stalino. There the horror of the famine turned him into a bitter critic of party policy. According to the accusations against him, Nechaev had demanded the dissolution of collective farms, the closure of special stores and cafeterias for the elite, and the convocation of a special congress of the party to review its "general line" and remove the leaders of the party and the government. Having witnessed many strikes and uprisings, he likened the situation to 1921, and declared that the masses of workers and peasants were not on the side of the party Central Committee and Stalin but on the side of Bukharin, Tomskii, Rykov, Zinov'ev, Uglanov, and Kamenev. One witness even contended that Nechaev had told him that if he caught sight of Stalin he would shoot him. Subsequently Nechaev recanted and attributed his "mistake" to temporary weakness under the influence of the Riutin "counterrevolutionary" group. Nechaev was expelled from the party as a traitor and arrested by the GPU.[154]

Similar incidents were legion. In February 1933 a group of local leaders in the Donbas was expelled from the party for appealing to the collective farms to strike and boycott state grain procurements: the state takes everything

armed guards there.
[151] P. P. Postyshev, *Stat'i i rechi* (Kharkiv, 1934), p. 271.
[152] See Martem'ian Riutin, *Na koleni ne vstanu* (Moscow, 1992), and *Reabilitatsiia. Politicheskie protsessy 30–50-kh godov* (Moscow, 1991), pp. 92–104 and 334–446.
[153] Starkov, "Utverzhdenie," ch. 4.
[154] DADO, f. R-835, op. 1sch, spr. 53, ark. 3–38.

and the people starve.[155] In Luhans'k, a certain Ponomarenko, a party member described as a Trotskyist, distributed fliers among the queues at a bakery: "The party is leading the country to destruction." Another member in Stalino, Dyminskii, openly declared at a Komsomol meeting that "all the grain has been exported abroad, and the people have been left to starve. The Soviet government and the party have led the peasants to the point where they have no choice but to organize into gangs [of plunderers]."[156]

A "Trotskyist group" in Artemivs'k led by the former party member E. V. Kuznetsov even succeeded in winning over workers. Kuznetsov was a teacher at a mine school, perhaps an elder, or a charismatic figure in the Artemivs'k mines, not unlike Konopliannikov, discussed in Chapter 3. In any case, in 1932 Kuznetsov and company began to accuse the party and the government of ruining the country: Stalin had imposed collectivization in order to facilitate robbing the peasants of grain; everything was being exported while the peasants were dying of hunger; the poor, hungry, and naked workers were no better off. He maintained, according to GPU records, that Trotsky was right: people lived in hunger while the higher-ups had become bureaucratized; the tempo of industrialization was beyond the means of the country; after all, it was impossible to build a socialist society in one country. The agitation of Kuznetsov was so successful that workers came to meet "all and any policies of the government" with hostility. They believed that the leading positions of the party were occupied by "alien elements" who had no compassion for the workers. According to the GPU, the Kuznetsov group said that peasant uprisings were inevitable, that poor, hungry, and naked workers would follow suit, and that the groups would fight, arms in hand. In the summer of 1933 nineteen people were arrested by the GPU: thirteen workers, five white-collar employees, and one teacher. The local GPU explained that the groups had not been uncovered and destroyed earlier because the groups maintained no connection with the Trotskyite center or with exiles, and therefore the GPU headquarters in Kiev had not been able to help its local agents.[157] The fate of the Kuznetsov group is not known.

In 1933 a similar "Trotskyite" group was also liquidated by the GPU in the city of Slov'ians'k. The group was charged with almost identical "crimes" as those of Kuznetsov and company. Indeed the indictment contended that the group sought to establish contact with the Artemivs'k "Trotskyite" organization.[158]

Were these affairs all fabricated by the GPU to preempt any independent political action? The answer is most likely in the affirmative, and many impli-

[155] Ibid., spr. 138, ark. 1–15.
[156] Ibid., f. 25p, op. 1, spr. 57, ark. 7.
[157] Ibid., spr. 105, ark. 62–67, spr. 139, ark. 66–68 and 78–81.
[158] Ibid., f. R-835, op. 1sch, spr. 79, ark. 136, 144–47, and 165–67.

cated in these cases have recently been cleared of criminal charges. Yet can one assume that, at a time when people were dying of hunger en masse, Soviet officials remained silent or harbored no doubts? Probably not, but many officials feared political complications, whatever their private feelings might have been. Thus, they mercilessly took grain from the peasants and forced the workers to work. Others took advantage of the difficulties to satisfy their greed or simply to survive under famine conditions. As is discussed in the next section, such people necessarily appeared as enemies to the powerless people.

Yet the assumption that all Soviet officials were either cowards, opportunists, plunderers, or true believers, fails to recognize the significance and complexity of popular anger and resistance. It is hard to believe that the extreme brutality committed during the civil war and the collectivization campaign paralyzed human reason and emotions. The GPU watched the people carefully precisely because it did not trust their allegiance. Indeed, the GPU took great trouble to uncover the politically suspect. Party members were not exempt. For example, in July 1933 the chief of the Donets'k *oblast'* GPU, V. Ivanov, compiled the political profiles of 175 suspect party members under surveillance. This is a truly interesting document.[159] One member, F. T. Kal'nitskii, for example, was said to have remarked on 18 March 1933 that "the politics of the party is fundamentally wrong. The peasants have been driven to destitution. . . . Stalin sits and commands with a small group of strong hands [*kulaki*] and laughs at us as we destroy ourselves. . . . Twenty-five percent of the collective farmers are famished, the general course of the party to build socialism is in fact babel."[160] Another member and an engineer, E. M. Andreev, was reported to have said on the anniversary of Lenin's death: "It'd be better if Stalin died. No one would be sorry for him." On another occasion Andreev was quoted as saying:

> War's inevitable in the [Far] East. I'm confident that the workers will kill everyone off, including the GPU. We engineers cannot stand aside. We have first of all to destroy the GPU because they are guilty of things such as have never been witnessed before on this earth.

On still another occasion in January 1933:

> There is violence here. A nightmare. Such as has never been seen in any of the capitalist countries. A gang of bandits has gotten together and is deliberately destroying our country. If an uprising takes place I'll fight against the Bolsheviks.[161]

A miner and party member named Horbatenko spoke among his fellow workers:

---

[159]Ibid., ark. 201–26.
[160]Ibid., ark. 214.
[161]Ibid., ark. 217.

> The Soviet government will fall sooner or later. The workers must create a
> true, proletarian government so that workers and peasants can be happy, a
> government not like this one.[162]

P. Sakhno, a former Red partisan, worker, and party member said openly
among the workers that "life in our country has become a true purgatory. We
must begin to make a second revolution." Another worker and party member, Nekhotiaev reportedly said that "Stalin is the gendarme of the Communist
Party."[163] The secret police file goes on and on in this fashion.

Other reports are equally illuminating. Some Communists were desperate.
At a meeting of collective farmers in the village Dmitriivka in Novo Aidar in
the Donbas, a certain Krinichnyi declared, "It's no use waiting any more. We
have to take a flag and go begging for alms, as, for example, Gapon did in
1905."[164] Another member in the village Shtormove, M. F. Chuprina, went to
the party secretary and asked:

> Comrade Secretary, please tell me what difference there is between the capi-
> talist system and its government and the socialist system and its government.
> In my view, the former destroyed humanity by war, and our government,
> while not wanting war, is destroying people with famine all the same.

Both Krinitskyi and Chuprina were summoned to the party bureau where they
turned in their party membership cards and declared that they were no longer
Communists.[165]

It was at this time of famine that loyal Communist Party members, for
the first time, began to be arrested and tried and some even executed. In
November 1932 the Politburo of the Ukrainian Communist Party had sanctioned, as special cases, the "immediate arrest and trial" of Communists in
responsible positions who were "politically dangerous."[166] Thus, among the
many arrested officials of collective farms in Ukraine were a large number of
Communists. In October–November 1932 nine members were sentenced to
death.[167] (How many nonparty officials were sentenced to be shot is not clear.
In Dnipropetrovs'k *oblast'*, for example, fifty-nine kolkhoz officials were sentenced to capital punishment in the same period. In one district of Donets'k
oblast' alone, twenty were given the death sentence.)[168] At the beginning of

[162] Ibid., ark. 220.

[163] Ibid., ark. 199 and 217.

[164] *Holod 1932–1933 rokiv na Ukraini*, p. 389. Gapon was an Orthodox priest from Ukraine who
on 9 January 1905, during the Russo-Japanese War, led a march of workers to the Winter Palace
to appeal to the tsar for labor and civil rights. The march was met with police fire. This Bloody
Sunday marked the beginning of the 1905 Revolution in Russia.

[165] Ibid.

[166] Ibid., p. 265.

[167] Ibid., p. 285.

[168] Ibid., p. 281, and T. Bespechnyi and T. Bukreeva, "Te tri koloska . . . ," *Sotsialisticheskii
Donbass*, 14 February 1991. For similar cases in the northern Caucasus, see E. N. Oskolkov,

Figure 5.4. "Let's transform the old Donbas into a new, mechanized [Donbas]," in the early 1930s. From *Plakaty A. Strakhova* (Kharkiv, 1936).

December 1932, according to the Central Committee of the Ukrainian Communist Party, 327 Communists were on trial. They were to be deported to the north along with the "kulaks."[169] Indeed, in the Donbas many party members were arrested alongside kulaks.[170] Communists could be treated just like "class enemies."

Communist bosses in the Donbas coal-mining industry came under similar attack.[171] In 1932–33 the industry fell into severe crisis, owing both to the famine and to problems associated with rapid mechanization. Huge investments had not yielded quick results. Stalin and his close associates impatiently sought to boost output by increasing machine utilization. They believed machines were not being used efficiently because of the lack of technical supervision. So they sought to drive reluctant engineers and technicians into the mines. This measure generated considerable resistance among the technical personnel who clung to the easier life above the ground. Moreover, they considered such a move as an "affront to their status." No doubt, they had reason

---

Golod 1932/1933. Khlebozagotovki i golod 1932/1933 goda v Severo-Kavkazskom krae (Rostov on the Don, 1991), pp. 47–51.

[169] *Holod 1932–1933 rokiv na Ukraini*, p. 293.

[170] T. Bespechnyi, "Golod 1932–1933 godov v Donbasse," *Sotsialisticheskii Donbass*, 13 December 1989.

[171] See Kuromiya, "The Commander and the Rank and File."

to fear as well. The underground was the province of the workers and out-siders were not welcome. Workers met the descent into the mines of their bosses with hostility: a Varangian attempt to impose a new order.[172] So, apart from the ever present danger of accident underground, the bosses feared the lawless world of darkness where the frightening possibility of violence was omnipresent.[173]

Communist managers, too, feared underground work for the same reasons. They, moreover, were largely technically illiterate political commissars rather than managers, and the absence of engineers and technicians from the office made the work of the managers (writing up reports, technical orders, produc-tion plans, etc.) impossible. From the viewpoint of the managers, the prob-lems in the coal-mining industry were not the result of poor management but of famine, but Moscow blamed the former while refusing to acknowledge the latter. Along with these attacks came the campaign to purge the party, which made the work of the managers even more difficult.

Faced with the coal crisis, Moscow responded with unprecedented severity, calling for "unconditional punishment of all those who smell remotely of sab-otage." It branded recalcitrant managers and engineers as "saboteurs," "wreck-ers," "enemies of the party," and "counterrevolutionaries with a party card in their pockets." Many were demoted or removed from their positions, expelled from the party, and some even arrested and imprisoned.[174] Frequent accidents in the mines also led the GPU to arrest many other Communist bosses.[175] Ar-rests made by the GPU meant almost certainly a political crime, and indeed cases were reported in which party members allegedly belonged to "wrecking organizations" in the Lysychans'k mines.[176] In these cases, hardly any distinc-tion was made between Communist "wreckers" and *spetsy* "wreckers."

All these incidents indicate that at this time of grave crisis an important change had occurred in the official image and meaning of the "enemy." In-creasingly, the representation of enemies came to be divorced of ideological content. Certainly, the old generic Marxist concept of "class enemies" was still used widely. Class-neutral concepts, too, such as wreckers and saboteurs had always been around. Previously, however, these terms were almost al-

---

[172] See *Sotsialisticheskii Donbass*, 20 May 1933. "Varangian" refers to the Scandinavians who were said to have come to rule Kievan Rus'.

[173] Ibid., 30 May and 8 September 1933. See also *V plenum Donetskogo obkoma KP(b)U. Mate-rialy* (Stalino, 1933), pp. 80–81.

[174] See, for example, *Sotsialisticheskii Donbass*, 9 September 1933. See also N. Kolotilin, *Otch-etnyi doklad o rabote Shakhtinskogo raikoma VKP(b)* (Shakhty, 1934), p. 49. F. T. Pugach was one case. He was sentenced to eight years as a saboteur and wrecker and, in the mid-1930s, worked on the Moscow-Volga Canal construction sites. Pugach denied all the charges. See A. Avdeenko, *Nakazanie bez prestupleniia* (Moscow, 1991), pp. 102, 111, and 117–27.

[175] See, for example, DADO, f. R-835, op. 1, spr. 77, ark. 33–37.

[176] Ibid., spr. 111, ark. 125.

ways used against non-Communists and "class enemies" such as *spetsy* and kulaks. Yet class-neutral representations were now applied to party members as well. Even though "wrecking" by old *spetsy* was occasionally reported in the Donbas,[177] by 1933 the distinction between the old *spetsy* and the growing number of Red experts or Communist managers was blurred in press reports on "wrecking." Some party members branded as wreckers and saboteurs were allegedly former kulaks, Makhnovites, or other anti-Communists, but many were genuine and devoted Communists without political blemish such as Red Army veterans of the civil war. Yet the party now began to declare that many party members, too, were enemies, and not simply wrongheaded diehards, misguided strayers, or incompetent or inept bureaucrats. Just whose enemies they were was still not clear. Phrases such as "enemies of the working class" and "enemies of the party" were used, but the distinction between them and the concept of "class enemy" had begun to blur, at least in the party's representation. When authentic Communists were demonstrated to be "enemies," they could hardly be characterized as "class enemies."

At the time, therefore, the concept of "enemy of the people" (*vrag naroda*), a class-neutral construction, began to emerge in official political discourse. The term was not new and had been used at least since 1917. It was at this time of crisis in 1932–33, however, that this class-neutral term began to gain currency, at least in the Donbas. In the summer of 1933, for example, a group of people working in the catering service in Makiivka was arrested for stealing millions of rubles' worth of foodstuffs. The group included "people with a party membership card in their pockets." They were branded as "enemies of the people." Four were sentenced to death.[178] A newspaper article called five mining officials in the Krasnodon coalfield who were accused of deliberately cutting workers' wages "Enemies of the people."[179]

The new construction of the enemy was politically convenient because it was supraclass and could apply to anyone, whether party member or not. It also promised to be popular with the *narod* who, literally famished, were eager to see enemies among the Communist rulers. Soon a new, also class-neutral image was to be applied: "fascist spies." In the meantime, "counterrevolutionary organizations" continued to be uncovered by the GPU in the Donbas. In March 1934 a Trotskyite group was liquidated at a Luhans'k institute. An instructor by the name of Gurevich was accused of "counterrevolutionary agitation": "We have party dictatorship, not proletarian dictatorship."[180] In April workers and students at the mines in Roven'ki were arrested for their "counterrevolutionary, right-deviationist" activity. They, according to the indictment, contended

---

[177] See, for example, Postolovskaia, "Osobennosti," p. 53.
[178] *Sotsialisticheskii Donbass*, 26 June and 8 July 1933.
[179] Ibid., 12 October 1933.
[180] Ibid., 5 March 1934.

that the famine was caused by the mistaken agricultural policy of the party and demanded the dissolution of collective farms.[181]

Who Is the Enemy?

This question became an important and obsessive theme in Soviet history in the 1930s, a theme that retained its power up to the final years of Soviet society and even thereafter. As in the prerevolutionary period, the questions *Kto vinovat?* (Who is to blame?) and *Chto delat'?* (What is to be done?) may have continued to preoccupy the politically conscious, but a new formula for political discourse was passed down from above. It merged with a similar construction surfacing from below.

To some the answer to Who is the enemy? was clear: class enemies. Leonid Likhodeev, for example, who grew up in Iuzivka (Stalino), has said that in 1932–33 enemies were evident everywhere in the city. Famished kulaks wandered around begging for alms. The police banned begging and arrested and dispatched them. Still, beggars would appear at his house. In the morning the dead could be found in dirty alleys. It was frightening because the police would ask him why a kulak corpse was found at his backdoor. People, including Likhodeev's mother, secretly gave the "enemies" alms. "We," Likhodeev has written, "were indignant with the beggars" because "we were certain that we were living on the threshold [from socialism to communism] and maybe under communism itself." Likhodeev did take pity on a woman and her child whom his mother helped, but he remained convinced: the kulaks carry children to get pity, but carry guns to kill Communists, Komsomols, and Pioneers; some of the kulaks carry dynamite wrapped in the form of a baby to explode factories and mines. He was taught at school about class enemies who "risked their lives to spoil our optimism [*peredovoe nastroenie*], our confidence in a bright future." "We believed," Likhodeev has explained, because "our favorite newspaper *Pionerskaia pravda* confirmed word for word" what was taught at school.[182]

Stalin suggested in 1933, however, that many of the enemies had become increasingly invisible. In January 1933 Stalin declared that

> the last remnants of moribund classes – private manufacturers and their servitors, private traders and their henchmen, former nobles and priests, kulaks and kulak agents, former White Guard officers and police officials, policemen and gendarmes, all sorts of bourgeois intellectuals of a chauvinist type, and all other anti-Soviet elements – have been tossed out.
>
> But tossed out and scattered over the whole face of the USSR, these

[181]DADO, f. 26p, op. 1, spr. 150, ark. 2–12.
[182]Leonid Likhodeev, *Pole brani, na kotorom ne bylo ranenykh* (Moscow, 1990), pp. 215–17.

"have-beens" have wormed their way into our plants and factories, into our government offices and trading organizations, into our railway and water transport enterprises, and, principally, into the collective farms and state farms. They have crept into these places and taken cover there, donning the mask of "workers" and "peasants," and some have even managed to worm their way into the party.

What did they carry with them into these places? They carried with them hatred for the Soviet regime, of course, burning enmity toward new forms of economy, life, and culture.

Then Stalin emphasized:

We must bear in mind that the growth of the power of the Soviet state will intensify the resistance of the last elements of the dying classes. It is precisely because they are dying and their days are numbered that they will go from one form of attack to another, sharper one, appealing to backward sections of the population and mobilizing them against the Soviet regime. . . . This may provide fuel for a revival of the activities of defeated groups of the old counterrevolutionary parties: the SRs, the Mensheviks, and the bourgeois nationalists of the central and border regions . . . the Trotskyites and right deviationists. . . .

This is why revolutionary vigilance is the quality most needed by the Bolsheviks at the present time.[183]

Three months later A. Ia. Vyshinskii maintained at the Metro-Vickers trial that, having lost the battle, the enemy now resorted to "methods known as quiet sapping" rather than direct frontal attack, and that the enemy sought to conceal its wrecking acts with all sorts of "objective reasons," "defects," and the contention that the incidents did "not seem to be caused by malicious human intent." Therefore, Vyshinskii emphasized, the enemy "becomes less detectable and hence it becomes less possible to isolate him."[184]

One might detect here genuine fears of the enemy on the part of Stalin and Vyshinskii. It would appear to be absurd not to fear the ghosts of those who had died en masse during collectivization, industrialization, dekulakization, and famine, and to fear the revenge of those millions of people whose families had survived state terror by fleeing to the cities, factories, mines, construction sites, and elsewhere. To them must be added, as Stalin made clear, political enemies of all sorts. It was logical that Stalin questioned whether in case of war these people would support him and his government, and the famine crisis coincided with the war scare.

There was more to it, however. Stalin was a past master of political manipulation. In this case, too, Stalin was actually promoting a political vigilance campaign by implying that enemies were hidden everywhere, even within the

[183]I. V. Stalin, *Sochineniia*, vol. 13 (Moscow, 1951), pp. 207 and 212.
[184]Kuromiya, *Stalin's Industrial Revolution*, p. 318.

party. Vyshinskii's remark that it had become less possible to isolate the enemy suggests that mass repression would become inevitable. One can detect here the political logic that it would be better to "isolate" one hundred people in the hope of finding one enemy among them than to allow that one to remain at large. This is of course dangerous logic. According to the testimony made in 1937 by G. G. Iagoda, in 1932–33 some GPU officials opposed the vigilance campaign: "Any talk of counterrevolutionaries is nonsense."[185] Yet, there were others who were eagerly vigilant, and the campaign went on all the same.

The free steppe of the Donbas continued to attract many freedom seekers; numerous hungry fugitives overcame obstacles and found a refuge in the Donbas. Thus many workers, students, and even some shopkeepers were former kulaks and their children who had fled to the Donbas and changed their identities.[186] Priests, who were lucky enough to be able to flee, also came to the Donbas; so did many Baptists.[187] Some former priests continued to perform religious rites secretly, for example, baptizing miners' children at the parents' request.[188] This stirred up the vigilance campaign in the Donbas. Already by April 1932 the Soviet officials were screaming for "vigilance, vigilance, and yet more vigilance."[189]

Throughout political, economic, and social turbulence the Donbas retained its reputation as the free steppe. In the view of Stalin and his associates, the freedom of the steppe with its Cossack past made it a potential base for anti-Moscow counterrevolution. Indeed, the Don, along with the Kuban, was one of the areas that put up the stiffest resistance to Moscow's grain procurement and consequently was severely punished by Moscow for its alleged sabotage and covert struggle against Soviet power.[190] The threat of war was far greater and real this time than on previous occasions (particularly 1927 and 1930), but even then the allegiance of the local population, particularly of the former White Cossacks, proved quite suspect. (From 1932 onward, and especially in 1937–38, time and again, Bukharin and his former associates were accused of having sought anti-Stalin support among the Don and Kuban Cossacks.)

[185]Quoted in O. V. Khlevniuk, *1937-i: Stalin, NKVD i sovetskoe obshchestvo* (Moscow, 1992), p. 24.

[186]For more cases of this, see Mace and Heretz, *Oral History Project*, vols. 1–3 (see especially 2:854); Kostiuk, *Zustrichi i proshchannia*, p. 680; and *Ukraina*, 1989, no. 12, p. 15.

[187]See, for example, Mace and Heretz, *Oral History Project*, 1:48–49, 2:875, and F. M. Putintsev, *Politicheskaia rol' i taktika sekt* (Moscow, 1935), p. 420.

[188]Bohdan, *Avoiding Extinction*, pp. 28–32.

[189]TsDAVO, f. 2605, op. 3, spr. 1129, ark. 857.

[190]There is a good firsthand account of the Don by M. Sholokhov: *Pisatel' i vozhd'. Perepiska M. A. Sholokhova s I. V. Stalinym. 1931–1950 gody. Sbornik dokumentov iz lichnogo arkhiva I V. Stalina* (Moscow, 1997). For letters from the Don, the Kuban, and other Cossack areas on the famine, see "Krestnaia nosha. Tragediia kazachestva," *Don*, 1990, no. 7.

In 1932–33 in the Donbas, as elsewhere, an internal passport system was introduced in the cities. By denying a passport to rural residents, the government sought to restrict population movement, more specifically to prevent a mass influx of famished people from the countryside to the cities, thereby shielding the cities from the impact of the famine. The introduction of passports also meant that urban residents without proper documentation could be expelled. (In the process, numerous faked documents were found, and their traders arrested.) In Stalino, for example, 220,661 passports were issued, but 10,465 persons were denied a passport. Of those denied, 45 percent were said to be kulak fugitives, 19 percent "parasites," and 14 percent the disenfranchised and former criminals. A certain Gorvulin, for example, was said to be a kulak who had made his way to the Donbas where he had joined the party and had been working as a coal hewer. Gorvulin was expelled from the party and disappeared from Stalino. Dziuba and Pakhon'ko, both hewers, were forced out of the city as former Makhnovites. There were at least 1,896 colliers and 1,150 metalworkers among the 10,465 who were denied passports.

Of these workers, however, 906 were allowed to remain in Stalino because of their importance to industry. This extraordinary permission symbolizes the freedom the Donbas had long signified to outlawed members of society. The remainder of the 10,465 were office workers and manual workers in the surrounding settlements.[191] In some mines, nearly 20 percent of workers were unmasked as kulaks.[192] There were many angry and worried people. At a mine in Stalino, a policeman in charge of issuing passports was shot by two men, but survived the assault. Workers in Stalino sought to defend their fellow workers by contending that they were all "dekulakized" and "disenfranchised" people" because, although they might have the right to vote, voting was meaningless.[193]

People who came from the border area were met with suspicion. For example, a Ukrainian born in Bukovina who had moved to the border on the Soviet side, came to the Donbas to work as a "common laborer." "Unfortunately at that time an arms factory was being built and the GPU was interested in newcomers, paying special attention to their place of origin. When they found out where this man had lived, they arrested him. He was held in prison for four months and then sent to labor camps."[194] War was lurking in the shadows and this man was isolated as a possible spy.

The passport system did not stop the tide of people. Many willingly took up heavy and dangerous work underground, and managers, always pressed for more laborers, willingly employed them without proper documents. For

---

[191] DADO, f. R-835, op. 1sch, spr. 78, ark. 7–10.
[192] Ibid., spr. 106, ark. 192–93.
[193] Ibid., spr. 78, ark. 13–14 and 17.
[194] *The Black Deeds of the Kremlin*, 1:119.

some administrators, former kulaks were much more valuable than, say, the Komsomol members recruited to work in the Donbas, because "the kulaks work harder."[195] Ordzhonikidze, who visited the famished Donbas in February 1933, told the workers that many sons of kulaks were working in the Donbas and engaged in wrecking. These enemies, he contended, were responsible for the "endless accidents." Then Ordzhonikidze declared: "Comrades, 1933 will be a year of bitter class struggle. Keep watch."[196] In June a newspaper article under the title "The Enemy" reported wrecking by a former tsarist army intelligence officer and exhorted the reader: "Look around you, don't you see class enemies hidden among you? Tear off their masks!"[197] Another article in a mining journal in the autumn of the same year presented this image of the enemy: "The more successes we have, the more desperately the class enemy resists. He's similar to a beast that's been injured but has not been finished off yet."[198]

Numerous accidents and technical problems made this image appealing to workers. They saw evil hands at work in the cutting of ventilation ducts, the placing of dynamite in heavily trafficked underground areas, the burning of motors, the hurling of bolts into machines, and many other incidents that threatened their lives. "Enemies" were almost invisible in the dark underground, and this peculiarity enhanced vigilance.[199]

The deteriorating food situation had the same effect on popular vigilance. Poor catering prompted many vigilantes to see enemy activity in workers' cafeterias, which, under famine conditions, often became the only source of subsistence. In the Donbas, 80 percent of the staff of Donnarpit (Donbas Public Catering) were said to be disenfranchised people. In none of the Donnarpit cafeterias was soap or a towel available. The only redeeming factor was that the Donnarpit office was next to the GPU: it was easy to drag Donnarpit officials there.[200]

Indeed, many seem to have been dragged to the GPU. In December 1932, for example, twenty men were indicted for disrupting the catering of the Smolianka, Rutchenkove, and Budenivka mines in the Stalino district by a systematic misappropriation of foodstuffs. The defendants were allegedly former kulaks, merchants, bakery owners, and a former army officer. Two were sentenced to be shot as "enemies of the people." Five others were given ten years of imprisonment each. The press reported that "The Enemies of the People

---

[195] *Sotsialisticheskii Donbass*, 9 May 1933.
[196] RTsKhIDNI, f. 85, op. 29, d. 47, ll. 4–5.
[197] *Sotsialisticheskii Donbass*, 21 June 1933.
[198] *Udarnik uglia*, 1933, no. 12, front inside cover.
[199] See, for example, cases of wrecking by enemies in *Sotsialisticheskii Donbass*, 15 September 1933 and 15 January 1934; *Udarnik uglia*, 1933, nos. 10–11, p. 11; and *Molot*, 23 March 1933.
[200] GARF, f. 7416, op. 1, d. 202, l. 63.

Figure 5.5. Audience at a trial of embezzlers in Stalino, 1934. From TsDKFFA, od. zb. 2-1540.

Have Got What They Deserved."[201] There followed many similar cases in 1933. Even when workers did eat, the food was often spoiled and resulted in food poisoning. Most likely, the caterers were not responsible: there was no soap, no towels! Yet the press published calls for death sentences for the "enemies of the people." Death sentences ensued.[202]

While many were falsely accused, under famine conditions much of the countryside did resist state grain procurements. Armed "bandits" were widely observed in the Donbas. One such group in Debal'tseve was composed of members of the former "counterrevolutionary organization 'The Sons of Offended Fathers.'" The ringleader, A. R. Radchenko, proclaimed in 1932 that war was inevitable in Manchuria and that, come war, the government would collapse. So he appealed: "And then, lads, forward." The Sons of Offended Fathers, according to police reports, attributed the state onslaught against the peasants to the Jews: "This government is anti-Christ. It's ruled by Yids [zhidy]. . . . They have exported all their gold and goods abroad."[203] In vari-

[201] Sotsialisticheskii Donbass na protsesse vreditelei rabochego snabzheniia, no. 2 (25 December 1932), and Sotsialisticheskii Donbass, 26, 28, 29, and 30 December 1932.

[202] DADO, f. R-835, op. 1, spr. 51, ark. 76–79, and op. 1sch, spr. 117, ark. 2zv.; and Sotsialisticheskii Donbass, 11 January, 30 August, and 11 September 1933.

[203] DADO, f. R-835, op. 1, spr. 59, ark. 9–15.

ous districts cells of an "insurgent army" were uncovered, their aim being to "arouse discontent" among the workers and soldiers by disrupting the food supply and staging armed uprisings.[204] In the summer of 1933 in a village in Rubizhne, the kolkhoz brigadier Kuleshov was removed from his job and labeled an "enemy." He then went after the new brigadier with an ax. Kuleshov was quoted as saying: "We have two classes, we cannot live together. This evening either you or I will have to die." Kuleshov did not challenge the indictment and was sentenced to be shot.[205] Under the extreme conditions of famine, the theft of grain and arson in grain storages were not infrequent. The press reported such incidents with captions like "The Kolkhoz in the Hands of Enemies of the People," and "No Mercy to the Enemies of the People."[206]

The "enemy of the people" was constructed not only from above but also from below. The brutal ways in which the country was governed in general and the handling of the famine in particular contributed to a popular creation of "enemy of the people." The Stalin leadership encouraged brutal terror in dealing with crises, but when the use of terror threatened the stability of the regime, it turned around and blamed those people directly involved in the terror. Now under famine conditions, Moscow suggested that many enemies were hidden even among the party's own members. This led to the escalation of random and unpredictable acts of violence against local officials, but also to violence as the recourse of choice for disputes among people. The enemy could be lurking anywhere.

Certainly, instances of abuse of power abounded. Beatings of farmers by collective farm officials were a common phenomenon in 1933.[207] As in the old days, farmers were subjected to humiliating punishment – whipping – for minor offenses such as napping in the field.[208] In the village Alekseev in the Donbas, the Soviet chairman often apprehended farmers who did not follow his orders, beat them, and threw them into the basement of the Soviet building. On the collective farm Chervona Zirka (Red Star), the board members caught five women who had stolen flax, beat them, stripped them, and carried them naked around the village.[209] In another village in Volodars'ke district, a judge, a public prosecutor, and another official, all party members, who came to investigate a case of theft of fodder, got drunk at the village Soviet and fired gunshots through the windows. The district official Shkpel', half naked, chased after kolkhoz women on their way home from work and was detained

[204] Ibid., spr. 79, ark. 10–11.

[205] Sotsialisticheskii Donbass, 29 June 1933.

[206] See, for example, ibid., 2 August, 12 November, and 3 December 1933, and 28 March 1934.

[207] See cases in DADO, f. R-835, op. 1sch, spr. 106, ark. 2.

[208] Ibid., spr. 84, ark. 75.

[209] Bespechnyi and Bukreeva, "Te tri koloska." For similar incidents elsewhere in the Donbas, see DADO, f. R-835, op. 1, spr. 35, ark. 17.

by a brigade of men. The collective farmers were "extremely indignant."[210]

Traditional rural forms of lynching (*samosud*) persisted. People were beaten and even killed for stealing.[211] The village of Komykivka in the Donbas is representative of the popularly sanctioned use of violence in this period. In the summer of 1933, three peasants suspected of horse theft had their homes searched, leading to the discovery of horsemeat. The party secretary S. I. Koz'menko beat them about the face and head with a stick and locked them up in a storeroom to obtain their confessions. Koz'menko arrested and killed another man V. on suspicion of stealing household items from a villager. (Another villager, E. N. Cherkassov, stole the shirt and the jacket off the dead man.) The villager E. E. Nesmashnyi beat D. A. Letuchaia, a mentally ill woman, for stealing milk from his house. Letuchaia set fire to Nesmashnyi's house in revenge. Nesmashnyi caught Letuchaia, beat her within an inch of her life, and threw her into a well with a stone tied around her neck.[212]

By far the most harsh official measure taken was the notorious 7 August 1932 law enacted to prevent famished people from stealing "socialist property" (which included watermelons in the field). The punishment was a mandatory death sentence or, in case of extenuating circumstances, ten years of imprisonment. According to this extraordinarily brutal law, between 7 August 1932 and 1 May 1933 in the Donbas 301 persons were sentenced to be shot, and 8,728 to various terms of imprisonment or forced labor.[213] Brutal as it was, the law seems not to have been applied strictly. The largest group of the punished were individual (middle and poor) peasants (3,461), followed by workers (2,077), and collective farmers (1,636).[214] Many of those spared life did not leave the Donbas, but engaged in forced labor in its various correctional facilities.[215]

Crime statistics alone do not accurately represent the extent of random everyday violence in the famished Donbas. For example, although fields and gardens were guarded by armed watchmen, many of the watchmen were killed by armed assailants. Sometimes the assailants were caught and killed, and then turned out to be party members or shock workers.[216] Women living by themselves (widows, soldiers' wives) became targets of violence. Village officials would break into their homes at night, rape them, and confiscate whatever foodstuffs were there.[217]

---

[210]DADO, f. R-835, op. 1, spr. 35, ark. 38.

[211]For a widespread practice of lynching in Luhans'k, see DALO, f. P-33, op. 1, spr. 18.

[212]DADO, f. R-835, op. 1sch, spr. 84, ark. 49–50. For other cases of lynching, see op. 1, spr. 92, ark. 10.

[213]Ibid., f. R-920, op. 1, spr. 9, ark. 50.

[214]Ibid.

[215]In Stalino, for example, a newspaper was published by these facilities. See *Perekovka*, nos. 1, 2, and 24–25 (1934).

[216]DADO, f. R-835, op. 1sch, spr. 106, ark. 21.

[217]See, for example, ibid., spr. 100, ark. 1.

Moscow became alarmed by the extensive application of the 7 August law and the extent of violence used to take grain from the peasants. On May 1933 Stalin and Molotov sent out a secret circular condemning indiscriminate arrests and deportations ("a saturnalia of arrests" and "repression on an extraordinary scale"), and called for a halt to mass arrests.[218] However, the "saturnalia of arrests" did not stop in the Donbas. Surprisingly, in its 28 October 1933 resolution the Central Committee of the Ukrainian Communist Party deplored the continuing violation of "revolutionary legality" and declared that the lawlessness was a result of the wrecking activity of White Guards, Makhnovites, nationalists, and other degenerates.[219] Certainly, there must have been some such elements among rural officials and party members, but in party discourse, too, some party members now came to be equated with "counterrevolutionary enemies." In the eyes of the peasants the collective farm system had come to resemble the serfdom of old. If the peasants considered themselves the "ordinary people" (narod), then the system with its managers became the enemy. The peasants' attitude is best reflected in their reading of the VKP (All-Union Communist Party) as Second Serfdom (Vtoroe Krepostnoe Pravo).[220]

The same construction of "the enemy of the people" operated among the industrial workers. They may have been better treated than the peasantry, but the world in which they lived was far from the paradise they had been promised. The new regime came increasingly to resemble the old regime. Managerial neglect of industrial safety, for example, constantly endangered workers' lives. The social, economic, and cultural divisions between the verkhi and nizy remained firm both literally and symbolically in the mining community. To many workers, their new, Communist bosses had long been new enemies. And now the party openly told them that indeed among their Communist bosses were many enemies. As the distinction between old and new enemies blurred, the traditional opposition between the people and their enemies became an appealing way to understand their world.

Alexei Gorchakov has recounted an illuminating episode that took place in the Donbas in the summer of 1932. He was taken there by his father who was "sent there by his trade union to give a series of lectures":

> The poverty and conditions under which the miners lived made a deep impression on me. Houses were leaning over, almost in a state of collapse. The faces of the miners, blackened by coal dust, were thin and emaciated. Near

---

[218]Ibid., op. 1. spr. 52, ark. 60. The circular is reproduced in Merle Fainsod, *Smolensk under Soviet Rule* (Harvard University Press, 1958), p. 187.

[219]DADO, f. R-835, op. 1, spr. 62, ark. 62. In August 1933 the Politburo had allowed "temporarily" capital punishment to be applied to the organizers and *aktiv* of armed "bandits" in Ukraine and elsewhere. *Stalinskoe Politbiuro v 30-e gody. Sbornik dokumentov* (Moscow, 1995), p. 64.

[220]For the best discussion of this attitude, see Sheila Fitzpatrick, *Stalin's Peasants: Resistance and Survival in the Russian Village after Collectivization* (Oxford University Press, 1994).

many a mine was a shining, new building – the miners' "Palace of Culture."

They were real palaces: parquet floors, tremendous meeting halls, and everywhere portraits of the leaders. But the miners sat in their tiny hovels, too tired and hungry to visit the palace.

"They build us palaces, but we don't even have a decent bathhouse, can't even wash the coal dust out of our skin," they said.

I have seldom since met such anger. I remember my father's very first lecture. Almost in a chorus the miners began yelling:

"Why tell us about Shakespeare? Is that all we need, fat. . . . "

The lecture was interrupted. Later the director of the Palace of Culture, an old Communist and hero of the Civil War, told us:

"You didn't get off so badly, we've had much worse."

I saw a different kind of life in the Donbas. Near one mine, apart from the regular miners' huts, there stood neat rows of white houses with tile roofs. Not far off, a herd of fat cows grazed in the pasture. These were the homes of German Communist miners who had come to work in the USSR.[221]

If Gorchakov had looked at the community more carefully, he would also have noticed "a very different kind of life," that of the managers and engineers. In 1932 the average living space of the engineering-technical personnel was at least two and half times as large as that of the miners.[222] The wives of engineers and technicians did not queue to obtain food. (These leisured wives, however, were said to be a major problem: they consulted fortune-tellers, and circulated rumors, such as the imminent advance of Cossacks and White Guards.)[223] Preferential food supply led the wives of the workers in one instance to a fistfight with the wives of the engineers and technicians. When the family of an engineer was put in workers' barracks either for lack of a suitable flat or by mistake, the wife of one of the workers brawled with the engineer's wife, and the worker himself struck the engineer, who hit back. Such incidents were observed in many parts of the Donbas.[224] In January 1933 there were even murder attempts against engineers and technicians at Mine 13/18 in Stalino.[225] In none of these cases was it discussed whether the engineers and technicians involved were old "bourgeois" *spetsy* or new, Communist experts (who were growing in numbers). This ambiguity makes a striking contrast with the previous years when the "bourgeois" *spetsy* were specifically identified and attacked as a group.

Experience of ill-treatment by managers meant that they were no better received by workers. At Mine Smolianka-11, Komlev, Malakhin, and other

[221] Louis Fischer, ed., *Thirteen Who Fled*, tr. Gloria Fischer and Victor Fischer (New York, 1949), pp. 60–61.
[222] GARF, f. 7416, op. 1, d. 226, l. 13.
[223] Ibid., ll. 31 and 50.
[224] Ibid., d. 224, ll. 20, 290b, and 48.
[225] DADO, f. R-835, op. 1sch, spr. 79, ark. 20.

managerial personnel frequently beat workers.[226] At Mine 2 Izvarino, S. Arte-
mov, a party member and *desiatnik* (equivalent of assistant foreman), often
brandished his Browning and fired it randomly. On 23 April 1933 he fired
at the workers' quarters repeatedly, scaring the women, and chasing them.[227]
At yet another mine, Volodarskii, the manager Samarskii shot his driver dead.
The reason is not recorded. Samarskii's successor Gagonin, for no apparent
reason, shot dead the manager of the mine shop Polianskii. At Mine 17/17
the assistant manager Kozlov sought unsuccessfully to sleep with the wife of
one Nimoshkodenko. When Kozlov threatened to fire the wife and her husband from the mine, Nimoshkodenko went to the administration office where
he was met by the manager Kovbas and ordered to leave. He resisted and was
slugged twice in the face by Kovbas with a Browning.[228]

Injuries and deaths were frequent in and around the mines. In the Donbas
coal mines, the number of deaths from accidents increased sharply from 539
in 1932 to 782 in 1933 and 826 in 1934 (during that period the average size
of the labor force remained more or less constant because of the ebb and flow
of workers).[229] Previously the *spetsy* had had to take responsibility, but the
Communist managers were no longer exempted from charges of willful negli-
gence. In many mines, managers were sentenced to harsh punishments of up
to ten years of imprisonment.[230] It was only one step from there to accusations
of "counterrevolutionary wrecking." The problem of frequent accidents was
to become an explosive issue in 1936–38.

Nor did the famous draconian decree of November 1932, which empow-
ered management to dismiss workers for even a single day's unjustified absence,[231] make management popular. The workers panicked. It is true that the
absenteeism law was not always enforced: it was difficult to dismiss workers
in a sellers' labor market. Yet there were numerous cases of workers' being
fired according to this law.[232] Managerial power thus appeared to workers to
be at once oppressive, callous, and arbitrary. At a Donbas mine, as one witness
has recounted, one day an eighteen-year-old collier named Petro Tereshchenko
became ill and did not report to work. The following day when he returned
to work, his boss, M. M. Piskovyi from the same village in Kiev *oblast'* as
Tereshchenko, said to him, "Go croak! Son of a bitch, you don't work here
any more." Piskovyi refused to allow him to return. Tereshchenko died nine
days later of starvation.[233]

[226] *Sotsialisticheskii Donbass*, 12 September 1933.
[227] DADO, f. R-835, op. 1sch, spr. 79, ark. 206.
[228] Ibid., spr. 84, ark. 37–38.
[229] RGAE, f. 7566, op. 1, d. 2701, l. 3.
[230] See, for example, *Sotsialisticheskii Donbass*, 9 and 12 December 1933, and 29 March 1934.
[231] Kuromiya, *Stalin's Industrial Revolution*, p. 306.
[232] See *Sotsialisticheskii Donbass*, 1933.
[233] Mace and Heretz, *Oral History Project*, 1:42.

The same witness recalls his horror at the mockery of the people. Once in 1934, when he and his fellow workers finished work, their boss, Piskovyi, probably the same Piskovyi just mentioned, asked one of them why he had produced so little coal, only two wagonloads, and told him to go get more. The exhausted collier folded his arms and said: "Where do you want me to go? I'm ready. Give me a cross, I'm ready [to die]." He was emaciated and thin as a stick. He said: "I'm ready. Give me candles and a cross. I won't go anywhere."[234] The food situation remained a serious problem. At a shipbuilding factory in Mariupol', for example, a man named Koliada, a party member, declared during the discussion at a general meeting of workers held on 10 July 1934: "Here we have workers' children and managers' children, one group lives well, and the other starves." Another man by the name of Sentiurin, a former party member, followed: "We don't trust anyone. Only the leaders live well, and they don't see how the working class lives. We don't need government inspections. They won't have any results. What's needed is for us to get down to business, walk out of work, and destroy the dining halls." Some party members were booed and not allowed to speak at the meeting, because they were "not our people" [ne nashi]. Out of the 150 or so workers present, only 60 participated in the vote that followed, the rest abstained.[235]

In the Donbas, power relations often involved ethnic factors. Numerous Ukrainian peasants have testified that the plenipotentiaries and other representatives were outsiders, largely Russians.[236] What is important is not so much whether this was true, as is their perception of Russians. Even when the enforcers of collectivization, dekulakization, and grain procurements were Ukrainians, they appeared to the villagers as people who were urbanized, that is, Russified. To the Ukrainian peasants, these assaults, which resulted in famine, were merely another attempt by Moscow to strengthen Russian rule. Moscow, in turn, feared Ukrainian nationalism as a separatist force, the mainstay of which, as in the time of revolution and civil war, was in the countryside where the majority of the Ukrainians still lived.

Other nationalities also suffered because of their ethnic origin. This may have been simply because there were more well-off farmers among them than among the Russians or Ukrainians. Yet this factor alone does not explain the extent of terror staged against national minorities if only because at this time the national minority districts as a whole began to be abolished. Thus, Greek and German farmers were dekulakized en masse. Nearly one-tenth of the Greek farmers were said to have been deported.[237] In one Greek district,

[234] Ibid., pp. 47–48.
[235] DADO, f. 26p, op. 1, spr. 150, ark. 13–13zv.
[236] Mace and Heretz, *Oral History Project*, 3 vols., and *The Black Deeds of the Kremlin*, 2 vols.
[237] B. V. Chyrko, "Natsional'ni menshosti na Ukraini v 20–30-kh rr.," *Ukrains'kyi istorychnyi zhurnal*, 1990, no. 1, p. 59, and L. D. Nasiedkina, "Hrets'ki natsional'ni sil'rady ta raiony v

30 percent of the population died of hunger.[238] Ethnic Russians resettled in the recently depopulated areas. As a result, as one historian has put it, by the mid-1930s the ethnic situation in the Donbas became "explosive."[239] How serious a threat the ethnic Greeks could have possibly posed to the regime is difficult to reckon.

The Ukrainians and Ukrainization did constitute a challenge to Russian political hegemony. Collectivization and industrialization propelled many ethnic Ukrainians to the Donbas, to the extent that their migration had changed the ethnic composition of the Donbas cities in favor of Ukrainians. This trend disquieted Moscow and encouraged the Ukrainian nationalists.[240] The proletarian and predominantly Russian cities in Ukraine now appeared inundated with Ukrainian peasants whose political allegiance was suspect at best. The countryside may have been the main support for Ukrainian nationalism, but it was the cities that provided ideology and resources. Urbanization and industrialization are usually associated with the rise of modern nationalism, and this was the case in the Donbas, too. People were always on the move and people from all social strata and geographical areas mixed in the cities. This made the issue of national consciousness particularly important in the Ukrainian cities.[241] Moscow now had to face a possible erosion of, to use its parlance, the proletarian cities not just by the petit bourgeois but also by the nationalist countryside.

Ethnic tensions were evident in the Donbas towns and settlements. Russians would insult Ukrainians as *khokhol*s and Ukrainians retaliated with remarks on *katsap*s.[242] Russians would tell Ukrainians to speak Russian, and be told that they were in Ukraine, not in Russia.[243] In Krasnyi Luch (formerly Krindachevka) there are records of Russian and Ukrainian miners having fistfights.[244] Ukrainization angered many Russians. By the late 1920s the Ukrainization of the Donbas was earnestly and seriously promoted. The writer Antonenko-Davydovych, who visited the Donbas in 1929, was truly impressed by the way Ukrainization was taking place in, for example, Iuzivka (Stalino), which had earlier "appeared hopelessly Russified." Even though he noticed

Ukraini (druha polovyna 20-kh–30-ti roky)," ibid., 1992, no. 6, pp. 69 and 71.

[238] 33-i: holod, p. 230.

[239] L. D. Nasedkina, "Grecheskie natsional'nye sel'skie sovety Ukrainy vo vzaimodeistvii natsional'noi i sotsial'noi politiki," in *Greki Ukrainy: istoriia i sovremennost'* (Donets'k, 1991), p. 126.

[240] Ukrainian nationalists believed that the Donbas workers were now "Ukrainian at heart." See Iaroslav S. Stets'ko, *30 chervnia 1941. Proholoshennia vidnovlennia derzhavnosty Ukrainy* (Toronto, 1967), p. 47.

[241] See George O. Liber, *Soviet Nationality, Policy, Urban Growth, and Identity Change in the Ukrainian SSR, 1923–1934* (Cambridge University Press, 1992).

[242] See, for example, *Trud*, 17 September 1930.

[243] See, for example, Mace and Heretz, *Oral History Project*, 2:654.

[244] *Visti VUTsVK*, 3 January 1930 and Bohdan Krawchenko, *Social Change and National Consciousness in Twentieth-Century Ukraine* (New York, 1985), p. 120.

that practically all of the signs in Ukrainian had errors, he sensed with exhilaration that Ukrainization was progressing from below, from the mines and factories.[245] When Russian schools were Ukrainized with teachers imported from the western parts of Ukraine, Russian workers staged rebellions.[246]

Whatever the case, an all-out attack on Ukrainization and Ukrainian national Communism began in 1933 at the apex of the famine crisis. Terror was directed not only at "bigwigs" in the cities and the countryside. Ukrainian teachers were fired and often arrested as "class enemies." In 1933 as many as 10 percent of teachers in the Ukrainian schools were branded as political enemies.[247] In the Donbas, the Ukrainian secondary schools were transformed wholesale to Russian-language instruction; technical schools used only Russian, treating Ukrainian as a foreign language. Many people involved in Ukrainization were repressed.[248]

Ukrainian workers in the Donbas were not free from this onslaught. Already by this time, those suspected of being Ukrainian nationalists were particularly harshly treated by the authorities. P. Lysenko, for example, a Donbas miner who was arrested in 1932 as a "Ukrainian insurgent," testified to being tortured by secret police officials. The chief of the police in Ordzhonikidze (formerly Ienakiieve), the city where he was arrested, "approached me and spat in my face." The tortures he had to endure were "indescribable":

> Three names in particular struck terror in the hearts of prisoners. They were: Dimitriev, a young skinny Russian of short stature and grey eyes, Tsukerov, a blonde, and Svirsky. These three butchers caused people to hang themselves in their cells, as did a young teacher Taranukha, a Ukrainian. Some cut their throats with pieces of tin. This happened to an agriculturalist Yaschenko, a Ukrainian, employed at the Voroshilov collective farm. He was married and had a family. Another young Ukrainian, 25 years of age, an agriculturalist from the Nikitowsk collective farm in Donbas was arrested as an insurgent and later charged also with causing livestock to die. The poor fellow could not stand any more torture and tried to hang himself, but the guard noticed it

---

[245] Borys Antonenko-Davydovych, *Zemleiu Ukrains'koiu* (Philadelphia, 1955, a reprint of the 1942 L'viv edition), pp. 146–150 and 152. For a similar testimony to Ukrainization from below, see Haidarivs'kyi, *A svit takyi harnyi*, p. iii. For Ukrainization in the Donbas, see also Andrii Khvylia, *Do rozv'iazannia natsional'noho pytannia na Ukraini* (Kharkiv, 1930), pp. 76–127, and S. Borisov, "Po Donetskomu Basseinu. Putevye ocherki," *Novyi mir*, 1929, no. 2, p. 128.

[246] Krawchenko, *Social Change*, pp. 88–89, and Postyshev, *Stat'i i rechi*, p. 318. In the mid-1920s, 20% of the Donbas schools used the Ukrainian language in instruction. See *2 sessiia Ts.I.K. 3 sozyva. Stenograficheskii otchet* (Moscow, 1926), p. 543.

[247] Heorhii Kas'ianov, *Ukrains'ka intelihentsiia 1920-kh–30-kh rokiv: sotsial'nyi portret ta istorychna dolia* (Kiev, 1992), p. 154 (V. P. Zatons'kyi's remark in December 1933). In November 1933 he was reported to say that 30% to 40% of the Ukrainian teachers were "class enemies." Quoted in "Sozdavaia sem'iu narodov. O praktike resheniia natsional'nogo voprosa na Ukraine v 20–30-e gody," *Pod znamenem leninizma*, 1989, no. 11, p. 53.

[248] Mace and Heretz, *Oral History Project*, 3:1434.

and cut him down. He was later sentenced to eight years in the concentration camps, though he was absolutely innocent.

When an orphan brought into the prison asked for more food, he was told by an inspector, a Russian:

> You fool, you should be satisfied that you have free board here. Your kind are dying from hunger on the streets and you're lucky you are here eating the ration of a Soviet official.[249]

Whether or not Moscow starved Ukraine to break its resistance, it is clear that the famine crisis brought about the end of Ukrainization and the beginning of direct Russian rule.

Anti-Semitism died hard in the Donbas. In November 1932 in Kramators'k in the northern Donbas, a worker and party member since 1917 by the name of Kotliarov, for example, harshly criticized the party leadership for the famine. He had fought for freedom, but "now one can't live." Then he blamed the Jews: "Yids [*zhidy*] occupy positions of power, particularly in the GPU. Why didn't we cut down the Jews before? All the same we'll beat them."[250] In 1933 at a mining school in Chystiakove, the assistant director and party member Butenko and other members of the party and the Komsomol, Rybal'chenko, Polishchuk, and Ievstaf'ev terrorized the best student Berenbek. They forced their way into his room at night, on one occasion making him drink gum arabic, then they beat him up in the dark; on another occasion they threw him out of bed, spat in his face, and kicked him out of the dorm into the street. They accused him of stealing vegetables, stood him against the wall, threatened him with a gun to his forehead, and locked him up in a room. When they were arrested and tried for anti-Semitism, people at the school said: "If this were done by Russians, there wouldn't be any trial. All they did was beat a Yid [*zhidiuga*], and they've been put on trial."[251]

As Communist rulers resorted to sheer brute force to overcome the famine, the traditional opposition between *narod* and *nachal'stvo* (authorities, bosses), or *verkhi* and *nizy*, or between "we" and "they" explained much of the world to the people.[252] Yet just like "enemy of the people," the "people" was a class-neutral, abstract construct that was understood in different ways. True believers, like Leonid Likhodeev mentioned earlier, believed in the omniscience of

---

[249] *The Black Deeds of the Kremlin*, 1:118–19.

[250] DADO, f. R-835, op. 1, spr. 62, ark. 16.

[251] Ibid., f. 326p, op. 1, spr. 103, spr. 10, and *Sotsialisticheskii Donbass*, 10 September 1933. For other cases, see, for example, *Sotsialisticheskii Donbass*, 4 and 5 December 1934. In 1934 the synagogue in Stalino was closed, to be reopened only in September 1990. (*Vechernii Donetsk*, 27 September 1990.)

[252] For an exploration of this issue, see Sarah Davies, " 'Us' against 'Them': Social Identity in Soviet Russia, 1934–1941," *Russian Review*, 56:1 (January 1997). Unfortunately, however, Davies treats the subject only from 1934 onward as if it were nonexistent before 1934.

the party leaders and the stupidity of the *narod*. The mythical *narod*, however, was deeply divided along the lines of nationality, religion (or irreligion), and many other factors such as professions, skills, and earnings. Within each group and subgroup, including the family, whatever unity there was was constantly undermined by denunciations. Likhodeev, for example, was fascinated by the story of Pavlik Morozov, who was said to have denounced his own father as an enemy. Likhodeev's father remarked that he was raising a Chekist (Cheka worker) in his own home.[253] His remark may have been a joke, but it symbolized the political atmosphere in which people lived.

From Stalin's perspective, it mattered little whether the enemy carried a party card or not. Challenges to his power came from both within and without the party, and the enemy was the enemy, be he a party member or not. There was no guarantee that the enemies would not resort to terror: there was a long tradition of political terrorism in Russia, and since 1928 security was sharply tightened for the party leaders. According to Molotov, at that time all it would have taken would have been to kill Stalin and two or three other leaders for everything to collapse.[254] Nor was there any assurance that some of the Bolsheviks, past masters of conspiracy, would refrain from intrigue to oust him. One cannot lightly dismiss the oft-quoted rumor that at the seventeenth party congress ("congress of victors") in January–February 1934 three hundred or so delegates voted against Stalin. Whatever the case, at the same congress, Stalin savagely attacked the "bigwigs" who, he contended, considered that party decisions and Soviet laws were "not written for them but for fools and that because they were irreplaceable, they could violate the decisions and laws with impunity." Then Stalin warned that the "overconceited bigwigs" would have to be "removed from the leading posts, irrespective of past services," and evoked cries from the audience: "Quite right."[255] The delegates had not understood that they would soon be removed en masse as "bigwigs."

Stalin had reason to fear the *"narod,"* too. A Luhans'k worker named Kolinov reacted to the July 1933 suicide of M. O. Skrypnyk, the chief architect of the Soviet Ukrainization program, with the hope that Stalin would follow suit: "If Com. Skrypnyk has worked to the point of shooting himself, then now one may expect that perhaps Stalin, too, will shoot himself."[256] However, the old tsar myth may also have survived, as the following song from Luhans'k suggests:

> Dear Father Stalin
> Come and see

---

[253]Likhodeev, *Pole brani*, p. 216. The Pavlik Morozov story is almost certainly a legend. In all likelihood, the secret police made up the story. For a chilling story of this, see Iurii Druzhnikov, *Voznesenie Pavlika Morozova* (London, 1988).

[254]*Sto sorok besed s Molotovym. Iz dnevnika F. Chueva* (Moscow, 1991), p. 300.

[255]Stalin, *Sochineniia*, 13:370.

[256]DALO, f. P-1, op. 2, spr. 180, ark. 1.

> We've lived long enough in the kolkhoz
> The house's collapsed, the barn leans
> And the mare has but one eye
> On the house the banner hovers
> In the chest the heart hardly beats
> On the banner are the sickle and hammer
> But in the house, only hunger and death.[257]

Yet this can also be interpreted as a reflection of angry desperation. People understood that Stalin was responsible for their misery:

> The sun rises
> And everything comes down
> From Father Stalin
> From Moscow, from the Kremlin.[258]

Close police surveillance pointed out the existence of widespread popular discontent and hostility; there were even occasional peasant uprisings or workers' strikes. Yet to gauge popular feeling was difficult because it had been driven underground. In 1933 in Ukraine the following "counterrevolutionary anecdote" was told: "Lenin always walked in shoes 'cause he worked neatly, but Stalin walks in boots 'cause he is sunk in mud up to the knees."[259] In the Donbas, an angry man who had served in Petliura's army and subsequently was dekulakized and fled to the Donbas, spit at the portraits of Stalin ("son of a bitch") and gouged out the eyes from the pictures. His grandchildren, watching this, followed suit.[260] When the famine subsided, people came back to their village to find few survivors. Hence they sang:

> No cows,
> No pigs –
> Only Stalin on the wall.[261]

This song may be no more than a show of cynicism and resignation by the people. However, one relegates everything to provocation only at the risk of underestimating popular resentment. No doubt there were enemies of Stalin. Exactly how many was difficult for anyone (including the secret police) to know.

[257] Quoted in *Novosti i sobytiia* (Donets'k), no. 21 (July 1993).
[258] From Mari'inka near Stalino. Quoted in *Holos Ukrainy*, 10 September 1993.
[259] DADO, f. R-835, op. 1sch, spr. 105, ark. 7.
[260] Mace and Heretz, *Oral History Project*, 2:876–77.
[261] Zaika, "Golodomor."

6   The Great Terror

THE GREAT TERROR took place against the background of the threat of war
from the West and the East. It was a preemptive strike against presumed enemies whose loyalty Stalin doubted. The Donbas, a haven for the disenfranchised, was terrorized in the process. Its political and economic leaders were
decimated and tens of thousands of innocent people were executed. Available
evidence suggests that the Donbas was the hardest hit in Ukraine. Yet at the
same time, the terror was mitigated by the fact that the Donbas was an industrial center of critical importance.

The terror against the "enemies of the people" was ultimately self-
defeating, because the concept of "enemy" had become all-inclusive. The terror had to stop before the entire population was destroyed.

The Three "Good" Years, the Kirov Murder,
and the Stakhanovite Movement

Overcoming the famine crisis gave rise to optimism. In a phrase aptly coined
by Naum Jasny many years ago, the years 1934–36 marked "the three 'good'
years" in which there was a vast increase in industrial production.[1] Part of
this rise was due to the Stakhanovite movement, a movement for productivity
launched in 1935, but there were grounds to believe that the huge investment,
wrought at an enormous cost to the nation, had finally come to bear fruit. According to official statistics, coal production in the Donbas, for example, increased from 51 million tons in 1933 to 80.7 million tons in 1938; the output
of pig iron and steel in Ukraine grew even more rapidly from 1932 to 1937:
from 3.9 to 8.8 million tons and 3.1 to 8.5 million tons respectively.[2] One

[1] Naum Jasny, *Soviet Industrialization, 1928–1952* (University of Chicago Press, 1961), p. 142.
[2] *Sotsialisticheskoe stroitel'stvo Soiuza SSR (1933–1938 gg.). Statisticheskii sbornik* (Moscow
and Leningrad, 1939), pp. 47 and 56–57.

has to take these statistics with a grain of salt, but the achievement, at least in quantity, was evident.

The end to the grave famine crisis gave rise to elation in party circles, as was discussed earlier. This feeling did not dissipate quickly. Clearly, the abolition of the rationing system in 1934–35 had had a positive effect. In the Donbas, as soon as bread rationing was abolished, people scrambled for bread, but as the bread supply became more reliable, they soon settled down.[3] The writer Konstantin Simonov recalled 1934 as "the year of the brightest hopes": the country had surmounted difficulties and it had become easier to live both spiritually and materially.[4] Some indeed contend that the years 1934–35 were "a spring" and a time of "perestroika." In the cities, the rationing system, which symbolized material hardships, had been abolished; in the countryside the notorious political departments were abolished and the new collective statutes, at least on paper, put the land at the disposal of farmers.[5] Elena Bulgakova, the wife of the writer M. Bulgakov, wrote in her diary on 31 December 1934 how happy that year had been: "Lord, if only it would be like this in the future too!" [*Gospodi, tol'ko by i dal'she bylo tak!*][6] The German refugee Wolfgang Leonhard recall similar optimism prevailing in the capital in 1935: " 'The worst is over now. Things are bound to get better. Even the political system will get more democratic – that's clear enough already from the proposal for a new constitution.' This was the key-note of many discussions during that year."[7]

By contrast, the international situation continued to pose a grave menace both from the West and from the East. Yet in this sphere, too, there were many good signs. In September 1934 the Soviet Union entered the League of Nations, the embodiment of the bourgeois order against which the country had long fought; in May 1935 it concluded an alliance with France, a major capitalist power; and by the summer of 1935 Stalin finally discarded the doctrine of "social fascism" and came to second firmly the "popular front." The country's "struggle for collective security," as Jonathan Haslam has aptly called it,[8] appeared successful thus far, and contributed to the general optimism of 1934–35.[9]

---

[3] James E. Mace and Leonid Heretz, eds., *Oral History Project of the Commission on the Ukraine Famine* (Washington, D.C., 1990), 2:862, 3:1390.

[4] Konstantin Simonov, *Glazami cheloveka moego pokoleniia. Razmyshleniia o I. V. Staline* (Moscow, 1988), pp. 45–46.

[5] M. Ia. Gefter, *Iz tekh i etikh let* (Moscow, 1991), pp. 260 and 354.

[6] Elena Bulgakova, *Dnevnik Eleny Bulgakovoi* (Moscow, 1990), p. 84.

[7] Wolfgang Leonhard, *Child of the Revolution*, tr. C. M. Woodhouse (London, 1957), p. 22. In early 1935 the need for a new constitution was proposed and in late 1936 the "Stalin Constitution" was adopted.

[8] Jonathan Haslam, *The Soviet Union and the Struggle for Collective Security in Europe, 1933–1939* (New York, 1984).

[9] See, for example, Gefter, *Iz tekh i etikh let*.

The assassination on 1 December 1934 of S. M. Kirov, the party boss in Leningrad, put a damper on the apparently optimistic social atmosphere. Simonov, for example, has maintained that his generation saw in the murder a very ominous sign.[10] Leonhard also has added that there "was often a frightened undertone in conversations about Kirov."[11] Yet, as Bulgakova and others have suggested, this ominous event did not destroy the overall bright social mood in the country.

Nevertheless, the Kirov assassination marked an important point in the development of political terror both in the country as a whole and in the Donbas. Whether Stalin and the secret police (reorganized as the NKVD) masterminded the murder of Kirov, Stalin's putative rival, has been a bone of fierce contention.[12] As is the case for John F. Kennedy, the Kirov incident has not been solved conclusively. Recent research tends to support the view of the murder as an act by a single assassin, L. V. Nikolaev, disgruntled with the Leningrad party organization and its boss.[13] Still, one cannot categorically exclude Stalin's involvement. What is clear is that Stalin took advantage of the incident to embark on the bold yet risky road toward eliminating any real or imagined enemies.

Immediately after the assassination Stalin singlehandedly enacted a law that legalized speedy executions of those accused of terrorism. Based on this law, according to one estimate, in December 1934 alone as many as 6,501 people were repressed in the country.[14] In Leningrad, the assassin Nikolaev as well as his wife and many others who had nothing to do with the murder were summarily sentenced to death and executed. It appears that when Stalin received the news of the Kirov murder, he decided to use the murder to decimate his enemies. Thus Stalin instructed Nikolai Ezhov, soon to be the NKVD head, to find the assassins among the Zinovievites.[15] According to Stalin's right-hand man, Molotov, there was no document to show the involvement of the Zinov'ev group.[16] When the NKVD agents appeared reluctant to follow Stalin's order,

[10] Simonov, *Glazami*, p. 49.

[11] Leonhard, *Child of the Revolution*, p. 23.

[12] Compare J. Arch Getty, *Origins of the Great Purges: The Soviet Communist Party Reconsidered, 1933–1938* (Cambridge University Press, 1985); Robert C. Tucker, *Stalin in Power: The Revolution from Above, 1928–1941* (New York, 1990), ch. 12. Also note recent discussion in *Pravda*, 4 November 1990 ("Vokrug ubiistva Kirova") and 28 January 1991 (A. Iakovlev, "O dekabr'skoi tragedii 1934 goda").

[13] See Alla Kirilina, *Rikoshet ili skol'ko chelovek bylo ubito vystrelom v Smol'nom* (St. Peterburg, 1993), and " 'Ia znala, chto predstoit ubiistvo Kirova': Versiia sekretnogo sotrudnika OGPU-NKVD," *Istochnik*, 1994, no. 2. See also a memorandum written by one of the NKVD investigators, G. S. Liushkov, "Stārin e no kōkaijō," *Kaizō* (Tokyo), 1939, no. 4.

[14] Vasilii Maslov and Nikolai Chistiakov, "Stalinskie repressii i sovetskaia iustitsiia," *Kommunist*, 1990, no. 10, p. 105.

[15] Quoted by Ezhov in *Voprosy istorii*, 1995, no. 2, p. 16.

[16] *Sto sorok besed s Molotovym. Iz dnevnika F. Chueva* (Moscow, 1991), pp. 310–11.

Stalin called Iagoda, then head of the secret police, and warned him: "Mind you, we'll slap you down."[17] In January 1935 Stalin circulated a closed letter to the party in which he linked the Zinovievites to a German fascist agent, equated the former oppositionists with the White Guard, and called for punishment appropriate for counterrevolutionaries.[18] Thus in January–February 1935, 843 former Zinovievites were arrested by the NKVD.[19] In the spring of 1935 A. G. Shliapnikov and other former members of the "Workers' Opposition" were arrested for allegedly conducting underground anti-Soviet activities.[20]

Why Stalin had to resort to terror tactics when the crisis was over and the country had come to enjoy a new political "spring" may seem puzzling. Yet it was precisely in overcoming the crisis that the stage was set for further political complications. One now had to ask what steps were to be taken once the crisis was over. The entire country and its administrative apparatus had to be put in order; the party, brutally purged during the famine crisis, had to be reorganized; foreign policy had to be adapted to the rapidly changing international climate. The "spring" of the mid-1930s created room for sincere discussion and therefore room for disagreement. Historians have shown recently how contradictory the political process of the country in the mid-1930s was.[21]

Of all the issues, the threat of war was the most critical. Just as Lenin and his supporters among the Bolsheviks had taken the defeatist position during World War I, it was quite conceivable at the time that some of Stalin's opponents would not support him in the coming war; moreover, there were millions of former "kulaks," many of whom were incarcerated, but unknown numbers of whom were hidden in the cities, in the factories and mines, on construction sites and collective farms. From Stalin's point of view, there was no guarantee that in case of war these people would fight for him. The linking of the Leningrad Zinovievites to foreign agents was not an accident. Indeed, in the subsequent years of the Great Terror, enemies were almost invariably presented

---

[17] See Ezhov's speech in *Voprosy istorii*, 1995, no. 2, p. 17. See also *Reabilitatsiia. Politicheskie protsessy 30–50-kh godov* (Moscow, 1991), pp. 123, 153, and 154.

[18] *Reabilitatsiia*, pp. 191–95.

[19] Ibid., p. 175.

[20] Ibid., pp. 104–22.

[21] For administration in general, see Gábor T. Rittersporn, *Stalinist Simplifications and Soviet Complications: Social Tensions and Political Conflicts in the USSR, 1933–1953* (Chur, Switzerland, 1991); for the party, see Getty, *Origins*; for penal policy, see Eugene Huskey, "Vyshinskii, Krylenko, and the Shaping of Soviet Legal Order," *Slavic Review*, 46:3–4 (Winter 1987); and for foreign policy, Haslam, *The Soviet Union*, and "Political Opposition to Stalin and the Origins of the Terror in Russia, 1932–1936," *Historical Journal*, 29:2 (1986). For the best work on the Great Terror in general, see Oleg Khlevniuk, "The Objectives of the Great Terror, 1937–1938," in Julian Cooper, Maureen Perrie, and E. A. Rees, eds., *Soviet History, 1917–53: Essays in Honour of R. W. Davies* (London, 1995).

as agents of fascist Germany and Japan. The theme of foreign espionage and terrorism became the leitmotif of the terror.

The Kirov murder provided Stalin with a golden opportunity for eliminating all the politically suspect as foreign agents, enemies of the people, and fifth columns. More immediately, Stalin had every reason to fear that a single bullet from a disgruntled element would end his life and power. As a former revolutionary, he must have been very aware that one of the legacies of the Russian revolutionary movement, political terrorism, had killed many officials and one tsar. What mattered, Stalin implied, was not the number of enemies. This message is evident in a speech Stalin made in March 1937: "To win a battle in war, several corps of Red Army soldiers may be needed, but to ruin the victory at the front a few spies will suffice somewhere in army headquarters or even in the division headquarters who can steal an operation plan and pass it to the enemy."[22] If the enemies were hidden and hidden enemies were more dangerous than openly hostile elements (who, according to Stalin, had basically been destroyed), then the search for these dangerous foes had to be extensive and thorough. The Kirov incident was a golden opportunity for this maneuver.

The whole question was, Who is the enemy? As is discussed in Chapter 5, the enemy category had already expanded since the famine crisis to include many tried and true Communists. From the Kirov murder onward, this trend became evident. Certainly, the old categories of class enemies persisted. Shortly after the assassination (in the first few months of 1935), for example, thirty thousand to forty thousand Leningraders were expelled from the city as "social aliens"; many of them were former nobles, tsarist officials, and their families.[23] In the Donbas, throughout the spring and summer of 1935, many individuals accused of being kulaks and bandits were executed.[24] Yet now the enemy category encompassed every group of the population, including the Bolsheviks. Even the armed forces were not immune from enemy hunting.[25]

By any measure, the organized opposition movement within the country was almost completely destroyed by ruthless repression. Contact among for-

[22] I. V. Stalin, *Sochineniia*, vol. 1 (14) (Stanford, Calif., 1967), p. 219.

[23] Anton Ciliga, *The Russian Enigma* (London, 1940), p. 71 (where he insists that these were "workers"); Iakovlev, "O dekabr'skoi tragedii"; and Simonov's story of his own relatives in his, *Glazami*, pp. 50 and 54. Molotov, in response to a protest by the famous Russian physiologist and Nobel Prize winner I. P. Pavlov, stated that the repression was related to the city's proximity to the border and the complex international situation. (*Stranitsy istorii KPSS. Fakty, problemy, uroki*, vol. 2 [Moscow, 1989], p. 650.) It is often said that the lists of the people to be expelled were made by comparing the prerevolutionary and the 1934 telephone directories.

[24] See, for instance, *Sotsialisticheskii Donbass*, 14 April; 1, 3, 9, and 14 June; 3 and 30 July; 2, 3, 8, and 9 August 1935.

[25] For repressions in the armed forces after the Kirov murder, see O. F. Suvenirov, "Narkomat oborony i NKVD v predvoennye gody," *Voprosy istorii*, 1991, no. 6, p. 27.

mer oppositionists was nil or too limited to assume any organizational force. This must have been clear to the secret police and Stalin. Moreover, the aftermath of the Kirov murder disarmed many oppositionists. The incident so frightened them that they morally capitulated to Stalin's terror and accepted guilt for crimes they had not committed.[26] Yet this state of affairs no more guaranteed Stalin's hold on power than the 3 June regime under Nicholas and Stolypin ensured the power of tsarism. After all, Stalin's archenemy, Trotsky, was still politically active abroad just as Lenin was on the eve of World War I.

Immediately after the Kirov murder, many party members were arrested, tried, and exiled. According to one set of statistics, in the Donbas, in 1934, 1935, and 1936 respectively, 120, 146, and 775 "Trotskyites" were subjected to such a fate.[27] In the Stalino metallurgical factory alone, no fewer than ten "Trotskyite" groups were uncovered in 1934–36.[28] In the first half of 1935, Old Bolsheviks in Donbas factories, mines, and railways were branded and "liquidated" as "Trotskyists," "Zinovievites," and "Workers' Oppositionists." Some of them were said to have organized the "Group of Old Bolsheviks," the "Union of Old Leninists," and the like and provided monetary help to those in exile.[29] (By summer 1935 both the Society of Old Bolsheviks and the Society of Former Political Prisoners were abolished by fiat.)[30]

This operation against former oppositionists was carried out by the NKVD with help from the party organizations.[31] Some assistants were so anxious to find enemies that in December 1935 the Central Committee of the Ukrainian Communist Party had to restrain the zealots. Yet it still continued to advocate repression of the enemies of the party and the government.[32] By all indications, Ukraine was hit hardest by this wave of repression: by far the largest numbers of "spies" were arrested in Ukraine in 1935.[33] Within Ukraine, the Donbas was subjected to the most intense crackdown: as of 1 December 1935, in connection with the verification campaign of party documents, 560 in Donets'k

---

[26] Iurii Feofanov, " 'My dumali, chto tak nado . . . ,' " *Nedelia*, 1988, no. 41, pp. 11 and 13, demonstrates this point well. It is based on an interview with A. N. Safonova, whose husband I. N. Smirnov was implicated in the Zinov'ev-Kamenev trial in 1936 and was executed.

[27] RTsKhIDNI, f. 17, op. 21, d. 5195, l. 121. Some cases were reported in the press. See *Sotsialisticheskii Donbass*, 20, 26, and 29 January; 2, 21, and 27 February 1935, etc. Iu. I Shapoval, *Ukraina 20-kh–50-kh rokiv: storinky nenapisanoi istorii* (Kiev, 1993), pp. 181–82, shows that the attack on the "counterrevolutionary work" of the remnants of nationalists and Trotskyites began in the autumn of 1934.

[28] RTsKhIDNI, f. 17, op. 21, d. 5195, l. 123.

[29] DADO, f. 326p, op. 1, spr. 304, ark. 49–50 and 129; f. 26p, op. 1, spr. 226a; and f. 424p, op. 1a, spr. 183, ark. 21.

[30] Robert Conquest, *The Great Terror: A Reassessment* (Oxford University Press, 1990), pp. 76–78.

[31] See RTsKhIDNI, f. 17, op. 2, d. 561, l. 161.

[32] Valerii Vasil'ev, "30-e gody na Ukraine," *Kommunist*, 1990, no. 17, p. 79.

[33] RTsKhIDNI, f. 17, op. 120, d. 181, l. 251.

oblast', 408 in Dnipropetrovs'k *oblast'*, 350 in Kharkiv *oblast'*, and 264 in
Kiev *oblast'* were arrested by the NKVD as "spies," "Trotskyites," "nationalists," "fascists and terrorists," and the like.[34] In the process, party membership
in the Donbas was halved between 1933 and 1936 (from 166,000 to 83,000).[35]

Particularly revealing of the war factor was the repression of ethnic minorities as potential fifth columns. Ukraine was the most vulnerable. Even
before the Kirov incident, Ukrainian officials expressed much fear that money
and other forms of aid from Germany to ethnic Germans, begun at the time
of the famine crisis, were in fact an "open fascist campaign."[36] Eight days
after the Kirov murder, on 9 December 1934, the Ukrainian Communist Party
Politburo, in response to a circular of the Central Committee of the party in
Moscow, sent a special secret telegram to the *oblast'*'s, ordering an elaborate review of German and Polish districts in Ukraine, threatening deportation abroad
or to remote areas of the country for "the slightest attempts at anti-Soviet activity or propaganda." Eight days later another telegram followed declaring a
purge of "anti-Soviet elements" from the border military zones.[37] Throughout
1935 tens of thousands of people "disloyal to the Soviet government," particularly ethnic Poles and Germans, were deported from the western border
areas.[38] "In 1935 there was a complete break in contacts between the Soviet
Germans and the outside world."[39] In April 1936 a secret order on the deportation of ethnic Poles in Ukraine followed.[40] Repression in the west was
matched by repression in the east against ethnic Koreans and Chinese accused
of being Japanese spies.[41]

After the Kirov murder many foreign political refugees were considered

---

[34] Ibid., f. 17, op. 120, d. 84, l. 1. See also ibid., d. 181, l. 73.

[35] *Sotsialisticheskii Donbass*, 9 October 1936.

[36] *Natsional'ni vidnosyny v Ukraini u XX st. Zbirnyk dokumentiv i materialiv* (Kiev, 1994),
pp. 212–16. "As early as 1934, as a result of the Nazis coming to power in Germany, the Central
Committee of the Communist Party decided to have full and accurate data collected on all Germans
working in industry and in administrative bodies, and to see to it that this survey should not be
publicly known." According to one who collected data, already at the end of 1934, the party "had
before it the most precise data on the numbers and occupations of all the Germans living in the
USSR. All the secret service work and repressions carried out later were guided by the data we
collected and arranged." Ingeborg Fleischhauer and Benjamin Pinkus, *The Soviet Germans: Past
and Present* (New York, 1986), pp. 34 and 91.

[37] TsDAHO, f. 1, op. 16, spr. 11, ark. 294–95 and 323.

[38] Ibid., spr. 12.

[39] Fleischhauer and Pinkus, *Soviet Germans*, p. 63.

[40] M. F. Buhai, "Deportatsii naselennia z Ukrainy (30–50-ti roky)," *Ukrains'kyi istorychnyi zhurnal*, 1990, no. 10, p. 34. As many as 35,820 ethnic Poles were deported according to this order.
V. I. Paliienko, "Nezakonni represii proty pol'skoho naselennia v Ukraini u 20–30-kh rokakh," *Za
mizhnatsional'nu zlahodu proty shovinizmu ta ekstremizmu* (Kiev, 1995), p. 82, and Ihor Vynnychenko, *Ukraina 1920–1980-kh: deportatsii, zaslannia, vyslannia* (Kiev, 1994), pp. 39 and
106–7.

[41] RTsKhIDNI, f. 17, op. 2, d. 561, ll. 129 and 153.

tantamount to enemies. Several hundred Polish refugees, both Communists and non-Communists, were arrested in Ukraine between December 1934 and 1936.[42] The Donbas hosted many such refugees and was hard hit by anti-Polish and anti-German repression. They were repressed as "spies" and "fascist agents."[43] From late 1934 to 1936 numerous German "counterrevolutionary" organizations were liquidated by the Donbas NKVD, including "Prolog," "Renegaty," "Filial," "Segment," "Redaktor," "Pereplet," "Azovtsy," "Kol'tso," "Pochtamt," and "Zheleznyi krest."[44]

From December 1934 onward, at Polish schools and institutes instruction in Polish was restricted or abolished.[45] The Greek schools in the Donbas were subjected to the same fate in 1936.[46]

Ethnic Ukrainians were far from immune to political repression. Within two weeks of the Kirov murder, thirty-seven Ukrainians were tried in Kiev as belonging to the Ukrainian White Guard terrorist Center. Twenty-three of the defendants were "widely known writers, cultural and social workers" (including the "young deaf-and-dumb poet" A. F. Vlyzko). Seven were Galicians "who had come to live in the Soviet Ukraine." Twenty-seven of the defendants, many of whom had never traveled abroad, were sentenced to be shot and executed for having crossed the border into Soviet Ukraine from Poland and Rumania with the "intention" of organizing terrorist acts.[47] Members of the former Ukrainian association of Orientalists were repressed en masse as Japanese spies.[48] Ukrainians from Galicia (then under Polish rule) became as suspect as ethnic Poles and Germans.[49] In the spring of 1935 seventeen former members of the Ukrainian Left Socialist Revolutionaries (*partiia borot'bistiv*) were arrested for underground counterrevolutionary activities (including po-

---

[42] *Istoricheskii arkhiv*, 1992, no. 1, pp. 114–17. In December 1935, Postyshev, then the Ukrainian party leader, contended categorically that 90% of the so-called political emigrants were Polish agents. RTsKhIDNI, f. 17, op. 2, d. 561, l. 162.

[43] TsDAHO, f. 1, op. 1, spr. 469, ark. 126, and RTsKhIDNI, f. 17, op. 120, d. 181, ll. 85–86 and 120–22.

[44] *Vechernii Donetsk*, 23 February 1990.

[45] TsDAHO, f. 1, op. 16, spr. 12, ark. 278, 304, and 313. See also Shapoval, *Ukraina*, pp. 160–61.

[46] *Greki Ukrainy: istoriia i sovremennost'* (Donetsk, 1991), p. 22.

[47] Hryhory Kostiuk, *Stalinist Rule in the Ukraine: A Study of the Decade of Mass Terror (1929–39)* (New York, 1960), pp. 98–101, and Shapoval, *Ukraina*, pp. 152–60. Repression against prominent Ukrainian writers continued into 1935 and 1936. B. D. Antonenko-Davydovych, for example, was arrested in January 1935, was sentenced to ten years in September 1935, for allegedly participating in a counterrevolutionary organization. TsDAHO, f. 1, op. 23, spr. 699, ark. 6. For other cases, for example, the "Terrorist Group of Professor Zerov" trial in January 1936, see Kostiuk, *Stalinist Rule*, pp. 101–2.

[48] Iu. I Shapoval, *Liudyna i systema. Shtrykhy do portretu totalitarnoi doby v Ukraini* (Kiev, 1994), pp. 31–32. The association was abolished earlier (in 1933).

[49] See, for example, RTsKhIDNI, f. 17, op. 120, d. 181, l. 74, and op. 2, d. 561, l. 162.

litical terrorism and organizing Ukrainian nationalists).[50] Some Communist Party members were arrested as Ukrainian nationalists. In the Donbas mines, workers were arrested for reading Ukrainian nationalist literature (by Vynny-chenko, Kulish) and for hanging the late Skrypnyk's portrait in the dormitory. Some in Kadiivka were repressed for protesting against use of Russian in meetings and for allegedly contending that "Ukraine is under [Russian] yoke."[51]

The former oppositionists and ethnic minorities were relatively easy to identify and isolate as putative enemies. It was far more difficult, as Stalin, Vyshinskii, and others had maintained since 1933, to uncover so-called hidden and masked enemies. Stalin took advantage of the Kirov murder to extend an intensive enemy hunt to every corner of the country. Even before the Kirov murder the secret police closely watched those whom it deemed politically suspect. After the Leningrad incident enemy hunters, particularly those in the secret police, zealously pursued enemies. The whole operation threatened to develop into mass terror: the more closely they watched society, the more hidden enemies seemed to appear.

The police painstakingly recorded numerous "counterrevolutionary" remarks, songs, and leaflets in the Donbas as elsewhere.[52] If one were to believe them, one would be tempted to conclude, as some NKVD vigilantes did, that "enemies" were ubiquitous.

This would be, however, a dangerous short circuit in logic. Certainly, there were occasional explosions of emotion or slips of tongue. But for the most part people had learned to keep silent and not utter dangerous remarks. All the more so, real enemies of the Soviet government, cognizant of the danger, tended to lie quiet, and that was why Stalin and others maintained that these hidden enemies were particularly dangerous. The secret police was thus forced to take extraordinary measures to unearth "enemies." In fact, many case documents in the former State Security Committee (KGB) archives in the Donbas show that the vast majority of the charges brought against alleged enemies were fabricated by enemy hunters and secret police provocateurs and informers who knew exactly what remarks and views would reflect the dreams and fantasies of hidden enemies. These were the people who spoke for the imagined enemies: in case after case, there is no evidence but second- and third-hand rumor or confessions extracted under duress.[53]

---

[50]Shapoval, *Ukraina*, ch. 10, and Kostiuk, *Stalinist Rule*, pp. 102–3.

[51]DADO, f. 424p, op. 1a, spr. 183, ark. 23 and 27. For other cases, see, for example, ibid., ark. 37–38, and *Sotsialisticheskii Donbass*, 4 February 1935.

[52]See, for example, Smolensk in Merl Fainsod, *Smolensk under Soviet Rule* (Harvard University Press, 1958), p. 422, and Sheila Fitzpatrick, *Stalin's Peasants: Resistance and Survival in the Russian Village after Collectivization* (Oxford University Press, 1994), pp. 291–92. See the case of Red Army soldiers, in B. A. Viktorov, *Bez grifa "sekretno." Zapiski voennogo prokurora* (Moscow, 1990), p. 201.

[53]I base this conclusion on numerous files I consulted in the former KGB archives in Donets'k

Numerous "dangerous" popular reactions to the Kirov murder were reported by the secret police. It is impossible to ascertain whether the alleged enemies were actually responsible for them or whether the police and informers had fabricated them. Soon after the assassination, a Komsomol named Dobyt'ko in the Donbas was arrested by the secret police for stating that "Kirov was killed; it's not enough, Stalin had to be killed" [*Ubili Kirova, etogo malo, nado bylo ubit' Stalina*].[54] A Luhans'k worker named Nesmachnyi was similarly apprehended for a conversation with his fellow workers in which he allegedly said: "Kirov was killed. It's a pity that Stalin wasn't [*Ubili Kirova, zhalko chto ne Stalina*]."[55] Colliers at the Horlivka mine were accused of singing "counterrevolutionary songs" to the effect that "Kirov was killed – food rationing was abolished; if Stalin is killed – people will begin to live" [*Kirova ubili – khlebnye knizhki otmenili, Stalina ub'iut – narody zazhivut*].[56]

Reaction among the Donbas youngsters set a particularly uneasy tone, according to the secret police. The Kirov incident prompted verbal attacks against the party leadership, direct criticism of Soviet policies, and sharp manifestations of anti-Semitism, Ukrainian nationalism, and hooliganism. Schoolchildren in Stalino would converse among themselves: "Now it's Stalin's turn, soon Stalin will be no more" [*Seichas ochered' za Stalinym, skoro Stalina ne budet*]. One boy, whose father had been expelled from the party, was said to have remarked gloatingly of the Kirov murder: "He deserved it" [*Tak emu i nuzhno*]. A certain Petrenko, a seventh grader of School 49 in Stalino and son of a Red partisan, during a discussion on the abolition of food rationing, was accused of saying, "Food rationing was abolished because they were scared after the Kirov murder; all the same the workers are eating rotten bread." Petrenko was further accused of claiming during class, "Our policemen are worse than fascists; they beat and mock workers, put them in labor camps and torture them." Petrenko, according to the secret police, was a terrorist who declared that Nikolaev (Kirov's assassin) was a hero and that he himself would like to go to Moscow and do the same.[57] The police carefully recorded even innocent remarks by schoolchildren in Horlivka such as "The more leaders were killed, the less schoolwork we would have to do." Komsomol members at the Artem Mine in Horlivka were said by the police to have entertained themselves by discussing how they would kill Stalin if they were dispatched to Moscow. Some cautioned that even if Stalin were killed, it would be all the same because Kaganovich would take over.[58] The Donbas secret police also reported

and Luhans'k.
[54]DADO, f. 326p, op. 1, spr. 304, ark. 34.
[55]Ibid., ark. 37.
[56]Ibid., ark. 20.
[57]Ibid., f. 424p, op. 1a, spr. 183, ark. 5–8.
[58]Ibid., ark. 10–11 and 14.

increasing numbers of attacks against Jews, Russians, and Tartars by Ukrainian children. Some in Horlivka circulated a poem for "beating of Yids, Bolsheviks, and Communists."[59]

Jokes and anecdotes became ever more dangerous. Young collective farmers in Rivne in the Donbas who had organized a drinking group, would sing while drinking:

> Lenin rides a sheep
> With an onion in his pocket
> And tempts [people] with herring
> To fulfill the five-year plan.[60]

The group was indicted as a counterrevolutionary group. In another case, M. A. Grebtsov, a party member since 1928 and director of a mine supply department, was accused of telling the following riddle while under the influence of alcohol: "What is the difference between Jesus Christ and Stalin?" When no one responded, Grebtsov is said to have replied: "Jesus Christ rode on a donkey and fed him, but Comrade Stalin rides on everyone and feeds no one." Grebtsov attributed the joke to someone else, but he was given three years.[61]

Even a slight manifestation of doubt about the body politic came to constitute state crime. In January 1936 eighteen youths (many of whom were miners) in Luhans'k were arrested for organizing a "counterrevolutionary economic union of vanguard youth" and advocating the creation of a new party. The alleged leader of the group, V. A. Anokhin, in fact wanted to create a mutual-help group. Among the confiscated personal material were found diaries, notes, and poems, which the secret police contended showed that Anokhin and others entertained some doubt about the way the country was being governed. Anokhin, for example, wrote to his friend: "One has to look life directly in the face. Basia, I don't understand why you are afraid of depicting life realistically in art . . . certainly I understand that to show real life is more difficult than to create a fairy tale about white steer." Fortunately for the defendants, it was still early 1936. Many of them fought back at the trial, denied charges of anti-Soviet propaganda, and some even resorted to hunger strikes. Others broke down and pleaded guilty. They were given terms of between two and seven years. The defendants were rehabilitated in 1959 except for P. F. Shirokov who, during the war, collaborated with the Germans.[62]

Shirokov's case is instructive. Apologists for state terror contend that ter-

---

[59] Ibid., f. 326p, op. 1, spr. 304, ark. 2, and f. 424p, op. 1a, spr. 183, ark. 4–13.

[60] DALO, f. 3747, op. 3, spr. 3-r. Onion and herring symbolized poor consumption. The living and working conditions in the Donbas were so poor that Spanish socialist miners who fled prosecution and emigrated to the "socialist motherland" in 1935 had almost without exception returned home by 1936. See *Istoricheskii arkhiv*, 1996, no. 2, pp. 133–41.

[61] DADO, f. 26p, op. 1, spr. 226a.

[62] AUSBULO, no. 7027-r, 9 vols.

ror was justified because people like Shirokov (who was released either by the
Soviet government before the war or by the Germans during the war) were
dangerous to state security and that indeed Shirokov, for example, did betray
the country during the war. If anything, according to the apologists, terror
should have been severer so as to eliminate any possibility of betrayal. Iagoda,
the secret police chief, contended at the time: "History dictates to us [the task
of] deciding whom to isolate rather than whom to release."[63] One may counter,
however, that it was the terror that embittered people like Shirokov and turned
them into traitors. The question of loyalty was still hypothetical in the mid-
1930s, but the state had every reason to fear unknown numbers of embittered
people. One would run the risk of underestimating human emotion by assum-
ing that the millions of people who were terrorized by the state entertained no
bitterness toward it.

It is likely that some of the allegations were indeed true. After the Kirov
murder, five wagonloads of Donbas miners were arrested and deported. Their
crime was remarks critical of Stalin and his government, including "Stalin
slaughters people without a knife"; "Pity Kirov. Maybe there are mistakes
in our policy, so they have begun to kill off our leaders." The writer Ivan
Uksusov who met these miners in prison has suggested that these were sincere
remarks.[64] Baptists in the Donbas, according to a 1935 police report, engaged
in counterrevolutionary agitation among the workers: "Hitler was placed in
power by God, and God helps him."[65] Some Donbas residents were arrested
in 1935 for praising Hitler and expressing that in case of war with Germany
they would fight for the defeat of the Soviet Union.[66] In Luhans'k leaflets were
dropped in 1935 openly calling for the overthrow of "slavery."[67] Terror against
innocent people in the wake of the Kirov murder added to the bitterness of the
Donbas population and disquieted party officials.[68]

The three good years did not save the industrial managers and engineers
from the enemy hunters. There were considerable numbers of former oppositionists, nobles, tsarist or White officers, and others of suspect origins working
in the Donbas as managers and in other capacities for industrial development.[69]

[63]See Ivan Uksusov, "58-ia stat'ia za 58 knig s avtografami," *Literaturnaia gazeta*, 16 November 1988.
[64]I. I. Uksusov, "Posle molchaniia," *Sovetskii shakhter*, 1989, no. 11, p. 10. See also Hryhorii
Kostiuk, *Zustrichi i proshchannia. Spohady. Knyha persha* (Edmonton, Canada, 1987), pp. 538–
39 and 546–47.
[65]DADO, f. 326p, op. 1, spr. 304, ark. 144.
[66]Ibid., f. 26p, op. 1, d. 226a.
[67]Ibid., f. 424p, op. 1a, spr. 183, ark. 2–3.
[68]See reports in ibid., f. 326p, op. 1, spr. 304, ark. 7–8. A Krasnoluch mine manager Khlevovoi
killed himself after dozens of his subordinates were arrested and he feared for more of his workers.
Ibid., ark. 16.
[69]For statistical data, see Oleg Khlevniuk, *1937-i: Stalin, NKVD i sovetskoe obshchestvo*

These people, like any other former oppositionists, were particularly vulnerable. During the famine crisis the party card barely saved them from the repressive hand of Moscow, but after the Kirov murder the party card lost all its function as a special indulgence or privilege.

Even before the Kirov murder, the managers were in a precarious position. Industrial accidents created much suspicion against the managers and engineers. In 1933, according to official statistics, 239 managers and engineers in the Donbas collieries were sentenced to various terms of imprisonment and forced labor for infringement of industrial safety rules, but the number increased to 451 in 1934, decreased to 373 in 1935, and then rose to 459 in 1936.[70] Some incidents were declared to be acts of diversion and wrecking, and the defendants were charged as terrorists.[71] Yet many managers skillfully shifted the responsibility to the middle and lower managerial personnel. More than half of the convicted were such people.[72] This situation gave rise easily to the suspicion that many innocent people were being convicted while many guilty enemies were at large.[73] The question naturally arose as to who the real enemy was.

The famous Stakhanovite movement launched in 1935 complicated this question. After the famine crisis, the two main industries – coal and steel – in the Donbas saw a steady increase. Yet the coal industry still experienced periodic slumps for seasonal and other reasons and remained a bottleneck and a source of irritation for Moscow. Not satisfied with the performance in good years, Ordzhonikidze, the commissar of heavy industry, used the famous record-breaking exploit by the Donbas collier, Aleksei Stakhanov, for a breakthrough. The norm-busting movement soon spread to all industry. One important implication of this assault against the old norm of management and labor was a renewal of industrial cadres.[74] This method of breaking ground was employed, for example, for the rapid industrialization drive in the late 1920s.

(Moscow, 1992), pp. 116–17.

[70]GARF, f. 9474, op. 1, d. 114, l. 56.

[71]See, for example, RTsKhIDNI, f. 17, op. 120, d. 181, ll. 2–3.

[72]GARF, f. 9474, op. 1, d. 114, l. 54. There were dozens of workers as well who were convicted for industrial accidents.

[73]Ibid., l. 46.

[74]For a very good treatment of the Stakhanovite movement, see O. V. Khlevniuk, *Stalin i Ordzhonikidze. Konflikty v Politburo v 30-e gody* (Moscow, 1993), pp. 55–66. For more detailed discussion, see Lewis H. Siegelbaum, *Stakhanovism and the Politics of Productivity in the USSR, 1935–1941* (Cambridge University Press, 1988); Robert Maier, *Die Stachanov-Bewegung 1935–1938. Der Stachanovismus als tragendes und verschärfendes Moment der Stalinisierung der Sowjetischen Gesellschaft* (Stuttgart, 1990); Gábor T. Rittersporn, "Heros du travail et commandants de la production. La campagne stakhanoviste et les stratégies fractionelles en U.R.S.S (1935–1936)," *Recherches*, nos. 32–33; Robert Thurston, "The Stakhanovite Movement: The Background to the Great Terror in the Factories, 1935–1938," in J. Arch Getty and Roberta T. Manning, eds., *Stalinist Terror: New Perspectives* (Cambridge University Press, 1993).

The movement, however, quickly turned into "political pogroms" against the managerial cadres.[75]

Ordzhonikidze and other industrial leaders used customarily harsh words against those who implicitly or explicitly opposed the new movement. They did not intend a violent attack against their own men, but given the political atmosphere of the time, such a turn of events was almost inevitable. Within a month after Stakhanov's wild norm-breaking on 31 August 1935, the press began to report cases of managerial cadres being removed from work and prosecuted as saboteurs.[76] On 26 September the Donets'k *oblast'* court held a special session at Mine 29 in Makiivka and heard a case against the former mine director Vishniakov and section director Fediaev. Five hundred workers and housewives attended the session. The defendants were accused of deliberately and repeatedly disrupting the work of Stakhanovite norm busters. The court sentenced the defendants to seven years of imprisonment and exile for their "counterrevolutionary sabotage of the Stakhanovite method of work." According to the press, the sentence was greeted with high approval by those present.[77]

If this episode from Makiivka is credible, workers' sentiment against their bosses ran high. True, the managers and engineers feared that even though the Stakhanovite norm busting might set spectacular records and increase production and productivity temporarily, concentration on record breaking would affect the overall work of mines and factories adversely. It was unavoidable that workplace safety would suffer for the sake of efficiency. Such a claim appeared to the industrial leaders as a classical example of managerial inertia and, what was worse, managerial maneuvering to hide the real production capacity of mines and factories to keep production targets low. The impatient political leaders presented this claim as counterrevolutionary sabotage. Yet not all workers supported the new productivity campaign. Apart from the ambitious who wanted to profit from it and those who genuinely hoped to improve productivity, many workers soon found that the movement did not necessarily improve their work or life. They feared that the movement would increase their output quotas and reduce their earnings. There was a host of other reasons as well for resenting yet another campaign. In the Donbas, leaflets attacking the movement as a new form of exploitation were dropped.[78] Some resisted the movement with physical violence against the Stakhanovites.[79] The Stakhanovite movement gave rise to sharp tension in the workplace.

[75]This expression comes from Khlevniuk, *Stalin i Ordzhonikidze*, p. 58.

[76]*Za industrializatsiiu*, 21 and 23 September 1935.

[77]*Sotsialisticheskii Donbass*, 28 September 1935.

[78]RTsKhIDNI, f. 17, op. 120, d. 272, ll. 14–16.

[79]Siegelbaum, *Stakhanovism*, ch. 5, and Donald Filtzer, *Soviet Workers and Stalinist Industrialization: The Formation of Modern Soviet Production Relations, 1928–1941* (New York, 1986), pp. 200–5.

Thus, the Stakhanovite movement made enemies of both managerial cadres and rank-and-file workers. The former were the more prominent victims of the enemy hunt. Outspoken workers, whose harsh attacks led to the downfall of their bosses,[80] were promoted to positions of responsibility. By the beginning of 1936, 156 cadres (including 26 mine directors and 23 chief engineers) were removed from the Donbas coal-mining industry. In turn, 300 Stakhanovites were promoted to positions of responsibility.[81] How many more were removed in 1936 is unknown. According to one statistic, more than 1,000 managerial and engineering personnel were prosecuted and, of them, more than 500 were convicted.[82] Whatever the case, the impact of the witch-hunt was already evident. The party and the highest managerial leaders in the Donbas made numerous groundless accusations against almost all commanders of production.[83] As a result, an impression was created that the Donbas managers were all saboteurs.[84] For the Donbas leaders, there was no other choice, however: the first secretary of the Donets'k Oblast' party committee, S. A. Sarkisov, was being pressed by the Ukrainian NKVD chief V. A Balits'kyi to find wrecking activities (*vreditel'stvo*), a more serious charge than sabotage, among the managerial cadres. Sarkisov defended them by insisting that there was sabotage but no wrecking.[85]

The managers had to adapt to new facts of life: they accepted, at least superficially, the Stakhanovite movement rather than face criminal charges. The serious charges of treason and espionage were as yet rare before the summer of 1936. Yet the nightmare soon began. Impressive production records were transitory, and the overall organization of work was undermined by the flashy Stakhanovite movement. This in turn opened the managers to charges of wrecking. Once, when some colliers complained to Stalin that their mine failed to provide a bath for them (and by implication to create favorable working conditions), Stalin declared: "The boss is an enemy of the people."[86]

The Bacchanalia of Terror

"Genghis Khan killed many people, saying, 'The deaths of the conquered are necessary for the conquerors' peace of mind" [*Smert' pobezhdennykh nuzhna*

[80]See my "Soviet Memoirs as a Historical Source," in Sheila Fitzpatrick and Lynne Viola, eds., *A Researcher's Guide to Sources on Soviet Social History in the 1930s* (Armonk, N.Y., 1990). The Stakhanovites were praised for their role. See, for example, *Za industrializatsiiu*, 1 April 1936.

[81]*Pervyi Vsedonetskii slet stakhanovtsev-masterov uglia. 7–10 ianvaria 1936 goda, Stalino. Sten. otchet* (Kiev, 1936), pp. 59–60, and Nikolai Troian, "'My pokoriaem vremia. . . .'" Stakhanovskoe dvizhenie: vzgliad s poroga 90-kh," *Donbas*, 1990, no. 1, p. 72.

[82]RTsKhIDNI, f. 17, op. 21, d. 4683, l. 20.

[83]Note a speech by the director of Stalino Coal, A. Khachatur'iants in *Za Industrializatsiiu*, 28 June 1936.

[84]Ibid., 8 May 1936.

[85]RTsKhIDNI, f. 17, op. 21, d. 5196, l. 290.

[86]*Sto sorok besed s Molotovym*, p. 295.

dlia spokoistviia pobeditelei]. Stalin underlined this phrase while reading a book on Russian history.[87] One is tempted to read here Stalin's rationale for the Great Terror. Indeed, it appeared that Stalin had conquered the whole nation and now was ready for the coup de grace.

The terror of 1936–38 is generally known as the Great Terror.[88] The terror is also referred to as Ezhov's time (*Ezhovshchina*), when the infamous secret police chief N. I. Ezhov managed the terror operation. In September 1936 Ezhov was installed by Stalin's fiat and was removed in November 1938. Ezhov was arrested in April 1939 and was executed in February 1940.[89] In urging the Politburo to accept Ezhov's appointment Stalin had contended that

> Yagoda [Iagoda] has definitely proven himself to be incapable of unmasking the Trotskyite-Zinovievite bloc. The OGPU is four years behind in this matter. This is noted by all Party workers and by the majority of the representatives of the NKVD.[90]

It was not that Ezhov's predecessor Iagoda refrained from terror, as is shown in the previous section of the present chapter. In March 1936 Iagoda even proposed to Stalin that all Trotskyites, convicted of terrorism, be executed. In May his proposal was realized by a Politburo decision.[91] It was during his tenure that the first Moscow trial was held in August 1936 and Zinov'ev, Kamenev, and other prominent former oppositionists were executed immediately thereafter. Yet, in the summer of 1936 when Iagoda was presented with confessions from former Trotskyites, clearly exacted by torture, asserting the existence of a "Trotskyite-Zinovievite bloc," Iagoda did not believe it: it was, in his words, "rubbish," "nonsense," "impossible."[92] Hence Iagoda's removal. He was implicated later in the 1938 Bukharin trial and was executed.

Even before the appointment, Ezhov, in his capacity as chair of the Party Control Commission, was deeply involved in the persecution of former oppositionists. In the summer of 1936 Ezhov drafted a secret circular in which he explicitly held a "Trotskyite-Zinovievite bloc" responsible for the Kirov murder. Stalin edited his draft, adding, for example, that the bloc aimed at killing Stalin, Voroshilov, Kaganovich, and others. The confidential circular, sent in

---

[87]O. Volobuev and S. Kuleshov, *Ochishchenie. Istoriia i perestroika. Publitsisticheskie zametki* (Moscow, 1989), p. 146.

[88]There is a substantial literature on the subject. For the latest Western literature, see Getty and Manning, eds., *Stalinist Terror*. For a critique of this book, see O. Khlevniuk, "Upravlenie gosudarstvennym terrorom," *Svobodnaia mysl'*, 1994, nos. 7–8, pp. 123–27.

[89]*Izvestiia TsK KPSS*, 1990, no. 7, p. 94, and *Istoricheskii arkhiv*, 1992, no. 1, pp. 123–31.

[90]Conquest, *Great Terror*, p. 138, and *Stalinskoe Politbiuro v 30-e gody. Sbornik dokumentov* (Moscow, 1995), pp. 149–50. The OGPU had been reorganized into the NKVD in 1934. Probably Stalin meant by "four years behind" the 1932 Riutin affair (see Chapter 5).

[91]*Reabilitatsiia*, pp. 216–17.

[92]Ibid., p. 179. See also Getty, *Origins*, pp. 121–22 and 245–46.

late July 1936, explicitly alleged a conspiracy by the bloc and foreign spies and hirelings.[93] Ezhov became Stalin's executioner.

In the view of Ezhov and Stalin, even formerly close comrades of Lenin were heinous criminals who were willing to sell the country and its people to foreign powers for the sake of their own political aims. Political terrorism and foreign espionage were the leitmotif of the Great Terror. Its victims were almost invariably branded as "enemies of the people." The class-neutral "enemy of the people" was a perfect construction to encompass all "terrorists" and "spies," regardless of their class backgrounds and ideological convictions. In June 1937 Stalin contended that literally everyone, even "our own people," needed to be examined as hidden enemies. In all spheres but one, according to Stalin, the Soviet government had defeated the international bourgeoisie, which, however, had beaten the Soviet government effortlessly in the area of intelligence operations. He therefore called for the strengthening of intelligence.[94] This was at a time when the secret police had already acquired a formidable reputation. In Stalin's view, if only 5 percent of the alleged enemies were indeed enemies, it was a big deal (*esli budet pravda khotia by na 5%, to i eto khleb*).[95] According to Khrushchev, Stalin "used to say that if a report [denunciation] was ten percent true, we should regard the entire report as fact."[96]

In almost no case was there hard evidence of terrorism and espionage by the alleged enemies of the people. The testimony of Molotov, who, along with Stalin, signed numerous execution orders, is instructive. For example, one of the charges against the defendants at the sensationally reported Kemerovo trial held in Novosibirsk in November 1936 was an assassination attempt against Molotov who had earlier toured the Siberian coal-mining region. Molotov recalled in 1972 that it was difficult to believe in the attempt but that there was talk and gossip to that effect.[97] Molotov also noted that the fantastic self-indictments of many of the defendants (such as Bukharin, Rykov, and Iagoda) at the show trials were ridiculous: they continued to fight against the party (i.e., Stalin) by making their confessions appear unbelievable.[98] Yet Stalin's terror against the "enemies of the people," according to Molotov, was justified for a fundamental reason: "if only to hold on to power" [*tol'ko by uderzhat' vlast'*].[99]

[93] *Reabilitatsiia*, pp. 185–86 and 196–210.
[94] His speech on 2 June 1937 in *Istochnik*, 1994, no. 3, p. 79.
[95] Ibid., 1994, no. 3, p. 80. See also *Reabilitatsiia*, p. 295.
[96] *Khrushchev Remembers*, tr. and ed. Strobe Talbott, introduction, commentary, and notes by Edward Crankshaw (Boston, 1970), p. 283.
[97] *Sto sorok besed s Molotovym*, p. 302.
[98] Ibid., p. 401. For the same view, see Feliks Chuev, *Tak govoril Kaganovich. Ispoved' stalinskogo apostola* (Moscow, 1992), p. 74.
[99] *Sto sorok besed*, p. 402.

It was true that Stalin was fighting to retain power in an increasingly menacing international situation. As Adam Ulam has correctly pointed out, the advance of Hitler's armed forces into the Rhineland on 7 March 1936 was a critical event. This move was a blatant violation of the Versailles treaty and gave a clear signal to the world that Hitler was bent on waging war in Europe.

It was this event that appears to have prompted Stalin and Ezhov to "seek out and uproot treason in a more systematic and wide-ranging way than hitherto." "It was foolish to imagine," as Ulam has noted, "that all those Zinovievs, Bukharins, and Radeks might not secretly feel the same way now" as Lenin and others had toward the tsarist government during World War I. Ulam has argued: "There is strong circumstantial evidence that the idea of physical liquidation of all his intra-Party opponents germinated in Stalin's mind following the Rhineland crisis."[100]

Stalin shied away from nothing to retain power. To hold on to power and to avert war for the time being, he went so far as to conclude a nonaggression treaty with his archenemy Hitler in 1939. Yet even before that, in 1936–37, at the height of his terror campaign against German and Japanese spies, he sent out a feeler to Germany for a possible rapprochement.[101] Simultaneously, he tried to convince the party that former comrades of Lenin were Hitler's hirelings. In an attempt to make his incredulous case more convincing, Stalin declared that the alliance of Trotsky and Zinoviev with Hitler showed that "there is nothing surprising in human life."[102]

Stalin appeared to have been in much the same position as the Russian tsars. According to G. Dimitrov's notes on his conversations with Stalin in November 1937, the Russian tsar did one good thing: the building and uniting of a huge state. Now the enemies of the people wished to sell Ukraine to Germany, Belarus to Poland, the Maritime Province to Japan, and the Donbas to France. Stalin declared that anyone who "makes an attempt on the unity of the socialist state by deed or by thought, yes, by thought too, will be destroyed mercilessly."[103] Any discussion of history related to terrorism became an anathema. In 1937 Kaganovich attacked an article on the 1881 assassination of Alexander II as a signal to the terrorists, the Trotskyites, and Zinovievites.[104]

Dimitrov's notes also suggest that Stalin intended to eliminate anyone con-

---

[100] Adam B. Ulam, *Stalin: The Man and His Era* (New York, 1973), pp. 404–7.

[101] Haslam, *The Soviet Union and the Struggle for Collective Security*, pp. 127–28.

[102] His remark at the February–March 1937 plenum of the party Central Committee in *Voprosy istorii*, 1992, nos. 4–5, p. 36.

[103] Anatolii Latyshev, "Riadom so Stalinym," *Sovershenno sekretno*, 1990, no. 12, pp. 18 and 19. For the same speech by Stalin on 8 November 1937, see also Tucker, *Stalin in Power*, pp. 482–83. Tucker's analysis is based on a "verbatim record."

[104] His remark at the February–March 1937 Central Committee plenum in *Voprosy istorii*, 1992, no. 10, p. 34.

nected to the "enemy" allegedly bent on undoing his empire: "We'll destroy any such enemy, be he an Old Bolshevik. We'll annihilate his clan [*rod*], his family. . . . For the complete destruction of all enemies, themselves and their clans."[105] Stalin used the term clan repeatedly in his speech. Surely, the Great Terror was a massive operation, entailing the repression of family, friends, and colleagues of alleged enemies.

In the Donbas, as elsewhere in the country, people were terrorized en masse in 1936–38. The pre-Ezhov repression was extensive in the Donbas, as has already been discussed. Yet Ezhov's appointment, according to the NKVD chief in the Donbas V. T. Ivanov, created an entire revolution by resurrecting the old traditions of the Cheka: "Without waiting for advice, sanctions, and directives, we smashed counterrevolution."[106] In June 1937 A. Ia. Vyshinskii, the prosecutor general, writing a series of articles in *Sotsialisticheskii Don-bass*, reminded Donbas residents of the 1928 Shakhty affair and reiterated his theme of the difficulty of uncovering enemies: "Of course, it's impossible to recognize a spy by his appearance. In fact, it's altogether difficult to write some kind of recipe valid for all, on how to identify the enemy who is so cleverly masked into the bargain."[107] If Lenin's closest colleagues proved "enemies," anyone could be an enemy.

The Donbas political elite were decimated by the Great Terror. Sarkisov, who had governed the Donbas for several years, and his entourage were killed in 1937. Sarkisov had had a confrontation with the Ukrainian NKVD honcho Balits'kyi earlier, but he could not continue to stand firm because of a blemish on his political past: he had been a Trotskyite. Therefore, on many occasions he was publicly humiliated. By December 1936 he could no longer contend that there were saboteurs but no wreckers; now he was forced to admit that those he had earlier dismissed as saboteurs had proved to be Trotskyite wreckers.[108] Still Sarkisov could not save his own life. In April 1937 he was removed from the party secretaryship and appointed director of Donbas Coal. In July 1937 he and his associates were arrested almost wholesale as enemies of the people and summarily executed.[109] Of the seventy-six full *oblast'* committee in May 1937, only six remained in June 1938.[110]

---

[105]Latyshev, "Riadom so Stalinym," p. 19. See also Tucker, *Stalin in Power*.

[106]RTsKhIDNI, f. 17, op. 21, d. 5166, l. 69. However, Ivanov, said to be an SR before the revolution, was arrested on 1 August 1937 and sentenced to be shot in July 1938. He had until then managed the terror operation in the Donbas, but, like Iagoda, he was suspected of leniency toward the former "Trotskyites" in the Donbas. See *Nashe Mynule*, 1 (6) (1993), pp. 82–85.

[107]*Sotsialisticheskii Donbass*, 27 June 1937.

[108]RTsKhIDNI, f. 17, op. 2, d. 574, l. 74.

[109]For Sarkisov, see his file in RTsKhIDNI, f. 589, op. 3, d. 2042.

[110]For details, see my "Stalinist Terror in the Donbas: A Note," *Slavic Review*, 50:1 (Spring 1991), pp. 157–62.

E. K. Pramnek, who succeeded Sarkisov, lived in fear and desperation.[111] In public he appeared belligerent. At the September 1937 plenum of the U-krainian Communist Party Central Committee, he declared: "Now for three months we've been cleansing and cleansing these 'loos' where the enemies hid, still it's quite impossible to rake out this refuse."[112] In private, however, according to the writer A. Avdeenko to whom Pramnek once intimated his difficulty, he found it impossible to work: "With whom to work? All the first and second secretaries of the city and district committees have turned out to be enemies of the people. Almost all members of the bureaus have been repressed. The directors of enterprises have proved to be wreckers or spies. The chief engineers, chief technicians, and even the chief doctors of some clinics and hospitals are also from the ranks of scum."[113] Pramnek was removed from his post in March 1938 and was soon arrested. A Latvian, he was accused of espionage for Latvia (then an independent country) and Germany. At trial he pleaded not guilty, but was executed in July of the same year.[114]

The Komsomol was terrorized at least equally harshly. In 1937 almost all members of the Ukrainian Komsomol Central Committee were arrested; the leaders of all the *oblast'* organizations turned out to be "enemies of the people"; so were the secretaries of all large cities, including Stalino, Makiivka, and Voroshylovhrad. All Komsomol newspapers from Kiev down to the *oblast'*'s turned out to be in the hands of "enemies."[115] Clearly, the whole Komsomol was annihilated in the Donbas.[116]

As a major industrial center, the Donbas was home to a large number of prominent industrialists. Many of them perished in the terror campaign. From the summer and autumn of 1936 onward, the protection that Ordzhonikidze, the commissar of heavy industry, and Donbas party leaders such as Sarkisov, had given to the managers became ineffective.[117] Ordzhonikidze suffered from the enormous pressure caused by the avalanche of terror against his men. He committed suicide in February 1937. The Donbas managers had been accused of sabotaging the Stakhanovite movement since 1935. Yet the movement had the side effect of aggravating on-the-job issues of life or death: the productivity

---

[111] A. O. Avdeenko, *Nakazanie bez prestupleniia* (Moscow, 1991), pp. 182–83.

[112] TsDAHO, f. 1, op. 1, spr. 539, ark. 40.

[113] Avdeenko, *Nakazanie*, p. 182. N. N. Blagoveshchenskii, a professor at the Medical Institute in Stalino, was arrested for allegedly spreading epidemics by bacteriological methods in order to disorganize the home front, weaken the strength of the country, and topple the government. See V. F. Burnosov, "Nekotorye stranitsy 1937 goda. Kak eto bylo," *Novye stranitsy v istorii Donbassa. Stat'i*, vol. 2 (Donets'k, 1992), pp. 110–14.

[114] See his file in RTsKhIDNI, f. 589, op. 3, d. 7588.

[115] TsKhDMO, f. 1, op. 23, d. 1237, l. 1.

[116] For the terror against the Komsomol in Ukraine, see D. V. Tabachnyk, V. A. Holoven'ko, and O. A. Korniievs'kyi, *Chorni roky Komsomolu Ukrainy* (Kiev, 1990).

[117] For Ordzhonikidze, see Francesco Benvenuti, "A Stalinist Victim of Stalinism: 'Sergo' Ordzhonikidze," in Cooper, Perrie, and Rees, *Soviet History*.

campaign did not allow the mines and factories to pay enough attention to workplace safety, which had not been commendable in the first place. This was an emotionally charged issue for everyone involved, particularly so in an accident-prone industry like coal mining and metallurgy. Enemy hunters made every effort to present the accidents as wreckers' deeds.

Accidents were frequent in the Donbas. All accidental deaths were re- ported to Moscow. Archival data show painful records. On 7 October 1936, a gas explosion killed five in Donbas Anthracite. Ten days later another gas explosion killed eleven colliers in Artem Coal. On 28 November, the collapse of a shaft left five miners dead.[118] (About a year later, on 17 November 1937, according to reports received by Moscow, deaths by accidents appeared to be ubiquitous in the Donbas. At one mine, a collier was crushed by a mine cage. At another, a miner was killed by a falling rock. At yet another, a worker was run over and killed by a wagon. In Makiivka Coal, a worker was electrocuted. In Artem Coal, a hewer was destroyed by a falling rock.[119]) By early 1937, the seemingly growing numbers of fatal accidents prompted Vyshinskii to re- view all cases of those indicted in industrial accidents since 1934 for possible enemy actions.[120] The review concluded that the increase in accidents was a consequence of "wrecking activities by enemies of the people."[121]

Even before the review was initiated, at the December 1936 plenum of the party Central Committee Ezhov contended that some Donbas colliery man- agers were wreckers intent on rousing workers' wrath against the Soviet gov- ernment by intentionally causing accidents. They regarded workers, accord- ing to Ezhov, as livestock whose lives were not to be pitied.[122] Deeply dis- turbed, Ordzhonikidze spoke to the Commissariat of Heavy Industry officials two weeks before he killed himself. He reminded them that in the old days, under the tsar, when a few people were killed, it caused a sensation even in the "Black Hundred state Duma"; many of those present ought to remember this because they were old revolutionaries. Yet now when twenty people were killed, their bodies were removed, buried, and the workers' mood was report- edly uplifted. There is no spirit, their minds are blunt. Accidents occur. No one accounts for the deaths. Then more people die.[123]

It was not that no one was held accountable. No one wanted to take re- sponsibility and as a result everyone was blamed. For fear of being accused of protecting enemies of the people, some industrial bosses, along with the court and the prosecutor's office, resorted to mass repression of managers,

[118]RGAE, f. 7566, op. 1, d. 2522, l. 33.
[119]Ibid., d. 2766, l. 21.
[120]See Vyshinskii's speech in *Sotsialisticheskii Donbass*, 16 May 1937.
[121]GARF, f. 9477, op. 1, d. 114, l. 44.
[122]RTsKhIDNI, f. 17, op. 2, d. 575, ll. 35 and 45.
[123]Ibid., f. 85, op. 29, d. 156, ll. 10–12.

engineers, and technicians. At one mine, all the managerial personnel were prosecuted.[124] This became so common that in May 1937 the party had to condemn the practice.[125] Many, some 70 percent of the prosecuted, were said to have been exonerated by the party's intervention.[126] Yet exoneration, in turn, was then declared to be a Trotskyite tactic to wreck mines and factories and then pass the buck to innocent people.[127] Thus, it became increasingly unclear who the real "enemies of the people" were. In other words, anyone could be the enemy. As Stalin had said, nothing was surprising in human life. By all accounts, labor discipline declined in 1937,[128] which further aggravated the problem of worker safety, and, in turn, encouraged the enemy hunters.

During the course of 1937–38, numerous managers fell victim to Stalin's terror. According to the head of the Ukrainian Communist Party, there were more remnants of "alien people" in Ukraine than anywhere else.[129] G. V. Gvakhariia, a thirty-six-year-old former Trotsky supporter and director of Makiivka Metallurgical Plant, was arrested in April 1937. After extended torture, he broke down, implicating some of his fellow managers, and was executed in September 1937 as an enemy of the people.[130] Ia. S. Gugel', forty-two-year-old director of Azov Steel Plant and former director of Magnitogorsk Metallurgical Plant, was implicated by Gvakhariia, arrested in August 1937, and executed two months later.[131] The chief engineer of the Donbas Coal Complex, V. M. Bazhanov, one of the few old ("bourgeois") Bolshevik engineers in the country to become the doyen of the Soviet coal-mining industry, was arrested in September 1937. His former boss, M. L. Rukhimovich, tortured in captivity, implicated Bazhanov in an "anti-Soviet terrorist, diversionist, wrecking organization of the right." Bazhanov, evidently under duress, pleaded guilty at the interrogation, but recanted his confessions, the only evidence of guilt, at his trial. All the same, he was sentenced to be shot and executed two months later. His wife O. S. Bazhanova, as wife of the alleged traitor, was given eight years' imprisonment.[132]

[124]Sotsialisticheskii Donbass, 21 May 1937.

[125]Sobranie zakonov i rasporiazhenii Raboche-Krest'ianskogo Pravitel'stva SSSR, 1937, no. 28, pp. 245–48. For this practice of wholesale repression, see also DADO, f. 26p, op. 1, spr. 237, ark. 13-15; GARF, f. 9474, op. 1, d. 111, ll. 13, 38, and 86; and Sotsialisticheskii Donbass, 16 May 1937 (Vyshinskii's speech) and 24 May 1937.

[126]Trynadtsiatyi z'izd Komunistychnoi partii (bil'shovykiv) Ukrainy, Bulletin, no. 3 (Kiev, 1937), p. 21. See also Za industrializatsiiu, 27 July 1937.

[127]See Vyshinskii's speech in Sotsialisticheskii Donbass, 16 May 1937.

[128]See, for example, Trynadtsiatyi z'izd Komunistychnoi partii, Bulletin 4 (Kiev, 1937), p. 10, and GARF, f. 7511, op. 1, d. 221, l. 26.

[129]Kosior's speech on 27 February 1937 (Voprosy istorii, 1993, no. 6, p. 7).

[130]See Priazovskii rabochii, 20 March 1992. For more detail on Gvakhariia, see Burnosov, "Nekotorye stranitsy," pp. 95–101, and on the terror in Makiivka, see Francesco Benvenuti, "Industry and Purge in the Donbass, 1936–37," Europe-Asia Studies, 45:1 (1993).

[131]Priazovskii rabochii, 20 March 1992.

[132]See his file RTsKhIDNI, f. 589, op. 3, d. 1124. For a short biography of Bazhanov, see

Bazhanov's successor, K. P. Epifantsev, was removed soon, in October 1937; his fate is unknown, but he appears to have died during an interrogation.[133] The thirty-one-year-old new Donbas Coal director, I. A. Fesenko, did not last long: he was arrested in June 1938.[134] Between May and August 1938, of the thirty-two highest officials of Donbas Coal, nineteen were repressed, twelve disappeared (almost certainly repressed), one was transferred to another job. Earlier in September 1937 the Coal Administration of the Commissariat of Heavy Industry was almost completely decimated. Because of extensive terror everywhere, statistics of this period are incomplete. According to a few sets of data, collected by the commissariat, which itself was subjected to brutal terror, between late 1936 and April 1938 (when the Great Terror had far from subsided) at least one-quarter of the Donbas mine managers and chief engineers were repressed as enemies of the people.[135] The metallurgical industry fared little better. At the Stalino Metallurgy Plant, the terror "cut down all but a handful of the more than two hundred engineers needed to run the factory. They just disappeared, and it was never clear whether they were shot."[136]

Many, like the Stalino engineers, simply disappeared. Some were forced to undergo a show trial. These Communist bosses were broken by the secret police and were tried as enemies of the people and fascist spies. One such trial was held in November 1937 against the managers and engineers of Budennov Coal. The issue of industrial accidents was the most explosive. At the trial, the chief prosecutor in the Donbas R. A. Rudenko (who went on to become the chief prosecutor from the Soviet Union at the Nuremberg trial, became the prosecutor general of the country, and even presided over the rehabilitation of victims of Stalin's terror after 1953) asked the director of the trust S. P. Volodarskii:

> *Rudenko*: Did your actions place the lives of many workers in danger?
> *Volodarskii*: Yes, they did.
> *Rudenko*: Did you do all this for the purpose of wrecking?
> *Volodarskii*: Yes.

Rudenko then asked another defendant, Iaroslavtsev, a mine director at Budennov Coal:

> *Rudenko*: Was the insult, maiming, and murder of workers one of the tasks of your counterrevolutionary organization?
> *Iaroslavtsev*: Yes.

Komandarm ugol'nogo fronta (Moscow, 1977). Rukhimovich himself was executed in 1938.

[133]*Ispytanie dolgom*, 3rd ed. (Donets'k, 1989), p. 165, which mentions that the director of Donbas Coal died during an investigation in 1937. The director was almost certainly Epifantsev.

[134]RGAE, f. 7566, op. 2, d. 114, l. 19.

[135]See my "Stalinist Terror in the Donbas." For the very high turnover rate among the Donbas managerial and technical cadres caused by the purges, see Khlevniuk, *1937-i*, p. 236.

[136]Kevin Klose, *Russia and the Russians: Inside the Closed Society* (New York, 1984), p. 60.

Then Rudenko presented to the court a letter by the wife of a worker named Gogolev killed in an accident. The angry wife, Gogoleva, stated that Iaroslavtsev and others made her husband work underground near the exposed electrical cable that killed him. Rudenko contended that these crimes had been committed to embitter workers against the Soviet government. Seven of the eight defendants were sentenced to be shot and were soon executed.[137]

Many Donbas residents, particularly the Stakhanovites, seemed to have genuinely believed in these grave accusations and confessions; they actively and savagely participated in the attacks against their bosses.[138] The writer A. Avdeenko, who worked in the Donbas at the time of the terror, says that he believed in the accusations then.[139] The charges were not new to anyone: the press and the political authorities had presented some (if not all) bosses as enemies of the people for some years already. Moreover, the show trials were carefully scripted so that the *narod* would believe in them. Even Western observers, including the American ambassador who attended the Moscow trials, believed in the charges against the defendants.[140] Still the testimonies of Stakhanovites and others have elements of ex post facto self-justification.

The whole nation was terrorized, but Stalin exhibited a peculiar populist appeal at the height of the Great Terror. At an October 1937 reception (in the Kremlin) of industrial managers (many of whom were to perish) and Stakhanovites from the coal-mining and metallurgy industries, for example, Stalin attacked "some managers" who had become enemies of the people and contended that the industrial leaders were not up to their task. Then he declared: "The leaders may come and go, but the people will stay and live forever" [*Rukovoditeli mogut prikhodit' i ukhodit', a narod ostaetsia i vsegda budet zhit'*].[141]

Some of the people did entertain the bitter feelings against their bosses attributed to them by Stalin. A *chastushka*, which was recorded in the Donbas in the summer of 1937 by an ethnographer, is demonstrative of the people's mood:

> Mine Committe Chairman[142]
> Don't put on airs

---

[137] *Sotsialisticheskii Donbass*, 1–5, 10 November, 3 December 1937. There were several similar show trials reported by the newspaper, particularly in July and August 1938.

[138] See particularly A. Stakhanov's memoir, *Rasskaz o moei zhizni* (Moscow, 1938). For an analysis of memoirs by Stakhanovites, see Kuromiya, "Soviet Memoirs as a Historical Source."

[139] Avdeenko, *Nakazanie*, p. 208.

[140] Joseph E. Davies, *Mission to Moscow* (New York, 1941).

[141] RTsKhIDNI, f. 558, op. 1, d. 3215, l. 13. The part of the speech that attacked the managers was deleted by Stalin for publication. At the same reception, Kaganovich stated that as a result of wrecking by Trotskyite-Bukharinite hirelings the coal-mining industry was now in a difficult situation. Stalin cut this part from publication. Ibid., l. 3.

[142] Refers to the trade-union chairman.

Treat the workers
Better, always better

Received my pay on time
On the twenty fifth
But the coll[ective] agreement says
Payday is the tenth

It's fun to work in the mine
It's possible to make money
A look at the Worker's Path [*raput'*][143]
Would make anyone sick

I went to the union committee
And asked for a pass [to a sanatorium]
Chairman says:
"That'll be five rubles."[144]

The Stakhanovite movement had made it easy for simple people to voice their grievances and attack their bosses openly.[145]

The ferocity with which people attacked their bosses reflected the deep gulf between the upper (*verkhi*) and the lower (*nizy*) strata, a fissure that in the Donbas was amplified further by the symbolic division between the safe and bright surface and dangerous and dark underground. Yet one sees little spontaneity in popular reaction at this time. The Stakhanovites knew exactly how to attack the supposed enemies because the scripts were readily provided from above. Show trials were limited in number, and the majority of the victims simply disappeared.

Not all official scripts worked perfectly. For example, the introduction in 1936 of the Stalin Constitution, touted as the most democratic in the world, caused some problems for Stalin's "populism." Some quasi-democratic principles, including contested elections, were to be introduced in the new elections to the Supreme Soviet, slated for December 1937. In the Donbas, these innovations met with opposition from the NKVD: "Hostile elements are preparing very energetically for the elections in order to insinuate their people into the Soviet organs."[146] In fact, few openly challenged the party dictatorship. When,

[143] *Raput'* is *rabochii put'*, which refers either to the trade-union organ or to workers' life in general or both.

[144] RF IMFE, f. 8-3/202, ark. 140–41. Recorded on 28 July 1937 from a collier at Il'ich Mine in the city of Sergo named D. D. Bobkin. Note that Bobkin sang in the voice of a woman.

[145] See Thurston, "The Stakhanovite Movement," and Sheila Fitzpatrick, "Workers against Bosses: The Impact of the Great Purges on Labor-Management Relations," in Lewis H. Siegelbaum and Ronald Grigor Suny, eds., *Making Workers Soviet: Power, Class, and Identity* (Cornell University Press, 1994).

[146] See, for example, a May 1937 speech by D. M. Sokolinskii, a high-ranking NKVD official in the Donbas, in *Sotsialisticheskii Donbass*, 20 May 1937. According to Ihor Kamenetsky, *The*

Figure 6.1. A meeting in Stalino celebrating the new election law, 1937. From TsD-KFFA, od. zb. 2-23456.

in the end, the "democratic" gestures were repealed by Moscow,[147] a sixty-four-year-old "citizen" (not a comrade) named P. I. Averin spoke out at an election meeting in Stalino: "Why is it that in 1917 there were many parties in the Constituent Assembly elections whereas now we have only one party?" Averin's speech was reported to be "counterrevolutionary agitation."[148] Such clear-cut cases were few and far between, but the secret police were quick to brand as "counterrevolutionary manifestation" subversive jokes like the following: a mine mechanic named Sobinov said, "We are overtaking the capitalist countries. If they work 10–10.5 hours [a day] there, we are working 12 hours."[149] It is very possible, however, that this "counterrevolutionary joke," like so many others, was fabricated by an NKVD agent.

Tragedy of Vinnytsia: Materials of Stalin's Policy of Extermination in Ukraine during the Great Purges, 1936–1938 (Toronto, 1989), pp. ix and xviii, Sokolinskii moved to Vinnytsia and committed the famous mass executions there in 1938. See also Robert Conquest, *Inside Stalin's Secret Police: NKVD Politics, 1936–1939* (London, 1985), pp. 4, 19, 60, 63, and 187. He was shot by the Soviets in 1942. V. Semystiaha, "Tse potribno i mertvym, tse potribno i zhyvym," *MH* (Luhans'k), 19 November 1991, p. 8.

[147]For an excellent discussion of this campaign, see J. Arch Getty, "State and Society under Stalin: Constitutions and Elections in the 1930s," *Slavic Review*, 50:1 (Spring 1991).

[148]DADO, f. 26p, op. 1, spr. 237, ark. 17. Surprisingly, he was not arrested, at least for the time being.

[149]RTsKhIDNI, f. 17, op. 21, d. 5196, l. 106.

Whatever the case, the innocent little people and nameless middle-level technical-administrative personnel were repressed en masse for the same charges of anti-Soviet propaganda, treason, wrecking, and other political crimes as their bosses. In short, people of all strata were terrorized. The terror may well have spared the politically useful Stakhanovites. Yet the mythical *narod* were far from immune from the terror against the enemies of the people (*vragi naroda, vorohy narodu*).

A few examples illustrate the case. T. G. Kadolba, a Ukrainian, sixty-two years of age, a timber hand in Mine 17/17bis, Stalino Coal, a non–party member, was arrested in November 1937 for allegedly spreading anti-Soviet Trotskyite propaganda among the miners. He was charged with purporting that the Soviet government was not for the workers and peasants, that Stalin should have been killed a long time ago, but that Stalin would be killed sooner or later. His file in the KGB archive contains only ten sheets. Kadolba was said to be of kulak origin. He was interrogated only once, on 19 November, when he categorically denied the charges. His file contains the record of the short investigation:

Q: Do you confirm this?

A: No, I did not conduct anti-Soviet agitation.

Q: You are telling a lie and untruth. The investigator insists that you talk honestly about your anti-Soviet agitation, directed against the party and the Soviet government.

A: Yes, I am telling the truth: I did not conduct anti-Soviet agitation.

Q: You are avoiding giving honest answers to the questions given you. It is known to the investigator that you spread rumors among workers about imminent war . . . , [after] which Ukraine will be independent, and people will get back their farms and work as before. The investigator insists that you give exhaustive answers about the essence of the questions given you.

A: I repeat that I did not engage in any anti-Soviet agitation.

Interrogation suspended.

The protocol of the investigation was read to me and written from my words, which I testify are true.

Kadolba

This file suggests that Kadolba was not very literate, barely able to sign his own name. Yet on 1 December 1937 he was sentenced to be shot and executed. Kadolba was posthumously rehabilitated in 1989.[150]

---

[150] AUSBUDO, no. 22096-pf.

Figure 6.2. A page from Kadolba's interrogation records, 19 November 1937. From AUSBUDO, no. 22096-pf, ark. 12.

I. I. Shraiber was fifty-five years of age, an ethnic German, said to be of kulak origin, a mine manager before the revolution, and mine foreman at Mine 152 in Krasnoluch at the time of arrest on 21 December 1937. Shraiber was accused of entering the party in 1930 by falsifying his past, of engaging in an anti-Soviet campaign, and of conducting religious services among the ethnic Germans. He denied the charges, but was sentenced to be shot on 12 January 1938 and was executed on the same day. In 1991 the evidence presented against him was found to be untrue and Shraiber was posthumously rehabilitated.[151]

D. A. Balashov was arrested on 27 March 1938 and on 19 April 1938 was sentenced to be shot and was executed. Balashov was thirty-five years of age, Russian, a hewer at the Stalin Mine in Voroshylovhrad, a party member, and from a poor peasant family. He may have been sympathetic toward the Trotskyites in the 1920s, but was recruited by the secret police later. He was charged to be a masked Trotskyite who misinformed the NKVD about other Trotskyites at the mine. Balashov was posthumously rehabilitated in 1989.[152]

I. V. Belikov was a twenty-seven-year-old non–party member and a roofing worker at the Ordzhonikidze Mine in Makiivka at the time of his arrest on 17 June 1938. He was said to be from a Ukrainian kulak family. Belikov was accused of intentionally roofing the mine shafts improperly and thus wrecking the mine. Belikov pleaded guilty. He was sentenced to be shot on 3 July 1938 and was executed on the same day. The accusations proved to be unfounded, and he was posthumously rehabilitated in 1989.[153]

I. E. Akol'zin, born in 1897, an unskilled horse hand at the Voroshilov Mine in Stalino, was arrested on 2 August 1938 for allegedly organizing a group of dekulakized Cossacks for wrecking purposes. (Akol'zin was alleged to be a dekulakized Russian Cossack.) In case of war, according to the charges, he intended to support the enemy of the country. He was sentenced to be shot and executed on 28 August 1938. In 1989 Akol'zin was posthumously rehabilitated for lack of evidence.[154]

The countryside fared no better. Numerous counterrevolutionary organizations were uncovered on collective farms, state farms, machine-tractor stations, land settlement offices, and everywhere. Fires (perennial rural problems), deaths of livestock, inadequate sowing or harvest, breakdowns of machinery, and all other major and minor problems led to the repression (very often execution) of people in responsible positions as enemies of the people.[155]

---

[151] AUSBULO, no. 19850-r.

[152] DALO, f. 3747, op. 3, spr. 1184-r.

[153] AUSBUDO, no. 21551-pf.

[154] Ibid., no. 21427-pf. For other cases of terror against the Donbas miners, see also Mace and Heretz, *Oral History Project*, 1:43-44, 3:789 (suicides to escape arrest), and 3:1154 (torture).

[155] *Sotsialisticheskii Donbass* carried numerous articles on these cases in 1937 and 1938. Roberta

Like ordinary workers, ordinary farmers fell victim to the terror alongside their bosses. A. M. Ianke, an ethnic German, fifty-three years of age, a shepherd on a collective farm near Stalino, was arrested on 26 August 1937 as an active member of a fascist organization. Ianke was accused of receiving money from the "fascists," presumably Germans. Ianke pleaded guilty. He was sentenced to be shot on 26 August 1937 and was executed on the same day. In 1989 Ianke was posthumously rehabilitated for lack of evidence.[156]

I. I. Klink, a forty-six-year-old Ukrainian (possibly an ethnic German) and a collective farmer in Krasnoarmiis'ke not far from Stalino, was arrested on 28 May 1938 as an active member of a fascist insurgent organization. Klink pleaded guilty. On 9 October 1938 he was executed on the same day as he was sentenced. In 1989 Klink was posthumously rehabilitated for lack of evidence.[157]

In the case of terror in the countryside, there was clear sanction from the center. On 2 July 1937, within a month after the sensational report on the execution of M. N. Tukhachevskii and other top military leaders, the Politburo of the party Central Committee adopted a resolution (signed by Stalin) on anti-Soviet elements. It noted that a large segment of former kulaks and criminals, who had returned to their homelands after exile in the north and Siberia, were the principal ringleaders of all kinds of anti-Soviet, diversionary crimes on collective and state farms (the resolution added transport and "some industries" as the theater of enemy actions). It ordered that the most hostile elements be arrested immediately and shot.[158]

On 30 July an operation order of the NKVD followed. The order made clear that the criminal elements included former members of the "anti-Soviet parties" (SRs and various nationalist parties) and White Guard Cossacks. The instruction is incomplete on Ukraine's quota, but a separate order stipulated that 8,000, of whom 1,000 were in the Donbas, were to be shot, and 28,800 arrested. In the country as a whole, except for Ukraine, 65,950 people were ordered shot.[159] Yet the Ukrainian NKVD, like the NKVD leaders elsewhere, soon requested permission for the repression of more people. Thus, by early 1938, in Ukraine 111,675 people were arrested.[160] The Ukrainian NKVD fur-

---

T. Manning's forthcoming work on Sychevka, Smolensk, paints a similar picture.

[156] AUSBUDO, no. 22253-pf.

[157] Ibid., no. 22093.

[158] "Rasstrel po raznariadke, ili kak eto delali bol'sheviki," *Trud*, 4 June 1992.

[159] Ibid. For Ukraine, see Iu. Z. Daniliuk, "Masovi karal'ni aktsii orhaniv NKVS v konteksti politychnykh represii v Ukraini v kintsi 30-kh rokiv," in *Shosta Vseukrains'ka naukova konferentsiia z istorychnoho kraieznavstva (m. Luts'k, veresen'–zhovten' 1993 r.)* (Luts'k, 1993), p. 11, and Oleh Bazhan and Viktor Voinalovych, "Viina proty vlasnoho narodu," *Literaturna Ukraina*, 29 July 1993.

[160] See Bazhan and Voinalovych, "Viina proty vlasnoho narodu." See also Oleg Mikhailov, "Limit na rasstrel," *Sovershenno sekretno*, 1993, no. 7. p. 5, and Nataliia Gevorkian, "Vstrechnye

ther requested permission to repress more "enemies." Between 19 September and 14 October 1938 alone, 22,508 people were sentenced to be shot.[161]

Torture was sanctioned by Stalin. On 21 July 1937 he gave clear instructions to apply torture, "as an exception," to those enemies of the people who refused to reveal their coconspirators. Stalin asked why the socialist secret service had to be more humane in applying torture against the agents of the bourgeoisie and the enemies of workers and peasants than the bourgeois secret services had been when torturing the representatives of the socialist proletariat.[162]

As the individual cases cited here suggest, certain ethnic groups were particularly vulnerable to the political terror. Indeed, the NKVD targeted them. There was sentiment among the powers that be that "All Germans in the USSR are spies": "If they are arrested, they won't be able to cause harm in case of war."[163] On 25 July 1937 the NKVD sent out an order to seek out and liquidate the organizations of "German fascists." On 11 August another order on the Poles followed. On 24 September the NKVD instructed that all visitors to the Polish consulate be arrested. As of 1 November 1937, 19,030 were arrested under the Polish operations; of them, 4,885 were sentenced to be shot. One of those Polish Soviet citizens was V. I. Petkevich, fifty, a roofer at the Gorky Mine in Stalino, who was shot on November 1938 on false charges of counterrevolutionary wrecking.[164] In 1937–38 nearly 50,000 Soviet Poles were thus repressed (arrested or shot).[165] In the same period more than 25,000 ethnic Germans fell victim to the terror. The Latvians were similarly targeted.[166]

Thus, in Stalino *oblast'* alone, between September 1937 and February 1938

---

plany po unichtozheniiu sobstvennogo naroda," *Moskovskie novosti*, 1992, no. 25, pp. 18–19. In Moscow and Leningrad, some of those sentenced to five, seven, or eight years of imprisonment became ill or invalid. To get rid of the burden imposed by them, the organ reviewed their cases and sentenced them to be shot. See *Vecherniaia Moskva*, 17 May 1991.

[161] Bazhan and Voinalovych, "Viina proty vlasnoho narodu."

[162] Mikhailov, "Limit na rasstrel."

[163] *Istoricheskii arkhiv*, 1992, no. 1, p. 119. In Moscow and elsewhere, many German Communists who sought refuge in the Soviet Union after Hitler's coming to power were arrested in hundreds. More members of the former Politburo of the German Communist Party fell victim to Stalin's terror than to Hitler's. (Herman Weber, *"Weißen Flecken" in der Geschichte. Die KPD-Opfer der Stalinischen Säuberrungen und ihre Rehabilitierung* [Frankfurt a.M., 1989], pp. 132–33.) In the Donbas, Thomas Miksch, an Austrian Communist refugee, working as a baking technical director, was arrested in October 1936 as a Gestapo spy. (Hans Schafranek, *Zwischen NKWD und Gestapo. Die Auslieferung deutscher und österreichischer Antifaschisten aus der Sowjetunion an Nazideutschland 1937–1941* [Frankfurt a.M., 1990], pp. 72–73 and 150–51.) Many sections of the Komintern were depleted by arrests. In 1938 the Polish Communist Party was disbanded by a Komintern resolution. See *Istoricheskii arkhiv*, 1993, no. 1, pp. 220–21.

[164] AUSBUDO, no. 22618-pf.

[165] Bazhan and Voinalovych, "Viina proty vlasnoho narodu."

[166] Ibid.

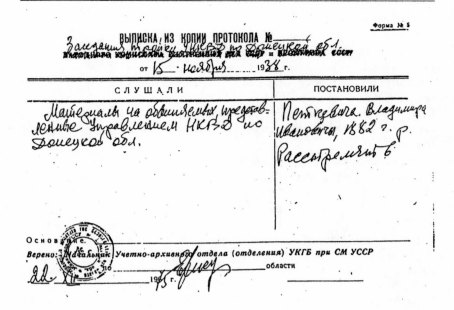

Figure 6.3. Excerpt (dated 22 December 1975) from a protocol of the Donets'k *oblast'* NKVD troika, 15 November 1938, the decision of which reads "Petkevich, Vladimir Ivanovich, b. 18812, to be shot." From AUSBUDO, f. 22618-pf.

at least 3,777 Poles were arrested; of them, 3,029 or 80.2 percent were executed.[167]

Similarly, numerous German "storm troops" were liquidated in the Donbas. Those ethnic Germans deported earlier from the western borders to the Donbas were particularly hard hit.[168] Well before the NKVD instruction was issued, however, ethnic Germans were terrorized. In January 1937 Sarkisov was told that sixty fascist organizations had been uncovered in the Donbas. Apparently to protect himself, Sarkisov contended that the Germans had to be deported from the Donbas: some exceptions could be made, but it was necessary to get rid of the Germans; "We don't need them."[169] In February 1937, according to the proud NKVD chief in the Donbas, one German collective farm near Khartsyz'k had lost all its men: they had proved to be "enemies."[170]

Individual cases illuminate the terror. In 1937 B. A. Leival'd, an ethnic

[167]V. M. Nikol'skyi, " 'Velyka chystka,' " in *Pravda cherez roky. Statti, spohady, dokumenty* (Donets'k, 1995), p. 29.

[168]RTsKhIDNI, f. 17, op. 21, d. 5197, l. 30, and d. 5195, l. 131.

[169]TsDAHO, f. 1, op. 7, spr. 517, ark. 132–33.

[170]RTsKhIDNI, f. 17, op. 21, d. 5196, l. 151.

German, twenty-two years of age, a cleaning woman at a school, was arrested as a German spy and was given twenty years.[171] P. P. Aisler, 33, an ethnic German collier at Mine 3 in Krasnoarmiis'ke, a non–party member, was arrested on 3 July 1938 on charges of causing eight accidents in the mine in 1937. He was alleged to be a member of a "diversionary organization." He had been born and grew up a poor peasant, but was branded a "kulak." Aisler was sentenced to be shot on 26 September 1938 and was executed on the same day. Nevertheless, in 1960, when his family inquired of the KGB about Aisler, they were told that Aisler had died of pneumonia in prison on 18 February 1945. He was rehabilitated in 1989.[172] Similar cases were legion.[173]

All in all, between September 1937 and February 1938, at least 4,265 ethnic Germans were arrested in Stalino *oblast'*. Of them, 3,608, or 84.6 percent, were executed.[174] Ethnic Germans accounted for 1.5 percent of the population in *oblast'*, but, according to one study, they composed 21.7 percent of the repressed.[175]

Other nationalities were also repressed because of their ethnicity. Many ethnic Greeks perished in the Donbas. In 1937 one village lost 600 Greeks to Stalinist terror on charges that they intended to separate the southern Donbas, much of the Don, the Kuban, and the northern Caucasus from the Soviet Union and establish a Greek Republic.[176] I. A. Sokolov, thirty-eight, a Greek peasant, and A. S. Shapurma, fifty-one, a stable man, both from Greek villages in the southern Donbas, were arrested on 17 December 1937. On 28 January 1938 they were executed as members of a counterrevolutionary Greek insurgent organization.[177] Most members of the Greek national theater troupe in Mariupol' were executed.[178] Thus, between September 1937 and February 1938, at least 3,628 ethnic Greeks were arrested and 3,470, or 95.6 percent, of them were executed.[179]

Jews were not targeted as an ethnic group, but some were repressed as

[171] *Luch-inform* (Amvrosiivka), 3 March 1993.

[172] AUSBUDO, no. 21978-pf.

[173] See, for example, the execution in October 1938 of four ethnic German colliers at Shevchenko Mine in Stalino. Ibid., no. 28478-pf.

[174] Nikol'skyi, " 'Velyka chystka,' " p. 29.

[175] Volodymyr Nikol'skyi, "Ukraintsi Donechchyny, represovani v 1937–1938 rr.: sotsiolohichnyi analiz statystyky," *Skhid* (Donets'k), no. 3 (November 1995), p. 39.

[176] Lev Iarutskyi, "Dopros v novogodniuiu noch'. Novoe o Georgii Kostoprave," *Donbas*, 1993, nos. 1–2. See also *Logos* (Donets'k), no. 1 (3) (4–10 February 1991).

[177] *Priazovskii rabochii*, 1 June 1993. For the repression of Greeks in the Donbas, see also Mace and Heretz, *Oral History Project*, 2:657–58, and L. D. Nasiedkina, "Stalins'ki represii proty hrekiv Ukrainy v 30-ti roky," in *Za mizhnatsional'nu zlahodu proty shovinizmu ta ekstremizmu*, p. 86.

[178] Anatolii Baldzhi, *Elliny Priazov'ia vchera, segodnia, zavtra. Grecheskoe natsional'noe dvizhenie v Ukraine glazami mariupol'skogo zhurnalista* (Mariupol', 1995), p. 13.

[179] Nikol'skyi, " 'Velyka chystka,' " p. 29.

"Zionists."[180] Like other groups, the Jews had suffered because they retained their own distinct culture. In Kiev, a Jewish choir was abolished ("it had such power over the people's souls," according to one observer; "it was high art, beautiful craftsmanship, and people were proud of it") and Jewish literature was destroyed: "It was all burned."[181] Many Gypsies also fell victim to Stalinist terror.[182] The Tartars in the Donbas were said to propagate Pan-Islamism, which was, according to Ivanov, the secret police chief, the work of German spies.[183]

While the Germans and Poles were repressed en masse in the west of the country, the Iranians, Kurds, and other nationalities were deported from the southern border and the Koreans and Chinese were deported from the Far East.[184] In the summer of 1937 all the Chinese disappeared from Kiev. The disappearance of Poles, Chinese, and others looked to one Kiev resident like an ethnic purge.[185] In all these purges, the intelligentsia, as the articulator of national sentiments and hence "nationalism," was terrorized particularly harshly.

In the Red Army, national formations as separate entities were abolished in March 1938.[186] By a June 1938 decree, the Commissariat of Defense dismissed 4,138 commanders and political workers of foreign origin as well as of German, Polish, Latvian, Lithuanian, Estonian, Bulgarian, and other national descent.[187]

Ethnic Ukrainians, who composed the largest ethnic group in the Donbas as in Ukraine in general, appeared to the enemy hunters as potential nationalists and hence potential separatists and enemies. (Khrushchev recalled later that Kaganovich "was fond of saying that every Ukrainian is potentially a nationalist.")[188] Like his predecessors, the people's commissar of enlightenment, V. P. Zatons'kyi, fell to Stalin's terror. In November 1937 he was arrested,

[180]Bazhan and Voinalovych, "Viina proty vlasnoho narodu."

[181]*Report to Congress: Commission on the Ukraine Famine* (Washington, D.C., 1988), pp. 301 and 307–8.

[182]M. Ivanesko, "Sovetskie tsigany," *Politika i vremia* (Kiev), 1991, no. 7, p. 82.

[183]RTsKhIDNI, f. 17, op. 21, d. 5196, l. 151.

[184]*Tak eto bylo. Natsional'nye repressii v SSSR. 1919–1952 gody*, vol. 1 (Moscow, 1993), pp. 87, 97, 111; Liu Khe and Kim En Un, comp., *Belaia kniga o deportatsii koreiskogo naseleniia Rossii v 30–40-kh godakh. Kniga pervaia* (Moscow, 1992); N. F. Bugai, "Vyselenie sovetskikh koreitsev s Dal'nego Vostoka," *Voprosy istorii*, 1994, no. 5; Haruki Wada, "Koreans in the Soviet Far East, 1917–1937," in Dae-Sook Suh, ed., *Koreans in the Soviet Union* (University of Hawaii Press, 1989); John. J. Stephan, " 'Cleansing' the Soviet Far East, 1937–1938," *Acta Slavica Iaponica*, 10 (1992); and Kim Chan-Jong, *Siruku rōdo no chōsenjin. Sutārin to nihon ni yoru 1937 aki no higeki* (Tokyo, 1990).

[185]N. Korzhavin, "V soblaznakh krovavoi epokhi," *Novyi mir*, 1992, no. 7, p. 192. The returnees from the Far East ("Kharbintsy") were also repressed en masse.

[186]Iu. I. Korablev and N. F. Makarov, "Obrazovanie SSSR: ukreplenie oborony strany," *Voprosy istorii*, 1982, no. 12.

[187]*Izvestiia TsK KPSS*, 1900, no. 1, p. 188 (statistics to the end of 1938).

[188]*Khrushchev Remembers*, p. 172.

charged falsely as a member of the "anti-Soviet Ukrainian Nationalist Center," and was shot in July 1938.[189] The Ukrainian Communist Party leadership was almost thoroughly purged. Of the 11 Politburo members elected at the May–June 1937 party congress, 10 were repressed; of 102 members and candidates of the Central Committee and 9 members of the Auditing Commission, 100 were repressed.[190] Not all of them were ethnic Ukrainians, but non-Ukrainians like Postyshev (Russian) and Kosior (Polish) were suspected of being spiritual captives of Ukraine. The Communist Party of Western Ukraine was dissolved in July 1938 "by the Comintern on Stalin's orders, and most of its members were 'invited' to Moscow, where they were executed."[191]

The Ukrainian intelligentsia, like the intellectuals of other ethnic groups, was targeted for savage terror. Writers were repressed en masse. Between 1930 and 1953 at least 80 percent of them had disappeared. Of the 259 writers whose records are available, 17 were shot, 8 committed suicide, 175 were thrown into the camps (where unknown numbers of them were shot or died), 16 simply disappeared without a trace, and only 7 died of natural causes.[192] The whole discipline of Ukrainian and regional studies (*kraieznavstvo*) was destroyed.[193]

Many ordinary workers, too, were repressed as nationalists. P. S. Panait, forty-seven, a Ukrainian plumber in Luhans'k, a non–party member, was arrested on 13 November 1937. He was accused of counterrevolutionary nationalist activities. He categorically denied all charges (which after Stalin's death were found to be fabricated). Yet he was executed ten days later. In 1955 he was rehabilitated, but the KGB told his widow that Panait had been sentenced to ten years of imprisonment and died of a heart attack in prison in 1944.[194] Another case involved K. N. Zarusinskii, a fifty-one-year-old Ukrainian, a carpenter at the Red Star Mine in Stalino, a non–party member. Zarusinskii was arrested on 14 June 1938. He was born in L'viv and apparently had some relatives in the city, then under Polish rule. He was accused of counterrevolutionary wrecking by order of the Polish secret service.[195] No comprehensive statistics exist, but in Ukraine, as many as 24,233 Ukrainians were arrested as nationalists in the first six months of 1938 alone.[196]

[189] *Pro minule zarady maibutn'oho* (Kiev, 1989), pp. 272–73.

[190] *Marshrutami istorii* (Kiev, 1990), p. 314, and Iu. I Shapoval, *U ti trahichni roky. Stalinizm na Ukraini* (Kiev, 1990), p. 119.

[191] David R. Marples, *Stalinism in Ukraine in the 1940s* (New York, 1992), pp. 72–73.

[192] Heorhii Kas'ianov, *Ukrains'ka intelihentsiia 1920-kh–30-kh rokiv: sotsial'nyi portret ta istorychna dolia* (Kiev, 1992), p. 162, and *Zhertvy repressii* (Kiev, 1993), p. 218. For the terror against the Ukrainian writers, see Iar Slavutych, *Rozstriliana muza* (Detroit, 1955; Kiev, 1992), and *Z poroha smerti: pys'mennyky Ukrainy – zhertvy stalins'kykh represii* (Kiev, 1991).

[193] See the very important study, *Represovane kraieznavstvo (20–30-i roky)* (Kiev, 1991).

[194] DALO, f. 3747, op. 3, spr. 1304-r.

[195] AUSBUDO, no. 23323-pf.

[196] Bazhan and Voinalovych, "Viina proty vlasnoho narodu."

Finally, religious groups were also targeted for terror. The adoption of the Stalin Constitution in December 1936 alarmed the secret police in the Donbas. The clergy began to act openly, maintaining that the new constitution had given them the right to open churches and perform services. According to a January 1937 speech by the Donbas NKVD chief Ivanov, the clergy immediately became "incredibly active" and even performed a liturgy on the adoption of the Stalin Constitution.[197] The Donbas had been a traditional haven for many sectarians, some of whom had secretly performed religious services (such as christenings) for the miners.[198] Ivanov emphasized a month later that nowhere did the clergy possess such vast material resources as in the Donbas.[199] In March Ivanov again sounded an alarm, declaring that, according to his data, at least 8,000 people in the Donbas were organized by various sects (Baptists, Evangelists, Adventists) and that there were "very many wandering monks, clergy without a parish, and other ruffians" working in the Donbas. "It's to our shame that they [clergy and sectarians] are strong precisely in the cities and industrial districts." They received material and moral support in the Donbas, because they had mesmerized, according to Ivanov, "the wives of some workers and sometimes the youth." Ivanov insisted that the clergy and sectarians were actively moving toward fascism.[200]

There is evidence that the party and the secret police were surprised to see how strong religious belief remained among the population. The 1937 population census, taken in early 1937 in the midst of raging terror, inquired of all residents of the country whether they were believers. One might expect that people would have answered in the negative in a census in an openly and terroristically atheistic state. Yet the census revealed that of the 29,937,843 "illiterate population," 25,139,192 (or 84 percent) were believers, and, of the 68,473,289 "literate population," 30,137,857 (or 44 percent) were.[201] The persistent attraction of spiritual "opium" must have astonished the atheists. In May 1937, M. M. Khataevich, a member of the Politburo of the Ukrainian Communist Party, told the Ukrainian party congress that more than half of the Ukrainian population proved to be believers. "This was a complete surprise to all of us," he declared, adding that "we have overestimated our success in the fight against religious prejudices."[202] No breakdown of data according to regions is available, but in the Donbas, a haven for the persecuted, the figure must have been at least as high as the Ukrainian average.

[197]RTsKhIDNI, f. 17, op. 21, d. 5195, l. 132.

[198]See, for example, Vladimir A. Bohdan, *Avoiding Extinction: Children of the Kulak* (New York, 1992), pp. 26–32, which discusses a clandestine clergy named Ihnat Rastchenko.

[199]RTsKhIDNI, f. 17, op. 21, d. 5196, ll. 150–51.

[200]Ibid., d. 5197, ll. 32–33.

[201]*Vsesoiuznaia perepis' naseleniia 1937 g. Kratkie itogi* (Moscow, 1991), pp. 106–7.

[202]*Trynadtsiatyi z'izd Komunistychnoi partii*, Bulletin, no. 6, p. 23. Note also Kosior's remark in *Voprosy istorii*, 1993, no. 6, p. 8.

There were many attempts in the Donbas as elsewhere to open churches by taking advantage of the freedom supposedly offered by the Stalin Constitution. The attempts led to massive repression. K. N. Veisman, sixty, a Russian from Novocherkassk who graduated from Don Ecclesiastic Seminar in 1897, father of seven children, was arrested in a village near Makiivka on 24 October 1937. He had collected signatures for the opening of a church. He categorically denied the charges of anti-Soviet propaganda, but was sentenced to be shot three days later and was executed on the same day.[203] M. I. Mukha, forty-five, a Ukrainian priest of an Autocephalous orientation who had returned from exile, was arrested in Mine Butovka in Stalino on 5 November 1937. He dismissed the charges of counterrevolutionary activities (including his alleged remarks that the "Soviet is Satan"). Mukha was categorical:

> *Q*: You are arrested as an activist and c[ounter]-r[evolutionary] agent for conducting anti-Soviet propaganda among working people. Do you confirm your anti-Soviet activity?
>
> *A*: I did not conduct any anti-Soviet propaganda among working people.
>
> *Q*: Upon arrival in the Donbas, in Stalino district, you got in touch with the c-r activist, the former nun Safronova [*sic*].
>
> *A*: Yes, upon arrival in Stalino I met Safonova at the church in the village of Shchyhliivka in June 1937. I became acquainted with her and stayed in her house where I lived until the day I was arrested.
>
> *Q*: Did you and Safonova hold illegal meetings of believers in your house?
>
> *A*: No, I did not hold meetings of believers.
>
> *Q*: Did you give Safonova orders to hold illegal meetings in believers' homes?
>
> *A*: No, I did not give Safonova such orders.
>
> *Q*: You are telling an untruth. The investigator possesses materials [to show] that you organized illegal groups of believers, and conducted among them anti-Soviet, defeatist, and fascist agitation. Do you confirm it?
>
> *A*: No, I do not. I maintain that I did not create any groups. . . .

Yet on 3 December 1937 Mukha was sentenced to death and was executed.[204]

It was easier to break organized religion than to eliminate religion driven underground. As Ivanov made clear, there were numerous "wandering priests" (*brodiachie popy*) working in the Donbas, a perfect place for underground activity. They organized youth circles and collective prayers and performed other religious services, moving from one place to another. Some were said to advise against military service and the Stakhanovite movement.[205] The secret police

[203] AUSBUDO, no. 21662-pf.
[204] Ibid., no. 21979-pf.
[205] *Sotsialisticheskii Donbass*, 6 and 26 July 1937.

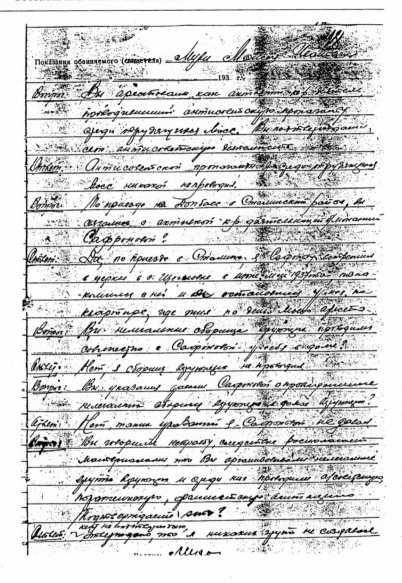

Figure 6.4. A page from Mukha's interrogation records, November 1937. From AUS-BUDO, no. 21979-pf, ark. 18.

characterized their activities as anti-Soviet and counterrevolutionary and the wandering priests as spies.[206] Thus the police arrested "very many" of them, but when someone was arrested, others soon appeared. The Baptists remained particularly strong in the Donbas.[207]

Self-Defeating Terror

Mass terror continued to the very end of 1938. In September 1938 in Voroshylovhrad alone at least 1,016 people were confirmed executed.[208] In Donets'k, 70 people were shot on 5 September 1938, 332 on 5 October, 295 on 10 October, 336 on 14 October, 237 on 14 November, 134 on 17 November, 84 on 19 November. The list continues.[209] On 19 December 1938, S. A. Gromov, forty-three, a collier in Amvrosiivka, was arrested and executed on the same day.[210] One could go on ad nauseum.

By late 1938 it became apparent to Stalin and his closest associates that the terror could not possibly continue at that pace: in due course the whole nation would be destroyed.[211] Stalin and Molotov signed numerous execution orders at a feverish pitch in 1937 and 1938.[212] It is far from clear whether Moscow authorized each and every case of execution. However, the Great Terror of 1936–38 was a terror campaign orchestrated by Moscow. It encouraged the secret police and other enemy hunters to find enemies, gave them "control figures" for each *oblast'* and republic, and sanctioned the counterplans from the provinces eager to overfulfill the control figures. In Donets'k *oblast'* (which was split into Stalino and Voroshylovhrad *oblast's* in 1938), the plan overfulfilled the original plan by fifteen times.[213] If this report is true, then at least fifteen thousand people were executed from July 1937 to the end of 1938 in the Ukrainian part of the Donbas alone. Terror on such a scale had to stop at some point lest the whole nation be eliminated.

There were at least two factors that made the Great Terror self-defeating. First, Stalin exercised little constraint on the escalation of terror. Since 1933, a time of grave internal crisis and mounting foreign threat from the West and

---

[206]See, for example, Sokolinskii's speech in *Sotsialisticheskii Donbass*, 11 January 1938.

[207]See RTsKhIDNI, f. 17, op. 21, d. 5167, l. 256. See also Bohdan, *Avoiding Extinction*, p. 32, for the disappearance of Father Rastchenko, who clandestinely christened the author Bohdan.

[208]*Komsomol'skaia znamia* (Kiev), 14 September 1990, p. 2.

[209]Vsevolod Orlov, "Den' gneva. Roman Rudenko. Kto zhe on – general'nyi prokuror ili general'nyi palach?" *Donetskie vedomosti*, no. 37 (September 1992), pp. 6–7.

[210]*Luch – inform* (Amvrosiivka), 17 February 1993.

[211]This danger is discussed in detail by Rittersporn, *Stalinist Simplifications*.

[212]See, for example, "Iosif Stalin: 'Vinovnykh sudit; uskorenno. Prigovor – rasstrel.' Rassekrechen lichnyi arkhiv vozhdia narodov," *Izvestiia*, 10 June 1992, and *Sto sorok besed s Molotovym*, pp. 439–40, where Molotov admitted that he and Stalin signed execution orders.

[213]Orlov, "Den' gneva."

East, Stalin had encouraged the hunting of the "enemies of the people." His instructions and signals were often vague enough to allow for local initiative. When he gave clear signals (at least one case is known – the July 1937 orders), the secret police and other enemy hunters responded eagerly. When they proposed even higher figures of "enemies" to be exterminated, Stalin willingly gave his approval.

There was danger in so momentous an operation. For one, some in the secret police would resist a mass terror campaign. Hence Stalin removed Iagoda and subsequently had him shot. At the February–March 1937 plenum of the party Central Committee, the report on "The Lessons of Wrecking, Diversion, and Espionage of Japanese-German-Trotskyite Agents in the NKVD" was discussed along with "The Lessons of Wrecking, Diversion, and Espionage of Japanese-German-Trotskyite Agents in the People's Commissariats of Heavy Industry and Transport."[214] In the late 1930s, more than twenty-three thousand NKVD officials were said to have been repressed for their opposition to the terror campaign.[215] Clearly in this case, as in the case of the Great Breakthrough (of rapid industrialization and wholesale collectivization), Stalin preferred excess to moderation to ensure the implementation of the policy. As was the case in 1930, once a breakthrough was made, he could shift the responsibility to others.

Many loyal NKVDists, who did much to terrorize the country, thus fell victim to Stalin's terror. For example, the Ukrainian NKVD chiefs disappeared in succession: V. A. Balits'kyi was arrested in July 1937 and shot in November;[216] I. M. Leplevs'kyi was arrested in April 1938 and shot in July;[217] A. I. Uspenskii, fearing arrest, vanished without trace in October 1938, but was caught later and shot in 1941 along with his wife.[218] In the Donbas, too, numerous NKVD officials, starting with Ivanov and then Sokolinskii, were repressed as Polish and German spies.[219] In November 1938 Stalin removed Ezhov and in February 1940 had him shot as a foreign spy. Later, according to the famous Soviet aviation designer A. S. Iakovlev, Stalin said:

> Ezhov is a scoundrel [*merzavets*]! A degenerate. Call him at the commissariat

---

[214] *Voprosy istorii*, 1992, nos. 2–3, p. 3.

[215] Dmitrii Volkogonov, *Triumf i tragediia. Politicheskii portret I. V. Stalina*, vol. 1, pt. 2 (Moscow, 1989), p. 284. In Ukraine, 1,199 "leading NKVD cadres" were executed in 1938. *Radians'ka Ukraina*, 9 August 1988 ("Na storozhi bezpeky Vitchyzny"). Ezhov later said, "I purged Checkists everywhere . . . as many as 14,000." See Vadim Bakatin, *Izbavlenie ot KGB* (Moscow, 1992), p. 30.

[216] V. A. Zolotar'ev and Iu. I. Shapoval, "V. A. Balyts'kyi. Na shliakhu do pravdy pro n'ioho," *Ukrains'kyi istorychnyi zhurnal*, 1993, nos. 7–8, pp. 64–66.

[217] *Nashe Mynule*, 1993, no. 1, pp. 56–59.

[218] *Shchit i mech*, 1991, no. 17, p. 12; *Khrushchev Remembers*, pp. 96–97; and *Istoricheskii arkhiv*, 1992, no. 1, pp. 130–31.

[219] See *Vechernii Donetsk*, 26 February 1990.

and they'll say, 'He's gone to the CC [party Central Committee].' Call the CC and they'll say, 'He's gone to work.' Send for him at home and it turns out that he lies drunk in bed. Many innocent people perished. We shot him for that.[220]

Yet on 12 December 1938, according to Dmitrii Volkogonov, after Ezhov's dismissal, Stalin and Molotov signed yet another execution order for as many as 3,167 people.[221]

There was another important factor that made the terror self-defeating in the end. In some respects it was the self-defeating mechanism of dictatorship itself. All but official forms of political expression were driven underground in the 1930s. Stalin's brutal policy of rapid industrialization and wholesale collectivization terrorized the bulk of the population. The terror against the supposed enemies was not unpopular among certain groups of workers, but the famine crisis was such that Stalin came to suspect the loyalty of even his own supporters in the party, let alone the millions of dekulakized and others. Because there was no way of gauging the political mood of the population (e.g., by free elections and polls), it was difficult to estimate the real strength of the hostile elements. This was why Stalin, Vyshinskii, and others contended that there were many hidden, masked enemies and that it was becoming more difficult than ever to recognize enemies in the seemingly loyal population.

The same question still poses enormous difficulties to historians. One has no "objective data" with which to study the popular mood. A close examination of the files of the repressed people clearly shows that the vast majority of the numerous anti-Soviet, anti-Stalin remarks and jokes attributed to them in this period were either fabricated by the secret police or were extracted by force from "witnesses."[222] The interrogators would boast that they uncovered so many counterrevolutionary organizations by "closely working with the arrested even though there were absolutely no data [on the existence of such groups]."[223] The vast majority of the population did not speak out, because the regime did not tolerate so much as a hint of disloyalty.

Stalin and his supporters, however, were not alone in seeing embittered elements in the population. For example, John Scott, an American, worked in Magnitogorsk (a giant metallurgical plant in the Urals) for several years in the 1930s, along with the dekulakized and other repressed people. Briefed by the American Embassy in Moscow, Scott wrote confidential reports to the

---

[220] A. S. Iakovlev, *Tsel' zhizni. Zapiski aviakonstruktora*, 5th ed. (Moscow, 1987), pp. 212–13.

[221] Volkogonov, *Triumf i tragediia*, p. 301.

[222] Based on my examination of dozens of personal files in the former KGB archives in Donets'k and Luhans'k.

[223] See, for example, the Donbas interrogator B. N. Spivakovs'kyi cited in Semystiaha, "Tse potribno i mertvym, tse potribno i zhyvym." See a story on another interrogator in Stalino in A. M. Samsonov, *Znat' i pomnit'. Dialog istorika s chitatelem* (Moscow, 1988), p. 219.

American State Department in 1938. In one of them Scott says: "I once saw an old peasant throw a crowbar into a large generator and then give himself up to the armed guards laughing gleefully." Scott thought: "In the event of a war, invasion or internal breakdown, serious trouble would probably arise from the kulaks. If no such crisis should occur within the next ten years, I believe that the group will gradually be absorbed by the community since the old members will soon die off and the youth will lose to a great extent their feeling of inferiority and bitterness"; "At present they [specialists] are terrorized but in the event of some crisis they might become dangerous to the dictatorship."[224]

The war factor was evident. In June 1938 L. M. Kaganovich, for example, addressed the Donbas party conference and contended that there had been many kulaks, enemies, and spies in the Donbas. If they had not been destroyed, he declared, "perhaps we would have had war already": Stalin, the party, and the NKVD had eliminated the enemies without fearing what would be said about it, thereby delaying war.[225]

Clearly, however, the contention of Stalin and his supporters of the ubiquitous existence of enemies was a political expediency. By making "enemies of the people" of his political opponents, Stalin destroyed them politically (and physically). Yet Stalin was not omniscient. He could not read the minds of his seemingly loyal supporters who, he suspected, might turn against him if chance arose. That was why he ended up killing so many of his own supporters. Here an analogy with the Inquisition is quite appropriate: "The more fiercely they [witches] were persecuted, the more numerous they seemed to become."[226]

Afterthoughts of Stalin's closest associates at the time of the Great Terror support this view. According to Kaganovich, for example, Stalin, if alive, would admit his mistakes. "We were to blame for going too far [*peresolili*], thinking that there were more enemies than there actually were." Yet the Great Terror was justified, Kaganovich implied, because there were fifth columns and, had they not been eliminated, the Soviet Union would have been beaten by the Nazis.[227] In an almost identical vein, Molotov also insisted that "Stalin played safe (*Stalin perestrakhoval*)." There was no hard evidence that, for example, Tukhachevskii was a German agent, but he was "dangerous," and "we were not sure whether he would stay firmly on our side in a difficult mo-

---

[224]John Scott, *Behind the Urals: An American Worker in Russia's City of Steel*, enl. ed. prepared by Stephen Kotkin (Indiana University Press, 1989), pp. 283, 284, and 288.

[225]RTsKHIDNI, f. 81, op. 3, d. 231, ll. 73 and 79.

[226]Adam Hochschild, *The Unquiet Ghost: Russians Remember Stalin* (New York, 1994), p. 173. For an excellent analogy with the Inquisition, see also Stephen Kotkin, *Magnetic Mountain: Stalinism as a Civilization* (University of California, 1995), pp. 336–38 ("Counterrevolution was a state of mind . . . it was necessary to employ clever and forceful methods to probe suspected people's consciences, thereby exposing a suspect's true inner thoughts" [p. 336]).

[227]Chuev, *Tak govoril Kaganovich*, pp. 35–36 and 101.

ment." Evidence was not so important, Molotov suggested, because "there is no smoke without fire." Molotov justified Stalin and himself: "Let an extra head fall and there will be no vacillation at the time of war and after the war." The terror of this period was necessary and inevitable, and, Molotov maintained, "it was impossible to conduct it without mistakes."[228]

As was the case in 1917 with the term *burzhui*, the terms "enemy," "enemy of the people," "Trotskyite," "German (or Japanese or Polish) spy," and "traitor" became all-inclusive. Manipulation was part and parcel of politics, and in this case, as was the case in 1917, these dangerous terms were manipulated from above. Yet people had their own thoughts and understood the terms in their own way. When rumor had it in the Donbas that Molotov and Kaganovich had been arrested, the residents began to remove the portraits of the "enemies."[229] The all-inclusive construction of enemy images made the operation dangerous and chaotic. Some could not believe in what was happening. In Moscow, a textile worker and old party member named O. I. Nikitina openly declared at a factory meeting in June 1937: "Say we are all traitors. Right, it was Lenin who had no eyes and failed to see the people around him." Nikitina got ten years.[230]

Particularly revealing of popular images of enemies is the following letter a worker named Petrov, in the city of Artemivs'k in the Donbas, wrote on 25 May 1937 (and signed by fourteen other workers) to the (nominal) head of the state M. I. Kalinin:

> Mikhail Ivanovich, I inform you that in our Artemivs'k something terrible is happening now. Who's a Trotskyite? – the City Party Committee Chairman Kopytin, who has stolen everything possible. They took the furniture to him. Zlatkin and Eskin pinched the whole housing construction for him and for Ol'khovskii, the chairman of the city Soviet. Kopytin and Ol'khovskii went to a village and arranged for drinking binges and orgies to conduct a meeting there. Makagon, Golovko, and Kostov were rewarded most generously for stealing everything – flour, butter, lard, chicken – and providing them to Kopytin, but those who ought to be rewarded he expelled [from the party] and now they are exiled. This is [not] just. In our city Plotnikov, Eratsenko, Bychkov, Abramov, Rabinovich, and many more have been expelled from the party and exiled by the order of Kopytin. They are the victims of Kopytin the Trotskyite, who raped girls and arranged drinking binges. Somehow he's all right. The workers demand that you wake up and look at what's happening here. Here is a nest of Trotskyites, yet uncovered. How can it be uncovered, when our NKVD chief does what Kopytin tells him to do. Is it really permissible that Sheluchenko helped Kopytin instead of watching as he expelled [others from the party]. There are many innocent victims in our city.

[228] *Sto sorok besed s Molotovym*, pp. 36, 392, 397, 413, 416, and 418.
[229] Vasil'ev, "30-e gody na Ukraine," p. 82.
[230] O. Khlevniuk, "1937 god: protivodeistvie repressiiam," *Kommunist*, 1989, no. 18, p. 107.

Petrov asked whether it was admissible to mock the Bolsheviks in "our republic of workers" and went on to say:

> I'll give you an example of how many Trotskyites are here: Sakhronov, Zoz, Borshchrv [sic], Lager', Ol'khovskii, Kuroedovivan, Peredernikov Andrei, Tkachev, Kopytin, Stasikevich, Entin, Zharkii, Vetkov, Bur'ian, Seleznev, Zubritskii, Orlik, Zelekman, Maksimenko, Pyslinko, Onyshchenko, and many more. I know that they haven't been arrested, jailed, because they are needed to eat up the old, loyal Bolsheviks. I wrote Petrovs'kyi [Ukrainian government head], no results. Those whom they jailed and exiled, their families were destroyed and reduced to beggary. Is this really permissible? This means, let the innocent suffer and the traitors walk around free. Why don't you send someone here to uncover the real nest. . . . Our traitors are walking around. Why is this? It has to be investigated, but it hasn't been, probably because traitors sit on the *oblast'* court. . . . They are all scoundrels and Trotskyites. . . . Did we Bolsheviks really fight to be imprisoned while the enemies can walk?[231]

Although subsequently Kopytin and other corrupt officials, the NKVD chief Sheluchenko, and the judges were likely to have been repressed, there is no information available on their fates. Whatever the term "Trotskyite" may have meant, in the minds of Petrov and his cosigners, it was coterminous with "enemy" and "traitor."

The old concept "class enemy" was still being used in this period, but it was no longer prominent in the vocabulary of the time. The images of enemies became class-neutral and demonized. They had no Marxist residue. It was no coincidence that the "guilt" of an "enemy of the people" was extended by law to his or her family members and relatives.[232] Guilt by association was a convenient tool with which to take family members as hostages in case the enemy refused to capitulate. Yet capitulation rarely spared them.

According to secret police data, in 1934 78,999 were indicted for "counterrevolutionary charges" in the country. The number rose rapidly to 267,076 in 1935, then slightly increased to 274,670 in 1936, rose sharply to 790,665 in 1937, fell somewhat to 554,258 in 1938, and dropped precipitously to 63,889 in 1939. The number of death sentences for these years were as follows:[233]

---

[231]GARF, f. 1235sch, op. 4sch, d. 200, l. 5. For popular images of "the omnipresent conspiracy," see Gábor Tamás Rittersporn's important work, "The Omnipresent Conspiracy: On Soviet Imagery of Politics and Social Relations in the 1930s," in Nick Lampert and Gábor T. Rittersporn, eds., *Stalinism: Its Nature and Aftermath. Essays in Honour of Moshe Lewin* (New York, 1992).

[232]This was enacted in June 1934. See *30-e gody. Vzgliad iz segodnia* (Moscow, 1990), p. 94.

[233]V. P. Popov, "Gosudarstvennyi terror v sovetskoi Rossii. 1923–1953 gg. (istochniki i ikh interpretatsiia)," *Otechestvennye arkhivy*, 1992, no. 2, p. 28. "Russia" in Popov's article refers to the Soviet Union as a whole.

1934	2,056
1935	1,229
1936	1,118
1937	353,074
1938	328,618
1939	2,552

In Ukraine, in 1937 and 1938 267,579 people were arrested, and 122,237 were sentenced to be shot.[234] In Stalino *oblast'*, there were at least 33,774 cases of political crime, the vast majority of them in 1937 and 1938.[235] Given that some cases included more than one person, the number of the repressed are likely to range from 40,000 to 50,000.[236] In Voroshylovhrad *oblast'*, there were about 40,000 cases.[237] How many were shot in the Donbas is unknown, but one local historian estimates that between 27,000 and 30,000 were executed in Stalino *oblast'*.[238] This may be too high. Yet a study, albeit very preliminary, shows that 74.2 percent of those repressed in Odessa in 1937–38 were given death sentences.[239] If this degree of severity applies to the Donbas as well, the death figures for Stalino *oblast'* just quoted appear plausible. In fact, an incomplete and preliminary examination of the 1937–38 repression in Stalino *oblast'* indicates that as many as 9,367 executions were accounted for by three national minorities alone (Germans, Poles, and Greeks).[240] Compute a similar rate of capital punishment in Voroshylovhrad *oblast'* and one reaches a total figure of nearly 50,000 death sentences in the Ukrainian Donbas.

It is far from clear, however, whether these figures on arrests and death sentences are comprehensive. In the case of the provinces, many cases were transferred to Kiev or Moscow, which makes the compilation of statistics even more difficult.

Yet if these figures on Ukraine and the Donbas are correct to any degree, it can be said, although very tentatively, that the Donbas (Stalino and Voroshylovhrad *oblast'*s) was indeed hit hardest in Ukraine: the Donbas accounted for up to one-third of the executed in Ukraine, whereas in 1937 only

[234]Ivan Bilas, *Represyvno-karal'na systema v Ukraini 1917–1953. Suspil'no-politychnyi ta istoryko-pravovyi analiz*, vol. 1 (Kiev, 1994), p. 379.

[235]V. M. Nikol'skyi, "Diial'nist' orhaniv DPU na Donechchyni u dzerkali statystyky kryminal'nykh sprav," *Ukrains'ka derzhavnist'. Istoriia i suchasnist'. Materialy naukovoi konferentsii. Sichen' 1993 r.* (Kiev, 1993), pp. 288–90.

[236]*Donechchyna*, 27 October 1993 ("Reabilitovani istoriieiu"). An official at AUSBUDO informed me on 28 July 1994 that the figure was about 40,000.

[237]*Luganskaia pravda*, 8 July 1990, and *Nasha gazeta* (Luhans'k), 4 November 1992.

[238]V. M. Nikol'skyi, who is on the commission to record all cases of repression in Stalino (now Donets'k) *oblast'*.

[239]O. V. Hontar and Zh. O. Smotrych, "Stalins'ki represii na Odeshchini," in *Shosta Vseukrains'ka naukova konferentsiia z istorychnoho kraieznavstva*, p. 303.

[240]Nikol'skyi, " 'Velyka chystka,' " p. 29.

16.1 percent of the Ukrainian population resided in the Donbas. Moreover, one would have to add repression in the Russian part of the Donbas to make the picture complete.

The terror in the Donbas could have been worse, given the fact that the Donbas had attracted so many fugitives with politically dubious pasts. Many came to the Donbas, changed their identities, and severed or hid their family ties. In fact, this alleviated the terror in the Donbas. The relatives of the "enemies of the people" were very often repressed, but in the Donbas, seeking them out was not an easy task. Many Donbas residents also believed that Moscow would have wiped out the Donbas had it been possible to do so without destroying its industry.[241] Even in the harshest times, the Donbas seems to have retained elements of the free steppe.

Whatever the case, as this chapter suggests, certain groups were harder hit than others: party and government officials, people with non-Bolshevik political records, industrial managers and engineers, ethnic minorities, intellectuals, and the clergy.[242] Men were far more likely to be repressed than women.[243]

There was no popular outburst of anti-Semitism recorded in this period, at least in the Donbas. Given the persistent ethnic prejudice, this is surprising. It was not that Jews were not repressed, and my data include many Jews among the repressed in the Donbas. A considerable number of Jews must have been among the repressed managers and engineers. According to one account, many Jews were in responsible positions in the Donbas, and the lack of safety and the Stakhanovite movement "created deep hatred toward Jews and communists."[244] Nevertheless, no cases of pogrom or pogromlike violence was reported. This may be yet another piece of evidence that the whole enemy-hunting operation was centrally administered. However, there is a dark side to this. There was a perception that, unlike on previous occasions of popular suffering, the Jews did not suffer from the terror more visibly than others. This

---

[241] Numerous Donbas residents with whom I have talked expressed this view. One interviewee (Interview 4), born in 1913 in the Donbas and dekulakized in 1929, suggested that the Donbas was saved to some extent by its having too many former kulaks. He fled from exile to the Donbas and managed to find a job.

[242] See Kuromiya, "Stalin's Terror in the Donbas." The case of the ethnic Ukrainians (the ethnic majority in Ukraine) is a complicated subject. (See Hiroaki Kuromiya, "Ukraine and Russia in the 1930s," forthcoming in *Harvard Ukrainian Studies*.) Generally, they were more vulnerable to repression than the ethnic Russians. In Stalino *oblast'*, however, the ethnic Ukrainians accounted for 34.4% of the repressed, whereas they constituted 59.4% of its overall population. See Nikol'skyi, "Ukraintsi Donechchyny, represovani v 1937–1938rr.," p. 39.

[243] My small database of 371 repressed in the Donbas includes only 4 women. For a similar conclusion (1,053 women arrested, of whom 61 were sentenced to be shot) derived from a much larger database (about 40,000); see V. M. Nikol'skyi, "Zhinky, represovani na Donechchyni u 1937–1938 rr.: zahal'na kharakterystyka zhertv," *Materialy nauchnoi konferentsii "Bogdan Khmel'nitskii: zhizn', deiatel'nost', istoriia i sovremennost'." 14–15 dekabria 1995 g.* (Donets'k, 1995), p. 24.

[244] Vladimir Bohdan's letter to the author (15 December 1993).

created a mistaken suspicion in the population that the Jews accounted for the majority of the NKVD interrogators responsible for the torture and death of innocent people.[245]

The bosses, or people in positions of responsibility, were repressed disproportionately. In all likelihood, however, the bulk of the "enemies of the people" (*vragi naroda, vorohy narodu*) will turn out to be "ordinary citizens," or *narod*.[246] According to a preliminary analysis, non–party members accounted for the vast majority of the repressed (78.3 percent in Stalino *oblast'* and 95 percent in Voroshylovhrad *oblast'*), and more than half of the repressed (53.7 percent and 66.4 percent in respective *oblast'*s) were workers and peasants (collective farmers).[247] Mass graves of victims have now been found in various places in the Donbas, accounting for at least thousands of nameless corpses in Donets'k alone.[248]

People lived in misery. A boy whose father was arrested in Mariupol' wrote out of desperation to Lenin's widow in Moscow in December 1937:

> Grannie Krupskaia for what do I and my 10-month-old brother suffer? Papa was taken by NKVD. don't know for what. he sits already for 3 months. don't know for what. Mama is sick in hospital. help my sorrow. Mama was raised in a children's home. do we really have to grow up in a children's home too? but we have Papa and Mama who have to bring us up.
> Vova Kozlov
> My address: S. I. Olada (district committee)
>   4 Quarter
>   Volodars'ke Village
>   Mariupol'
> Papa sits in the city of Mariupol'.[249]

[245]This explanation has been offered to me privately on a number of occasions, in both Russia and Ukraine. See also *Report to Congress*, p. 300, a testimony by a Ukrainian on the terror in Kiev: "I have to emphasize that I am not an anti-Semite; in fact, I am against anyone who dislikes the Jews and is against the Jews. I do not count myself among those who do. I had wonderful friends in Kiev who happened to be Jews. But to my great consternation, I have to confirm that in 1937 and 1938, the majority of interrogators in the NKVD were Jewish Communists, and if they happened to get their hands on a Ukrainian who spoke Ukrainian, then to them it was a foregone conclusion that this person was a Petliurist. He might have had nothing at all to do with Petliura in any way, but if he happened to speak Ukrainian, then he had to be a Petliurist and was tortured in hideous ways. Later, in 1939, after the Ukrainian intelligentsia had been destroyed at the hands of the Jews, it was their turn to be destroyed. All the Jewish interrogators were shot, destroyed."

[246]See Kuromiya, "Stalinist Terror in the Donbas."

[247]Nikol'skyi, "Ukraintsi Donechchyny, represovani v 1937–1938 rr.," p. 40, and "Obviniteli i obviniaemye," in *Vozvrashchenie imeni i chesti. Ocherki, vospominaniia, informatsionnye i spravochnye materialy* (Luhans'k, 1995), p. 284. See also Zinaida Lykholobova, "Naibil'sha 'chystka' v Donbasi," *Z arkhiviv VUChK-HPU-NKVD-KHB*, 1995, nos. 1–2, p. 184.

[248]See Kuromiya, "Stalin's Terror in the Donbas" for Donets'k, and *Prapor peremohy* (Luhans'k), 28 February and 14 October 1990, and *Komsomol'skaia znamia* (Kiev), 30 January, 29 May, and 14 September 1990 for Luhans'k, which suggest another several thousand corpses.

[249]GARF, f. 7523, op. 23, d. 56, ll. 91–92. When children went to school and found some-

Figure 6.5. Excavation of a mass burial site in Rutchenkove, Donets'k, 1989. From Donets'kyi kraieznavchyi muzei.

Vova Kozlov even forgot to mention his father's name. This letter was merely one of tens of thousands of such letters received by Krupskaia. She had little power. It is not clear whether this letter reached her at all. In any case, no action was taken. Kozlov's letter was simply archived.

Once, while reviewing a list of those to be executed, Stalin noted: "Who will remember all these scoundrels [*negadiai*] in ten–twenty years? Who remembers now the names of the boyars [Ivan] The Terrible removed? No one. . . . People must know: they remove their own enemies. In the end, each got what he deserved." Molotov then responded: "People understand [you], Iosif Vissarionovich, they understand and support [you]."[250] Ten years later, when he criticized Ivan the Terrible in a conversation with Sergei Eisenstein and Nikolai Cherkassov, Stalin was most likely justifying himself:

> Ivan the Terrible was very ruthless. One can show that he was ruthless. But you must show why IT WAS NECESSARY TO BE RUTHLESS. One of Ivan the Terrible's errors was that he failed to knife through five large feudal families. Had he wiped out these five families, there would have been no Time of Troubles. But Ivan the Terrible executed someone and then he felt

one absent, they immediately concluded that his or her father had been arrested. *Put' Oktiabria* (Tel'manovo), 24 February 1993.

[250] Volkogonov, *Triumf i tragediia*, p. 245.

Figure 6.6. Skulls of victims of the 1937–38 terror excavated in Rutchenkove, Donets'k, 1989. From Donets'kyi kraieznavchyi muzei.

sorry and prayed for a long time. God hindered him in this matter. Tsar Ivan should have been even more resolute.[251]

Clearly God did not hinder Stalin from being even more resolute than Ivan the Terrible.

[251] *Moscow News*, 1988, no. 32, p. 8 (a transcript of the conversation on 25 February 1947 by Eisenstein and Cherkassov, who played Ivan the Terrible in Eisenstein's film on the tsar). Emphasis in the original. Tucker has a detailed analysis of Ivan and Stalin in his *Stalin in Power*, pp. 276–82 and 482–86.

7   The War

HITLER DEEMED the Donbas with its mineral resources indispensable to his war efforts. The occupation of the Donbas in 1941 and 1942 followed a period of terror by the Soviet government, succeeded by further atrocities inflicted on the population by the occupation forces, and then again by the Soviet authorities after the German retreat. The war, however, created political alternatives to the Soviet government for those in occupied territory. Apart from the Communist (Soviet) and Nazi (German) ideologies, a third alternative – Ukrainian nationalism – entered the political scene in the Donbas. Yet the Donbas did not accept it unconditionally. Some of the Ukrainian nationalists dispatched to rally the Donbas instead converted themselves to a democratic conception of the body politic. The extreme conditions of war, which allowed for no neutrality, had created alternatives, all unsafe.

The Specter of War

The infamous Soviet-German agreement was a marriage of convenience. When the Molotov-Ribbentrop pact was signed in the Kremlin in August 1939, Stalin toasted Kaganovich, then people's commissar of transport. Like Stalin, Joachim von Ribbentrop walked up to Kaganovich and clinked glasses. Kaganovich, a Jew, enjoyed this bit of Stalin's mischief. When they left the banquet hall, Stalin told Kaganovich: "We have to gain time."[1]

To many others, however, the rapprochement was a surprise, a shock, and a betrayal. Up until that moment Stalin had had hundreds of thousands of people executed on charges of spying for Nazi Germany and Japan. Now Stalin had become Hitler's partner. Anti-Nazi propaganda disappeared from everywhere, including the Donbas.[2] *Sotsialisticheskii Donbass*, for example, reprinted the

---

[1] Feliks Chuev, *Tak govoril Kaganovich. Ispoved' stalinskogo apostola* (Moscow, 1992), p. 90.
[2] Everyone but one former Komsomol member I interviewed in the Donbas confirmed this

24 August 1939 *Pravda* editorial about the pact on 26 August not on the front page but on page two and with no comment at all.

One might well have asked who the real "enemies of the people" were, although there is little evidence that people were able to ask this question openly at the time. It was awkward at best for Stalin and others to urge the nation to do so. The hunt for "enemies of the people" (whatever the term might have meant) continued in a subdued fashion. Restoration of order and discipline became Stalin's chief concern, as is discussed later.

The threat from the East eased eventually: Japan decided to go south rather than north against the Soviet Union. The spring 1941 nonaggression treaty with Japan was a blessing for Stalin. Stalin was so pleased and so anxious for Japan to observe the treaty that he even took the trouble to see Japanese Foreign Minister Matsuoka off at a rail station. Such a courtesy surprised everyone present. Stalin is reported to have proclaimed to Matsuoka that they were both Asians. Then he embraced the German Ambassador Schulenberg and told the German military attaché Hans Krebs: "We will remain friends with you in any event."[3]

In August 1940 Stalin succeeded in eliminating his most dreaded political foe, Trotsky. Stalin had long feared that Trotsky would attempt a political comeback, particularly in the case of war, even if it meant allying with the devil.

By contrast, with the war threat looming ever larger, some of the bitterest enemies of Bolshevism came to regard Stalin, with awe and respect, as a statesman. Stalin's apparent identification with Russia and the Russian raison d'état disarmed many of his opponents. His brutal policy made him appear to them as a staunch defender of Russia's state interests. There had been a movement among the émigrés toward reconciliation with the Soviet Union since the 1920s. Now, as the very existence of Russia (which practically meant the Soviet Union) was being threatened, Stalin became the defender of its land. One of the best examples of rapprochement was Pavel Miliukov, formerly a Cadet leader and bitter enemy of Bolshevism, who came to accept Soviet Russia by the time the war broke out.[4]

Stalin must have asked himself, however, whether the people would fight

change. This Komsomol member also insisted that she was unaware of the terror of 1936–38. She admitted, however, that people simply disappeared, not an unusual phenomenon in the mobile Donbas. Interview 3.

[3] Adam B. Ulam, *Stalin: The Man and His Era* (New York, 1973), p. 532, and Isaac Deutscher, *Stalin: A Political Biography* (Oxford University Press, 1949), pp. 452–53. For Stalin's treatment of Matsuoka, see also *Sto sorok besed s Molotovym. Iz dnevnika F. Chueva* (Moscow, 1991), pp. 29–30.

[4] See Jens Petter Nielsen, *Miliukov i Stalin. O politicheskoi evoliutsii Miliukova v emigratsii (1918–1943)* (Oslo, 1983). Miliukov believed in the accusations against the defenders at the Moscow trials.

for him. The Molotov-Ribbentrop pact gave rise to disorientation and cynicism among soldiers. The Polish campaign of 1939 exposed Soviet soldiers to a different, "bourgeois" society, enticing them to make feverish purchases of "nonessential goods in large amounts, including alarm clocks, tablecloths, and ladies' shoes."[5] On the home front, the situation was not any better. In Slov'ians'k in the Donbas, for example, at the time of the Polish campaign, two Red Army soldiers who were posted to guard munitions to be shipped by rail disappeared with the munitions. They were never found.[6]

The Red Army did fight in the Winter War against Finland (November 1939–March 1940), but not very satisfactorily. After the war, the army was reorganized, and more traditional forms of military ranks were reintroduced. Harsh disciplinary measures were imposed, but their efficacy was questioned by military leaders. With the memory of the Great Terror still fresh, military commanders wavered between two extremes: on the one hand, the terror made them hesitant in applying disciplinary measures; on the other hand, fearful of being repressed for not being authoritarian enough, they applied punishment indiscriminately.[7]

In civilian as in military life, draconian regulations became the order of the day. In December 1938 dismissal and eviction from company housing became mandatory for three offenses of tardiness for work. In 1939 labor books were introduced to control the labor force. In June 1940 the much celebrated achievement of the Soviet system, the seven-hour working day, was abolished by fiat: the working day was increased to eight hours without any compensation. Moreover, the working population was chained to the workplace: leaving work without permission was outlawed, punishable by two to four years of imprisonment. Tardiness without permission also became a crime; offenders were subject to up to six months of corrective labor.[8] As if the law were not harsh enough, another order followed soon, stipulating even harsher measures for minor offenses.[9]

According to the people's commissar of armaments, this measure was demanded by industrial commissars who were not able to control the mobile labor force and enforce discipline at work. The Great Terror had had an adverse effect on the authority of commanders in the workplace. Stalin, according to B. L. Vannikov, people's commissar of armaments, reluctantly agreed to the

---

[5]Mark von Hagen, "Soviet Soldiers and Officers on the Eve of the German Invasion: Towards a Description of Social Psychology and Political Attitudes," *Soviet Union/Union Soviétique*, 18:1–3 (1991), pp. 98–99.

[6]RGVA, f. 25900, op. 6, d. 19, l. 216.

[7]O. S. Suvenirov, "Voinskaia distsiplina: uroki istorii. 'Prikaz otmeniat' ne budem," *Voenno-istoricheskii zhurnal*, 1989, no. 4, pp. 32–39.

[8]See O. Khlevniuk, "26 iiunia 1940 goda: illiuzii i real'nosti administrirovaniia," *Kommunist*, 1989, no. 9.

[9]*30-e gody. Vzgliad iz segodnia* (Moscow, 1990), p. 26.

new law.[10] Whatever the case, Stalin was aware that the sacrifices demanded of the working population could not be popular.[11]

Indeed, the laws were imposed on a population already struggling daily for survival under harsh living and working conditions. Molotov subsequently maintained that the government had demanded "colossal sacrifices of workers and peasants." People lived poorly, but all resources were spent on war preparations, and no housing construction was allowed. The workday was increased and the workers were bound to their workplace. The peasants were paid little for their labor and produce, because there was very little with which to pay them.[12]

Vladimir Bohdan recalls that at the end of the decade the Donbas coal-mining community

> teemed with all kinds of diseases. Sanitation facilities were nonexistent; there were no rest rooms. Food supplies were sporadic, and in wintertime vegetables and fruit became unobtainable. Scurvy, rickets, and other vitamin deficiency maladies killed children of all ages right and left. My younger sister, Natasha, caught a bad case of impetigo and her little body was covered with boils and ointment for two weeks before this contagious disease somehow bypassed the rest of our family. A 50 percent survival rate was considered good for most families.[13]

Poverty persisted. Bohdan's neighbor, Katerina Rykhina, had four children. They had no father, and Rykhina worked in a mine. The two little girls, Zoia and Marya,

> craved attention and had a remarkable talent for showing up to play at whatever house where the food was on the table for a meal, to which they hoped to be invited also. Their older brother, Elko, who was twelve, no doubt trained them in this art, at which he was also an expert. This youngster was the epitome of the survivor. He traded, borrowed, bullied, bought, stole, and did everything to help that family survive; and he had no qualms about doing it, either! My mother, and other people, had seen him at his machinations many times. Like the time he stole carrots and radishes from our neighbor old Evdokia. In spite of Evdokia's vigilance in sitting and watching her garden, Elko still got the vegetables right from under her nose. Watching from the side, my mother found it both amusing and heartrending to observe this struggle for survival.[14]

The life of women in the Donbas was particularly hard. At School 20 in Stalino, a child named Falin would always arrive in a slovenly state. His teacher

---

[10] B. L. Vannikov, "Iz zapisok narkoma," *Novaia i noveishaia istoriia*, 1988, no. 1, p. 88, and "Zapiski narkoma," *Znamia*, 1988, no. 2, pp. 148–49.

[11] See Khlevniuk, "26 iiunia 1940 goda," p. 88.

[12] *Sto sorok besed s Molotovym. Iz dnevnika F. Chueva* (Moscow, 1991), pp. 36–37.

[13] Vladimir A. Bohdan, *Avoiding Extinction: Children of the Kulak* (New York, 1992), p. 38.

[14] Ibid., pp. 41–42.

summoned his mother, Falina. Falina told the teacher that she worked all day, that she had six children, and that she had little time to look after him. The teacher blamed Falina: "Why did you bear so many children and bring them up to beg?" Falina angrily responded that she had already had twelve abortions (some of which were no doubt illegal, because abortion was banned in 1936). She was told that she should have had more abortions.[15]

As military expenditures increased, food supplies declined. This, too, adversely affected labor discipline. In April 1940, shortly before the June law was enacted, the commissar of coal mining V. Bakhrushev bitterly complained to the government that the food supply in the Donbas was too unreliable for labor to be stable. Since January, almost no macaroni, groats, flour, or buns had been available. Some of the working families did not even have bread. At the canteen of Mine 5 in Artemivs'k, for example, the main course consisted of tea. Bakhrushev warned that such a state of affairs had created an "unsound mood among the workers."[16] Bakhrushev then traveled to the Donbas, whence he bombarded Moscow with telegrams requesting a large sum of money (many colliers had not received their wages for some time) and various material supplies to keep production going.[17]

The June 1940 law, discussed earlier, had a devastating effect everywhere. An acute observer in Moscow has noted:

> The factory directors were in a panic of terror themselves. The number of those prosecuted or condemned to disciplinary educational work reached astronomical figures. . . . These events [violations of labor legislation] came to occupy so central a position in the life of every inhabitant of the Soviet Union that others were hardly noticed at all. The collapse of France, the air battles over England, the occupation of the Baltic States by Soviet forces and their conversion into Republics of the U.S.S.R., the annexation of Bessarabia and the northern part of Bukovina to the Soviet Union – all paled into insignificance in comparison with the struggle against so-called shirkers, idlers and disruptive elements.[18]

For fear of tardiness, people would dash into the streets at night to ask the time of someone who happened to pass by.[19] The same was almost certainly true of the Donbas.

In fact, within two months, as many as 12,150 people were sent to the court in Stalino *oblast'* alone, in accordance with the June 1940 law. Of them, 1,049 were imprisoned and 7,440 were sent to corrective labor with a 25 percent

[15]DADO, f. 424p, op. 1, spr. 172, ark. 3–4.
[16]RGAE, f. 8225, op. 1, d. 83, ll. 7–11.
[17]Ibid., f. 8225, op. 1, d. 805, ll. 3–40, and d. 153, ll. 12–18.
[18]Wolfgang Leonhard, *Child of the Revolution*, tr. C. M. Woodhouse (London, 1957), pp. 93–94.
[19]*30-e gody*, p. 36.

pay cut.[20] Thousands of surface workers were forced to work underground as punishment.[21] This could not have improved worker safety, a perennial problem in the Donbas. How many more people were punished in the Donbas after the summer of 1940 is not known. In the country as a whole, from June 1940 till June 1941 3 million people, or approximately 8 percent of the working population, were prosecuted; of them half a million were sentenced to imprisonment.[22]

This was a massive repression by any standard. It has been argued, most notably by Donald Filtzer, that managers, judges, and prosecutors often conspired to circumvent this unreasonably harsh law.[23] Both the press and archives provide ample evidence of this.[24] With labor in short supply, industry could not afford to lose people for minor offenses. (N. M. Ivantsova, a member of the future "Young Guard" partisan group in Krasnodon, testified that her father, a deputy director of Mine 1bis, was arrested in September 1940 for protecting tardy workers. He was given two years of forced labor at a factory in Voroshylovhrad. Then he was taken elsewhere. Ivantsova never saw her father again.)[25] Managers, judges, and prosecutors, like military commanders, had to protect themselves from possible repression. Ivantsova's father had been lenient, but other bosses punished all of their workers for fear of being accused of "rotten liberalism." Often the same person went from one extreme to the other, a tendency that had long been displayed by people in responsible positions who feared taking responsibility.[26] There is ample evidence in the press and archives of widespread abuse of power. In August 1940 at the Dzerzhyns'k Mine in Dzerzhyns'k, for example, the director Trofimov sent the machine operator Starovoitov to court for violation of labor discipline. Starovoitov was ill in the hospital at the time. Still he was sentenced to a year of imprisonment. When he came back to work after recovery, he was arrested and put in jail. At the same mine, a hewer was given four days of leave for his wife's illness. He had to absent himself two extra days to bury her. He did so with permission.

---

[20]DADO, f. 326p, op. 1, spr. 1763, ark. 1–2.

[21]RGAE, f. 8225, op. 1, d. 150, l. 4.

[22]Oleg Khlevniuk, "Prinuditel'nyi trud v ekonomike SSSR. 1921–1941 gody," *Svobodnaia mysl'*, 1992, no. 13, p. 81, and "GULAG v gody Velikoi Otechestvennoi voiny," *Voenno-istoricheskii zhurnal*, 1991, no. 6, p. 17. For a detailed analysis of the "criminalization of labor infractions," see Peter H. Solomon Jr., *Soviet Criminal Justice under Stalin* (Cambridge University Press, 1996), ch. 9.

[23]Donald Filtzer, *Soviet Workers and Stalinist Industrialization: The Formation of Modern Soviet Production Relations, 1928–1941* (Armonk, N.Y., 1986).

[24]See *Sotsialisticheskii Donbass*, summer–autumn 1940, and GARF, f. 8225, op. 1, d. 150, ll. 6–7.

[25]DALO, f. 179p, op. 4v, spr. 4501, ark. 4.

[26]See Hiroaki Kuromiya, "*Edinonachalie* and the Soviet Industrial Manager, 1928–1937," *Soviet Studies*, 36: 2 (April 1984).

Yet the court sentenced him to four months of imprisonment.[27] Such cases were common.[28]

As a result of the June 1940 law, many migrant workers began to boycott the Donbas, severely curtailing the flow of labor from traditional suppliers in Russia and Ukraine. From the first to the second half of 1940, the labor supply declined sharply by a factor of three to one.[29] The Donbas badly needed workhands. Facing boycott by the Russian and Ukrainian heartland, the Donbas managers turned to the newly annexed areas. In the second half of 1940, as many as 38,000 came to work in the Donbas from Bessarabia and the northern Bukovina. Many did not understand Russian and, as a result, frequently fell victim to the June 1940 law. Of 13,023 for whom there are statistics, 3,238 were prosecuted for the violation of the June 1940 order, with 2,076 given a prison sentence. Managers often failed to explain safety rules to the newcomers, and therefore accidents, including fatal ones, were frequent among them.[30] This was a baptism by fire for the new Soviet citizens.

Thousands of new arrivals from western Ukraine fared no better in the Donbas.[31] After 1933, people of western Ukrainian origin were politically suspect almost by default and untold numbers of them had perished because of their origins alone. Now they, like those from Bessarabia and the northern Bukovina, were needed for labor in the Donbas. These new arrivals were closely watched by the police, for fear of Ukrainian nationalist influence. (The Donbas police continued to repress Ukrainians, though in a more circumspect fashion than just a few years earlier. For example, a teacher and a longtime resident of Makiivka, Arsen Pogorodnyi, was a loyal Stalinist and supporter of the death penalty for "enemies of the people," right up until his arrest in 1940, when he was accused of belonging to the Union for the Liberation of Ukraine [SVU] and of wearing a Ukrainian embroidered shirt.)[32] Like their fellow workers from Bessarabia and the northern Bukovina, the western Ukrainians soon fell victim to the harshness and brutality of life in the Donbas. "After the initial wave, voluntary departures [from western Ukraine to the Donbas] ceased, and soon a mocking rhyme about the experience became part of street folklore: 'Hopsa sasa do Donbasa, a z Donbasa na golasa [Hey, ho, cheerfully to Donbas, and from Donbas back – stripped naked].' "[33]

[27]TsKhSD, f. 6, op. 6, d. 592, l. 34.

[28]See, for example, DADO, f. 326p, op. 1, spr. 1765, ark. 17.

[29]RGAE, f. 8225, op. 1, d. 700, l. 16.

[30]TsKhSD, f. 6, op. 6, d. 593, ll. 1–6.

[31]See numerous reports in *Sotsialisticheskii Donbass*, for example, 26 October, 1 November, and 3 December 1939.

[32]"Spovid' staroho vchytelia," *Donechchyna* (Donets'k), 26 November 1992.

[33]Jan T. Gross, *Revolution from Abroad: The Soviet Conquest of Poland's Western Ukraine and Western Belorussia* (Princeton University Press, 1988), p. 192. Apart from the voluntary arrivals, there were numerous involuntary departures to the east. About 10% of the population

Neither was the new, harsh order a cause for celebration among the Soviet population, despite press reports of the working population welcoming the June 1940 law. A collier named Bogovolov at Mine 8 in Horlivka was reported to have openly declared that "At the end of April [1940] they raised output quotas, in mid-May they raised food prices, and in June they increased the working hours. Here is the face of our rulers. They are the same capitalists as those who were here before 1917."[34] It is not clear whether this remark was fabricated. If that is the case, the informers knew what the authorities expected of them. The rulers were well aware that the new order was harsh and feared and expected such sentiments arising among the population.

Political sentiments were not allowed to surface openly among the population. Yet there is evidence of their existence. People sang about the Molotov-Ribbentrop pact which deprived them of much of their produce which was being sent to Germany:

> Ukraine is arable [*khliborobna*]
> She has given grain to the Germans
> And herself goes hungry.[35]

In her memoirs of the period Halina Ruscheva, whose father was a chauffeur for Ia. S. Gugel' (former director of Azov Steel) and was repressed in 1937 along with Gugel', recalls singing a song praising Stalin in a school choir. She sang the song to her mother (who had survived by changing her identity) at home. Her mother turned pale, clutched her shoulders, and said: "Never sing about Stalin. He destroyed your father. He destroyed our life as well."[36]

Stalin's terror did not help the nation to prepare for war. Nor did the Molotov-Ribbentrop pact. "Enemies of the people" were still being arrested and many executed. By then people almost certainly had asked themselves, if

in western Ukraine and western Belarus was repressed for political reasons between 1939 and 1941; most of those repressed were forcibly deported to the east (Kazakhstan and elsewhere). All nationalities were affected in this wave of repression. (See V. S. Parsadanova, "Deportatsiia naseleniia iz Zapadnoi Ukrainy i Zapadnoi Belorussii v 1939–1941 gg.," *Novaia i noveishaia istoriia*, 1989, no. 2, p. 44, and Iu. I. Shapoval, *U ti trahichni roky. Stalinizm na Ukraini* [Kiev, 1990], p. 128.) Among them were 15,000 Polish military officers and police officials; several thousands were interned in Starobil's'k in the northern Donbas. They were executed summarily in the spring of 1940. The more famous massacre took place in Katyn near Smolensk. (See *Katynskaia drama. Kozel'sk, Starobel'sk, Ostashkov: sud'ba internirovannykh pol'skikh voennosluzhashchikh* [Moscow, 1991]). Disenchantment with Soviet life was such that even "large masses of Jews" who fled to the Soviet zone from the advancing German forces subsequently chose to return to the former Polish territory occupied by the openly anti-Semitic German forces. See Gross, *Revolution from Abroad*, pp. 206–7.

[34]DADO, f. 326p, op. 1, spr. 1765, ark. 5.

[35]James E. Mace and Leonid Heretz, eds., *Oral History Project of the Commission on the Ukrainian Famine* (Washington, D.C., 1990), 2:1165. The word *khliborobna* could be a typographical error for *khliborodna*. In that case, this line should be "Ukraine is fertile."

[36]See her memoir in *Priazovskii rabochii* (Mariupol'), 16 April 1989.

not in public, then in private, who the enemies of the people were if they were not German spies. Stalin did not publicly address this awkward question. Yet the implication of the political repression of "enemies of the people" was that the enemies were not patriots but traitors. The issues patriotism posed were many for Stalin and the Bolshevik party. For example, during a "political conversation" just ten days before the war with Germany broke out, a Communist and NKVD official named Shatilov in Krasnodon declared in response to a question about the Bolsheviks and the "imperialist war" of 1914: "The Bolsheviks supported the war."[37] The police report pointed out that this showed how ignorant some Communists were. Shatilov was not entirely wrong because not all Bolsheviks had opposed the war. Yet it is quite probable that this question was meant as a provocation and that Shatilov was trying to protect himself. Had he told the truth, he might well have been accused of propagating defeatism, this time a defeat not of tsarist Russia but of Stalin's Russia.

War and Occupation

German troops invaded the Soviet Union on 22 June 1941 in violation of the Soviet-German nonaggression pact. War with an external enemy provided the ultimate test for distinguishing friends from foes within the country. The test seemed straightforward enough: would one fight for or against the enemy? In fact, the test was much more complicated. The war proved to be extraordinarily brutal both at the front and on the home front. The entire Donbas was occupied by enemy forces, and its population suffered from violence by both sides.

The Germans advanced quickly. The initial stage of the war was a disaster for the Soviet forces. Stalin had a number of military commanders executed for the debacle.[38] Between 22 June and 10 October 1941, 657,364 military servicemen who left or deserted their units were detained by the NKVD. Some sought a haven in the Donbas by working in collieries. Most deserters were sent back to the front, but 25,875 were arrested on various charges (espionage, diversion, treachery, desertion, etc.). Of those arrested, as many as 10,201 were executed, 3,321 in front of the ranks.[39]

As the Red Army retreated, many important cities fell one after another. Kiev fell on 19 September 1941, and by the end of September the two capitals

---

[37]DALO, f. P-179, op. 3, spr. 48, ark. 2 and 8.

[38]I. I. Kuznetsov, "Generaly 1940 goda," *Voenno-istoricheskii zhurnal*, 1988, no. 10, pp. 31–32, and *Skrytaia pravda voiny: 1941 god. Neizvestnye dokumenty* (Moscow, 1992), pp. 343–45 (which lists the names of the repressed).

[39]See an archival document quoted in *Rodina*, 1993, no. 4, p. 78. For cases of their hiding in the Donbas, see DALO, f. 3747, op. 3, spr. 608-p.

were in danger of direct attack by German forces. In October, much of the government evacuated to Kuibyshev. The German advancement, particularly in Ukraine, was aided in part by the large number of residents who welcomed the enemy forces. This was particularly true in western Ukraine, which had recently been incorporated into the Soviet Union, and where the Ukrainian nationalists had deeper roots among the population than in the Soviet east. The repression that had followed the incorporation did not help the residents to adapt to the Soviet regime, a difficult proposition to begin with. The massacres the Soviet secret police committed before retreating further east only benefited the German forces and their allies (Hungarian, Rumanian, and Italian troops). In L'viv alone, well over 10,000 were said to have been executed by the Soviets.[40]

The occupiers proved to be no less brutal and savage than the Soviets, however. No doubt Nazi racist ideology contributed to the atrocities committed by the Germans.[41] The most notable of their crimes was the infamous Babi Yar (Babyn Iar) massacre: on 29–30 September alone 33,371 Jews were executed in the Babi Yar ravine in Kiev, and tens of thousands more Jews, Gypsies, and others were subjected to the same fate in the days following.[42] The Ukrainian nationalists, most of whom had supported the German forces initially, soon had to face a harsh reality. Their dreams of an independent Ukraine were dashed by the Germans and many were arrested or forced to go underground.[43]

The initial reaction of the Soviet population to the war was generally positive from the government's point of view. Although the outbreak of war did cause a run on the market and, as in 1914, there were many instances of drinking binges, the mood among the mobilized was said to be "brave and confident." Many women asked to enlist, and some mines and factories in Voroshylovhrad were not able to replace the mobilized men, which led to a slowdown in production output.[44] Patriotism, particularly Russian patriotism, became a catchphrase for the war effort. The government called the war

[40] Gross, *Revolution from Abroad*, pp. 179–81.

[41] For this, see Omer Bartov, *The Eastern Front, 1941–45: German Troops and the Barbarisation of Warfare* (London, 1985). For German occupation in general, see the most detailed treatment by Alexander Dallin, *German Rule in Russia, 1941–1945: A Study of Occupation Policies*, 2nd ed. (Boulder, Colo., 1981).

[42] For an absorbing account of this event, see A. Anatoli (Kuznetsov), *Babi Yar: A Document in the Form of a Novel*, tr. David Floyd (New York, 1970). For recent documents, see "Babyn Iar (veresen' 1941–veresen' 1943 rr.)," *Ukrains'kyi istorychnyi zhurnal*, 1991, nos. 9 and 12.

[43] See John A. Armstrong, *Ukrainian Nationalism*, 3rd ed. (Englewood, Colo., 1990). For the relations between Germany and Ukraine during the war, see Volodymyr Kosyk, *Ukraina i Nimechchyna u druhii svitovii viini* (Paris, 1993).

[44] *Izvestiia TsK KPSS*, 1990, no. 6, p. 211 (28 June 1941 report). Within ten days of the outbreak, as many as 240,000 men, or nearly 8% of the 1939 population, of Stalino *oblast'*, went to the front. Of them 42,000 were party members and 97,000 Komsomol ones. See *Sil'ska Donechchyna*, 7 June 1991.

the "Great Patriotic War" after the "Patriotic War" in which the Russians had defeated the Napoleonic invaders. Even in Ukraine, Ukrainianness came to be emphasized by the party. On 6 July 1941, for example, three days after Stalin's famous speech, Khrushchev, an ethnic Russian and then the Ukrainian party leader, addressed the Ukrainians "Comrades, workers, peasants, and intelligentsia of the great Ukrainian people": "Brothers and Sisters! Sons and daughters of great Ukraine!"[45]

Perhaps surprisingly, the Gulag population also appears to have stood behind the government. According to reports from the Gulags, only an insignificant part of those incarcerated in the labor camps hoped to be released by the Germans; patriotism prevailed among the majority of the Gulag population.[46] It is instructive that the productivity of Gulag labor in 1943 increased by 80 percent from 1941 and doubled in 1944 in comparison with 1941.[47] During the war, as many as 975,000 prisoners were transferred to the Red Army from the Gulags, including 43,000 Poles and 10,000 Czechoslovaks who then formed their own national military units.[48] At the same time, the execution of political prisoners accelerated in the autumn of 1941.[49]

Stalin may have privately wondered whether he had had too many people executed and arrested. Yet he may also have felt reassured that no serious uprisings against the Soviet government took place at the outbreak of the war. In the virtual information blackout, however, rumors circulated everywhere. Some were openly anti-Soviet and anti-Semitic. Many were fabricated, but it also appears certain that there were people who entertained doubts about Stalin and his leadership.[50] When war broke out, an elderly mechanic in Slov'ians'k angrily intimated to his friend that the country's leaders were "brave and courageous [only] when they fight with us [people]."[51] Then he shut up. He was

---

[45]TsDAHO, f. 1, op. 23, spr. 17, ark. 11–15.

[46]V. N. Zemskov, "GULAG (istoriko-sotsiologicheskii aspekt)," *Sotsiologicheskie issledovaniia*, 1991, no. 6, p. 25. There was a report that anti-Soviet activity within the Gulags became "significantly active" since the first days of the war. The Gulag authorities actively recruited inmates as informers. Hundreds of "insurgent" groups were exposed. See "Gulag v gody voiny," *Istoricheskii arkhiv*, 1994, no. 3, pp. 74–78, and Edwin Bacon, *The Gulag at War: Stalin's Forced Labour System in the Light of the Archives* (London, 1994), pp. 155–56. For concrete cases, see *Resistance in the Gulag: Memoirs, Letters, Documents* (Moscow, 1992), pp. 72–76 and 84–87.

[47]"GULAG v gody Velikoi Otechestvennoi voiny," p. 22.

[48]"Gulag v gody voiny," pp. 64–65.

[49]P. N. Knyshevskii, "Gosudarstvennyi komitet oborony: metody mobilizatsii trudovykh resursov," *Voprosy istorii*, 1994, no. 2, p. 55.

[50]For the popular mood in Moscow, see "Moskva voennaia. 1941 god. . . . (novye istochniki iz sekretnykh arkhivnykh fondov)," *Istoriia SSSR*, 1991, no. 6; "Iz istorii Velikoi Otechestvennoi voiny," *Izvestiia TsK KPSS*, 1991, no. 4, pp. 210–14; and John Barber, "Popular Reactions in Moscow to the German Invasion of June 22, 1941," *Soviet Union/Union Soviétique*, 1991, nos. 1–3.

[51]Hryhorii Kostiuk, *Zustrichi i proshchannia. Spohady. Knyha persha* (Edmonton, Canada,

Figure 7.1. Peasants returning to their village burned down by the German Luftwaffe, Luhans'k *oblast'*, 15 August 1941. From DALO, f. P-7118, op. 1, spr. 702.

fortunate because his friend did not inform on him. Yet many others were not as fortunate. Stalin's logic was consistent: he sacrificed all 100 if he suspected that there were 5 enemies among them. The number of death sentences against political criminals increased sharply from 1,649 in 1940 to 8,011 in 1941 and to 23,278 in 1942.[52] Nevertheless, these numbers were far lower than those of 1937–38.

Had the Red Army repelled the enemy, the Soviet population would have had little opportunity for considering its own fate and that of their country. The contrary was the case. The Germans and their allies rapidly advanced on the Donbas. According to General Eric von Manstein, the Donbas had a special significance in Hitler's mind: the Donbas had "played a fundamental part in Hitler's operational calculations as far back as 1941, for he considered possession of it to be of vital importance to the outcome of the war." The Germans "extracted substantial quantities of Donetz [Donbas] coal for our own [i. e., German] use," but "all the bunker coal for the railway supplying this vast territory had to be brought out from Germany because Donetz coal did not suit

1987), p. 682.
    [52] V. P. Popov, "Gosudarstvennyi terror v sovetskoi Rossii. 1923–1953 gg. (istochniki i ikh interpretatsiia)," *Otechestvennye arkhivy*, 1992, no. 2, p. 28.

our [German] locomotives." The fighting capability of the Soviet forces even long after much of the Donbas was lost failed to dissuade Hitler from his belief in the absolute importance of the Donbas to the German war effort.[53] Whatever the case, Stalino, the city that bore the name of Hitler's archenemy, fell to the Germans on 20 October 1941 and Artemivs'k on 31 October. Voroshylovhrad and its surrounding areas withstood German attacks longer, but the city fell on 17 July 1942 and Krasnodon on 20 July.

The advance of the Germans provided the Donbas population, like that of other occupied areas, with political alternatives, options of which the Soviet population as a whole had long been deprived. In Slov'ans'k, where more ethnic Russians than Ukrainians lived, one former political activist recalled that there was no one inclined to defend the country.[54] Clearly this is an exaggeration, but as the Germans approached the Donbas in September, people began to take actions that had been inconceivable just a few months earlier.

On 1 September, at the Komsomolets Mine in Horlivka, bread rationing was introduced. For various reasons some workers were left without coupons. Angry workers and their wives demanded bread. They began to break the windows of the party committee office and attacked the assistant party organizer Karpetchenko, who was seriously injured and taken to the hospital. On 3 September similar disturbances took place at the Lenin Mine 5 in Artemivs'k. Wives of workers who had been sent to "special tasks" (most likely construction works) at the front demanded food ration cards. The women, with the help of a few men, began to destroy the flat of the party organizer Leonov. Leonov and the mine director Larchenko were beaten by the group. The party organizations of both mines failed to keep the workers informed of the internal and international situation and to explain to the women why their men were being sent to the front lines. Moreover, the officials introduced the ration cards without warning and at night. The women's actions were said to have been incited by kulaks and criminal elements. The NKVD arrested four at Komsomolets and seven at the Lenin Mine. Their fate is unknown.[55]

In some collieries, workers and housewives dared to remove explosives implanted in the mines by their bosses in preparation for German advancement and thus prevented the destruction of their workplace. At the Kam'ianka (Kamenka) Mine in Kadiivka, a group of angry workers attacked the mine director and the city NKVD official. At Mine 1bis, colliers and housewives destroyed a warehouse, a vegetable storage, a hospital, and crèches, places frequented by their bosses. Some of the ringleaders were alleged to be kulaks and criminals

[53]Erich von Manstein, *Lost Victories*, ed. and tr. Anthony G. Powell, with a foreword by B. H. Liddell Hart (London, 1958), pp. 399 and 412.

[54]Ivan Maistrenko, *Istoriia moho pokolinnia. Spohady uchasnyka revoliutsiinykh podii v Ukraini* (Edmonton, Canada, 1985), pp. 327–28.

[55]TsDAHO, f. 1, op. 23, spr. 47, ark. 14, and RTsKhIDNI, f. 17, op. 22, d. 3420, ll. 307–12.

and were executed. On 21 October, the leaders of the city Horlivka panicked in the face of advancing German forces and left the city immediately. They did so after blowing up a bread factory and flour storages, leaving the population to starve.[56]

In the Donbas countryside, the farmers took actions of their own. In the villages near Krasnyi Lyman, for example, an order was given to evacuate within twenty-four hours, but no transport was provided. All of the livestock of the collective farms was evacuated by the army as if it were more important than the humans. "Counterrevolutionary, anti-Soviet elements" took advantage of the situation, mobilized the farmers, and attacked the policemen and the army officers. The ringleaders were executed.[57] Similar incidents took place in various other districts and villages.[58]

When enemy forces were rapidly advancing on the coveted Donbas, two divisions made up of colliers (in all likelihood elderly workers) for the defense of the Donbas mutinied. The armed miners returned home. It was said that the rebellion facilitated the entry of Italian forces into Stalino *oblast'* on 15 September 1941.[59]

Popular actions against Soviet officials and their neglect of citizens' needs took place elsewhere as well, most notably in Ivanovo at that time (in September–October 1941).[60] Yet the grave situation in the Donbas disquieted Moscow so much that the Central Committee of the party sent its representatives there. They found the Donbas far from reorganized in a wartime fashion. The party leadership was weak, and "In the *oblast'* and districts," their report emphasized, "there isn't [a strong] enough dictatorship, or resolute power; there isn't enough organization and discipline; there are many meetings but there is little [assumption of] responsibility for the execution of decisions by the center or for their own decisions."[61]

It was not that repressive measures were not applied in the Donbas. In fact, many of the alleged ringleaders of the disturbances described earlier were executed. There were many other cases of savage terror against the population. In the summer of 1941, P. I. Vasil'ev, a railway inspector in Krasnyi Lyman, was sentenced to be shot for "provocative rumors about workers' living conditions in the USSR" and for comparing labor in the USSR to serfdom and

---

[56]"U rik vazhkykh vyprobuvan': svidchat' dokumenty," *Arkhivy Ukrainy*, 1991, no. 2, p. 13.

[57]TsDAHO, f. 1, op. 23, spr. 195, ark. 10–12.

[58]Ibid., ark. 6–8.

[59]Tamara Saidak, "Donets'kyi kriazh. Spohad pro pidpil'nykiv," *Ukrains'ki visti* (Neu Ulm, Germany), 15 August 1954, p. 3.

[60]See "Smiatenie oseni sorok pervogo goda. Dokumenty o volneniiakh ivanovskikh tekstil'shchikov," *Istoricheskii arkhiv*, 1994, no. 2, pp. 111–36, and G. A. Bordiugov, "Velikaia Otechestvennaia: podvig i obmanutye nadezhdy," *Istoriia otechestva: liudi, idei, resheniia. Ocherki istorii Sovetskogo gosudarstva* (Moscow, 1991), pp. 259–62.

[61]See the 4 October 1941 report to Stalin in *Izvestiia TsK KPSS*, 1990, no. 12, pp. 208–9.

appealing to workers for collective protest. Another railway worker Pan'kov was also sentenced to be executed in the summer for his "counterrevolutionary agitation of a defeatist nature" regarding the invincibility of Hitler's army.[62] In the summer of 1941, when the Red Army was retreating, two workers of retirement age in a Luhans'k factory drank and discussed the war situation on a payday. They sung:

> Our pilots are brave,
> But our planes are paper-made. . . . [63]

The two were given ten years. In August A. F. Pervoi, a schoolchild at Middle School 37 in Stalino, was arrested. Pervoi was alleged to have told his friend to remove Stalin's portrait, circulated rumors that the Soviet government would fall, and praised Germany. Pervoi was in fact a believer in Stalin. The accusations had been fabricated by a girl who was angry with him. Pervoi was tortured but did not plead guilty. He was sentenced to death, in any case, but by miracle his sentence was commuted to ten years in labor camp. He was sent to Siberia ten days before Stalino fell. He survived the war there.[64] Faced with the question of life or death as the Germans advanced, the Moscow representatives seemed to believe that terror was the only solution.

Here and there the party began to lose authority. There were numerous cases of party members destroying their cards or refusing to serve in the Red Army.[65] At the Ordzhonikidze Mine in Makiivka, in September the majority of party activists were mobilized for the military. Nevertheless, their absence from the mines in a time of great danger aroused suspicion among the workers. Ever since the outbreak of war, the secretary of the party district committee had failed to show up in the office or at meetings. When rumor circulated that the party organizer Kuznetsov (who had indeed been mobilized for special tasks) had abandoned the mine, fifteen to twenty women came to Kuznetsov's wife to confirm the rumor. They began to knock on the door and windows and were dispersed by the police. The Komsomol was described as nonexistent as an organization. At the mine, only a sick girl remained in the Komsomol and no one else was to be seen. One party candidate was reported to have refused to pay his party membership fee: "What a fool I am, why did I join the party at all?" Another candidate: "I left my candidate membership card at home and my baby tore it up, so I ask the party to expel me."[66]

In Makiivka, Kostiantynivka, and Kramators'k, many workers, hungry for

[62] *Istochnik*, 1994, no. 5, pp. 108–9.

[63] "Nashi letchiki otvazhnye, / A samoletichi bumazhnye. . . . " Henadyi Kravchenko, "A u khati – smert' ta holod . . . ," in *Novosti i sobytiia* (Donets'k), no. 21 (July 1993), p. 4. The two were Kravchenko's neighbors.

[64] *Vechernii Donets'k*, 1 September 1989.

[65] See, for example, DALO, f. P-179, op. 1, spr. 250, ark. 24, spr. 247 and 248.

[66] DADO, f. 326p, op. 1, spr. 1897, ark. 2–3.

information on the war, would appear at meetings, but the party secretaries failed to appear. Panic prevailed, and many questions were raised: "Why don't they evacuate our children? Do they really mean to get away at the last moment and leave us to the looters?" In Debal'tseve, the city prosecutor was closely watched by everyone. When it was known that he had instructed a chauffeur to have a lorry ready at all times near his house, there was much resentment. In the city, a large, highly desirable apartment building where many city dignitaries had lived was now empty, because the residents had left for smaller flats so as not to be so visible. When one boss evacuated his family, an uproar arose. It was reported that the situation was demoralizing even party members. In Slov'ians'k, the secretary of the city party committee Poliakov went around to the flats of Communists, asking whether they were pickling vegetables for the winter. A negative answer meant that the Communist planned to evacuate. When a Communist pickled vegetables, then his neighbors followed his example.[67]

It was a fact that families of local Donbas dignitaries were evacuated first and that the local authorities abused their power to supply their families in refuge with foodstuffs designated for the local residents. Naturally the people left behind were angry.[68]

Not surprisingly, the evacuation of factories in the Donbas went poorly[69] and much energy was spent on the destruction both of the industrial plants and of the prisoners held in the Donbas. In Stalino explosions of mines and factories continued incessantly for three days from 19 October.[70] One witness recalled: "Another rumble shook the ground around Cold Ravine [name of a mine] as black smoke billowed up with fresh intensity. We didn't see any fire, just smoke. You could actually see the glow at night, but in daylight only smoke was visible."[71]

At Mine 4/21 in Stalino, workers, women (many of whose husbands were at the front), and children protested the mining of their coalfields. NKVD forces and Red Army soldiers were called in. The soldiers refused to shoot, so the NKVD detachment fired at the protestors. Mass arrests followed. Among them was an elderly collier named Nikulin. When he asked an NKVD man for a cigarette, he was shot dead on the spot. Many of the arrested were taken farther from the front to Voroshylovhrad. Along with an estimated fifteen hundred prisoners (mostly Red Army deserters and soldiers who complained about

[67] Ibid., ark. 5, 9, 13, 14–15.

[68] See, for example, Mykhailo Kobal' and Liudmyla Kondratenko, "Komu viina, a komu . . . ," *Vitchyzna*, 1996, nos. 1-2, pp. 112–13.

[69] See G. A. Kumanev, "Sovetskaia ekonomika i evakuatsiia 1941 goda," *Soviet Union/Union Soviétique*, 1991, nos. 1–3, p. 170. See also *Komsomolets Donbassa*, 6 May 1990.

[70] *Donetskii vestnik*, 22 January, 12 February, and 14 June 1942.

[71] Bohdan, *Avoiding Extinction*, p. 48. For another eyewitness account, see Louis Ernst, "Inside a Soviet Industry," *Fortune* (Chicago), October 1949, p. 177.

the lack of munitions), they were executed before the Soviet forces retreated from the city.[72] In Stalino itself, the killing of prisoners (among whom were Stakhanovites) continued for several nights in October 1941. Among the killed were also wounded Red Army soldiers who could not be evacuated.[73] One resident later recalled:

> In this city in the NKVD prison factory the communists executed 180 persons and buried them in two holes dug in the prison yard. The corpses were liberally treated with unslaked lime, especially the faces.
>
> My brother was sentenced to three months in jail for coming late to work. After serving 18 days in the factory prison he was set free, and a month later was drafted into the Red Army because this was in July 1941.
>
> Later, his wife and my mother found him among the corpses, identifying him by the left hand finger, underwear and papers he had on him.[74]

Some Stalino prisoners were taken to Snizhne in the east of Stalino, away from the approaching Germans. Under armed escort they were transported to a gully where they were forced to dig holes. (A witness, then a boy, recalls their tormented and sad faces even today.) Then they were shot.[75]

Most Stalino residents refused, or at least were unable, to leave their city.[76] The evacuation of the Soviet forces and local authorities created "complete panic and disorder everywhere."[77] Many residents came out to the streets in hopes of finding foodstuffs and were shot by drunkards and policemen roaming the city. Once all the authorities disappeared, "open looting and banditry" by marauders and hooligans ensued.[78] According to one witness in Slov'ians'k, they destroyed everything just as the Soviets had done before they retreated.[79] The same scenes of looting and disorder were seen in other Donbas cities as well. Those who remained were regarded by the authorities as

[72] Note the story by A. T. Tyzhnenko (who was arrested, then shot along with others, and yet survived by feigning death) in *Donetskii vestnik*, 23 November 1941. See also *Luganskaia pravda*, 8 July 1990.

[73] *Vechernii Donetsk*, 2 March and 15 September 1990. See also *Donetskii vestnik*, 22 August 1942.

[74] Andriy Vodopyan, "Crime in Staline," in *The Black Deeds of the Kremlin: A White Book*, vol. 1, *Book of Testimonies* (Toronto, 1953), p. 121.

[75] *Zven'ia*, vol. 1 (Moscow, 1991), p. 44.

[76] For a case of refusal in the Donbas, see Mace and Heretz, *Oral History Project*, 2:877. For a vivid description of the occupation, see N. N. Kozlova and I. I. Sandomirskaia, *"Ia tak khochu nazvat' kino." "Naivnoe pis'mo": Opyt lingvo-sotsiologicheskogo chteniia* (Moscow, 1996), pp. 89ff.

[77] AUSBUDO, no. 35462-pf, t. 2, ark. 430zv.

[78] *Donetskii vestnik*, 15 November 1941 and 22 January 1942. Some of these may have been common criminals from the western parts where they fled from prison in the confusion of the evacuation. See V. M. Kuritsyn, "Prava i svobody grazhdan v gody Velikoi Otechestvennoi voiny," *Sovteskoe gosudarstvo i pravo*, 1987, no. 5, p. 129.

[79] Maistrenko, *Istoriia moho pokoliniia*, p. 332.

"traitors" and were terrorized by remaining Soviet units ("partisans").[80] Whatever the case, of the 465,000 people of the city of Stalino, according to the city authorities under German occupation, no more than 65,000 left the city.[81]

When the German forces came, many residents were said to have welcomed them in Stalino and elsewhere.[82] At least, according to some firsthand accounts, people hoped to live under the Germans. As soon as the Germans and their allied forces arrived, however, they rounded up a large number of men. The Russians and Jews never came back. Many ethnic Ukrainians, whom the occupiers considered more politically sympathetic toward themselves, were identified and then released.[83]

The Donbas, unlike much of Ukraine, was put under military administration by the Germans, owing largely to its proximity to the front. Within the Donbas itself, the mood of the local population often depended on where the front stood. The closer the town and the countryside to the front, the less harsh the German military regime tended to be. In those areas located close to the front, people, particularly collective farmers, tended to help the Germans and met the Red Army soldiers with hostility when they returned. The farmers refused to give drinking water to the Soviet fighters, on the grounds that they breathed more freely under the Germans than under the Bolsheviks.[84]

Many Communists, like many non–party members, chose to remain in the Donbas or were unable to leave for a variety of reasons. If they were not killed outright by the Germans, they were obliged to register with them. Those who refused to do so, be they Ukrainian or Russian, were executed.[85] In Krasnodon, in August 1942 shortly after it was occupied, thirty colliers who were Communist Party members were buried alive for failing to appear for registration.[86] Others were killed as traitors by Soviet "partisans" (who, in these cases, were most likely to be NKVD extermination squads).[87] To complicate matters, as will be discussed later, some of the police working for the Germans were in fact NKVD infiltrators assigned to eliminate those Communist Party members and others considered traitors.[88] Exactly how many remained under occupa-

---

[80] Ibid., p. 331 (Slov'ians'k). In one village in Novoaidar in the north of Voroshylovhrad, the retreating authorities gave orders to lynch the politically suspect. One collective farmer was thus shot. TsDAHO, f. 1, op. 23, spr. 58, ark. 8.

[81] *Donetskii vestnik*, 15 November 1941. In 1940 the population of Stalino was 507,000. *Donetsk. Istoriko-kraevedcheskii ocherk* (Donetsk, 1981), p. 198.

[82] See, for example, TsAMO, f. 359, op. 6015, op. 13, l. 86 (Krasnoarmiis'k).

[83] Interview 1.

[84] TsDAHO, f. 1, op. 23, spr. 685, ark. 9–11 and 18–20 (January 1943 report).

[85] Ibid., spr. 3839, ark. 62–63 (Stalino).

[86] Ibid., op. 22, spr. 24, ark. 1.

[87] Ibid., op. 23, spr. 160, ark. 11. For NKVD activities behind the front line, see also John A. Armstrong, ed., *Soviet Partisans in World War II* (University of Wisconsin Press, 1964), pp. 78–80.

[88] See Maistrenko, *Istoriia moho pokolinnia*, pp. 328 and 334.

tion is far from clear. In Voroshylovhrad *oblast'*, there were 46,222 party members and candidates in 1940. In 1944, after liberation, the number was only 11,140. Of them, 7,365 stayed under the Germans, and 3,457 of those registered with the police and Gestapo.[89] K. F. Chernichenko, fifty years of age and a party member since 1932, was one who did so, according to his own account, in order to "remove from himself the title of party member," because he believed that "there won't be a Soviet power any more. The Germans have strong technology, while the Red Army has naked soldiers and no technology."[90] Others managed to hide. Some did so by burning their cards.[91]

The Jews and Gypsies in the Donbas as elsewhere were targeted for total extermination, according to Nazi ideology. Clearly many Jews did not or could not evacuate. The Soviet government did not inform them of the systematic killings committed by Germans elsewhere in Ukraine and other occupied territory.[92] The government also kept from the population information on how close the front stood. According to a former resident of Stalino, "But we, in the middle of this storm, did not even know where the front was!"[93] When the Germans came, the population was helpless.

The occupiers required all Jews to wear a David's star insignia. Soon they were executed en masse. These crimes were committed by Germans with the explicit and implicit help of local residents, both Russians and Ukrainians, both party and non–party members.[94] In October 1941, eight thousand (according to some accounts, nine thousand) Jews in Mariupol' were told to report for transport to Palestine but were liquidated instead.[95] What happened in Mariupol' in October was almost an exact replica of events in Babi Yar in Kiev. Sarra Gleykh, who miraculously survived the mass killings, left the following 20 October entry in her diary:

[89]TsDAHO, f. 1, op. 23, spr. 335, ark. 43, and DALO, f. P-179, op. 3, spr. 185, ark. 9.

[90]TsDAHO, f. 1, op. 23, spr. 689, ark. 34.

[91]Ibid., spr. 59, ark. 48.

[92]In Slov'ians'k, Jews stayed on the assumption that they would be all right because they were not Communists. One day all Jews were executed. One Ukrainian, whose wife was a Jew, thought that he could save her because he was not a Jew. Instead the Germans killed both. Maistrenko, *Istoriia moho pokolinnia*, pp. 330–31.

[93]Bohdan, *Avoiding Extinction*, p. 47.

[94]For a discussion of the participation of non-Jews in the Holocaust in Ukraine, see Philip Friedman, "Ukrainian-Jewish Relations during the Nazi Occupation," in *YIVO Annual of Jewish Social Science* (New York), 12 (1958–59), and M. V. Koval', "Natsysts'kyi henotsyd shchodo ievreiv ta ukrains'ke naselennia (1941–1944 rr.)," *Ukrains'kyi istorychnyi zhurnal*, 1992, no. 2. There is little evidence that one particular group, for example, the Ukrainians, participated in the Holocaust more actively than others. There are numerous cases of Ukrainians risking their lives to save Jews. For such a case in the Donbas, see Iakiv Suslens'kyi, *Spravzhni heroi. Pro uchast' hromadian Ukrainy u riatuvanni ievreiv vid fashysts'koho henotsydu* (Kiev, 1993), pp. 129–30.

[95]YIVO Archives, Reports on the Activities of the Einsatzgruppen in the USSR, 001833, and Itskhak Arad, ed., *Unichtozhenie evreev SSSR v gody nemetskoi okkupatsii (1941–1944). Sbornik dokumentov i materialov* (Jerusalem, 1992), p. 16.

Our turn arrived, and the horrible image of a senseless, a wildly senseless and meek death was before our eyes as we set off behind the barns. The bodies of Father and Mother were already there somewhere. By sending them by truck, I had shortened their lives by a few hours. We were herded toward the trenches which had been dug for the defense of the city. These trenches served no other function than as receptacles for the death of nine thousand Jews. We were ordered to undress to our underwear, and they searched for money and documents. Then we were herded along the edge of the ditch, but there was no longer any real edge, since the trench was filled with people for half a kilometer. Many were still alive and were begging for another bullet to finish them off. We walked over the corpses, and it seemed to me that I recognized my mother in one gray-haired woman. . . . Fanya [sister] did not believe that this was the end: "Can it be that I will never again see the sun and the light?" she said. Her face was blue-gray, and Vladya [little brother] kept asking: "Are we going to swim? Why are we undressed?" . . . I held my head and began to scream in a wild voice. I seem to remember that Fanya had time to turn around and say: "Be quiet, Sarra, be quiet." At that point everything breaks off.

When I regained consciousness, it was already twilight. The bodies lying on top of me were still shuddering; the Germans were shooting them again to make doubly sure that the wounded would not be able to leave. At any rate, I understood the Germans to say that. They were afraid that there were many who had not been finished off, and they were right; there were many like that. These people were buried alive, since no one could help them even though they screamed and called for help. Somewhere above the corpses babies were crying. Most of them had been carried by their mothers and, since we were shot in the backs, they had fallen, protected by their mothers' bodies. Not wounded by the bullets, they were covered up and buried alive under the corpses.

I began to crawl out from underneath the corpses. . . . [96]

After "a month of wandering in the steppe," Gleykh was able to escape to the Soviet side.[97]

Massacres took place everywhere. In Debal'tseve, Jews were confined to a town square and crushed to death by German tanks.[98] In December 1941 all Jews in Makiivka were killed.[99] In January 1942 all Jews and Gypsies were annihilated in Artemivs'k: children were poisoned; some adults were shot, others gassed or thrown down mine shafts alive. Communists and others

---

[96]Ilya Ehrenburg and Vasily Grossman, eds., *The Black Book: The Ruthless Murder of Jews by German-Fascist Invaders throughout the Temporarily-Occupied Regions of the Soviet Union and in the Death Camps of Poland during the War of 1941–1945*, tr. John Glad and James S. Levine (New York, 1981), pp. 74–75. A more complete version of the diary was published in *Neizvestnaia chernaia kniga* (Jerusalem and Moscow, 1993), pp. 211–22.

[97]Ehrenburg and Grossman, *The Black Book*, p. 76.

[98]*Neizvestnaia chernaia kniga*, p. 164.

[99]TsDAHO, f. 1, op. 22, spr. 511, ark. 59.

politically suspect were killed in a similar fashion. Some had their eyes poked out and noses cut off. Altogether the victims in the January massacre accounted for three thousand.[100]

In Stalino, killings began in December 1941 and continued into the spring of 1942.[101] Gas vans were extensively used in the operations there. A German perpetrator later recalled killings on Easter Monday in Stalino:

> The Jews had to climb into the van fully clothed. There was no sorting out. Men, women and children all had to get in together. I estimate that about sixty people had to get in each time. They had to climb up some steps to get into the van. It did not seem as if the Jews knew that they were about to be gassed. After the doors had been closed we then drove to a disused coal shaft. I do not remember whether the shaft was in front of the van or whether we had to turn round. The gas-van could not be driven right up to the shaft and we had to pull the bodies out of the vans and drag them to the shaft, which was about eight metres away, and then throw them in. . . .
>
> When the doors were opened a cloud of smoke wafted out. After the smoke had cleared we could start our foul work. It was frightful. You could see that they had fought terribly for their lives. Some of them were holding their noses. The dead had to be dragged apart. It was while doing this that I first found out how heavy a human being can be.[102]

All in all, up to 15,000 Jews were killed in Stalino.[103]

In January 1942 the Jews in Kramators'k were sent to what the Germans called Palestine (i.e., the other world).[104] In September 1942, all Jews (about 40) and "political activists" were rounded up, shot, and thrown down a mine shaft in Kransodon.[105] In Ienakiieve 280 Jews were shot.[106] In Voroshylov-hrad, on 1 November 1942, all Jews in the city were ordered to report for deportation. They were instead taken outside the city and shot. Children were poisoned by a substance put on their lips. On this day alone 3,000 Jews perished in the city.[107] More killings followed in December; they were shot, poisoned, or gassed to death.[108] In all, 8,000 Jews and others were killed in this fashion in Voroshylovhrad.[109] The Jews had suffered ever since coming to

---

[100] Ibid., ark. 54, and op. 23, spr. 3839, ark. 77.

[101] Ibid, op. 23, spr. 3839, ark. 75.

[102] Ernst Klee, Willi Dressen, and Volker Riess, *"The Good Old Days": The Holocaust as Seen by Its Perpetrators and Bystanders*, tr. Deborah Burnstone (New York, 1991), pp. 72–73.

[103] TsDAHO, f. 1, op. 23, spr. 3839, ark. 75.

[104] See a letter written by a Jew who fled from the massacre in Ehrenburg and Grossman, *The Black Book*, pp. 550–52.

[105] AUSBULO, no. 26518, t. 1, ark. 156, and t. 3, 269.

[106] TsDAHO, f. 1, op. 23, spr. 336, ark. 1, 4.

[107] DALO, f. R-693, op. 5, spr. 1, ark. 1 and 158.

[108] *Sovetskie evrei pishut Il'e Erenburgu 1943–1966* (Jerusalem, 1993), pp. 123–24.

[109] *Ukrains'ka RSR u Velykii Vitchyznianii viini Radians'koho Soiuzu 1941–1945 rr.*, vol. 1 (Kiev, 1967), p. 363.

the Donbas, but the Holocaust during the war was by far the most systematic and most deadly blow, annihilating the Jews wholesale.

Many Donbas residents initially regarded German occupation as an alternative to the Soviet regime. Yet the Germans immediately proved no better. As Alexander Dallin has shown, their racial ideology contributed much to the brutality with which they ruled the occupied territory.[110] They killed innocent residents everywhere. They looted the cities and the countryside.[111] For various offenses of the rules imposed, people were lashed just as in the old days.[112] The Germans allowed private trade to operate, renamed some cities (Stalino became Iuzovka or Iuzivka again) and streets (Rosa Luxemburg Street became Oil Street), and privatized some lands. Yet, to the disappointment of many farmers, they never dissolved the collective farms on any large scale. The collective farm system was useful for the Germans, just as it was for the Soviet government, to collect grain and other produce. People had to live in hunger. (Harsh punishments, including public executions, notwithstanding, the Germans could not control the wave of crime in the cities.)[113] Within a few months, the mood of the local residents turned against the occupiers: the Soviet regime now began to appear better than foreign occupation. Some had set up icons at home, prayed, and waited eagerly for the Germans. When the Germans looted their houses, however, they realized what occupation meant. So they declared that they no longer believed in God.[114] Others held on to the icons because they thought that in case the Whites came back, they would be safer with icons.[115]

Another important operation by the German occupants contributed to the problems they faced in the Donbas. They exported hundreds of thousands of people from the Donbas to forced labor in Germany. Occupation newspapers carried numerous articles describing how inhuman labor under the Soviet regime was and exhorted the residents to go to work in the Reich, where paradise was awaiting them. They also carried reports on how enthusiastically people were responding to the appeal to go to Germany.[116] Initial recruits were largely volunteers, but the terrible treatment they met on their way to and in Germany soon became known. The subsequent recruitments were forced.

---

[110]Dallin, *German Rule in Russia.*

[111]See, for example, TsAMO, f. 359, op. 6015, d. 15, ll. 39–41.

[112]See, for example, TsDAHO, f. 1, op. 22, spr. 87, ark. 84.

[113]See Evgenii Iasenov, "Poslevoennoe Stalino: vodka deshevle khleba," *Gorod* (Donets'k), no. 43 (11 November 1993), p. 10.

[114]TsAMO, f. 359, op. 6015, d. 3, l. 101 and l. 91 (November 1941 report), and TsDAHO, f. 1, op. 23, spr. 538 (no pagination).

[115]TsDAHO, f. 1, op. 70, spr. 11, ark. 20 (June 1942 report from Voroshylovhrad).

[116]See, for example, *Donetskii vestnik* (Stalino) and *Nove zhyttia* (Voroshylovhrad) for 1942. See also Ulrich Herbert, *Fremdarbeiter. Politik und Praxis des "Ausländer-Einsatzes" in der Kriegswirtschaft des Dritten Reiches* (Berlin and Bonn, 1985), pp. 158-59.

The Germans would "seize people in the market place" and dispatch them to Germany.[117] The German operations contributed to growing anti-German sentiment.[118]

The Donbas played an important role in human export. Initially the Germans targeted 50,000 industrial workers from Stalino for export.[119] It is symbolic that it was in the Donbas (Stalino) that the first official transport of civilians took place (in January 1942): 1,100 were dispatched to the Reich.[120] Altogether, more than 300,000 Donbas residents (252,239 from Stalino *oblast'*, or more than 8 percent of its 1939 population, and 74,047 from Voroshylovhrad *oblast'*, or 4 percent of its 1939 population) were taken to Germany.[121] They were among the estimated nearly 5 million Soviet people drafted as forced laborers to the Reich.[122]

During the war, savage terror was inflicted on soldiers and civilians alike by both sides. According to the latest estimates of population loss during the war, nearly 8 million Soviet soldiers and up to 20 million civilians were killed or died of hunger, diseases, injuries, and other war-related causes.[123] Among them were nearly 2 million civilian Jews targeted for total extermination.[124] In Voroshylovhrad *oblast'* 45,649 civilians were said to have been killed by the occupiers.[125] In Stalino *oblast'*, which was occupied longer, the number of victims was higher, 279,000, of whom about 100,000 were accounted for by the city of Stalino, or more than 20 percent of the residents who remained under occupation.[126] As many as 75,000 were thrown dead or alive into Mine

---

[117]See Lewis H. Siegelbaum and Daniel J. Walkowitz, *Workers of the Donbas Speak: Survival and Identity in the New Ukraine, 1989–1992* (State University of New York Press, 1995), p. 46.

[118]Dallin, *German Rule in Russia*, p. 430. See also Viktor Andriianov, *Pamiat' so znakom OST. Sud'ba "vostochnykh rabochikh" v ikh sobstvennykh svidetel'stvakh, pis'makh i dokumentakh* (Moscow, 1993), pp. 28–29 and 45.

[119]Herbert, *Fremdarbeiter*, p. 158.

[120]Pavel Polian, " 'Ost'y – zhertvy dvukh diktatur," *Rodina*, 1994, no. 2, p. 52.

[121]TsDAHO, f. 1, op. 23, spr. 1477, ark. 1, and spr. 1478, ark. 7.

[122]V. I. Zemskov, "K voprosu o repatriatsii sovetskikh grazhdan 1944–1951 gody," *Istoriia SSSR*, 1990, no. 4, p. 26.

[123]The numbers vary, but see A. A. Sheviakov, "Gitlerovskii genotsid na territoriiakh SSSR," *Sotsiologicheskie issledovaniia*, 1991, no. 12, and "Zhertvy sredi mirnogo naseleniia v gody Otechestvennoi voiny," ibid., 1992, no. 11.

[124]Of them nearly 1 million were on pre-1939 Soviet territory. In western Ukraine, of 870,000 Jews only 17,000 or 2% survived the war. See Lucjan Dobroszycki and Jeffrey S. Gurock, eds., *The Holocaust in the Soviet Union: Studies and Sources on the Destruction of the Jews in the Nazi-Occupied Territories of the USSR, 1941–1945* (Armonk, N.Y., 1993), pp. 3 (Zvi Gitelman) and 212 (Sergei Maksudov); Aharon Weiss, "Jewish-Ukrainian Relations in Western Ukraine during the Holocaust," in Peter J. Potichnyj and Howard Aster, eds., *Ukrainian-Jewish Relations in Historical Perspective* (Edmonton, Canada, 1990), p. 409.

[125]Sheviakov, "Zhertvy sredi mirnogo naseleniia v gody Otechestvennoi voiny," p. 10. The list on p. 9 somehow shows 19,373.

[126]TsDAHO, f. 1, op. 22, spr. 511, ark. 53 and 66, and op. 23, spr. 3839, ark. 74. The data on Stalino *oblast'* are not included in Sheviakov's study for some reason.

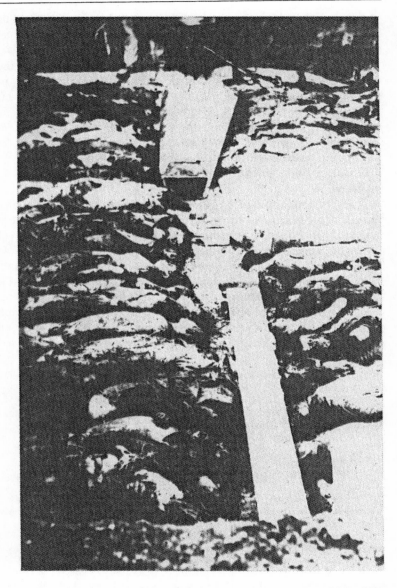

Figure 7.2. Bodies of people murdered by the German forces, recovered from Mine 3/3bis in Kadiivka, 1943. From DALO, f. P-7118, op. 1, spr. 704.

4/4bis in Stalino.[127] In the city of Shakhty in the Russian part of the Donbas, 13,854 civilians and 10,260 Soviet POWs were exterminated.[128]

While the majority of the killings were perpetrated by the Germans and their allies, these figures almost certainly include victims of Soviet terror as well.[129] The Great Terror of the Soviets was followed by waves of destruction.

Alternatives

War creates an extreme circumstance in which one can be only an ally or an enemy. At least this was the ideology and practice promoted by the Soviet government. As Stalin consolidated his power and geared up for war, the concept of enemy underwent a transformation from "class enemy" to class-neutral "enemy of the people." Terrorized, people had to live in the country on terms dictated by the government. When the war began, people had to decide their own fates. For millions of men, there was no choice but to be drafted into the ranks of the Red Army. Many gave their lives, but some chose to desert the front and many of them were executed for their choice. Millions of citizens chose to evacuate to the east to avoid the rapidly advancing enemy, but many more people chose to remain under the occupiers. No doubt, many civilians, unable to make a decision for a variety of reasons, found themselves living under occupation, just as millions of soldiers unwillingly became prisoners of war. Still, once under occupation or in captivity, they determined their own fates to the extent that circumstances allowed. The war appeared to allow for no alternatives, but it actually accorded options to the Soviet citizens, however difficult it was to choose among them. As M. Ia. Gefter has appropriately remarked, "This [1941–42] was a period of *spontaneous de-Stalinization*. We were in full crisis. Stalin's totalitarian system had fallen apart in the face of the invasion and occupation. People were suddenly forced to make their own decisions, to take responsibility for themselves. Events pressed us into becoming truly independent human beings."[130]

---

[127]RTsKhIDNI, f. 17, op. 88, d. 1005, l. 48.

[128]Sheviakov, "Zhertvy sredi mirnogo naseleniia v gody Otechestvennoi voiny," p. 6.

[129]For the most critical analysis, see Michael Ellman and S. Maksudov, "Soviet Deaths in the Great Patriotic War: A Note," *Europe-Asia Studies*, 46:4 (1994). Of the sixteen eastern *oblast*'s in Ukraine, Stalino and Voroshylovhrad *oblast*'s accounted for the greatest population loss in proportionate terms from January 1941 to July 1946, 25% and 23% respectively. See A. L. Perkovs'kyi and S. I. Pyrozhkov, "Demohrafichni vtraty narodonaselennia Ukrains'koi RSR u 40-kh rr.," *Ukrains'kyi istorychnyi zhurnal*, 1990, no. 2, p. 17.

[130]Quoted in Nina Tumarkin, *The Living and the Dead: The Rise and Fall of the Cult of World War II in Russia* (New York, 1994), p. 65 (emphasis in the original). See also M. Ia. Gefter, *Iz tekh i etikh let* (Moscow, 1991), pp. 418–22.

Foreign occupation was not new to the Donbas. Those residents, and there were many, who had stayed in the occupied Donbas during the terrible years of the civil war were villified in innuendos for their choice, whereas those working people who had remained in the city of, for example, Petrograd, were touted as true proletarians. As the subsequent two decades show, the Donbas was very difficult to control politically and was subjected to harsh terror by Moscow. Facing abandonment by the Soviet authorities in the autumn of 1941, many residents in the Donbas chose to determine their own fate in untoward circumstances. To them, "the [Soviet] scorched-earth tactic amounted to a sentence of cruel punishment often followed by starvation. It also made one wonder who was really the enemy."[131]

Although German occupation proved deadly for most, those who had been repressed under the Soviet regime were treated by the occupation forces favorably as likely allies. Thus many of them acquired alternatives that would have been impossible under the Soviet regime. Exiled kulaks began to return to their native villages in the Donbas. More noticeably, many dekulakized or otherwise repressed people, who were numerous in the Donbas, began to return to their villages under occupation. Massive migrations were not new to the Donbas. Hunger accelerated the movement westward. People traveled to Poltava, to Dnipropetrov'sk, and even to the Right Bank. The number of migrating people was said to be nearly one million.[132] When one Ukrainian family returned to its village in Chernihiv from the Donbas after a harrowing five-hundred-mile journey on foot, "the word got around the village that some Bohdans had come back from the coal mines. . . . Our kinfolks looked at us as though we were resurrected from the dead, and their joy was boundless."[133]

The church revived under occupation. Many of the clergy who had hidden underground in the Donbas began to return to their former parishes. People filled the churches.[134] According to Hans Koch, a German counterintelligence officer in charge of Ukrainian religious affairs,

> Those who emerged from hiding under the Soviets were far too few to take care of the many reopened churches. Priests were "exhumed," but the demand far exceeded the supply; yet more than I had expected did turn up –

[131] Bohdan, *Avoiding Extinction*, p. 47.
[132] Ievhen Stakhiv, "Natsional'no-politychne zhyttia Donbasu v 1941–1943 rr. (na osnovi osobystykh sposterezhen')," *Suchasna Ukraina* (Munich), 12 August 1956 (the author worked in the Donbas during the German occupation). For the migration, see also E. Pavliuk, "Borot'ba ukrains'koho narodu na skhidno-ukrains'kykh zemliakh 1941–1944 (spomyny ochevydtsia i uchasnyka)," in *Kalendar Provydinnia Stovaryshennia Ukraintsiv Katolykiv v Amerytsi na zvychainyi rik 1947* (Philadelphia, 1947), p. 51, and Lev Shankovs'kyi, *Pokhidni hrupy OUN* (Munich, 1958), pp. 43 and 164–65. For those who joined the mass migration, see Maistrenko, *Istoriia moho pokolinnia*, 335–39, and Mace and Heretz, *Oral History Project*, 2:1154.
[133] Bohdan, *Avoiding Extinction*, p. 65.
[134] See, for example, Mace and Heretz, *Oral History Project*, 1:48–49. See also Bohdan, *Avoiding Extinction*, p. 68.

many had spent years as workers in the Donbas, had sung as basses in factory choirs, etc.[135]

Some of them engaged in a bitter campaign against the Soviet government with the encouragement of Germans.[136] Still the activity of the Orthodox Church in the Donbas remained limited. Instead, sectarians, particularly Baptists who had traditionally been numerous in the Donbas, became very active again.[137]

Things Ukrainian, if not Ukrainian nationalism, also began to attract people's attention even in such a heavily Russified place as the Donbas. In a peculiar way, by incorporating western Ukraine and northern Bukovina in 1939, Stalin had united much of Ukraine, which had for nearly three centuries been divided. The export of labor from the newly incorporated areas to the Donbas brought the two groups of Ukrainians with very distinct historical backgrounds closer together. When war broke out, Moscow began to make concessions to various social forces it had repressed as hostile elements. The church is one example, as reflected in a 1943 concordat between the Kremlin and the Russian Orthodox Church.[138] National sentiments and traditions were another. Stalin's growing identification with Russia was already evident in the 1930s. As Khrushchev's speech on 6 July 1941 suggests, concessions, at least as a formality, were also being made to Ukrainian national sentiment.[139] In any case, the war quickly separated the whole of Ukraine from Russia.

Ukrainian nationalism was one alternative that became available to Donbas residents. The ideology came mainly from western Ukraine. The question of the relations between Nazis and Ukrainian nationalists (particularly the Organization of Ukrainian Nationalists, or OUN, founded in western Ukraine in 1929) is complex and emotional. Some of the Ukrainian nationalists were as racist and fascist as their counterparts in Germany, Italy, and elsewhere.[140] They were unmistakable Nazi collaborators.[141] The Nazis used the Ukrainian

---

[135] Harvey Fireside, *Icon and Swastika: The Russian Orthodox Church under Nazi and Soviet Control* (Harvard University Press, 1971), pp. 153–54.

[136] See the case of Metropolitan of Kharkiv Feofil who went to Voroshylovhrad after the church was closed in Kharkiv in 1937. Arrested many times, he survived the Great Terror. When Kharkiv was occupied, he assumed the church administration under which the Donbas was also placed. See TsDAHO, f. 1, op. 23, spr. 90, ark. 48–49.

[137] TsDAHO, f. 1, op. 22, spr. 87, ark. 104. See also Ievhen Stakhiv, "Natsional'no-politychne zhyttia Donbasu v 1941–1943 pp.," *Suchasna Ukraina*, 23 September 1956, p. 6.

[138] See Fireside, *Icon and Swastika*, pp. 177–78.

[139] According to Yuri Slezkine, "The USSR as a Communal Apartment, or How a Socialist State Promoted Ethnic Particularism," *Slavic Review*, 53:2 (Summer 1994), there were contradictions between the form and the content of Soviet nationality policy throughout the Soviet period.

[140] See John A. Armstrong, "Collaborationism in World War II: The Integral Nationalist Variant in Eastern Europe," *Journal of Modern History*, 40:3 (September 1968).

[141] See B. F. Sabrin, *Alliance for Murder: The Nazi-Ukrainian Nationalist Partnership in Genocide* (New York, 1991). This is a work of passionate and partisan condemnation. For a dialogue between Ukrainian and Jewish historians, see Potichnyj and Aster, *Ukrainian-Jewish Relations*,

nationalists as a counterweight to the Soviets. Yet once it became clear that the Nazis would not allow for independent Ukrainian statehood and had begun to repress Ukrainian nationalists, many of the nationalists turned against the Nazis and fought a double-front war against Germany and Russia.[142] During the war, nationalists came from the west to build a political base in the industrial center of Ukraine.

In the 1930s Ukrainians with nationalist backgrounds had been almost completely destroyed in the Donbas. However, the peasants in the Donbas, as elsewhere in Ukraine, had frequently changed camps in the civil war of 1918–20, allying with the Ukrainian nationalists when that suited their needs. The secret police would have had to repress almost everyone to eradicate the least hint of political deviation in Ukraine. Volodymyr Sosiura, who subsequently became a famous Soviet-Ukrainian poet, was but one such example (see Chapter 3). One witness testified that one still could meet former Petliura supporters in the German-occupied Donbas during World War II.[143] Mykola Stasiuk, a minister in the Ukrainian Central Rada in 1918, "had managed to survive the Soviet period by working as a park attendant," and during the occupation assumed the editorship of the new Ukrainian newspaper *Mari'iupil'ska Hazeta*. He helped the OUN-B (OUN faction of followers of S. Bandera), and Mariupol' became the stronghold of Ukrainian nationalists in the Donbas.[144] In Stalino, the wife of the former Petliura government minister Shymanovycha, who had returned from Siberia, helped in the Ukrainian underground.[145]

Arrests and executions of Ukrainian nationalists were frequent in the Donbas. On one day, for example, twenty OUN activists were executed by the Germans in Mariupol'.[146] Nevertheless, the OUN was able to place its activists in Horlivka, Kostiantynivka, Mariupol', Stalino, i Hryshyne, Slov'ians'k, Kramators'k, and elsewhere in the Donbas.[147] In Kramators'k groups of "Prosvita," traditional organizations for the promotion of Ukrainian culture and education, were set up.[148] In Mariupol', the head of the school system "proposed to stress

sec. V, and Michael Berenbaum, ed., *A Mosaic of Victims: Non-Jews Persecuted and Murdered by the Nazis* (New York University Press, 1990), chs. 10–13.

[142] See Armstrong, *Ukrainian Nationalism*, and Kosyk, *Ukraina i Nimechchyna*.

[143] Saidak, "Donets'kyi kriazh." See also a report by OUN in TsDAVO, f. 3833, op. 1, spr. 113, ark. 4.

[144] Armstrong, *Ukrainian Nationalism*, p. 208. See also Ievhen Stakhiv, "Ukrains'ke revoliutsiine pidpillia v Donbasi v rr. 1941–43 (dopovnennia do statti Tamary Saidak)," *Ukrains'ki visti*, 3 October 1954, p. 3, and *Kriz' tiurmy, pidpillia i kordony. Povist' moho zhyttia* (Kiev, 1995), pp. 114–19.

[145] Stakhiv, "Natsional'no-politychne zhyttia Donbasu v 1941–1943 rr." (23 September 1956), p. 6.

[146] Stakhiv, "I v Krasnodoni diialo natsionalistychne pidpillia," *Ukraina moloda* (Kiev), no. 66 (21 August 1992), p. 3.

[147] Stakhiv, "Ukrains'ke revoliutsiine pidpillia v Donbasi v rr. 1941–43."

[148] TsDAVO, f. 3833, op. 1, spr. 113, ark. 4. See also Armstrong, *Ukrainian Nationalism*, p. 199.

the native language, love of the fatherland, and respect for elders."[149] "Almost everywhere" in the Donbas under occupation, a "quiet war" went on between Ukrainians and Russians for influence in local administration.[150] As early as November 1941 a Soviet military intelligence officer in the Donbas noted that "everywhere I went I heard that some Stepan Bendera [*sic*], a 'scholar,' would head the government in Ukraine."[151] Stepan Bandera was already by this time a well-known Ukrainian nationalist.

The OUN activists from Galicia, according to Soviet intelligence reports, attracted mainly intellectuals, teachers, medical doctors, and youth, who made up "considerable groups" in the Donbas.[152] (The secret police's "considerable" may have meant a dozen or so people here and there, however. For example, "a group of twelve members of the OUN-B in Kramatorskaia [Kremators'ka] in the Donbas is referred to by one of the leaders of the party in that area as a 'big' cell.")[153] Some Red Army deserters also joined their forces, so did an anti-Soviet battalion of Soviet POWs organized and dispatched by Germany to Stalino.[154] People often traveled elsewhere in Ukraine for barter and came back with nationalist literature. Among themselves they began to speak about Ukraine.[155] The slogan "Ukraine was and will be independent" [*Ukraina bula i bude nezalezhnoiu*] began to appear in the Donbas countryside.[156] The eighty-year-old Metropolitan of Kharkiv Feofil, who worked in the occupied Donbas, passionately declared in the newspaper *Nova Ukraina*: "In the old days, in the heyday of culture in Ukraine, when Ukraine was much more cultured than Russia and its culture stood at the level of Western states, the church in Ukraine was the center of culture. . . . Build in Ukraine the best, most blessed, peaceful, and contented life."[157]

Yet there is little compelling evidence that Ukrainian nationalism was embraced enthusiastically in the Donbas as a whole. Initially the OUN-M (followers of A. Mel'nyk, an OUN leader) came to Stalino. They organized the police in the city administration, which had been created by Russians under occupation. The nationalists forced the police to wear the Ukrainian coat of arms, the

[149] Armstrong, *Ukrainian Nationalism*, p. 171.

[150] Stakhiv, "Natsional'no-politychne zhyttia Donbasu v 1941–1945 rr." (12 August 1956), p. 6.

[151] TsAMO, f. 359, op. 6015, d. 13, l. 92.

[152] TsDAHO, f. 1, op. 23, spr. 3839, ark. 46–47 and 56–61. See Armstrong, *Ukrainian Nationalism*, pp. 182–83, for a similar observation on local Ukrainian leaders in general. Ievhen Stakhiv, however, has maintained that in the Donbas, unlike elsewhere, the OUN supporters were workers and youth. See his "Natsional'no-politychne zhyttia Donbasu v 1941–1943 pp.," *Suchasna Ukraina*, 23 September 1956, p. 6.

[153] Armstrong, *Ukrainian Nationalism*, p. 162.

[154] TsDAHO., f. 1, op. 23, spr. 3883, ark. 34–49, and Ie. Pavliuk, "Donbas u borot'bi z nimtsiamy," *Litopys polytv'iaznia* (Munich), 1947, nos. 1–2, pp. 47–48.

[155] TsDAVO, f. 3833, op. 1, spr. 113, ark. 1.

[156] Ibid., spr. 453, ark. 16.

[157] Ibid., spr. 90, ark. 57–58.

Trident and the blue-and-yellow shoulder bandage, on their uniforms. Under the Ukrainian coat of arms, they carried out the most brutal orders given by the Germans. The OUN-M delegates lasted for only two weeks in Stalino: they were sent back to L'viv.[158] The OUN-B (Bandera supporters) from Galicia fared a little better. Yet when they came to the Donbas and gave people books by Dmytro Dontsov, an ideologue of integral Ukrainian nationalism and an eastern Ukrainian himself, by birth, the Donbas residents called the literature fascist.[159]

One immediate problem for the Galicians was the lack of a common language. Because, unlike their predecessors, the Bandera supporters attempted to build a popular political base in the Donbas, the problem of communication became critical. The Galician dialect of Ukrainian was hardly understood in the heavily Russified Donbas. Those residents who did speak Ukrainian did not admit that they spoke Ukrainian, insisting that they spoke a "local language." They were probably right, because their language was a mix of Russian and Ukrainian.[160] Forced to use the Russian language, which they did not know well, the OUN activists made many linguistic mistakes.[161] Communication was difficult and consequently the number of converts small. In Stalino, according to a nationalist teacher who worked under the OUN leader in the Donbas "Ievhen" (most likely Ievhen Stakhiv), there were only about seven activists in his cell.[162] V. G. Gladkii (V. H. Hladkyi), a chief mechanic in the Stalino metallurgical factory, was later accused of assisting the OUN. Gladkii, a Ukrainian, admitted that he had helped the OUN because the OUN appealed to the population to fight against the Germans.[163]

Contemporary reports from OUN activists in the Donbas are contradictory. On the one hand, the reports paint a glowing picture of their growing influence in the Donbas: people were ready for an immediate revolution.[164] On the other, they were desperate: the Donbas population had never heard of UPA (Ukrainian Insurgent Armies, i. e., partisans); more than half of the male urban population were speculators, "self-seekers," army deserters, and the like who, afraid of the return of the Bolsheviks, wished for the victory of Germany; the women just wanted the war to end and their men to come back; the majority of the peasants would be happy to forget everything if the tsar came down from heaven with a return to "the peaceful Nicolaevian life" and if the devil gave them some land and promised no taxes; the village youth were opportunistic,

---

[158] Stakhiv, "Natsional'no-politychne zhyttia Donbasu v 1941–1943 rr." (12 August 1956), p. 6.
[159] Stakhiv, "I v Krasnodoni diialo natsionalistychne pidpillia."
[160] Stakhiv, "Natsional'no-politychne zhyttia Donbasu v 1941–1943 rr." (26 August 1956), p. 5.
[161] TsDAVO, f. 3833, op. 1, spr. 113, ark. 1 (OUN report from the Donbas).
[162] AUSBUDO, no. 35462-pf, t. 1, ark. 274–75 (I. P. Svechinskii's testimony).
[163] Ibid., t. 2, ark. 364–68.
[164] Ibid. See also ark. 29.

pro-German when the Germans were victorious and pro-Soviet when the Soviets were winning the battle; one village might be very nationalist, while all the surrounding area knew nothing of nationalist ideas.[165]

Postwar Ukrainian nationalist literature overstates the influence the nationalists managed to exert on the Donbas population. One of the OUN leaders in the Donbas has fondly recalled how people, even ethnic Russians, protected him, a total stranger from Galicia, at the risk of their lives.[166] The OUN reports repeatedly note that the Donbas population wanted a third path, neither Bolshevik nor German. By the spring of 1943, when the Germans were already retreating, "almost everyone" in Stalino wished for the victory of a third force, which meant Ukrainian independence. Yet people believed that "the Ukrainians would not be able to accomplish anything without foreign help and would not be able to deal with the remnants of the Bolsheviks." Some were convinced that the Americans and British would help them and that the British would certainly come to the Donbas, because Hughes and other Englishmen had organized industry in tsarist times in the Donbas. Upon reflection, a minority said that the Germans were better than the Bolsheviks, and the majority that the Russians were preferable because they were "our people" and the Germans foreign.[167]

The Ukrainian alternative attracted non-Ukrainians in the Donbas as well: Russians, Greeks, Tartars, and Caucasian people. In Rutchenkove, there was an underground group of Russian workers (*hrupa Moskaliv-robitnykiv*) working with the OUN. They believed they were citizens of Ukraine and wanted to fight jointly against the Germans and Bolsheviks.[168] Yet they were ambivalent about the OUN version of Ukrainian nationalism. In fact, some workers in the Donbas are known to have put forth independent slogans at that time: "Ukrainian Soviet power without the Bolsheviks" and "Soviet Ukraine without the Bolsheviks and without the dictatorship of the Communist Party."[169] Stakhiv himself later recalled that the foremost concern of the Donbas population was social ills, upon the solution of which their participation in the Ukrainian liberation movement depended. Yet these problems were merely secondary to the OUN activists. The ultimate reason for the OUN's failure

[165]TsDAVO, f. 3833, op. 1, spr. 113, ark. 1–21 and 54 (spring–summer 1943 reports).

[166]"Iakby Oleha Koshevoho ne stratyly nimtsi – stratyly b bil'shovyky," *Vechirnii Kyiv*, 6 March 1993.

[167]TsDAVO, f. 3833, op. 1, spr. 113, ark. 3 and 20.

[168]Ibid., ark. 54; Pavliuk, "Borot'ba ukrains'koho narodu," p. 53; and Stakhiv, "Natsional'no-politychne zhyttia Donbasu v 1941–1943 rr." (26 August 1956), p. 5, and "Evoliutsiia ukrains'koho natsionalizmu – vid total'taryzmu do demokratiii: Dumky pro OUN (banderivtsiv)," in *Ukrains'ka Povstans'ka Armiia i natsional'no-vyzvol'na borot'ba v Ukraini u 1940–1950 rr. Materialy Vseukrains'koi naukovoi konferentsii (25–26 serpnia 1992 r.)* (Kiev, 1992), pp. 80–81.

[169]Stakhiv, "Natsional'no-politychne zhyttia Donbasu v 1941–1943 rr." (9 September 1956), p. 6. Note also Iaroslav S. Stets'ko, *30 chervnia 1941. Proholoshennia vidnovlennia derzhavnosty Ukrainy* (Toronto, 1967), p. 107.

to embrace the Donbas workers and youth was that it adhered to the extreme ideology of Dontsov. By the time they abandoned it, according to their own account, it was too late.[170]

Late though it may have been, the OUN's abandonment of its nationalist ideology in the Donbas was truly remarkable. Stakhiv, who had idealized Spain's Franco regime, was told by the Donbas people that his nationalism was fascist. In his interaction with them, Stakhiv abandoned a narrowly defined Ukrainian nationalism and embraced the ideal of a democratic Ukraine without discrimination against its national minorities. To this day Stakhiv is grateful to the Donbas people for his conversion.[171] The proselytizing power of the Donbas best represents the fiercely independent thinking of the free steppe.

Finally, the alternative of collaboration was readily available. The Germans targeted non-Russians and the politically repressed for recruitment. The ethnic Germans (*Volksdeutsche*) were at the top of the list for their knowledge of the German language and their supposed enmity toward the Soviet regime.[172] It is not known how many ethnic Germans were in the Donbas when it was occupied. Even though there was no significant activity of Ukrainian Germans as fifth columns,[173] Soviet repression of them intensified as German troops advanced: *Volksdeutsche* were arrested and exiled, often on fabricated charges or simply for being German.[174] In August 1941 ethnic Germans were deported wholesale from Ukraine and the Volga.[175] There must have been few ethnic Germans left in the Donbas at the time of occupation.[176] The occupiers were disappointed by the "unsuitable quality" of what few *Volksdeutsche* remained in Ukraine for "the administration and economy of the country."[177] Still the *Volksdeutsche* were favored, and the majority of them, according to Meir Buchsweiler, collaborated with the conquerors to one degree or another,

[170]Stakhiv, "Natsional'no-politychne zhyttia Donbasu v 1941–1943 rr." (26 August 1956), p. 5, and (23 September 1956), p. 6.

[171]Stakhiv, *Kriz' tiurmy, pidpillia i kordony*, pp. 133–34 and 308.

[172]M. V. Koval' and P. V. Medvedok, "Fol'ksdoiche v Ukraini (1941–1944 rr.)," *Ukrains'kyi istorychnyi zhurnal*, 1992, no. 5, p. 15.

[173]Meir Buchsweiler, *Volksdeutsche in der Ukraine am Vorabend und Beginn des Zweiten Weltkriegs – ein Fall doppelter Loyaliät?* (Stuttgart, 1984), pp. 337–41.

[174]See some personal files in DALO, f. 3437, op. 3, spr. 19-r, 1191-r, etc.

[175]*Istoriia rossiiskikh nemtsev v dokumentov (1763–1992 gg.)* (Moscow, 1993), pp. 160–61; Koval' and Medvedok, "Fol'ksdoiche"; V. N. Zemskov, "Spetsposelentsy (po dokumentatsii NKVD-MVD SSSR)," *Sotsiologicheskie issledovaniia*, 1990, no. 11, p. 8.

[176]Dallin, *German Rule in Russia*, p. 290. Koval' and Medvedok, "Fol'ksdoiche," cite a figure of 44,000 for Stalino *oblast'*, but it must have included many pretenders. The burgomaster of Kramators'k, V. V. Shopen, an engineer who conducted many arrests, was said to be an ethnic German. (Pavliuk, "Borot'ba Ukrains'koho narodu," p. 53.) According to *Kramatorskaia pravda*, 20 June 1964, Shopen's real surname is Shopin, an ethnic Ukrainian, then (in 1964) said to be living in Canada. Which version is true is not known.

[177]Dallin, *German Rule in Russia*, p. 290, and Koval' and Medvedok, "Fol'ksdoiche," p. 17.

ranging from passive collaboration to active participation in war crimes.[178] They retreated en masse with the Germans as the tide of the war turned.[179]

Other groups, particularly Cossacks, both local Don Cossacks and those who had returned from abroad, served as policemen.[180] (Curiously, according to Nazi ideology, the Cossacks were not *Untermenschen*, or subhumans.) Many Uzbeks were also found in the police. The Cossacks were happy to be given back their arms. Yet, according to an OUN report from Stalino, their commitment to the Germans was purely opportunistic: they would work with the Germans as long as the Germans were strong; they would desert the Germans when they lost power.[181] The same may have been true of the "Ukrainian Cossack battalions" formed in the Donbas and elsewhere: they were given the option of starving to death or fighting alongside the Germans. Some of them proved sympathetic to the Ukrainian nationalist cause.[182]

Former kulaks were another group favored by the Germans. Many kulaks returned to the Donbas countryside under occupation and reclaimed their former property, usually with the help of the village elders and Germans.[183] Some worked for the police, participating in the arrest and interrogation of Communists and their sympathizers.[184]

That those who were repressed under the Soviet regime worked for the Germans is not surprising. Stalin made every effort to destroy or isolate those who were even remotely suspect politically. Because many of those who actively assisted the Germans fled with them, it is difficult to analyze exactly who the collaborators were. Still the Soviet secret police investigated the question.

The Voroshylovhrad NKVD, for example, reached a preliminary conclusion that kulaks and repressed people accounted for an insignificant percent of the 450 traitors the NKVD arrested shortly after the liberation of Voroshylovhrad. The majority, according to the NKVD, were those who at first glance

---

[178]Buchsweiler, *Volksdeutsche in der Ukraine*, pp. 364–83. For concrete cases in Kransoarmiis'k in the Donbas, see TsAMO, f. 359, op. 6015, d. 13, l. 39.

[179]Dallin, *German Rule in Russia*, p. 292, and Koval' and Medvedok, "Fol'ksdoiche," p. 27.

[180]See AUSBULO, no. 10399, t. 1. Hundorivs'ka (Gundorovskaia), just north of Krasnodon, was a famous Cossack village, which produced, among others, White Army General P. N. Krasnov. Krasnov and another White general, A. G. Shkuro, returned to this area in 1942. See A. G. Shkuro, *Zapiski belogo partizana* (Moscow, 1991), pp. 6–7, and *Istoriia rabochikh Donbassa*, vol. 2 (Kiev, 1981), p. 46. As active German collaborators, both generals were taken back to the Soviet Union after the war and executed (hanged) in 1947.

[181]See TsDAVO, f. 3833, op. 1, spr. 113, ark. 21. For Cossacks, see also *Donetskii vestnik*, 19 February 1942.

[182]TsDAHO, f. 1, op. 23, spr. 115, ark. 25, 31, and 32, and Pavluk, "Borot'ba ukrains'koho narodu," p. 55. See also note 154.

[183]See numerous cases in DALO, f. R-1307sch, op. 2, spr. 206.

[184]See, for example, DALO, f. R-693, op. 5, spr. 1, ark. 174. Some returned to their native villages and sought revenge against their former enemies. In one village in Poltava, villagers stoned the collective farm chairman Lisovyi to death. See Mace and Heretz, *Oral History Project*, 3:1456.

had no reason to be disaffected.[185] In fact some party members were found among them – for instance, N. I. Tkachenko and P. I. Kotliarov, the burgomaster and the police chief respectively in Lysychans'k.[186] How subsequent arrests of more traitors changed the preliminary conclusion drawn by the Voroshylovhrad NKVD is not known.

The NKVD's profiles of collaborators suggest at least four possibilities. First, the police had repressed the wrong people and missed the real enemies of the Soviet government before the war. Second, many of the traitors were merely forced by circumstances to work for the Germans. Third, the war gave people alternatives inconceivable in peacetime and they chose to work against the Soviet government. Fourth, the traitors the police arrested were innocent. There is an element of truth to all four interpretations. Concrete examples will illustrate how complex the whole issue of collaboration was and how indiscriminately the police treated those who stayed under the Germans.

There were many levels of collaboration.[187] In fact, the Germans had different categories for those who worked for them. At the same time some active collaborators worked against the Germans. For example, the burgomaster of Hryshyne, Valerii Iakubovych, who later emigrated to Canada, assisted the Ukrainian underground activists.[188]

A trial held in Stalino after its liberation is instructive. Twelve traitors were put on trial in the autumn of 1944 by the military tribunal of the NKVD. They did not or could not flee with the Germans and were hunted down and arrested by the security police. "Almost all" were said to be from kulak families or repressed families, although none of them seem to have been repressed themselves. The father of the defendant V. I. Skorod'ko had been repressed; the father of another defendant N. M. Diusar was dekulakized; I. D. Zvigunov, former chief engineer at Mine 11, was said to be the son of a kulak and had a brother-in-law who had been repressed; G. A. Maliutin was accused of having fought on the side of the White Army during the civil war, when, in fact, he had sold himself as a former White Guard to gain the confidence of the Germans; Iu. Iu. Shcherbakov's father had been repressed; S. S. Vasil'ev was accused of having worked for the White Army.[189]

The prosecutors wished to portray the traitors as no ordinary Soviet citizens, but as criminals and enemies of the Soviet people embittered by the "legitimate" terror inflicted on their families. Many of these charges (son of a kulak, and the like) were of course mere fabrications. However, some charges were undoubtedly true given the fact that the Donbas attracted numerous out-

[185]DALO, f. P-1790, op. 1, spr. 262a, ark. 9.

[186]TsDAHO, f. 1, op. 23, spr. 689, ark. 35.

[187]For a thoughtful discussion, see Sergei Kudriashov, "Predateli, 'osvoboditeli' ili zhertvy voiny? Sovetskii kollaboratsionizm (1941–1942)," *Svobodnaia mysl'*, 1993, no. 14.

[188]Stakhiv, "Ukrains'ke revoliutsiine pidpillia v Donbasi v rr. 1941–43."

[189]*Sotsialisticheskii Donbass*, 29 September–1 October 1944.

lawed elements. If one reasonably assumes that the terror had affected more or less every family in one way or another, one would have to conclude that the defendants were just "ordinary citizens."

The defendants were accused of working for the SD, the German security service. No defendant seems to have denied the charges, according to the press. At least two were chauffeurs, who drove gas vans (*dushegubki*) in which Jews were gassed to death. It is a sad reminder of Soviet life to read that one defendant drove a gas van in return for boots, trousers, and hats, which were in acutely short supply under the Soviet regime. The court depicted the defendants as cheap, greedy criminals who helped Germans murder tens of thousands of Soviet people. Other defendants were charged with active participation in the torture of Soviet citizens, charges they did not deny. When Skorod'ko was asked how in the world he could have dealt with Soviet citizens so savagely, he responded: "I have never been a Soviet man" [*Ia nikogda ne byl sovetskim chelovekom*].[190] Whether Skorod'ko's father was actually repressed is not known, but Skorod'ko was wholly alienated from the Soviet regime. This remark was the last stand Skorod'ko took against the Soviet government. All twelve defendants were sentenced to be shot and executed.[191]

The case of the burgomaster of Voroshylovhrad is also instructive. A. P. Zubovskii, born in 1895 in Mogilev into a clergy family, a medical doctor in the city since 1922, became burgomaster of the Voroshylovhrad city administration after a brief stint as the director of health. Zubovskii fled with the Germans, but was arrested by the Soviet forces in Odessa in April 1944. Zubovskii was accused of assisting the German occupation forces, particularly helping them to identify and execute Jews, Communists, and other suspect elements in Voroshylovhrad. Zubovskii failed to help fifteen Jewish doctors, former colleagues of his, who were helpless under German occupation. When Dr. M. L. Kats asked him for advice the day before the massacres took place in November 1942, he merely told Kats not to comply with the order to report to the Germans. When another Dr. Raisa Broitman asked Zubovskii to protect her small baby from the Germans, he merely brought it to a nursery. All fifteen doctors were executed in November 1942, along with three thousand other Jews of the city.[192] Zubovskii pleaded guilty at a trial held in the city in October 1944.[193] On 3 January 1945 he was executed.[194]

Zubovskii's case reveals a man who had suffered deeply under the Soviet regime, even though he survived the worst phase of terror in 1936–38. The secret police documents in his criminal file are contradictory. One document

[190]Ibid., 30 September 1944.
[191]Ibid., 6 October 1944.
[192]AUSBULO, no. 4846, t. 1, ark. 81 and 214zv. and t. 2, ark. 132–34 and 234–34zv.
[193]Ibid., t. 3, ark. 228.
[194]Ibid., t. 2, ark. 266.

indicates that his father had twice been arrested by Soviet authorities. Yet another explicitly states that no member of his family had ever been repressed.[195] Zubovskii himself was arrested in February 1931 and charged with belonging to a counterrevolutionary, insurgent organization of doctors. Five months later he was freed. In the meantime he was recruited by the secret police and obliged to report on his fellow doctors. Subsequently in 1944 he told the investigators that in fact he did very little work for the GPU-NKVD. He even wrote favorable reports on his colleagues who were true enemies of the Soviet regime. Zubovskii confessed that until his arrest in 1931, he had regarded himself as a supporter of the Soviet regime, but that after his release he became an enemy of the Soviet government. He believed that his 1931 arrest was unjust, but more important was the tragedy caused by his arrest: his wife killed herself while he was held in detention in 1931.[196] In the summer of 1942 he concluded that the defeat of the Soviet Union was inevitable and decided not to evacuate.[197] Then followed his story of collaboration. One can conclude that the Soviet regime created its own enemy in this case.

Another case involved I. I. Mel'nikov who had been a hewer at Mine 2/4 in Krasnodon until it was occupied. Mel'nikov, an ethnic Russian, born in 1912 into a peasant family in Rostov *oblast'*, a non–party member with only one year of elementary education, had never been repressed under the Soviet regime. He was accused of participating in the torture and execution of many people in Krasnodon (including the famous Young Guard partisans, who will be discussed later). He fled with the Germans, but was captured in the autumn of 1944 in Odessa by the Red Army. Hiding his past, he fought with the Red Army and was even awarded a medal "For the Victory over Germany." More than twenty years later, in May 1965, however, Mel'nikov was arrested on a collective farm in Odessa, where, remarried, he was working as a farmer.[198]

Prosecutors charged that Mel'nikov tortured particularly brutally the former Communist bosses of the mine as if there were some personal accounts to be settled.[199] Mel'nikov pleaded guilty to charges of arrest, torture, transport of prisoners and their bodies, but he denied the charges of having participated directly in executions. Clearly Mel'nikov was a minor policeman in Krasnodon under occupation; many of the major figures, who were directly involved in the killings of Soviet citizens, fled abroad and were not brought to justice. Mel'nikov maintained that he worked for the police, because he had a family to support. (He later confessed that he fled from Krasnodon with the Germans because his children did not interest him.) He had been taken prisoner by the

[195] Ibid., t. 1, ark. 67zv. and t. 2, ark. 227.
[196] Ibid., ark. 68zv.–70.
[197] Ibid., ark. 78.
[198] AUSBULO, no. 26518.
[199] Ibid., t. 1, ark. 157.

Figure 7.3. Mel'nikov at trial, Krasnodon, 1965. A still reproduced from a documentary film, TsDKFFA, P-3551.

Germans when they occupied Krasnodon, and five days later he volunteered to work for the police. No one forced him to do so. Mel'nikov maintained at his trial held in December 1965 that he did not know what police work would involve. When the killings began, he understood what he was doing. Mel'nikov testified that he simply did not think about the fate of the motherland.[200] He was sentenced to be shot. His appeal for clemency based on his repentance and his service in the Red Army was turned down. On 4 April 1966 Mel'nikov was executed.[201]

A very similar case involved V. P. Podtynnyi, alias V. D. Podtynnyi. Born in 1917 into a peasant family in Luhans'k, Podtynnyi, an ethnic Ukrainian, had never been repressed under the Soviet regime. He served in the Red Army from 1937 to August 1941 (apparently discharged for injury) and from February 1944 to October 1946. He was awarded three orders and three medals for his bravery in the war. He became a party member in 1949. Yet he was arrested in April 1959 for his alleged participation with the police in Krasnodon under German occupation. Podtynnyi was accused of torturing and executing

[200] Ibid., t. 8, ark. 91–101.
[201] Ibid., ark. 209.

Jews, Communists, and partisans. During the occupation he served the Germans and, when the Red Army retook the Donbas, he fled with the Germans. In Odessa he registered with the Red Army by changing his patronymic and birth date and place and marched all the way to Berlin. At a trial held in June 1959, Podtynnyi pleaded guilty to some of the charges. The *oblast'* court in Stalino sentenced him to fifteen years of corrective labor. Yet in December 1959 the Ukrainian Supreme Court rejected the verdict and had him retried in Luhans'k in February 1960. Podtynnyi was sentenced to be shot and was executed.[202]

These were difficult cases because Mel'nikov and Podtynnyi appeared to combine both hero and villain. The death sentences were probably politically motivated, because there is at least one other very similar case in the Donbas in which a war criminal was not touched by the security organ on the grounds that he was a Red Army hero.[203] A number of others, who had escaped the draft into the Red Army and worked for the German police in Krasnodon, were tried but were not given death sentences.[204] (These occurred before 1947 when capital punishment was temporarily suspended.)

There were many other cases, however, in which the lines between heroes and villains blurred in a different sense. Many *politsai* (*Polizei*), those who worked in the German police units, were actually NKVD agents. This was a dangerous game so widely practiced throughout occupied territories that one historian has maintained that "the number of people who participated voluntarily in these institutions is thus considerably reduced."[205] Whatever the case, the Communist infiltration of the Gestapo and the German police was said to have been directed at identifying and eliminating traitors.[206] As a result, even the pro-German residents avoided collaborators who joined the police force. Another function of the Communist infiltrators was "to provoke the Germans into taking reprisals against the population." The logic was: "The more brutal the actions of the Germans, the more hatred they would generate, and the more willing the population would be to support the [Soviet] partisans."[207] Yet many innocent citizens refused to believe that these savage "traitors" (infiltrators) were actually "heroes."

[202] AUSBULO, no. 26499, especially ark. 4–5, 55–57, 72–74, and 91. There was no record of execution in this file, but I confirmed it in Luhans'k.

[203] See *Edinozhdy priniav prisiagu . . . Rasskazy o chekistakh* (Donets'k, 1990), pp. 101–12.

[204] See AUSBULO, no. 6606 (D. M. Zhukov), no. 8136 (G. S. Retivov), no. 8962 (P. F. Zimin), etc.

[205] Bohdan Krawchenko, "Soviet Ukraine under Nazi Occupation, 1941-4," in Yury Boshyk, ed., *Ukraine during World War II: History and Its Aftermath. A Symposium* (Edmonton, Canada, 1986), p. 25.

[206] Maistrenko, *Istoriia moho pokolinnia*, pp. 328, 332, 334, and 340. For other cases, see Stakhiv, "Natsional'no-politychne zhyttia Donbasu v 1941–1943 rr." (9 September 1956), p. 6.

[207] Alexander Dallin and Ralph S. Mavrogordato, "Rodionov: A Case Study in War-Time Redefection," *American Slavic and East European Review*, 18:1 (February 1959), p. 32.

One interesting case involved the Ukrainian V. A. Kovshik. A non–party member, fifty-seven years of age, and a shop director, Kovshik was left behind the front line in 1942 by the Soviet secret police to eliminate traitors. In April 1943 he succeeded in infiltrating the German police in the village of Almazna in Voroshylovhrad *oblast'*. He managed to save many Communists from the Germans and had many traitors executed by the Germans as Communists. He even converted the police agents to the partisan movement when the Germans were about to retreat in September 1943. Yet Kovshik was arrested immediately after liberation by Smersh, the counterintelligence unit of the Soviet secret police. People testified against him. It took Smersh considerable effort to confirm that Kovshik was indeed a Soviet security police agent. From his personal file, it appears that even his wife did not know for whom Kovshik was actually working. Kovshik was released in January 1944.[208]

Another case concerned A. A. Shvedov. In December 1941 the Soviet secret police sent the thirty-year-old agent to Stalino to organize partisan groups. He was not able to do much work in enemy territory before he was caught in August 1942 (some sources say May 1942) by the Germans. He was tortured by a Russian interrogator and three "Cossacks." After the Red Army reoccupied Stalino, he and his comrades were arrested and tried by the Soviets in 1944. Shvedov was accused of breaking down and helping the Germans to identify and execute Soviet secret agents and partisans. Shvedov was sentenced to be shot and executed.[209] Yet when local people did painstaking work to establish what actually happened, it became clear that Shvedov did not betray the country: he had been shrewd enough to name only those who had already been exposed as Soviet agents. As a German "agent," Shvedov tried to confuse the Germans and even succeeded in recruiting agents for the Soviets and converting traitors back to the Soviet camp. In 1973 Shvedov was rehabilitated: even though at the trial Shvedov overstated his success, he had committed no crime under German occupation; the 1944 court had ignored important facts and distorted his activity.[210] Shvedov was a victim of the suspicion cast by the Soviet government on those who risked their lives to fight the enemies.

There were numerous cases in the Donbas in which heroes were turned into traitors. The group organized by G. I. Tkachenko in Voroshylovhrad *oblast'* was a very successful partisan unit. When local party leaders deserted, the partisans operated on their own. The Red Army commanders' testimonies to that effect did not help. Tkachenko and his heroic comrades were tortured and forced to confess that they had actively collaborated with the Germans. It appears that the same local party leaders who had deserted returned after the

[208]DALO, f. 3747, op. 3, spr. 1355-r.
[209]TsDAHO, f. 1, op. 23, spr. 3839, ark. 45zv–46zv and DADO, f. 5000-p, op. 1, spr. 115, ark. 3–9, 39.
[210]DADO, f. 5000-p, op. 1, spr. 115, ark. 52–56.

liberation and had the partisans tried as collaborators. In the summer of 1943 fourteen of the partisans were thus executed.[211]

The case of the Krasnodon partisan group " Young Guard," immortalized by A. A. Fadeev's famous novel of the same name (1945), is also illuminating. When Krasnodon was occupied in the summer of 1942, the party and the secret police left a group of Communists and agents. The leaders of the group fled with a large sum of money and gold, intended for partisan activity, and secret documents on the group were lost in the process. Of those people who remained, some conducted no underground activity while others were said to have become active collaborators with the Germans.[212] In the meantime, young Komsomol patriots, trapped in Krasnodon, began to organize themselves into partisan groups. One of these groups was the Young Guard. They had had little contact with party organizations, which were absent or at best utterly inactive in the occupied Krasnodon. Some of the youth were inexperienced in underground activity and were soon exposed. Nearly all members of the group were arrested, tortured, and executed by the Germans. After the liberation of Krasnodon, a Soviet commission concluded that Kashuk, or O. Koshovyi, was the leader of the partisan group and that V. I. Tret'iakevych was a traitor who sold out his comrades. (Both men had been murdered by the Germans.) Koshovyi's mother contributed to this version of events, casting one as a hero and the other as a villain. Both Fadeev and the party leaders who returned from the safe home front accepted this version. Several survivors of the group were not allowed to speak up.[213]

In fact, Tret'iakevych, trained and dispatched to Krasnodon by the NKVD, was the leader who had organized the group and defended it.[214] It is not clear whether there were any traitors in the group. Some, including Koshovyi, may have been unwittingly trapped by the police.[215] According to one survivor (who knew Tret'iakevych personally and was subsequently tried as a "traitor"), some members, including Koshovyi, were thieves and speculators, who were caught selling foodstuffs stolen from a German lorry; they did not even see

[211]TsDAHO, f. 1, op. 22, spr. 192. The information on the torture is based on several conversations I had with the Luhans'k historian V. F. Semystiaha.

[212]Volodymyr Semystiaha and Iurii Kozovs'kyi, "Shche zh bulo u Krasnodoni?" *Molod' Ukrainy*, 12 September 1992, and Vladimir Semistiaga, "Kak voznikaiut mify," *Donbas*, 1992, nos. 9–10, pp. 237–38.

[213]Semystiaha and Kozovs'kyi, "Shcho zh bulo u Krasnodoni? Mif druhyi," *Molod' Ukrainy*, 18 September 1992, and "Ego nazyval' 'Kashuk'? 'Molodaia gvardiia' v svete real'nykh faktov i svidetel'stv," *Pul's* (Luhans'k), 1992, no. 20, pp. 4–5.

[214]V. Semystiaha, "'Na zv'iazok ne vyishov'," *Bakhmuts'kyi shliakh* (Luhans'k), 1995, nos. 1–2, pp. 33–34.

[215]Semystiaha and Kozovs'kyi, "Shcho zh bulo u Krasnodoni? Mif Druhyi"; idem, "Shcho zh bulo u Krasnodoni? Mif tretii," *Molod' Ukrainy*, 22 September 1992; and idem, "Ego nazyvali 'Kashuk.' "

that the lorry carried weapons as well.[216] Whatever the case, Soviet officials conspired to perpetuate the myth of Fadeev's story. Tret'iakevych was rehabilitated in 1960. Still the whole episode was not made public. In the meantime the Tret'iakevych family was harassed by those who believed the official version. Only recently have local historians begun to expose the incident on the basis of documents from the former KGB archives.[217]

Bitter toward those who remained under occupation, Soviet authorities hunted down traitors among the few survivors once Krasnodon was liberated. In September 1943, in connection with the Young Guard debacle, three persons were publicly executed in the city in the presence of a huge crowd: M. E. Kuleshov, forty-five, a Russian lawyer who had worked for the city administration set up by the Germans; V. G. Gromov, fifty-one, Russian, a party member, assistant director at Mine 1bis before the war, and an ordinary timber hand under the Germans; G. P. Pocheptsov, twenty-one, Russian, and a former member of the Hummer (*Molot*) (partisan group similar to the Young Guard).[218]

Kuleshov had a blemish on his political record: during the civil war he had been mobilized by the Denikin army and fought among the ranks of the White Army. Yet in 1941 he fought in the war against the Germans, was wounded, and returned to Krasnodon. As German troops approached the city in 1942, he was not able to evacuate because no transport was provided, so he had no option but to stay. With the Germans came former Cossacks who had been in hiding or returned from exile. He got involved in the Cossack movement, which, according to Kuleshov, was rather miserable, manned mainly by old, frail men. Kuleshov admitted that he voluntarily worked for the Germans, because he believed that the Soviet government was no more and feared that he would otherwise be punished for having worked for the Soviet government. He maintained, however, that he had never been an enemy of the Soviet government, and that he had honestly worked for it. When the Red Army came to repel the invaders, he fled with the Germans, but then he decided to come back voluntarily to "atone for his crime." At the trial held (in part in closed sessions) in August 1943, Kuleshov pleaded guilty to working for the Germans. Yet he denied the most serious charges that he participated in the killings of the Young Guard members and that he had been sent back to Krasnodon by the German

---

[216]Stepan Kuryliak, "Khto ie khto," *Zona* (Kiev), 1992, no. 3, pp. 204–5. Ievhen Stakhiv has claimed that Koshovyi and others fought for the Ukrainian democratic cause or that at least they were national Communists. (Stakhiv, "Natsional'no-politychne zhyttia Donbasu v 1941–1943 rr.," [26 August 1956], p. 6; idem, "I v Krasnodoni diialo natsionalistychne pidpillia," and idem, "Iakby Oleha Koshevoho ne stratyly nimtsi – stratyly b bil'shovyky.") There is no evidence to support his claim. (See *Ukraina moloda*, 25 September 1992, p. 3.) In fact, in his recent memoirs, Stakhiv did not repeat this important contention. See his *Kriz' tiurmy, pidpillia i kordony*, pp. 135–36.

[217]See the several articles by Semystiaha and Kozovs'kyi cited earlier, and idem, "Zhizn', smert' i bessmertie Viktora Tret'iakevicha," *Zhizn' Luganska*, no. 39 (September 1993).

[218]AUSBULO, no. 10399, t. 2, ark. 344, and TsDAHO, f. 1, op. 23, spr. 684, ark. 63–67.

intelligence. He contended at his trial that he had been forced by interrogators to admit to crimes he had not committed. All the same, he was executed.[219]

Gromov was also accused of selling out the Young Guard and Krasnodon Communists to the Germans and of staying under the Soviets to spy for Germany. At the trial he recanted his confession at preliminary hearings: he had been tortured into incriminating himself by interrogators. He did work for the Germans, which he admitted was a crime. He had been encircled by enemy forces during the evacuation and had had no choice but to return to Krasnodon at the risk of his life. To save his life, he, a Communist, reported everyday to the Germans. Believing that the Soviet government was no more, he began to work for the Germans as an ordinary timber hand. He did denounce G. S. Retivov, who was working for the German police, to the Germans. Because he knew that Retivov was an enemy of the Soviet government, he wanted to have him arrested by the Germans. Before the war Gromov voted Retivov out of the party, and now he let the Germans know that Retivov had applied to enter the party before the war. Retivov was arrested by the Germans but apparently managed to survive and run away with the Germans.[220] Gromov was also executed.

Pocheptsov, a stepson of Gromov's, pleaded guilty to the same charges of selling out the Young Guard and spying for the Germans. Under German arrest, he had denounced the Young Guard to save his life. Yet, as it turned out later, it did not help the Germans because the Young Guard had already been exposed. Subsequently Pocheptsov was released by the Germans. Gromov cursed Pocheptsov for what he had done, but did not report Pocheptsov's crime to the Soviet authorities when they returned to Krasnodon.[221] Pocheptsov was also executed.

There was yet another defendant at the trial, I. T. Chernyshev, twenty-one, Russian, a worker and a former member of the Komsomol. He, too, could not evacuate when Krasnodon fell to the Germans. Chernyshev was arrested by the Germans but managed to get released by agreeing to work for them. He worked in a mine but then hid in the city. When the Soviets returned, he assisted the Soviet secret police in exposing the *politsai*. Afterward he was arrested by the Soviet secret police. At the trial he pleaded guilty to staying behind in Krasnodon to spy for Germany. Even so, he was acquitted by the

---

[219]AUSBULO, no. 10399, t. 1 and t. 2, ark. 315–16. Note that in these and other files on war criminals, most documents, including trial proceedings, are written in longhand. Only those which recorded their (forced) confessions of crimes are typed. This suggests that the police typed selected documents to please the local authorities as well as Moscow and Kiev.

[220]Ibid., t. 1, particularly ark. 51 and 238–39, and t. 2, ark. 308–16. Retivov fled with the Germans and was absent from Krasnodon at the time of the trial. He was repatriated in 1945 from Germany, tried in 1946, and sentenced to ten years of corrective labor. AUSBULO, no. 8138, ark. 68–76.

[221]AUSBULO, no. 10399, t. 2, ark. 315, and t. 3, ark. 407.

court![222] Chernyshev survived the Soviet regime to testify that he had been forced by Soviet interrogators to incriminate himself (and, no doubt, others as well).[223]

In 1991–92 the court reviewed the cases of Kuleshov, Gromov, and Pocheptsov, but did not rehabilitate the three men.

The war had provided the Donbas population with alternatives. In actuality, however, each alternative involved danger. To save their lives, people had to be cunning, resourceful, and opportunistic. The dividing line between bravery, heroism, and crime was not easy to draw. Still, the Soviet security police continued to divide people into heroes and villains, sometimes mistakenly and other times deliberately.

The case of the "association of engineers" in Stalino is another good example. In February 1947 three engineers and one worker were tried in Stalino for their alleged treacherous acts under German occupation: organizing an anti-Soviet association of engineers and operating the Stalino Metallurgical Plant for the Germans. The four were non–party members: K. V. Messerle, born in 1889 in Kursk into a Swiss merchant family, assistant director of the Donets'k Industrial Institute, and chief engineer at the plant during the occupation; V. G. Gladkii (V. H. Hladkyi, who has been mentioned earlier), forty-one years of age at the time of the trial, son of a clergyman, chief mechanic at the plant during the occupation; O. A. Grechko (Hrechko), born in 1900, director of mechanical equipment at the plant before the war, director of supply during the occupation, soldier in the Red Army from 1944 to 1945, wounded in battle, and awarded a medal "For the Victory over Germany"; N. I. Chumachenko, a worker of twenty-four years of age, who served as an interpreter. All but Messerle were Ukrainians. Messerle and Gladkii were condemned to twenty years of corrective labor, and Grechko and Chumachenko to ten years.[224]

At the trial all pleaded guilty of working for the Germans and of other relatively minor crimes (in Messerle's case, refusing to evacuate from Stalino; in Gladkii's case, having contact with Ukrainian nationalists; or, in Grechko's case, having served in the White army during the civil war). Yet they denied other, more serious charges of exposing partisans and Communists to the Germans. Some kind of deal had been struck before the trial (probably admission of guilt in exchange for a light sentence). The unexpected sentences of long prison terms upset the defendants. So they fought back after they were incarcerated through appeals to the court. Messerle recanted his admission that he had stayed deliberately in Stalino to wait for the Germans. He did not deny explicitly that the association ever existed, but insisted that it had never met and never conducted any agitation. He claimed that he had been forcibly taken

[222] Ibid., t. 2, ark. 140–41, 180–82, and 336.
[223] See Semistiaga and Kozovs'kyi, "Zhizn', smert' i bessmertie Viktora Tret'iakevicha."
[224] AUSBUDO, no. 35462-pf, 2 vols.

to Germany with the retreating German troops, but voluntarily reported to return to the motherland. He had never been an enemy of the Soviet Union. He committed the crime of working for the Germans, but only because there was no alternative.[225]

Gladkii contended that he had first heard about the association from the interrogator and that it could not have existed. His request to confront Messerle was never granted. He claimed that he had been forced by the Germans to work. Then he was taken by force to Germany, where he broke off all contact with Ukrainian nationalists and carefully preserved his Soviet passport: "I have always been a Soviet citizen." He had originally become interested in the OUN because of its call for resistance to the Germans. In a 1955 appeal Gladkii noted that he had been beaten and threatened by interrogators into admitting crimes he had not committed.[226]

In a similar vein Grechko sent appeals from the Gulags. He maintained that he had worked to evacuate the plant and people as the Germans approached Stalino, as a result of which he was trapped in the city. Initially he refused to work for the Germans, but he was forced to do so. He was coerced into retreating with the Germans, but hid in Odessa and, when the Red Army came, volunteered for the Red Army. He had never served in the White Army during the civil war of 1918–20. He contended in his appeals that his case had been fabricated.[227]

Chumachenko also appealed from the Gulags. He, like many Stalino residents, could not evacuate through no fault of his own. He had gone into hiding, but could not hide forever. So as not to be sent to Germany as forced labor, he began to work as a loader at a German food storage. Then he was forced to serve as an interpreter because of his knowledge of German. When the Germans retreated, they put a gun to his head and forced him to flee with them. In Germany he refused to serve as an interpreter, for which he was punished. He maintained that he had voluntarily come back to the Soviet Union.[228]

The appeals of the four were turned down several times. It is not clear whether they have been rehabilitated since.[229]

The Soviet security police was deeply concerned that the war and the evac-

---

[225] Ibid., t. 2, ark. 319–20.

[226] Ibid., ark. 372.

[227] See, for example, ibid., ark. 355–63.

[228] Ibid., ark. 430–34.

[229] *Ispytanie dolgom. Vospominaniia chekistov*, 3rd ed. (Donets'k, 1989), pp. 173–92, which portrays the "association" in detail, still maintains that the accused and many other engineers were traitors and enemies of the people. There were other people like these defendants who were subjected to the same fate. See Lev Vakhtin in Marcel Sztafrowski, *Direction Stalino. Un Polonais dans les camps soviétiques* (Paris, 1987), pp. 74–76. For a list of engineers who were accused of organizing a similar association "Vostok" and collaborating with the Germans in Stalino, see TsDAHO, f. 1, op. 23, spr. 3839, ark. 27–41.

uation had annulled party rule and created political alternatives. Clearly they admitted the existence of both heroes and villains. However, no middle ground was allowed. Kuleshov, Gromov, Messerle, Gladkii, and their company, according to the Soviet doctrine, ought to have crossed the lines to the Soviet side at any cost or to have engaged in anti-German underground activity. Just as in the 1930s, mere suspicion, not proof, was often enough to destroy individuals. (Some of those who had been safely ensconced somewhere during the war actively hunted down suspects when they returned to the liberated Donbas.) Yet paradoxical as it may appear, the postwar experience suggests that the war changed the nature of Soviet state terror: Stalin had to come to terms with the fact that it was not possible to terrorize tens of millions of people who had been exposed to political alternatives during the war (Chapter 8).

8   The Postwar Years

STALIN FEARED new political ferment in the wake of the war. His power had not been directly challenged, but the liberating impact of the war was evident in the Donbas as elsewhere. Like a magnet, the Donbas attracted people, providing opportunities to fortune hunters and refuge to fugitives, such as the Ukrainian nationalists, and Jews who had been spurned elsewhere. In the post-Stalin years, the Donbas gave rise to independent labor movements, but their independence (regarded as a narrow-minded self-interest) was accepted neither by anti-Communist liberals nor by nationalist dissidents. The Donbas workers struck repeatedly in the perestroika and post-Soviet era, continuing to demonstrate their independence and thus incurring the wrath of the political centers.

Victory and Famine

The end of the long and brutal war was a cause for celebration for many Soviet citizens. One American diplomat has written of "the almost indescribable joy of the Soviet people on V-E Day."[1] Another recalled V-E Day in Moscow:

> The news reached the Soviet people early on May 10, a day none of us in the United States Embassy in Moscow will forget.
>
> Red Square was aswirl with people milling, smiling, congratulating anyone in uniform. The uniformed Americans who went out of the Embassy's chancery, across from the Kremlin, were carried off to Red Square on the shoulders of exultant Muscovites. A civilian attaché, I joined the crowd in the square. My most vivid memory is of a Red Army major looking toward me and saying to no one in particular, "Now it's time to live!". . . .
>
> The throng held up no placards and shouted no slogans. It wasn't an

[1] Frederick C. Barghoorn, "The Soviet Union between War and Cold War," *Annals of the American Academy of Political and Social Science*, 263 (May 1949), p. 6.

official event. It was something almost unthinkable in Stalin's Russia – a spontaneous popular demonstration.[2]

Similar scenes prevailed everywhere in the Soviet Union. In the Donbas, all the streets in towns and villages were filled night and day with people of all ages. They hugged, sang, and danced. In Druzhkivka, twenty thousand people demonstrated spontaneously on the streets of the city with portraits of party and government leaders.[3]

Even if the end of bloodshed was a cause for celebration, the liberation of the Donbas, which preceded the final victory, and the return of the Soviet security police were not a cause for rejoicing for everyone. Luhans'k was liberated as early as February 1943, as was Krasnodon. Donets'k and Artemivs'k were taken back by the Soviet forces in September 1943. There is no way of knowing how many Donbas residents retreated voluntarily with the Germans. Subsequently some people returned of their own volition; some were repatriated unwillingly. Those who had chosen to stay behind under the Germans had reason to fear the returning Soviet power, which had made it known that such a choice was tantamount to treason. When the NKVD returned to Lysychans'k, they arrested everyone who had worked for the Germans. The prisons soon filled with people. Those who "had worked for the sake of the people" (whatever this may have meant) were released, while others were dispatched eastward. In Kramators'k, the NKVD shot twenty women who had married or been intimate with Germans.[4] In Slov'ians'k, Kramators'k, Kostiantynivka, and elsewhere Soviet women who had borne children to Germans were murdered by the secret police along with their children.[5] The victory was not a liberation for all Soviet citizens. According to an American engineer, in 1945 in the Donbas "stories that the Americans or British were to take over the Ukraine were current and caused much jubilation."[6]

Although no records remain to attest to the fact, it appears that as in France and elsewhere, there were cases of summary executions in the Donbas and elsewhere in the Soviet Union.[7] The secret police came quickly to control the liberated areas. The western Ukraine was an exception. There numerous Ukrainian nationalists continued to fight against the Soviet forces well into the late 1940s, with tremendous casualties on both sides.[8]

[2] Robert C. Tucker, "V-E Day, Moscow: 'Time to Live!'" *New York Times*, 11 May 1985.
[3] DADO, f. 326p, op. 2, spr. 923, ark. 65 and 70.
[4] TsDAHO, f. 3833, op. 1, spr. 113, ark. 3.
[5] Volodymyr Kosyk, *Ukraina i Nimechchyna u druhii svitovii viini* (Paris, 1993), p. 337.
[6] Louis Ernst, "Inside a Soviet Industry," *Fortune* (Chicago), October 1949, p. 177.
[7] According to one study, "At least four and a half thousand summary executions took place in France in the months following the Liberation"; many more were unrecorded. Peter Novick, *The Resistance versus Vichy: The Purge of Collaborators in Liberated France* (London, 1968), pp. 71 and 202–8. For summary executions in Vinnytsia, see Amir Weiner's forthcoming work on postwar Vinnytsia.
[8] Ivan Bilas, *Represyvno-karal'na systema v Ukraini 1917–1953. Suspil'no-politychnyi ta istoryko-pravovyi analiz*, 2 vols. (Kiev, 1994), 2:604. For extensive operations of the NKVD

Brutal though postliberation rule was, Moscow could not possibly have resumed the kind of terror it had used against the population in the prewar years. Before the war mere casual contact with a German national was considered suspicious and could lead to execution. After the liberation, Moscow would have had to terrorize the whole population of the occupied territories. In fact, Stalin did deport wholesale small nations (Crimean Tartars, Chechens, Ingushes, Kalmyks, Karachaevs, and many others) whom he held responsible collectively for the collaboration of some of their members with the Germans.[9]

Terror did continue in various forms. In Stalino *oblast'*, less than two months after liberation, 2,569 people were arrested as German spies, traitors, and collaborators.[10] An unknown number of people were executed.[11] In the first seven months of 1946 the Ukrainian court tried 21,412 people as political criminals (traitors, spies, burgomasters, etc.). Of them, 452, or about 2 percent, were sentenced to death, 15,512 to ten years of imprisonment, 4,922 to hard labor, and 524 to terms shorter than ten years. Some people had their sentences commuted because of their repentance and subsequent service in the Red Army.[12] How many people were falsely accused is not known.[13] Harsh as the sentences were, they appeared lenient in comparison with those of the Great Terror period.

The war experience made the binary division of people into friends and foes no longer sustainable even in the eyes of the Soviet secret police. It is instructive that the elder of a village near Artemivs'k was not arrested by the Soviet security organ despite his alleged collaboration. He had written favorable reports to the Germans on those Communists who had dekulakized him, thereby saving the lives of twenty-two Communists. The villagers would not allow him to be arrested.[14]

Repatriates appeared dangerous to the Soviet regime: they may have gone abroad of their own will; at the very least they had been exposed to different

in this period in western Ukraine, see Iu. I. Shapoval, *Liudyna i systema. Shtrykhy do portretu totalitarnoi doby v Ukraini* (Kiev, 1994), pp. 43–69.

[9] See the classic by A. Nekrich, *The Punished Peoples* (New York, 1978), and S. U. Alieva, comp., *Tak eto bylo. Natsional'nye repressii v SSSR 1919–1952 gody. Repressirovannye narody segodnia*, 3 vols. (Moscow, 1993).

[10] TsDAHO, f. 1, op. 23, spr. 3839, ark. 48.

[11] The prominent historian and archaeologist S. O. Loktiushev, who protected valuable items in museums in Luhans'k under occupation, was reported to have died in prison. In fact, he was shot. See V. F. Semystiaha, "S. O. Loktiushev," in *Shosta Vseukrains'ka naukova konferentsiia z istorychnoho kraieznavstva (m. Luts'k, veresen'–zhovten' 1993 r.)* (Luts'k, 1993), p. 262.

[12] TsDAHO, f. 1, op. 17, spr. 3, ark. 60–62.

[13] F. I. Perel'man, a Jewish worker in Slov'ianoserbs'k near Voroshylovhrad, was falsely accused of refusing to evacuate and selling Jewish doctors to the Germans. Perel'man changed his name to Peremanov and survived the German occupation. Then he served in the Red Army and was wounded. Yet he was arrested in 1945 and given five years of imprisonment. He was subsequently rehabilitated. DALO, f. 3747, op. 3, spr. 12353-r.

[14] TsDAHO, f. 1, op. 17, spr. 37, ark. 293.

societies, cultures, and politics. Among the Soviet civilian laborers abroad, about 70 percent were said to have wished to return to the Soviet Union; 5 percent chose not to return; and 25 percent vacillated out of fear of repression. The Soviet POWs were said to have inclinations similar to their civilian counterparts.[15] In the repatriation process, mistakes were made by the Western powers involved: some were repatriated against their will; some (mainly non-Soviet citizens who had emigrated to the West before the war) were illegally returned to the Soviet Union. Among the repatriated were war criminals. As of 1 March 1946, 272,867, or 6.5 percent of the total expatriates, were handed over to the Soviet security police. The majority, 57.81 percent, were allowed to return home, 33.56 percent were taken by the army and the Defense Ministry, and 2.13 percent were at "transit points."[16]

In this respect, too, those who, in the view of the security organ, were politically suspect by default, survived much more successfully after the war than in the 1930s. Overall, according to official data, the execution of political criminals declined in the postwar years: 4,252 in 1945 (a sharp increase from 3,029 in 1944), 2,896 in 1946, 1,106 in 1947, and 0 in 1948, when the death sentence was temporarily suspended.[17] If these figures reflect the actual scale of repression to any degree at all, the majority of the repatriates who were handed over to the security police seem to have survived. In July 1949, according to police data, 131,394 former "Vlasovites," 95,552 OUN members, and 2,277 collaborators (*nemetskie posobniki*) had been sent into special exile.[18] No doubt they included, in their numbers, those arrested inside the Soviet Union. Yet they do reflect the postwar change in state terror: more than 200,000 who almost certainly would have been executed in the 1930s were allowed to live.[19]

Quickly superseded by the brutality of everyday life, the joy of victory did not last long. Many repatriates, even those at large, had to live with the opprobrium of being "traitors."[20] Repatriates were often robbed on their way

---

[15]V. N. Zemskov, "K voprosu o repatriatsii sovetskikh grazhdan 1944–1951 gody," *Istoriia SSSR*, 1990, no. 4, p. 27.

[16]Ibid., p. 36. Those repatriated very early (before the victory) may have been treated by the Soviet authorities more harshly than those repatriated later en masse. See Hans Fröhlich, *In der vierten Nachtwache. Erlebnisberichte aus der Deportation* (Munich, 1977), p. 56.

[17]V. P. Popov, "Gosudarstvennyi terror v sovetskoi Rossii. 1923–1953 gg. (istochniki i ikh interpretatsiia)," *Otechestvennye arkhivy*, 1992, no. 2, p. 28.

[18]V. N. Zemskov, "Spetsposelentsy (po dokumentatsii NKVD-MVD SSSR)," *Sotsiologicheskie issledovaniia*, 1990, no. 11, p. 12.

[19]This may have been some kind of political amnesty, but the actual amnesty benefited mainly criminal offenders, not political prisoners. See *Resistance in the Gulag: Memoirs, Letters, Documents* (Moscow, 1992), p. 86.

[20]For the bitterness one repatriate entertained about the way they were treated by the Soviet government, see, for example, Viktor Andriianov, *Pamiat' so znakom OST. Sud'ba "vostochnykh rabochikh" v ikh sobstvennykh svidetel'stvakh, pis'makh i dokumentakh* (Moscow, 1993), pp. 100–1.

back home. Then they were left out in the cold on the Donbas steppes.[21] Upon returning from captivity to Luhans'k, M. G. Belozerov, a former Red Army officer, was fortunate to land a job at a factory. Yet he lived in dire privation and in fear of arrest for having been in Germany as a POW. In January 1947, in the midst of famine, out of despair he killed his wife and daughter and hanged himself.[22]

Crime shot up. For the reconstruction of Donbas industry, many criminals were brought in and left unsupervised. In 1945 nearly a hundred thousand repatriates were said to have been mobilized to the Donbas mines. Some local officials complained that the mobilized were "former traitors" and "Vlasovites." Whatever the case, the Donbas, with its vast need for manpower in reconstruction, attracted all kinds of people.[23] Everyone was said to participate in robbery. Even in public areas in the Donbas, people were frequently beaten about the head and robbed in plain view. Trains were favorite targets for robbers. Every night people were terrorized by the sound of incessant shots from automatic rifles. The presence of large numbers of street waifs added to crime.[24]

The image of the free steppe, for all its problems, revived in the Donbas in the postwar years. Like a magnet, the Donbas began to attract all kinds of criminals and adventurers. In the postwar years one out of every ten Stalino residents landed in prison. The Donbas became known as a place for "making a quick buck." Marketplaces were areas where people gathered and were robbed. Here and there fights broke out. In Stalino, Assyrians returned to monopolize the shoe business, and Jews the barber's.[25] Life was dangerous and hungry. The acute population imbalance between the sexes caused by the war made women's lives particularly difficult.[26] Many children were left fatherless. Nevertheless, the children managed to play in this bleak world, using German skulls as footballs and digging up German graves in hopes of finding something valuable, particularly crosses. In spite of the real possibility of being attacked, people walked about the city for lack of other entertainment.[27]

If the Donbas maintained elements of the free steppe, then it was no surprise that the Donbas appeared even to the Ukrainian nationalists as a place of refuge. At the end of 1947, when the Ukrainian Insurgent Army faced de-

---

[21] TsDAHO, f. 1, op. 23, spr. 1479, ark. 8, and spr. 1477, ark. 49.

[22] Ibid., op. 17, spr. 4, ark. 51.

[23] DADO, f. 326-p, op. 2, spr., 850, ark. 4–9.

[24] Ibid.

[25] Evgenii Iasenov, "Poslevoennoe Stalino: vodka deshevle khleba," *Gorod* (Donets'k), no. 43 (11 November 1993), p. 10.

[26] The vast majority of divorces were initiated by men whose scarcity made them more valuable. Of the 481 cases arbitrated by the court in Stalino between 1945 and 1949 I have examined, 365 or 76% were initiated by husbands. See files in DADO, f. 3410, op. 2.

[27] Iasenov, "Poslevoennoe Stalino."

feat in its fight against the Soviet government in western Ukraine, "the UPA command ordered them [its members] to escape, either by posing as workers being resettled in the Donbas or by fighting their way to the American occupation zones in Germany and Austria."[28]

In the Donbas, as elsewhere, the victory over Germany reinforced anti-Semitism. The evacuation of Soviet officials believed to be Jewish during the war raised popular suspicion that Jews avoided fighting and took refuge before anyone else.[29] When the Soviet security police returned to the Donbas later in the war, Ukrainian nationalists in the Donbas reported that it was "interesting to note that the NKVD was composed exclusively of Jews" and that residents spoke of the secret police being composed of Jews alone.[30] Even the famous film director O. Dovzhenko was secretly recorded by the police during the war complaining that Ukrainian culture was being harmed by Jews, who "hated us, hate us, and will hate us" and "seek to worm their way in everywhere and take everything into their hands."[31] After the war, when Jews returned from the front or the evacuation, they were greeted with hostility by other residents. When Jews wished to regain their former flats and property, anti-Semitism often exploded into open confrontation. Thus, in almost all cities in Ukraine, anti-Semitism became sharper than before. According to official reports, this was related in part to the erroneous perception that there were proportionately fewer Jews in the Red Army than any other ethnic group.[32] The report also noted that anti-Semitism strengthened Zionism among the Ukrainian Jews.[33]

As it turned out, the postwar years were not a "time to live." As Sheila Fitzpatrick has argued, hopes for a return to "normalcy" were bound to be dashed because the Soviet Union had no model of normalcy to which to return.[34] As Robert C. Tucker, who was stationed in the American Embassy in Moscow at that time, later recalled, it was time

> to gear up for another great war whose strong possibility was lodged, Stalin said on Feb. 9, 1946, in the nature of "imperialism." Hence, three or four

[28] John A. Armstrong, *Ukrainian Nationalism*, 3rd ed. (Englewood, Colo., 1990), p. 221.

[29] DADO, f. 326p, op. 1, spr. 1897, ark. 5–15. For a firsthand observation of acute anti-Semitism elsewhere in Ukraine in 1941, see James E. Mace and Leonid Heretz, eds., *Oral History Project of the Commission on the Ukraine Famine* (Washington, D.C., 1990), 2:654 and 700.

[30] TsDAVO, f. 3833, op. 1, spr. 113, ark. 3.

[31] TsDAHO, f. 1, op. 23, spr. 685, ark. 82. For Dovzhenko's anti-Semitism before the war, see Marco Carynnyk, "Alexander Dovzhenko's 1939 Autobiography," *Journal of Ukrainian Studies*, 19:1 (Summer 1994), p. 27.

[32] TsDAHO, f. 1, op. 23, spr. 1363. This perception was not substantiated by data, which show a very high rate of Jews' participation in combat. See Maiia Aleksenitser and Semen Averbukh, "Statistika evreiskogo geroizma v gody Velikoi Otechestvennoi voiny," in *Evreis'ka istoriia ta kul'tura v Ukraini. Materialy konferentsii. Kyiv. 8–9 hrudnia 1994* (Kiev, 1995), p. 4.

[33] TsDAHO, f. 1, op. 23, spr. 1363.

[34] Sheila Fitzpatrick, "Postwar Soviet Society: The 'Return to Normalcy,' 1945–1953," in Susan J. Linz, ed., *The Impact of World War II on the Soviet Union* (Totowa, N.J., 1985).

more five-year plans ("five-year plan" symbolized sacrifice) would be needed to guarantee against "all contingencies." A Russian in whose apartment I was sitting when Stalin's speech came over the radio lay his head on his folded arms when he heard those words. All over Russia, I believe, people did the same. It was the end of expectations for a postwar life free of the tension and privation experienced throughout the 1930s. The postwar period was being prefigured as a potential new prewar period. The cold war was on.[35]

The end of the war and the onset of the cold war were accompanied by severe famine in the country.

The famine of 1946–47 affected much of Ukraine, including the Donbas and Moldova, Western Siberia, the southern Urals, the lower and middle Volga, and much of the Black Earth Region. Unlike the 1932–33 famine, this famine also affected the non–Black Earth Region and major cities such as Moscow, Leningrad, Novosibirsk, and others. The famine and the diseases related to it took a heavy toll of 1 million lives.[36] In Stalino *oblast'*, according to incomplete data, in 1947 2,703 deaths from hunger were recorded. (Many more died of famine-related diseases.) Of them, 60 percent took place in the cities. Those least provided for (sick people, retirees, invalids) accounted for the majority (65 percent) of the deaths. More men (60 percent of the victims) died than women.[37]

Several factors combined to create this tragedy in the wake of victory. The administration of agriculture changed little after the war. It was rigidly planned and controlled from the center for state procurements of grain and other agricultural produce. To fulfill the plans, collective farms used the farmers as if they were slave laborers subject to military discipline. Such a system seemed like militarized serfdom to a boy who fled from a dreadful famine in Stalino to a collective farm. (He was later arrested for speaking among his friends of serfdom in the countryside.)[38] To create sufficient grain reserves, the government imposed unrealistically high procurement targets on a collective farm system weakened by years of war. When the collective farms desperately needed animal and man power, they were not aided but were forced to part with more grain than they could possibly afford. There was not much incentive to increase tilled areas. Little was paid to the farmers, in any case. They were therefore more interested in tilling their private plots, which enabled them to survive. The number of farmers who failed to perform the minimum number

[35] Tucker, "V-E Day, Moscow."

[36] V. F. Zima, "Golod v Rossii 1946–1947 godov," *Otechestvennaia istoriia*, 1993, no. 1, pp. 35 and 43. For a detailed analysis of the famine, see Zima, *Golod v SSSR 1946–1947 godov: proiskhozhdenie i posledstviia* (Moscow, 1996).

[37] A. I. Zadneprovskii, "Zhertvy goloda 1946–1947 gg. v Donbasse," *Letopis' Donbassa. Kraevedcheskii sbornik*, vol. 1 (Donets'k, 1992), pp. 56–58. The data seem to include those deaths which took place in one district in Voroshylovhrad *oblast'*.

[38] Interview 1.

of labor days (*trudodni*) reached a record level in 1946.[39] To make matters worse, large areas of the country, including the Donbas, were assaulted by a severe drought. In Stalino *oblast'* a yield of 9.5 centner (1 centner = 100 kilograms) of grain per hectare was planned for 1946, but the actual yield was only 6.6 centner. Yet the procurement plans were raised.[40]

In the autumn of 1946, when the countryside was suffering from the ill effects of the drought and the high procurement quota, the government annulled food rationing for twenty-eight million rural residents.[41] People starved. Many despaired. T. M. Tsigar'ov, a worker at the Evdokievka Mine in Stalino, was reported to have declared to his fellow workers that "life is becoming worse and worse every day. I don't know how I can go on living any more."[42] Many people believed that the country was starving because of the aid given to Poland and other eastern European countries. A collier at Mine 9 in Stalino, Ivan Tokarev, was quoted by informers as having contended that "I don't believe that there are no grain reserves for us in the Soviet Union. This [famine] is because our government helps the democratic countries [i.e., countries of 'people's democracy']."[43]

Tokarev was right in that the government possessed enough grain reserves to feed the hungry population. Yet it was loath to part with them. In the autumn of 1947, after a relatively good harvest, which eased the famine, the government even increased the grain reserves by 80–90 percent.[44] It did so to abolish food rationing in the cities and enact a currency reform with the aim of stabilizing the economy. (The reform, however, devalued the ruble and wiped out much of the savings of the population.) The day rationing was abolished (17 December 1947), famished people in the Donbas rushed to buy bread. "A large number of deaths" were recorded on the happy day: people swallowed bread a loaf at a time and died of volvulus.[45] Bread became freely available, but it was in short supply and, as before, people had to queue for bread for hours. Even after rationing was abolished, the famine continued in many parts of the country.[46]

[39] I. M. Makoviichuk and Iu. H. Pyliavets, "Holod na Ukraini u 1946–1947 rr.," *Ukrains'kyi istorychnyi zhurnal*, 1990, no. 8, p. 19.
[40] A. I. Zadneprovskii, "Golod 1946–47 gg. v selakh Donechchyny," *Novye stranitsy v istorii Donbassa. Stat'i*, vol. 2 (Donets'k, 1992), p. 117, and Mokoviichuk and Pyliavets, "Holod na Ukraini."
[41] Zima, "Golod v Rossii," p. 35.
[42] DADO, f. 326-p, op. 4, spr. 375, ark. 139.
[43] Ibid., ark. 140. Clearly "democratic countries" referred to eastern European countries that Stalin endeavored to keep under the Soviet influence. For this perception of the Soviets suffering because of Poland and other states, see also A. Strelianyi, "Poslednii romantik," *Druzhba narodov*, 1988, no. 11, p. 227. Note also Interview 1.
[44] Zima, "Golod v Rossii," p. 49.
[45] G. Gorbunev, "Golodnyi 1947-i," *Enakievskii rabochii*, 22 September 1993.
[46] Zima, "Golod v Rossii," pp. 49–50, and Zadneprovskii, "Golod 1946–47 gg. v selakh Donechchyny," pp. 132–33.

Unlike 1932–33, the government did not deny the existence of famine. It accepted foreign aid (from the United Nations, the Red Cross, the Russian Relief in the United States, and others), which helped to alleviate the crisis.[47] When Khrushchev reported famine in Ukraine, Stalin said, "You're being soft-bellied! They're [i.e., Ukrainians are] deceiving you. They're counting on being able to appeal to your sentimentality when they report things like that. They're trying to force you to give them all your reserves." Khrushchev understood that Stalin knew of the famine: "Apparently Stalin had channels of information which bypassed me and which he trusted more than my own reports." Stalin did take the matter to the Central Committee. Reluctant and stingy though they were, Stalin and the Soviet government did divert some grain to the famished areas, because, according to Khrushchev, Stalin said, "The Ukraine is being ruined, which could be a disaster for our whole country."[48] The relief was not sufficient to solve the problem.

Like the Ukrainian party leader Khrushchev, many local leaders did fight to save the famished. Having learned a lesson from the 1932–33 famine, some collective farm chairmen risked their lives to hoard grain to feed the farmers. To make procurements impossible, the head of the R. Luxemburg Farm in Stalino gave an order to break a drying machine. The leaders of Amvrosiivka district in Stalino *oblast'* even forbade the collective farms from surrendering grain to the state without their written permission. Similar independent actions of local leaders to cope with the famine crisis were observed widely elsewhere.[49]

The consequence of such actions was repression. Koval'ov, of the Stakhanov collective farm in Krasnoarmiivs'k, Stalino *oblast'*, was sentenced to seven years of imprisonment for "squandering" grain (which referred to paying the peasants for their work and using grain for consumption on the farm). In 1946 and in the first quarter of 1947, one out of every sixteen kolkhoz chairmen in Ukraine was prosecuted for his technically illegal actions. Among this group were former Red Army veterans and war invalids who assumed the administration of farms upon demobilization.[50] According to a Soviet historian, "at no time in the history of collective farm building did the number of changes in farm chairmen assume such a scale as in 1946–1947."[51] Harsh as these punishments were, one may be struck by the contrast with the 1930s when actions against state orders led often to executions.

---

[47] Zima, "Golod v Rossii," pp. 47–49.

[48] *Khrushchev Remembers*, tr. and ed. by Strobe Talbott, introduction, commentary, and notes by Edward Crankshaw, (Boston, 1970), pp. 235 and 240–41.

[49] Markoviichuk and Piliavets, "Holod na Ukraini," pp. 21 and 23.

[50] Ibid., pp. 24–25. Many were prosecuted for stealing grain according to the infamous 7 August 1932 law. DALO, f. R-2295, op. 3, has numerous files on these cases.

[51] I. M. Volkov, *Trudovoi podvig sovetskogo krest'ianstva v poslevoennye gody: Kolkhozy SSSR v 1946–1950 gg.* (Moscow, 1972), p. 232.

While the leaders were assailed, the famished areas were plagued by crime. Khrushchev received reports of murder and cannibalism in Ukraine.[52] In November 1946, a worker at Ordzhonikidze Coal in Ienakiieve, F. I. Nezhyvykh, killed his wife and their son, three months of age. He survived on their meat for a while. Then he became acquainted with H. Kozhevnykova, who met the same fate as Nezhyvykh's wife in January 1947. On 20 January Nezhyvykh was arrested.[53] In February 1947, a railway worker in Krasnyi Lyman in Stalino *oblast'*, A. I. Sapel'nykov, and his wife received neither rationing cards nor any material help from the administration. Driven by hunger, Sapel'nykov killed his wife and fed himself for an extended period on her meat.[54] Between 11 January and 5 February 1947, there were five more cases of murder and cannibalism of family members in Stalino and two in Voroshylovhrad *oblast'*.[55]

Murders and armed robberies of grain took place frequently in the famished Donbas. On 2 April 1947 three hundred kilograms of grain were stolen from the storage of the collective farm Krasnyi Kut. Its guardsman Pankov was found dead in a nearby mine shaft. The Komsomol secretary named Goliak, at the Krasnyi Partisan collective farm in Iasynuvata district, Stalino *oblast'*, was shot dead on 28 August 1948. It turned out that the chairman I. L. Kosmatenko, a party member, and his company had murdered Goliak for having discovered that Kosmatenko and his wife had "squandered" the property of the collective farm. It is not known whether Kosmatenko simply diverted grain to feed the hungry collective farmers or plundered the kolkhoz's grain for himself.[56] The party Central Committee in Kiev had to send a special circular to the Donbas warning of political terrorism by enemy forces.[57] It is instructive that in 1947 the prisons in Stalino and Voroshylovhrad accommodated three times more inmates than their capacities, and that even in 1949, to cope with crime, the Ukrainian Ministry of Internal Affairs had to allocate the largest and third largest contingents of its staff to the two Donbas *oblast'*s of all the *oblast'*s in Ukraine.[58]

Famine once again challenged the very raison d'être of collective farms. It was not that the collective farm system itself failed to produce enough food for the country. In fact, during the war, the system had managed to feed the country and millions of soldiers. Stalin and the party leadership never doubted the rationale for collective farms. Molotov even contended that the "success of collectivization is more significant than victory in the Great Patriotic War":

[52] *Khrushchev Remembers*, pp. 234 and 240.
[53] Bilas, *Represyvno-karal'na systema*, 1:347–48.
[54] TsDAHO, f. 1, op. 17, spr. 5, ark. 156–58, and Bilas, *Represyvno-karal'na systema*, 1:348–49.
[55] Bilas, *Represyvno-karal'na systema*, 1:348.
[56] TsDAHO, f. 1, op. 23, spr. 4961, ark. 1, 126–27, 136, 161–63, etc.
[57] Ibid., spr. 4960, ark. 186–92.
[58] Ibid., f. 1, op. 17, spr. 7, ark. 17, and Bilas, *Represyvno-karal'na systema*, 1:351, 2:682–83.

without collectivization the country would not have won the war.[59] Even the Germans had made no or only halfhearted efforts to disband the collective farms in occupied territory, because the collective farm system facilitated grain collection.

Both before and after the war, rhetoric about the collective farm system being a new serfdom had illicitly circulated widely in the country. The famine crisis led party leaders to look for solutions in the prerevolutionary practice of rural administration. Once the worst of the famine was over, Khrushchev proposed a measure to bolster the collapsing collective farm system. In his memorandum of 10 February 1948 to Beria, he noted:

> In tsarist Russia there was a law, according to which peasant communities could pass sentences for the removal from the village of individuals, "whose further existence in this milieu threatens local welfare and safety" (Russian Empire Code of Laws, vol. IX, article 683). It is clear that this law protected private property and was directed against people socially dangerous for the tsarist-landowner regime.
>
> In our time it would be in order for the protection of socialist property to issue a law, according the general meetings [of collective farms] the right to pass sentences for the eviction beyond the borders of the [Ukrainian] republic of the most dangerous, antisocial, and criminal elements, who stubbornly refuse to join in socially useful labor.[60]

Moscow met his request. On 21 February 1948 an order was issued for "the eviction from the Ukrainian SSR of individuals, intentionally avoiding work activity in agriculture and living an antisocial and parasitic way of life." Within a month and a half more than 2,000 people were thus evicted from the eastern part of Ukraine. Moreover, in June Moscow issued a secret order to the same effect that applied to the whole country. Between 1948 and 20 March 1953, 33,266 people were exiled by these orders, and 13,598 family members followed them into exile.[61]

The famine of 1946–47, unlike that of 1932–33, affected the Donbas urban population at least as badly as it did the rural population. The reconstruction of ruined mines and factories was carried out at enormous cost in workers' lives. As before people continued to be killed by inadequate safety measures

---

[59] *Sto sorok besed s Molotovym. Iz dnevnika F. Chueva* (Moscow, 1991), p. 383.

[60] "Neizvestnaia initsiativa Khrushcheva (o podgotovke ukaza 1948 g. o vyselenii krest'ian)," *Otechestvennye arkhivy*, 1993, no. 2, pp. 35–36.

[61] Ibid., pp. 31 and 37–38. See also Zima, *Golod v SSSR 1946–1947 godov*, ch. 7. Between 1948 and July 1950, 11,991 sentences to deportation beyond the border of Ukraine were passed by collective farms. See Iu. I. Shapoval, *Ukraina 20–50-kh rokiv: storinky nenapysanoi istorii* (Kiev, 1993), p. 273. See also Ihor Vynnychenko, *Ukraina. 1920–1980-kh: deportatsii, zaslannia, vyslannia* (Kiev, 1994), pp. 72–75. For many tragedies caused by these deportations, see A. I. Zadneprovskii, "Vyselenie krest'ian iz Donbassa v 1948 g.," *Novye stranitsy v istorii Donbassa. Stat'i*, vol. 3 (Donets'k, 1994).

at mines. Little was done to alleviate the chronic problem of water shortage in the Donbas. People had no choice but to use dirty water, and the healthy and the sick had to share the same tap and bucket, further risking infection. Moscow was not responsive to cries for help. Wages were often not paid for a month or longer, leaving workers without any means to feed themselves and their families.[62]

As before, therefore, people were on the move in the Donbas. In 1949 in Ukraine 75,134 people were reported to have left their workplaces without permission, a criminal offense. "Many people were running away from here [the Donbas]," a former miner has testified. "People were arrested for such things in those days."[63] The Donbas (Stalino and Voroshylovhrad *oblast*'s) alone accounted for as much as 74.6 percent of desertion offenses in Ukraine.[64]

In the same vein, the Donbas accounted for a large percent of those prosecuted for "hooliganism" in Ukraine. (Hooliganism referred to minor criminal offenses, but it could also include murder.) According to one set of data, the number of criminal prosecutions in Ukraine increased steadily after the war: from 4,545 in 1947, to 7,718 in 1948, to 9,798 in 1949, to 10,757 in 1950, and to 6,154 in the first half of 1951. In 1951, the largest numbers (1,319) were recorded in Stalino *oblast'*, and the second largest (701) in Voroshylovhrad *oblast'*. The Donbas thus accounted for 32.8 percent of the total. The majority of the offenders were young workers, many of whom lived in terribly overcrowded dormitories.[65]

De-Stalinization

According to James R. Millar, "the economic cost of the war was equal to, and possibly even somewhat greater than, the total wealth created during the industrialization drive of the 1930s."[66] However, unlike his British counterpart Winston Churchill, who lost his power in the postvictory elections, Stalin continued to rule the Soviet Union until his death in 1953. True, unlike Churchill, Stalin did not have to face free elections. Still, as Millar has appropriately noted, no other nation or state in modern times "has withstood such terrible costs in war and survived intact as a political and economic system."[67]

---

[62]For example, see the December 1948 letter from women workers at the Kalinin Mine in Artemivs'k to the minister of the coal-mining industry in RGAE, f. 8628, op. 1, d. 884, ll. 90–95.

[63]Lewis H. Siegelbaum and Daniel J. Walkowitz, *Workers of the Donbas Speak: Survival and Identity in the New Ukraine, 1989–1992* (State University of New York Press, 1995), p. 50.

[64]TsDAHO, f. 7, op. 5, spr. 499, ark. 22.

[65]Ibid., spr. 585, ark. 60–61 and 64, and f. 1, op. 1, spr. 1120, ark. 229.

[66]James R. Millar, "Conclusion: Impact and Aftermath of World War II," in Linz, *Impact*, p. 283. See also Susan J. Linz, "World War II and Soviet Economic Growth," and Wassily Leontieff, "Capital Reconstruction and Postwar Development of Income and Consumption," in Linz, *Impact*.

[67]James R. Millar, *The ABC of Soviet Socialism* (University of Illinois Press, 1981), p. 43.

Clearly Stalin had won over some of his former skeptics. Typical of attitudes expressed during the war is that of former opponents of Stalin's rapid industrialization program: "What would we have done without our *pyatiletki* [Five-Year Plans] against a Germany that is fighting us with all the industry of western Europe?"[68] Private conversations among members of the Ukrainian Academy of Sciences in evacuation were secretly recorded by the secret police during the war. One member, named Popov, was quoted as having noted in 1942: "I think of Stalin and kneel before his intellect."[69] In the Donbas, as elsewhere, many diehard Stalinists became even more staunch supporters of Stalin.[70]

Historians may be tempted to ask whether the Soviet Union won the war because of Stalin or in spite of Stalin. Like many other questions, this one cannot be answered by quantification. Yet, as was the case with the famine crisis of 1932–33, the victory created at least two contradictory political trends. On the one hand, Stalin appeared to consolidate his power: as a leader, Stalin had pulled the country out of a grave crisis and led it to a resounding victory, whatever the costs. Many people appeared to believe that no other leader would have been able to do so. On the other hand, Stalin committed grave mistakes and coped with the resulting crisis with characteristic brutality. The cost both material and human proved unfathomable. The war inevitably posed questions about Stalin's leadership for everyone concerned.

Stalin himself appeared to be ambivalent on the war experience. On the one hand, soon after the victory he elevated himself to the rank of "generalissimus" – "the superlative general."[71] In February 1946 Stalin declared publicly that "our victory means above all that our social system has won and that the Soviet social system has successfully withstood the test of the fire of war and demonstrated its full viability."[72] Stalin seemed to take for himself the credit for the victory.

On the other hand, the war experience constantly reminded Stalin of the many painful mistakes he had made. Soon after the victory, on 24 May 1945, Stalin noted frankly that "our government has made many mistakes. We had some desperate moments in 1941–42. . . . "[73] He "found it necessary to clear the streets of cripples whom he saw as ugly vestiges of the war." Wishing to "leave the war aside," in 1947 Stalin "demoted Victory Day from a state holiday to a regular working day." He even prohibited the publication of, or reference

[68] Maurice Hindus, *Mother Russia* (New York, 1943), p. 165.

[69] TsDAHO, f. 1, op. 23, spr. 685, ark. 5. For the same point, see P. V. Volobuev, in E. Iu. Zubkova, *Obshchestvo i reformy 1945–1964* (Moscow, 1993), p. 190.

[70] Interview 3. The interviewee has until today remained a firm believer in Stalin.

[71] Robert H. McNeal, *Stalin: Man and Ruler* (London, 1988), p. 264.

[72] I. V. Stalin, *Sochineniia*, vol. 3 (16) (Stanford, Calif., 1967), p. 6.

[73] Ibid., vol. 2 (15) (Stanford, Calif., 1967), pp. 203–4.

to, the infamous orders issued during the war: Military Order 270 (16 August 1941), "which equated being taken prisoner with treason and stipulated that the families of prisoners of war would suffer dire consequences"; and Order 227 (28 July 1942), the "not one step back" order. Stalin feared exposure through art and literature of his mistakes. However, the war experience remained so much a part of the life of the people that Stalin's government "could not realistically place a taboo on the theme of the war [in art and literature] as it had on the purge and terror of the thirties, over which there reigned a malignant silence."[74]

What was clear to Stalin was that the war and the victory brought new concerns into domestic and international politics. Although he surely did not have full control over world affairs, he successfully fought to keep eastern Europe, liberated by the Red Army, under Soviet influence. He did so by waging the cold war internationally and launching another Five-Year Plan domestically. Internally Stalin appeared at times to adapt to the new postwar order and at other times to fight against it.

The most important factor was "the problem of the impact of Western culture on Soviet people," as Frederick C. Barghoorn has suggested:

> While this had always existed, wartime contacts were so unfavorable that they constituted a new major problem. The only thing remotely comparable in Russian history was the intellectual ferment among Russian officers after the Napoleonic wars, leading to the December uprising.[75]

It is difficult to imagine that Stalin, a man so keen on Russian history, would not have been aware of the evident analogy with the Napoleonic Wars.[76]

Stalin had every reason to fear the military leaders. The postwar misery in the triumphant country did prompt some military commanders to adopt a sharply critical stance to the country's political leadership, although there is little evidence that the military commanders ever even dreamed of a Decembrist rebellion.[77]

The prestige the Red Army and its leaders acquired through the victory posed another problem for Stalin: Stalin now had some formidable competition. It was G. K. Zhukov and other military commanders, as much as Stalin,

---

[74]Nina Tumarkin, *The Living and the Dead: The Rise and Fall of the Cult of World War II in Russia* (New York, 1994), pp. 100–4.

[75]Barghoorn, "Soviet Union," p. 2. The December uprising refers to the 1825 rebellion by Russian officers against the tsar. In fact, the Napoleonic War is known in Russia as the Fatherland War, and World War II as the Great Fatherland War, so named after the Fatherland War.

[76]As early as February 1942, in fear of a new Decembrist movement, the political administration chief of the Second Belorussian front, Okorokov, explicitly discussed this analogy. See E. S. Seniavskaia, *1941–1945. Frontovoe pokolenie. Istoriko-psikhologicheskie issledovaniia* (Moscow, 1995), pp. 202–3.

[77]There were critical elements in the military. For an especially illuminating case, see "Podslushali i rasstreliali," *Izvestiia*, 16 July 1992.

who had saved the country from the initial fiasco and eventually led the country to victory. Marshall Zhukov, the man who led the Soviet army to Berlin, enjoyed so much prestige among the military and so much popularity in the population that he became an immediate threat to Stalin. Thus, the "trip to the United States which Zhukov apparently planned never materialized."[78] In the Donbas, a collective farmer named Tat'iana Kaban was reported to have declared in July 1947 that "after the demobilization of the Red Army, our country will be led by Marshall Zhukov, and Stalin will retire. Zhukov will disband the collective farms, and the people will live individually."[79] In early 1946 in an anti-Semitic fit a worker named Emel'ian Makarenko in the Donbas even made Zhukov an anti-Semitic crusader: "Zhukov has recently been a guest of Stalin's. In his conversation with Stalin he declared: we've won, now we're afraid of nothing, but our life will improve only when we annihilate the Yids."[80]

Zhukov was recalled from Berlin in March 1946. A group of military leaders had been arrested; one of them was forced to write a denunciation of Zhukov, claiming that he was power-hungry and that he had made remarks against Stalin, and the like. Zhukov was presented as a Bonapartist contender for power.[81] Subsequent developments in the case are unprecedented. In June 1946 Stalin convened the Supreme Military Council to which he also invited all the members of the Politburo, marshals, and generals. Although Molotov, Beria, and Bulganin, and General P. I. Golikov attacked Zhukov, the majority of the marshals stood in his support. Marshal I. S. Konev, in particular, spoke up and categorically denied the charges against Zhukov. When Stalin retorted with charges of Zhukov's alleged usurpation of war glory, Konev responded: "Well, it's a trifle." Konev later related this episode and explained his courage: at that time he thought that if he and others did not defend Zhukov, there would be a repeat of 1937, and that, besides, during the war, he and others had become more courageous than before. Stalin had to accept this remarkable change, a process of de-Stalinization. Reminding Zhukov of the modesty of the great Russian military commanders of the past such as Suvorov, Kutuzov, and Skobelev, Stalin scolded Zhukov for his alleged lack of modesty and simply demoted him.[82]

---

[78] Barghoorn, "Soviet Union," p. 6.

[79] DADO, f. 326p, op. 2, spr. 924, ark. 44. See also RTsKhIDNI, f. 17, op. 88, d. 688, l. 30.

[80] TsDAHO, f. 1, op. 23, spr. 3880, ark. 26.

[81] "Donos. Sekretnye dokumenty zagovora protiv Marshala Sovetskogo Soiuza Georgiia Zhukova," *Sovershenno sekretno*, 1993, no. 2, pp. 10–11.

[82] Ibid.; Anatolii Ponomarev, "Marshaly. Kak delili slavu posle 1945-go," *Rodina*, 1995, no. 1, p. 78; Konstantin Simonov, *Glazami cheloveka moego pokoleniia. Razmyshlennia o Staline* (Moscow, 1988), pp. 419–21; and Zhukov's own recollections in G. K. Zhukov, "Korotko o Staline," *Pravda*, 20 January 1989. See also Arkadii Vaksberg " 'Delo' marshala Zhukova: nerazorvavshaiasia bomba," *Literaturnaia gazeta*, 5 August 1992, p. 12.

The war gave birth to a critical mind, widening mental horizons and encouraging people to think differently. The fact that tens of millions of Soviet citizens had lived under the Germans and that millions of soldiers, POWs, and forced laborers had seen and experienced the West injected a totally new factor into Soviet political life. Critical thinking, however, did not lead to any discussion of a viable alternative to the victorious Soviet regime.[83] No Decembrist rebellion took place. Nevertheless, people demanded a better life and became less inhibited in their political expression. Marshal Konev was brave enough to oppose Stalin in defense of the seemingly defenseless Zhukov. Few were perhaps as brave as Konev,[84] but archival material suggests that Soviet citizens became more vocal after the war than they had been before.

Repatriated citizens were scrutinized upon their return from Germany, and their correspondence was monitored and intercepted by the secret police. Still it appears that they discussed and wrote what they would not have in the 1930s. A nineteen-year-old collective farmer Vera Zolotareva in Voroshylovhrad reported her disappointment upon her reaching her motherland in 1945: "When I entered Soviet territory, I felt as if I had fallen into a dirty hole."[85] V. V. Gaidar, twenty-five years of age, similarly noted: "The Germans didn't insult me, I could have continued to work there. I regret very much having left."[86] Anna Shelemskaïa was angry: "It was better in the German camp than here at home."[87] A worker named Ul'ianov at Mine 2/2 in Bokovo-Antratsyt echoed Shelemskaïa's disappointment and anger: "Work in the Donbas is penal servitude and deception of workers. When I worked in Germany, the work conditions were better than this."[88] V. Polovnik, a collective farmer and twenty years of age, had a solution to the food problem: "In Germany there are no collective farms. The Germans live better. Were it not for collective farms here, there would be more grain."[89] V. I. Noreiko, who worked at Stalin Coal, reported after being repatriated from Germany: "In foreign countries elections have long been held. There is real democracy, because several parties freely propose their candidates. Our elections won't be democratic, because there is only one party."[90]

---

[83] Zubkova, *Obshchestvo i reformy*, pp. 16–32.

[84] Konev, however, "later showed an inclination to dabble in political intrigue." He seems to have supported Stalin's "Doctors' Plot" in 1953. *Khrushchev Remembers*, p. 286.

[85] TsDAHO, f. 1, op. 23, spr. 1479, ark. 7.

[86] Ibid., ark. 8–9.

[87] Ibid., ark. 7. For similar sentiments, see also Fröhlich, *In der vierten Nachtwache*, p. 56. There were cases in which former repatriates deserted the Donbas, intent on reaching the American zone in Germany. In almost all cases, they fell far short of their goal and were arrested by the Soviet authorities. TsDAHO, f. 1, op. 23, spr. 4961, ark. 94.

[88] DALO, f. P-179, op. 3, spr. 307, ark. 9.

[89] TsDAHO, f. 1, op. 23, spr. 1479, ark. 7.

[90] RTsKhIDNI, f. 17, op. 88, d. 456, l. 63.

Others seemed to be equally vocal. A worker named Ovcharenko at Chystiakove Anthracite was quoted as declaring in July 1945:

> The foolish soldiers surrender their weapons and go back home when demobilized. They should take up their weapons and demand an answer from Stalin: why did we fight and shed blood? For 100 grams of ration allocated to the invalid?[91]

N. P. Strel'tsov, a worker in Voroshylovhrad, was very pessimistic:

> We can't see life now, even before the war there wasn't life, just torment. We saw a bit of life before the beginning of the five-year plans, then began the five-year plans, then the war, and now again a five-year plan, and so it will be for us until death. No one cares for the people.[92]

A teacher named I. E. Kolomoitsev in Voroshylovhrad declared in October 1945:

> As long as the Soviet government exists and the current leader sits at its helm, our life will be the same. Only his death will save the people from Soviet slavery.[93]

One must view these statements with a certain amount of skepticism, because, as in the 1930s, the police and informers may have fabricated some of them. As before the war, the Soviet surveillance apparatus operated vigorously. Yet it is significant that there is no evidence that these people were immediately arrested, as would have been the case in the 1930s. Few were branded as enemies of the people in the secret reports, which, after the war, tended to note their "subversive" utterances as a matter of fact. This was a remarkable change.

It was not that terror had disappeared. On the contrary, according to official data, the number of people prosecuted for political crimes was substantial:[94]

1945	123,248
1946	123,294
1947	78,810
1948	73,269

---

[91] DADO, f. 326p, op. 2, spr. 924, ark. 45.

[92] TsDAHO, f. 1, op. 23, spr. 1477, ark. 53.

[93] Ibid., ark. 54.

[94] The 1945 and 1946 figures are higher than those of 1934, 1940, or 1941 (78,999, 71,800, and 75,411 respectively). The death sentence was suspended in 1948. When it resumed in 1950, 475 sentences of capital punishment were passed; the number rose to 1,609 in 1951, to 1,612 in 1952, and dropped sharply to 198 in the first half of 1953. See Popov, "Gosudarstvennyi terror v sovetskoi Rossii," p. 28. A large number of them in the immediate postwar years appear to have been war-related crimes such as those of Vlasovites, Ukrainian nationalists, and collaborators.

1949	75,126
1950	60,641
1951	54,775
1952	28,800

Stalin instituted various kinds of discrimination against repatriates and those who lived under the Germans, relegating them to second-class citizenship. Yet the difference from the 1930s is evident. In 1937–38, as discussed earlier, mere casual contact with a foreigner often led to death. Yet, in the postwar years, the wartime exposure of tens of millions of Soviet citizens to foreign regimes made it practically impossible for Stalin to liquidate or isolate them.

After the war, moreover, people in the Donbas as elsewhere began to listen furtively to the radio broadcasts of the Voice of America and the BBC. (The BBC quickly gained a reputation for broadcasting full and objective accounts in contrast to Soviet media.)[95] Ironically, the Gulags, which embraced hundreds of thousands of foreign POWs (Germans, Japanese, Poles, and others), also became a place of exposure to foreign culture: Soviet and foreign citizens mixed there even though close contact was dangerous.[96]

In other areas, too, while Stalin behaved like a dictator, he was forced to compromise. The film director L. Lukin's case is instructive. His 1941 film *Bol'shaia zhizn'* on the Donbas colliers won the Stalin Prize. Lukin produced a sequel to the film in 1946, but it never mentioned the name of the Great Leader. It is said that when Stalin previewed the film, he walked out in anger. Stalin had the film banned and Lukin condemned, but Lukin continued to work.[97]

Stalin's position on Ukrainian national aspirations was not one of unconditional repression. Although deeply skeptical, Stalin had understood well that some concessions to Ukrainian national feelings were needed to win the war. In 1944 Stalin took the trouble of convening a Politburo meeting to discuss O. Dovzhenko's film scenario *Ukraina v ohni* (Ukraine in flames). Stalin openly attacked Dovzhenko's work as anti-Leninist (the scenario did not even mention Lenin) and as nationalistic. This would have meant death for Dovzhenko in the 1930s. Dovzhenko felt utterly devastated, but he neither acknowledged an error nor asked Stalin for mercy, and yet, like Lukin, "the nationalist" Dovzhenko was allowed to continue to work.[98] In 1944, perhaps as a maneuver to secure

[95] DALO, f. P-179, op. 5, spr. 550, ark. 129 (report for 1956). For the Voice of America, see a 1951 report in TsDAHO, f. 1, op. 17, spr. 37, ark. 255.

[96] For example, Marcel Sztafrowski, *Direction Stalino. Un Polonais dans les camps soviétiques* (Paris, 1987), pp. 59 and 78, and Jacques Sandulescu (a Romanian who worked in Donbas mines as a prisoner), *Donbas* (New York, 1968).

[97] See Alla Afinogenova, "Bol'shaia zhizn' donetskikh shakhterov," *Iskusstvo kino*, 1989, no. 9.

[98] I. V. Stalin, "Ob antileninskikh oshibkakh i natsionalisticheskikh izvrashcheniiakh v kinopovesti Dovzhenko 'Ukraina v ogne,'" *Iskusstvo kino*, 1990, no. 4, and "Z ohnennym bolem u sertsi," *Literaturna Ukraina*, 1990, no. 27, p. 5. The same was true of the writers M. M.

the representation of Ukraine in the new United Nations as a separate republic,[99] Stalin even suggested that a separate Ukrainian Ministry of Defense be created. It was created, and then was ignored by Stalin. It had no power.[100] Stalin presented Ukraine as a legitimate republic on the international scene, an unprecedented event for Ukraine. Moreover, by forcibly incorporating western Ukraine into the Ukrainian Soviet Republic, Stalin united much of Ukrainian territory for the first time since the seventeenth century.

Whether or not his actions represented a compromise on Stalin's part, he had to live with the consequences. After the liberation of the Donbas from the Germans, several Ukrainian nationalist organizations in the Donbas were eliminated quickly by the Soviet security organ.[101] Yet after the war tens of thousands of western Ukrainians were mobilized for, or sought work, in the Donbas.[102] In 1953 the party leader in the Donbas noted with pride that its working class was "Ukrainized."[103] At the same time, this massive immigration afforded a valuable opportunity for the Ukrainian nationalists to intensify their activity in the Donbas. In 1951 the MGB (successor to the prewar NKVD) complained that it could not recruit informers from among the numerous Ukrainians in the Donbas.[104] In the end, many western Ukrainians, repelled by the harsh living and working conditions in the Donbas, returned to their homeland. "A significant number" of armed underground Ukrainian nationalists were among them.[105]

Stalin and his government battled against the armed Ukrainian separatist nationalists, mainly in the politically less stable western Ukraine. This was an uncompromising war that took heavy casualties: from January 1944 to June 1945 alone there were 93,166 military deaths on the Ukrainian nationalist side, and more than 10,000 on the Soviet side.[106] The war continued for several

Zoshchenko and Anna Akhmatova and the historians I. I. Mints and N. L. Rubinshtein, all of whom were subjected to harsh attack by the party. See Nikolai Barsukov, "Na perelome. Sovetskoe obshchestvo v poslevoennye desiatiletiia," *Svobodnaia mysl'*, 1994, no. 6, p. 98.

[99] Stalin demanded this at the Yalta Conference in February 1945 where he intimated to Roosevelt that he "felt his position in the Ukraine was difficult and insecure. A vote for the Ukraine was essential . . . for Soviet unity." See Edward R. Stettinius Jr., *Roosevelt and the Russians: The Yalta Conference* (New York, 1949), p. 187.

[100] V. A. Hrynevych, "Utvorennia Narkomatu oborony URSR u 1944 r.: z istorii odniiei politychnoi hry," *Ukrainskyi istorychnyi zhurnal*, 1991, no. 5, pp. 29 and 36–37.

[101] TsDAHO, f. 1, op. 23, spr. 3883, and Bilas, *Represyvno-karal'na systema*, 1:367. For nationalist activity in the Donbas in 1944–45, see also Taras Hunczak, ed., *Litopys Ukrains'koi Povstans'koi Armii. Tom 7. UPA v svitli nimets'kykh dokumentiv. Knyha druha: cherven' 1944–kviten' 1945* (Toronto, 1983), pp. 140–41.

[102] TsDAHO, f. 1, op. 1, spr. 1120, ark. 132–33 indicates that in 1945–53 more than ten thousand western Ukrainians moved to the Donbas.

[103] Ibid., ark. 133.

[104] Ibid., f. 1, op. 17, spr. 37, ark. 334–35.

[105] Ibid., op. 1, spr. 1120, ark. 135.

[106] Bilas, *Represyvno-karal'na systema*, 2:604–5 and 608–609. The Soviet side included civil-

more years. The Greek Catholic Church clergy in Ukraine was subjected to mass arrests and in 1946 the church itself was disbanded by the Soviet government.[107] In 1946 the old Ukrainian national Bolshevik O. Ia. Shums'kyi was assassinated by the Soviet security organ for attempting to return to Ukraine.[108]

Separatism was anathema, and Stalin fought against it with brute force but, at the same time, he had to accommodate the national sentiments of Ukrainians, which he had exploited during the war. This accommodation manifested itself, in part, in the growing "Ukrainization" of political leaders in Ukraine. In 1940 the proportion of Ukrainians in the Central Committee of the Ukrainian Communist Party was 40 percent, but the number rose sharply to 68.8 percent.[109] Likewise, the representation of Ukrainians among the party congress rose from 55.4 percent in 1940 to 60.9 percent in 1949 and to 66.2 percent in 1952.[110] This trend was also observed in local representation as well.[111] The core of the new Ukrainian elite, according to Amir Weiner's study, was made up of veterans who legitimated their postwar dominance by their participation in the war. "Ukrainization" was a reflection of the shift "from a class-based to a nation-based polity," and this increase in national representation helped the new elite both to "divert Ukrainian nationalist sentiments and [to] resist Russification." In a word, one might call this new politics "Soviet Ukrainian nationalism."[112]

A somewhat different trend, which was not incompatible with "Soviet Ukrainian nationalism," also operated in eastern Ukraine, including the Donbas: territorial patriotism, or regionalism. According to John A. Armstrong,

ians. However, some civilians may well have been murdered by the Soviet side, which engaged in extensive provocative acts.

[107] Vasyl Markus, "Religion and Nationality: The Uniates of Ukraine," in Bohdan R. Bociurkiw and John W. Strong, eds., *Religion and Atheism in the U.S.S.R. and Eastern Europe* (London, 1975), pp. 104–6.

[108] Pavel Sudoplatov and Anatolii Sudoplatov with Jerrold L. and Leona P. Schecter, *Special Tasks: The Memoirs of an Unwanted Witness – A Soviet Spy Master* (Boston, 1994), p. 249. See also Shapoval, *Liudyna i systema*, pp. 151–52. For the wartime national awakening of some Ukrainian intelligentsia whom the security organ closely watched, see M. V. Koval', "Pid 'kovpakom' beriivs'koi derzhbezpeky," *Ukrains'kyi istorychnyi zhurnal*, 1992, nos. 10–11.

[109] Yaroslav Bilinsky, *The Second Soviet Republic: The Ukraine after World War II* (Rutgers University Press, 1964), p. 233.

[110] John A. Armstrong, *The Soviet Bureaucratic Elite: A Case Study of the Ukrainian Apparatus* (New York, 1959), p. 16.

[111] Bilinsky, *Second Soviet Republic*, p. 233.

[112] Amir Weiner, "Wartime Experience and Political Discourse: Representations of War in the Vinnytsa Region" (unpublished paper, 1994), and "The Making of a Dominant Myth: The Second World War and the Construction of Political Identities within the Soviet Polity," *Russian Review*, 55:4 (October 1996). The Ukrainian film director O. Dovzhenko represented this very well. His diaries show his attachment to Ukraine, dreaming of dying on Ukrainian soil. Yet, despite Stalin's attack on his work in 1944, Dovzhenko continued to admire Stalin, the "great leader-conqueror." See his diary, Oleksandr Pidsukha, "Dovzhenkove vsevydiashcheie oko," *Dnipro*, 1989, no. 4, and Oleksandr Dovzhenko, "Storinky shchodennyka," *Dnipro*, 1989, nos. 5, 6, 7, 8, and 9.

the population in eastern Ukraine was "attracted by the concept of territorially decentralized government."[113] The extent to which regionalism in eastern Ukraine concerned Stalin (who was preoccupied with western Ukraine) is not known. Yet, surely, it was one consequence of the war during which time Ukraine lived outside Moscow's control. Moreover, territorial patriotism was not confined to Ukraine. The relative independence which Leningrad's leaders had acquired during the war and sought to maintain after the war disquieted Stalin. Stalin fought back, and in 1950 six prominent party figures associated with Leningrad were executed and more than two thousand people dismissed from party and governmental posts in Leningrad.[114] Still Stalin could not have decimated (and did not decimate) regional political leaders as he had come close to doing in the 1930s.

Another notable consequence of the war and occupation was religious revival, seeming both to strengthen and to erode Stalin's rule. This was particularly important in the Donbas, where unorganized religions had traditionally been as strong as the organized churches.

When Soviet forces liberated the Donbas from the Germans, the government did not proceed to close the churches that had been open under occupation. (Few clergy left with the Germans.) This tolerance won over "a significant segment of the clergy" to the Soviet side.[115] Few new churches were allowed to open, and some churches were closed, under the avowedly atheist government, which set up a special commission and closely followed church activity. Yet the government refrained from any open attack. In Voroshylovhrad *oblast'*, for example, 126 churches were opened under the Germans; in 1944, after liberation, 2 more churches were allowed to open and register with the Soviet government. The number of registered churches increased to 129 in 1947, then decreased somewhat to 123 in 1949 and 120 in 1953.[116]

Some clergy regarded the apparent accommodation of the churches by the government as a "betrayal of Orthodoxy" and "a service to the antichrist." They began to organize illegal sects and live a nomadic style of life.[117] Some presented themselves as holy fools (*iurodivye*), possessing the divine gift of prophecy. These people were subjected to repression (arrest, exile, imprison-

---

[113] Armstrong, *Ukrainian Nationalism*, p. 218.

[114] See *Reabilitatsiia. Politicheskie protsessy 30–50-kh godov* (Moscow, 1991), pp. 311–22. Of course, the specific charges of political crimes were fabricated by those who intrigued against N. A. Voznesenskii, A. A. Kuznetsov, Ia. F. Kapustin, and P. G. Lazutin, and torture was used in the investigations of the accused.

[115] See, for example, a 1945 report on Voroshylovhrad in DALO, f. P-179, op. 3, spr. 307, ark. 16–17.

[116] DALO, f. 2673s, op. 1, spr. 2s, ark. 12; spr. 4s, ark. 63; spr. 8s, ark. 52; spr. 12s, ark. 82; and f. P-179, op. 5, spr. 294, ark. 2–4.

[117] Ibid., f. P-179, op. 3, spr. 307, ark. 16–17, and f. R-2673sch, op. 1, spr. 2sch, ark. 6.

ment).[118] Still in 1951 one observed many "wandering priests" in Voroshylov-hrad going from house to house, christening children, performing funeral services, and consecrating wells and houses.[119]

The free Donbas had traditionally attracted many religious minorities. They were mercilessly repressed by the Soviet government in the 1930s. By the beginning of the war, the government "completely destroyed" all sectarian organizations in Voroshylovhrad.[120] Yet the sectarians were past masters at secret activity and they revived under German occupation. After the liberation, the Soviet government arrested many leaders for their alleged anti-Soviet activity. V. V. Zhuravlev in Krasnyi Lyman declared in 1945 that "Stalin won't lead the country. He will soon be killed." Brother Siguta would appeal to the Donbas Baptists: "Let us pray for our brothers and sisters, who sit in jail for truth and for God's words."[121] In 1948–50, it was reported that religious organizations spread "anti-Soviet leaflets" in the Donbas.[122] The police confiscated and burned the Bibles and Psalms. The persecution of sectarians continued at least until Stalin's death.[123] Still the sectarians, particularly the Baptists, maintained a strong presence in the Donbas. Industrial workers made up the core of the Baptist groups. Many war veterans were observed among them.[124]

The war and its aftermath brought new concerns into Soviet political life, but one crucial issue remained constant even after the war: despite an extensive intelligence network, Stalin could not gauge exactly how strong elements critical of his regime were.[125] This was a weakness inherent in a dictatorship that allowed for no free political expression. Stalin may have comforted himself with the belief that the voluminous reports by the secret police on anti-Soviet activity were exaggerated or that such people were a tiny minority and could easily be contained by execution or incarceration. Other reports suggested deep apathy among the population. The sentiments of Lev Vakhtin, an engineer who was imprisoned after the war for working for the Germans in the occupied Donbas, is representative of this apathy. Vakhtin reportedly believed that another cataclysm such as war or revolution would bring no good to the country: Hitler replaced Stalin, who then replaced Hitler: "For us, History has been merely a succession of traps."[126]

---

[118]Ibid., f. P-179, op. 3, spr. 307, ark. 18, and TsDAHO, f. 1, op. 23, spr. 3881, ark. 1–4.

[119]DALO, f. P-179, op. 5, spr. 6, ark. 34.

[120]Ibid., f. 2626sch, op. 1, spr. 5, ark. 48.

[121]TsDAHO, f. 1, op. 23, spr. 3881, ark. 5–11.

[122]*Edinozhdy priniav prisiagu . . . Rasskazy o chekistakh* (Donets'k, 1990), pp. 128–33.

[123]DALO, f. P-179, op. 5, spr. 6, ark. 45; and f. 2626sch, op. 1, spr. 3, ark. 24–25, and spr. 5, ark. 4.

[124]Ibid., f. 2626sch, op. 1, spr. 3, ark. 15 and 17 (for 1946); and f. P-179, op. 5, spr. 6, ark. 42 (for 1951–52).

[125]Zubkova makes the same point in Zubkova, *Obshchestvo i reformy*, p. 77.

[126]Sztafrowski, *Direction Stalino*, p. 76. Sandulescu has spoken of former Russian POWs work-

In a recent interview one resident in Stalino, responding to the question of what people thought of Stalin and his government in the postwar Donbas, claimed that "everyone lived a dual life at that time."[127] Because critical elements did exist however covertly, suspicion ran high and repression never stopped. A resident in Luhans'k, who boasted that he had worked for the Soviet secret police in the old days, asserted that there was no political repression in the postwar Donbas where he worked as a mine engineer and administrator. Yet, he went on to say that although people kept politically silent, they sometimes opened their hearts among their confidants. He added that they were arrested as a result. One incident remained particularly strong in his memory. "A brilliant student named Petrov" at a Donbas mining institute was denounced by a colleague named Smirnov: Petrov once told fellow students (who were studying "Stalin's nationality policy") that there was no such thing as "Stalin's nationality policy": Stalin had simply copied everything from Lenin. Petrov disappeared suddenly. It became known later that Petrov was sentenced to ten years of imprisonment.[128]

In a society in which the war had created fissures as much as a unity, Stalin did seek and find allies. According to Vera S. Dunham,

> Accommodation and settlement were being used at the same time that millions suffered because of Stalin's paranoia. Despite the spread of terror, the dictatorship had to decide whether to honor wartime promises to the people – some stated, but most implicit. The risky alternative was to tear up the wartime treaty with the people. The regime chose instead a long-term middle course, and this course was that it modified its wartime treaty with *all* the people in favor of a new treaty with *some* of the people.[129]

Dunham has called this alliance "The Big Deal," an alliance with the Soviet middle class (party officials, industrial managers, engineers, and the like), backed up by both material compensation and social prestige guaranteed by the state. The Big Deal thus "reflected the embourgeoisement of the entire system." In other words, "where Nicholas II failed, Stalin succeeded."[130]

Dunham's argument may require some qualification: "all the people" did not include certain nationalities. During the war many nationalities were deported almost wholesale to the east and north as potential fifth columns or as a punishment for the conduct of some of their members under occupation.

---

ing in the Donbas mines: "There was a lot of bitterness among them, which was understandable. A few were still full of life, glad that the war was over. Others didn't care one way or the other." Sandulescu, *Donbas*, p. 122.

[127]Interview 8.

[128]Interview 6.

[129]Vera S. Dunham, *In Stalin's Time: Middleclass Values in Soviet Fiction* (Cambridge University Press, 1976), p. 13 (emphasis in the original).

[130]Ibid., pp. 15 and 18.

After the war, Stalin targeted one group of people for destruction for their alleged lack of allegiance to the Soviet Union: the Jews.[131] This is the famous "anticosmopolitan" campaign. Stalin represented the Jews as enemies of the Soviet people, just as wartime allies became enemies in the cold war.

This was a complete reversal from the wartime policy toward the Jews. During the war, Stalin allowed the Soviet Jews to organize in order to mobilize them for his war effort and to win the support of the international Jewish community. Thus the Jewish Anti-Fascist Committee (EAK) formed in 1942.[132] Prominent Soviet Jews led the committee: Shlomo Mikhoels, famed Yiddish actor, Shakhne Epshtein, prominent Soviet journalist, and Isaak S. Fefer, Soviet Yiddish poet. Its members included the old Bolshevik S. A. Lozovskii, well-known writers such as Il'ia Ehrenburg and Vasilii Grossman, and even the wife of Molotov, Pavlina Zhemchuzhina. Stalin's plan was successful. In the United States, 2,230 Jewish committees were organized in response to the call of the Soviet Jews to help the Soviet Union.[133]

The EAK soon assumed the function of representing the interests of the Soviet Jewry. Even during the war, this new role of the EAK invited suspicion from among the party leadership.[134] "Mikhoels's actions on behalf of displaced Jews not only annoyed Stalin, they made him deeply suspicious of Mikhoels."[135] After the war, particularly after it became clear that the Soviet Union could expect neither Western Jewish funds for reconstruction nor a pro-Soviet Jewish state in Palestine, the EAK lost all its importance for Stalin.

One event appears to have deeply disquieted Stalin. When Golda Meir, ambassador to Moscow from the newly created Israel, visited a synagogue in Moscow on Rosh Hashanah in 1948, she reports being met by a crowd of Moscow Jews. The street in front of the synagogue

> was filled with people, packed together like sardines, hundreds and hundreds of them, of all ages, including Red Army officers, soldiers, teenagers and babies carried in their parents' arms. Instead of the 2,000-odd Jews who usually came to the synagogue on the holidays, a crowd of close to 50,000 people was waiting for us. For a minute I couldn't grasp what had happened – or even who they were. And then it dawned on me. They had come – those good, brave Jews – in order to be with us, to demonstrate their sense of

[131] According to Stettinius, *Roosevelt and the Russians*, p. 278, Stalin observed at the Yalta conference that "the Jewish problem was extremely difficult."

[132] For EAK, see Shimon Redlich, *Propaganda and Nationalism: The Jewish Antifascist Committee in the USSR, 1941–1948*, East European Monographs, no. 108 (Boulder, Colo., 1982).

[133] Aleksandr Vaisberg, "Novye istochniki po istorii Evreiskogo antifashistskogo komiteta v SSSR (EAK)," in *Istoricheskie sud'by evreev v Rossii i SSSR: nachalo dialoga. Sbornik statei* (Moscow, 1992), p. 210. For the success in the United States, see also Redlich, *Propaganda and Nationalism*, pp. 100–4.

[134] Vaisberg, "Novye istochniki," pp. 211–16.

[135] Sudoplatov and Sudoplatov, *Special Tasks*, p. 295.

> kinship and to celebrate the establishment of the State of Israel. . . . I was on
> the verge of fainting, I think. But the crowd still surged around me, stretching
> out its hands and saying *Nasha Golda* (our Golda) and *Shalom, shalom,* and
> crying.[136]

This was an unprecedented spontaneous action by the Jewish community. Having observed this incident, Isaak S. Fefer, a former EAK leader, told his wife: "They will never forgive us for this."[137] Fefer was soon arrested and executed.

Although the Jews in the Donbas were not as active as the Moscow Jews, there was no shortage of popular anti-Semitism. In popular imagination, the Jews had occupied but one category of enemies, but now, for the first time in Soviet history, they were officially presented as enemies who had colluded with imperialism and Zionism. Public discourse turned sharply against the Jews. Remarks such as "What did the Russian people fight for? For the freedom of Jews?" typified anti-Semitism observed in liberated territories.[138] In Voroshylovhrad, from 1945 onward Jews repeatedly requested to be allowed to open a synagogue, but their requests were consistently rejected by city authorities on the grounds that the existence of a synagogue in the city was "politically inexpedient."[139] The press intentionally ignored the contribution the Jews had made to the war effort, while emphasizing Jewish deserters, criminals, and the like. By the early 1950s local journalists were explicitly instructed that "no articles would be published that showed Jews in a positive light."[140]

Even the "anti-Soviet" idealistic youth organization in Stalino, "Democratic Youth of Russia and Ukraine," was anti-Semitic. In 1949 several Russian and Ukrainian workers from the organization were arrested in Stalino for advocating an "active struggle against the Soviet government for the improvement of workers' lives." One worker at Stalino Coal, I. V. Solzhenko, twenty, son of a worker and war veteran, had turned against the government out of sympathy with fellow workers who lived in destitution: four years had passed since the end of the war and their lives ought to have been better. Solzhenko and his company, according to a police report, regarded the Jews as an "unjust people" who "lived off Russians."[141] The group appears to be representative of a long history of anti-Semitism in the Donbas worker movement.[142]

---

[136]Golda Meir, *My Life* (New York, 1975), pp. 250–51.

[137]Quoted in Vaisberg, "Novye istochniki," p. 217.

[138]See, for example, DADO, f. 366-p, op. 2, spr. 924, ark. 44, and RTsKhIDNI, f. 17, op. 88, d. 688, l. 30.

[139]DALO, f. 2626sch, op. 1, spr. 3, ark. 2, 24, and spr. 5, ark. 42; and f. P-179, op. 5, spr. 6, ark. 44–45.

[140]Jerusalem Post, *Anatoly and Avital Shcharansky: The Journey Home* (San Diego, 1986), p. 9.

[141]TsDAHO, f. 7, op. 5, spr. 427, ark. 45–51.

[142]The report may have been fabricated, but one ought to consider the fact that the police knew well at that time that anti-Semitism was an official policy and, therefore, the group's anti-Semitism was no state crime.

Isaak Fefer's fears after the demonstration for Golda Meir proved correct. Stalin began to accuse the Jews as a group of "cosmopolitanism" and "Zionism," or a lack of loyalty to Stalin and his government. All Jews became "rootless cosmopolitans" and "Zionists." Stalin sponsored the anticosmopolitanism campaign as a way to reverse the wartime opening of Soviet society to the outside world.[143]

Already by January 1948 Stalin had had the EAK leader Mikhoels assassinated under the guise of an accident. During 1948 Stalin had other EAK leaders arrested (including Zhemchuzhina, Molotov's wife) and the EAK itself was disbanded as an "anti-Soviet organization that had collaborated with foreign intelligence." Jews began to be arrested everywhere. In the Donbas, the security police "actively engaged" in uncovering "Jewish nationalists, formerly Trotskyites." Yet the Stalino police complained in 1951 that it had "almost no qualified agents" on Jewish affairs, because the police itself had been purged of Jews.[144] In 1952 fifteen EAK leaders were tried on fabricated charges of foreign espionage and nationalist activity. Of them thirteen, including Lozovskii and Fefer, were sentenced to be shot. They were executed shortly after the trial.[145]

Their trial was followed in January 1953 by the announcement that a terrorist group of doctors, many of whom were Jews, had been uncovered. The group of prominent doctors who worked at the Kremlin hospital was accused of foreign espionage and the assassinations of Soviet dignitaries such as A. A. Zhdanov and A. S. Shcherbakov.[146] People feared that a new Great Terror was imminent and that all Jews would be deported to Siberia.[147]

The "Doctors' Plot" announcement officially encouraged anti-Semitism. The Stalino police, for example, reported extreme, "pogromlike" moods in the city: "Jews live off the Russian people. They are parasites, don't want to work. They have to be strangled." A hewer named Bazik at the Kochegarka Mine declared that all Jews had to be beaten.[148] At Middle School 22 in Makiivka, fifth

---

[143]According to Sudoplatov, already in 1947 Stalin prohibited Jews from being enlisted "as officers in the state security organs." See Sudoplatov and Sudoplatov, *Special Tasks*, p. 295.

[144]TsDAHO, f. 1, op. 17, spr. 37, ark. 251–52, 260, and 345.

[145]*Reabilitatsiia*, pp. 322–26, and *Nepravednyi sud. Poslednii stalinskii rasstrel. Stenogramma sudebnogo protsessa nad chlenami Evreiskogo antifashistskogo komiteta* (Moscow, 1994). At the trial the 1948 demonstration in the Moscow synagogue was cited as a crime (p. 232).

[146]For the so-called "Doctors' Plot," see Ia. L. Rapoport, *Na rubezhe dvukh epokh. Delo vrachei 1953 goda* (Moscow, 1988). Stalin sanctioned torture to get confessions out of the doctors. Stalin told the state security chief S. D. Ignat'ev, "If you don't obtain confessions from the doctors your head will be taken." *Reabilitatsiia*, p. 53.

[147]Shapoval, *Ukraina 20–50-kh rokiv*, pp. 289. According to V. Nikol'skii, "Osoba, priblizhennaia k imperatoru, zhila v Stalino," *Komsomol'skaia pravda* (Donetskii vypusk), 8 May 1993, in 1952–53, all the cases of the former political criminals still alive were reexamined "owing to new circumstances."

[148]DADO, f. 326-p, op. 8, spr. 1030, ark. 2 and 24.

graders beat a Jewish schoolgirl named Rozenberg and chased after another, Keifman, calling her "Yid [*zhidovka*]." The teacher Brino, a Jew, could not give a lesson because some pupils constantly disrupted the class, yelling "Yid" at her. At Middle School 1 in Horlivka, however, when two boys tried to beat their classmate, Gol'denberg, others protected the Jewish boy.[149] There were cases in which patients refused to be seen by Jewish doctors and parents kept their children from being inoculated by Jewish doctors. In Alchevs'k, patients beat Jewish doctors with sticks.[150] In Kostiantynivka, people asked why the Jews had not been deported like the Tartars and Germans.[151] The engineer I. A. Vitenburg at the Kirov Factory in Makiivka could not work because of "frightening anti-Semitism."[152]

Many Jews refused to be intimidated. As Konev noted, people had become more courageous during the war than they had been before. For example, when the statement of the arrest of Kremlin doctors was read at a scientific conference held at Hospital 3 in Horlivka, F. D. Ostromukhova, a Jew, "demonstratively left the auditorium."[153] Stalin terrorized the Jews, but the postwar era was no longer 1937 or 1938 when people were too terrorized to put up a fight. At least the party withstood Stalin's onslaught well. War veterans, who composed a large part of the party membership, were able to defend themselves by their participation in the war.[154] According to T. H. Rigby, "the Jews have continued to do well in the CPSU [Communist Party of the Soviet Union] membership, in spite of the vicissitudes of the Soviet Jewish community in the postwar years."[155]

After Stalin

Although not immediately apparent to all, Stalin's death in March 1953 saved the lives of many. At first Jews in Stalino, for example, feared that pogroms would follow Stalin's death: when the future Soviet dissident Anatoly Shcharansky (who grew up in Stalino) returned home on the day Stalin's death was announced, he found his mother crying, and "only later did I learn the real reason for her tears: she was afraid of pogroms":

> Earlier that day, Mama had been in the [Stalino] town square, where people gathered to listen to the news. As Mama watched in horror a man walked

[149] Ibid., ark. 3, 25, and 49.
[150] Ibid., ark. 3, 7, and 34.
[151] Ibid., ark. 42.
[152] Ibid., ark. 25.
[153] Ibid.
[154] Weiner has argued this point convincingly (see n. 112).
[155] T. H. Rigby, *Communist Party Membership in the U.S.S.R., 1917–1967* (Princeton University Press, 1968), p. 386.

up to an old Jewish woman and slapped her in the face. "Damn kikes," he shouted. "You killed our Stalin and now you're crying?" Nobody came to her defense, and my brother and I weren't allowed to leave the apartment for days.[156]

On the other hand, Stalin's death brought relief to Shcharansky's father, a war veteran. He told his sons, according to Shcharansky, that Stalin "killed many innocent people" and persecuted Jews: "we were very fortunate that this terrible butcher was dead. Papa warned us not to repeat these comments to anyone."[157]

Still people wept over the death of the dictator. In recent interviews in Donets'k and Luhans'k everyone has testified that the whole city appeared to be weeping at the news. According to one man, he had been horrified because he did not know what would happen to him and to the country without Stalin.[158] Another, who had returned from forced labor in Germany, "felt sorry, because I had been accustomed to his rule."[159] Yet another interviewee, who was a schoolgirl in 1953, admitted, "We [kids] were very pleased that we would have an extra holiday."[160]

The subject of de-Stalinization in the Donbas requires a book of its own. However, a few pages on the post-Stalin era will suffice to complete this story of freedom and terror in the Donbas.

In 1956, Khrushchev's famous "secret report" on Stalin's crimes and uprisings in eastern Europe encouraged more vocal criticism than before. M. N. Skorvenko, a collier at the Il'ich Mine in Kadiivka, was reported to have openly declared to his fellow workers, in connection with the Hungarian Revolution, that "over there Western democracy is probably being restored, as in America, where people enjoy full freedom." N. F. Dudenko, a barber in Luhans'k, noted, according to a party report, that "this is the beginning of the end of the socialist system. It's good that the Hungarians rose up. Let them beat the Communists. Others will follow the Hungarians." G. A. Ringel', a worker at the Voroshylov Plant in Luhans'k, uttered to a group of workers:

> The Soviet government impudently deceives the whole world. So workers and peasants in Hungary have risen against Communism and are fighting against socialist society, because the workers and peasants have experienced the Communist yoke. The Hungarians lived well before the Soviets came, but when the Soviet Union brought democracy to their country, this democracy led the Hungarian people to poverty and ruin.

[156]Natan Sharansky, *Fear No Evil*, tr. Stefani Hoffman (New York, 1988), p. x.
[157]Ibid.
[158]Interview 5. For similar testimonies, see Siegelbaum and Walkowitz, *Workers*, pp. 19 and 26–27.
[159]Interview 7.
[160]Interview 8.

People in the Donbas gathered information by listening to the BBC. Remarkably, reports refer to such comments as those just quoted simply as "negative views," not as "counterrevolutionary agitation."[161]

The postwar reconstruction of the Donbas attracted many people to the free steppe, as was noted earlier. The population grew much more rapidly in the Donbas than elsewhere. In 1945 the population of Stalino *oblast'* was 1,998,000, but it had more than doubled to 4,262,000 by 1959, and in the same period Voroshylovhrad (Luhans'k) *oblast'* had also nearly doubled its population from 1,244,000 to 2,452,000. The population of Ukraine (excluding the Crimea) rose much less rapidly: 49 percent.[162] People with nowhere to go tested their luck in the Donbas. Such was the case with the father of Anatoly Shcharansky, who could not work in Odessa because of a quota imposed on Jews and was told to go to the Donbas: "Try your luck in Stalino." He and his family moved to Stalino in 1947.[163] Many idealistic youths also came to the Donbas to help in its reconstruction and development. Alexei Nikitin from Briansk was one such example: "With a gift for tools and machinery, Nikitin found himself drawn irresistibly to Donetsk and the mines."[164] Yet the conditions in which they were forced to live and work eventually dampened their enthusiasm. The chief of KGB in Stalino *oblast'*, S. A. Lukin, warned in 1957 that these idealistic youths "with patriotic intentions" turned to "crime," including anti-Soviet activity, in the Donbas.[165] In May–June 1957 many disaffected youths resorted to riots in several settlements in the Donbas.[166]

Such was the case in Khrestivka (now Kirovs'k), Khartsyz'k district, Stalino *oblast'*, where a rebellion took place in June 1957. One day a hewer was killed at a mine face. No coffin large enough was available, so the body was bent to fit a small coffin. The collier was buried in working clothes. The mine officials drank the money appropriated for his funeral and apparel. They took advantage of the funeral, set up stools, and sold various things they had stolen from the mines to people who gathered for the funeral. At the time, with

---

[161] DALO, f. P-179, op. 5, spr. 550, ark. 129–31. Note also the attack by the party leadership against the police use of agents provocateurs in the Donbas. See TsDAHO, f. 1, op. 17, spr. 67, ark. 54–69.

[162] For 1945, see A. L. Perkovs'kyi and S. I. Pyrozhkov, "Demohrafichni vtraty narodonaselennia Ukrains'koi RSR u 40-kh rr.," *Ukrains'kyi istorychnyi zhurnal*, 1990, no. 2, p. 17, and for 1959, see *Itogi Vsesoiuznoi perepisi naseleniia 1959 goda. Ukrainskaia SSR* (Moscow, 1963), p. 16.

[163] Jerusalem Post, *Anatoly and Avital Shcharansky*, p. 6.

[164] Kevin Klose, *Russia and the Russians: Inside the Closed Society* (New York, 1984), p. 57. Nikitin subsequently became a famous defender of workers' rights and died for his cause. This will be discussed later in this chapter.

[165] TsDAHO, f. 1, op. 53, spr. 639, ark. 183.

[166] Ibid., spr. 658, ark. 39. An indifferent attitude of mine administrators to workers' deaths and their funerals had often caused strong indignation among the miners. See, for example, a 1953 case in Kadiivka in ibid., op. 17, spr. 58, ark. 232. Beatings of workers by the police were common. See DADO, f. 326-p, op. 10, spr. 847, ark. 72–73.

nearly twenty thousand youths living in crowded barracks, a second death was enough to trigger a rebellion. The police arrested a young Muscovite Komsomol, who then died in custody. When it became known that he had been beaten to death by the police, the young men in Khrestivka, including Komsomol members, took over the town. Women destroyed the local police station completely. Some took weapons and hid them. Several hundred rioters were armed with iron bars. The police reinforcements sent from Khartsyz'k were easily beaten back by a crowd of several thousands. After a platoon of soldiers arrived, they shot into the crowd. Thirty people, including some women, were wounded. Even then the youths took care of the wounded, stopping cars on the road and having them carry the victims to hospitals. In the end, three hundred youths were put on trial. They were accused of organizing a "counterrevolutionary uprising."[167]

Some of the rioters were "those exiled from western Ukraine" and former "counterrevolutionaries." The presumed leader of the riot, Boris Lugovoi (Borys Luhovyi), twenty-three, continued to fight from prison; he was accused of organizing a Ukrainian "nationalist organization" in prison and was given an extra term of imprisonment.[168] Whatever the case, soon after the Khrestivka incident, the KGB liquidated a number of "anti-Soviet" youth organizations in the Donbas.[169] The most prominent was the Realistic Worker Group of Democrats (Realistychnyi robitnychyi hurtok demokrativ), allegedly organized by the eighteen-year-old E. G. Donichenko, a fitter in Stalino. Donichenko, according to Lukin, the KGB chief in Stalino, under the influence of anti-Soviet Western radio broadcasts, organized the youth group after coming to recognize the lack of democracy in the Soviet Union.[170] The group distributed antigovernment leaflets in many cities in the Donbas; Donichenko boldly sent letters to Moscow, urging the government to release political prisoners.[171]

The Donbas, as before, attracted many sectarians. The case of M. M. Levchuk, in Petrovs'k district in Stalino, is instructive. In 1954, Levchuk, a nineteen-year-old Pentecostal, was conscripted into the Soviet army. Yet, on grounds of his religious belief, Levchuk refused to take an oath to the army. He was imprisoned for "anti-Soviet" conduct. For his good behavior in prison, Levchuk was released in 1956. Working as a work brigade leader at Mine

---

[167]TsDAHO, f. 1, op. 53, spr. 658, ark. 39, and spr. 655, ark. 23; DADO, f. 326-p, spr. 847, ark. 72–75; and an eyewitness account by Vadym Peunov, "Za mezheiu terpinnia," *Vitchyzna*, 1990, no. 1, pp. 156–57.

[168]TsDAHO, f. 1, op. 53, spr. 658, ark. 39, and spr. 639, ark. 222–23.

[169]Ibid., spr. 639, ark. 220–23.

[170]Ibid. According to Anatolii Rusnachenko, "Sprotyv robitnytstva ta robitnychi protesty v U
kraini (kin. 50-kh–poch. 80-kh rr.)," *Rozbudova derzhavy*, 1996, no. 4, p. 55, the group followed the example of the 1956 worker uprising in Poznań in Poland.

[171]Ibid. In the summer of 1996, my request to consult the Donichenko case files was rejected by AUSBUDO.

4/21, he continued his religious activity. To the alarm of the local KGB, in March 1957, Levchuk even succeeded in being elected as deputy to the district Soviet.[172] In 1961, more than 20 percent of newborn babies were baptized in Luhans'k *oblast'*. In 1980 the proportion of baptized newborn babies was even higher: "almost one-third."[173]

The free steppe, however, was also a land of persecution. The Baptists, in particular, continued to be persecuted "because they do not accept preachers sent by an atheist plenipotentiary of the state, but prefer their own." In January 1964 the local authorities put some Baptists on trial in Mykytivka, Donets'k (formerly Stalino) *oblast'*. One of the defendants was "Bazbei, father of *nine* children, a miner who had never received any support from the Union committee at his pit because he was a Baptist." The police isolated one of his daughters from her parents and had her testify against him. At the trial, however, she retracted her testimonies against her father: "The interrogator dictated what I had to say himself." Zhenya Khloponina closed her statement with the following:

> Instead of going to the cinema or to dances, I used to read the Bible and say my prayers – and just for that you are taking my freedom from me. Yes, to be free is a great happiness, but to be free from sin is a greater still. Lenin said that only in Turkey and Russia did such shameful phenomena as religious persecution still exist. I've never been in Turkey and know nothing about it, but how things are in Russia you can see for yourselves.

Khloponina was cut short. "The defendants accepted their sentences [three to five years in the camps] *joyfully*, and said a prayer."[174]

As for official anti-Semitism, it became less explicit after Stalin. Even though the Donbas attracted many Jews in the postwar years, their population was still smaller than before the war because of the Holocaust: the number of Jews in Stalino (Donets'k) *oblast'* declined from 65,556 in 1939 to 42,501 in 1959, while the Jewish population in Voroshylovhrad (Luhans'k) *oblast'* dropped from 19,949 to 13,939 in the corresponding years.[175] Yet on a popular level anti-Semitism persisted.

Anatoly Shcharansky's experience in Stalino (Donets'k) is instructive:

> Donetsk was a city that gave full expression to the endemic Russian suspicion and hatred of Jews, which stemmed from the belief that Jews were the killers of Jesus and were unrepentant heretics. Anatoly's moment of truth came at seventeen [in 1965] when some boys he had regarded as friends beat him up. A year later, his best friend called him a "dirty Yid." . . . The second incident

---

[172]TsDAHO, f. 1, op. 53, spr. 639, ark. 225–26.

[173]Ibid., spr. 2725, ark. 121, and op. 54, spr. 5638, ark. 38.

[174]Aleksandr I. Solzhenitsyn, *The Gulag Archipelago, 1918–1956: An Experiment in Literary Investigation, V-VII*, tr. Harry Wills (New York, 1978), pp. 515–17 (emphasis in the original).

[175]*Vsesoiuznaia perepis' naseleniia 1939 goda. Osnovnye itogi* (Moscow, 1992), pp. 68–70, and *Itogi Vsesoiuznoi perepisi naseleniia 1959 goda. Ukrainskaia SSSR*, p. 174.

came as a particular shock, from someone he felt close to. It was an epiphany of sorts: for at that moment, Anatoly recognized that the Union of Soviet Socialist Republics was not his home.[176]

In the Donbas, as elsewhere, even today one hears latent anti-Semitism in private conversations.[177] In 1994, when Jews from the homeland of John Hughes visited Donets'k with medical equipment and other humanitarian aid, two city residents yelled at them: "Yids, beat it!" and then slung potatoes at the visitors.[178]

Similarly, the Ukrainian issue in the Donbas was not done away with by the rapid Russification process in the postwar years. As Yuri Slezkine has discussed, there was a fundamental contradiction between rhetoric and substance or content in Soviet nationality policy.[179] While the government acknowledged national distinctions as if they were permanent, it never ceased to promote Russification. In the 1960s this ambiguity prompted two Donbas miners, N. V. Yankov'sky and N. I. Pavlyuchenko, to ask the party daily *Pravda* for clarification. They inquired as to the party's views on whether the Ukrainian language should develop or disappear:

> We would like to speak Ukrainian, but we don't know whether this will be correct. Won't this be a survival of the past, won't we slow down the correct march of development, won't we do harm to internationalist feelings? Yet we love all nationalities, including our own Ukrainian one.[180]

The party never responded to the two colliers. In the 1960s and 1970s local intellectuals strove to promote the Ukrainian language in the Donbas only to be arrested.[181] As before, the Donbas lived between Ukraine and Russia without commitment to either.

Two other sources of trouble continued to plague the Donbas, as if nothing had changed since the revolution or even since the prerevolutionary years:

[176]Jerusalem Post, *Anatoly and Avital Shcharansky*, p. 16. See also Avital Shcharansky, with Ilaha Ben-Joseph, *Next Year in Jerusalem*, tr. Stefani Hoffman (New York, 1979), p. 26.

[177]Siegelbaum and Walkowitz, *Workers*, p. 94, refer to the same point.

[178]"Gosti iz Barneta v Donetske," *Alef* (Donets'k), no. 3 (26) (April 1994).

[179]Yuri Slezkine, "The USSR as a Communal Apartment, or How a Socialist State Promoted Ethnic Particularism," *Slavic Review*, 53:2 (Summer 1994).

[180]Ivan Dzyuba, *Internationalism or Russification: A Study in the Soviet Nationalities Problem*, 2nd ed. (London, 1970), pp. 190 and 192.

[181]See, for example, the case of O. I. Tykhyi in " 'Livishe sertsia – Ukraina!' " and his "Dumky pro ridnyi Donets'kyi krai" in *Donbas*, 1991, no. 1, and "Shche raz pro 'Dumky . . . ' Oleksy Tykhoho," ibid., 1993, nos. 1–2. (For the 1977 trial in the Donbas of Tykhyi and Mykola Rudenko, see Lesya Verba and Bohdan Yasen, eds., *The Human Rights Movement in Ukraine: Documents of the Ukrainian Helsinki Group, 1976–1980* [Baltimore, 1980], pp. 203–50.) For other cases, see also *Ukrains'ka inteligentsiia pid sudom KGB. Materiialy z protsesiv V. Chornovola, M. Masiutka, M. Ozernoho ta in.* (Munich, 1970), pp. 194 and 231; *Ukrains'kyi visnyk* (Munich), vol. 3 (October 1970), pp. 37–38 and 70, and vol. 4 (January 1971), p. 156; and "Pravo zhyty," *Donbas*, 1993, nos. 1–2, p. 35.

poor living and working conditions and rude treatment by bosses. The chronic shortage of water, for example, did not allow colliers even to wash up.[182] In 1962–63 a wave of strikes assaulted the Donbas[183] (following the famous riot in Novocherkassk, south of Shakhty in which twenty-three people were killed by the army.)[184] A hike in food prices was one of the major causes of the strikes. In Donets'k leaflets circulated and posters appeared with the battle cry: "They cheated and still cheat us. Let's fight for justice."[185] "Justice" (*spravedlivost'*) was a keyword. Not only workers, but also youngsters in the Donbas, acted on it at the time: they were reported to organize unofficial (non-Pioneer) "councils of justice."[186] In the winter of 1963–64, because of the strikes, according to a report from the Donbas, white bread began to appear there. In other areas of the country where people did not strike, white bread was not to be seen.[187] Still, food shortage remained a perennial problem in the Donbas, causing the hungry workers to "grumble openly."[188]

Nothing, not even violent strikes and protests, seemed to change the way people were treated in their workplace. Kevin Klose, an American correspondent who observed the Donbas in the late 1970s and early 1980s, has noted some characteristic incidents:

> Tatiana Ivanovna [a coal sorter working in Butovka-Donets'k Mine for twenty years whose husband also worked as a carpenter in the same mine] told us how she had recently asked her shift supervisor in the coal-sorting department at Butovka to give her an owed day off on her husband's birthday. "If you try to take it," the supervisor replied, "we'll fire you. So go ahead and try it." She said she later felt like a fool for even asking, since her request had given the supervisor an opportunity to humiliate her.[189]

Klose has another story to tell about Olga Grigorevna Famina, eighty, who "had worked for sixteen years as a coal-sorter and retired when she was 57,"

---

[182]See, for example, TsDAHO, f. 1, op. 53, spr. 3052, ark. 42, 57, 84.

[183]Rusnachenko, "Sprotyv robitnytstva," pp. 53–54.

[184]"Novocherkasskaia tragediia, 1962," *Istoricheskii arkhiv*, 1993, nos. 1 and 2.

[185]*Neizvestnaia Rossiia. XX vek*, vol. 3 (Moscow, 1993), pp. 148 and 152, and *Istoricheskii arkhiv*, 1993, no. 1, p. 112.

[186]TsDAHO, f. 1, op. 53, spr. 2620, ark. 98.

[187]*Posev* (Frankfurt a.M.), 18 January 1963 and 5 March 1965. Cornelia Gerstenmaier, *Voices of the Silent* (New York, 1972), pp. 97–98, contends that there was an organized opposition in the Donbas.

[188]Note, for example, the food shortage problem in 1968, the year of the "Prague Spring," recorded by the Ukrainian Communist Party chief: P. E. Shelest, *Da ne sudimy budete. Dnevnikovye zapisi, vospominaniia chlena Politbiuro TsK KPSS* (Moscow, 1995), p. 408. For independent worker movements in the 1960s to 1980s, see Oleh Bazhan, "Zrostannia nevdovolennia sered ukrains'koho robitnytstva iak odyn z faktoriv formuvannia opozitsii radians'komu totalitaryzmu v 60–80-kh rokakh (na materiialakh Pivdnia Ukrainy)," *Rozbudova derzhavy*, 1996, no. 3.

[189]Klose, *Russia*, p. 41.

but was living in destitution with a meager pension. Famina

> had gone to the regional party committee and asked them for help, explaining that she lived in someone else's apartment in the New Colony community and thought she deserved something better.
> "Do you have a table?" the official asked her.
> "I have."
> "Do you have a bed?"
> "I have."
> "That's enough for you! Get out of here!"
> She fainted on the street outside and spent a month recuperating from nervous strain in a city hospital.[190]

In yet another story, Klose relates how Donets'k authorities treated the labor activist Alexei Nikitin. Nikitin was a former party member and mining engineer who had in the 1970s been expelled from the party and imprisoned in psychiatric hospitals for criticizing the inadequate safety measures in the Donbas mines. The city party chief, A. A. Kubyshkin, raged at Nikitin's activity:

> "So you defend the people, do you?" he screamed at Alexei. "Well, you're a literate fellow, you've read your history and in the history books it's written that those who tried to lead the masses – they lost their heads!"

Kubyshkin equated Nikitin with Cossack rebel leaders such as Stenka Razin and Emelian Pugachev who were executed by Moscow tsars. Yet Nikitin fought back: "I grew up amid the people and if defending them means losing my head, I'm ready!" Nikitin was further threatened by Vladimir Degryarev, *oblast'* party chief: "If you stick your nose into our business, I'll mix coal with your blood and take your body and grind it into fertilizer!"[191] Luckily Nikitin was not turned into fertilizer, but in 1980 he was again arrested and imprisoned in a psychiatric hospital. In 1984 he was released only to die.[192]

In the 1970s the Donbas provided a large number of members of the Free Trade Union Association of the Soviet Working People, composed of labor activists from various parts of the country.[193] Like Nikitin, its leader, Vladimir Klebanov, also a mining engineer in the Donbas, had since the late 1960s fought for the betterment of the mining community and was repeatedly impris-

---

[190]Ibid., pp. 50–51. These and other episodes are also described in David Satter, *Age of Delirium: The Decline and Fall of the Soviet Union* (New York, 1996), pp. 124–47.

[191]Klose, *Russia*, p. 65. Degryarev was regarded by the Donbas people as a regional tsar. "'Whatever he wanted, he did, and he built a European city,' said one elderly woman who had never been to Europe and who despised the Soviet regime. 'People trembled when they spoke of him . . . he was a great chief,' she acknowledged with grudging respect" (ibid., p. 60).

[192]*Washington Post*, 19 April 1984, p. C6.

[193]Victor Haynes and Olga Semenova, *Workers against the Gulag: The New Opposition in the Soviet Union* (London, 1979), pp. 45–72, which lists 16 members from Donets'k, Makiivka, and Luhans'k out of the total of 156.

oned in psychiatric hospitals for his activity.[194] How much interest the Donbas workers as a whole showed in organized action is not known, but every attempt at organization was crushed by the party and the police. As one former Donbas collier has recalled, no one was interested in politics, because once interested one would immediately be put behind bars (like Nikitin and Klebanov).[195] The security police (KGB) and the Soviet government in Moscow considered it expedient not to publicize Klebanov's unions in any way at all in the country or abroad.[196] They could have staged a defamation campaign but instead chose to ignore him and his cause completely.

In both rhetoric and substance, Nikitin, Klebanov, and others merely demanded "normal" (or "just," as they claimed) living and working conditions, obstinately refusing to politicize their fights. Klebanov's straightforwardness and single-mindedness did not impress political dissidents in the capitals. The champion of the Soviet human rights movement, Andrei Sakharov, was said to have refused to get involved in his movement. "Klebanov's bitter conclusion" was: "He [Sakharov] knows very little about how average people live." Sakharov and his wife, according to the *New York Times* correspondent, David K. Shipler who interviewed them, appeared to support the official propaganda that Klebanov and others were mentally ill: "Klebanov is not entirely healthy."[197]

In September 1979, as if to punish the Donbas, the government exploded a nuclear bomb in the Iunkom Mine in Ienakiieve. All residents were temporarily evacuated, but the day after the experiment, all colliers had to work

---

[194]*Chronicle of Current Events*, no. 48 (London, 1978), pp. 164–66; V. Chalidze, ed., *SSSR – rabochee dvizhenie?* (New York, 1978), p. 36; and Walter D. Connor, *The Accidental Proletariat: Workers, Politics, and Crisis in Gorbachev's Russia* (Princeton University Press, 1991), pp. 225–32. For Klebanov and Nikitin, see also John Cunningham, *Klebanov and Nikitin: The Story of Two Ukrainian Miners' Fight against the Soviet Bureaucracy* (Oxford, n.d.) (My thanks to Taras Kuzio for a copy of this pamphlet.) The court records of the Klebanov case are held at the Donets'k *oblast'* court. In the summer of 1996 the court did not meet my request for permission to consult the records.

[195]Mykola Muratov, "Okrovavlene vuhillia Donbasu," *Derzhavnist'* (L'viv), 1993, no. 2, p. 31. Those very few interested in politics included two Mariupol' brothers (V. N. Zerkal'tsev and A. N. Zerkal'tsev) who openly came out to criticize the Communist Party rule in 1981. They were declared mentally ill and confined in psychiatric hospitals and prisons. See *Priazovskii rabochii*, 28 June 1995.

[196]*Arkhivy Kremlia i Staroi ploshchadi*, 1993, no. 3, p. 67.

[197]David K. Shipler, *Russia: Broken Idols, Solemn Dreams* (New York, 1983), pp. 207–8. Sakharov remained negative about Klebanov's movement. See his interview in *Der Spiegel* (Hamburg) 41:2 (5 June 1987), p. 99. (Both the Sakharov Archive at Brandeis University and the Sakharov Foundation in Moscow have informed me that no document on the meeting of Klebanov and Sakharov can be found in their document collections.) Another Ukrainian dissident, Leonid Pliushch, noted in 1982 that he was not certain whether a national factor played a role at all in Klebanov's cause: "The worst exploitation obtains in the Donbas – that was the basis [for the Klebanov movement]." Karl Schlögel, *Der renitente Held: Arbeiterprotest in der Sowjetunion 1953–1983* (Hamburg, 1984), p. 243.

in the mine. Even twelve years later the radiation level of the city was three to four times higher than the natural level.[198] Similarly, the 1985 Chernobyl' (Chornobyl') nuclear reactor explosion had a large impact on the Donbas miners. Stalino *oblast'* had only 980 Afghan war veterans, but its Chernobyl veterans, those miners and others who had been mobilized or volunteered to contain radiation in Chernobyl and were exposed to very high radiation while working virtually without any protection, numbered as many as 22,000.[199]

The explosion of the strike movement in 1989 appeared to contemporary observers as a surprise, but with hindsight, it appears a natural reaction to events after the loosening of the reins of the party and the government under perestroika. As early as 1981, David Satter, Moscow correspondent for the *Financial Times* who visited the Donbas with Kevin Klose in late 1980, reported: "In four days of conversations at bus stops, in the barren parks outside mines and in communal flats with water dripping from the ceiling, the [Donbas] miners clearly indicated that all the conditions which led to worker unrest [the Solidarity movement] in Poland exist in more extreme form in the Soviet Union."[200] The 1989 miners' strikes in the Donbas were spontaneous and extensive, with, for example, all the mines in the city of Donets'k joining in the walkout.[201] Their main grievances were economic, ranging from the lack of consumer goods to low wages to poor housing. They rejected the Communist Party, kicking out party cells here and there and forming strike committees, but they showed no or little interest in "forming 'a second party' or an alternative trade union of the [Polish] *Solidarnosc* type." At the very beginning of the strikes, various political groups sent representatives to the Donbas to influence the striking colliers for political gain. The Ukrainian groups were also active. From the first day of the strikes, for example, the Ukrainian Helsinki Union worked in the Donbas. Rukh, or the Ukrainian Popular Movement for Perestroika, did the same. Yet the anti-Moscow Ukrainian groups, like others, were rejected by the Donbas miners.[202] In 1990 a Rukh leader still found the Donbas miners very indifferent to its cause and referred to them as "sausage

[198]"Iadernyi vzryv v Donbasse byl," *Izvestiia*, 26 June 1992.

[199]Vadim Peunov, "Chto dal'she? ili zhe razmyshleniia o tom, chto dala nam pervaia shakhterskaia zabastovka," *Donbas*, 1990, no. 6, p. 136.

[200]*Financial Times* (London), 9 January 1981.

[201]For the strikes, see A. N. Rusnachenko, "Stachka shakhterov na Ukraine v iiule 1989 goda," *Otechestvennaia istoriia*, 1993, no. 1; Theodore Friedgut and Lewis Siegelbaum's account in their "Perestroika from Below: The Soviet Miners' Strike and Its Aftermath," *New Left Review*, 181 (May–June 1990); and Stephen Crowley, "Between Class and Nation: Worker Politics in the New Ukraine," *Communist and Post-Communist Studies*, 28:1 (1995). See also a documentary film on the strike *Perestroika from Below* (1990, produced by Siegelbaum and Walkowitz with Barbara Abrash).

[202]Rusnachenko, "Stachka shakhterov na Ukraine v iiule 1989 goda," p. 74, and Friedgut and Siegelbaum, "Perestroika," pp. 29–30.

people": one miner had declared, "It's all the same to us what language we speak, as long as there is sausage."[203]

By 1991 the mood of the Donbas workers, at least those in the Ukrainian Donbas, had shifted, swinging sharply in favor of Ukrainian sovereignty and eventually Ukrainian independence. Their sense of profound alienation from Moscow, as well as the feeling that Moscow simply exploited the Donbas, inclined the Donbas workers to think that they would be better off in an independent Ukraine – that an independent Ukraine would not exploit the Donbas as much as Moscow had done.[204] In the referendum held in December 1991, against the background of the imminent collapse of the Soviet Union in the wake of the August coup attempt in Moscow, a Russified Donbas with a large Russian population voted overwhelmingly for the independence of Ukraine. In Donets'k (formerly Stalino) *oblast'*, the turnout was 76.7 percent, and 84 percent of the voters supported independence. In Luhans'k (formerly Voroshylovhrad) *oblast'*, the corresponding figures were 80.7 and 83.9 percent.[205]

Independence did not lead to economic betterment, however. Euphoria over independence was soon replaced by profound disappointment in the dismal economic decline of independent Ukraine. By 1993–94, the Donbas swung sharply away from Kiev, which, like Moscow, appeared to exploit the Donbas. Now the Donbas demanded regional independence and a free economic zone, voting in the Communists whom they had earlier kicked out of the government offices.[206] Yet there was little sign that the Donbas was against an independent Ukraine, even though it pressed for closer ties with Russia. Nor was it evident at all whether the Donbas constituencies subscribed to old-style Communist economic management; in fact, their demand for a free economic zone was a rejection of the old, centrally planned economy.[207] The disobedience of the Donbas became one of the most serious political challenges to Kiev.

---

[203] Satter, *Age of Delirium*, p. 364.

[204] See Crowley, "Between Class and Nation." See also, Lewis H. Siegelbaum and Daniel J. Walkowitz, " 'We'll Remain in This Cesspool for a Long Time': The Miners of Donetsk Speak Out," *Oral History Review*, 20:1–2 (spring–fall, 1992). In the summer of 1990 one "independent union leader for miners" said, "Ukraine is very rich. It has enormous potential. The Donbas workers will support sovereignty and independence for Ukraine if it makes economic sense." Taras Kuzio and Andrew Wilson, *Ukraine: Perestroika to Independence* (Edmonton, Canada, 1994), p. 110.

[205] Kuzio and Wilson, *Ukraine*, pp. 189 and 198.

[206] See Crowley, "Between Class and Nation," and Andrew Wilson, "The Growing Challenge to Kiev from the Donbas," *RFE/RL Research Report*, 2:33 (20 August 1993).

[207] For a very interesting analysis of local elections in the Donbas in 1994, see "Nomenklatura oboshla na mestnykh vyborakh i 'levykh' i 'pravykh,' " *Donetskii kriazh*, no. 77 (29 July–4 August 1994).

The Donbas has remained a problem child for both Moscow and Kiev. It has retained the reputation and, to a degree, the substance of the free steppe where people, far away from the political metropolis of Moscow or Kiev, fiercely defend their own interests, often behaving like opportunists or mercenaries to safeguard their freedom. Paradoxically, the Donbas has also retained elements of the wild field where a wild exploitation of people was the norm.

It is not accidental that the mining industry has played a central political role in the Donbas. It is in this industry that a sense of exploitation, reinforced by the deep division of the actual and symbolic world into the dark netherland and the bright open field, has remained keenest among the workers. Life somehow is not "normal," whatever "normal" may mean. According to a member of the strike committee in Donets'k, in the Donbas "the average life expectancy for the main occupations, tunnel cutters, machinists, coal cutters and other miners, is about thirty-eight years. People live to be just thirty-eight years old."[208] In recent strikes, the miners have repeatedly demanded a "normal, human life" and showed a profound resentment for the lack of respect, sympathy, and care on the part of their bosses.[209] Their demands are a cry stemming from their sense of moral order. True, as Stephen Crowley has demonstrated, "they themselves have proved unable to find a viable alternative" to the existing system.[210] To some people the miners are simply "muddled."[211] Yet if the issue concerns nonnegotiable matters of respect, care, and human dignity, they are not at all muddled.

Many observers have found it difficult to understand Donbas politics. Sakharov considered Klebanov, the protector of Donbas colliers, insane. Indeed, there were (and are) many contradictions in the Donbas. The free steppe was also a land of exploitation and intolerance. Had Trotsky lived to see the recent events in the Donbas, he might have said again as he did earlier: "One can't go to the Donbas without a [political] gas mask."

---

[208] Siegelbaum and Walkowitz, " 'We'll Remain in This Cesspool,' " p. 85. Similarly, the Donbas's infant mortality rate was the highest in Ukraine. See Peunov, "Chto dal'she?" p. 122.

[209] This was what people in the Donbas, miners and nonminers alike, told me again and again. See also the interviews in Siegelbaum and Walkowitz, *Workers in the Donbas Speak*. In July 1989, the miners at the Iasinovskaia-Glubokaia Mine in Makiivka closely followed the miners' strike in the Kuzbass in Russia. They did not intend to strike. When problems arose with mine transport and miners asked the director A. Siniavskii for assistance, he responded by yelling at the miners. The miners exploded in anger and struck, demanding basic necessities of life, such as a regular supply of water and gas. See *Stroitel'naia gazeta* (Moscow), 19 July 1989, p. 4.

[210] Crowley, "Between Class and Nation," p. 65.

[211] " 'Liudei sbili s tolku . . . ,' " *Politika* (Moscow), no. 3 (April 1991), p. 5.

Conclusion

"CLASS" AND "NATION," the two major concepts of political thought that arose in reaction to the Enlightenment,[1] did not and do not apply comfortably to Donbas politics. The Marxists had a very difficult time in the Donbas even at the time of "proletarian revolution" and civil war (or "class war") in 1917–20; so did nationalist parties at a time when they thrived elsewhere in the wake of the collapse of both imperial Russia and the Soviet Union.

What has defined Donbas politics was (and still is) a fierce spirit of freedom and independence. Independence did not preclude the possibility of a pragmatic alliance with foes and outsiders, behavior that often appears to observers as unprincipled, mercenary, and lacking in perspective. This spirit is a historical product. The Donbas belongs to an area that used to be called the "wild field," a no-man's-land. No-man's-land attracted freedom seekers, and the wild field became a free, Cossack steppe land. Even after the free steppe was conquered, the frontiers closed, the Zaporozhian Cossackdom abolished, and the Don Cossacks incorporated into the Russian Empire, the metropolis's hold on the former frontier region remained weak, and the spirit of freedom endured.

Industrial development from the latter half of the nineteenth century onward, in particular, opened the region to massive migration, thereby recreating frontiers in a symbolic sense. The Donbas began to attract all sorts of freedom seekers, as well as fortune hunters, en masse.

Even in the Stalinist 1930s and beyond, the Donbas never lost its reputation as a safe haven for fugitives. Both before and after World War II, the Donbas attracted numerous people who sought to live new lives there. Such was the case with the numerous disenfranchised people such as the "kulaks" and clergy as well as Jews such as Shcharansky's father who tried his luck in Stalino. Moscow even helped the Donbas to remain the "free steppe" by dumping

---

[1] For an excellent discussion on these two competing ideologies, see Roman Szporluk, *Communism and Nationalism: Karl Marx versus Friedlich List* (Oxford University Press, 1988).

335

undesirable social elements there in an attempt to safeguard the metropolises from them. Such was the case in 1939–40 when people from areas newly incorporated into the Soviet Union were sent to the Donbas as cheap labor and in the postwar years when the Donbas accepted all sorts of refugees, criminals, POWs, and the like.

The Donbas was imagined by the Soviet people to be an "exit," to use Albert Hirschman's concept, and it functioned to a large extent as such.

The free steppe was not free for everyone, however. Pernicious ethnic tension and wild economic exploitation were facts of life. As Shcharansky has noted, for example, anti-Semitism, among other ethnic prejudices, had tough roots in the Donbas; and, as the post-Stalin labor movements in the Donbas indicate, it was blatant economic exploitation and disregard for human lives, and not nationalism or liberal democracy, that ignited the Donbas colliers in political struggle. Yet the reputation of the Donbas for discrimination and exploitation did not discourage people from seeking freedom and fortune there, much as the United States – the New World, a land of freedom and opportunities – continues to attract all kinds of immigrants, notwithstanding widespread racism and crime.

Terror was another fact of life on the free steppe. The brutality of everyday life in the Donbas astonished metropolitan visitors and other "respectable" people. In a sense, the prevalence of violence was a reflection of the weakness of governmental authority and control from without. Violence was further compounded by modern industrial development which intensified traditional anti-Semitism, deepened old social rifts, and created new ones. In 1917 social tension exploded into violence. The disappearance of any effective political authority during the civil war unleashed a bacchanalia of political terror by all parties concerned.

Stalin used well the unhealed wounds of the terror for his own political purposes. In this respect, the Donbas served Stalin's politics. Nevertheless, because of its function as a refuge for freedom seekers, the Donbas remained politically suspect and was indeed hit hard by Stalin's Great Terror. World War II led to more waves of carnage, perpetrated by both sides. These turbulent years brought about unimaginable human suffering and tragedy in the Donbas, as this book has shown.

The German occupation of the Donbas made it all the more suspect in the eyes of Moscow after the war. After liberation, terror was inflicted again upon the people of the Donbas by the Soviet government. Still, the kind of massive terror Stalin used in the 1930s was no longer feasible, given the fact that the whole population, who lived and worked under occupation, had become suspect. Even though Stalin had the option of exercising, and the ability to exercise, massive terror, the futility and danger of such an exercise had become apparent. People, too, had learned to take stands against what they considered to be unjust. After the war, unlike in 1937–38, people were not easily intimidated and refused, even under duress, to admit to crimes they had not committed. The Donbas, which had experimented with political alternatives during World War II and had attracted and accepted all kinds of "undesirable elements" (former Ostarbeitern, Soviet and foreign POWs, Ukrainian nationalists, as well as criminals and freedom seekers) after the war, played an important role in the postwar de-Stalinization process.

The independence of the Donbas posed a dilemma not just for Moscow, but for Kiev, the political metropolis of Ukraine, as well. In 1917–20, although Moscow's grip loosened and then was lost, Kiev never succeeded in influencing the Donbas. When Moscow lost power again during World War II, the Donbas assumed a special significance for Ukrainian nationalists. Yet the population of the Donbas did not accept their narrowly defined nationalist ideologies and influenced them instead to abandon their views in favor of democratic ideals.

Postwar Donbas labor activists such as Nikitin and Klebanov remained obstinately independent, refusing to politicize their cause, much to the dismay of Moscow dissidents and Ukrainian nationalists.

When the Soviet Empire collapsed, the Donbas immediately became the most troublesome spot for Kiev. The problem is not just that the Donbas has a large Russian population or that it is highly Russified linguistically and culturally. Whenever Kiev has attempted to build a nation, the Donbas has acted like an antimetropolitan Cossack land, resisting Kiev's nation building. This presents an ironic political difficulty for Kiev, inasmuch as the Cossack myth is at the core of modern Ukrainian nation building and the Donbas appears to be the most "Ukrainian" of all the regions in Ukraine.[2]

The situation may change in the next few years or in a few decades. Like Peter Sahlins's Catalans in the Cerdanya ("a valley in the eastern Pyrenees divided between Spain and France"),[3] the people in the Ukrainian Donbas may in due course develop their own national (Ukrainian) identity, just as the people in the eastern Donbas may have no choice but to become good citizens of Russia. But for now there is little sign that Kiev's or Moscow's difficulty with the Donbas will disappear any time soon.[4] If, as some observers have noted critically, people in the Donbas have never developed a large (national)

[2] For this difficulty, see Hiroaki Kuromiya, *Kuchma, Kravchuk, and Ukrainian Nationbuilding: An Essay* (Washington, D.C.: National Council for Soviet and East European Research, 1995).

[3] Peter Sahlins, *Boundaries: The Making of France and Spain in the Pyrenees* (University of California Press, 1989) (quotation from p. xv).

[4] For a more optimistic view, see Sarah Birch and Ihor Zinko, "The Dilemma of Regionalism," *Transition* (1 November 1996), pp. 22–25 and 64. For a comparison, note the case of regionalism in Italy, a country that grew out of disparate regions, in Rudolf Lill, "The Historical Evolutions of the Italian Regions," in Malcolm Anderson, ed., *Frontier Regions in Western Europe* (London, 1983), pp. 109–22.

perspective, it is simply because they have rejected it or, at the very least, it has not been their main concern.

This history of freedom and terror is not entirely unique to the Donbas. It may apply, in various ways, to other parts of left-bank Ukraine that belonged to the free, Cossack land.[5] Yet during the Stalin years no other Ukrainian land came even close to the Donbas as an attractive haven for freedom seekers. While a close examination of other frontier regions in the former empire – Siberia, for example – may yield a similar story, the vast and inhospitable Siberia was as inaccessible as it was inescapable and remained as much a land of confinement as a land of freedom.

The present book is a product of regional studies, but I have also paid considerable attention to the relations between the Donbas as the political frontier and Moscow and Kiev as the political metropolises. My analysis of the Donbas suggests several important points of relevance to national politics.

First, Stalin enacted the Great Terror. Many people around him in Moscow as well as people, both big and small, in Kiev, the Donbas, and elsewhere, were no doubt partners in his operations. Indeed, it was well-nigh impossible to be a political outsider in a society in which political passivity was a crime. Yet it was Stalin who ordered the terror explicitly or implicitly.

Second, the 1932–33 famine crisis was instrumental to the development of Stalin's terror. From that time onward, the targets of enemy hunting shifted from "class enemies" to class-neutral, or supraclass "enemies of the people," clearing the way for mass terror. The question of Who is the enemy? became the focus of political discourse and practice both in Moscow and in the provinces, including the Donbas. The Great Terror was a massive operation enacted from above to eradicate any potential enemies, both Communists and non-Communists alike.

Third, the terror operation revealed a weakness inherent in a mighty political dictatorship. Whether the Soviet system was "totalitarian" or not, the state did aspire to a total control of society, including the last "frontier," the minds of the people. Because the Stalinist system deprived itself of any independent means by which to gauge (and verify) the mood of society (which was driven underground), it institutionalized ubiquitous surveillance.[6] Yet the very lack of any checking mechanism created much room for error and arbitrariness and hence for uncontrollable terror. The terror itself became self-defeating. Prob-

[5]Charters Wynn, for example, has treated the Donbas and the Dnieper area together in his *Workers, Strikes, and Pogroms: The Donbass-Dnepr Bend in Late Imperial Russia, 1870–1905* (Princeton University Press, 1992).

[6]Historically speaking, the issue of surveillance is much more complex and the Soviet practice was far from unique. See Peter Holquist, " 'Information Is the Alpha and Omega of Our Work': Bolshevik Surveillance in Its Pan-European Context," *Journal of Modern History*, 69 (September 1997), pp. 415–50.

ably this lesson was not entirely lost on Stalin, who did not resort to terror on this scale again (although, toward the end of his life, he may have been contemplating a similar operation against the Jews).

The state's wholesale intervention in society ultimately undermined the state itself; by contrast, Muslim nations, with similarly weak civil societies but without the wholesale intervention of the state in society (particularly in the economic sphere), have proved more enduring as political entities.[7]

It is not that the Stalinist regime enjoyed little social support. It was not merely a terroristic regime. A generation of social historians has examined how much support there was and exactly what kind of people supported the regime. There were various reasons why people supported the regime. Subscription to the state ideology was one. In my previous work on industrialization I myself discussed social support for terror against the "enemies" as evidence of the ideology's popularity.[8]

Historians have recently begun to examine the subjective side of individuals in detail (based on formerly inaccessible sources such as diaries), indicating how difficult or impossible it was for individuals under Stalin to develop a subjective, private world apart from or independent of the official world.[9] This may have been true of some citizens, but the crux of the matter for Stalin and his secret police (or, for that matter, historians) was that there was no sure way of ascertaining this, because freedom of expression did not exist.[10]

Popular support for terror was more than ideological. Many other factors were involved: starvation, greed, fear, hatred, prejudice, anger, revenge – that is, those factors which ideologies or world views can not easily subsume into themselves. This is part of the reason why the "enemy of the people," a concept not constrained by any ideology, became so inclusive and hence so dangerous.

The present book on the Donbas has emphasized the importance of regional studies. Works focused on Moscow or Leningrad tend to assume that the Soviet regime lasted for seventy-some years uninterruptedly. In the case of the Donbas, and other western regions of the former Soviet Union, this was not the case: the regime did collapse during the war. At that time, people had to decide their own fates, however few and unattractive available options may

[7]I owe this point to Ernest Gellner. See his "Islam and Marxism: Some Comparisons," *International Affairs* (London), 67:1 (January 1991), pp. 1–6, and *Conditions of Liberty: Civil Society and Its Rivals* (London, 1994).

[8]Hiroaki Kuromiya, *Stalin's Industrial Revolution: Politics and Workers, 1928–1932* (Cambridge University Press, 1988).

[9]Note Jochen Hellbeck's important work, *Tagebuch aus Moskau 1931–1939* (Munich, 1996).

[10]Even in the case of Stepan Podlubnyi, the author of the diary Hellbeck has edited (n. 9), he came to entertain doubts about the regime with which he had identified himself. As the editor emphasizes, even then Podlubnyi could not express himself except by official discourse, but one can imagine that this fact hardly mattered to the powers that be. Indeed, he, too, was arrested, albeit not for a political crime. Ibid., p. 279.

have been. Moreover, there is no evidence to show that even at the peak of the Great Terror, people did not imagine alternatives to Stalinism. Whether the numerous "counterrevolutionary remarks" allegedly uttered by Soviet citizens and recorded painstakingly by Stalin's secret police, and quoted in profusion in this book were real or not, at least someone (police agents, informers, interrogators) imagined them. Stalin himself did not believe that people could not imagine such possibilities. As Stalin intimated to Dimitrov in 1937, he meant to exterminate all those who appeared to be against his regime, even "by thought." Stalin's terror was a trial of conscience. Because the Donbas was a haven for the outlawed, there was every reason for him to believe that anything was possible there. Stalin terrorized the Donbas because it symbolized freedom.

Sources

The most important sources for this book come from the previously closed archives in Ukraine and Russia. I have not been able to have access to the most secretive of all archives – the so-called Presidential Archive and the former KGB archives in Moscow and Kiev. However, I have been able to gain more than ample data in those open "archives" in the capitals and in the Donbas, as well as the former KGB archives in Donets'k and Luhans'k,

The published sources are found in major libraries in the West, Moscow, or Kiev, except for many local publications, which can be consulted at provincial libraries in the Donbas, the catalogs of whose *Viddil kraieznavtva* are treasure troves for the study of the Donbas.

Archival Sources

Archives are mostly cited by their acronyms with the following notations: f. (*fond*), op. (*opis'*, *opys*), d. (*delo*) or spr. (*sprava*), l./ll. (*list/listy*) or ark. (*arkush/arkushi*), and ob. (*oborot*) or zv. (*zvorot*) for Russian and Ukrainian archives.

AUSBUDO: Arkhiv Upravliniia Sluzhby bezpeky Ukrainy po Donets'kii oblasti (Donets'k, Ukraine), formerly the KGB archive in Donets'k.

AUSBULO: Arkhiv Upravlinnia Sluzhby bezpeky Ukrainy po Luhans'kii oblasti (Luhans'k, Ukraine), formerly the KGB archive in Luhans'k.

DADO: Derzhavnyi arkhiv Donets'koi oblasti (Donets'k, Ukraine), which includes the former Communist Party archive in Donets'k *oblast'*.

DALO: Derzhavnyi arkhiv Luhans'koi oblasti (Luhans'k, Ukraine), which includes the former Communist Party archive in Luhans'k *oblast'*.

GARF: Gosudarstvennyi arkhiv Rossiiskoi Federatsii (Moscow, Russia), formerly Tsentral'nyi gosudarstvennyi arkhiv Oktiabr'skoi revoliutsii Soiuza Sovetskikh Sotsialisticheskikh Respublik (SSSR).

Neveu Documents: Archives of the Assumptionist General House (Rome, Italy).

RF IMFE: Rukopysni fondy Instytutu mystetstvoznavstva, fol'kloru ta etnohrafii AN Ukrainy (Kiev, Ukraine).

RGAE: Rossiiskii gosudarstvennyi arkhiv ekonomiki (Moscow, Russia), formerly Tsentral'nyi gosudarstvennyi arkhiv narodnogo khoziaistva SSSR.

RGVA: Rossiiskii gosudarstvennyi voennyi arkhiv (Moscow, Russia), formerly Tsentral'nyi gosudarstvennyi arkhiv Sovetskoi Armii SSSR.

RTsKhIDNI: Rossiiskii tsentr khraneniia i izucheniia dokumentov noveishei istorii (Moscow, Russia), formerly the Communist Party archive (Tsentral'nyi partiinyi arkhiv).

TsAMO: Tsentral'nyi arkhiv Ministerstva oborony Rossiiskoi Federatsii (Podol'sk, Moscow *oblast'*, Russia).

TsDAHO: Tsentral'nyi derzhavnyi arkhiv hromads'kykh ob"iednan' Ukrainy (Kiev, Ukraine), formerly the Communist Party archive (Partiinyi arkhiv Institutu istorii partii pry TsK Kompartii Ukrainy).

TsDAVO: Tsentral'nyi derzhavnyi arkhiv vyshchykh orhaniv vlady ta upravlinnia Ukrainy (Kiev, Ukraine), formerly Tsentral'nyi derzhavnyi arkhiv Zhovtnevoi revoliutsii Ukrains'koi Radians'koi Sotsialistychnoi Respubliky (URSR).

TsDIA: Tsentral'nyi derzhavnyi istorychnyi arkhiv Ukrainy (Kiev, Ukraine), formerly Tsentral'nyi derzhavnyi istorychnyi arkhiv URSR.

TsDKFFA: Tsentral'nyi derzhavnyi kinofotofonoarkhiv Ukrainy (Kiev, Ukraine), formerly Tsentral'nyi derzhavnyi arkhiv kinofotofonodokumentiv URSR.

TsKhDMO: Tsentr khraneniia dokumentov molodezhnykh organizatsii (Moscow, Russia), formerly the Komsomol archive (Arkhiv Tsentral'nogo komiteta Vsesoiuznogo leninskogo kommunisticheskogo soiuza molodezhi).

TsKhSD: Tsentr khraneniia sovremmenoi dokumentatsii (Moscow, Russia), the so-called Staraia ploshchad', formerly the Communist Party Central Committee archive (Arkhiv Tsentral'nogo Komiteta Kommunistichekoi partii Sovetskogo Soiuza).

VMA: Vrangel' Military Archive, Hoover Institution Archive (Stanford, Calif.).

WKP: "Records of the All-Union (Russian) Communist Party, Smolensk District, Record Group 1056," or the so-called Smolensk Archive, widely available on microfilm from the U.S. National Archives (Washington, D.C.).

YIVO Archives: YIVO Institute for Jewish Research Archives (New York).

Interviews

All interviews were conducted by the author in Russian and Ukrainian. The author promised anonymity to all the interviewees. Many more interviews were conducted in Donets'k, Luhans'k, and Khartsyz'k in 1989, 1990, 1991, 1992, 1993, 1994, and 1996 than listed here. Many other attempts at interviews failed because people often did not wish to discuss their past. Even those interviewees listed here declined to respond to many questions posed to them.

1: A Ukrainian couple in Donets'k on 22 October 1989. The husband was born in 1931, as was his wife. Both lived in Donets'k under German occupation during the war. The husband was arrested in 1951 for "anti-Soviet propaganda."

2: An elderly Russian man in Donets'k on 3 July 1991.

3: An elderly Russian woman in Donets'k on 5 July 1991. A former Komsomol activist in the 1930s, she withdrew to the Urals during the war.

4: A Ukrainian man in Luhans'k on 28 July 1993. He was born in 1913 near Luhans'k, dekulakized in 1929, then exiled to Perm', but soon fled back to the Donbas. He fought in the war and became a party member in 1942.

5: A Ukrainian man in Luhans'k on 28 July 1993. Born into a skilled construction worker's family near Luhans'k in 1925, he lived in Luhans'k during the German occupation.

6: A 65-year-old man (ethnicity unknown) in Luhans'k on 30 July 1993. He came to the Donbas from Irkutsk in 1943–44 as a miner, studied in a technicum, and later became a chief mechanic and mine director in various mines in the Donbas. He boasted of having worked for the KGB.

7: A 66-year-old man (ethnicity unknown) in Luhans'k on 18 July 1994. He was taken to Germany as a forced laborer in 1942. His father was killed in the war.

8: A 53-year-old woman (ethnicity unknown) with a Jewish husband in Donets'k on 28 July 1994. Her father was killed in the war.

Frequently Cited Newspapers and Periodicals

Arkhivy Ukrainy (Kiev)
Diktatura truda (Stalino)
Donbas (Donets'k)
Donechchyna (Donets'k)
Donetskii proletarii (Kharkiv)
Donetskii proletarii (Luhans'k)
Donetskii shakhter (Kharkiv)
Donteskii kriazh (Donets'k)
Donteskii vestnik (Stalino)
Gornorabochii (Kharkiv, Moscow)
Gornotrud (Kharkiv)
Gornozavodskoe delo (Kharkiv)
Istochnik (Moscow)
Istoricheskii arkhiv (Moscow)
Istoriia SSSR (Moscow)
Izvestiia (Moscow)
Izvestiia TsK KPSS (Moscow)
Khoziaistvo Donbassa (Kharkiv)
Kochegarka (Artemivs'k)
Letopis' revoliutsii (Kharkiv)
Literaturna Ukraina (Kiev)
Litopys revoliutsii (Kharkiv)
Luganskaia pravda (Luhans'k)
Makeevskii rabochii (Makiivka)
Narodnoe khoziaistvo (Moscow)
Nasha gazeta (Luhans'k)
Otechestvennaia istoriia (Moscow)
Prapor peremohy (Luhans'k)
Pravda (Moscow)
Priazovskii rabochii (Mariupol')
Proletarskaia revoliutsiia (Moscow)
Rodina (Moscow)

Sotsialisticheskii Donbas (Stalino)
Suchasna Ukraina (Munich)
Ukrains'kyi istorychnyi zhurnal (Kiev)
Vechernii Donetsk (Donets'k)
Voprosy istorii (Moscow)
Z arkhiviv VUChK-HPU-NKVD-KHB (Kiev)
Za industrializatsiiu (Moscow)

Books and Articles

The full reference is given on the first citation in notes to each chapter. The following bibliography is selective.

Collections of Documents

Anriianov, Viktor. *Pamait' so znakom OST. Sud'ba "vostochnykh rabochikh" v ikh sobstvennykh svidetel'stvakh, pis'makh i dokumentakh.* Moscow, 1993.
Ehrenburg, Ilya, and Vasily Grossman, eds. *The Black Book: The Ruthless Murder of Jews by German-Fascist Invaders throughout the Temporarily-Occupied Regions of the Soviet Union and in the Death Camps of Poland during the War of 1941–1945.* Tr. John Glad and James S. Levine. New York, 1981.
Holod 1932–1933 rokiv na Ukraini: ochyma istorikiv, movoiu dokumentiv. Kiev, 1990.
Meller, V. L., and A. M. Pankratova, eds. *Rabochee dvizhenie v 1917 godu.* Moscow, 1926.
Natsional'ni vidnosyny v Ukraini u XX st. Zbirnyk dokumentiv i materialiv. Kiev, 1994.
Neizvestnaia chernaia kniga. Jerusalem and Moscow, 1993.
Pravda cherez roky. Statti, spohady, dokumenty. Donets'k, 1995.
Reabilitatsiia. Politicheskie protsessy 30–50-kh godov. Moscow, 1991.
Shosta Vseukrains'ka naukova konferentsiia z istorychnoho kraieznavstva (m. Luts'k, veresen'–zhovten' 1993 r.) Luts'k, 1993.
Sovteskie evrei pishut Il'e Erenburgu 1943–1966. Jerusalem, 1993.
Vozvrashchenie imeni i chesti. Ocherki, vospominaniia, informatsiinye i spravochnye materialy. Luhans'k, 1995.
Zlepko, D., ed. *Der ukrainische Hunger-Holocaust.* Sonnenbuehl, 1988.

Memoirs and Other Personal Accounts

Antonenko-Davydovych, Borys. *Zemleiu Ukrains'koiu.* Philadelphia, 1955.
Avdeenko, A. O. *Nakazanie bez prestupleniia.* Moscow, 1991.
Baitalsky, Mikhail. *Notebooks for the Grandchildren: Recollections of a Trotskyist Who Survived the Stalin Terror.* Tr. Marilyn Vogt-Downey. Atlantic Highlands, N.J., 1995.
The Black Deeds of the Kremlin: A White Book, vol. 1, *Book of Testimonies.* Toronto, 1953.
The Black Deeds of the Kremlin. A White Book, vol. 2, *The Great Famine in Ukraine 1932–1933.* Detroit, Mich., 1955.
Bohdan, Vladimir A. *Avoiding Extinction: Children of the Kulak.* New York, 1992.
Borodin, N. M. *One Man in His Time.* London, 1955.

Chuev, Feliks. *Tak govoril Kaganovich. Ispoved' stalinskogo apostola.* Moscow, 1992.

Croghan, Patrick A. *The Peasant of Makeyevka: Biography of Bishop Pius Neveu, A.A.* Worcester, Mass., 1982.

Fenin, Aleksandr I. *Coal and Politics in Late Imperial Russia: Memoirs of a Russian Mining Engineer.* Tr. Alexandre Fediaevsky and ed. Susan P. McCaffray. Northern Illinois University Press, 1990.

    Vospominaniia inzhenera. K istorii obshchestvennago i khoziaistvennago razvitiia Rossii (1883–1906 g.g.). Prague, 1938.

Fischer, Louis, ed. *Thirteen Who Fled.* Tr. Gloria Fischer and Victor Fischer. New York, 1949.

Frölich, Hans. *In der vierten Nachtwache. Erlebnisberichte aus der Deportation.* Munich, 1977.

Grigorenko, Petro G. *Memoirs.* Tr. Thomas P. Whitney. New York, 1982.

Haidarivs'kyi, Vasil'. *A svit takyi harnyi. . . .* Buenos Aires, 1962.

Haimson, Leopold, in collaboration with Ziva Galili y Garcia and Richard Wortman. *The Making of Three Russian Revolutionaries: Voices from the Menshevik Past.* Cambridge University Press, 1987.

Haydon, W., ed. *Russia as Seen by Two Tilmanstone Miners: A Record of a Tour to the Donetz Basin in Aug.–Sept., 1929.* Dover, 1929.

Hellbeck, Jochen, ed. *Tagebuch aus Moskau 1931–1939.* Munich, 1996.

Ispytanie dolgom. Vospominaniia chekistov. 3rd ed. Donets'k, 1989.

Khelemendyk-Kokot, Antonina. *Kolhospne dytynstvo i nimets'ka nevolia. Spohady.* Toronto, 1989.

Khrushchev Remembers. Tr. and ed. Strobe Talbott. Introduction, commentary, and notes by Edward Crankshaw. Boston, 1970.

Khrushchev Remembers: The Glasnost Tapes. Tr. and ed. Jerrold L. Schecter with Vyacheslav L. Luchkov. Foreword by Strobe Talbott. Boston, 1990.

Khrushchev Remembers: The Last Testament. Tr. and ed. Strobe Talbott. Foreword by Edward Crankshaw and introduction by Jerrold L. Schecter. Boston, 1974.

Klee, Ernst, Willi Dressen, and Volker Riess. *"The Good Old Days": The Holocaust as Seen by Its Perpetrators and Bystanders.* Tr. Deborah Burnstone. New York, 1991.

Klose, Kevin. *Russia and the Russians: Inside the Closed Society.* New York, 1984.

Kostiuk, Hryhorii. *Zustrichi i proshchannia. Spohady. Knyha persha.* Edmonton, Canada, 1987.

Kozlova, N. N., and I. I. Sandomirskaia. *"Ia tak khochu nazvat' kino." "Naivnoe pis'mo": Opyt lingvo-sotsiologicheskogo chteniia.* Moscow, 1996.

Kravchenko, Victor. *I Chose Freedom: The Personal and Political Life of a Soviet Official.* New York, 1946.

The Life of a Chemist: Memoirs of Vladimir N. Ipatieff. Stanford University Press, 1946.

Likhodeev, Leonid. *Pole brani, na kotorom ne bylo ranenykh.* Moscow, 1990.

Mace, James E., and Leonid Heretz, eds. *Oral History Project of the Commission on the Ukrainian Famine.* 3 vols. Washington, D. C. 1990.

Maistrenko, Ivan. *Istoriia moho pokolinnia. Spohady uchasnyka revoliutsiinykh podii v Ukrainini.* Edmonton, Canada, 1985.

Our Journey through Russia: A First-Hand Account by Two British Working-Men of a Journey through Russia. London, 1929.

Paustovsky, Konstantin. *The Story of a Life.* Tr. Joseph Barnes. New York, 1964.
Rudenko, Mykola. *Ekonomichni monolohy. Narysy katastofichnoi pomylky.* Munich, 1978.
Samsonov, A. M. *Znat' i pomnit'. Dialog istorika s chitatelem.* Moscow, 1988.
Sandulescu, Jacques. *Donbas.* New York, [1968].
Sharansky, Natan. *Fear No Evil.* Tr. Stefani Hoffman. New York, 1988.
Shcharansky, Avital, with Ilaha Ben-Joseph. *Next Year in Jerusalem.* Tr. Stefani Hoffman. New York, 1979.
Shipler, David K. *Russia: Broken Idols, Solemn Dreams.* New York, 1983.
Shkuro, A. G. *Zapiski belogo partizana.* Moscow, 1991.
Siegelbaum, Lewis H., and Daniel J. Walkowitz. *Workers of the Donbas Speak: Survival and Identity in the New Ukraine, 1989–1992.* State University of New York Press, 1995.
Sosiura, Volodymir. "Tretia rota." *Kyiv,* 1988, no. 1.
Stakhiv, Ievhen. *Kriz' tiurmy, pidpillia i kordony. Povist' moho zhyttia.* Kiev, 1995.
Sto sorok besed s Molotovym. Iz dnevnika F. Chueva. Moscow, 1991.
Sztafrowski, Marcel. *Direction Stalino. Un Polonais dans les camps soviétique.* Paris, 1987.
Terekhov, R. *Storinky heroichnoi borot'by. Spohady staroho bil'shovyka.* Kiev, 1963.
33-i: holod. Narodna knyha-memorial. Kiev, 1991.
Tschebotarioff, Gregory P. *Russia, My Native Land.* New York, 1964.
Uksusov, Ivan Il'in. "Posle molchaniia." *Sovetskii shakhter,* 1989, no. 11.
Voroshilov, K. E. *Rasskazy o zhizni. Vospominaniia. Kniga pervaia.* Moscow, 1968.

Statistical publications

Abramov, A. *Zhilishchno-bytovoe stroite'stvo Donbassa.* Moscow and Leningrad, 1930.
Donbas v tsifrakh. Statisticheskii spravochnik. Stalino, 1936.
Itogi sploshnoi podvornoi perepisi Donetskoi gubernii (ianvar'–fevral' 1923 g.). Vol. 1. Kharkiv, 1923.
Itogi Vsesoiuznoi perepisi naseleniia 1959 goda. SSSR (Svodnyi tom). Moscow, 1962.
Itogi Vsesoiuznoi perepisi naseleniia 1959 goda. Ukrainskaia SSR. Moscow, 1963.
Kirzhner, D. M. *Gornaia promyshlennost' v tsifrakh. Kratkii spravochnik.* Moscow, 1926.
Materialy k serii 'Narody Sovetskogo Soiuza'. Ch. 5. Perepis' 1939 goda. Moscow, 1990.
Pervaia vseobshchaia perespis' naseleniia Rossiiskoi imperii, 1897 g. Vols. 12 and 13. St. Petersburg, 1904–5.
Statisticheskii spravochnik Stalinskogo okruga. Stalino, 1928.
Statistika neschastnykh sluchaiev s rabochimi gornoi i gornozavodskoi promyshlennosti iuzhnoi Rossii za 1908–1904 [sic] gg. Kharkiv, 1910.
Voprosy tekhniki bezopasnosti i travmatizma v gornoi promyshlennosti SSSR. Doklady gornoi sektsii II Vsesoiuznogo s"ezda po profgigiene i tekhnike bezopasnosti. Moscow, 1928.
Vsesoiuznaia perepis' naseleniia 1937 g. Kratkie itogi. Moscow, 1991.
Vsesoiuznaia perepis' naseleniia 1939 g. Osnovnye itogi. Moscow, 1992.

Index

Printed in the United States
18453LVS00002B/157-168